Certification and Security in Health–Related Web Applications:
Concepts and Solutions

Anargyros Chryssanthou
Hellenic Data Protection Authority, Greece

Ioannis Apostolakis
National School of Public Health, Greece

Iraklis Varlamis
Harokopio University of Athens, Greece

MEDICAL INFORMATION SCIENCE REFERENCE

Hershey · New York

Director of Editorial Content: Kristin Klinger
Director of Book Publications: Julia Mosemann
Acquisitions Editor: Lindsay Johnston
Development Editor: Dave DeRicco
Publishing Assistant: Milan Vracarich Jr.
Typesetter: Michael Brehm
Production Editor: Jamie Snavely
Cover Design: Lisa Tosheff

Published in the United States of America by
Medical Information Science Reference (an imprint of IGI Global)
701 E. Chocolate Avenue
Hershey PA 17033
Tel: 717-533-8845
Fax: 717-533-8661
E-mail: cust@igi-global.com
Web site: http://www.igi-global.com

Library of Congress Cataloging-in-Publication Data

Certification and security in health-related web applications : concepts and
solutions / Anargyros Chryssanthou, Ioannis Apostolakis and Iraklis Varlamis,
editors.
     p. cm.
  Includes bibliographical references and index.
  Summary: "This book aims to bridge the worlds of healthcare and information
technology, increase the security awareness of professionals, students and
users and highlight the recent advances in certification and security in
health-related Web applications"--Provided by publisher.
  ISBN 978-1-61692-895-7 (hardcover) -- ISBN 978-1-61692-897-1 (ebook) 1.
Medical informatics--Security measures. 2. Medicine--Databases--Security
measures. 3. Medicine--Databases--Certification. 4. Internet in medicine--
Security measures. I. Chryssanthou, Anargyros, 1979- II. Apostolakis,
Ioannis, 1961- III. Varlamis, Iraklis, 1974-
  R859.7.S43C47 2011
  610.285--dc22
                          2010016324

British Cataloguing in Publication Data
A Cataloguing in Publication record for this book is available from the British Library.

All work contributed to this book is new, previously-unpublished material. The views expressed in this book are those of the authors, but not necessarily of the publisher.

Table of Contents

Section 1
Access Control

Chapter 1

Alejandro Enrique Flores, University of Wollongong, Australia
Khin Than Win, University of Wollongong, Australia
Willy Susilo, University of Wollongong, Australia

Chapter 2

Efstratia Mourtou, St. Andrew General Hospital, Greece

Section 2
Increasing the Flexibility of Access Control Mechanisms

Chapter 3

Eleni Mytilinaiou, University of Piraeus, Greece
Vassiliki Koufi, University of Piraeus, Greece
Flora Malamateniou, University of Piraeus, Greece
George Vassilacopoulos, University of Piraeus, Greece

Section 3
Certification and Evaluation of Security

Section 4
Trust in Healthcare Networks (and Communities)

Detailed Table of Contents

Section 1
Access Control

Chapter 1
Alejandro Enrique Flores, University of Wollongong, Australia
Khin Than Win, University of Wollongong, Australia
Willy Susilo, University of Wollongong, Australia

A shared care environment is a complex setting where keeping a patient's information confidential proves a challenging task as issues, such as correct identification of users, assigning of access permissions and resolution, arise when data need to be exchanged among health care providers. Traditional access control models such as MAC (Mandatory Access Control), DAC (Discretionary Access control) and RBAC (Role-Based Access Control) are not always the most competent solution for protecting medical information, especially in shared care environments. This chapter describes how attribute-based encryption can be used for protecting the confidentiality of patients' information during the exchange of electronic health records among healthcare providers. The use of attribute-based encryption reinforces access policies, reduces the risk of unauthorized access to sensitive information and provides a set of functionalities, which are described using a case study.

Chapter 2
Efstratia Mourtou, St. Andrew General Hospital, Greece

Hospital Information Systems (HIS) are designed in order to support healthcare activities, are fed with confidential medical data and have a twofold role: to support doctors and health professionals in their daily activities and to keep patients' data confidential - accessible only by authorized people. This requires an effective information security policy, which sets the rules and procedures that must be followed in order to provide access to people in heterogeneous settings while preserving confidentiality of medical data. This chapter explores access control issues of healthcare information systems by reviewing potential threats and vulnerabilities as well as basic attributes of a hospital's security plan. As a shield to the security threats the chapter presents a hierarchical access control model, which refers to data ownership and access control issues.

Section 2
Increasing the Flexibility of Access Control Mechanisms

Chapter 3

    Eleni Mytilinaiou, University of Piraeus, Greece
    Vassiliki Koufi, University of Piraeus, Greece
    Flora Malamateniou, University of Piraeus, Greece
    George Vassilacopoulos, University of Piraeus, Greece

The authors of this chapter assume a process-oriented PHR system and present a security framework which deals with authorization and access control issues that arise in IT-enabled, patient-centric, modeled systems, whose scope is to provide shared care among heterogeneous healthcare providers working in different settings and using different sets of rules. The framework, which the authors propose, ensures that users are provided with tight, just-in-time permissions, in order that authorized users are able to access specific objects according to the current context. If the context changes then the users' permissions are modified according to the changing context. In this way, compromising medical information integrity during task executions has reduced risk likelihood.

Chapter 4

    Rafae Bhatti, Oracle Corp, USA
    Tyrone Grandison, IBM Almaden Research Center, USA

This chapter presents a privacy protection architecture called PRIMA, which attempts to increase the usability of healthcare applications without compromising the security of patient information. The components of the PRIMA architecture guarantee policy definition, auditing of actions and restrictions throughout the clinical process and refinement of the original policies per case. As a result, the security policies and exceptions are more precise and realistic and fit to the clinical workflow instead of impeding it, thus enabling improved privacy protection for the patient and increased usability of the clinical workflow.

Chapter 5

    Boleslaw Mikolajczak, University of Massachusetts, USA

The chapter deals with design and analysis of healthcare workflow systems and provides a solution that improves their structural and behavioral flexibility. Giving emphasis on flexibility, without neglecting security, security in careflow systems is conceptually modeled using Petri nets and colored Petri nets. In this model, security and flexibility are covered separately and incrementally in sequential order. Dynamic change, case handling and mainly worklets are employed for increasing workflow flexibility in design and run time and consequently security models are applied in each step of the careflow system.

Section 3
Certification and Evaluation of Security

This chapter provides an overview of information security management standards in the context of health care information systems and focuses on the most widely accepted ISO/IEC 27000 family of standards for information security management. The chapter is a guide for developing a complete and robust information security management system for a health care organization, which mentions special implications that are met in a health care organization, as well as special considerations related to health related web applications. The guide is based on special requirements set by ISO/IEC 27799:2008.

The chapter capitalizes on the quality and reliability issues of web information systems in healthcare. It presents how a wrong security policy decreases the reliability of the system and consequently deteriorates its overall quality and suggests several statistical models for evaluating the reliability of software. The modelling and study of the reliability of an EHR, especially when it is based on a service-oriented architecture, is performed with statistical models and measures called web metrics which assess the performance of health related applications and alert when reliability reaches critical levels.

Section 4
Trust in Healthcare Networks (and Communities)

This chapter focuses in e-health networks and privacy protection. Since e-health networks can improve the efficiency and quality of care, they set a major requirement for security, privacy and trust management in a systematic manner. The chapter suggests Federated Identity Management and a single sign on framework in order to control access to patient data, as well as an auditing and reporting mechanism in order to validate and ensure compliance to security policies.

Chapter 9

Charalampos Doukas, University of the Aegean, Greece
Ilias Maglogiannis, University of Central Greece, Greece
Aristotle Chatziioannou, National Hellenic Research Foundation, Greece

The chapter discusses certification and security issues in biomedical grid portals and presents the security infrastructure of GRISSOM (Grids for In Silico Systems biology and Medicine) platform. GRISSOM consists of a web-based portal and a Web Service that enables statistical data analysis over a grid infrastructure. The chapter presents the security infrastructure that manages user authentication and access issues and offers data encryption, Grid secure access and Web Service Security.

Chapter 10

Anastasius Moumtzoglou, P&A Kyriakou Children's Hospital, Greece

The chapter examines security of health related web applications under the collaborative prism of Medicine 2.0 and Health 2.0. The virtual interactions between patients and health professionals raise concerns about disintermediation and magnify the need for privacy and information security. The chapter considers the key debates that occur in the literature with respect to the terms Medicine 2.0 and Health 2.0 and examines all potential solutions to security and privacy issues from a patient-centered aspect.

Section 5
Security in Wireless and Mobile Healthcare Applications

Chapter 11

Konstantinos Siassiakos, University of Piraeus, Greece
Athina Lazakidou, University of Peloponnese, Greece

This chapter studies the issues of collecting and transferring patient information using mobile devices. The study refers to TETRA networks and examines how simply a healthcare professional can collect physiological data from mobile and/or remote patients and how securely and reliably health information can be transferred from emergency places to hospitals. The chapter gives an overview of the TETRA technology and analyses the characteristics of TETRA calls.

Section 6
Legal Aspects of Security in Healthcare

Chapter 12

Eleni Tzoulia, LL.M. Heidelberg, Germany

The aim of this chapter is to examine several issues of online advertising in relation to medicinal products and health related services. The chapter clearly shows that the marketing of medicinal products over the internet puts consumers at a number of risks related to both their privacy and their health and studies whether the existing EU legislation can efficiently protect the individual, who may be induced to disclose his/her health related information.

Section 7
Case Studies: How Healthcare Professionals and Students Perceive Security

Chapter 13

Ana Ferreira, Cintesis, Portugal & University of Kent, UK
Ricardo Correia , Cintesis, Portugal
David W. Chadwick, University of Kent, UK
Henrique Santos, University of Minho, Portugal
Rui Gomes, Hospital Prof. Doutor Fernando Fonseca, Portugal
Diogo Reis, Hospital S. Sebastião, Portugal
Luis Antunes, Instituto de Telecomunicações, Portugal

In this chapter authors present a cross sectional case study of how healthcare professionals actually deal with password authentication in typical real world scenarios. The chapter compares the professionals' actual practice with what they feel about password sharing and what are the most frequent problems associated with it and suggests how to solve or minimize some of these problems by using both technological and social cultural mechanisms.

Chapter 14

Stelios Daskalakis, National and Kapodistrian University of Athens, Greece
Maria Katharaki, National and Kapodistrian University of Athens, Greece
Joseph Liaskos, National and Kapodistrian University of Athens, Greece
John Mantas, National and Kapodistrian University of Athens, Greece

The chapter presents a case study on behavioral factors toward the applicability of security measures and practices in healthcare applications and investigates human attitudes in regards to security consciousness and familiarity. The study empirically assesses the intention of undergraduate nursing students to apply security concepts and practices and concludes that the perceived benefits, the general security orientation and self-efficacy of nursing students in applying security concepts and practices is more significant than a series of other constructs.

Foreword

Over the last few years, the immense need to develop and organize new ways for providing accessible, responsive, timely, effective, safe, qualitative and efficient health care, has fortunately been accompanied by significant advances in the field of information and communication technology. The application of these advances in most areas of health care delivery had truly dramatic and revolutionary effects. In fact there are major progresses in the health care sector over the past years, but the realm of health information technology is unique.

Specifically, health care information and communication technology is indispensable for overcoming fragmented systems and services and for achieving cost savings, as well as productivity and efficiency gains in the organization and funding of health care. In addition, it ensures the timely and accurate collection, exchange and availability of data, which are critical for the provision of safe, qualitative and effective care. Furthermore, it facilitates online access to clinical guidelines and drug databases, provides health care practitioners with evidence-based clinical information at the point of care and facilitates their interaction with patients and other stakeholders. On the other hand, it also gives patients the ability to obtain information to better manage their condition and to communicate with the health system, a fact that could also improve the efficiency and quality of care.

Technology has recently made it possible to exchange health data over the internet or thought web and wireless systems and applications, a technical evolution which raises significant challenges with regards to the credibility, accountability, safety, confidentiality, integrity, availability and privacy of services, information and resources. In this light, a main challenge relates to the fact that the sector struggles with inconsistent medical terminology, clinical records and data storage, as well as a multiplicity of schemes introduced to facilitate interconnection and communication between specific information systems. This fragmentation and the rapidly evolving nature of technological solutions, in the absence of agreed industry-wide standards, expose providers investing in technological infrastructure to high risks of failure and poor returns. The interoperability of the systems is dependent upon adopting common standards and achieving compliance with them.

Moreover, another significant challenge relates to enabling robust and reliable privacy and security frameworks. Specifically, because of the sensitivity of health information and the generalized uncertainty on how existing legal frameworks apply to health information technology systems, privacy concerns constitute one of the most difficult barriers in the wider implementation of information technology. Health information can be extremely sensitive, while professional ethics in health care demands a strict adherence to strict confidentiality and legal rules. Hence, there appears to be a generalized need for clear and enforceable systems and rules on these sensitive issues.

In light of the above mentioned, the present book represents a significant contribution in the field, which provides relevant and newest theoretical frameworks and references to the most recent empirical research findings in this area. In particular, it deals with the issue of access control and secure exchange of health information over the internet through web healthcare and related information systems. It attempts to deal with issues relating to certification and security procedures, to identify open threats and emerging needs and to provide solutions to the various challenges. Indeed, it constitutes a valuable tool for every professional intending to develop or support a health related application over the internet or participate in such an application. As such a tool, this book will increase the interaction between health care, health administration and health information technology professionals and all other interested parties.

Nikos Maniadakis
National School of Public Health, Greece

Nikos Maniadakis *is Chair at the Department of Health Services Management at the National School of Public Health in Greece and Director of the corresponding MSc programme. He holds a BSc in Economics from the University of Athens, an MSc in Health Economics from the University of York and a PhD in Business Studies from Warwick Business School. He was Research Fellow at Oxford and Warwick University and Senior Manager at the pharmaceutical companies Pharmacia and Eli Lilly. He also served as a CEO and President of the University Hospitals of Patras and Heraklion in Greece. He has been advisor to many private, governmental and European organisations and is member of several professional societies and referee to prominent journals in health services research. He is co-author to several articles in peer reviewed journals, has presented to a number of international conferences and lectures health care management in several international schools.*

Foreword

The healthcare sector is an indicative example of an application area that can benefit a lot from the development of a Web-based infrastructure. E-health networks enable integrated healthcare services in the form of electronic health records accessible via Internet technology. During the last years, with the adoption of Electronic Health Records, a steadily increasing number of health-related Web applications have been made available to providers, practitioners, researchers and patients. While this development offers important benefits, there are security and privacy concerns integral to the process of electronic healthcare delivery. Ensuring secure access to Electronic Healthcare Records and protecting the privacy of patient information are two issues of paramount importance when it comes to the design of health related web applications. Efficiency and effectiveness of information security policy is crucial, especially when dealing with applications that may affect patients' rights and interests. One of the biggest challenges in implementing e-health concepts is convincing the individuals sharing their electronic health records that their data will be safe and secure. This book discusses theoretical issues as well as empirical findings and case studies in health related web applications. Divided into seven parts including fourteen chapters, this volume addresses the most aspects of this area.

The first section (chapters 1-2) deals with access control: The authors of Chapter 1 present an approach based on attribute-based encryption to protect the confidentiality of patients' information during the exchange of electronic health records among healthcare providers. In Chapter 2 the authors review possible threats and vulnerabilities and present a hierarchical access control model that, from a security policy perspective, refers to data ownership and access control issues.

Section 2 (chapters 3-5) refers to the goal of increasing the flexibility of access control mechanisms. In Chapter 3 a context-aware authorization model is presented, which ensures provision of tight, just-in-time access according to the current context. The main contribution of Chapter 4 consists in the proposed privacy protection architecture called PRIMA aiming at reconciling security and privacy policies with the actual healthcare workflow, while the purpose of Chapter 5 is to present an interplay of flexibility and multi-level security, perceived as important structural and behavioral features of robust intelligence in careflow systems.

The third section (chapters 6-7) deals with evaluation and certification of security measures. With focus on ISO/IEC 27000:2009, Chapter 6 offers an overview of information security management standards in the context of healthcare information systems and provides a guide to develop a complete and robust information security management system for healthcare organizations. Chapter 7 focuses on reliability features of Electronic Health Records and emphasizes the need to develop a Web security vulnerabilities framework reflecting the service deployment environment.

Section 4 (chapters 8-10) is about the issue of trust in healthcare networks and communities. Chapter 8 highlights the necessity to address issues around security, privacy and trust in a systematic manner and tackle legal, business and technical issues that arise when providing electronic healthcare services. Chapter 9 deals with certification and security issues in biomedical grid portals and presents the security infrastructure of GRISSOM (Grids for In Silico Systems biology and Medicine) platform. Chapter 10 discusses the key debates with respect to Medicine 2.0 and Health 2.0 and possible privacy concerns about disintermediation between patients and health professionals and over reliance on virtual interactions.

The issue of security in wireless and mobile healthcare applications is dealt with in Section 5. Chapter 11 studies the issues of secure collection and transfer of physiological data from mobile or remote patients through a TETRA network.

Section 6 (chapter 12) deals with legal aspects of security. It discusses the issues of online advertising of health related products and services and stresses the risks for the privacy and safety of consumers, while presenting the EU legal framework.

The last section (Section 7 – chapters 13 and 14) refers to the perception of security by healthcare professionals. Password sharing is a common practice in the health sector which simultaneously constitutes a crucial security problem when providing electronic healthcare services. Chapter 13 suggests some solutions to the problem of password authentication using both technological and social cultural mechanisms. By empirically assessing the intention of and the attitude of nursing students in relation to security practices, Chapter 14 highlights the significant effects of perceived benefits, general security orientation and self-efficacy to behavioral intention of nursing students in applying security concepts and practices.

This volume deals with one of the most crucial issues in the area of e-health. Adopting a holistic approach this book attempts to close the gap between theory and praxis, between a pure technological approach and other aspects of security in web-based health related applications. The authors provide relevant theoretical frameworks and the latest empirical research findings. In this perspective this volume achieves its aim and increases interaction between members of the medical community, researchers, IT professionals and all other interested parties, such as patient organisations etc. The readers will be stimulated in their own research in the field of security in Electronic Health Records and the relevant web-based applications. It is also a highly educational text for anybody who wants to understand this area. Covering many security and certification issues and discussing case studies, this volume is a valuable reference book for security in web based health related applications.

Lilian Mitrou
University of the Aegean, Greece

Lilian Mitrou *is Assistant Professor at the University of the Aegean-Greece (Department of Information and Communication Systems Engineering) and Visiting Professor at the Athens University of Economics (Postgraduate Studies Program). She teaches information law and data protection law. She has served as a Member of the Hellenic Data Protection Authority (1999-2003) and as an Advisor to the former Prime Minister K. Simitis in sectors of Information Society and Public Administration (1996 - 2004). From 1998 till 2004 she was the national representative in the EC- Committee on the Protection of Individuals with regard to the Processing of Personal Data. She served as member of many Committees working on law proposals in the fields of privacy and data protection, communications law, e-government etc. Her professional experience includes senior consulting and researcher positions in a number of private and public institutions on national and international level. Her research interests include: Privacy and Data Protection; e-Democracy and eGovernment services; Internet Law. L. Mitrou published books and chapters in books (in Greek, German and English) and many journal and conference papers.*

Preface

CERTIFICATION AND SECURITY IN HEALTHCARE

Advances in telecommunications and informatics have provided humanity with the opportunity to provide advanced services to people world-wide. One of the areas that have most benefited from information technology is the health sector. Health-related web applications have provided advanced services, such as telemedicine, to patients and doctors. However, these applications have brought along several responsibilities: to record, process and store medical information by following standard and lawful procedures, to protect medical data from unauthorized access, to ensure continuity and constant availability of healthcare services, etc.

The Web attracted more patients in this way increasing the popularity of freely available medical advice and knowledge. The abundance of web sites that offer medical content affected the way patients face their doctors, gave them a second opinion and increased their awareness. Its' successor, Web 2.0, was built on the same technologies and concepts, but also added a layer of semantic abstraction, offered a network as a platform sensation and gave a social networking aspect to healthcare and medical applications.

The web offers access to many databases that contain medical information, and has significantly changed the way patients seek medical help. According to recent surveys, 50% of patients access medical information via the internet before visiting their doctor and this information affects their choice of treatment. The assistant role of virtual communities for patients who seek for medical help and advice is undeniable. Researchers, practitioners, medical industry and patients jointly contribute their findings, products and experiences, to the community's knowledge base. The information transferred inside a health related virtual community and the stockpiled knowledge must be carefully protected from unauthorized use and validated in order to be qualitative and useful.

With the use of web-based healthcare applications, such as telemedicine, tele-healthcare, tele-homecare etc, doctors are able to provide medical services to patients in distant and isolated areas. All these applications assume that medical data, such as vital signs and a patient's medical profile, are transferred securely and reliably over the complex infrastructure of the World Wide Web. Moreover, they assume the trustfulness of the source and destination of medical data.

Till now, the most widely used service is the distribution of informative content (i.e. medical documents, surveys, medical advices, news etc.). Content should be easily located and retrieved from patients. In order to facilitate new users, content can be forwarded to patients via appropriate services. However, information dissemination inside a medical community needs to be secured and certified. For example, dissemination via mailing lists requires security measures to be taken, in order to ensure the safe transfer of medical data, while medical rss feeds require validation and certification concerning their sources. In the former case (website transmission) cryptographic protocols, such as SSL (Secure Socket Layer), can be used by a member to communicate with the community site, whereas in the latter case a respectful healthcare association is required to certify the feed sources.

In the case of telemedicine systems, for example, a patient's medical profile and other medical information are transferred over the network from the examination lab to the doctor's office in order for the doctor to be able to perform a diagnosis. According to the CIA model (confidentiality, integrity and availability), the medical information transferred across the network should be encrypted, secured and protected until it reaches its final destination. Patients' medical profiles should be accessible by their doctors in order to support diagnosis and care, but must be invisible to other patients, medical companies or individuals who don't have the appropriate privileges. Moreover, medical data should be preserved for future use and must always be available, although protected from unauthorized alterations. The use of standards in the whole process of collecting, transferring, storing and managing sensitive medical data is a requirement and should be accompanied by auxiliary auditing and monitoring services in order to build a trust model between patients and doctors.

Security in Health-Related Web Applications has many aspects such as: a) authentication, which guarantees that medical data and consultation are genuine, b) authorization, which assures that medical data are accessed by appropriate right holders, thus reinforcing trust between the partners of a medical transaction, c) non-repudiation, which guarantees that both trustees will fulfill their obligations to a contract and will acknowledge all conducted transactions, thus gradually enhancing the bonds between partners, d) risk management which refers to the ongoing iterative process of assessing web based applications for vulnerabilities, reinforcing them against threats and implementing appropriate security controls.

Certification is an addition to traditional aspects of security and is a means of guaranteeing that medical data are exchanged and processed appropriately. It requires auditing and ensures appropriateness of the medical process in terms of information security and compliance to suitable standards and regulations (ISO/IEC 27000 series, HIPAA directions and data protection laws).

Methodologically, taking security measures may maintain integrity, ensure availability and protect confidentiality however it does not guarantee the "ultimate" level of computer security. In the case of transferring medical data across complex computer networks, it might not suffice to secure the exchanging endpoints. Throughout its lifecycle, medical data is vulnerable to unauthorized access, alteration or manipulation, which without any security checks or presence of auditing procedures can easily go undetected, and weaken its reliability. In a secure lifecycle, medical data is managed and protected so that it remains authentic, reliable and useable, while retaining its integrity. These attributes of medical data can be preserved by implementing an effective Information Security Management System (ISMS) for Medical Information that ensures all three aspects of the aforementioned CIA model by implementing policies and procedures, allocating human and machine resources for all physical, personal and organizational aspects. Implementing an ISMS is not just putting measures in place, it means also auditing the system, evaluating its effectiveness and correcting it based on any identified security vulnerabilities or pitfalls, whether a security problem is caused from a human mistake or a manufacturer error.

Certification in web applications springs from the need to verify the accurate, impervious and protected exchange of data across the web. The persons accessing medical data, as well as the exchanging parties during transfers of medical data need to be accurately identified. Certifying these issues means that an auditing body can track down responsibilities and identify the culprit responsible for any breach of security, in any of the following areas: confidentiality, integrity, availability, authorization, non-repudiation.

These issues are of extreme importance when applied to medical virtual communities and the assistant role they provide to patients who seek for medical help and advice. In such communities it is important that the information transferred inside the community and the stockpiled knowledge is carefully protected from unauthorized access or use and validated in order to be qualitative and useful.

Summarizing all the above issues, any health-related web application (tele-medicine, tele-healthcare, tele-consultation etc.) must be examined under the prism of certification, security and confidentiality, but also fulfill authentication and non-repudiation requirements, thus providing a holistic approach in building trust within a networked web of medical information and tele-services. Developers of web based medical applications should also consider how certification applies in their applications. In the following section we depict the critical issues on building, maintaining, securing and certifying health related applications and summarize the available solutions.

SECURITY RISKS AND COMPLIANCE TO STANDARDS

As telemedicine applications evolve, the amount of sensitive information that travels through the World Wide Web increases and subsequently more strict security measures need to be taken in order to protect this information from unauthorized access. The measures can vary from simple password encryption policies to advanced cryptographic methods such as elliptic curves. For example a medical web community can employ Virtual Private Network technology as an access control measure for its users. A Virtual Private Network (VPN) is a private data network that makes use of the public telecommunication infrastructure, maintaining privacy through the use of a tunneling protocol and security procedures. Since the users of the health community connect to the application via an encrypted tunnel, any conducted communication is private and therefore secure. However, this is not always sufficient to build trust between the users of the community, thus certification is another step forward.

The ISO/IEC 27000 series of standards intends to cover all the different levels and aspects of security, such as auditing of the data transfer process, assessment of information security risks, implementation of information security controls and continuous monitoring, maintenance and improvement of information security. Data protection authorities can associate the level of provided protection with the applied security measures and certify whether an organization is providing adequate level of protection for medical data. It needs to be examined whether an authoritative party, such as a national health association, the world health organization or the EU, is providing specific guidelines for taking appropriate security measures for medical data and achieving an adequate level of protection.

An integral part of the ISO/IEC 27000 series in regards to health information systems, is the ISO/IEC 27799:2008 standard, which defines guidelines to support the interpretation and implementation of ISO/IEC 27002:2005 in health informatics. It specifies a set of detailed controls for managing health information security and provides health information security best practice guidelines. Healthcare organizations that comply with this standard ensure a minimum level of security and maintain confidentiality, integrity and availability of personal health information. Although the development of a security management system, which follows the ISO 27799:2008 directives, is a complicated task it is the first step in providing secure and trustful web based healthcare applications. Defining a clear and concise ISMS policy, which leads to the implementation of information security policies, is the real source pool for hardening the strength of a security management system. These policies can be systemic (e.g. access control policy), data (e.g. privacy policy) or human related (rules of conduct).

The Health Insurance Portability and Accountability Act of 1996 is an attempt to use federal law in order to protect the privacy of medical records. The implementation of the HIPAA privacy regulations proved to be costly, inconsistent, and frustrating to both physicians and patients. Moreover, healthcare applications on the web usually cross national borders and as such, they face several legal issues, such as licensing, accreditation, concerns of identity theft and dependency, which are difficult to be properly addressed by legislative entities.

The opt-out policy adopted by the U.S. Government defines that companies cannot collect consumer's data if the consumer asks for it. Concerning medical information, U.S. laws assume total confidentiality in several issues (i.e. abortions, contraception or psychological diseases) but delegate decisions to the state laws in others. European Union has adopted an opt-in model for all personal data, which assumes that all personal information is classified until their owner grants access on them. According to the EC directive for medical data protection (95/46/EC), only health professionals can access medical information and are responsible for protecting confidentiality. According to the Recommendation (97) 5, medical data can be collected without user consent, only for preventing a real danger or in the case of a criminal offence. Moreover, if the law provides for this, data may be collected and processed in order to preserve vital interests of the data subject, or of a third person. In the case of genetic data this includes the members of the data subject's genetic line.

TARGET AUDIENCE

Students of management of healthcare systems and healthcare managers in general will use this book as a companion that helps them avoid design pitfalls and provides a walkthrough towards building trustful healthcare applications. More specifically, managers will understand what is critical and what is not, always in terms of security, and will be facilitated when taking strategic decisions that concern the Health Information Systems.

Medical professionals will use the book as a reference, a gateway which can lead to potential solutions for issues, which just lurk in the background. More specifically, they will learn how to protect their patients and themselves, from loss or theft of information and they will better understand the needs of the medical community. Furthermore, they will be able to identify the need for a security oriented mentality which will prohibit them away from dwelling into security pitfalls with even legal consequences.

Members of the pharmaceutical profession will identify the value of security when using health web applications and learn the pitfalls that lurk in the World Wide Web when not being able to identify the requestor of medical information or the providing hand of pharmaceutical products by means of internet pharmacies.

Security professionals working in medical institutions will be able to identify the specific requirements of the medical community, learn how medical practitioners perceive security and thus implement the proper measures to achieve an adequate level of security for medical data.

Security auditors, who aim to audit healthcare organizations, can identify by reading this book the security problems of health information systems in general and health web applications in particular, in order to build a concrete methodology in their line of work in regards to medical applications.

Computer science and medical students will get informed on the new advances in security, certification and building of trust in a healthcare community.

This book aims to bridge the two worlds of healthcare and information technology, to increase the security awareness of professionals, students and users from both worlds and to highlight the recent advances in certification and security in health related web applications.

THE CHAPTERS

The book includes fourteen chapters that cover many different aspects of security and certification in health related web applications, ranging from the legal and ethical issues that concern the use and dissemination of medical data to different flexible data access control models and to the difficult task of increasing security awareness of users.

In the first chapter, entitled *Secure Exchange of Electronic Health Records*, the authors examine the traditional approaches in data access control, such as Mandatory Access Control, Discretionary Access control and Role-Based Access Control in terms of a shared care environment, where many medical professionals cooperate and exchange patient information. After a comparison of access control policies, the authors conclude that a shared care environment must define which information is collected, stored and accessed and suggest a flexible access control mechanism that protects privacy of patients and guarantees authorized access to stored data. The attribute-based encryption model allows the encryption of different sections of an electronic health record, which can be decrypted only by the owners of the proper key. Patients grant access to their doctors, who consequently are able to delegate access to collaborating physicians.

In the second chapter, entitled *Modeling Access Control in Healthcare Organizations*, the authors examine the security of hospital applications. They first explore issues in managing access control and security of healthcare information and review the possible threats and vulnerabilities for a hospital security plan, such as hardware or software failure, weak passwords and password stealing, misuse and abuse of the hospital information system etc. The paper introduces a hierarchical access model, which covers data ownership and access control issues and discusses the security issues that arise.

In chapter three, *A Context-Aware Authorization Model for Process-Oriented Personal Health Record Systems*, authors assume a process-oriented approach in Patient Health Records management and present a security framework that addresses several authorization and access control issues. The proposed framework capitalizes on tight and just-in-time authorization in order to guarantee that only authorized users get access to patient data and only for performing a specific task. A set of permissions, which is continuously adjusted in order to adapt to the changing context, reduces the risk of compromising information integrity during task execution.

The fourth chapter, entitled *Improving Security Policy Coverage in Healthcare*, presents a privacy protection architecture called PRIMA, which attempts to increase the usability of healthcare applications without compromising the security of patient information. The components of the PRIMA architecture guarantee policy definition, auditing of actions and restrictions throughout the clinical process and refinement of the original policies per case. As a result, the security policies and exceptions are more precise and realistic and fit to the clinical workflow instead of impeding it, thus enabling improved privacy protection for the patient and increased usability of the clinical workflow.

The fifth chapter, entitled *Flexibility and Security of Careflow Systems Modeled by Petri Nets*, deals with design and analysis of healthcare workflow systems and provides a solution that improves their structural and behavioral flexibility. Giving emphasis on flexibility, without neglecting security, security in careflow systems is conceptually modeled using Petri nets and colored Petri nets. In this model, security and flexibility are covered separately and incrementally in sequential order. Dynamic change, case handling and mainly worklets are employed for increasing workflow flexibility in design and run time and consequently security models are applied in each step of the careflow system.

Chapter six, *Information Security Standards for Health Information Systems: The Implementer's Approach*, provides an overview of information security management standards in the context of health care information systems and focuses on the most widely accepted ISO/IEC 27000 family of standards for information security management. The chapter is a guide for developing a complete and robust information security management system for a health care organization, which mentions special implications that are met in a health care organization, as well as special considerations related to health related web applications. The guide is based on special requirements set by ISO/IEC 27799:2008.

Chapter seven, *Statistical Models for EHR Security in Web Healthcare Information Systems*, capitalizes on the quality and reliability issues of web information systems in healthcare. It presents how a wrong security policy decreases the reliability of the system and consequently deteriorates its overall quality and suggests several statistical models for evaluating the reliability of software. The modelling and study of the reliability of an EHR, especially when it is based on a service-oriented architecture, is performed with statistical models and measures called web metrics which assess the performance of health related applications and alert when reliability reaches critical levels.

Chapter eight, entitled *Identity Management and Audit Trail Support for Privacy Protection in E-Health Networks*, focuses in e-health networks and privacy protection. Since e-health networks can improve the efficiency and quality of care, they set a major requirement for security, privacy and trust management in a systematic manner. The chapter suggests Federated Identity Management and a single sign on framework in order to control access to patient data, as well as an auditing and reporting mechanism in order to validate and ensure compliance to security policies.

The ninth chapter, which is entitled *Certification and Security Issues in Biomedical Grid Portals: The GRISSOM Case Study*, discusses certification and security issues in biomedical grid portals and presents the security infrastructure of GRISSOM (Grids for In Silico Systems biology and Medicine) platform. GRISSOM consists of a web-based portal and a Web Service that enables statistical data analysis over a grid infrastructure. The chapter presents the security infrastructure that manages user authentication and access issues and offers data encryption, Grid secure access and Web Service Security.

Chapter ten, *Health 2.0 and Medicine 2.0: Safety, Ownership and Privacy Issues*, examines security of health related web applications under the collaborative prism of Medicine 2.0 and Health 2.0. The virtual interactions between patients and health professionals raise concerns about disintermediation and magnify the need for privacy and information security. The chapter considers the key debates that occur in the literature with respect to the terms Medicine 2.0 and Health 2.0 and examines all potential solutions to security and privacy issues from a patient-centered aspect.

The eleventh chapter, entitled *Securing and Prioritizing Health Information in TETRA Networks*, studies the issues of collecting and transferring patient information using mobile devices. The study refers to TETRA networks and examines how simply a healthcare professional can collect physiological data from mobile and/or remote patients and how securely and reliably health information can be transferred from emergency places to hospitals. The chapter gives an overview of the TETRA technology and analyses the characteristics of TETRA calls.

Chapter twelve, *Online Advertising in Relation to Medicinal Products and Health Related Services: Data & Consumer Protection Issues*, examines several issues of online advertising in relation to medicinal products and health related services. The chapter clearly shows that the marketing of medicinal products over the internet puts consumers at a number of risks related to both their privacy and their health and studies whether the existing EU legislation can efficiently protect the individual, who may be induced to disclose his/her health related information.

In chapter thirteen, *Password Sharing and How to Reduce It*, authors present a cross sectional case study of how healthcare professionals actually deal with password authentication in typical real world scenarios. The chapter compares the professionals' actual practice with what they feel about password sharing and what are the most frequent problems associated with it and suggests how to solve or minimize some of these problems by using both technological and social cultural mechanisms.

Finally, chapter fourteen, *Behavioral Security: Investigating the Attitude of Nursing Students Toward Security Concepts and Practices*, presents a case study on behavioral factors toward the applicability of security measures and practices in healthcare applications and investigates human attitudes in regards to security consciousness and familiarity. The study empirically assesses the intention of undergraduate nursing students to apply security concepts and practices and concludes that the perceived benefits, the general security orientation and self-efficacy of nursing students in applying security concepts and practices is more significant than a series of other constructs.

CONCLUSION

The main aim of this book is to enlighten the path for building secure and trustful healthcare applications for the web, which is expected to serve patients' and practitioners' aims. This holistic approach comprises several actions, such as:

- To alert patients and practitioners in regards to security issues, and more specifically,
- To raise the level of security awareness of: a) IT professionals, who develop, maintain or contribute to health related communities, b) patients that reveal their privacy to a doctor over the web and make use of medical advices shared by other patients, c) medical professionals that use web based applications and may not understand the special issues that arise when accessing medical data across huge and potentially unsecured computer networks, d) pharmacists that use the World Wide Web to acquire medical information or pharmaceutical products or to supply pharmaceutical services of their own by means of internet pharmacies,
- To propose a set of technologies, which can under circumstances ensure that patients and medical professionals benefit from using community services while minimizing the risk of phishers, spammers, hackers and crackers exploiting potential security holes,
- To form a methodology for certifying the validity of exchangeable medical data, exchanging parties and the exchange process.
- To review the certification and security procedures through collaboration, to identify open threats and emerging needs and to provide solutions.
- To cover as many security and certification issues as possible and provide practical solutions and case study applications.
- To identify the need for frequently revisable security plans and periodical risk assessments in order to update the overall security of health information systems.

This holistic solution can be summarized to a flexible security management system, which complies with standards, takes into account all the restrictions imposed by law and continuously evolves and strengthens against potential risks. The gains from a certified security management solution are multifold both for patients and medical professionals: (1) the availability of healthcare information is valuable for the effective operation of healthcare organizations, (2) the protection of the personal and healthcare information, promotes the trust among patients and the healthcare professionals, (3) minimizing risk from the medical law point of view protects healthcare enterprises and organizations from legal sanctions – penalties and reduces negotiation overhead between the healthcare organization and the patient.

This book provides a novel aspect of security of medical applications, which covers both security and certification. It touches several legal and ethical issues that relate to the use of health information and introduces a new perspective on the security of healthcare information systems which relates to the acceptance of security policies and technologies by the medical community members. It is an excellent source of comprehensive knowledge and literature on the topic of certification and security in e-health applications and we hope that readers will find it useful when endeavoring in their line of work.

Anargyros Chryssanthou
Hellenic Data Protection Authority, Greece

Ioannis Apostolakis
National School of Public Health, Greece

Iraklis Varlamis
Harokopio University of Athens, Greece

Acknowledgment

First of all, we would like to thank the Editorial Board Members, authors, readers, and reviewers for their great help and support in this book and we look forward to collaborate again in future projects. Special thanks go to Dr. Anastasia Kastania and Dr. Athina Lazakidou for their useful advices concerning the preparation of this book.

Finally, we would like to thank IGI Global for giving us the opportunity to publish this work and for supporting us throughout the whole process.

Anargyros Chryssanthou
Hellenic Data Protection Authority, Greece

Ioannis Apostolakis
National School of Public Health, Greece

Iraklis Varlamis
Harokopio University of Athens, Greece

Section 1
Access Control

Chapter 1
Secure Exchange of Electronic Health Records

Alejandro Enrique Flores
University of Wollongong, Australia

Khin Than Win
University of Wollongong, Australia

Willy Susilo
University of Wollongong, Australia

ABSTRACT

Protecting the confidentiality of a patient's information in a shared care environment could become a complex task. Correct identification of users, assigning of access permissions, and resolution of conflict rise as main points of interest in providing solutions for data exchange among health care providers. Traditional approaches such as Mandatory Access Control, Discretionary Access control and Role-Based Access Control policies do not always provide a suitable solution for health care settings, especially for shared care environments. The core of this contribution consists in the description of an approach which uses attribute-based encryption to protect the confidentiality of patients' information during the exchange of electronic health records among healthcare providers. Attribute-based encryption allows the reinforcing of access policies and reduces the risk of unauthorized access to sensitive information; it also provides a set of functionalities which are described using a case study. Attribute-based encryption provides an answer to restrictions presented by traditional approaches and facilitate the reinforcing of existing security policies over the transmitted data.

INTRODUCTION

In a shared care paradigm, remote access to distant data repositories along with the exchange of relevant electronic health records (EHRs) becomes essential for providing integral health care

services. Internet is the natural platform to support such functionalities. However, the insecure nature of the network and the increased amount of health information transmitted through it raise the concern over the secure exchange of EHRs (Ohno-Machadoa, Silveira, & Vinterbo, 2004). In fact, the disclosure, transmission and use of a patient's data for delivering health care services

DOI: 10.4018/978-1-61692-895-7.ch001

are an expanding practice that concerns the interest of health institutions, physicians and patients. In a dynamic and demanding environment, such as health care, a patient's confidentiality can only be guaranteed by incorporating security services and mechanisms along with common security policies and/or conflict resolution policies to protect the data at any given point (Lopez & Blobel, 2009). Additionally, EHR systems not only should assure the protection of patients' privacy and confidentiality but also guarantee the reliability and integrity of the information gathered by health care professionals (Conrick & Newell, 2006). Therefore, it is essential that health information systems consider the privacy and integrity of the data and also allow the safe retrieval of information for primary and secondary uses, especially in an interconnected health information scenario (Lusignan, Chan, Theadom, & Dhoul, 2007).

In this context, projects centered in the interconnection of health information systems, such as national health information initiatives or multi-domain EHR systems, not only confront information and functional requirements, such as the development and implementation of standardized communication protocols, standardized vocabulary and homogeneous development frameworks, but also privacy and security requirements. Protection of a patient's privacy and the secure disclosure of health information are crucial functionalities that should be embedded within the specifications of modern and reliable electronic health record systems (Conrick & Newell, 2006; Ohno-Machadoa, et al., 2004; Safran, et al., 2007). Moreover, to guarantee the secure transmission and release of health information in a shared care paradigm, the protection of a patient's privacy has to be conceived as an issue which combines the secure transmission of data, correct user authentication, access control and security policies, either at the point of origin or at the destination of the communication channel.

During the exchange of EHRs, even when the transmission has been between trusted parties,

access permission can be violated under specific circumstances. Consider a scenario in which health care institutions A and B are trusted parties during the exchange of information. Using public key technologies both institutions can transmit information using a secure channel. The secure channel guarantees confidentiality and integrity of the transmitted information. However, the existence of different access policies may lead to a violation of access permissions either at the point of origin or when the information reaches its destination. Blobel et al. have suggested the definition of common domain policies to address differences or conflicts rising from disparities in the definition of security and access policies existing among health care organizations (Blobel, Nordberg, Davis, & Pharow, 2006). However, implementing this approach requires the existence of standardized vocabularies and common policy structures, which is limited in the actual health information infrastructure. There is also a virtual agreement that for communication of medical information and posterior access to the data, access policies based on role-based access control models may facilitate the overcoming of possible violation of access permission (Blobel, et al., 2006; Gritzalis & Lambrinoudakis, 2004). However, role-based access control models also present issues that may increase the risk of unauthorized access to sensitive medical data (Alhaqbani & Fidge, 2008).

This chapter aims to address the issues of secure transmission of data, access control and user privileges and propose a specification for an information exchange model that allows a secure and safe approach for the exchange and release of EHRs in a shared care scenario. Assuming that transmission of medical information is maintained over insecure channels, we propose a policy reinforcement model based on attribute-based encryptions and incorporate security mechanisms in order to protect patients' privacy during the exchange and release of the information.

BACKGROUND

An electronic health record should not only be considered as a replacement for paper-based medical records but also as means to facilitate the quicker/easier access to relevant health information. EHRs also facilitate the implementation of information architectures to provide support to shared care environments, where communication between the staff involved in imparting care to a patient as well as remote access to data repositories are essential activities. In general, the historical information maintained within the health repositories can also be used as a supporting knowledge base for continuing treatment of the patient, a base of information for further treatment of the same patient, and as base-knowledge for advanced research and medical education.

Security and Privacy of Patients' EHRs

The nature of a medical record can be described as information provided by a uniquely vulnerable human being, worried in some manner about the core of his/her very existence, to a trusted person with superior knowledge (Eddy, 2000). In fact, modern electronic health records contain extremely personal and sensitive information regarding not only health history but also the dietary habits, sexual orientation, sexual activities, employment status, income, eligibility for public assistance and family history of a patient (Choi, Capitan, Krause, & Streeper, 2006). Therefore, sharing EHRs raises concerns over the legal and ethical implications associated to the unauthorized access and release of personal information, and the effects that this may cause to the patient (Anderson, 2007; Conrick & Newell, 2006). Patients understand the importance of retaining medical information to support and improve the delivery of health care even when they recognize both the sensitive nature of the collected data and the fact that information contended by computerized

health information system becomes more accessible to health professionals, administrative and medical staff, and third parties (Conrick & Newell, 2006). Patients expect secure health information systems in which personal data is protected and any disclosed information would be used only for health care purposes (Grain, 2006).

Safe access and exchange of electronic health information requires not only the secure transmission of data but also to ensure that information will be disclosed only to those with the correct access privileges. This implies that protection of patients' privacy needs to be conserved at the source point, when it is transmitted and when it reaches the destination point. In order to protect sensitive medical data, the principles of "need to know" and relevance apply. Under this premise users should be allowed to access a patient's EHR in order to obtain the relevant information to carry out a task in concordance with the access and security policies of the organization in which the patient has been treated (Blobel, 2004; Garson & Adams, 2008). The principle of need-to-know is driven by the relevance that the accessed information has in the support of the patient care. However, relevancy is an ambiguous concept that depends on the context in which the information is generated and the purposes for which the data has been released. Consequently, the information accessed by a physician should be relevant but also sufficient to provide health care services (van der Linden, Kalra, Hasman, & Talmon, 2009).

Securing medical information is not only a social, ethical and technological matter, but is also about the establishment of well defined privacy policies and legislation. The legal duty of confidentiality is embedded in the professional relationship between physician and patient, and therefore, an essential aspect to be considered when exchanging medical records. From a perspective in which the mobility of patients as well as the exchange of information becomes more usual, the definition of means to protect the privacy and confidentiality of the patients in an efficient way becomes even more necessary. Both security services and mechanisms are essential for allowing access to authorized users as well as for protecting sensitive medical information during the exchange of data (Blobel, et al., 2006). Therefore, it is essential for health information systems to consider both the protection and privacy of patients' data but also the safe and authorized retrieval of information. At this point, it is important to consider that adding excessive security measures could lead to inefficient, more time demanding and less user friendly access control methods. Defining the correct balance between security requirement and availability of information is a critical goal in a complex environment such as health care (Lopez & Blobel, 2009).

Security and Privacy in a Shared Care Paradigm

In a shared care environment, different health care units (HCU) are involved in the care process as well as in maintaining accurate medical records. Indeed, in modern healthcare environments different care services are offered by different HCU within the organization or in a healthcare network that involves multiple organizations. This requires the communication and cooperation among all actors involved in the administration of patients' care (Choi, et al., 2006). Internet turns into a natural environment for such functionalities by allowing the exchange of EHRs and the interconnection of medical applications, thus facilitating better management of medical services as well as faster treatment of patients (Gritzalis & Lambrinoudakis, 2004).

As in paper-based health records, physicians have an ethical obligation of protecting patient information in order to prevent potential harm to an individual. Nevertheless, the nature of EHRs has transformed the duty of physician-patient confidentiality to a complex task. Despite the personal nature of health records, EHRs make patient's information potentially available to

anyone with access to a health information system (Anderson, 2007). Therefore, the responsibility of protecting patient privacy has moved from an individual/local responsibility to a duty shared among the different entities that share the information. This tendency is altering the preexisting conception of the doctor–patient confidentiality and is threatening the quality of health care (Choi, et al., 2006). These apprehensions are also shared by the public whose primary concern is security, privacy, confidentiality and protection of their personal health information (Goldschmidt, 2005; Rash, 2005).

In a shared care paradigm defining what is considered sensitive information as well as what access permissions are granted to users becomes uncertain. In fact, each participating institution of a health network would have different approaches for defining the level of sensitivity associated to the information, access rights and the level of security required to protect privacy of patients (Blobel, et al., 2006). Those approaches not only depend on legal restrictions but also are built based on the accumulated experience and the culture of organizations. Since the conception of security and protection of a patient's privacy differ from one organization to another, methods for interconnecting health information systems should include comprehensive understanding of the complexity of requirements involving the secure exchange and release of medical data. In general, an electronic health record system able to secure and protect the confidentiality of patients should not only incorporate security requirements but also guarantee the flow and availability of the information.

Implementing a shared care environment has several implications not only in how the information is managed or which technology can be used but also in the way in which information is collected, stored and accessed. The exchange of information in a shared care environment exceeds the needs of a locally integrated health information system and requires the definition of a new set of requirements. Even more, it requires a different approach to overcoming technical, legal and ethical issues that rise from exchanging highly sensitive information. In a shared care paradigm, the number of specialists that can have access to EHRs increases and the information contained by EHRs can be broken down among different health information systems within the organization or among different healthcare providers, increasing the possibility of a security breach. In general, the implementation of the share care paradigm not only requires the support of standardized information systems architectures, data exchange protocols and common vocabularies but also protecting the privacy of patients, guaranteeing authorized access to stored data and protecting the integrity of the information (Blobel, et al., 2006).

Securing the Exchange of EHRs

Secure exchange and disclosure of electronic health records over insecure channels such as internet requires the implementation of comprehensive security policies and technologies that allows the exchange of data whilst the protection of a patient's privacy is guaranteed (Choe & Yoo, 2008). These policies and technologies should provide mechanisms for access control and define access privileges for information management and protection of data privacy (Blobel, et al., 2006; Ohno-Machadoa, et al., 2004). During the electronic exchange of medical data, a patient's sensitive information always has to be protected; especially the information considered sensitive due to the legal and ethical consequences that unauthorized releases could carry. Unauthorized access and release of sensitive information are considered a breach of confidentiality and could lead to issues of public concern such as discrimination, embarrassment or economic harm (Ohno-Machadoa, et al., 2004). At this point, several issues have to be considered: (1) the origin of the information, (2) the reason for its release, (3)

secure transmission of data and (4) protection of a patient's privacy.

The origin of the information refers to who and where the data has been collected. Health information can be collected by different organizations and can serve a variety of purposes, and its storage can be local or external. Information locally stored can be promptly available and can normally be accessed by users at any time and location within the organization. On the contrary, external health data is usually retrieved from information systems that do not provide direct access rights to users. In this case, access rights are provided based on common agreements between the organizations involved (Lopez & Blobel, 2009; van der Linden, et al., 2009).

The reason for the disclosure of information is an important element in defining an efficient security strategy. Detailed and grained information is normally required to offer primary services such as the treatment of a subject of care. On the contrary, information required for secondary uses should not be linkable to the patient (Agrawal & Johnson, 2007). The destination of the information also affects the definition of a security strategy. Local security needs substantially vary from the requirement of a shared care scenario (van der Linden, et al., 2009). Locally, standard security measures and standardized messages allow the secure access and disclosure of information. However, the secure exchange and release of information among different health providers not only depends on secure and standardized electronic mechanisms but also on standardized security and access policies (Lopez & Blobel, 2009).

PROTECTING PATIENT'S PRIVACY AND CONFIDENTIALITY

Social, Ethical and Legal Perspective

The benefits of electronic health records and how the use of this technology could impact in society are still open for debate. Nonetheless, the general perception is that incorporating EHRs to medical practice provides support in the delivery of health care by facilitating access to historical medical data (Agrawal & Johnson, 2007; Anderson, 2007). EHRs provide an instrument to maintain non-fragmented and actualized health information.

The information collected in EHRs has a historical character and corresponds to the lifelong medical records of an individual. A perfect EHR would be a complete health history of the patient's encounters with health system (Berner, 2008). However, having the complete medical history raises concerns over how the confidentiality of the information would be protected. Traditionally, protecting confidentiality of information has been the responsibility of the physician and/or the institution that holds the patient's medical records. In a shared care setting, the provision of health care services becomes a multitask activity in which the interaction of multiple actors is required not only for providing health care but also in protecting the confidentiality of health records.

Under this complex scenario countries such as U.S., Canada, Japan and the member of the European Union have incorporated laws and regulations that aim to reduce fraud and abuse as well as protect patients' information (Anderson, 2007). International regulations such as that imposed by HIPAA (Health Insurance Portability and Accountability Act) and the European Data Protection Directive (Agrawal & Johnson, 2007; Lusignan, et al., 2007) demand the highest level of security and protection during accessing, processing and exchanging information that involve sensitive data of individuals. Australia also possesses a set of privacy principles that regulates the collection, use and disclosure of personal information. Additionally, Australian legislation protects and provides a legal body for people that have suffered harm as a product of unauthorized disclosure or use of private information.

Challenges of Securing Electronic Health Records

Securing electronic health records, in a scenario where information is potentially accessed by multiple actors, could become a complex and costly activity. To provide a framework for secure maintenance and release of health care information, the European Committee for Standardization has released a set of information security standards for health information systems (CEN-ENV, 2000a, 2000b, 2000c). CEN standards recognize four global security needs that any health information system should accomplish: availability, confidentiality, integrity and accountability (CEN-ENV, 2000a).

Availability of information is a key factor for functional electronic health record systems; users with the right to access information should be allowed to do so in order to perform their duties. However, to protect confidentiality of information, access to patient's data should be carried out under the principles of relevance and need-to-know (Garson & Adams, 2008). The principle of relevance prevents the information overload and protects the patient's privacy by restricting the release of information to the relevant data required to support the health care process (Berner, 2008; van der Linden, et al., 2009). In the same way, the principle of "need-to-know" guarantees that only personnel who required the information and have the access privileges will be allowed to extract the data. Defining the correct balance between availability of information and security requirement is a critical goal in a complex environment such as health care.

A security breach poses a threat for protecting the integrity of electronic health records as well as for providing reliable information for accountability purposes. Integrity of information is not only guaranteed by incorporating additional security mechanisms within the system or for securing a communication channel, when information is exchanged between systems, but also by ensuring that only authorized users can have access, add or alter stored data. In shared care environments controlling who is accessing the information turns into a complex and time demanding task. Indeed, the solo fact that existing authentication methods, such as PIN or passwords, allows unauthorized delegation of access permissions threatens the integrity and validity of the information (Heckle & Lutters, 2007; Shin, et al., 2008). Accountability of information also becomes less accurate when non-authorized users are able to access and manipulate data regardless of the fact that they do not have the privileges to execute such activities.

Analysis of Traditional Methods

In a shared care context the concepts of privacy, confidentiality, and security become essential for secure exchange of electronic health records. To provide a secure, safe and reliable environment for co-operation and communication, several security requirements need to be taken into consideration. Security may not only consider the services that will be implemented to avoid unauthorized access to sensitive information but also mechanisms that prevent unauthorized release of patient's data.

Existing authentication and access control models require safekeeping PINs, passwords or smartcards in order to provide access to restricted facilities and information. However the nature of the activities executed by physicians and medical personnel requires mobility and multiple accesses to different terminals within the organization or even remotely in the case of web based health information systems or integrated multi-domain systems (Garson & Adams, 2008; Shin, et al., 2008). Considering that access to different systems may require multiple authentication methods, it is usual to find that PINs and passwords are stored on computer terminals used by physicians or written on stick papers in the office, laboratories, medical consult or at home, or become a simple combination of well known numbers or digits such as phone extension, date of birth or pseudonyms which are

easy to remember but also relatively less efficient in avoiding security breaches (Garson & Adams, 2008; Shin, et al., 2008). The use of smartcards also may present certain disadvantages such as deterioration and accidental lost. Additionally, if physicians forget their PIN/passwords or misplace their smartcards a reissuance process must take place (Shin, et al., 2008). Consequently, existing models become inappropriate and less reliable for a medical environment.

Another issue associated to the use of traditional model are medical disputes generated by delegation of authentication codes (Chen, et al., 2008; Heckle & Lutters, 2007). Delegation of private authentication codes is generated when a member of a hospital's medical staff delegates his PIN/password or other authentication feature to other physician or nurse to access, modify or add information on behalf of the owner of the private authentication codes (Heckle & Lutters, 2007; Shin, et al., 2008). The delegation of access rights may grant access to sensitive information to a non-authorized user by breaking established policies of information privacy and confidentiality (Heckle & Lutters, 2007; Shin, et al., 2008). This also may have legal repercussions when restricted information is leaked to third parties without the proper authorization of the patient or when the addition of erroneous information compromises the safety of patients.

Traditional Access Control Models

In the following pages traditional access control models, such as discretionary access control (DAC), mandatory access control (MAC), role-based access control (RBAC), will be presented. In order to do so, a paradigm will be used (see Figure 1), where a doctor working in a particular institute needs to acquire information regarding a patient's medical history from foreign institutions in order to handle the patient's case. Figure 2 presents a graphical representation of the relation and flow of information of the actors historically involved

Figure 1. Case analysis

68 years old lady 'A' was admitted to the hospital 'HA' with abdominal pain and doctor 'DC' has been assigned to her case. The patient has indicated having a history of chronic diseases. 'A' has been previously hospitalized at hospital 'HB' for chest pain and followed up treatment with the cardiologist 'C' for Atrial Fibrillation, Hypertension and Recurrent Angina. Radiological information of the patient is also maintained in the hospital records. Additionally, she has been diagnosed with diabetes for 20 years and has been visiting clinic 'CL' for her regular medical treatment. She has checked her blood according to the doctor's order at the local pathology 'P' regularly. 'A' has also been seen by the Dietitian 'D', Ophthalmologist 'O', podiatrist 'PO', Exercise Physician 'EX' for her diabetes and diabetes related complications. She visited gynecologist 'G' for postmenopausal symptoms 2 years back and had an episode of knee pain 3 weeks ago having taken an x-ray at the Radiology 'R'. She is on several medications for different conditions. As an elderly lady with multiple pathologies, the doctor 'DC' has decided to trace back her history from her healthcare providers. The patient has also given consent for the doctor to do that.

Figure 2. Case analysis, interaction and expected flow of information

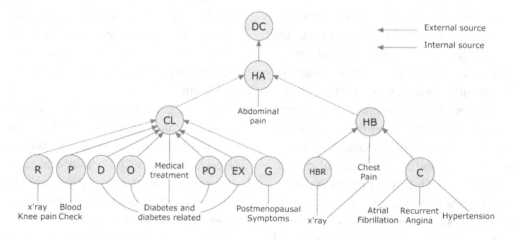

in the treatment of patient 'A', as described in Figure 1. The paradigm used presents difficulties that arise in providing health care in today's interconnected medical environments. These difficulties require the existence of efficient access control mechanisms in order to ensure security. In the scenario discussed, for example, only doctor 'DC' who has the patient's consent, accesses the patient's medical data. Traditional access control models try to cope with these kinds of difficulties giving access to a patient's EHR only to the rightful owner.

Mandatory Access Control

Mandatory access control polices (MAC) govern access based on classification of subjects and objects within a system. The access control decision is made by a centralized authority that determines, on one hand, the level of security required for each object and, on the other hand, the trustworthiness level of subjects for accessing the protected information (R. S. Sandhu & Samarati, 1994). Access control is based on comparing security levels, which indicate how sensitive data is and is performed by assessing security clearances, which indicate the entities that are allowed to access such data. To access the information a subject should have at least a level of security clearance equal to the security level of the object being accessed (Stallings & Brown, 2008). MAC policies established that users cannot delegate access rights in this way enforcing protection at the data "level", which guarantees the confidentiality of the accessed data (Stallings & Brown, 2008). MAC policies also allow the establishment of fine-grained access rights over data and, at the same time, reinforce established access restrictions. However, MAC policies are rather rigid which makes them unsuitable for a shared care environment, especially considering that in MAC more than one security level cannot be assigned to the same data object (Hafner et. all, 2008).

For example, in our previous mentioned paradigm, a situation where information of patient 'A' is maintained under MAC policies, doctor 'DC' will be required to provide the necessary clearances to retrieve the data from clinic 'CL' and hospital HB information systems. In this case, the data fields confining patient 'A' information would be maintained labelled with different levels of security accordant with the sensitivity of the information. Doctor 'DC' would be able to retrieve the data that reflect the access right provided by the clearances that he possesses. In fact, to maintain the principles of need-to-know and relevance 'DC' would only have access to the relevant information needed to perform the task. However, a physician with the same security clearances as 'DC' would also be allowed to access the retrieved data, which would not reflect the consent provided by patient 'A' to doctor 'DC'. MAC policies are centered on the level of sensitivity of the information rather than on rights and permissions that users or user groups have to access the data, which does not allow discriminating among users with the same clearances.

Furthermore, in a shared care context where data can be exchanged between multiple organizations, delegated and accessed by multiple users

in a need-to-know base, users can play different roles and have access to information under different contexts (Alhaqbani & Fidge, 2008). However, delegation of information and establishing hierarchies of access permissions are not allowed by MAC policies. In general, although MAC policies are less complex to define and allow the establishment of fine-grained access permissions based on the sensitivity of the information, they are extremely rigid for a health care environment, especially in managing users and user groups and delegating access permissions (Hafner, Memon, & Alam, 2008).

Discretionary Access Control
Discretionary access control (DAC) is based on the identity of the requestor (user or system process) and on access rules, which establish what the requestor is allowed to do. Access will be granted to the user accordantly to the permissions that the user has over the object at the moment of accessing it. DAC policies allow users to provide access permissions to another entity (user or system process). However, they do not impose restriction on how information will be managed when it is received by a user. In fact, a user could pass the data to another user not authorized to access it.

A key element of DAC is the ownership of the information, especially because owners are allowed to grant access to the stored data. However, in health care ownership of the information is not always clear. In fact, EHRs belong to a patient but are created and modified by health care professionals and the information is not only shared but could also be maintained by different health organizations which could claim ownership of the data (Alhaqbani & Fidge, 2008; Hafner, et al., 2008). Considering the situation of patient 'A', the data retrieved by doctor 'DC' from clinic 'CL' and Hospitals 'HA' and 'HB' correspond to her personal health information; however ownership of the data is not clear. In the case of patient 'A', contents of her electronic health records have been created and accessed by physicians of the three organizations. Simultaneously, information has been collected from other external sources (radiology results and postmenopausal symptoms in the case of clinic 'CL'). Additionally, patient's 'A' electronic health records are distributed in the information systems of all three organizations, which, in principle, have different access principles and security policies. The example shows that information could be created by various collaborative partners that could not claim complete ownership of the data.

Although, DAC access policies are flexible, the model lacks the ability of supporting dynamic change of access rights. Additionally, fine-grained access privileges are difficult to be managed, especially when users are allowed to grant access right to other users. DAC is centered in users rather than user groups; however, if the model is extended by including categories or group definitions, group management is possible.

In general, DAC policies are less complex to implement if compared to RBAC, are also flexible but still restricted for a shared care environment and increase the complexity of defining fine-grained access to stored data. Implementing DAC in shared care settings could result in additional security problems (R. S. Sandhu & Samarati, 1994; Stallings & Brown, 2008).

Role-Based Access Control and Exchange of EHRs

Most of the existing researches consider role-based access control (RBAC) as a mechanism to guarantee authorized access to electronic health resources, especially during the exchange of EHRs. Role-based access control (RBAC) is used to protect information resources from unauthorized access based on the roles that a user could have or perform within an organization. RBAC was first introduced by David Ferraiolo and Richard Kuhn in 1992 as a mean to provide manageable access privileges to identifiable groups of users (Ferraiolo & Kuhn, 1992). The Ferraiolo-Kuhn model was later integrated with the framework proposed by

Sandhu et al.(R. S. Sandhu, Coynek, Feinsteink, & Youmank, 1996) and published as the NIST RBAC model in 2000 (R. Sandhu, Ferraiolot, & Kuhnt, 2000). The integrated framework proposed by Ferraiolo, Sandhu and Richard was adopted as ANSI/INCITS standard in 2004.

The central idea of the RBAC model is that users can perform multiple roles and roles can be associated to multiple access permissions. In RBAC permissions are represented by the relation existing between resources and operations over those resources (Lee, Kim, Kim, & Yeh, 2004). In practice, RBAC models are based on access policies defined in terms of permissions that are associated with roles assigned to users. Permissions will determinate the operations that a role is able to perform on information resources and, therefore, all users that have assigned that specific role (Kim, Ray, France, & Li, 2004).

Even though the RBAC model has been successfully implemented in several domains, in the healthcare it presents several issues that need to be considered. Some of these issues are described in the following situations which are described using the case presented in Figure 1.

Definition of Roles

A role can be defined based on the structure of the organization or the functions that members perform within the organization. This could lead to an ambiguous definition of an access permission that can generate security issues when information is exchanged among organizations. Since in RBAC models operations are generically assigned to roles, it is difficult to separate into individual access permissions. However, when the patient 'A' is admitted to 'HA', the assignation of the access permission is done based on the consent given by the patient and not on the access privileges that could be associated to roles. For example, the patient will be treated by Cardiologist 'CA-A' but not by Cardiologist 'CA-B'. Therefore, even though both Cardiologists could have the same role, only cardiologist attending A should be allowed to access the patient's information. Furthermore, in a shared care environment the team of physicians taking care of patient 'A' should be the only ones with access to his medical records. In this case roles are not sufficient to determine access privileges, while the function of the physician within the team or being part of the team is. In reality access to health information is given to the members of the 'team' treating the patient and not to all physicians with similar roles within the organization. Under these conditions, role-based access control will not provide a suitable solution to the problem of restricting access to those users that are not taking part of the patient treatment.

Since in role-based access control models access permissions are determined by the role assigned to a user, the control that the patient has over the access to specific and sensitive information will be intrinsically limited. In fact, in a conventional RBAC model patient 'A' would not have control whatsoever over permission assigned to his medical records.

Combining and Extending Access Control Models

Alhaqbani and Fidge proposed a security access control protocol based on a three level access security model (Alhaqbani & Fidge, 2008). The proposed protocol combines Discretionary Access Control (DAC), Mandatory Access Control (MAC) and Role-Based access control in an hierarchically layered security mechanism, which determines access to data depending on a set of rules and policies evaluated at each level. According to the access hierarchy of the model, access to sensitive information will be determined by a Mandatory Access Control Policy, which provides a solution to the previously described scenario. However, implementation of this model in a shared care environment would be rather complex. The complexity of EHRs would limit the usability of DAC in a shared care setting since role definitions can differ among health providers. Moreover, the

complexity of all models could be reduced by reinforcing the policy that allows/restrict access to information stated as sensitive.

Motta and Furuie proposed a Contextual Role-Based Access Control (C-RBAC) model which extends the conventional RBAC definitions by including contextual information to determine access permissions to patients' data (Motta & Furuie, 2003). In this case, the model allows the statement of pacific restriction by adding contextual data to restrict the access to the information. Context information such as physicians assessing of patient, location and time can be used to determine if a user can be granted with access to information. The model was developed to be flexible in granting fine-grained access privileges in large health care centers using RBAC. Nonetheless, its' definition and structure limits the model to local environments, which made the model unsuitable for shared care environments with participation of multiple health care providers.

Peleg et. al proposed a solution based on contextual RBAC which considers definition of scenarios, which are called situations, in which a user would be allowed to access EHRs. Situations are described and classified, and each classification would define a pattern that can be applied when a user is requesting access to information (Peleg, Beimel, Dori, & Denekamp, 2008). The Situation Role-Based Access Control (S-RBAC) model could also be used to manage access permissions over remote repositories by applying patterns that define situations in which inter-institutional exchange of information is allowed. However, the model was developed using a patient centric approach which did not directly consider requirements of all possible stakeholders. Additionally, since the model is based on RBAC, conflicting roles and access policies would be expected when data is exchanged among different health care providers, which will increase the complexity in defining situational patterns for data exchange and release. Also, if additional health providers and all possible stakeholders'

Table 1. Comparison of access control policies

	MAC	DAC	RBAC	C-RBAC	S-RBAC
Complexity	Low	Low	Medium	High	High
Multiple users	Restricted	Restricted	Possible	Possible	Possible
Policy management	Rigid/Restricted	Flexible/Restricted	Applicable	Applicable	Applicable
Fine-Grained access	Applicable	Restricted	Restricted	Applicable	Applicable
Pros	Guarantees protection over accessed data Allow Fine-Grained access restrictions	Policies are Flexible	Allows management of access rights at group level Facilitates the management of access rights in large organizations	Considers the contextual information to determine fine-grained access to medical records	Considers the contextual information to determine fine-grained access to medical records Is designed for share care settings
Cons	Protection policies are centered on the information rather than on user or user groups. Difficult to implement in large organization with multiple users and groups accessing the data	Establishment of ownership over the data is rather difficult in shared care environments. The model lacks the ability to support dynamic change of access rights It is limited and difficult to manage in a shared care scenarios	Lacks the ability to specify fine-grained access rights for users Constraints are not flexible Different role definitions could be present when information is exchanged among health providers	Is not designed for share care settings	Model is mainly patient centered, and does not consider all stakeholders Level of complexity potentially increases with the inclusion of additional situations Different role definitions could be present when information is exchanged among health providers

scenarios are described and included, the number of patterns would potentially increase as well as the complexity of managing access permissions.

Attribute-Based Encryption

Attribute-based encryption (ABE) has its origins in Identity-Based Encryption (IBE) schemes, firstly proposed in by Boneh & Franklin in 2001 (Boneh & Franklin, 2001). The IBE scheme allows a sender to encrypt a message using an identity without incorporating a public key infrastructure (Sahai & Waters, 2005; Shamir, 1985). In this case, the identity is viewed as a string of characters (e.g. user's name, an email address, or telephone number) which serves as a user's public key (Liu, Guo, & Zhang, 2009). A private key, which is provided

by a trusted private key generator (PKG), is used to decrypt the data. The private key is provided only if the user has been successfully identified by the PKG (Au, et al., 2008).

Sahai and Waters (Sahai & Waters, 2005) introduced the notion of attribute-based encryption (ABE) as a new mechanism for reinforcing access control. The attribute-based encryption approach allows a ciphertext to be decrypted by more than one recipient, unlike the traditional public key cryptography methods (Bethencourt, Sahai, & Waters, 2007). In its place, both the users' private keys and ciphertexts are associated with a set of attributes or policies that are used to grant access to the encrypted data. Attributes are defined as a set of strings, in this case represented by access policies, which are associated to an access structure applied to the encrypted data. A user would be able to decrypt the encrypted data only if he/she possesses a private key with attributes that overlap the attributes used in the ciphertext(Bethencourt, et al., 2007; Ibraimi, Tang, Hartel, & Jonker, 2009). In other words, to allow a user to decrypt a ciphertext, at least k attributes must overlap between the identity used to generate the ciphertext and his private keys. Note that not all but k attributes are sufficient to grant access to the encrypted data, which is represented as an error-tolerance in the model. This error-tolerance allows the implementation of Fuzzy Identities or Attribute-Based Encryption schemes for biometric technology (Sahai & Waters, 2005).

In this section, we will present and describe an Attribute-Based Encryption scheme and how it can be applied to protect the information of parties during the exchange and release of EHRs.

An Approach for Securing EHRs Exchange and Applications

Considering the case in Figure 1, Hospitals 'HA', 'HB' and Clinic 'CL' have previously agreed on a set of principles that allows them to exchange information. Those principles have been set on contracts that permit the transference of any relevant data regarding health history which can be required during the treatment of a patient. All institutions have defined independent security approaches and mechanism for protecting the information that is managed on their system, HA and HB being public hospitals and according to the health policy guidelines for a public hospital, CL, being a General Practice, following the guideline for security from the General Practice Computing Group. Therefore, there could be differences in access control, security and information release polices. To avoid controversies a policy reinforcing method is used during the exchange and release of information. The method proposed is reinforcing security policies by using attribute-

based encryption scheme. In this case, the access policies are used to encrypt the information that has been exchanged, allowing only users with the correct access privileges to decrypt and access the information.

Data Encryption

Considering the scenarios described previously, the exchanged information is maintained encrypted until an authorized user, with the sufficient k attributes, proceeds to decrypt the message completely or partially. In this case, a secret key, *SK*, is used to decrypt the ciphertext encrypted with the initial attribute set (access policies), Ap, if and only if the attributes that the user possesses are sufficient as measured by the "set overlap" distance metric for the security policies used to encrypt the data (Sahai & Waters, 2005). To decrypt the message, a private key is also needed. The scheme requires of a trusted authority, known as the Private Key Generator (*PKG*), with the task of generating the private key (SK). The PKG will provide such a private key only after the user has been successfully identified (Au, et al., 2008). The generated key can then be used to decrypt the ciphertext originally received from the sender (see Figure 3). In the following, k denotes the minimal number of attributes that the user must have in order to decrypt the message or part of it.

This approach guarantees that only users that have access privileges would be allowed to access the encrypted data. The access privileges are described by the security policies used to encrypt the data. A user that does not have the attributes required to decrypt the data will not be able to access the information. If the security policies attached are hierarchically associated to information, the access could be provided at different levels for different users. In this case, user will be able to access different level or contents within the encrypted data depending on the attributes associated to their access privileges.

Figure 3. Attribute-based encryption

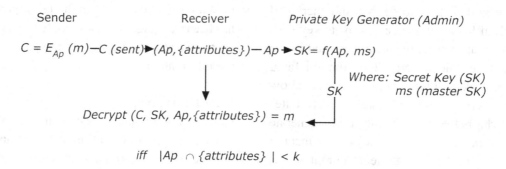

Figure 4. Case use scenario 1

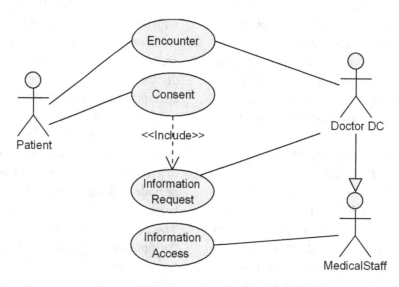

Enforcing of Access Control Policies and Secure Transference of Data

Information Exchange

After patient 'A' is admitted to hospital 'HA' and her first encounter with physician 'DC', doctor 'DC' starts recollecting patient's 'A' historical medical data. The recollection starts with the remote request of data from clinic 'CL' and hospital 'HB' health information systems. To guarantee the confidentiality of the information, the data is encrypted using attributes associated to physician 'DC'. Since the transference of data is done by reinforcing access policies only doctor 'DC' will

initially be authorized to decrypt the data provided by clinic 'CL' and hospital 'HB'. Considering that patient 'A' will not only be treated by physician 'DC' but also by a team of physicians and medical staff, the access permissions will eventually be modified in order to provide access to all personnel involved in patient's 'A' care. This can be done by providing a private Key to each member of the staff assuming responsibility with patient's 'A' care; each member will be allowed to retrieve the information depending on the access policies described by the attributes associated to their private keys. For example, physician treating patient 'A' will have access to all relevant medical history of the patient, on the contrary nurses

Figure 5. Access tree patient's data

$$P_{(Mrpitt)} = (Pat.A) \lor (Doc.DC \land Depto.ME \land Hosp.HA)$$

M

⟨∨⟩

{Pat.A}   {Doc.DC, Depto.ME, Hosp.HA}

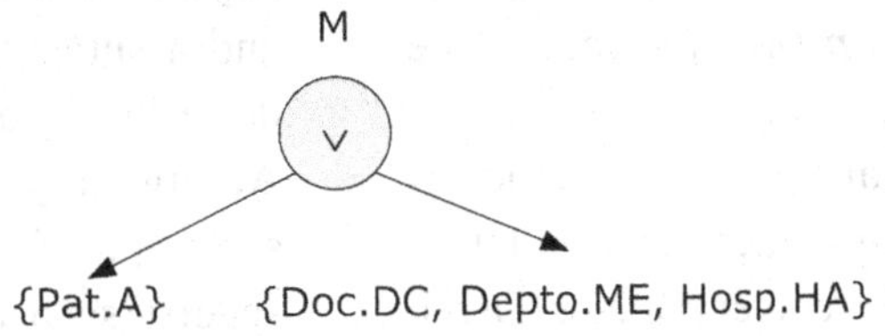

Figure 6. Sequence diagram scenario 1

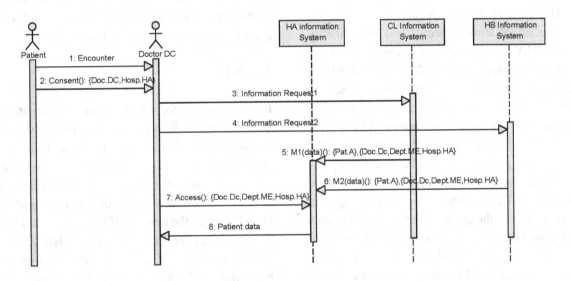

and administrative staff will be provided with restricted access to the data.

Analysis

This case presents a normal patient-physician encounter in which the historical information of patient 'A' can only be accessed by the primary physician at hospital 'HA' by Doctor 'DC'. To simplify the analysis let us assume that the consent policy has been created during the first encounter (steps 1 and 2 in Figure 6). As it has been described previously, the policy defines a set of attributes that establishes who would be able to access the medical information of patient 'A'. In this case a

set of attributes (*{Pat.A},{Doc.GP, Clinic.CL})* is used to describe the access permission to patient's 'A' information.

Even when the patient has progressed through the health system, the information gathered from encounters as well as reports can be shared using electronic communication. An information request made by doctor DC would start the process as shown in steps 3 and 4 of Figure 6. The information in the EHRs of hospital 'HB' and clinic 'CL' can be encrypted using the attributes (*{Pat.A},{ Doc.DC, Depto.ME, Hosp.HA })* and send directly to the electronic health record system in hospital HA, which is shown in steps 5 and 6 of Figure 6. In this case the access policy for the data is described as $M_{(data)} = (Pat.A) \lor (Doc.DC \land Depto.ME \land Hosp.HA)$. Since the patient cannot possess a private key that includes the attributes *{Doc.DC, Depto.ME, Hosp.HA }* the access tree has only two possible outcomes.

In this scenario, the transfer of information is directly managed between sender ('HB' and 'CL' information systems) and receiver (Doctor 'DC'). Since the information is shared between organizations the attribute *{ Doc.DC, Depto.ME, Hosp. HA }* is applied to encrypt the relevant medical information associated to patient A, and then sent to 'HA''s information system.

The information collected and sent directly to the 'HA' systems, can be accessed by 'DC', as illustrated in steps 7 and 8 of Figure 6. At this point, the transferred data has been protected using an enforced access policy approach; therefore the information can only be accessed by Doctor 'DC'. To provide access to other members of the staff access permissions can be modified by associating a new access key to the encrypted data, by allowing Cardiology 'CA-A', for example, to have access to the patient medical history. This delegation of access to specific users is possible because attribute-based encryption supports partial delegation of access permissions. To enforce that only 'CA-A' is able to access the data the information the following attributes will be incorporated to the access permissions ({ *Doctor. DC, Depto.ME*}).

Access Delegation and Patient Control Over Data Access

Now consider the situation presented in role definition. According to the access and security policies of hospital 'HA' only a member of the team attending the patient can have access to his EHRs. Since originally the information was requested and collected by doctor 'DC' of Medicine department the data could be encrypted using the flowing attribute set $M_{(data)} = (Pat.A) \lor (Doctor. DC \land Depto.ME)$. However, to allow other phy-

sicians access to patient's 'A' data, a new set of attributes needs to be incorporated. In this case, physicians could be provided with a private key and assume specific responsibilities, which are described by a specific set of attributes (policies). Additionally, information could be restricted in some specific cases, which can be described by a specific set of attributes (policies). Each specialist will be able to decrypt the data, which is under his responsibility, but will not be able to decrypt the data that has been restricted. This provides a solution for restricting access only to members of the team treating the patient and to achieve patient's control over access permissions.

Analysis

Initially only doctor 'DC' has access to the patient information. To allow access to cardiology 'CA-A' a new set of attributes can be added to the access policy of patient 'A', which will incorporate attributes associated to 'CA-A'. Since cardiology 'CA-A' works the Cardiology department of hospital 'HA', the new set of attributes would be $M_{(data)} = (Pat.A) \lor (Doctor.DC \land Depto.ME) \lor (Doctor.CA-A \land Depto.CAR)$. No other cardiologist will have the attributes *{Doctor.CA-A, Depto.CAR}* associated to their access privileges, therefore no one else but CA-A will be allowed to access and manipulate patients 'A' data. The new access tree has only three possible outcomes:

When patient A provides consent to Doctor 'DC' to collect his historical medical information, he could state that only a physician involved in his case would have access to his psychiatric history, denying access to other physicians and personnel of hospital 'HA'. In this case the access Key of other physicians and personnel will not allow them access to the psychiatric history of patient 'A'. Access to information is stated according to the consent of the patient and the access policies. Access then will incorporate the restrictions over information access, making some of the information inaccessible by other physicians

Figure 7. Access tree considering access to cardiologist CA-A

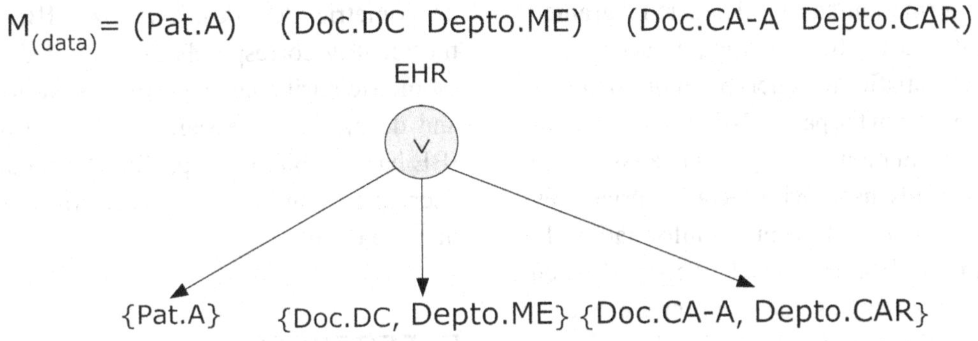

$M_{(data)}$ = (Pat.A) (Doc.DC Depto.ME) (Doc.CA-A Depto.CAR)

EHR

∨

{Pat.A} {Doc.DC, Depto.ME} {Doc.CA-A, Depto.CAR}

even when they could have access to the patient's EHR.

CONCLUSION

Health information systems, especially Electronic Health Records (EHR), are considered crucial sources of information for healthcare professionals and an essential instrument for delivery of health care services. Nevertheless, the level of accessibility provided by health information systems raises concern over the secure access and release of information, especially in share care environments. In shared care context protecting the confidentiality of patients becomes the focus of attention and a key element to be considered in the implementation of information interfaces for data exchange among health care providers. Functional and reliable inter-domain EHRs require the consideration of shared concepts as well as standardized terminology and standardized information architectures.

At the application level, the main security issues presented in approaches based on MAC and DAC are inflexibility of policies, complexity in determining ownership of the information, difficulty in implementing large shared care environments and restriction considering delegation and hierarchical access permissions to the data. Implementation based on RBAC models present

security issues associated to the ambiguities that exist in the definition of roles and access privileges among organizations, the non-existence of a common and/or standardized framework for defining roles and access privileges, lacking the ability of fine-grained access to information. Extensions to RBAC have allowed the fine-grained definition of access rights to data but at the same time increased the complexity of the models. The proposed approaches have failed to provide suitable solutions for exchange of data in scenarios that involve more than one health care provider.

In this chapter, we presented a security approach which reinforces access policies using attribute-based encryption schemes. Attribute-based encryption allows the encryption/decryption of data based on policies, which are represented as attributes associated to the information. The approach allows an independent but secure method to protect the privacy and confidentiality of patients' information transmitted over insecure channels. The model is flexible in providing access to multiple users based on security policies, which describe the access permissions over encrypted data. The use of attribute-based encryption allows:

1. Control over access permissions of transmitted data: only a user with the private access key that satisfies the encryption protocol will be able to decrypt the exchange information.

2. Delegation of access permission: Access to information can be delegated / granted to other users by providing an access key which satisfies the encryption protocols.

3. Protection of the patient's data: the transmitted information is encrypted in a fashion in which only users with the appropriate key will be able to decrypt the information. In addition, data can only be accessed when a user possesses the appropriate access permissions, and information is provided considering the principles of need-to-know and relevance.

4. Hierarchical access to rumpled data: user can access the complete information or part of it, depending on the attribute set associated to the private key.

In conclusion, attribute-based encryption offers several security advantages over traditional methods and can also be used for different purposes. In fact, it provides a flexible access control mechanism that can be implemented under different circumstances.

FUTURE RESEARCH DIRECTIONS

Future work in this area is to explore and provide a suitable and scalable solution for complex health care environments. The complexity of modern EHR systems requires flexible solutions that can be adapted in a variety of settings. In addition, the growing quantity and variety of information collected by EHR systems along with its' potential uses demand scalable solutions. Moreover, in a shared care environment the number of interconnected systems and the potential number of users increase the demand for secure mechanisms that can cope with an increasing need for highly sensitive information.

Attribute Identity-Based Encryption also allows the use of biometric profiles as attributes for data encryption. In this case encryption of

a message is done by using fuzzy inputs, such as biometric identities. In a Fuzzy IBE scheme, the identity corresponds to a set of descriptive biometric attributes that will be used to encrypt and decrypt the message. Utilization of Fuzzy IBE base on biometric profiles for medical data encryption is an alternative that can also be studied in more detail.

REFERENCES

Agrawal, R., & Johnson, C. (2007). Securing electronic health records without impeding the flow of information. *International Journal of Medical Informatics*, *76*, 471–479. doi:10.1016/j.ijmedinf.2006.09.015

Alhaqbani, B., & Fidge, C. (2008). *Access Control Requirements for Processing Electronic Health Records*. (. *Lecture Notes in Computer Science*, *4928*, 371–382. doi:10.1007/978-3-540-78238-4_38

Anderson, J. G. (2007). Social, Ethical and Legal Barriers to E-health. *International Journal of Medical Informatics*, *76*, 480–483. doi:10.1016/j.ijmedinf.2006.09.016

Au, M., Huang, Q., Liu, J., Susilo, W., Wong, D., & Yang, G. (2008). Traceable and Retrievable Identity-Based Encryption. In Bellovin, S.M., Gennaro, R., Keromytis, A.D., Yung, M. (eds.) *ACNS 2008*. (LNCS, vol. 5037, pp. 94–110). Heidelberg: Springer-Verlag.

Berner, E. (2008). Ethical and Legal Issues in the Use of Health Information Technology to Improve Patient Safety. *HEC Forum*, *20*(3), 243–258. doi:10.1007/s10730-008-9074-5

Bethencourt, J., Sahai, A., & Waters, B. (2007). *Ciphertext-Policy Attribute-Based Encryption*. In Proceedings of the 2007 IEEE Symposium on Security and Privacy. Oakland, California.

Blobel, B. (2004). Authorisation and access control for electronic health record systems. *International Journal of Medical Informatics, 73*(3), 251–257. doi:10.1016/j.ijmedinf.2003.11.018

Blobel, B., Nordberg, R., Davis, J. M., & Pharow, P. (2006). Modelling privilege management and access control. *International Journal of Medical Informatics, 75*(8), 597–623. doi:10.1016/j.ijmedinf.2005.08.010

Boneh, D., & Franklin, M. (2001). Identity-Based Encryption from the Weil Pairing. In *Advances in Cryptology - CRYPTO 2001,*(LNCS 2139, pp. 213-229). Heidelberg: Springer-Verlag.

CEN-ENV (2000a). *Health informatics - Security for healthcare communication - Part 1: Concepts and terminology.* Published Standard CEN ENV 13608-1:2000: European Committee for Standardization.

CEN-ENV (2000b). *Health informatics - Security for healthcare communication - Part 2: Secure data objects.* Published Standard CEN ENV 13608-2:2000: European Committee for Standardization.

CEN-ENV (2000c). *Health informatics - Security for healthcare communication - Part 3: Secure data channels.* Published Standard CEN ENV 13608-3:2000: European Committee for Standardization.

Chen, Y.-C., Chen, L.-K., Tsai, M.-D., Chiu, H.-C., Chiu, J.-S., & Chong, C.-F. (2008). Fingerprint verification on medical image reporting system. *Computer Methods and Programs in Biomedicine, 89*(3), 282–288.

Choe, J., & Yoo, S. K. (2008). Web-based secure access from multiple patient repositories. *International Journal of Medical Informatics, 77*(4), 242–248. doi:10.1016/j.ijmedinf.2007.06.001

Choi, Y. B., Capitan, K. E., Krause, J. S., & Streeper, M. M. (2006). Challenges Associated with Privacy in Health Care Industry: Implementation of HIPAA and the Security Rules. *Journal of Medical Systems, 30*(1), 57–64. doi:10.1007/s10916-006-7405-0

Conrick, M., & Newell, C. (2006). Issues of Ethics and Law. In Conrick, M. (Ed.), *Health Informatics: Transforming Healthcare with Technology.* Melbourne, Australia: Thomson Social Science Press.

Eddy, A. (2000). A Critical Analysis of Health and Human Services' Proposed Health Privacy Regulations in Light of the Health Insurance Privacy and Accountability Act of 1996. *Annals of Health Law, 9,* 1–72.

Ferraiolo, D., & Kuhn, R. (1992). *Role-Based Access Control.* In proceedings of the 15th National Computer Security Conference, Balmy, Baltimore, USA.

Garson, K., & Adams, C. (2008). *Security and privacy system architecture for an e-hospital environment.* In proceedings of the 7th symposium on Identity and trust on the Internet. Gaithersburg, Maryland: ACM, Goldschmidt, P. G. (2005). HIT and MIS: implications of health information technology and medical information systems. *Communications of the ACM, 48,* 68–74.

Grain, H. (2006). Consumer issues in Informatics. In Conrick, M. (Ed.), *Health Informatics: Transforming Healthcare with Technology.* Melbourne, Australia: Thomson Social Science Press.

Gritzalis, D., & Lambrinoudakis, C. (2004). A security architecture for interconnecting health information systems. *International Journal of Medical Informatics, 73*(3), 305–309. doi:10.1016/j.ijmedinf.2003.12.011

Hafner, M., Memon, M., & Alam, M. (2008). Modeling and Enforcing Advanced Access Control Policies in Healthcare Systems with SECTET. In H. Giese (ed.), *MoDELS Workshops,*(LNCS, Vol. 5002, pp132-144). Heidelberg: Springer-Verlag.

Heckle, R. R., & Lutters, W. G. (2007). *Privacy implications for single sign-on authentication in a hospital environment*. In Proceedings of the 3rd Symposium on Usable privacy and security. Pittsburgh, Pennsylvania. USA.

Ibraimi, L., Tang, Q., Hartel, P., & Jonker, W. (2009). *Efficient and Provable Secure Ciphertext-Policy Attribute-Based Encryption Schemes*. (LNCS, Vol. 5451, pp. 1-12) Berlin: Springer.

Kim, D.-K., Ray, I., France, R., & Li, N. (2004). *Modeling Role-Based Access Control Using Parameterized UML Models*. In proceedings of the 7th International Conference Fundamental Approaches to Software Engineering, FASE 2004, Barcelona, Spain.

Lee, G., Kim, W., Kim, D.-k., & Yeh, H. (2004). *Effective Web-Related Resource Security Using Distributed Role Hierarchy*. In proceedings of the 5th International Conference on Advances in Web-Age Information Management, WAIM 2004. Dalian, China.

Liu, S.-l., Guo, B.-a., & Zhang, Q.-s. (2009). An identity-based encryption scheme with compact ciphertexts. *Journal of Shanghai Jiaotong University (Science)*, *14*(1), 86–89. doi:10.1007/s12204-009-0086-3

Lopez, D. M., & Blobel, B. F. M. E. (2009). A development framework for semantically interoperable health information systems. *International Journal of Medical Informatics*, *78*(2), 83–103. doi:10.1016/j.ijmedinf.2008.05.009

Lusignan, S. d., Chan, T., Theadom, A., & Dhoul, N. (2007). The roles of policy and professionalism in the protection of processed clinical data: A literature review. *International Journal of Medical Informatics*, *76*(4), 261–268. doi:10.1016/j.ijmedinf.2005.11.003

Motta, G. H. M. B., & Furuie, S. S. (2003). A contextual role-based access control authorization model for electronic patient record. *IEEE Transactions on Information Technology in Biomedicine*, *7*(3), 202–207. doi:10.1109/TITB.2003.816562

Ohno-Machadoa, L., Silveira, P. S. P., & Vinterbo, S. (2004). Protecting patient privacy by quantifiable control of disclosures in disseminated databases. *International Journal of Medical Informatics*, *73*(7-8), 599–606. doi:10.1016/j.ijmedinf.2004.05.002

Peleg, M., Beimel, D., Dori, D., & Denekamp, Y. (2008). Situation-Based Access Control: Privacy management via modeling of patient data access scenarios. *Journal of Biomedical Informatics*, *41*(6), 1028–1040. doi:10.1016/j.jbi.2008.03.014

Rash, M. C. (2005). Privacy concerns hinder electronic medical records. *The Business Journal of the Greater Triad Area*. Retrieved 10/1/2010 from http://www.bizjournals.com/triad/stories/2005/04/04/focus2.html.

Safran, C., Bloomrosen, M., Hammond, W. E., Labkoff, S., Markel-Fox, S., & Tang, P. C. (2007). Toward a National Framework for the Secondary Use of Health Data: An American Medical Informatics Association White Paper. *Journal of the American Medical Informatics Association*, *14*(1), 1–9. doi:10.1197/jamia.M2273

Sahai, A., & Waters, B. (2005). *Fuzzy Identity-Based Encryption Advances in Cryptology*. In proceedings of the 24th Annual International Conference on the Theory and Applications of Cryptographic Techniques (Eurocrypt 2005). LNCS, 3494, 457-473. Aarhus / Denmark.

Sandhu, R., Ferraiolot, D., & Kuhnt, R. (2000). *The NIST Model for Role-Based Access Control: Towards A Unified Standard*. In Proceedings of the 5th ACM Workshop on Role Based Access Control, Berlin, Germany.

Sandhu, R. S., Coynek, E. J., Feinsteink, H. L., & Youmank, C. E. (1996). Role-Based Access Control Models. *IEEE Computer*, *29*(2), 38–47.

Sandhu, R. S., & Samarati, P. (1994). Access control: principles and practice. *IEEE Communications Magazine*, *32*(9), 40–49. doi:10.1109/35.312842

Shamir, A. (1985). *Identity-Based Cryptosystems and Signature Schemes*. In Proceedings of Crypto'84 and In G. R. Blakley and D. Chaum, (ed.), Advances in Cryptology, LNCS 196, 47–53. Berlin:Springer–Verlag.

Shin, Y. N., Lee, Y. J., Shin, W., & Choi, J. (2008). *Designing Fingerprint-Recognition-Based Access Control for Electronic Medical Records Systems*. In Proceedings of the 22nd International Conference on Advanced Information Networking and Applications Workshops, AINAW 2008. Okinawa, Japan.

Stallings, W., & Brown, L. (2008). *Computer security: principles and practice*. Upper Saddle River, NJ: Pearson international ed.

van der Linden, H., Kalra, D., Hasman, A., & Talmon, J. (2009). Inter-organizational future proof EHR systems: A review of the security and privacy related issues. *International Journal of Medical Informatics*, *78*(3), 141–160. doi:10.1016/j.ijmedinf.2008.06.013

KEY TERMS AND DEFINITIONS

Attribute-Based Encryption (ABE): an approach to restricting access in which both the users' private keys and ciphertexts are associated with a set of attributes or policies that are used to grant access to the encrypted data. Attributes are defined as a set of strings, in this case represented by access policies, which are associated to an access structure applied to the encrypted data.

Contextual Role-Based Access Control (C-RBAC): model which extends the conventional RBAC definitions by including contextual information to determine access permissions to patients' data.

Discretionary Access Control (DAC): is based on the identity of the requestor (user or system process) and on access rules, which establish what the requestor is allowed to do. Access will be granted to the user accordingly to the permissions that the user has over the object at the moment of accessing it.

Identity-Based Encryption (IBE): The IBE schema allows for sender to encrypt a message by using an identity without accessing a public key certificate.

Mandatory Access Control Policies (MAC): an approach to restricting system access based on comparing security levels, which indicate how sensitive data is and is performed by assessing security clearances, which indicate the entities that are allowed to access such data. To access the information a subject should have at least a level of security clearance equal to the security level of the object being accessed.

Role-Based Access Control (RBAC): is an approach to restricting system access based on the role of the user within the organization. Users can perform multiple roles and roles can be associated to multiple access permissions. In RBAC permissions are represented by the relation existing between resources and operations over those resources.

Shared Care Paradigm: In a shared care environment different health care units (HCU) are involved in the care process as well as in maintaining accurate medical records. Indeed, in modern healthcare environments different care services are offered by different HCU within the organization or in a healthcare network that involves multiple organizations.

Situation Role-Based Access Control (S-RBAC): solution based on contextual RBAC which considers definition of scenarios, which are called situations, in which a user would be allowed to access EHRs. Situations are described and classified, and each classification would define a pattern that can be applied when a user is requesting access to information.

The Fuzzy Identity-Based Encryption: is an application of Identity-based Encryption (IBE) which enables the encryption of a message by using fuzzy inputs, such as biometric inputs as identities. In the Fuzzy IBE scheme, the identity corresponds to a set of descriptive attributes that will be used to encrypt and decrypt the message. Fuzzy IBE scheme describes an error tolerance which allows the use of biometric as an identity attribute.

Chapter 2
Modeling Access Control in Healthcare Organizations

Efstratia Mourtou
St. Andrew General Hospital, Greece

ABSTRACT

Since Hospital Information Systems (HIS) are designed to support doctors and healthcare professionals in their daily activities, information security plays a vital role in managing access control. Efficiency and effectiveness of information security policy is crucial, especially when dealing with situations that affect the status and life-history of the patient. In addition, the rules and procedures to follow, in order to provide confidentiality of sensitive information, have to focus on management of events on any table of the HIS. On the other hand, control and statement constraints, as well as events and security auditing techniques, play also an important role, due to the heterogeneity of healthcare professionals' roles, actions and physical locations, as well as to the specific characteristics and needs of the healthcare organizations. This chapter will first explore issues in managing access control and security of healthcare information by reviewing the possible threats and vulnerabilities as well as the basic attributes of the hospital's security plan. The authors will then present a hierarchical access model that, from a security policy perspective, refers to data ownership and access control issues. The authors conclude the chapter with discussions of upcoming security issues.

INTRODUCTION

This chapter considers perhaps the most important topic in the acceptance of Information and Communication Technology (ICT) systems in healthcare. This topic covers the security from unauthorized access, the secure availability, the trust and the privacy protection of the HIS. The issues are discussed and a model access system – implemented in a Greek hospital – is presented. By understanding the key challenges and adopting strategies to improve security control policy between the user and the data of the HIS, hospi-

DOI: 10.4018/978-1-61692-895-7.ch002

talists could significantly improve the quality of healthcare. First we present the context.

In today's world there is high demand for improving both the quality of healthcare and the overall health status of individuals. National healthcare systems are facing a number of challenges in the coming years and pose great opportunities to IT professionals. Although the preservation of human life and the improvement of its quality are the subject areas of utmost importance to healthcare professionals, the provision of IT applications from research to practice, from medical procedures to palliative care and from health restoration to health preservation are some of the greatest challenges.

Health care providers are looking to IT not only to improve quality, but also to reduce costs, with efforts well under way to integrate it into the healthcare systems. For example, the Information Society in Greece (2005) reports that the West Greece sanitary district has spent € 2.570.000, 00 to implement an integrated HIS for 11 amenable hospitals and healthcare centers. However, there are many gaps in hospitals' use of IT that vary by institutional size and accreditation status. Almost 90 percent of Greek hospitals, for example, reported that they use HIS for administration transactions across a number of departments, but not in the area of clinical process and activity-based analysis. Nearly 4.87 percent of hospitals use electronic medical records and a 46,34 percent partly uses electronic lab results (Mourtou, 2007). Electronic medical records lag behind other types of hospital IT, not only because of implementation, cost, and integration difficulties, but also due to the absence of acceptance and trust by the healthcare workers.

Users' acceptance is one of the key components for success of an HIS from various perspectives. Among others, some of them are: (a) the system must become a help, not a hindrance, to all the healthcare workers (b) the system must allow fast and easy data retrieval and analysis and (c) the system must assure data quality, since clinical decisions are based on them. On the other hand a number of considerations are raised in healthcare environment, like confidentiality, privacy and ethical issues that must be properly faced. Since the patient-physician relationship depends on very high levels of trust, without proper organizational, ethical, and technological safeguards, patient information would be easily accessible to unauthorized users with intent on stealing, altering, or destroying the information contained in the HIS. In addition, important ethical questions surround the use of Electronic Medical Record (EMR) and thus, the security of HIS should be provided and used in such a manner that the rights and legitimate interests of patients are respected. Mediated access puts control policy between the user and the data and, thus, illustrates a general point that all healthcare managers should bear in mind: sound health information privacy and security access include a range of controls (Wiederhold & Bilello, 1998). Some of the security controls include:

1. Users' actions that specify what is to be done, if a situation of interest occurs
2. Roles that assign specified permissions to users to perform specific actions and rules that comprise specific conditions for actions. As Blobel & Roger-France, 2001) pointed out, "to handle any kind of user-related issues, the management of users including their specification of their possible roles and the rules applied to fulfill a security policy is needed as basis for all other application and communication security services".
3. Access levels that determine what kind of data any user can view, register and edit.

However, "access levels vary from access to the entire health record of a patient, to fine grained access definitions at the level of medical concepts" (Linden et al., 2009). Concepts in the medical domain spans levels of precision, complexity, and breadth of participation that makes the access problem more challenging than that in any other domain. The levels of access depend on the whole chain of hospital care that involves multiple participants such as medical doctors, general practitioners, nurses, ward clerks, pharmacists, administrative staff and laboratory technicians. For instance, "thousands of patients with thousands of items per patient could be shared between some of several thousands of health professionals and this exchange has to be bound on direct or indirect contributions to the patient's care leading to different rights and duties related to that information" (Blobel, 2004). On the other hand, the frequent transitions of nurses between medical departments –according to the nursing levels of the wards, and the allocation of part-time service personnel (Miyazaki & Masuda, 2005)– demand a control strategy that can provide different types of access and different privileges in order that patient information is accessible upon demand by an authorized person in a timely coordinated manner.

Even if security controls are properly managed, and maintained, there may still be some more issues to be considered. For example, events that commonly occur during the execution of procedures, may pose sound threats to hospital data security, if they are not accurately detected. The term "event" in the context of database means anything than may happen on database procedures, on accesses to tables, on performance, and on servers at a specific point in time (Heimrich & Specht, 2002). As the volume of patient data grows and database events are often complex, IT professionals are faced with the challenge of raising and registering them, by granting event-related privileges to all parts of the security system. In addition, it is essential to be sure that specified classes of security events are properly recorded in audit files for later analysis. In other words, security auditing alarms must be enabled, in order to cause a security record to be written to the audit log files.

On the other hand, the management of deadlocks inside the Hospital Database is a very important issue aiming to reduce overflow chains,

especially focusing on hashing (Knuth, 1973) and row locking techniques (Gornshtein & Tamarkin, 2004). The term "deadlock" bears a lot of meanings that mostly include situations that occur during transactions in transactional databases, but more generally "a deadlock is a stopping status of the flow of a marking due to a resource waiting, and it usually appears in contain subsystem which is run in parallel and resources share places" (Sanghwan, 2006). Hash tables, in comparison to other associative data structures (e.g., heap and b-tree structures), are most useful in HIS, due to the capacity of information to be stored, and especially if the size of the data set can be predicted (Wirth, 1986). Also problems such as the slow execution of queries or reports are crucial, especially when dealing with situations that affect the status and walk of life of the patient.

Concerning this cutting edge technology, there are a lot of technical issues: techniques, practices and mechanisms that provide a minimum security level for the Hospital Database must be addressed (Gritzalis et al., 2005). For example, an improper fill factor –it specifies the percentage of space filled on index data pages when an index is initially created (Schumacher, 2005)– could impair performance and fragment the storage of the data in a table, while the extension of the Data Base in alternative locations on different disks could protect the data, and also allow maximum performance. However, it is very important to understand that hospital information technology affects both human behavior and tolerance, such as work environment and work satisfaction as well as human activity coordination. Thus, it is consequently necessary to face security issues in terms of change management and also have sufficient flexibility to allow for the inevitable changes in practice that occur inside hospitals (Kara & Kayis, 2004). Thereby, apart from defining an access control model, the flexibility of the HIS must be evaluated in order to be easily adjusted to any of the aforesaid changes.

This chapter will first explore issues in managing access control and security of healthcare information by reviewing the possible threats and vulnerabilities as well as the basic attributes of the hospital's security plan. We will then present a hierarchical access model that, from a security policy perspective, refers to data ownership and access control issues. This model has been implemented in a Greek public hospital and it also illustrates some considerable issues in the implementation of rules for several types of control as well as in the events management and the security auditing, which are of major importance to healthcare environment. The chapter closes with some upcoming security issues that require more analysis and development to comply with the defined policy of new integrated information systems.

OVERVIEW OF ACCESS CONTROL

The term "access control" bears many meanings that mostly refer in providing secure handling of the sensitive information, especially concerning the complexity of diagnosis and treatment follow-up, not only for the inpatient but also for the outpatients. Moreover, personal data that constitute the informational basis of the EMR should be treated according to the law, with respect and protection of human dignity (HDPA, 2006). On the other hand, most healthcare professionals are seriously concerned about the validity and reliability of the handling of patient information, due mainly to the heterogeneous and non standardized type of data. For example, information is sometimes unstructured, and in many cases textual, while measurement units are often missing and terminology codes are occasionally used without specified coding schemes (Linden et al., 2009).

Generally, to secure access information within a system, three steps are usually required: "identification (where a user says who he is, e.g. with a login username); authentication (where a user proves his identification given in the first

step, e.g. with a password or a PIN number); and authorization (where access rights are given to the user)" (Ferreira et al., 2007). Blobel (2004) pointed out that "access control in distributed health information systems has to deal with policy description and negotiation including policy agreements, authentication, certification, and directory services but also audit trails, altogether forming the privilege management infrastructure". For example, user registration and the process of certification are playing an important role in the security administration, while the assessment of the confidence and security of the system have to be seriously considered. From this point of view, it is generally accepted that any information system is considered as secure and trusted, if it is has been proved that it satisfies all its characteristics. Pilot phases of access control indicate that significant benefits and performance improvements could be achieved through the secure use of IT inside healthcare organizations, where several procedures and complex processes are taking place at the same time. This entire complexity has an instant influence on the sort of access control that has to be designed to properly support both employees and activities. For example, some users may have access to medicine ordering and no access to medical procedures, while others may only have access to administrative procedures. The picture of access control in healthcare is not helped by the fact that since standard differences exist both within and across countries, it is impossible to refer to standards, but rather follow generic access recommendations that fit more suitably with the HIS (Swanson et al., 2003). Also, within healthcare organizations depending on their size and their complexity, different access levels can be obtained that can be step-by-step upgraded. For example, permissions are classified according to the type of objects they affect, while procedure permissions are associated with proportional rules and constraints.

However, considering that a major part of hospitals implementation initiatives in ICT were mostly concentrated on removing resistance to change through educational programs and patterns of behavior, a proper comprehensive management is essential to face all the security issues that access control policy creates for the HIS.

MODELING ACCESS CONTROL

Meeting the challenge of improving efficiency and quality of healthcare, sound precautions need to be taken to respect and protect the privacy and security of patient information. Unauthorized access and disclosure of personal and often sensitive information could compromise the patient privacy. In addition, the dramatic increase in accessibility of information provided by the internet brings with it the danger of revealing patient data that might threaten security and privacy related issues. A number of cases show the inappropriate disclosure of individually identifiable data that has resulted in harm to the individual. For example, "a computer that contained the files of people with AIDS and other sexually transmitted diseases was put on sale..." (Wager et al., 2005).

The basic scope of a proper access control is to provide a set of techniques, tools and practices that provide as many as possible of the critical elements that are required for the HIS. According to Blobel (2004), "the model for authorization and access control in distributed HIS has to deal with policy description and negotiation including policy agreements, authentication, certification, and directory services but also audit trails, altogether forming the privilege management infrastructure". In other words, critical elements should describe security control objectives and essential techniques should accomplish the security performance goals. The goals of security performance are:

1. Ensuring individual users have the right access control to view and manage the development of personal data in patient records.

2. Developing the policies and rules that govern access control and user privileges (in conjunction with user groups).
3. Implementing event and security auditing to facilitate tackling problems.

To start the definition and implementation of an access control model, a qualitative risk analysis has to be performed, that involves not only the identification of the most probable threats for a hospital, but also an analysis of the related vulnerabilities and the overhanging factors to these threats (Wold & Shriver, 1994).

Within healthcare organizations, risk analysis should be developed by a hospital security commission, which includes all specialties such as doctors, nurses, paramedics, and administrative staff, as well as the informatics department. Likewise, meetings with the members of the outsourcing organizations must be frequently arranged, in order to enforce the procedures during systems' evaluation and users' interaction. In addition, ad-hoc conversations with the users of the system are a fundamental necessity, since the users are objectively able to reveal the real requirements as well as the underlined content of their daily workflow.

The main task of the commission is to create a security plan, which has to delineate the specific actions, roles, access levels and responsibilities that are required for every user of the HIS. A general understanding of the security plan can be obtained by understanding the most relevant security requirements, to provide legal evidence of responsibility of principals involved. First we review some definitions of these requirements, as stated in ISO/TS 18308:

- **Data Integrity:** preserving the accuracy and consistency of data regardless of changes made (Grimson et al., 1998). In practice, information integrity simply means that data have not been altered or destroyed in an unauthorized manner.

- **Data Confidentiality:** It is defined as the assurance that information is accessible only to those authorized to have access (ISO/IEC-17799, 2005). Another definition is given by NCSC as "the concept of holding sensitive data in confidence, limited to an appropriate set of individuals or organizations" (NCSC, 1998).

- **Data Availability:** Data availability in the context of HIS means that the patient information is available when needed. Kohavi (1995) states that "a limited availability of data often makes estimating accuracy a difficult task".

- **Authenticity:** It is defined as the ability to be certain that medical records have been created by the person they say they are, when they say they are and containing true (or perceived to be true) information as related to their context.

- **Non-repudiation:** It is the property that ensures that the actions on an entity may be traced uniquely to the entity (ISO 7498-2, 1989). Depending on the non-repudiation policy of hospitals, and the national healthcare legislation, additional information may be required to complete the non-repudiation information, such as evidence about occurrence or non-occurrence of some event or action (Blobel, 2002). Simply trying to obtain proof for an entity or an action among hundreds is a challenge to confirm the integrity and origin of a data item.

- **Accountability:** It is defined as "the ability to audit the actions of all parties and processes which interact with the information and to determine if the actions are appropriate" (Berman, 2002). As Blobel (2002) pointed out "the accountability service concerns providing responsibility for medical data assuring the data origin is provable without repudiation".

Before considering the proposed access control model, the vulnerabilities of the HIS that make it more prone to attacks, such as incorrectly filtered input of the users in an application or the erroneous Structured Query Language syntax, have to be designated. For example, the incursion of some queries could probably disrupt the concurrency control of the Database. The major vulnerabilities are reviewed next, in order to acknowledge how the proposed access model copes with them.

Threats to a Hospital Information System

Data involved in HIS do not have the same degree of vulnerability as any other organization, due to the complex communication context. The chain of hospital care usually involves multiple participants such as doctors, paramedics, specialist practice and general practitioners, and administrative staff, thus creating a need not only for data protection from attackers but also from legitimate users. The degree of vulnerability depends mostly on the value of information that is possessed by a third party (Katsikas, 1995). In a similar way, information may employ a significant value in case that there is a possibility of changing it. Information may attract a lower value if it is not possible to be available to the concerned individuals. Many components are involved to the information assessment, like the possible benefits, the correlation of the information with some social values and the possibility to use this information for malign actions.

Gritzalis (1994) states that two types of data vulnerability can be assigned: (1) the intrinsic vulnerability, which is not dependent on the information system but it is directly dependent on the social system and (2) the intrinsic and total vulnerability, which is not dependent on the information system but stands for every individual, regardless the social system. The second one is obviously reflected by the laws that protect the personal data (Law 2472/1997. The Protection of Individuals with regard to the Processing of Personal Data, as amended by Laws 2819/2000 and 2915/2001). Therefore, the designation of the possible threats that can affect the security of the HIS is the essential requirement to handle properly the security plan. According to Gritzalis (2000) "a threat is defined as a possible action or an event that may cause the loss of one or more than one security properties on an information system". Considering the range of healthcare environments, where integrated patient information and clinical and laboratory and administrative interaction is involved, a list of threats can be traced, such as (Katsikas et al., 1997):

- **Hardware failure:** Hardware failure could compromise data integrity. For example, during the event of a single storage device failure, uncommitted transactions may be lost. The loss of power during sensitive work, like printing the results of medical tests, can easily result in the loss of many files. One of the most commonly stated reasons for hardware failure is the resource conflicts in the case that some devices are not properly configured to ensure they are not interfering with each other. In addition, users occasionally bring in their own files on flash devices that could probably convey viruses, thereby causing local hardware failures.

- **Application failure:** Sometimes, during the interaction of the application software with the Database Management System (DBMS), a recent out-of-date connection may occur, or it is possible to experience a failure of an application start up if the Structured Query Language (SQL) server has not recovered. In addition, access to patient data may be prohibited in cases that barcode readers do not read properly the blood samples and in cases of deadlocks. Deadlocks occur when each process is waiting for an event that only another pro-

cess in the set can cause. Thus all the processes are waiting, none of them will ever cause any of the events that could wake up any of the other members of the set, and all the processes continue to wait indefinitely. A similar problem is the concurrency of queries that involve transactions that have remained in an open state during the transaction execution. An application failure may also occur if lock timeout strategies are implemented counter to user interactions.

- **Weak passwords:** A weak password is the key to access patient personal information that it is stored on the hospital database as well as to cause authentication problems. In the healthcare environment, especially in hospital laboratories, it is very common for the same password to be used for all the staff and based on the lab manager's personal information. This password may not only easily be guessed by anyone, but also it does not provide the responsibility log of any user action. Weak passwords may seriously affect the evidence of the electronic medical records authenticity and the judgment of the health professionals' activity.

- **Password stealing:** A major problem that many healthcare professionals confront is the handling of password stealing, which can arise for several reasons. Typical reasons include users' carelessness, since it is fairly common that many users keep their login names and passwords on self sticking labels on their computers. Not very often, passwords are stored on a networked computer and so they may be easily found by malicious users. The situation becomes more serious after an attack by a dynamic intruder, who could probably use either a brute force attack, a sniffing method or an Address Resolution Protocol (ARP) spoofing (Hornig, 1984). After a password is stolen then a lot of elements of information security are compromised including data integrity, confidentiality, authenticity and non-repudiation. An important consequence of this masquerade is that some messages seem different than their real source.

- **Trap doors exploitation:** Trap doors or back doors are defined as system vulnerabilities that allow the breakthrough of security mechanisms and tend to evade logging procedures. In a large part, users are mostly responsible for the trap doors, so that they can use unauthorized software that may comprise with bugs, or to overcome their lost password. While backdoors are difficult to detect, they may be installed for accessing a variety of services, and thus they provide interactive access inside the local hospital network, especially in cases that standard services protocol are running, such as Telnet and File Transfer Protocol (Zhang & Paxson, 1998).

- **Spoofing Attacks:** In general, a spoofing attack is defined as the acceptance of unauthorized access to a local computer or a network by making it appear that a malicious message has come from a trusted machine by the "spoofing method". There are many types of this kind of attack, like blind and non-blind spoofing, and all of them are highlighted in the Internet Protocol (IP) address of the computer accessing that machine (Tanase, 2003). An IP spoofing is defined as the creation of TCP/IP packets using somebody else's IP address, and so a person or a program may successfully be masqueraded as another by falsifying data (Gantz & Rochester, 2005). In addition, spoofing involves the transparent splitting of a TCP (Transmission Control Protocol) connection between the source and destination by some entity within the network path (Ishac & Allman, 2001). Routers use the "destination IP" address in order to

forward packets through the Internet, but ignore the "source IP" address. That address is only used by the destination machine when it responds back to the source (Allman, 2000).

- **Unauthorized modification:** In some cases, like password stealing, unauthorized users with malicious intend may have access to the HIS and so they are able to modify the patient data. In particular, they may insert, update, and delete demographical and clinical information, thus, undetected concerning the data integrity and the systems reliability.

- **Denial of Service:** A denial of service is defined as a situation that a user is deprived of the services of a resource they would normally expect to have. For example, users could unfavorably, temporarily or indefinitely, affect the availability of printing and scanning operations, or they may deliberately disrupt connections between two computers of the same domain, thereby preventing access to a service and resulting in the reduction of the efficiency of the HIS. The situation is more serious in the case of a distributed denial-of-service attack, in which a multitude of compromised systems attack a single target, thereby denying service to the system to legitimate users (Mirkovic et al., 2004).

- **Misuse of resources:** An employee or any other insider may threaten the HIS, by misuse of computing resources, and so affecting access and performance of the service for authorized users. For example, some users could use the bandwidth for non-hospital-related internet surfing, or download media content or hazardous software, or copy patient files to portable storage devices without authorization, thus exposing the healthcare organization to violation liabilities. On the other hand, since physicians must have access to up-to-date epidemiological information that could give them a useful insight on important exogenous factors that influence the health status of a person – and thus access the internet and use computing resources - in some cases they unwittingly are causing misuse of resources.

- **Spamming:** Spamming and specifically, e-mail spam, is the practice of sending unwanted e-mail messages, frequently with commercial content, in large quantities to an indiscriminate set of recipients. Gyongyi and Garcia-Molina (2005) state that "the term spamming (also, spamdexing) refers to any deliberate human action that is meant to trigger an unjustifiably favorable relevance or importance for some web page, considering the page's true value". In the healthcare environment, spamming is a great problem, in the case when the hospital's servers and workstations are not automatically updated and properly configured, due to the frequently use of the Web for the users entertainment and not for their work.

Consequently, the handling of patient information that comes in ever increasing volumes inside the healthcare organizations brings forward large and interesting problems in resolving the security and access control to the end user. The implementation of a hierarchical security system into the hospital environment is of crucial importance for effective and optimal use of the Electronic Medical Record, not only for the hospital staff but mostly for the patient community. The next section presents a general hierarchical model that can map actions, roles and rules to the HIS's users. This approach is quite general and applicable to many healthcare organizations due to its simplicity. We will also present algorithms that are designed to make simple the creation of queries and events inside the hospital data base in an attempt to improve on the model.

The Hierarchical Access Model

What makes the design of an access control model more complex is that according to the World Wide Web Consortium (W3C), many different components must be included: policy agreements, authentication, certification, directory services, and audit trails (Blobel, 2004). Several studies have investigated the development of security-related models: the domain model, the policy model, the role model, the privilege management model, the authorization model, the access control model as well as the information distance model (Blobel & Holena, 1997). In our approach, in order to tackle the heterogeneous needs of the hospital, we have implemented a two-level hybrid approach that incorporates the Role Based Access Control (RBAC) model – it associates rights to users according to their roles -, and the Identity Based Access Control (IBAC) model – it associates rights to users depending on their needs -(Ferreira et al., 2007).

Before going further, it is useful to understand the concept of hierarchy in the access model. Most of us have a common understanding of the term hierarchy as an arrangement of items (e.g. objects, names, values, etc.) in which the items are represented as being "above", "at the same level as" or "below" one another and with only one "neighbor" above and below each level, and all classifications are made with regard to rank, importance, seniority, power status or authority (Simpson & Weiner, 1989). Applying the appropriate level of the hierarchy is very important for the maintenance of security and access control in the HIS. But before this hierarchy can be identified, we have to be able to designate all the parties bound by the hierarchy and, then to apply it into the HIS. Since healthcare professionals belong to more than one professional group, they should be given access in different applications and with different access levels. For example, training doctors belong to more than one medical department, so they need different access level to each one of them, and similar doctors work on a

Figure 1. The flow of hospital information

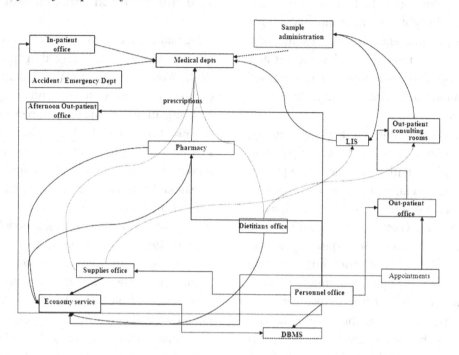

general medical ward as well as on an intensive or coronary care unit. In addition, administration staff may frequently change posts, and working hours, depending on the hospital's requirements, thus increasingly the end-user demand for access not only to database tables built for preconceived purposes, but also to a range of tables and queries, built for more specialized applications, in order to provide the required information. For instance, the Greek afternoon hospital out-patients sessions constitute a kind of "private consulting room" with distributed hospital locations and functions that are different from usual outpatient management: the staff needs access to different applications (Mourtou, 2009).

Access to different applications may also arise as a result of private hospitals takeovers and public hospital evolution and interactions, thus needing shared access to different information sources to deal with common situations. In a similar way, hospital processes involve many departments, such as in-patients office, out-patients office, afternoon out-patients office, personnel office,

pharmacy, supplies office, labs, and individual medical departments, thus, a number of legal aspects and a cohesive relationship between all departments need to be properly addressed. Yet, there is a need to be specific and precise when exploring the different levels of hierarchy, how they are defined and how they can be represented.

Assume that a patient is first admitted to the in/out/afternoon-patients office, and then examined by a physician. Examination involves a number of procedures: medical/radiology tests, prescriptions. After the examination, the patient may be hospitalized or not, depending on diagnosis. In the first case a ward of a medical department is assigned and a daily treatment (medication, physiotherapy, diet and medical supplies) is followed. During the treatment, various procedures are involved: Medical departments and labs must be supplied by the pharmacy and the supplies office, and more decisions must be taken. Figure 1 illustrates the flow of hospital information.

There are many key questions such as: Who is the owner of the patient digital radiograms, e.g.

Table 1. The access levels

1.	Patient charges to Insurance companies are permitted only to administrative staff of the In/Out patient office
2.	Patient demographics and registration number can only be allocated by an administrative member of staff of the In/Out patient office
3.	Every user is given by the Database Administrator a unique login name, and a strong password and one or more role passwords for specific access in applications
4.	Login names and passwords are given to users by strictly controlled administrative hospital procedures to prevent and detect any fraud, waste and abuse inside the hospital
5.	Login names and passwords and role passwords have well-defined expiration date, and the users are prompted with a password expiration notice
6.	In case that a user is transferred to a different department, then s/he has to be immediately removed from their existing group and added to their new group, while the original login names and passwords must be instantly removed
7.	Trainee doctors have temporary read and write access rights to the system for any patients they care for, while physicians have full access to the whole clinical record of patients registered within their department, but only read access to clinical records of patients belonging to other departments
8.	Nurses are granted read access to the clinical activity of the patients registered within their department and read and write access to medication and to the appropriate consumables
9.	Laboratory personnel are granted only read access to requests for medical tests
10.	Full access to the system is provided only by the staff of the hospital department of Informatics, which is responsible for the HIS management, (e.g. the integration of the existing data bases, the local network establishment and maintenance, the management of information security issues, the reinforcement of the application of data warehouse, the terminal equipment installation and technical support, and the system backups, and on the job training)

should it be the radiologist or the orthopedic clinician? Who is responsible for updating the patient medical record when the patient leaves the hospital, e.g. should it be the ward clerk or the medical secretary? Should specific medical information be stored together with patient charges? Who can access demographic patient information, and make additions and changes to it in case that the patient insurance has expired? Who is responsible for the changes in the barcode labels when a patient is transferred from one medical department to another? Is there any ability to download and save files on a local computer, or other storage devices and under what circumstances? Does laboratory staff have access and what kind of access should they have to the clinical record? Who is responsible for creating events that enable an application to notify other applications that a specific event has occurred?

To facilitate effective sharing of medical and administrative information on an ongoing basis,

the access levels are defined by the hospital security commission and they are listed in table 1.

From a security policy perspective, data ownership and access control issues are mainly related to the levels of hierarchy, which are the following:

- **Public:** This refers to access privileges that all users of the system have. Consider that access of insert is given to anyone but only to a subset of data of the table 'nurse'. Then a view that provides the necessary restrictions must be created and the appropriate permissions for this view have to be granted to public. Suppose this view is designated as 'nurseview'. Then if insert on 'nurseview' to public is granted, then all users may insert to the subset of data of the table 'nurse'.

- **Group:** This is an identifier that can be used to apply permissions to a list of users, through the associated functions "create with password", "alter" and "remove group". In this model, groups are designated according to the hospital departments, and users are being given a default group membership to one or more groups. For example, doctors of the group "orthopedics" are given also access to the group "emergency unit", but they have no access to the group "Psychiatry". In the proposed model, groups consisting of more than one user are initially defined and privileges are assigned to individual groups so that they can be easily granted to a large list of users. In addition, for each group a group identity is specified, leading to an efficient implementation across the hospital data base.

- **User:** A user is permitted to perform specific actions, according to the assigned privileges and permissions. Due to the frequent transitions of healthcare professionals between medical departments, special permissions and privileges have to be assigned to individual users, in order to fit to the group rights. In many cases, permission may involve the collection of the medical documents or information of the in-patient office and the proportional registration back into the HIS, with the associated validation. Therefore, it is a necessity to give employees access to the different applications with various access levels, in order to perform their job properly. Generally, users are given explicit permission to use the tables and procedures, but they are not given permission to create database objects even in the database to which they have access.

- **Role:** A role is an identifier that can be used as a connection between permissions and applications, and for testing purposes on the terminal monitor invocation line (Mourtou, 2007). Roles provide a means to indirectly assign privileges to individuals and they are "crucial issues in privilege

management and access control (Blobel, 2004). In other words, roles assign specified permissions to users to perform specific functions and they are created with an additional password authentication. In the medical domain, integration of multiple different passwords for general practitioners, medical departments, technicians and administrative staff is of crucial importance for effective security and data confidentiality. Therefore, after accessing the HIS with a login password, users are required to input another password to access a specific role to allow them for tasks performance. In addition, the authorization hierarchy is of critical importance in hospital applications, due to the highest precedence of the role toward the user and group.

For example, if a user logins in the system and specifies both group and role identifiers, even if the query row limit of the role has been defined less than the row limit for the group, the limit defined for the role is enforced because it has the highest order of precedence in the authorization hierarchy that ensures that structures are represented clearly and unambiguously. The access model also permits dynamic restructuring, such as altering or removal of roles, while a univocal relationship of the type "one user – one role" is developed, where one role corresponds through a relationship of the type "one-to-many" with more than one group. Figure 2 illustrates the major components of the hierarchical structure of the access model.

Specific roles associate permissions with applications, allowing for data access to be restricted in several ways every time the applications start. There are many classes of permissions related to tables, procedures, events and the database. Permissions may apply to all users (i.e. public), a single user, a group of users or a role. However, database and event permissions are given only to the Database Administrator and to the Operating

Figure 2. The major components of the access model

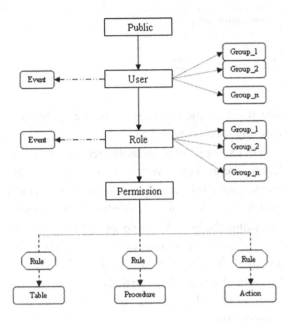

System Administrator, who both belong to the hospital department of informatics. Table permissions may allow access to any field of a specific table or to limited number of rows and columns, depending on local optimizations.

In addition, actions are specified by rules, referring to the database procedures, such as insert, update, or delete data of a specific table. Transactions are also represented conveniently in the access model, yet requiring the proper handling of both tables and queries. However, many problems may arise in the case that a transaction is left in an 'open' state for long, while the transaction fragments are executed on multiple nodes. Then a deadlock may occur, and so the problem is becoming rather worse, thus demanding concurrency resolution strategies, such as hashing and row locking techniques, or more local optimizations.

In order to provide the readers with a concrete sense of rule contexts, in the next section, we discuss the development of rules and constraints that have been deployed in the HIS.

The Development of Rules

The basis for most database system architectures must represent respectively all integrity constraints and rules that can lead to an efficient implementation across the access control model. Generally, rules are mechanisms or conditions that are implemented for several purposes, while constraints ensure the integrity of the hospital database in representing the world of interest. It has become critically important to not only understand the concept of rules developments in relational databases, but to also be able to define and implement a plurality of user-defined rules that contain security constraints for secure accessing of the medical information and receiving a request at a user interface.

Before continuing further, a few definitions are necessary: A rule is defined as a condition on the hospital database which specifies an action or an execution of a procedure to be taken when a particular condition occurs (Dodds, 1982). An action may be an insert, an update, or a delete on a specified table. As Heimrich and Specht (2002) pointed out, actions may specify what is to be done, if a situation of interest occurs, such as events and conditions evaluate to true. If a procedure associated with one rule is executed, then the respective rule is fired. However, only the Database Administrator as the owner of the tables has the ability to create rules for these tables, while users who are granted permission to access these tables may – via a procedure - fire the rule. In the case that a procedure invoked by a rule does not exist then the rule cannot be created against any table.

The implementation of rules is very important because they impose a consistent behavior on the HIS in many situations where external and internal resource controls must be applied. The following example, according to Ingres Administration Guide (1998) illustrates how a rule can be used to notify for the minimum value of a group of medicines in the table 'drugs': The rule 'order_cipro' fires whenever the number of quinolone antibiotics that contain the active ingredient "ciprofloxacin" in the table 'drugs' is reduced to value 50 (table 2).

Another example shows two rules that invoke two procedures, issuing an o_log file: this file logs the update information with the user name (oname). Consider a nurse has been transferred from the orthopedics to the neurology department. Then an action of insert must occur into the table 'neurology_nurse' after the action of update on the table 'orthopedics_nurse'. Both actions are specified by two rules which are called 'insert_ nurse' and 'update_nurse' and they respectively invoke two procedures by the name 'old_nurse' and 'new_nurse'. Table 3 depicts the rules creation algorithm.

However, instead of creating the two afore-mentioned rules, it is preferable to create only one rule that invokes an update procedure in the 'orthopedics_nurse' table after an insert action that occurs into the 'neurology_nurse' table. To do that it is necessary to have a general constraint to describe the relationship between both tables, and then a rule can be used to enforce the described relationship. Rules, which have been created to enforce general integrity, are a preferable solution in cases where data derived from one table must be maintained in another.

In addition, rules are applied in order to en-force referential integrity between tables with a relationship of the "parent–child" type. Referen-tial integrity is a relational database concept that ensures that relationships between tables remain consistent. When one table has a foreign key to another table, the concept of referential integrity states that no action of insert to the table that contains the foreign key is permitted, unless there is a corresponding record in the linked table (Ingres, 1998). Therefore an enforced relation-ship ensures each value entered in a foreign key column matches an existing value in the related primary key column. Rules can be created for both child and parent tables, to fire procedures

Table 2. The rule 'order_cipro'

```
create rule order_cipro
after update (in_drugs) of cipro
where cipro.in_drugs < 50
execute procedure order_ciproflaxin
(id = cipro.id,
cipro_left = cipro.in_stock);
```

that need to check and prevent the users from entering inconsistent data.

For example, suppose table 'neurology_nurse' has a foreign key that points to a field in table 'personnel'. Referential integrity would prevent a user from insert action to table 'neurology_nurse' that cannot be linked to table 'personnel'. In addi-tion, referential integrity rules are fired whenever any modification of the value of a linked field in 'personnel' occurs, in order that all related records in table 'neurology_nurse' will also be modified accordingly.

Furthermore, in addition to integrity enforce-ment, rules may be applied for other types of controls, such as cases of limitation in some rows and fields. Choosing a proper rule creating methodology is very important for healthcare environment, considering for example the limita-tions of the number of in-patient inside the wards. Suppose that the number of the in-patients of the ward A is been raised to some maximum value (let it be x), thereby any new in-patient must be placed in ward B. In that case the rule 'ward_b' is created that fires whenever the number of the in-patients of the ward_a is greater than x. Table 4 depicts the rule creation algorithm.

It will be noted that the rules technique, used in the hospital database, may also extend the permission system by ensuring that rows in op-eration code tables cannot be modified by unau-thorized users. In a similar way, "rules are used as security checkers on high priority tables that carry security labels as well as to define user transactions, and to arrange locks on resources, so that within a transaction, no new transactions can be issued" (Stonebraker, 1992). However,

Table 3. The rules creation algorithm

```
create procedure old_nurse
begin
        update orthopaedics_nurse
        set nurse = nurse - 1
        where name =:oname;
        insert into o_log values ('orthopaedics_nurse: ' +:oname + ', Deleted nurse: ') ;
end;
create rule update_nurse
after delete from orthopaedics_nurse
execute procedure old_nurse
        (oname = old. orthopaedics_nurse);
create procedure new_nurse
begin
        update neurology_nurse
        set nurse = nurse + 1
        where name =:nname;
        end;
create rule insert_nurse
        after update (nurse) of orthopaedics_nurse
        where old.nurse + 1 = new.nurse
        execute procedure new_nurse;
```

problems of overhead may arise in case that multiple rules are triggered on a specific table, and problems of dropping some rules in some cases may become very serious.

Under controlled circumstances a rule may be dropped and becomes unavailable as soon as it is completely removed from the database system. However, inevitably dropping rules can be very complex because the healthcare environment itself is very complex. For some clinical situations, medical information must be accessed by users whose roles do not readily grant access. Perhaps it is impossible to determine accurately whether a rule must be dropped from a physician who is being asked to give, for example, an extra opinion for a surgical in-patient. Unfortunately in some cases rules have to be disabled, for instance, when a utility that uploads a database must be used. In any case, for a fast-growing domain such as hospital informatics, it is valuable to be able to understand the advantages of rules from a variety of perspectives. Ceri and Widom (1998) observed that "many of the activities that would normally be coded in each application program to support these data management policies are centralized and abstracted using rules".

Table 4. The rule creation algorithm

```
create rule ward_b
after update (in_ patients) of patients
where patients.in_ patients.ward_a >x
execute procedure ward_b;
```

In addition to defining and creating rules, the creation of events and event-related privileges is of major importance to the security and maintaining of the hospital database. In the next session these additional issues will be discussed for better managing of health information and security.

Events and Security Auditing

As Heimrich and Specht (2002) pointed out, "an event is something that occurs at a specific point in time". According to the Ingress Administration Guide an event is something that occurs during the execution of a procedure. There are many classes of events, such as events on database procedures, events on accesses to tables, events on performance, server events and session events, among others. According to Ingres Visual DBA User guide, an event on a database may give rise to an application to notify some other application that a specific event has occurred. (Ingres, 1998). From a management perspective, a security event could be any use of procedures or access to tables or changes to user and group information.

In the proposed access control model, any event-related privilege may be granted to all parts of the security system (e.g. groups, users, and roles), in order to raise or register an event. In many cases, all types of access by all users of an application need to be logged for later analysis to find out and correct problems or possible threats. Apart from this, run time verification of groups and user names plays an important role in system security.

In order to implement security auditing, triggers are being placed on a number of tables to detect user illegal access operations, such as delete or update on a particular table, and e-mail exchange, among others. Triggers represent a set of actions that are executed when a database event occurs on a specified table, thus helping data integrity enforcement. They also give a chance to update related data and calculated fields whenever source data changes, preventing so something to "slip through the cracks" (Adams & Beckett, 1998). A single table may also contain more than one trigger, but all of them should relate to the same event.

For example, the table "medication" for inpatients must not be updated and no insert or delete are permitted, after a prescription has been completed by the pharmacy. Consequently, a security alarm statement, to define the conditions that will trigger the alarm, is created by the database administrator, through the statement of the form (Ingres, 2008):

Create security_alarm on table medication when insert, update, delete;

Thereby, whenever a user inserts a row in the table "medication", then the trigger fires and useful information is returned, as an audit file that contains any details about this action. To receive this log file, an appropriate table statement must be also applied to the table "medication", regardless of the trigger creation. The log file registers the event of insert that occurred in the specific table, such as the user name, the time at which the event took place, and the status and the type of the event, together with a text description of the event (Ingres, 2008).

The security auditing is of major importance to the healthcare environment not only to protect patient private medical information, but also to minimize the likelihood of harm from illegal actions. Several cases through the chain of public hospitals all over the world have been reported, involving incomplete and inefficient management of medication and supplies through staff illegal interventions (Mourtou & Pavlidis, 2005). Therefore, any previous security incidents at the healthcare environment should seriously be reviewed in order to overcome the possible weak points and to successfully develop a security audit plan under the current conditions. For example, it has been noticed that some users of the inpatient office register incorrectly the patient insurance company, thus restraining the patient charges. Moreover, considering that all necessary documents for the reimbursement of hospital charges must be submitted to the insurance company within six months after the date of hospitalization, otherwise the submission of such documents is considered overdue, the problem becomes more serious. Thereby, apart from log files that report events and actions, a user audit file is been created into the proposed accessed control model, that directly traces a specific user. Thus, when the director of the in-patient office is aware of the problem, s/he immediately asks the database administrator for reporting the users audit files and then he proceeds according the law and the hospital regulations. It is expected that further development and deployment of security auditing and better understanding of events, will increase the use of triggers at more levels.

FUTURE RESEARCH DIRECTIONS

The proposed access control model has been implemented since 2003, and in collaboration with the Centre of Computers of Social Services in the information system of a Greek Public hospital focusing on reaching the first level of a minimally functional EMR. The HIS and the access control model are both developed within Ingres II Enterprise Edition, which provides transparent access for application development, connectivity, and open information access across the Database Management System. In addition, the hospital database is running on the operating system Sco-Unix that offers a number of services to applications and users, although no graphical user interface has been applied yet. Although the windows style of user interface has given much to overcome users' difficulties and adaptation to computers, the usage of a command line interface is not becoming a real problem that could prevent the easy data transfer between running applications. Recently, Sco OpenServer Release 6.0 has been applied featuring large file support and easy to manage applications platform and also obtaining better support services. Moreover, a redundant array of inexpensive disks technology (RAID) is been applied to allow users to achieve high levels of storage reliability and to provide more security through an overall backup strategy (Patterson, et al., 1988).

It will be noted that before the access model implementation, login names and passwords were applied only through the operating system, hence without authorization to remote users. After the access model implementation, remote users are authorized for access through installation passwords that offer some advantages over user passwords: they indicate the user password will be authenticated by an external authentication mechanism. According to Ingres 9.2 Security Guide (2008), "by setting up an installation password to authorize access to a server installation from a remote client installation without setting up an operating system

account on the server, the user retains his identity as defined on the client instance". In other words users on the client do not require login accounts on the server. Furthermore, to face the need for identification and authentication of users when accessing their computers, a Telnet connection has been applied in order to transmit data via a TCP (McKenzie, 1973).

However, due to the increasing number of the users of the HIS and the growing of the demands, some tables and queries are growing all the time. On the other hand, according to Measure 2.6 (Information Society in Greece, (2005)) of the ICT applications in health and welfare during the Information Society Operational program, the completion of the introduction of health information technologies is provided, in order that health and welfare services systems will be based on operational data. Thereby, actions related to the preparation, selection, monitoring and assessment of activities of the projects of the Operational program must be provided, in order that demographic and clinical data for each hospital patient are transferred from the HIS of the same Region to the Integrated HIS (Information Society in Greece, 2005). Since transition constitutes a very complex task and must be managed from a lot of aspects, the central question arises: how flexible is the HIS to successfully allow the data transition.

For future work, there are still some issues that need to be taken into account, in the concept of access level and rules that require more analysis and development to comply with the defined policy of the new Integrated HIS. For example, special rule techniques could be used to allow the execution of some queries in more than one way, so increasing the degree of freedom of the possible options and therefore the flexibility index of the model could be increased (Mourtou, 2009). In this case, however, tables on which queries statistics are created are possibly not locked, so reducing the model reliability. Further, the nature and extent of security issues and plans surely vary greatly from hospital to hospital even of the same region.

CONCLUSION

For a fast growing domain such as HISs, it is crucial to be able to develop the efficiency and effectiveness of information security policy, especially when dealing with situations that affect the status and quality of life of the patient. In addition, the rules and procedures to follow in order to provide confidentiality of sensitive information have to focus on management of events on any table of the hospital database. The vast amounts of patient information must be efficiently and systematically protected in a variety of perspectives, requiring the provision of a set of techniques, tools and practices for the development of the critical elements that are required for a proper access control model. This model was designed in the context of the HIS and implements the four main issues presented in this work: the possible threats that can affect the security of patient information, the access control issues that are mainly related to the levels of hierarchy, the development of rules that may be applied for several types of control, and the implementation of events and security auditing.

Although there are numerous severe usability problems associated with the login procedures and with roles altering or removal, we believe that the proposed access control model not only helps the evolution of electronic healthcare security, but also is modular enough to take into account the heterogeneity of healthcare professional roles and actions, and thereby to be correctly adapted for other hospitals. Although this model is being successfully tested against several threats, new safeguards must be developed into the control process. For example, the wide use of the Internet within the hospital, and the use of mobile devices create specific threats to authentication and to confidentiality layers that have to be more carefully addressed. It is also noteworthy that the field of security control objectives presents a number of exciting challenges and opportunities for hospital administration and information scientists. In addition, an important and often neglected area in

HIS broadly is the security and access control, since the majority of public hospitals developed only administrative applications that have failed to be successfully deployed in the patient aspects of data confidentiality and integrity.

We believe that close examination of the secure access processes used in the proposed model could facilitate similar implementation efforts in other hospitals. Meanwhile, we think that identifying and clarifying the core concepts and relationships of the security issues will contribute to improve the sharability of existing security mechanisms as well as the hospital users transaction that rely on them.

ACKNOWLEDGMENT

I am grateful to Keith Jeffery and George Jonah Mourtos for fruitful discussions that contributed to my understanding of these issues. I also wish to acknowledge the helpful suggestions made by anonymous reviewers.

REFERENCES

Adams, D., & Beckett, D. (1998). 4D Triggers 2000. *Summit*, *98*, 2–17.

Allman, M. (2000). A Web Server's View of the Transport Layer. *ACM Computer Communication Review*, *30*(5), 10–20. doi:10.1145/505672.505674

Berman, J. J. (2002). Confidentiality Issues for Medical Data Miners. *Artificial Intelligence in Medicine*, *26*(1-2), 25–36. doi:10.1016/S0933-3657(02)00050-7

Blobel, B. (2002). *Information Systems. Studies in Health Technology and Informatics. Analysis, design and implementation of secure and interoperable distributed health information systems* (*Vol. 89*). Amsterdam: IOS Press.

Blobel, B. (2004). Authorisation and access control for electronic health record systems. *International Journal of Medical Informatics, 73*, 251–257. doi:10.1016/j.ijmedinf.2003.11.018

Blobel, B., & Holena, M. (1997). *Comparison, evaluation, and possible harmonisation of the HL7, DHE, and CORBA middleware*. In Dudeck, J. Blobel, B. Lordieck, W. Bórkle, T. (Eds.), New technologies in hospital information systems, Series Studies in Health Technology and Informatics, vol. 89, pp. 40—47, Amsterdam: IOS Press.

Blobel, B., & Roger-France, F. (2001). A systematic approach for analysis and design of secure health information systems. *International Journal of Medical Informatics, 62*(3), 51–78. doi:10.1016/S1386-5056(01)00147-2

Ceri, S., & Widom, J. (1998). Applications of active databases. In Widom, J., & Ceri, S. (Eds.), *Triggers and Rules for Advanced Database processing* (pp. 259–261). San Francisco, California.

Dodds, D. J. (1982). Reducing dictionary size by using a hashing technique. [New York: ACM Press.]. *Communications of the ACM, 25*(6), 368–370. doi:10.1145/358523.358547

Ferreira, A., Cruz-Correia, R., Antunes, L., & Chadwick, D. (2007). *Access Control: How can it improve patient's healthcare? Medical and Care Compunetics 4* (pp. 65–77). Amsterdam: IOS Press.

Gantz, J., & Rochester, B. J. (2005). *Pirates of the Digital Millennium*. New Jersey: Prentice Hall.

Gornshtein, D., & Tamarkin, B. (2004). *Locking conflicts resolution in Oracle RAC environments. A Technical White Paper*, WisdomForce Technologies, Revision 1.0, Retrieved 1/1/2010, from http://www.wisdomforce.com/resources/docs/locking.rac.pdf.

Grimson, J., Grimson, W., Berry, D., Stephens, G., Felton, E., & Kalra, D. (1998). A CORBA-based integration of distributed electronic healthcare records using the synapses approach. *IEEE Transactions on Information Technology in Biomedicine, 2*, 124–138. doi:10.1109/4233.735777

Gritzalis, D. (1994). *Information System Security in high vulnerability environments*. Doctoral dissertation, University of the Aegean, Greece.

Gritzalis, D. (2000). *Security and Reliability in ICT. Laboratorial exercises 1.5*. Computer Science Laboratory. Athens University of Economics and Business.

Gritzalis, D., Lambrinoudakis, C., Lekkas, D., & Deftereos, S. (2005). Technical guidelines for enhancing privacy and data protection in modern electronic medical environments. *IEEE Transactions on Information Technology in Biomedicine, 9*(3), 413–423. doi:10.1109/TITB.2005.847498

Gyongyi, J., & Garcia-Molina, H. (2005). *Web spam taxonomy*. In proceedings of the First International Workshop on Adversarial Information Retrieval on the Web (AIRWeb). In the 14th International World Wide Web Conference *Nippon Convention Center (Makuhari Messe), Chiba, Japan.*, New York: ACM Press.

Heimrich, T., & Specht, G. (2002). Enhancing ECA Rules for Distributed Active Database Systems. A.B. Chaudhri et al. (Eds.). Web Databases and Web Services 2002, LNCS 2593, (pp. 199–205). Berlin Heidelberg 2003:Springer-Verlag.

Hellenic Data Protection Authority (HDPA). (2006). *Law 3471/2006.*

Hornig, C. (1984). *A Standard for the Transmission of IP Datagrams over Ethernet Networks*, Retrieved June 13, 2009, from http://www.ietf.org/rfc/rfc894.txt.

Information Society in Greece. (2005). *ICT applications in health and welfare*, Action Line Measures, Technical Report of Measure 2.6, Retrieved November 27, 2008, from http://www.infosoc.gr/infosoc/en-UK/epktp/priority_actions/customerservice/hiddenchannel01/metro6.htm.

Ingres 9.2 Security Guide. (2008). *Introduction to Ingres Security: User Authentication Remote Users Installation Passwords*. pp.9.

Ingres II Enterprise Edition. (1998). *Database Administration's Guide. Release Notes for Ingres Release 2.0/9808* (pp. 328–333). Computer Associates International, Inc.

Ishac, J., & Allman, M. (2001). *On the performance of TCP spoofing in satellite networks*. NASA/TM—2001-211151.

ISO 7498-2. (1989). *Information processing systems — Open Systems Interconnection — Basic Reference Model — Part 2: Security Architecture*. Retrieved February 12, 2009, from http://webstore.iec.ch/preview/info_isoiec13888-2%7Bed1.0%7Den.pdf.

ISO/IEC 17799. (2005). *Information technology-Security techniques-Code of practice for information security management*. Retrieved February 12, 2009, from http://www.iso.org/iso/en/prods-services/popstds/informationsecurity.html.

Kara, S., & Kayis, B. (2004). Manufacturing flexibility and variability: an overview. *Journal of Manufacturing Technology Management, 15*, 466–478. doi:10.1108/17410380410547870

Katsikas, S. (1995). *The administration of risk in Information Systems. Information security, technical, legal and social issues*. Athens: EPY Editions.

Katsikas, S., Gritzalis, S., Spinellis, D. et al. (1997). *Trusted Third Party Services for Health Care in Europe*. CEC/DG XIII/INFOSEC, Project 20820, final report.

Knuth, D. (1973). *The Art of Computer Programming, Sorting and Searching*. Addison Wesley Series in Computer Science and Information Processing. 3, 506-542. Reading, MA: Addison-Wesley.

Kohavi, R. (1995). *A Study of Cross-validation and Bootstrap for Accuracy Estimation and Model Selection*. In Proceedings of the 14th International Joint Conference on Artificial Intelligence,(pp. 1137-1 143). San Francisco:Morgan Kaufmann.

Linden, H., Kalra, D., Hasman, A. & Talmon, J. (2009). Inter-organizational future proof EHR systems. A review of the security and privacy related issues. *International journal of medical informatics, 7 8*pp. 141–160.

McKenzie, A. M. (1973). *TELNET Protocol Specification*. Retrieved 1/1/2010, from ftp://ftp.rfc-editor.org/in-notes/rfc495.txt.

Mirkovic, J., Dietrich, S., Dittrich, D., & Reiher, P. (2004). *Internet Denial of Service: Attack and Defense Mechanisms*, pp. 19-20, 45, 51-52, and 297, New Jersey: Prentice Hall.

Miyazaki, S., & Masuda, M. (2005). Methods of Transposition of Nurses between Wards. *JSME International Journal Series C, 48*(1), 2–7. doi:10.1299/jsmec.48.2

Mourtou, E. (2007). *The technological innovation in the management of intra hospital procedures and the implementation of innovation on patient electronic medical record*. Doctoral dissertation, University of Patras, Greece.

Mourtou, E. (2009). An Evaluation of the Flexibility of the Information Management System in a Greek Public Hospital. *The Journal on Information Technology in Healthcare, 7*(5), 304–314.

Mourtou, E., & Pavlidis, G. (2005). Coding of Medical and Surgical Equipment and Supplies in Pharmacies of Greek Public Hospitals. *Proceedings of the 10th International Symposium on Health Information Management - iSHIMR 2005* pp. 150-159) Thessalonica, Greece: South East European Centre.

NCSC. (1998). *Glossary of Computer Security Terms.* In Aqua Book. Retrieved 20/5/2009, from http://www.marcorsyscom.usmc.mil/ sites/ia/ references/national/NCSC-TG-004% 20Glossary.html.

Patterson, A. D., Gibson, G., & Katz, H. R. (1998). *A case for redundant arrays of inexpensive disks (RAID).* University of California Berkley.

Sanghwan, K., Sangho, L., & Jongkun, L. (2006). *Computational Engineering in Systems Applications, IMACS Multiconference on Beijing (Vol. 1,* pp. 59–64). Deadlock Analysis of Petri Nets Based on the Resource Share Places Relationship.

Schumacher, R. (2005). High Performance SQL Server DBA. In Ed. Burleson D. Kittrell (Eds.) *Tuning & Optimization Secrets,* NC: Rampant TechPress.

Simpson, J. A., & Weiner, E. S. C. (1989). *Oxford English Dictionary.* Oxford, UK: Oxford University Press.

Stonebraker, M. (1992). The Integration of Rule Systems and Database Systems. *IEEE Transactions on Knowledge and Data Engineering, 4*(5), 415–423. doi:10.1109/69.166984

Swanson, M., Bartol, N., Sabato, J., Hash, J., & Graffo, L. (2003). *Security Metrics Guide for Information Technology Systems, NIST Special Publication 800-55, Computer Security Division, Information Technology Laboratory, National Institute of Standards and Technology.* Gaithersburg, MD: U.S. Department of Commerce, Technology Administration, National Institute of Standards and Technology.

Tanase, M. (2003). *IP Spoofing: An Introduction.* Retrieved 10/4/2009, from http://www.security-focus.com/infocus/1674.

Wager, K., & Wickham, L. F. Gloser. P.J. (2005). *Managing Health Care Information Systems. A practical Approach for Health Care Executives.* (pp. 81-83). San Francisco: Jossey-Bass.

Wiederhold, G., & Bilello, M. (1998). *Protecting Inappropriate Release of Data from Realistic Databases.* In Proceedings of DEXA '98 Workshop on Security and Integrity of Data Intensive Applications.

Wirth, N. (1986). *Algorithms and Data structures,* Prentice-Hall series in automatic computation, 257-279., London: Prentice-Hall.

Wold, G. H., & Shriver, R. F. (1994). Risk analysis techniques. *Disaster Recovery Journal, 7*(3), 46–52.

Zhang, Y., & Paxson, V. (1998). *Detecting Backdoors.* Retrieved May 20, 2009, from http://www.icir.org/vern/papers/backdoor/.

KEY TERMS AND DEFINITIONS

Accountability: The ability to audit the actions of all parties and processes which interact with the information and to determine whether actions are appropriate.

Access Levels: Determine what kind of data any user can view, register and edit.

Authenticity: The ability to be certain that medical records have been created by legitimate persons, have a valid timestamp and contain true (or perceived to be true) information as related to their context.

Data Availability: Patient information is available when needed (in the context of Hospital information systems.

Data Confidentiality: The assurance that information is accessible only to those authorized to have access.

Data Integrity: Preserving the accuracy and consistency of data regardless of changes made.

Deadlock: A stopping status of the flow of a marking due to a resource waiting.

Event: Something that occurs at a specific point in time.

Non-Repudiation: The property that ensures that the actions on an entity may be traced uniquely to the entity.

Rule: The specification of an action to be taken or a procedure to be executed in the hospital database, when a particular condition occurs.

Threat: A possible action or an event that may cause the loss of one or more than one security properties on an information system.

Trigger: An action that is executed when a database event occurs.

Section 2
Increasing the Flexibility of Access Control Mechanisms

Chapter 3
A Context–Aware Authorization Model for Process–Oriented Personal Health Record Systems

Eleni Mytilinaiou
University of Piraeus, Greece

Vassiliki Koufi
University of Piraeus, Greece

Flora Malamateniou
University of Piraeus, Greece

George Vassilacopoulos
University of Piraeus, Greece

ABSTRACT

Healthcare delivery is a highly complex process involving a broad range of healthcare services, typically performed by a number of geographically distributed and organizationally disparate healthcare providers requiring increased collaboration and coordination of their activities in order to provide shared and integrated care. Under an IT-enabled, patient-centric model, health systems can integrate care delivery across the continuum of services, from prevention to follow-up, and also coordinate care across all settings. In particular, much potential can be realized if cooperation among disparate healthcare organizations is expressed in terms of cross-organizational healthcare processes, where information support is provided by means of Personal Health Record (PHR) systems. This chapter assumes a process-oriented PHR system and presents a security framework that addresses the authorization and access control issues arisen in these systems. The proposed framework ensures provision of tight, just-in-time permissions so that authorized users get access to specific objects according to the current context. These permissions are subject to continuous adjustments triggered by the changing context. Thus, the risk of compromising information integrity during task executions is reduced.

DOI: 10.4018/978-1-61692-895-7.ch003

INTRODUCTION

Healthcare delivery is a highly complex process involving a broad range of healthcare services (e.g. in-patient, out-patient, emergency), typically performed by a number of geographically distributed and organizationally disparate healthcare providers requiring increased collaboration and coordination of their activities in order to provide shared and integrated care (Koufi & Vassilacopoulos, 2008). As healthcare providers are mostly hosting diverse and disparate information systems, it is difficult to obtain a complete picture of a person's healthcare record at the point of care when needed.

Recently, there has been a remarkable upsurge in activity surrounding the adoption of Personal Health Record (PHR) systems (Tang et al., 2006). A PHR is a consumer-centric approach to making comprehensive electronic health records (EHRs) available at the point of care while protecting patient privacy (Lauer, 2009). Unlike traditional EHRs which are based on the 'fetch and show' model, PHRs' architectures are based on the fundamental assumptions that the complete records are held on a central repository and that each patient retains authority over access to any portion of his/her record (Lauer, 2009; Wiljer et al., 2008). Thus, there is no need for interoperable virtual patient record architectures since storing and retrieving essential patient data is no longer fragmented. Hence, quality and safety of patient care is enhanced by providing patients and health professionals with relevant and timely information when and where needed, while ensuring protection and confidentiality of personal data.

Providing patients with access to their electronic health records offers great promise not only to improve patient health and satisfaction with their care but also to enhance professional and organizational approaches to health care (Wiljer et al., 2008). In particular, much potential can be realized if cooperation among disparate healthcare organizations is expressed in terms of cross-organizational healthcare processes, where information support is provided by means of PHR systems.

Healthcare processes are fundamentally different from those of other domains for a number of reasons including: (a) patient care requires availability of an extensive amount of medical data (medical images and free texts, XML documents, medical charts, etc), (b) ad hoc collaborative work and high degree of communication between healthcare professionals is an integral part of activities surrounding patient care, (c) each healthcare professional is involved in the care of several patients in parallel and (d) healthcare professionals are working in a mobile environment where their availability status is subject to rapid change due to the constant interruptions anytime, anywhere. Moreover, the computing environment in healthcare organizations is becoming increasingly complex as multiple heterogeneous technologies are employed and highly interactive user applications are supported. In such an environment, privacy and security of personal health information are considered critical factors in advancing the interests of both healthcare providers and consumers (Atluri & Huang, 1996; Wu, Sheth, Miller & Luo, 2002). Thus, one important consideration in the development of process-oriented PHR systems is to secure personal information against unauthorized access, collection, use, disclosure or disposal by ensuring a tight matching of permissions to actual usage and need. To this end, the least privilege principle should be enforced which, in turn, requires continuous adjustments of the sets of user permissions to ensure that, at any time, users (e.g. healthcare professionals) assume the minimum set of permissions required for the execution of each task of a healthcare process.

In healthcare processes, however, certain user permissions depend on the process execution context. That is, contextual information available at access time, such as user-to-patient proximity, location of attempted access and time of attempted access, can influence the authorization decision regarding task execution. This enables a more flexible and precise access control policy specification that satisfies the least privilege principle.

This chapter assumes a PHR-based architecture whereby healthcare processes are automated using the Web Services Business Process Execution Language (WS-BPEL, or BPEL for short) and presents an agent-based security framework that addresses authorization and access control issues arisen in process-based PHR systems. In particular, a context-aware authorization model and mechanism is presented that incorporates the advantages of broad, role-based permission assignment and administration across object types, as in role-based access control (RBAC) (National Institute of Standards and Technology, n.d.), and yet provides the flexibility for adjusting role permissions on individual objects at BPEL process enactment according to the current context. Thus, during the execution of a process instance, changes in contextual information are sensed to adapt user permissions to the minimum required for completing a job.

BACKGROUND

Healthcare delivery is undergoing radical change in an attempt to meet increasing demands in the face of rising costs. In turn, this requires providing the technological infrastructure that supports the coordination and integration of healthcare services across settings of care and among providers of care. To deal with these challenges, an IT-enabled, patient-centric model has emerged which can integrate care delivery across the continuum of services, from prevention to follow-up, and also coordinate care across all settings (Alberta Health Services, n.d). This model can be realized by means of PHRs. The original goal of PHRs was to transfer the control of health information from the hospital system or care site to patients, allowing information to be more portable across health systems. However, PHR technology is

evolving well beyond providing a consolidated patient record – in ways that make it more widely applicable and valuable to health systems. In particular, when integrated with workflow technology, PHR systems have the potential to stimulate transformational changes in healthcare delivery by (Alberta Health Services, n.d):

- *"Enabling access to comprehensive real-time patient data for clinicians and administrators across various care settings and facilities.*
- *Providing clinicians with tools to improve their partnership and coordination across different care settings.*
- *Achieving a level of integration that will allow data to flow seamlessly across the health system to enable the required tools and capabilities."*

For all the potential benefits, PHR systems have also perceived risks. One of them is related to health information security. In particular, consumers consistently rank concerns about security and privacy of health information above concerns for all other information, including financial (Chilmark Research, 2008). Hence, the need for suitable access control mechanisms preventing abuses and ensuring appropriate use of resources becomes imperative. RBAC constitutes a very attractive solution for providing security features in several computing infrastructures (Zhang & Parashar, 2004; Feinstein et al, 1996). Although the RBAC models vary from very simple to pretty complex, they all share the same basic structure of subject, role and privilege (Zhang & Parashar, 2004; Feinstein et al, 1996). Other factors such as time and location, which may be part of an access decision, are not considered in access control decision making (Zhang & Parashar, 2004; Feinstein et al, 1996).

During the last few years, research efforts regarding the development of highly adaptive security systems to achieve real-time, accurate and effective access control have been on the rise. Some involve the extension of the RBAC model, in order to enable the enforcement of more complex rules and the inclusion of context information in access control decisions. Zhang and Parashar have proposed a Dynamic RBAC model that extends the role based access control model and dynamically adjusts static Role Assignments and Permission Assignments based on context information (Zhang & Parashar, 2004). In (Kapsalis et al, 2006) a context-aware access control architecture is presented, in order to support fine-grained authorizations for the provision of secure e-services. The proposed architecture is based on a RBAC model, which incorporates dynamic context information in the form of context constraints. The latter involve the evaluation of both simple and composite context conditions. In (Byun et al., 2005) access control relies on the well-known RBAC model as well as on the notion of conditional role which is based on the notions of role attribute and system attribute. The role attributes can be viewed as cached user information that is relevant to the specific roles, and the role attribute values of a user should be updated if the user information changes. In (Hung, 2005) a framework of RBAC with privacy-based extensions is proposed. This framework aims at tackling the need for confidentiality of personal identifiable information and protected health information such as EHRs in e-Healthcare services. In (Kulkarni & Tripathi, 2008) a context-aware RBAC (CARBAC) model for pervasive computing applications is presented. In this access control model, dynamic context information is used in role admission policies, in policies related to permission executions by role members and in policies related to access of dynamically interfaced services by role members. In (Lia et al, 2009) a group-based RBAC model (GB-RBAC) is proposed for secure collaborations. This model is based on RBAC96 and extended with the group concept to capture dynamic users and permissions. Thus, global or system level management by system administra-

tors is supported as well as local or group level management by group administrators.

In this chapter, a security framework is proposed which addresses access control issues in the context of a process-oriented PHR system. The proposed framework allows for the definition of flexible and precise security policies that reflect real-time access control requirements. To this end, the traditional role-based model is enhanced by adding context-awareness features thus leading to an individualized security system for the regulation of access over tasks and data objects.

MOTIVATING SCENARIO

To illustrate the main principles of the proposed system architecture and implementation, an example of a cross-organizational healthcare process is described. As patient referrals are usually made among various healthcare providers (e.g. for hospitalization, for inpatient/outpatient consultation or for performing specialized medical procedures), there is a need to ensure that automated healthcare processes can be executed remotely and integrated patient information can be accessed through the execution of these processes by authorized users where and when needed. Thus, the sample process considered here is concerned with patient referrals issued by healthcare professionals to a clinical department of the same or another hospital.

Suppose a healthcare delivery situation where a hospital's physician, while on a ward round, visits one of his/her patients. While assessing the patient's condition, at the point of care, the physician needs to access the patient's medical record and to request a medical consultation from a cardiologist. After receiving the request, the consulting cardiologist assesses the patient's condition by taking into account the relevant portions of his medical record. In order to inform the referring physician of his medical findings, he sends him a consultation report. In turn, the

Figure 1. Consultation process model using IBM WebSphere workflow

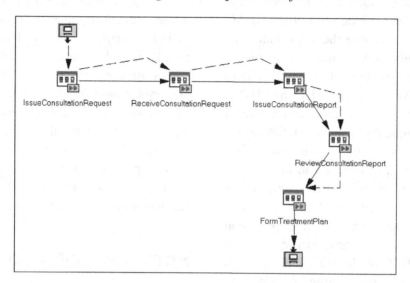

referring physician forms a suitable treatment plan for his patient.

Figure 1 shows a high-level view of the healthcare process pertaining to consultation management using the IBM WebSphere Work-flow build-time tool (IBM Corporation, 2005). In the sample healthcare process, two hospital departments are involved: Department of General Medicine and Department of Cardiology. Two of the participating roles in the healthcare process are: Physician (PH) and Cardiologist (CR). Table 1 shows an extract of authorization requirements regarding task execution and related data access privileges.

From an authorization perspective, the healthcare process of Figure 1 surfaces several requirements with regard to task execution and related data access privileges. These requirements include the following:

- **Task execution:** In certain circumstances the candidates for a task instance execution should be dynamically determined and be either a sub-group of the authorized users or only one, specific authorized user. For example, the request for a consultation from a cardiologist (issued by a physician) should be routed only to the sub-group of cardiologists who hold the relevant sub-specialty (e.g. interventional or echocardiography) and the consultation report (issued by a cardiologist) should be routed only to the requesting physician.

- **Data access:** Given that a role holder can execute a specific task, he/she should be allowed to exercise a dynamically determined set of permissions on certain data objects only. For example, during the execution of the "IssueConsultationRequest" task, a physician is allowed to read patient record data and to issue (write, edit and send) consultation requests only for his/her patients while on duty and within the hospital premises.

- **Permission propagation:** Some role holders should receive additional permissions on certain data objects in order to effectively execute a task but these permissions should be revoked upon successful execution of the task. For example, for an effective execution of the "IssueConsultationReport" task with regard to a patient, in response

Table 1. Extract of authorization requirements for the healthcare process of Figure 1

	Authorization Requirement
1.	PHs may issue consultation requests for their patients only (IssueConsultationRequest).
1.1	PHs may write consultation requests for their current patients.
1.2	PHs may edit consultation requests for their current patients before sent.
1.3	PHs may send consultation requests for their current patients to physicians who hold the relevant specialty/sub-specialty.
1.4	PHs may cancel consultation requests for their current patients after sent.
1.5	PHs may write and read PHRs of their current patients but they may read-only past PHR versions of their patients.
2.	CRs may issue patient consultation reports on request by PHs (IssueConsultationReport).
2.1	CRs may read patient consultation requests issued by PHs
2.2	CRs may read-only certain portion of the PHRs of patients they are requested to issue consultation reports for.
2.3	CRs may write patient consultation reports for their current patients.
2.4	CRs may edit patient consultation reports for their current patients before sent.
2.5	CRs may send patient consultation reports for their current patients to the requesting PHs only.
2.6	CRs may cancel patient consultation reports issued by them after sent.
2.8	CRs may read past patient consultation reports prepared by them.
3.	PHs may form treatment plans for their patients after having received the consultation reports issued by CRs on request by them (Prepare_Patient_Proposal).
3.1	PHs may read-only consultation reports issued by CRs only if requested by them.
3.2	PHs may form a treatment plan for their current patients.
3.3	PHs may alter a treatment plan for their current patients before putting it on the patient.
3.4	PHs may write and read PHRs of their current patients.

to a request submitted by a physician, a consulting physician (e.g. the cardiologist) should receive the permission to read the patient's record but he/she should not be allowed to retain this permission after successful task execution.

The above requirements suggest that certain data access permissions of the healthcare process participants depend on the process execution context. In particular, contextual information available at access time, such as user-to-patient proximity, location of attempted access and time of attempted access, can influence the authorization decision regarding task execution and, given this permission, associated web service invocation to access the relevant data objects. This enables a more flexible and precise access control policy specification that satisfies the least privilege principle by incorporating the advantages of having broad, role-based permissions across process tasks and data object types, like RBAC, yet enhanced with the ability to simultaneously support the following features: (a) predicate-based access control, limiting user access to specific data objects, (b) a permission propagation function from one role holder to another in certain circumstances, and (c) determining qualified task performers during a process instance based not only on the role-to-task permission policy, specified at process build time, but also on application data processed during the process instance. In addition, the model should not incur any significant administrative overhead and should be self-administering to a great extent.

Figure 2. System architecture

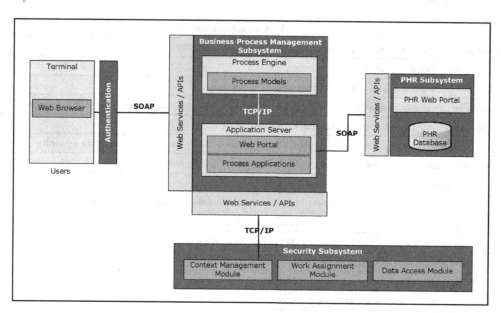

SYSTEM ARCHITECTURE

The prototype system described here facilitates remote execution of automated healthcare processes and, in turn, access to comprehensive patient information which is stored in a central repository. In this environment, a robust security framework is in place in order to ensure that health information follows patients throughout their care in a secure manner and that comprehensive information is made available to appropriate people anywhere, anytime.

Figure 2 illustrates a high-level view of the system architecture, which consists of three subsystems, namely the business process management (BPM) subsystem, the PHR subsystem, and the security subsystem.

BPM Subsystem

The BPM subsystem is responsible for managing healthcare processes. Apart from the process modeling tools, a core component of this subsystem is the Process Engine, a robust platform for executing process-based applications. Interactions with

the Process Engine are performed by means of a customized web portal which has been developed in order to establish secure access to healthcare processes and the web services invoked by them. To this end, digital signatures are utilized for certain parts of the messages exchanged during a BPEL process enactment. For example, each request for a task execution results at a request for a web service invocation. This request is performed by means of a SOAP message, parts of which (SOAP body and/or header) are digitally signed using the private key of the user's X.509 certificate. Thus, integrity of information exchanged in each transaction is ensured. Likewise, the web service response is digitally signed to ensure data integrity.

PHR Subsystem

The PHR subsystem supports both patients by enabling them to actively manage their own health and authorized healthcare professionals by ensuring quick and secure availability of patients' health data. The PHR subsystem comprises:

- A central repository where the complete patient records are held,
- A web portal through which a patient can access and manage his/her lifelong health information and make appropriate parts of it available to those who need it, and
- A number of web services which comprise a uniform interface to the central repository.

In a typical PHR system, authorization for access to medical information contained in the patient's PHR is exclusively granted either by the record owner (consumer or patient) or by an assigned "gatekeeper" (e.g. next of kin) (ICW eHealth Framework, n.d.; Power, 2009).

Security Subsystem

The security subsystem is responsible for regulating access to BPEL process tasks and associated web services. There is one security subsystem installed in each healthcare institution. Each one of these subsystems consists of three modules that cooperate to ensure that security policies are faithfully and consistently enforced. These modules are the Context Management Module (CMM), the Work Assignment Module (WAM) and the Data Access Module (DAM). The CMM acquires contextual information influencing authorization decisions and communicates it to WAM and DAM which are responsible for regulating access over BPEL process tasks and PHR data objects respectively. A more detailed description of this subsystem will be provided in the next two sections.

ACCESS CONTROL MODEL

User interactions are currently not covered by WS-BPEL which is primarily designed to support automated business processes that orchestrate activities exposed as web services (Kloppmann et al., 2005). However, the spectrum of activities that make up general purpose processes, including healthcare processes, is broader than this, because people participate in the execution of business processes. In particular, a healthcare process comprises disparate and distributed pieces of logic performed by a large number of personnel. For each piece of logic (i.e. task) authorization decisions cannot be made during design time as there is not enough information about the context on which the decision should be based. More specifically, in a healthcare process, role-based authorization is often based on a combination of contextual constraints imposed on each task and user roles, information that is not available during process modeling.

Within a process-oriented PHR system there is a need to address authorization in a centralized manner in order to enforce the least privilege principle. In turn, this requires ensuring that access permissions with regard to process tasks and associated web services are only awarded dynamically, thus allowing users to assume the absolute minimum role required for task executions and web service invocations. Hence, there is a need to enforce context-aware authorization constraints regarding BPEL task executions and associated web service invocations that result in accesses to PHR information.

Process Execution Context

Context can be defined as any information which is available at run time and is considered relevant to the resource accesses considered (Emig et al, 2006). Thus, it may be assumed that a context is defined by an evaluation of a relevant set of context types that may be divided into two main classes: static and dynamic. Static context types are those whose values are known at design time and are not subject to change during a BPEL process execution (e.g. physician's identity and specialty). Dynamic context types are those whose values are determined at runtime and are subject to constant

Figure 3. A subrole example

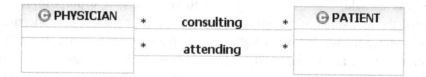

change during a BPEL process execution. For example, information related to the environment (e.g. spatio-temporal) and the "proximity" relationship between a physician and a patient (i.e. physician X is an attending physician to patient Y).

In a typical RBAC environment, roles are often defined as named collections of capabilities and privileges intended to perform healthcare functions and are assigned to users at design time through a many-to-many relationship. Users acting on a role are automatically assigned all the access permissions encapsulated in that role (Casati et al, 2001). However, these permissions may be more than those required for process task executions and web service invocations. Hence, to enforce the least privilege principle, context-based derivative roles are defined which, at any time, encapsulate the minimum sets of permissions that are tailored to run time access needs of users, so that users are provided with tight, just-in-time permissions when needed (Liu & Shen, 2003).

On these grounds, the new concept of subrole is introduced, which supplements the role concept of the typical RBAC model. Roles correspond to existing organizational structures and define the division of work and the lines of authority based on job functions and seniority (e.g. "physician" and "cardiologist"); they are specified during process design and may be taken on by users at run time, possibly subject to a number of contextual constraints such as spatio-temporal (Marjanovic, 2005). On the other hand, subroles are derived from one or more roles based on certain contextual constraints (e.g. "attending physician" and "consulting physician") and may be assigned to and revoked from individuals at run time on the

occurrence of specific events. It should be noted that a subrole is not assigned to a user but to a relationship (see Figure 3). For example, the subrole "consulting cardiologist" for a patient is derived from the roles "cardiologist" and "patient" and is taken on by a cardiologist when he/she is assigned to provide consultation in response to a request issued by the "attending physician" of that patient. In addition, it may be perfectly acceptable for a user holding the subrole "attending physician" for a patient to modify or cancel a submitted request for consultation before the latter is performed by a user holding the subrole "consulting cardiologist" for that patient, but certainly not after it has been performed. Hence, the subrole "consulting cardiologist" for a patient is revoked on the occurrence of the event that earmarks the performance of the consultation procedure.

Within the proposed system, the context information influencing authorization decisions is related to the users, the objects (i.e. tasks and associated web services) and the environment. In particular:

- The user context, as indicated by its name, is related to the user (i.e. healthcare professional) and consists of static attributes (e.g. identity, specialty) and dynamic attributes (e.g. physician's location, workload and availability)
- The object context is related to process tasks and associated web services and consists of static attributes (e.g. patient-determined policies on PHR data accessed by web services) and dynamic attributes (e.g. object status)

- The environmental context, as indicated by its name, is related to the environment and consists of dynamic attributes (e.g. time of attempted access)

Context-Aware Permission Assignment

In the proposed system, context-based subroles are used for controlling access to process tasks (execution) and associated web services (invocation). Hence, a subrole is translated into task execution permissions and given these permissions into web service invocation permissions (i.e. data access permissions). In particular:

1. Upon request for a task execution, the relevant context is evaluated and if certain conditions are met the user is assigned a subrole which he holds throughout task execution.

2. Given that the user has been assigned a subrole (i.e. has received the permission to execute a task), the corresponding permissions for invoking the associated web service (i.e. to access the relevant portion of the patient's PHR) are also assigned to him provided that certain conditions are met.

In both cases, whether required conditions are met is determined through the evaluation of relevant contextual constraints. For example, in the healthcare process of Figure 1, an authorization requirement may specify that "A physician can issue requests for consultation from within a hospital, between 8am to 5pm and for his/her patients only". This requirement contains three contextual constraints: (a) "for his/her patients only" which describes a physician-to-patient "proximity" relationship between a physician and a patient that can be expressed by the subrole "attending physician", (b) "from within a hospital" (location), and (c) "between 8am to 5pm" (temporal). All these constraints are taken into account in deciding whether an attempted access by a user can be permitted or denied. Hence, the above requirement can be expressed as follows: "An attending physician to a patient can execute the "IssueConsultationReport" process task and invoke the associated web service from within a hospital and between 8am to 5pm".

ACCESS CONTROL MECHANISM

As shown in Figure 2, the three modules of the security subsystem cooperate upon each request for BPEL task execution and associated web services invocation in order to determine the relevant permissions. All three modules are agent-based. In particular, each module implements the core functionality of a corresponding agent which is responsible for performing a certain task. In our prototype system, three types of agents have been defined, namely Context Acquisition Agent (CAA), Work Assignment Agent (WAA) and Data Access Agent (DAA).

- **Context Acquisition Agent (CAA):** it is responsible for capturing the runtime context and communicating it to the relevant agents handling permission assignments (either for a task execution or for web service invocation).

- **Work Assignment Agent (WAA):** it is responsible for assigning to each user the required permissions for a task execution. In particular, upon creation (initiation) of a process instance a WAA is automatically created. WAA tracks task initiations and terminations by receiving relevant messages by the process instance that created it. When WAA receives a task initiation message, it evaluates the context recorded by the CAA against the security policies it implements and identifies the subgroup of users who are eligible to execute the task. For each one of these users, the list of pending tasks is updated so as to include the new task. When a member of the subgroup accepts to undertake the execution of a task, the WAA is informed and alters the state of the task to unavailable in the work lists of the rest of the members of the subgroup. When the WAA receives a task termination message, it revokes all permissions assigned earlier.

- **Data Access Agent (DAA):** it is responsible for assigning to each user the required permissions for a web service invocation that results in data access. After a user picks a task for execution, a request for the invocation of the associated web service is placed. A DAA is then created which evaluates the runtime user context, that is, time of access, location of the user and other environmental variables and according to the policy rules it implements it determines the permissions the user should acquire in order to invoke the relevant web service. When a task is terminated the DAA revokes all permissions granted to the user.

PROTOTYPE IMPLEMENTATION

To illustrate the functionality of the proposed security model a prototype consultation request management system was implemented in a laboratory environment.

Implementation Issues

The system was developed as a web application using the Apache/Tomcat as Web/Application Server. The platform used for the generation of sample patient PHRs is Care2X Integrated Healthcare Environment. Care2X can store patient's complete medical information in one convenient and secure location (Care2X Integrated Healthcare Environment, n.d.). In addition, it supports the definition of static authorizations on each PHR.

In particular, a patient can authorize healthcare providers to access his/her record and assign to them specific access privileges (Care2X Integrated Healthcare Environment, n.d.). Access to data stored in Care2X repository is achieved by means of web services which make use of the Care2X Application Programming Interface (API).

The security subsystem was implemented as a distributed, multi-agent system using the Java Agent Development framework (JADE) as a construction and execution environment (Bellifemine et al., 2007; Java Agent Development framework, n.d.). JADE is an open-source software framework, aiming at assisting the development and execution of agent-based applications in compliance with the Foundation for Intelligent Physical Agents (FIPA) specifications for interoperable multi-agent systems (The Foundation for Intelligent Physical Agents, n.d.). In the security subsystem agents are held in four containers, namely the main container and three peripheral containers. Containers are activated by a BootDaemon process and container agents are then employed to process each transaction of a healthcare professional with the BPM subsystem and, in turn, with the PHR subsystem. The main container holds three JADE-specific agents, the Agent Management System (AMS), the Directory Facilitator (DF) and the Configuration Agent (CFA). The AMS represents the authority in the platform, namely it is the only agent that can activate platform management actions such as creating/killing other agents, killing containers and shutting down the platform (Java Agent Development Framework, n.d.). The DF implements the yellow pages service by means of which the other agents advertise their services and find other agents offering services they need (Java Agent Development Framework, n.d.). The CFA is responsible for interacting with the boot daemons and controlling the application lifecycle. Each one of the peripheral containers of the security subsystem holds a JADE-specific agent, namely Controller Agent (CA), and one of the three application-specific agents mentioned

Figure 4. Security architecture

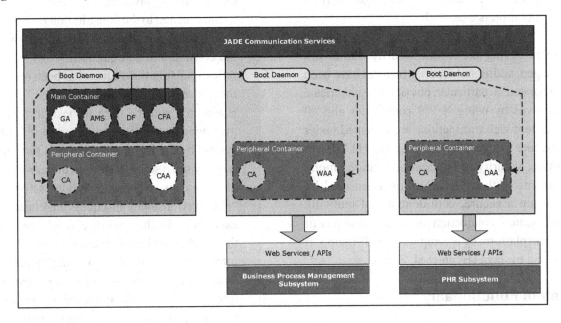

above, namely CAA, WAA and DAA as illustrated in Figure 4.

Agents execute tasks periodically or stimulated by an event or a message. These tasks are carried out within operations called behaviours. Several behaviours are executed concurrently by each agent. When there are no tasks available for execution, the agent's thread goes to sleep in order not to consume CPU time. The thread is woken up again once a task becomes available for execution after a stimulus. Agents communicate with each other using FIPA Agent Communication Language (ACL) (The Foundation for Intelligent Physical Agents, n.d.) over a specific protocol based on asynchronous message passing. Each agent has a 'mailbox' (the agent message queue) where the JADE run-time posts messages sent by other agents. Whenever a message is posted in the mailbox, the receiving agent is notified. The communication of the agents with the BPEL process is accomplished in two steps:

1. WSIF (Web Services Invocation Framework) enables the connectivity of BPEL processes with resources other than web services by describing each resource in WSDL even if it is not a web service. In the case of Java Classes, WSIF provides bindings for BPEL processes. The data exchange between BPEL and the Java classes requires data transformation. Because BPEL variables are XML and Java variables are not, a mapping between XML and Java is required. For that reason XML façades are utilized. XML façades are a set of Java interfaces and classes through which data stored in BPEL variables can be accessed using get/set methods (Juric et al., 2006).

2. JADE agents can be started from an external application. The JADE runtime is created to host them. These external applications are Java classes that can communicate with the BPEL process with the help of WSIF. Data is transferred in the Java class, and an agent is created in order to send a message containing the data and the requested operation, to the mailbox of the appropriate

agent. Depending on the message, the right operation is executed.

In achieving the robust security framework envisaged, additional security features have been incorporated. In particular, physicians authenticate themselves by using X.509 certificates and all subsequent web transactions are executed under the Secure Socket Layer (SSL) via HTTPS. In addition, security in the communication among the agents of the agent platform is ensured by setting up a secure, confidential and mutually authenticated, connection amongst containers of the agent platform by leveraging TLS/SSL support provided by Java (Byun et al, 2005).

System Functionality

Suppose that a hospital's physician, while on a ward round, needs a medical consultation from a cardiologist for one of his/her patients. To this end,

1. The physician initiates the relevant BPEL process for his/her patient, that is the BPEL process that corresponds to the healthcare process illustrated in Figure 1. In turn, the "IssueConsultationRequest" task of the new process instance is initiated and the BPM subsystem sends a relevant message to the security subsystem. Then, the WAA is created and contacts the CAA in order to obtain the contextual information required for making an authorization decision regarding the specific task execution. This information includes the time and location of attempted access as well as the patient ID. If the physician is on duty and within the hospital premises, the WAA generates a new subrole, namely "attending physician", based on the contextual information obtained by the CAA and makes the physician member of this role. In this way, the physician receives the required permissions to execute the task. During the task instance

execution, the physician provides the information related to the consultation requested (e.g. type of consultation, patient for whom the consultation is requested).

2. After a consultation request has been issued, the "ReceiveConsultationRequest" task is initiated and the relevant task initiation message is submitted to the security subsystem by the BPM subsystem. In turn, the security subsystem determines the sub-group of physicians who are candidates for the "ReceiveConsultationRequest" task instance execution. To this end, the WAA contacts the CAA in order to obtain the contextual information required for making an authorization decision regarding this task execution. This information includes specialty of consulting physician, current workload and availability of physicians who hold the relevant specialty/sub-specialty. Following that, the WAA generates a new subrole, namely "consulting cardiologist", based on the specialty of the consulting physician (i.e. cardiologist) and the other contextual information obtained by the CAA and makes the sub-group of physicians holding the relevant specialty/sub-specialty members of this role. Then, the Process Engine routes the "ReceiveConsultationRequest" task instance to the work lists of the physicians holding the subrole "consulting cardiologist". Some of the rules that need to be adhered to, while determining the members of the new subrole, are:

    a. The cardiologists must be available for the period of time required for the fulfillment of the consultation requested for each specific patient.

    b. The cardiologists having less workload will constitute candidates for the fulfillment of the consultation request.

    As soon as one of the members of the subrole "consulting cardiologist" picks the "ReceiveConsultationRequest" task instance for execution, the task instance is removed from the work lists of the rest of the members. In turn, an XML/SOAP message is created containing, among others, the patient ID. This message is sent to the appropriate web service, which will use these parameters as input for its method execution that retrieves the relevant parts of the patient's PHR. Upon request for this web service invocation, the DAA acquires the required context captured by the CAA in order to determine the specific permissions of the user requesting the web service invocation. If the user (i.e. the consulting cardiologist) has the required authorization the web service is invoked.

3. After the task "ReceiveConsultationRequest" has been executed (i.e. "consulting cardiologist" has examined the patient), the "IssueConsultationReport" task instance is initiated and a relevant message is submitted to the security subsystem by the BPM subsystem. Then, the WAA assigns the execution of "IssueConsultationReport" task instance to the same consulting cardiologist that executed the "ReceiveConsultationRequest" task. Thus, the consulting cardiologist can issue a consultation report for the patient, by executing the "IssueConsultationReport" task instance. Upon request for this task execution a task initiation message is submitted to the security subsystem by the BPM subsystem. The security subsystem, in turn, determines whether the consulting cardiologist has the permission to execute this task instance. In particular, the WAA contacts the CAA in order to obtain the contextual information required for making an authorization decision regarding this task execution. This information includes time and location of attempted access. If the consulting cardiologist is on duty and tries to execute the task from within the hospital premises, the task is executed, he/she provides all the required information (i.e. consultation report and any

relevant files) and an XML/SOAP message is created containing all this information. This message is sent to the appropriate web service which will use this information as input for its method execution that stores information in the patient's PHR. Prior to the web service invocation the DAA acquires the required context captured by the CAA in order to determine the specific permissions for the consulting cardiologist requesting the web service invocation. If he/she has the required permissions the web service is invoked. When the task execution is completed a relevant message is submitted to the security subsystem. Then, all permissions granted to the consulting cardiologist regarding "IssueConsultationReport" task execution and the associated web service invocation, are revoked by the WAA and the DAA, respectively. In addition, the WAA deletes the subrole "consulting cardiologist". At the same time, the WAA assigns the execution of the "ReceiveConsultationReport" task instance to the attending physician who had requested the consultation for his/her patient.

4. Upon request for the execution of the "ReceiveConsultationReport" task instance, the BPM subsystem submits a task initiation message to the security subsystem. The WAA contacts the CAA in order to obtain the contextual information required for making an authorization decision regarding this task execution. This information includes time and location of attempted access and patient ID. If the physician is on duty and within hospital premises and holds the subrole "attending physician" for this specific patient, the task is executed and an XML/SOAP message is created containing, among others, the patient ID. This message is sent to the appropriate web service which will use these parameters as input for its method execution that retrieves consultation reports

Figure 5. Sequence diagram for "IssueConsultationReport" task execution

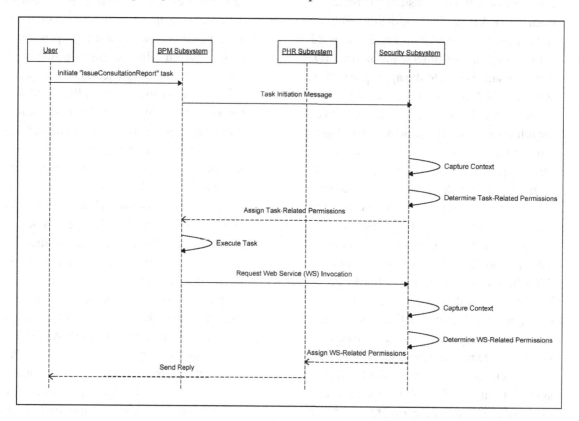

from the PHR data repository. Upon request for this web service invocation, the DAA acquires the required context captured by the CAA in order to determine the specific permissions for the attending physician requesting to invoke the web service that provides access to relevant parts of the patient's PHR. When the task execution is completed a relevant message is submitted to the security subsystem. Then, all permissions granted to the attending physician regarding "ReceiveConsultationReport" task execution and the associated web service invocation, are revoked by the WAA and the DAA, respectively. In addition, the WAA deletes the subrole "attending physician".

The sequence of actions taking place upon request for a task execution of the healthcare

process of Figure 1 (i.e. "IssueConsultationReport" task) is illustrated in Figure 5, by means of a sequence diagram.

CONCLUDING REMARKS

Process-oriented PHRs offer significant potential to stimulate transformational changes in healthcare delivery as they can meet collaboration requirements among health professionals and address healthcare information needs by providing a complete copy of each patient's medical record. In such environments, new challenges and new opportunities with respect to protecting the privacy and security of health information are created. Hence, it is essential to provide an effective access control mechanism that meets the requirements imposed by the least privilege principle. In turn, adherence to the least privilege principle requires continuous adjustments of user permissions in order to adapt to the current situation. This chapter presents a process-oriented PHR system that facilitates authorized access to healthcare processes. To this end, agent technology is used for the implementation of a fine-grained access control mechanism which regulates user access to BPEL process tasks and associated web services resulting is PHR data accesses. Thus, a tight matching of permissions to actual usage and need is ensured.

FUTURE RESEARCH DIRECTIONS

During the last few years, several health systems around the world have recognized the transformative potential of PHRs as well as the barriers to realizing this potential (Tang et al, 2006). As with EHR adoption, the impediments to PHR adoption are not limited to technical ones. In addition to the economic and technological challenges, organizational and behavioral issues can delay PHR adoption (Tang et al, 2006). Barriers exist both at the environmental level and at the level of individual health care professionals and consumers (Tang et al, 2006). On the one hand, developers of PHR systems must have a full understanding of individuals' and clinicians' mental models of healthcare processes and related workflows. Nowadays, workflow models for both providers and patients are poorly understood. For example, while informaticians have studied clinical workflow models in settings of care, they are rarely concerned with describing patient flow in the community and fitting the PHR into it. On the other hand, healthcare consumers must understand and accept their roles and responsibilities related to their own healthcare. An individual's PHR can only be useful if the person understands the importance of maintaining and coordinating health-related documentation and activities with health care providers. Breaking down these barri-

ers is an issue of outmost importance and, as such, it suggests directions for further work.

REFERENCES

Alberta Health Services. (n.d). Engaging the Patient in Healthcare: An overview of Personal Health Record Systems and Implications for Alberta, *White Paper*.

Atluri, V., & Huang, W. (1996). *An Authorization Model for Workflows*. Paper presented at the 4th European Symposium on Research in Computer Security, (. *Lecture Notes in Computer Science*, *1146*, 44–64.

Bellifemine, F., Caire, G., & Greenwood, D. (2007). *Developing Multi-Agent Systems with JADE*. Wiley Series in Agent Technology, John Wiley & Sons. doi:10.1002/9780470058411

Byun, J. W., Bertino, E., & Li, N. (2005, June). *Purpose Based Access Control of Complex Data for Privacy Protection*. Paper presented at the 10th ACM Symposium on Access Control Models and Technologies (SACMAT'05), Stockholm, Sweden.

Care2X Integrated Healthcare Environment (n.d.). Retrieved July 15, 2009, from http://www.care2x.org/.

Casati, F., Castano, S., & Fugini, M. (2001). Managing workflow authorization constraints through active database technology. *Information Systems Frontiers*, *3*(3), 319–338. doi:10.1023/A:1011461409620

Chilmark Research. (2008). *iPHR Market Report: Analysis & Trends of Internet-based Personal Health Records' Market*. Retrieved November 25, 2009, from http://chilmarkresearchstore.com/iphr-market-report-2008.html.

Corporation, I. B. M. (2005). *IBM Websphere Workflow - Getting Started with Buildtime V. 3.6.* Retrieved October 20, 2007, from http://publibfp. dhe.ibm.com/epubs/pdf/h1262860.pdf.

Emig, C., Schandua, H., & Abeck, S. (2006). *SOA-aware authorization control*. Paper presented at the International Conference on Software Engineering Advances, Papeete, Tahiti, French Polynesia.

Feinstein, H., Sandhu, R., Coyne, E., & Youman, C. (1996). Role-based access control models. *IEEE Computer*, *29*(2), 38–47.

Hung, P. C. K. (2005). *Towards a Privacy Access Control Model for e-Healthcare Services*. Paper presented at the 3rd Annual Conference on Privacy, Security and Trust. The Fairmont Algonquin, St. Andrews, New Brunswick, Canada.

ICW eHealth Framework. (n.d.). *Lifesensor*. Retrieved July 15, 2009, from http://idn.icw-global. com/solutions/lifesensor/lifesensor.html.

JADE. (n.d.). *Java Agent DEvelopment Framework*. Retrieved July 17, 2009, from http://jade. tilab.com.

FIPA. (n.d.). *The Foundation for Intelligent Physical Agents Agent Communication Language Specifications*. (n.d.). Retrieved July17, 2009, from http://www.fipa.org/repository/ aclspecs.html.

(FIPA). (n.d.). *The Foundation for Intelligent Physical Agents* Retrieved July 17, 2009, from http://www.fipa.org/.

Juric, M. B., Mathew, B., & Sarang, P. (2006). *Business Process Execution Language for Web Services*. Packt Publishing Ltd.

Kapsalis, V., Hadellis, L., Karelis, D., & Koubias, S. (2006). A dynamic context-aware access control architecture for e-services. *Journal of Computer Security*, *25*, 507–521. doi:10.1016/j. cose.2006.05.004

Kloppmann, M., Koenig, D., Leymann, F., Pfau, G., Rickayzen, A., von Riegen, C., et al. (2005). *WS-BPEL Extension for People - BPEL4People, IBM Corporation and SAP AG*. Retrieved November 30, 2009, from http://download.boulder.ibm. com/ibmdl/pub/software/dw/specs/ws-bpel4peo-ple/BPEL4 People_white_paper.pdf.

Koufi, & V., Vassilacopoulos, G. (2008). *HDG-Portal: A Grid Portal Application for Pervasive Access to Process-Based Healthcare Systems*. Paper presented at the 2nd International Conference in Pervasive Computing Technologies in Healthcare, Tampere, Finland.

Kulkarni, D., & Tripathi, A. (2008). *Context-Aware Role-based Access Control in Pervasive Computing Systems*, Paper presented at the 13th ACM Symposium on Access Control Models and Technologies (SACMAT'08). Estes Park, Colorado, USA.

Lauer, G. (2009). *Health Record Banks Gaining Traction in Regional Projects*. Retrieved December 9, 2009, from http://www.ihealthbeat. org/features/2009/health-record-banks-gaining-traction-in-regional-projects.aspx.

Lia, Q., Zhangb, X., Xua, M., & Wu, J. (2009). Towards secure dynamic collaborations with group-based RBAC model. *Journal of Computer Security*, *28*, 260–275. doi:10.1016/j. cose.2008.12.004

Liu, D. R., & Shen, M. (2003). Workflow modeling for virtual processes: An order-preserving process - view approach. *Information Systems*, *28*(6), 505–532. doi:10.1016/S0306-4379(02)00028-5

Marjanovic, O. (2005). Towards IS supported coordination in emergent business processes. *Business Process Management Journal*, *11*(5), 476–487. doi:10.1108/14637150510619830

National Institute of Standards and Technology (NIST). (n.d.). *Role Based Access Control (RBAC) and Role Based Security*. Retrieved December 10, 2009, from http://csrc.nist.gov/groups/SNS/rbac/.

Power, K. (2009). Global Mobile Healthcare An Electronic Framework for Portability of Health Records, *Medical Tourism Magazine*. Retrieved October 20, 2009, from http://www.medicaltourism-mag.com/issue-detail.php?item=223&issue=10.

Tang, P. C., Ash, J. S., Bates, D. W., Overhage, J. M., & Sands, D. Z. (2006). Personal Health Records: Definitions, Benefits, and Strategies for Overcoming Barriers to Adoption. *Journal of the American Medical Informatics Association, 13*(2), 121–126. doi:10.1197/jamia.M2025

Wiljer, D., Urowitz, S., Apatu, E., DeLenardo, C., Eysenbach, G., & Harth, T. (2008). Patient accessible electronic health records: exploring recommendations for successful implementation strategies. *Journal of Medical Internet Research, 10*(4), e34. doi:10.2196/jmir.1061

Wu, S., Sheth, A., Miller, J., & Luo, Z. (2002). Authorization and Access Control of Application Data in Workflow Systems. *Journal of Intelligent Information Systems, 18*(1), 71–94. doi:10.1023/A:1012972608697

Zhang, G., & Parashar, M. (2004, January). *Context-Aware Dynamic Access Control for Pervasive Applications*. Paper presented at the Communication Networks and Distributed Systems Modeling and Simulation Conference (CNDS 2004). San Diego, California, USA.

ADDITIONAL READING

Basson, G. (2009). *Process-oriented Systems Paradigm for the Process Age*, BPMInstitute.org. Retrieved December 27, 2009, from http://www.bpminstitute.org/articles/article/article/process-oriented-systems-paradigm-for-the-process-age.html.

Bellifemine, F., Caire, G., & Greenwood, D. (2007). *Developing Multi-Agent Systems with JADE*. Wiley Series in Agent Technology, Wiley. doi:10.1002/9780470058411

Casati, F., & Sham, M. C. (2002). Event-Based Interaction Management for Composite E-Services in eFlow. *Information Systems Frontiers, 4*(1), 19–31. doi:10.1023/A:1015374204227

Dadam, P., & Reichert, M. (2000). *Towards a New Dimension in Clinical Information Processing*. Paper presented at Medical Informatics Europe Conference (pp. 295-301). Amsterdam: IOS Press.

Detmer, D., Bloomrosen, M., Raymond, B., & Tang, P. (2008). Integrated Personal Health Records: Transformative Tools for Consumer-Centric Care. *BMC Medical Informatics and Decision Making, 8*, 45. doi:10.1186/1472-6947-8-45

Dumas, M., van der Aalst, W., & ter Hofstede, A. (2005). *Process-aware Information Systems*. Wiley. doi:10.1002/0471741442

Framinan, J. M., Parra, C. L., Montes, M., & Pérez, P. (2006). Collaborative Healthcare Process Modelling: A Case Study. In Camarinha-Matos, L. M., Afsarmanesh, H., & Ortiz, A. (Ed.), *Collaborative Networks and Their Breeding Environments, Vol. 186. IFIP TC5 WG 5.5 Sixth IFIP Working Conference on VIRTUAL ENTERPRISES* (pp. 395-402). Springer-Verlag.

Gritzalis, D., & Lambrinoudakis, C. (2004). A security architecture for interconnecting health information systems. *International Journal of Medical Informatics, 73*, 305–309. doi:10.1016/j.ijmedinf.2003.12.011

Groen, P. J. (2008). *Personal Health Record (PHR) Systems and Return on Investment (ROI)*. Virtual Medical Worlds. Retrieved December 25, 2009, from http://www.hoise.com/vmw/09/articles/vmw/LV-VM-01-09-1.html.

Groen, P. J., Goldstein, D., & Nasuti, J. (2007). *Personal Health Record (PHR) Systems: An evolving challenge to HER systems*. Retrieved December 8, 2009, from http://www.hoise.com/vmw/07/articles/vmw/LV-VM-08-07-26.html.

Jennings, N. R., Sycara, K. P., & Wooldridge, M. (1998). *A Roadmap of Agent Research and Development. Autonomous Agents and Multi-agent Systems* (pp. 275–306). Amsterdam: KluwerAcademic Publishers.

Kulkarni, D., & Tripathi, A. (2008, June). *Context-Aware Role-based Access Control in Pervasive Computing Systems*. Paper presented at the Symposium on Access control Models and Technologies (SACMAT'08). Estes Park, Colorado, USA.

Lemos, R. (2001), *Medical Privacy Gets CPR*. ZDNet. Retrieved December 25, 2009, from http://www.zdnet.com/zdnn/stories/news/0,4586,2667243,00.html.

Raisinghani, M. S., & Young, E. (2008). Personal Health Records: Key Adoption Issues and Implications for Management. *International Journal of Electronic Healthcare, 4*(1), 67–77. doi:10.1504/IJEH.2008.018921

Samarati, P., & Vinmercati, S. (2001). Access Control: Policies, Models, and Mechanisms. In Focardi, R. & Gorrieri, R. (Ed.), *Lecture Notes In Computer Science, Vol. 2171*. Revised versions of lectures given during the IFIP WG 1.7 International School on Foundations of Security Analysis and Design on Foundations of Security Analysis and Design: Tutorial Lectures (pp. 137–196). Springer - Verlag.

Sandhu, R. (1998). Role-based Access Control. In Zelkowitz, M. (Ed.), *Advances in Computers* (*Vol. 46*). New York: Academic Press.

Sandhu, R. S., Coyne, E. J., Feinstein, H. L., & Youman, C. E. (1996). Role Based Access Control Models. *IEEE Computer, 29*(2), 38–47.

Schilit, B., Adams, N., & Want, R. (1994, December). *Context-Aware Computing Applications*. Paper presented at the 1st International Workshop on Mobile Computing Systems and Applications. Santa Cruz, California.

Shortliffe, E. (1999). The Evolution of Electronic Medical Records. *Academic Medicine: Journal of the Association of American Medical Colleges, 74*(4), 414–419.

Sullivan, J. M. (1998). Process modeling for health care organizations. *College Review (Denver, Colo.), 15*(2), 85–103.

U.S. Department of Health and Human Services. Personal Health Records and Personal Health Record Systems (2006). A Report Recommendation from the National Committee on Vital and Health Statistics. Washington D.C.

Varadharajan, V., Kumar, N., & Mu, Y. (1998). *Security Agent Based Distributed Authorization: An Approach*. Paper presented at National Information Security Systems Conference. Hyatt Regency - Crystal City, Virginia.

Vila, V., Schuster, A., & Riera, A. (2007). Security for a Multi-Agent System Based on JADE. *Computers & Security, 26*(5), 391–400. doi:10.1016/j.cose.2006.12.003

Volonino, L., & Robinson, S. R. (2004). *Principles and practice of information security: Protecting computers from Hackers and Lawyers*. Upper Saddle River, NJ: Prentice Hall Inc.

Win, K. T., Susilo, W., & Mu, Y. (2006). Personal Health Record Systems and their Security Protection. *Journal of Medical Systems, 30*, 309–315. doi:10.1007/s10916-006-9019-y

KEY TERMS AND DEFINITIONS

Agent: A complex software entity that is capable of acting with a certain degree of autonomy in order to accomplish tasks on behalf of its user

Business Process Execution Language: An emerging standard for specifying business process behavior based on Web Services.

Electronic Health Record (EHR): It is a longitudinal electronic record of patient health information generated by one or more encounters in any care delivery setting. Information stored in EHRs include patient demographics, progress notes, problems, medications, vital signs, past medical history, immunizations, laboratory data and radiology reports.

Java Agent Development Environment (JADE): An open-source software framework, aiming at assisting the development and execution of agent-based applications in compliance with the Foundation for Intelligent Physical Agents (FIPA) specifications for interoperable multi-agent systems.

Least Privilege Principle: A principle whereby users are being assigned no more permissions than is necessary to perform their job function.

Personal Health Record (PHR): An electronic application through which individuals can access, manage and share their health information, in a private, secure, and confidential environment. Healthcare professionals can also access health information of others given that they are authorized to do so.

Process-Based Healthcare System: A healthcare system where collaboration of individual caregivers and departments, as well as coordination of their activities is achieved by means of processes.

Role-Based Access Control: A method of regulating access to resources based on the roles of individual users within an enterprise.

Treatment Plan: It usually follows a diagnosis and outlines the set of actions that need to be performed on or by a patient in an attempt to remedy a health problem.

Chapter 4
Improving Security Policy Coverage in Healthcare

Rafae Bhatti
Oracle Corp, USA

Tyrone Grandison
IBM Almaden Research Center, USA

ABSTRACT

With the adoption of Electronic Medical Records (EMRs), an increasing number of health-related Web applications are now available to consumers, providers and partners. While this transformation offers huge benefits, there are security and privacy concerns integral to the process of electronic healthcare delivery. In this work, the authors first survey the body of evidence to emphasize the design of appropriate security solutions for electronic healthcare applications. The successful solutions will always comply with the prime directive of healthcare - "nothing should interfere with delivery of care" (Grandison and Davis, 2007). The authors then formally present the problem of reconciling security and privacy policies with the actual healthcare workflow, which we refer to as the policy coverage problem. They outline a technical solution to the problem based on the concept of policy refinement, and develop a privacy protection architecture called PRIMA. They also offer guidelines for electronic healthcare applications to ensure adequate policy coverage. The ultimate goal is that electronic healthcare applications should be made secure without compromising usability.

INTRODUCTION

The use of Clinical Information Systems (CIS) in healthcare is gaining prominence, and several government-led mandates and incentives have driven the push toward the implementation of Electronic Medical Records (EMRs). As a re-

sult, the CIS managed by healthcare providers has gradually evolved from an isolated database system to an online information portal; offering a new range of possibility in health-related Web-applications to consumers, providers, and partners. While this transformation offers huge economic and technological benefits to the healthcare industry and community, there are security and privacy concerns integral to the delivery of

DOI: 10.4018/978-1-61692-895-7.ch004

care. The adoption of Web-based CIS applications therefore accentuates these concerns, which must be adequately addressed if these applications are to be adopted by patients and used long term. While security solutions for distributed systems abound, a one-size-fits all approach does not suit CIS. This is because healthcare applications have very low tolerance for impediments in the process of healthcare delivery. In contrast to typical online applications where it is reasonable to fit generic security controls to restrict access, healthcare applications require security controls designed specifically with consideration of the healthcare workflow.

Currently, security and privacy management is one of the main inhibitors of the deployment, adoption and use of EMR in the healthcare industry. There has been a recent push in the direction of increasing security and privacy for the health information of patients. The U.S. Healthcare Information Technology Standards Panel (HITSP) is developing standards for EMR that balance patient's rights to control their information and keep it confidential against the needs of healthcare providers and other stakeholders (Wagner, 2009). Leading privacy rights advocates agree that patients should have complete control of their medical records (Wagner, 2009). Several privacy laws and regulations have also emerged around the world in the past few years (Wong 2006), such as the Personal Data Protection Law (JMIA-CICP, 2003) in Japan, the Health Insurance Portability and Accountability Act (HIPAA) in the United States (HHS, 1996) and the Personal Information Protection and Electronic Documents Act (OPCC, 2010) in Canada. For American healthcare, HIPAA is normally assumed to provide the baseline for privacy compliance for healthcare entities.

While HIPAA and other healthcare-related privacy laws and regulations make it mandatory for organizations to specify and publish privacy policies regarding the use and disclosure of personal health information, recent media and academic reports about healthcare privacy (Pear, 2007)

(Rostad and Edsburg, 2006) indicate that there is not necessarily a strong correlation between the use of privacy policies and adequate patient privacy protection for electronic healthcare applications. A key reason for this discrepancy is the current state of CIS. Though today's clinical systems may be adequate in handling decision support, that is only one component of a CIS, and it does not account for patient-provider interactions, which permeate the healthcare domain (Malin et al., 2009). The authors in (Rothschild et al., 2005) emphasize the importance of designing information systems that are better aligned with the clinical workflow to allow integrated and patient-centered healthcare delivery. As noted in the literature (Grandison and Davis, 2007) (Malin et al., 2009), the design of CIS should take into consideration the specific constraints related not only to procedural policies but also to the access policies. While the former are related to timely delivery of healthcare information, the latter mandate particular disclosure rules for patients and healthcare providers. Patrick (2009) observes that any disruptions in clinical workflow caused by the technology designed to enforce either procedural or access policies can actually result in reduced overall efficiency and satisfaction, which is the opposite of the original intent of these technologies.

It is a direct result of the shortcomings in current healthcare systems that enforcing the disclosure rules often comes in the way of delivery of healthcare; with the result being that privacy protection policies are often bypassed and are flagged as exception-based accesses in order to deliver care (Rostad and Edsburg, 2006). The primary conclusion from all these observations in the field is that the models used and the policies in place to ensure security of health information and protect privacy of patients are being rendered effectively useless (Grandison and Davis, 2007). Secondly, there is an over-reliance on a secondary infrastructure comprising of audit logs to record exception-based accesses, as opposed to the system being able to incorporate legitimate accesses into the policy (Grandison and Davis, 2007). In such a system, over time the audit log becomes a more realistic representation of the security state of the system than the initially designed policy. As the access check is bypassed in favor of post-access audit, the system is also unable to prevent real time policy violations.

These observations intimate the existence of a general state of affairs in healthcare applications where circumventing data security and privacy controls is the rule and not the exception. This trend is alarming because it negates the existence and efficacy of policy. In this state, the policy does not precisely represent or embody the actual level of data protection afforded to the patient, i.e. the policy is no longer a genuine reflection of the privacy practices of the application.

Additionally, it undermines the notion of empowering the patient, as his consent may no longer be valid because the policy is no longer valid. While these observations may appear to reflect negatively on healthcare application providers, these scenarios are in fact a direct result of applying prior technology without considering the nuances of the clinical workflow. In light of the recent push to electronic health records (HIMSS, 2009), this conundrum will multiply in effect.

In the wake of these concerns, it is imperative that we shift our focus to the design of security solutions for healthcare applications and systems that fit into the clinical workflow, as opposed to requiring the workflow to fit them. In healthcare-related applications, disallowing access during service delivery is not an option because it may lead to grim consequences for the patient. Thus, what is traditionally thought of as an exception is a natural occurring phenomenon that must be facilitated. However, the premise of our work is that repeated exceptions should eventually be incorporated into the policy to make it consistent with the actual security and privacy state of the system as much and as quickly as possible.

It is our belief that it is possible to leverage artifacts from the actual clinical workflow to inform and construct appropriate privacy protection mechanisms for patients. We purport that policy refinement, which we will define as the process of improving the rules that define the level of protection, can be employed to gradually and seamlessly embed meaningful privacy controls into the clinical workflow based on the actual practices of the organization. This concept is the base construct for PRIMA, a PRIvacy Management Architecture, which also leverages data mining (Hand et al, 2001) and Hippocratic Database technology (Agrawal et al, 2002). In particular, the architecture builds upon the Active Enforcement (IBM, 2007) and Compliance Auditing (IBM, 2007b) components of the Hippocratic Database technology set, and leverages standard data analysis techniques. PRIMA's policy refinement helps mitigate the above stated conundrum by (i) improving the design of the policies, which should elevate the level of privacy protection afforded to the patient, and (ii) better aligning the system policies with the actual privacy practices of the organization to improve the coverage of the privacy policy. To the best of our knowledge, no prior work on policy refinement for electronic healthcare applications has been undertaken.

The rest of the paper is organized as follows. We will provide some background from a regulatory standpoint regarding use and disclosure of personal health information. Then we will analyze the rationale for stated privacy policies not being actual representations of patient privacy protection. We will describe the PRIMA architecture and technical details and then illustrate the use of PRIMA in a healthcare scenario. Finally, we will provide guidelines for electronic healthcare applications to ensure adequate policy coverage.

BACKGROUND

Privacy and security requirements for EMR are now well recognized across various countries in the world, and the healthcare systems in many advanced countries are beginning to address these requirements using advanced technologies in their healthcare applications. However, the privacy protection in healthcare applications is based on principles outlined in laws applicable to delivery of electronic healthcare which, though specific to each country, are generic enough to allow CIS designers to understand and meet those requirements through appropriate use of technology.

The privacy and security legislations in the healthcare industry are based on the notions captured in the OECD Data Protection Principles (Wong, 2006). For the purposes of exemplification, and without loss of generality, we ground our discussion on privacy protection in the healthcare sector by examining the Limited Use and Disclosure provision of the HIPAA Privacy Rule. The motivation and arguments for this provision can be extrapolated to the other similar legislation, regulations and laws around the world. With respect to the HIPAA Privacy Rule, covered entities refer to health plans, healthcare providers and healthcare clearinghouses, and Protected Health Information (PHI) refers to all individually identifiable health information held or transmitted by a covered entity or its business associate, electronically, on paper, or orally. The limited use and disclosure provision requires that covered entities must use or disclose the minimum necessary PHI for a specific purpose and ensure the development and implementation of policies and procedures governing access and use.

In accordance with the purpose specification provision in privacy regulations, a privacy policy statement normally contains specific purposes for which data can be used or disclosed. However, the defined purposes tend to be very broad in scope (Rostad and Edsburg, 2006). For example, many real-world policies mention collecting information for the purpose of "administering healthcare". This granularity is coarse enough to subsume many information uses and disclosures. We recognize that this practice may not be performed with mal-intent, but may be a function of reducing the complexity of policy specification, which reduces the size of the rule base.

It has also been observed that organizations had difficulty defining specific employee categories (i.e. useful roles) (Rostad and Edsburg, 2006), which define the authorizations for viewing specific patient data categories (Blobel, 2004). Typically, the collected information is available to all "members of medical staff", which effectively results in an umbrella authorization. Again, we recognize that the transition from the generalist school of medicine to the specialist school of medicine over the last few decades has meant that the number of healthcare professionals involved in the delivery of care to a single patient, has increased significantly and that categorizations may be hard because roles are so fluid and cannot be assumed to be mutually exclusive. Additionally, the primary purveyors of healthcare tend to be the nursing staff and it is understandable that authorization difficulties may exist. However, there are still clearly defined lines, at least legally, on who should be able to view and use particular aspects of patient data. Thus, role delineation and categorization is necessary and critical. For a few years now, the broader community has realized and advocated the need for fine-grained access control. This view is shared by both academic researchers (Anderson, 1996, Bhatti et al, 2006, Weaver et al, 2003) and medical professionals (IHE, 2006 and Blobel, 2004).

From the previous discussions, it is clear that, despite the underlying reasons, the limited use and disclosure provision in the HIPAA Privacy Rule has not been interpreted and implemented very well in existing healthcare informatics systems. Our view is that healthcare is an industry that will always require customized mechanisms to balance privacy and operational considerations.

In order to not be disruptive and to automate this process of customization, PRIMA attempts to gradually embed policy controls in the system by analyzing the information already existing in the system and informing the new state that the system needs to evolve to. Thus, the overall goal is to bridge the disparity between intended and achieved levels of privacy protection.

FORMAL MODEL

For an arbitrary healthcare organization, *HO*, the policy that they define for their IT systems embodies the regulations, legislation, laws and organizational mandates that they must follow. This represents what they would ideally like to happen, i.e. their ideal workflow *WIdeal*.

The studies discussed earlier state that after a period of operation, the audit trails of system accesses, which represents *HO's* real workflow *WReal*, is primarily filled with exception-based access statements.

In order to build healthcare applications that are truly useful, secure and privacy-enabling, these applications must adhere to *WReal*. Otherwise, the security and privacy controls will be circumvented and the applications decommissioned either by the management of the healthcare institution or by the public outcry from patients. The potential financial loss and the potential damage to brand reputation are significant deterrents from developing non-compliant healthcare applications. The first step in constructing these applications is to have a formal comprehension of the phenomenon that we have to be in compliance with.

Core Constructs

Let's formalize the underlying notions and the goal of the PRIMA system, which is the reduction of the gap between real and ideal workflows. We assume that the HO has chosen a privacy specification notation and has a mapping from the terms used in this notation to the artifacts that the IT system will manipulate. Hereafter, we refer to these artifacts as the privacy policy vocabulary (or vocabulary, for short). The formal representation

of the policies relies on the key concepts that make up a policy, namely *RuleTerm* and *Rule*.

Definition 1. *(RuleTerm): A RuleTerm (RT) is a tuple with two literal-valued elements, attr and value. It is written as RT = (attr, value). The two elements of RT are accessed as RT.attr and RT.value.*□

A *RuleTerm* models the assignment of an attribute in a policy rule. For example, demographic data is represented as (data, demographic) and telemarketing purposes as (purpose, telemarketing). *RuleTerm* is the fundamental construct for our formalism in order to ensure that the model is applicable to any arbitrary specification notation.

Definition 2. *(RuleTerm Types): A RuleTerm, RT, is considered **ground** (written as $\underline{RT}$) if its attribute value (RT.value) is an atomic-valued literal, with respect to the privacy policy vocabulary used. Otherwise, it is **composite** (written as $\overline{RT}$).*□

Let's define $RT1 =$ (data, demographic), $RT2 =$ (data, address), and $RT3 =$ (data, gender). The particular policy vocabulary used here is depicted in Figure 1. In this example, $RT3$ can be considered a ground *RuleTerm* since it contains the attribute value "gender", which cannot be further divided into multiple *RuleTerm*s according to the chosen vocabulary. On the other hand, $RT1$ is unequivocally a composite *RuleTerm* since demographic information could be further divided into information about address and gender. In fact, both $RT2$ and $RT3$ are subsumed by $RT1$.

For each composite *RuleTerm* $\overline{RT}$, we assume the existence of a special set, written as $\underline{RT'}$, that contains all the ground rule terms $\underline{RT}_1, ..., \underline{RT}_n$ that can be derived from $\overline{RT}_n$ using the chosen privacy policy vocabulary. In the example shown in Figure 1, the set $\underline{RT'}_1$ for $\overline{RT}_1$ is shown to comprise of four ground *RuleTerms*.

Figure 1. A sample privacy policy vocabulary

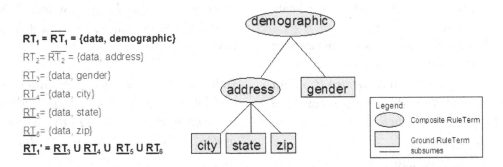

Definition 3. *(Existence of Ground RuleTerm): Given a composite RuleTerm $\overline{RT}$ and a privacy policy vocabulary, it can always be transformed to a corresponding ground RuleTerm $\underline{RT}$. Formally, $(\forall x : RT(x \in RT)) \rightarrow (\exists y: RT(y \in x'))$.[1]* □

An important notable notion is that of the equivalence of *RuleTerms*. Given a privacy policy vocabulary or set of vocabularies, the equivalence notion allows for the comparison of *RuleTerms*.

Definition 4. *(Equivalence of RuleTerms): Two RuleTerms, RTi and RTj, are considered equivalent, written RTi≈RTj, iff $\exists$ x, y: RT(x ∈ $\underline{RT_i}$) ∧ (y ∈ $\underline{RT_j}$) ∧ (x.attr = y.attr) ∧ (x.value = y.value)).* □

In the example in Definition 1, both *RT*2 and *RT*3 are equivalent to *RT*1 because there exist ground *RuleTerms* $\underline{RT_2}$ and $\underline{RT_3}$ belonging to the set $\underline{RT'_1}$.

Definition 5. *(Rule): A Rule, Ri, is a conjunction of RuleTerms. It is written as Ri = { RT1 ∧ ... ∧ RTn}; n ≥ 1. The number of RuleTerms of a Rule, n, is referred to as the cardinality of the Rule, written as #R.* □

A *Rule* models a specific combination of attribute assignments, which represents individual statements in a policy. For example, "nurses are authorized to see insurance information for billing purposes" may be represented as *{(data, insurance) ∧ (purpose, billing) ∧ (authorized, nurse)}*.

A *Rule*, *Ri*, is said to be a ground rule (written as $\underline{R_i}$) if all *RuleTerms* in *Ri* are ground. *Ri* is a composite rule (written as $\overline{R_i}$) if there exists at least one *RuleTerm* that is a composite *RuleTerm*.

Corollary 1. *(Existence of Ground Rule):* From Definition 3, it follows that for any *Rule Ri*, there always exists a corresponding *Rule $\underline{R_i}$*.

Definition 6. *(Equivalence of Rules): Two Rules, R1 and R2, are said to be equivalent, written as R1 ≈ R2, iff (#$\underline{R_1}$ = #$\underline{R_2}$) ∧ ($\forall x$: RT (x ∈ $\underline{R_1}$) → ($\exists y$: RT (y ∈ $\underline{R_2}$) ∧ (x ≈ y)).* □

Essentially, rules are equivalent when they have the same number of terms and every term in one rule is equivalent to another in the other rule.

Definition 7. *(Policy): A policy, Px, is a collection of rules that is symbolically tied to a data store x, where x can be either the policy store, PS, or the audit logs, AL. A policy is written as Px = $R^1 x$, ..., $R^m x$, m ≥ 1. The number of Rules in the Px, m, is referred to as the cardinality of Px, which is written as #Px.* □

For our purposes, we equate *WIdeal* to *PPS* and *WReal* to *PAL*. This is a simplification that holds true because the artifacts under investigation are the workflows relating to healthcare data disclosure and use.

Given that *RuleTerm*s and *Rule*s can be either ground or composite, a *Policy* can be too. A *Policy*, *Px*, is a ground policy (written $\underline{P_x}$) if all *Rules* are ground *Rule*s. If there is at least one composite *Rule* in *Px*, then it is a composite policy (written $\overline{P_x}$).

For each composite policy $\overline{P_x}$, we assume the existence of a special set, written as $\underline{P'_x}$, that contains all the ground rules that can be derived from the composite rules in *Px* using the chosen privacy policy vocabulary. The existence of this set follows from Definitions 3, 5, and 7.

Corollary 2. *(Existence of Ground Policy):* From Corollary 1, it follows that for any Policy Px, there always exists a corresponding Policy $\underline{P_x}$.

Policy Coverage

The concept of policy coverage builds upon the idea of comparing the real state of the system P_{AL}, as represented by the audit logs, with the ideal state of the system P_{PS}, as represented by the policy store that contains the rules specified by some system administrator, privacy officer, etc. We recognize that the P_{PS} will normally be specified at a high level of abstraction (and later mapped to low-level control statements), and that P_{AL} will be low-level information gathered by the system in its normal operation. Thus, in order to perform a meaningful comparison, we must transform both to the lowest common denomination, i.e. ground policies, and then do our evaluation.

Definition 8. *(Range): Given a policy Px, its range, $Range_{P_x}$, is the set containing all the rules in P'x.* □

The cardinality of the *Range* is the number of elements in the set $Range_{P_x}$, written # $Range_{P_x}$. Given this definition, we can now define policy coverage.

Definition 9. *(Coverage): Given two policies Px and Py, and a privacy policy vocabulary V, the coverage of Px in relation to Py, written Coverage$^{Px}_{Py}$, is given by #($Range_{P_x}$ ∩ $Range_{P_y}$) ÷ # $Range_{P_y}$.*

Here, the intersection is computed using the equivalence of rules as defined in Definition 6. Informally, the policy coverage in a given system is defined as the amount of overlap between the real and ideal representations of the system state, namely *PPS* and *PAL*. The coverage of *Px* with respect to *Py* is computed as a ratio using the algorithm ComputeCoverage given below.

The overall goal of the PRIMA system is to move towards a state of complete coverage, which is defined below. It is acknowledged that complete coverage may not be attainable given the human component, but higher levels of coverage should be a realistic goal. The process of improving the policy coverage is visually shown in Figure 2.

Definition 10. *(Complete Coverage): Given two policies Px and Py, and a privacy policy vocabulary V, Px completely covers Py iff $Range_{P_x}$ ∩ $Range_{P_y}$ = $Range_{P_y}$.* □

Algorithm 1. *ComputeCoverage (Px, Py, V)*

```
Require: ∃ getCardinality(S) (returns
the cardinality of a set S)
Require: ∃ getRange(P; V) (returns
the range of the policy P according
to the policy vocabulary V)
1: coverage ←0
2: rangex[]← getRange(Px; V)
```

Figure 2. Simplified Visual Representation of Policy Coverage

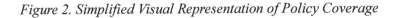

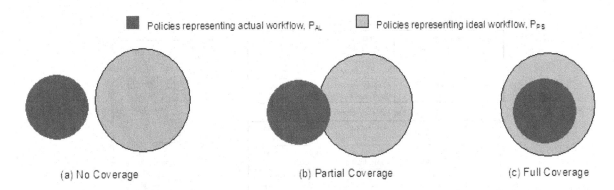

(a) No Coverage   (b) Partial Coverage   (c) Full Coverage

```
3: rangey[]← getRange(Py; V)
4: my ← getCardinality(rangey)
5: overlap[]← rangex ∩ rangey
6: mo ← getCardinality(overlap)
7: coverage = mo ÷ my
8: returncoverage
```

Illustrative Example

Let's look at a simple example that demonstrates coverage calculation. Consider the policy store shown in Figure 3(a). Let the policy tied to this policy store be denoted as P_{PS}. The top table shows the abstract-level composite policy, $\overline{P_{PS}}$, which comprises of three rules. The bottom table shows a portion of the ground policy, $\underline{P'_{PS}}$.

Now consider the audit logs shown in Figure 3(b). Let the policy tied to the audit logs be denoted as P_{AL}. By default, this policy is a ground policy, $\underline{P_{AL}}$, and it comprises of six rules. We observe that rules 1, 2, and 5 in $\underline{P_{AL}}$ are matched by rules 1a, 1b, and 3a, respectively, in $\underline{P'_{PS}}$, but rules 3, 4, and 6 in $\underline{P_{AL}}$ are not matched by any rules in $\underline{P'_{PS}}$. This indicates that exception-based accesses were utilized to access the data in a situation which not was allowed by the policy.

These exception scenarios are pointed out in the figure.

To elaborate, the reason for rule 3 not being matched is that a *nurse* needed to access *referral* data for *registration* purpose, but the policy allows the use of such data only for *treatment* purpose. The reason for rule 4 not being matched is that a *nurse* needed to access *psychiatry* data for *treatment* purpose, but the policy allows such data to be accessed only by a *physician*. Lastly, the reason for rule 6 not being matched is that a *clerk* needed to access *prescription* data for *billing* purpose, but the policy allows the use of only *demographic* data for this purpose. These scenarios indicate the customary practices during the clinical workflow which should be incorporated in the privacy policy of the system.

Invoking *Compute Coverage(P_{PS}, P_{AL}, V)* on this system, the policy coverage of P_{PS} with respect to P_{AL} in this system is found to be 50%, i.e. #($Range_{P_{PS}} \cap Range_{P_{AL}}$)/# $Range_{P_{AL}}$ is 3/6.

PRIMA: The System

The discussion on policy coverage is useful in formally understanding the goal of PRIMA. However, a significant consideration, from the clinical standpoint, is the design of the PRIMA system in a way that aligns with, and not impedes, the clinical workflow. PRIMA attempts to improve policy coverage by gradually embedding new policy statements, which were discovered

Figure 3. Example scenario illustrating coverage computation

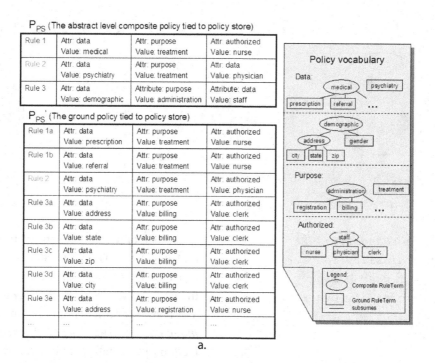

through the process of policy refinement, into the clinical system.

Figure 4 provides a high-level view of PRIMA. *Stakeholders* define the privacy policies for the *HO*, which is embedded in *privacy controls* that are integrated into the clinical environment. One of these privacy controls is an auditing function that automatically generates entries for the system's audit logs. These logs are either periodically replicated or PRIMA-enabled, by the construction of a consistent consolidated view of them. In the simplest case, there is just one log.

We will discuss desired features of audit controls in upcoming sections. At regular intervals or at the request of the stakeholders, the *Policy Refinement* component extracts input from the *Audit Management* component and the *Privacy Policy Definition* component and outputs a list of

Figure 4. The PRIvacy Management Architecture (PRIMA)

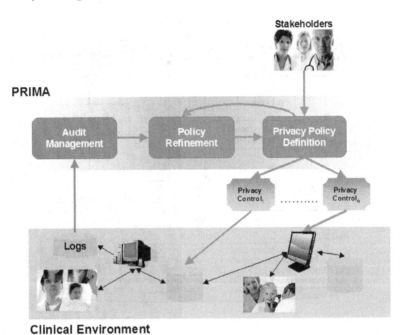

definitions, if any exist, that should be included in the policy definitions. Let's discuss each of these components in more depth.

Privacy Policy Definition

In this context, we assume that input is gathered by all the *stakeholders*, i.e. patients, medical practitioners, payers etc., and a representative uses this information to specify the *HO*'s policy. At an abstract level, PRIMA may leverage any arbitrary privacy policy definition tool that has the facility to create privacy controls that can be embedded into the clinical workflow. As a proof of concept, the initial instantiation utilizes the HDB Active Enforcement (IBM, 2007) and HDB Compliance Auditing (IBM, 2007b) components (Figure 5), which produces augmented database interfaces that both enforce fine-grained policy and patient consent and create minimal impact, storage and performance efficient logs. Our user would use the HDB Control Center to enter fine-grained

rules, patient consent information and specify what needs to be auditable.

The HDB components (Figure 5) operate at the middleware layer between the clinical database and the end user query interface. When the AE component receives user queries, it rewrites the queries so that only data consistent with policy and patient preferences is returned. The rewritten request gets sent to the database for execution and is also stored along with the query issuer, purpose, time and date in the audit log.

Audit Management

Retroactive controls, such as audit trails, and the threat of inevitable violation detection and prosecution are prevalent in healthcare information systems. Unfortunately, there are a series of concerns that may stem this approach. The first concern is the impact on the existing infrastructure, i.e. the degradation in system performance and the increased storage demand. The second is the nature of the technology's use, i.e. the logs tend

Figure 5. Combined Architecture of HDB Active Enforcement (AE) and Compliance Auditing (CA)

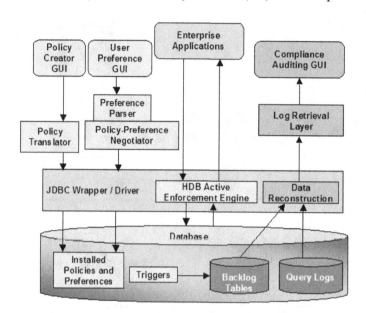

to be used only when someone raises a red flag about an improper data disclosure, not as a part of a continuous, proactive process. Finally, not all the necessary contextual information may have been logged with the request. The first and third concerns translate into requirements for auditing systems within the clinical environment.

Use of HDB Compliance Auditing in the clinical workflow allows us to meet these two requirements. The schema for an audit entry is $\{(time,t_j), (op,X_j), (user,u_j), (data,d_j), (purpose,p_j), (authorized,a_j), (status,s_j)\}$, where t_j is the entry's timestamp, X_j is either 0 (disallow) or 1 (allow), u_j is the entity that requested access, d_j is the data to be accessed, p_j is the purpose for which the data is accessed, a_j is the authorization category (e.g. role) of the entity that requested access, and s_j is either 0 (exception-based access) or 1 (regular access). The status s_j of access would in practice be recorded at the time the user either chooses or manually enters the purpose of access, where former corresponds to a regular access and latter to an exception-based access. We realize that this model could be augmented with the inclusion of conditions. However, the techniques that will be

used on the core elements presented are also applicable to augmentations of the model.

The PRIMA *Audit Management* component acts as a consolidation for the audit systems in the clinical environment. In the first instantiation, we use DB2 Information Integrator as the federation technology in the PRIMA *Audit Management* component to create a virtual view of all the audit trails. Alternative methods may be used that can consolidate all audit data in one place for subsequent analysis.

Irrespective of the mechanism used to populate the P_{AL} used by PRIMA, we must be cognizant that the audit logs may contain different kinds of information. There may be data on attempts to break into the system, i.e. possible violations or data breaches, or information that represents undocumented, informal clinical practice. We need to differentiate between violations and informal practice entries in the refinement process.

Policy Refinement

Refinement is based on the premise that a feedback loop is required between real and ideal policy;

in order to create policy that (i) more accurately represents the covered entity's intent and behavior, and (ii) more adequately represents the level of privacy protection afforded to the patient.

The pseudocode for the refinement process is given in Algorithm 2. The function is provided with (i) the policy store, P_{PS}, (ii) the policies in the logs, P_{AL}, and (iii) the privacy vocabulary, V, being used by this particular covered entity. P_{AL} is filtered to remove prohibitions, analysis is performed on the resulting set to create a set of patterns (if any exist), which are then pruned based on the coverage of P_{PS} with respect to P_{AL}.

Algorithm 2. *Refinement* (*PPS, PAL, V*)

Require: ∃ *Filter*(P) (returns the non-prohibitions in policy P)
Require: ∃ *extractPatterns*(P) (returns the rules that may be undocumented patterns)
Require: ∃ *Prune*(*Patterns; PPS; V*) (returns the patterns to be incorporated into the system's current policy)
1: *Practice*[]← Filter(*PAL*) (see Algorithm 4.3)
2: *Patterns*[]← extractPatterns(*Practice; V*) (see Algorithm 4)
3: *usefulPatterns*[]← Prune(*Patterns; PPS; V*) (see Algorithm 6)
4: **return***usefulPatterns*

Algorithm 3. *Filter* (*P*)

Require: ∃ *getCardinality*(P) (returns the cardinality of P)
Require: ∃ *getRule*(P; i) (returns the ith rule of policy P)
Require: ∃ *getStatus*(R) (returns the value for the status attribute in rule R)

Require: ∃ *appends*(R;Rset) (appends Rule R to the set of rules Rset)
1: *Practice* ← []
2: *n* ← *getCardinality*(P)
3: for *i* = 1 to *n* do
4: *Ri* ← *getRule*(P; i)
5: if *getStatus*(Ri) == 0 then
6:    append(Ri; Practice)
7: end if
8: end for
9: **return***Practice*

Algorithm 4. *extractPatterns* (*P; V*)

Require: ∃ *dataAnalysis*(P, A, f, c) (Given a policy P, an Audit Schema (or a subset thereof) A, a frequency f and a condition c, perform data analysis)
1: *A* ← *get attributes from Audit Schema* (may also be sent to any subset of Audit Schema)
2: *f* ← *system-defined threshold frequency* (by default set to 5)
3: *c* ← *system defined condition* (by default set to *COUNT(DISTINCT(User) > 1*)
4: *Patterns* ← []
5: *Patterns*[]← dataAnalysis(P, A, f, c)(see Algorithm 5)
6: **return***Patterns*

Algorithm 5. *dataAnalysis* (*P, A, f, c*)

Require: ∃ *executeQuery*(SQL) (executes SQL statement and returns results)
1: *Split A into* (Attr1, …, Attrn)
2: *statement* ← (SELECT Attr1, …, Attrn FROM *P's* table GROUPBY Attr1, …, Attrn HAVING *COUNT(*)* > f AND c)
3: *results*[]← executeQuery(statement)
4: **return** results

Algorithm 6. *Prune (Patterns, PPS, V)*

```
Require: ∃ getCardinality(S) (returns
the cardinality of a set S)
Require: ∃ getRange(P; V) (returns
the range of the policy P according
to the policy vocabulary V)
Require: ∃getComplement(Sx, Sy) (re-
turns the `set complement'of Sx and
Sy)
1: rangex[]← getRange(PPS; V)
2: rangey[]← getRange(Patterns; V)
3: usefulPatterns[] =
getComplement(rangex; rangey)
4: returnusefulPatterns
```

Even though refinement is an ongoing process, we assume that there is a *training period*, where a reasonable amount of information is collected in the audit log. This training period is totally dependent on the particular healthcare entity deploying the system.

Filter Algorithm 3 outlines the filter process. Given the schema previously presented and the policy under examination, this process removes all rules that are not exception-based access entries. Given a more restrictive or totally different schema, the problem of separating violations from useful exceptions in an audit trail may require more sophisticated algorithms and even further research.

Extract Patterns In this step, the exceptions provided by the *Filter* phase, referred to as *Practice* in Algorithm 3, are analysed using a standard *data analytics* technique. The process is outlined in Algorithm 4. To perform the data analytics, a simple routine is called that takes a set of attributes, A, which is (a subset of) our audit schema, a minimum frequency, f, and a simple condition, c, translates it into a SQL statement and executes it on *Practice* to retrieve a list of entries that have occurred at least f times and satisfy condition c (Algorithm 5). The technique finds the exact rules that have occurred more than f times. The data analysis routine has a well-defined interface that

allows the *extractPatterns* algorithm to evolve and be easily customizable.

Prune Not all the patterns produced from the extraction phase may be good candidates for inclusion into P_{PS}. As a first step in determining these useful patterns, we implement a prune mechanism, Algorithm 6, which removes the patterns that are already present in P_{PS}. This is where our implementation of prune ends, because we recognize that some patterns may represent behavior that needs to be stopped. This implies that human input is prudent at this stage to determine which patterns are actually good practice and which should be investigated or terminated.

USE CASE SCENARIO

We will now illustrate the use of PRIMA in a realistic healthcare use case scenario. We will refer to the system for which the policies are tied to the policy store and audit logs have already been described.

We have already defined the basic audit trail schema as *{(time,t$_j$), (op,X$_j$), (user,u$_j$), (data,d$_j$), (purpose,p$_j$), (authorized,a$_j$), (status,s$_j$)}*. Building on the policy store P_{PS}, audit logs P_{AL} and policy vocabulary V previously articulated, the audit trail generated by the system is shown in Table 1. Here we assume that the audit logs have been maintained for a period sufficient to be considered as the training period for this system and none of the exceptions reported in the logs are violations.

Invoking *ComputeCoverage(P$_{PS}$, P$_{AL}$, V)* on this snapshot of the audit logs reveals that the coverage has actually dropped to 30%. This is because the ratio of matching rules to total rules between P_{PS}, as per Figure 3, and P_{AL}, as per this snapshot, is now 3/10. In order to improve the coverage, we will run the *Refinement* algorithm. At line 1 of this algorithm, the *Filter(P$_{AL}$)* function filters out the log entries which are marked as non-exceptions, and therefore the *Practice* array

Table 1. Audit trail, P_{AL}, for the system described in Figure 3

Time	Op (1:allow)	User	Data (Category)	Purpose	Authorized (Role)	Status (0: Exception)
t1	1	John	**Prescription**	**Treatment**	**Nurse**	**1**
t2	1	Tim	**Referral**	**Treatment**	**Nurse**	**1**
t3	1	Mark	Referral	Registration	Nurse	0
t4	1	Sarah	Psychiatry	Treatment	Doctor	0
t5	1	Bill	**Address**	**Billing**	**Clerk**	**1**
t6	1	Jason	Prescription	Billing	Clerk	0
t7	1	Mark	Referral	Registration	Nurse	0
t8	1	Tim	Referral	Registration	Nurse	0
t9	1	Bob	Referral	Registration	Nurse	0
t10	1	Mark	Referral	Registration	Nurse	0

now contains only the entries recorded at *t3*, *t4* and *t6* - *t10*.

The next step is to run data analytics to get the patterns that are candidate for inclusion in the policy. This is done at line 2 of Algorithm 2, when *extractPatterns(P_{AL}, V)* algorithm is called. As first steps in this algorithm, the relevant variables are set to enable data analysis (*A = {data, purpose, authorized}, f=5, c="COUNT(DISTINCT(User))* > 1"). The output of the *dataAnalysis (P_{AL}, A, f, c)* routine returns those (*data, purpose, authorized*) tuples in P_{AL} that occur at least 5 times. In this instance, the pattern is *Referral*: *Registration*: *Nurse*, i.e. tuples *t3* and *t7-t10*.

As the last step, in line 3 of the *Refinement* algorithm, *Prune(Patterns, P_{PS}, V)* is called to obtain the useful patterns from the ones in *Patterns*. The prune algorithm works by taking the ranges of both P_{PS} and *Patterns* and then getting the `set complement' of their intersection. This resulting set effectively contains those patterns that are not covered by existing rules in the policy store.

Thus, at the end of the *Refinement* algorithm, *Patterns* contains *Referral*: *Registration*: *Nurse* which is recorded in entries at *t3* and *t7-t10*. This reveals that a Nurse accesses the Referral data for a patient too frequently for Registration reasons using the exception mechanism. Assuming that

this is not a negative trend then it suggests that a rule should be included in the policy stating that Nurses may be allowed to access patient Referral data for Registration purposes.

We are cognizant that the criterion used for pattern extraction, such as the threshold frequency of rules and numbers of users involved, is clearly subjective and this scenario only serves to illustrate our approach and is not meant to be a definitive solution. The PRIMA systems will need to be configured and tuned as per the requirement specifications of the target environment. Secondly, simple data analytics techniques may not be sufficient in all cases. In order to enable a bit more sophisticated inference, we propose to leverage the frequent pattern mining algorithm (Agrawal and Srikant, 1994) in our future work to detect correlations between attribute pairs that are not discovered by simple SQL queries.

Guidelines for Electronic Healthcare Applications

Like other health information technology, health-related web applications must be secure and privacy-preserving without compromising usability or the user experience. Not meeting this requirement will ensure that they will not be effective or deemed useful by healthcare practitioners. For existing and emerging web-based health technology, we recommend achieving this goal in one of two ways.

The first is to utilize the PRIMA system, as done in the HDB case (Fig. 5). With this configuration, web-based healthcare applications treat the PRIMA system as a standard disclosure API that handles security and privacy considerations on behalf of the application. This approach has the advantage of providing a single, consistent disclosure platform, while allowing the healthcare application to focus on its core function, without introducing security and privacy complexity.

The second way is to enable the goal of increased policy coverage natively, without the application user knowing. This means that the healthcare application implements the concepts previously presented. To make this goal possible and painless, we provide a template, which comprises of a set of guidelines that in future can be coded as a script that can be run against the application to automatically evaluate coverage.

The following are the codified guidelines used to help to ensure that applications are going in the direction of better policy coverage:

1. **Record policy coverage at pre-set intervals:** Choose an interval that best meets your usage scenario and application requirements. Ideally it should not be more than every few weeks.

2. **Save initial coverage logs, and analyze:** For coverage below ideal (say 80%), take following actions:
   - find the rules present in audit logs but not in policy store
   - record them separately in a log file (say A)

3. **Compare coverage of each subsequent interval with the one prior:** If coverage below ideal (say 80%), take following actions:
   - find the rules present in audit logs but not in policy store
   - record them separately in a log file (say B)
   - compare log files A and B

4. **Estimate progress or evaluate further action:** Depending on the overlap between two logs, take following actions:
   - if complete overlap (100%), reconciliation is not working, troubleshoot the system (alert system administrator)
   - if significant overlap (say > 50%), reconciliation requires manual inspection of policies (alert security administrator)
   - if not so significant overlap (say < 50%), reconciliation is working. return to #3

5. **Reassure via regular consumer and user feedback:** Ensure that the goals of the system of not comprising usability are being qualitatively met by seeking patient and medical staff satisfaction survey. Reassurance is based on whether or to what extent the clinical workflow was impeded. Flag negative responses, and follow up.

Throughout this chapter, we have demonstrated how guidelines 1 to 4 can be implemented. However, guideline 5 requires a socio-technological solution that has to be carefully implemented by a team of healthcare professionals, social scientists and computer scientists.

FUTURE WORK

Our reference implementation of PRIMA leverages proprietary technologies. It is our hope to develop an open source reference implementation with a well-defined API for integrating into arbitrary applications and systems. This would enable maximum impact on the field; allowing any technologist who wishes to use and improve our technology.

To deepen our work, we plan to do a comparative analysis, with the help of healthcare clients, of the data analysis algorithms that can be used to uncover patterns in the audit log. Our aim is to find the algorithm or a set of algorithms that produce the best results and characterize why they exhibit the behavior that they do, i.e. high accuracy. It is our hope that researchers with an interest in audit log mining may find it useful to leverage our results to create more novel and better algorithms that could have more far-reaching applicability, e.g. could be used as a starting point for efficient, medical fraud detection algorithms.

While emerging healthcare organizations leverage relational database systems, legacy systems employ hierarchical, XML-like structures. Thus, the natural evolution for our work is to adapt the core concepts and technology to the tree-based structures of legacy systems. We would also like to validate and expand our guidelines by observing the use of PRIMA in other deployments through collaborative efforts with healthcare practitioners.

Our work makes the assumption that legislative policy has corresponding technical counterparts that embody the "spirit" of the law or regulation. However, after interactions with lawmakers and healthcare professionals, this is probably not the case in many circumstances. We aim to investigate the extent of this phenomenon and modify our notions accordingly to reflect the state of the real world.

CONCLUSION

In this paper, we surveyed the requirements for security and privacy protection in clinical workflows using healthcare technology such that it does not disrupt the delivery of care, which is the prime directive of healthcare industry. Toward this goal, we formally introduced the notion of *policy coverage* in healthcare applications, which emerges from the over-reliance on the bypassing of security controls to access sensitive medical information - a phenomenon referred to in the medical community as *Break The Glass*. Our formalization is supported by PRIMA, a PRIvacy Management Architecture for healthcare systems, which addresses this problem of the circumvention of policy. PRIMA utilizes the actual practices of the organizations (embodied in the audit logs) to perform policy refinement. The system's advantages are that (i) it fits to the clinical workflow and does not require the workflow to fit to it, i.e. it does not impede the clinical workflow, (ii) it enables precise (or rather more realistic) definitions of purposes, criteria for exception-based accesses and categories of authorized users, and (iii) it enables improved privacy protection for the patient. We also provided guidelines for electronic healthcare applications to ensure adequate policy coverage with the goal of making them secure without compromising on usability.

REFERENCES

Agrawal, R., Kiernan, J., Srikant, R., & Xu, Y. (2002). *Hippocratic databases*. Proceedings of the 2002 Very Large Data Bases. Hong Kong, China.

Agrawal, R., & Srikant, R. (1994). *Fast algorithms for mining association rules*. Proceedings of the 1994 Very Large Data Bases. Santiago, Chile.

Anderson, R. (1996). *A security policy model for clinical information systems*. The Proceedings of the 1996 IEEE Symposium on Security and Privacy. Oakland, CA.

Bhatti, R., Moidu, K., & Ghafoor, A. (2006). *Policy-based security management for federated healthcare databases (or RHIOs)*. In Proceedings of the 2006 International Workshop on Healthcare Information and Knowledge Management. Arlington, VA.

Blobel, B. (2004). Authorisation and Access Control for electronic health record systems. *International Journal of Medical Informatics, 73*(3), 251–257. doi:10.1016/j.ijmedinf.2003.11.018

Grandison, T., & Davis, J. (2007). *The Impact of Industry Constraints on Model-Driven Data Disclosure Controls.* The Proceedings of the 2007 International Workshop on Model-Based Trustworthy Health Information Systems. Nashville, Tennessee.

Hand, D. J., Mannila, H., & Smyth, P. (2001). *Principles of Data Mining (Adaptive Computation and Machine Learning).* MIT Press.

HIMSS. (2009). *Patient Identity Integrity.* A White Paper by the HIMSS Patient Identity Integrity Work Group. Retrieved 10/1/2010 from http://www.himss.org/content/files/PrivacySecurity/PIIWhitePaper.pdf.

IBM. (2007a). *Hippocratic Database Active Enforcement (Version 1.0): User's Guide.* Retrieved 10/12/2009 from http://www.almaden.ibm.com/cs/projects/iis/hdb/Publications/papers/HDBEnforcementUserGuide.pdf.

IBM. (2007b). *Hippocratic Database Compliance Auditing (version 1.0): User's Guide.* Retrieved 10/12/2009 from http://www.almaden.ibm.com/cs/projects/iis/hdb/Publications/papers/HDBAuditingUserGuide.pdf.

IHE. (2006). *IHE Patient Care Coordination Technical Framework: Basic patient privacy consents.* Retrieved 10/12/2009 from http://wiki.ihe.net/index.php?title=Basic_Patient_Privacy_Consents.

Japanese Ministry of Internal Affairs, Communications Information, and Communications Policy. (JMIA-CICP) (2003). *Personal Data Protection Law.* Retrieved 10/12/2009 from http://www.kantei.go.jp/jp/it/privacy/houseika/hourituan/index.html.

Malin, B., Mathe, J., Duncavage, S., Werner, J., Ledeczi, A., & Sztipanovits, J. (2007). *Implementing a Model-Based Design Environment for Clinical Information Systems.* Proceedings of the 2007 ACM/IEEE International Workshop on Model-Based Trustworthy Health Information Systems. Nashville, TN.

NEMA. (2004). *Break-glass - an approach to granting emergency access to healthcare systems.* Retrieved from http://www.medicalimaging.org/documents/Break-Glass_-_Emergency_Access_to_Healthcare_Systems.pdf.

Office of the Privacy Commissioner of Canada (OPCC). (2010). *Personal Information Protection and Electronic Documents* Act. Retrieved 10/1/2010 from http://www.priv.gc.ca/information/02_05_d_08_e.cfm.

Patrick, J. (2009). *A Critical Essay on the Deployment of an ED Clinical Information System Systemic Failure or Bad Luck?* Retrieved 10/12/2009 from http://www.it.usyd.edu.au/~hitru/essays/The%20Story%20of%20the%20Deployment%20of%20an%20ED%20Clinical%20Information%20System6.0.pdf.

Pear, R. (2007). *Warnings over privacy of US Health Network.* Retrieved 10/1/2010 from http://www.nytimes.com/2007/02/18/washington/18health.html.

Rostad, L., & Edsburg, O. (2006). *Proceedings from 2006 Annual Computer Security Applications Conference.* Miami Beach, FL.

Rothschild, A. S., Dietrich, L., Ball, M. J., Wurtz, H., Farish-Hunt, H., & Cortes-Comerer, N. (2005). Leveraging systems thinking to design patient-centered clinical documentation systems. *International Journal of Medical Informatics, 74*(5), 395–398. doi:10.1016/j.ijmedinf.2005.03.011

USA Department of Health and Human Services (HHS). (1996). *Health Insurance Portability and Accountability* act. Retrieved 10/1/2010 from http://www.hhs.gov/ocr/hipaa/.

Wagner, M. (2009). *Electronic Medical Records: The Good, Bad, And Ugly*. Retrieved 10/12/2009 from http://www.darkreading.com/shared/print-ableArticle.jhtml?articleID=222002718.

Weaver, A. C., Dwyer, S. J., III, & Snyder, A. M. (2003). *Federated, secure trust networks for distributed healthcare it services*. Proceedings of the 2003 IEEE International Conference on Industrial Informatics. Alberta, Canada.

Wong, R. (2006). *An overview of Data Protection Laws around the world*. Retrieved 10/1/2010 from http://pages.britishlibrary.net/rwong/dpa.html.

ADDITIONAL READING

Agrawal, R., Grandison, T., Johnson, C. M., & Kiernan, J. (2007). Enabling the 21st century health care information technology revolution. *Communications of the ACM, 50*(2), 34–42. doi:10.1145/1216016.1216018

Ardagna, C. A., Capitani di Vimercati, S. D., Grandison, T., & Jajodia, S. Pierangela & Samarati, P. (2008). *Regulating Exceptions in Healthcare Using Policy Spaces*. The Proceedings of the DBSec 2008. London, England.

Grandison, T. (2008). *Privacy Controls for Electronic Health Records Systems*. The Proceedings of the 2008 American Medical Informatics Association (AMIA) Spring Congress. Phoenix, Arizona.

Grandison, T., & Bhatti, R. (2010). *Regulatory Compliance and the Correlation to Privacy Protection in Healthcare. International Journal of Computational Models and Algorithms in Medicine - Special Issue on Privacy and Security Issues for Medical Data*. IGI Global.

Grandison, T., Ganta, S. R., Braun, U., & Kaufman, J. (2007). *Protecting Privacy while Sharing Medical Data Between Regional Healthcare Entities*. Proceedings of the 2007 MedInfo. Brisbane, Australia.

Grandison, T., Grant, C., Liu, K., Bhagwan, V., & Thakur, T. (2009). *Leveraging Online Data To Deliver Better Decision Support For Personalized Chronic Disease Management*. The Proceedings of the American Medical Informatics Association (AMIA) Spring Congress. Orlando, Florida.

Mathe, J., Duncavage, S., Werner, J., Malin, B., Ledeczi, A., & Sztipanovits, J. (2007). Towards the security and privacy analysis of patient portals. *ACM SIGBED Review, 4*(2), 5–9. doi:10.1145/1295464.1295467

KEY TERMS AND DEFINITIONS

Healthcare: The maintaining and restoration of health by the treatment and prevention of disease especially by trained and licensed professionals

HIPAA: Acronym that stands for the Health Insurance Portability and Accountability Act, a US law designed to provide privacy standards to protect patients' medical records and other health information provided to health plans, doctors, hospitals and other health care providers.

Privacy Management: Privacy Management involves the strategies and safeguards used to protect the privacy of an organization's records that include resources, restricted assets, personnel, client and customer personally identifiable information.

Refinement: The result of refining; an improvement or elaboration.

Regulatory Compliance: Describes the goal that corporations or public agencies aspire to in their efforts to ensure that personnel are aware of and take steps to comply with relevant laws and regulations.

ENDNOTE

[1]   Note that x' is a set.

Chapter 5
Flexibility and Security of Careflow Systems Modeled by Petri Nets

Boleslaw Mikolajczak
University of Massachusetts, USA

ABSTRACT

The purpose of this chapter is to present an interplay of two important structural and behavioral features of robust intelligence in careflow systems, called flexibility and multi-level security. The chapter deals with design and analysis of careflow systems, i.e. workflow systems with applications in broadly understood healthcare industry. The authors focus on providing a robust intelligence to such systems in a form of structural and behavioral flexibility. They analyze several forms of design and run-time flexibility. However, the authors focus on case handling systems, exception handling, and on careflow systems with sub-processes called worklets. They also present how to model multi-level security within careflow systems that already have desired forms of flexibility. This implies that flexibility and security are conceptually independent and can therefore be modeled with Petri nets separately and incrementally in sequential order, first flexibility and then security. The authors apply Petri nets and colored Petri nets as conceptual modeling tool. They use example of Cutaneous Melanoma (CM) to illustrate some of our considerations.

INTRODUCTION

Recently (Arrow et al., 2009) a report of a group of healthcare professionals was published that formulates eight principles based on which a reform of American healthcare system must be based. Principle number 4 states: *"Develop a health information technology infrastructure with national standards of interoperability to promote data exchange."* This and remaining recommendations of the report address predominantly issues of healthcare databases and their interoperability. However, they do not address even more important issue of computerization of healthcare processes that are based on published medical guidelines for various disease, chronic healthcare, and medical

DOI: 10.4018/978-1-61692-895-7.ch005

procedures. Computerization of such processes can reduce the number of medical errors caused by medical personnel and, as a result, can improve performance and cost of the overall healthcare system.

This chapter deals separately with two important features of modern Healthcare Information Systems (HCIS): flexibility in design and execution of clinical procedures, and security of patient's medical and personal information. We focus on a special class of HCIS called Careflow (CF) systems, which are workflow systems applied to healthcare domain. Flexibility and security are conceptually unrelated, i.e. one can first develop a flexible careflow Petri net model that is later augmented with desired security features. As a result, flexibility and security can be modeled incrementally within the Petri net paradigm (Girault and Valk, 2003). Taking into account the fact that Petri nets can be directly implemented in hardware or software this allows direct deployment of careflow systems that are both flexible and possess desired multi-level security (Gami and Mikolajczak, 2007a).

Flexibility (Adams et al., 2005) is important for healthcare providers because it offers a desired change to otherwise hardwired workflow definition. It also equips healthcare (HC) providers with a "sense of being in control" of the medical and clinical procedures that are otherwise completely controlled by related software or information technology (IT) environment. Flexibility can be perceived and implemented as static (at design time) or dynamic (at run time). We consider both aspects of flexibility within the Petri net modeling framework.

Security in HCI systems refers both to secure access as well as to integrity of patients' medical and personal information. Quite often security in HCI systems is multi-leveled and includes changing reading and writing privileges to various healthcare providers (physicians, nurses, administrative assistants, etc). For this reason we use Multi-level Security (MLS) models in our considerations.

Our objectives for this chapter are threefold: to show how Careflow systems are modeled by Petri nets, to show how various security features can be incorporated into the Petri net models of Careflow systems, and to show how flexibility can be modeled and represented within the Petri net modeling framework. We address both design time flexibility and run time flexibility.

BACKGROUND

Desired features of future HCI systems are: personalized health care, careflow processes that produce data and adopt themselves to changing realities, and participatory decision making, among others. These HCI requirements lead to expectation of change in careflow systems' definition. Careflow processes that have desired change characteristics include: dynamic careflow processes, adaptive careflow processes, and, in general, flexible careflow processes.

Flexibility can be informally defined as an ability of the careflow process to execute on the basis of a loosely, or partially specified model, where the full specification of the model is made at run time, and may be unique to each instance of the careflow process. Modeling framework that offers true flexibility has to take into account factors, which influence the paths of unique instances together with the careflow process definition. We advocate an approach that aims at making the process of change as part of the careflow process itself. We use the notion of an open instance that consists of a core careflow process and several pockets of flexibility. We present a framework based on this notion – it makes use of special build activities that provide functionality to integrate the process of defining a change, into the open careflow instance. Adaptive careflows can be represented by Petri nets. In such case they are called Adaptive Careflow nets (Schonenberg et al., 2007). Desired features of Adaptive Careflow Nets include:

1. **adaptivity:** ability of a process to modify itself on-the-fly,
2. **adaptability:** ability of a process to be modified by an external party, for instance medical personnel with proper security and role capabilities,
3. **separation of concerns:** every process has an owner who executes all steps of the careflow process.

Careflow processes should not only be adaptive but also adaptable. Adaptive Petri nets are introduced and discussed within Careflow systems. Similarly, Extended Careflow Nets, Nested Nets for Adaptive Systems, Global History Nets, History-dependent Petri nets, Token Nets, and Owner of Token Nets are also considered to be net models to represent flexibility and adaptability. Modeling Careflow processes with Adaptive nets involves three-layered system:

1. top level that includes main process and strategic goal,
2. protocol layer defined by main care provider or delegated care provider; labs, test, etc.
3. task layer where individual tasks can be modeled by more detailed Petri net based models.

Expected properties of Adaptive Care processes include (Rinderle et al., 2004):

1. **soundness:** every process terminates properly from any reachable state from initial state,
2. **circumspectness:** every exception can be taken care by a higher layer, i.e. every exception has its owner, and
3. **consistency:** the modeled careflow process corresponds directly and uniquely to original specification.

In this chapter we use Petri net based modeling of careflow systems. Petri Nets are based on several sound principles that we present here (Girault and Valk, 2003):

The Principle of Duality for Petri Nets

PN elements Petri net name terms Entities of the real world

P-elements State elements, places interpreted as passive elements: conditions, places, resources, waiting pools, channels, etc.

T-elements Transition elements, transitions interpreted as active elements: events, transitions, actions, executions of statements, transmission of messages, etc.

The Principle of Locality for Petri Nets

The behavior of transition exclusively depends on its locality, which is defined as the totality of its input and output objects (pre- and post-conditions, input and output places) together with the element itself.

The Principle of Concurrency for Petri Nets

Transitions having disjoint locality occur independently (concurrently).

The Principle of Graphical Representation for Petri Nets

P-elements are represented by rounded graphical symbols (cycles, ellipses, …).

T-elements are represented by edged graphical symbols (rectangles, bars, …).

Arcs connect each T-element with its locality, which is a set of P-elements.

Additionally, there may be inscriptions such as names, tokens, expressions, guards.

The Principle of Algebraic Representation for Petri Nets

For each graphical representation there is an algebraic representation containing equivalent representation. It contains the set of places, transitions, and arcs, and additional information such as inscriptions.

In short, Petri nets support locality of actions, concurrency, graphical and algebraic representation, can model conflict for resources, can model and detect confusion (an interplay between conflict and concurrency, allow modeling of abstraction and refinement using the concept of Petri net morphisms (Mikolajczak and Wang, 2003).

REQUIREMENTS FOR PROCESS-ORIENTED CLINICAL INFORMATION SYSTEMS

Information Systems that give instant access to an Electronic Patient Record (EPR) would be very valuable in terms of saving time and workload of the medical personnel. However, the online access to patient data will not dramatically improve the situation because data have to be interpreted in terms of patient's history and placed in context of specific medical guidelines. Therefore knowledge-based systems, fed with comprehensive medical knowledge, could help much more. This implies that knowledge-acquisition, knowledge-maintenance, and potential legal problems with respect to responsibilities, are of great importance.

A clinical Information System (IS) should concentrate on the support of organizational procedures; i.e., it should assist the medical personnel in doing their work at the right point in time and, by providing the appropriate information, support them in taking the right decisions. But even if one concentrates on organizational procedures, the problem of flexible assistance still occurs. For clinical processes, it is almost impossible to pre-model all possible task sequences and all

exceptions in advance. If a physician comes to the conclusion that an additional measure which has not been anticipated in the process template becomes necessary, the process-oriented IS must not prevent him to perform this measure. Taking all these aspects together one can formulate the following list of requirements for a process-oriented clinical IS.

- It must offer a WorkFlow (WF) meta-model that is expressive enough to capture all relevant aspects of a process in an integrated and consistent way; e.g., control/data flow, resource constraints, temporal constraints, organizational ramifications, and flexibility expectations.

- High reliability and consistency are key requirements for such a system. The WF model must enable formal verification for the absence of any unexpected system behavior at run-time (such as deadlocks, lost updates, invocation of task programs with wrong or missing input parameters, or temporal inconsistencies).

- It must support ad-hoc deviations from the pre-modeled WF template at the WF instance level (i.e., to omit or postpone steps, to change the sequence of steps, or to insert new steps). Such dynamic changes must not violate the data consistency, the specified temporal constraints, or the robustness of the system. All changes must be properly integrated, especially with respect to access control (discretionary, mandatory, role-based) and documentation.

- To deviate from the WF template must not be complicated for users. All the complexity associated with the re-mapping of the input/output parameters of the components affected by a change, the problem of missing input data due to the deletion of steps, or the problem of deadlocks must be hidden to a large degree from them. Instead, users must be able to define a dynamic change at a high semantic level, without requiring that they are familiar with WF description formalism or a WF editing tool. In order to be able to realize application-specific user interfaces, the system must offer advanced programming interfaces to developers.

- The system must support temporal aspects. Besides deadlines, it should know about the externally fixed dates for steps and about temporal dependencies (e.g., minimal / maximal time distances) between them. It should monitor the WF execution with respect to these constraints and inform the user about potential problems during runtime (e.g., due to delays). Temporal aspects include ability to model and to simulate a delay of action as well as duration of action. Temporal aspects may be attached to actions or to data objects as timestamps.

- For the efficient support of hospital-wide and cross-hospital processes, scalability of the process support system is a must. The system must run with acceptable performance, even if the number of users and concurrently active WF instances becomes very large.

Further important aspects concern the evolution of WFs, including the adaptation of in-progress instances, the handling of inter-workflow dependencies or the problem of mobility with respect to data entry and retrieval. The WF meta-model should support cyclic tasks. This requirement, in conjunction with availability of dynamic changes, is not trivial. The same applies to temporal constraints. If both, dynamic changes and temporal constraints are supported then the addition of a new step or the change of pre-modeled task sequence, may lead to temporal inconsistencies. Finally, the support of dynamic changes should not negatively influence the performance of the system. Concepts which have been developed to achieve scalability must also work in conjunction with dynamic changes.

Medical guidelines serve as starting points that allow formal specification of the careflow processes with features such as case handling careflow systems, use of Petri nets in careflow systems: run time modification of algebraic high level nets, smooth integration of decision support and resource allocation, hierarchical and timed colored Petri Nets, adaptivity: graph grammars and Petri net transformation techniques as well as high-level nets with nets and rules as tokens (Adams et al, 2007). Current approaches to workflow flexibility include: under specification (placeholders) with late binding, adaptive nets: nested nets for adaptive systems, checking properties of adaptive workflow nets, worklets, a service-oriented implementation of dynamic flexibility in workflows; pockets of flexibility in workflow specification with late binding (Rinderle et al, 2004).

IMPLEMENTING WORKFLOW FLEXIBILITY

Experiences with workflow technology show that it is relatively easy to support structured processes. However, processes involving people and organizations tend to be less structured.

The lack of flexibility is often perceived as an inhibitor for the successful application of workflow technology. This is especially true in application domains with participation of highly professional human agents, such as in healthcare and human resources management. In addition, in real world different types of flexibility may be needed. This raises the question whether different forms of flexibility can be mixed and integrated into one system. One solution is Flexibility as a Service approach, inspired by the Service Oriented Architecture (SOA) and the taxonomy of flexibility. Activities in the process are linked through common interfaces to services. Different services may implement the corresponding activities using different workflow languages. As a result different styles of modeling may be combined and nested.

We adopt the taxonomy where four types of flexibility are distinguished (Schonenberg et al., 2007):

1. flexibility by design,
2. flexibility by deviation,
3. flexibility by under-specification, and
4. flexibility by change (both at type and instance levels).

This taxonomy shows that different types of flexibility exist. Moreover, different paradigms may be used, i.e., even within one flexibility type there may be different mechanisms that realize different forms of flexibility. For example, flexibility by design may be achieved by adding various modeling constructs depending on the nature of the initial language. To address the need for flexibility and to take advantage of SOAs, we adopt Flexibility as a Service (FAAS) (van der Aalst et al., 2009). The idea behind FAAS is that different types of flexibility can be arbitrarily nested using the notion of a service. The crux of the FAAS idea is to agree on the interfaces between engines supporting different languages. Activities in one workflow can act as service consumers while subprocesses, people, and applications act as service providers. Therefore different forms of flexibility are complementary and can be merged.

Flexibility by Design is the ability to incorporate alternative execution paths within a process definition at design time such that selection of the most appropriate execution path can be made at runtime for each process instance. For instance, parallel processes are more flexible than sequential processes, e.g., a process that allows for A and B to be executed in parallel, also allows for the sequence B followed by A and vice versa, and thus offers some form of flexibility. In this way, many of the workflow patterns (van der Aalst et al, 2003) can be seen as constructs to facilitate flexibility by design. A constraint-based language

provides a completely different starting point, i.e., anything is possible as long as it is not forbidden.

Flexibility by Deviation is the ability for a process instance to deviate at runtime from the execution path prescribed by the original process without altering its process definition. The deviation can only encompass changes to the execution sequence of activities in the process model for a specific process instance; it does not allow for changes in the process definition or the activities that it comprises. Many systems allow for such functionality to some degree, i.e., there are mechanisms to deviate without changing the model or any modeling efforts. The concept of case handling allows activities to be skipped and rolled back as long as people have the right authorization. (Ferraialo et al, 2007), Flexibility by deviation is related to exception handling as exceptions can be seen as a kind of deviation.

Flexibility by Under-specification is the ability to execute an incomplete process specification at runtime, i.e., one which does not contain sufficient information to allow it to be executed to completion. Note that this type of flexibility does not require the model to be changed at run time, instead the model needs to be completed by providing a concrete realization for the undefined parts. There are basically two types of under-specification: late binding and late modeling. Late binding means that a missing part of the model is linked to some pre-specified functionality (e.g., a sub-process) at runtime. Late modeling means that at runtime new (i.e., not predefined) functionality is modeled, e.g., a sub-process is specified. Worklets allow for both late modeling and late binding (Sadiq et al, 2001).

Flexibility by Change is the ability to modify a process definition at runtime such that one or all of the currently executing process instances are migrated to a new process definition. Unlike the previous three flexibility types the model constructed at design time is modified and one or more instances need to be transferred from the old to the new model. There are two types of flexibility by change:

1. *momentary change* (also known as change at the instance level or ad-hoc change): a change affecting the execution of one or more selected process instances, and
2. *evolutionary change* (also known as change at the type level): a change caused by modification of the process definition, affecting all new process instances.

The following definition from (van der Aalst et al., 2009) conceptualizes the main idea of "*workflow orchestration*" which consists of two types of services: workflow services and application services.

Definition 1. A workflow orchestration is a tuple *WO=(WFS; AS; W),* where

-   *WFS* is the set of workflow services,
-   *AS* is the set of application services
-   S=WFS ∪ AS is the set of services,
-   for any s ∈ WFS, we defined the following functions:
    -   *lang(s)* is the language used to implement the process,
    -   *act(s)* is the set of activities in s,
    -   *logic(s)* defines the process logic, i.e., the causal dependencies between the activities in *act(s)* and expressed in *lang(s),* and
    -   *impl(s)* ∈ *act(s)* → S defines the implementation of each activity in s,
-   from the above we can distill the following wiring relation:

$W=\{(cons, prov) \in WFS \times S | \exists_a \in_{act(cons)}$
$impl(cons)(a) = prov\}.$

YAWL (Yet Another Workflow Language) (van der Aalst and ter Hofstede, 2005) provides comprehensive support for control-flow patterns and thus is considered as a highly expressive language. Symbols used in YAWL can be seen in Figure 1. SyThis support was achieved by taking Petri nets as a starting point and by observing that Petri nets have the following shortcomings in terms of control flow patterns support:

1. It is hard to capture cancellation of (parts of) a workflow;
2. Dealing with various forms of synchronization of multiple concurrent instances of the same activity is difficult;
3. There is no direct support for a synchronization concept which captures the notion of "waiting only if you have to".

YAWL extends Workflow nets with concepts for the OR-split and the OR-join, for cancellation regions, and for multiple instance tasks. In YAWL terminology transitions are referred to as tasks and places as conditions. As a notational abbreviation, when tasks are in a sequence they can be connected directly (without adding a connecting place). The expressiveness of YAWL allows for models that are relatively compact as no elaborate workarounds for certain patterns are needed. Therefore the essence of a model is relatively clear and this facilitates subsequent adaptation should that be required. Moreover, by providing comprehensive pattern support YAWL provides flexibility by design and tries to prevent the need for change, deviation, or under-specification.

Typically workflow management systems are unable to handle unexpected or developmental change occurring in the work practices they model, even though such deviations are a common occurrence for almost all processes. Worklets (Adams et al., 2006) provide an approach for dynamic flexibility, evolution and exception handling in workflows through the support of flexible work practices, based not on proprietary frameworks, but on accepted ideas of how people actually work.

A worklet is in effect a small, self-contained, complete workflow process, designed to perform (or substitute for) one specific task in a larger

Figure 1. Symbols used in YAWL; from www.yawl-system.com/resources/lexicon.html

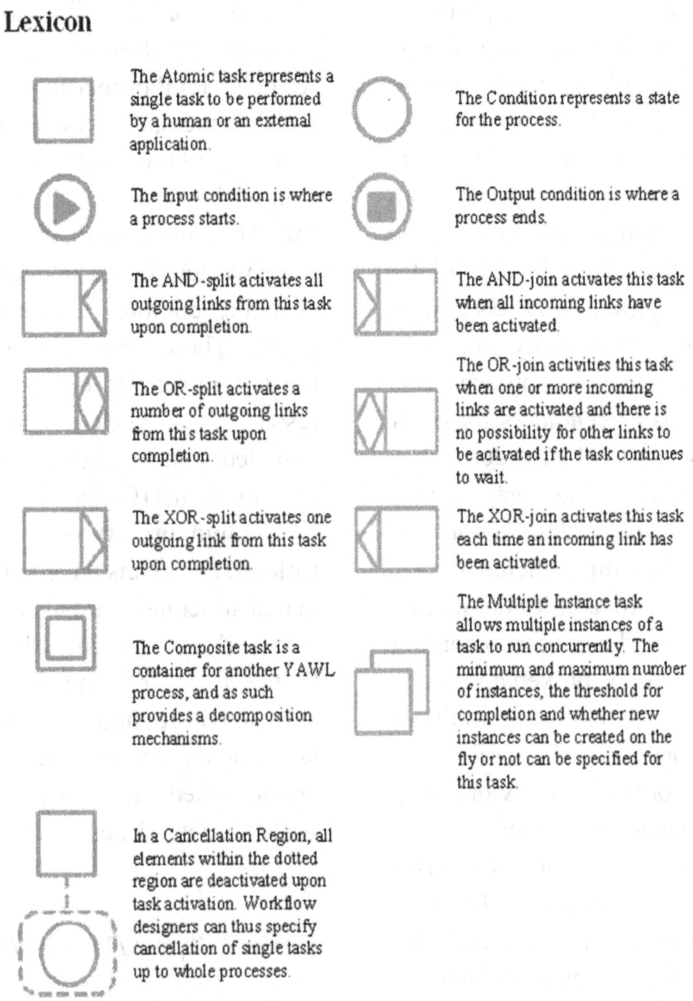

Lexicon

⬜	The Atomic task represents a single task to be performed by a human or an external application.	◯	The Condition represents a state for the process.
▶	The Input condition is where a process starts.	◉	The Output condition is where a process ends.
	The AND-split activates all outgoing links from this task upon completion.		The AND-join activates this task when all incoming links have been activated.
	The OR-split activates a number of outgoing links from this task upon completion.		The OR-join activities this task when one or more incoming links are activated and there is no possibility for other links to be activated if the task continues to wait.
	The XOR-split activates one outgoing link from this task upon completion.		The XOR-join activates this task each time an incoming link has been activated.
	The Composite task is a container for another YAWL process, and as such provides a decomposition mechanisms.		The Multiple Instance task allows multiple instances of a task to run concurrently. The minimum and maximum number of instances, the threshold for completion and whether new instances can be created on the fly or not can be specified for this task.
	In a Cancellation Region, all elements within the dotted region are deactivated upon task activation. Workflow designers can thus specify cancellation of single tasks up to whole processes.		

parent process. The worklets approach provides each task of a process instance with the ability to be associated with an extensible repertoire of actions (worklets), one of which is contextually and dynamically bound to the task at runtime.

ADAPTIVE WORKFLOWS WITH WORKLETS AND EXCEPTION HANDLING

One of the most important aspects of any healthcare system is ensuring that the appropriate careflow process is followed for a patient. Improper treatment has a much greater impact in the health industry than in any other. In this sense careflow systems belong to a category of mission-critical software systems. However, compounding this problem is the fact that deviations from the set process are the norm, rather than the exception. Each patient may require individual treatment and customization, seemingly rendering any sort of rigid workflow useless. However, this is not the case. A carefully designed careflow system with flexibility in mind can both provide a framework for medical personnel to work from and at the same time help to prevent iatrogenic mishaps. Another important observation to any proposed workflow system is that the healthcare professionals using it must be able to make changes in a simple fashion, without being unnecessarily proscribed from taking action. If workers must go outside the scope of the system, then valuable institutional information is lost and the changes they make will not be reflected in later cases. One proposed solution is the enactment of a "worklet" system. Conceptually similar to an object-oriented language, this approach treats steps in the workflow as placeholders for other objects, called worklets. A worklet is defined as *"a small, self-contained, complete workflow process which handles one specific task in a larger, composite process."* For example, there will be a linear high-level sequence for admitting a patient from the ER and diagnosing them before preparing a treatment. Each step may be broken down into further detailed sequences, involving multiple actors and resources. Since the overall scheme is represented in abstract form, each individual step can be altered or customized as needed.

One method of handling exceptions in cases is by "Ripple Down Rules", or shortly RDRs, a tree-based rule system used in many artificial intelligence applications. An example can be found in Figure 2. Each rule is modeled by a node on a binary tree, with branches corresponding to true and false clauses. Additional rules can then be easily added and modeled with additional true/false clauses. By integrating such a system into a careflow system, additional institutional knowledge will be added, allowing health care professionals to easily change the workflow if it becomes apparent that one method becomes superior to another, or is being performed more often. Thus, the previous exception, which would be handled "off system" in a different WFMS, resulting in wasted time and hassle for staff, instead replaces the original procedure.

Of course, significant modeling before enacting a careflow system may also reduce the num-

ber of exceptions required. For this, Colored Petri Nets, or CPNs for short, is desirable, since correctness of these workflow nets can be verified for behavioral properties such as soundness, circumspectness, and consistency. CPNs allow the modeling of the careflow system using an extension of the Standard ML language, called CPN-ML. This allows mathematical discrete functions to be written for the allocation of resources, for checking complex conditional statements and guards. These nets also enable simulations to be run beforehand, to pinpoint gridlock scenarios, resource bottlenecks, or other behavior such as boundedness, livelocks, fairness, and existence of home states (Girault and Valk, 2003). This allows rapid prototyping of careflow systems. Colored Petri Nets have led us to the conclusion that abstract tasks are also a desirable feature of any workflow system. Abstract tasks allow activities to be left undefined up until run-time, allowing professionals to dictate their implementation as the situation requires, rather than as a pre-described series of actions. Another alternative is an abstract task being selected from a predefined

Figure 2. Ripple Down Rules – example

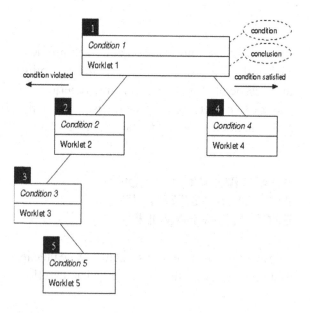

set. Thus, a patient entering the ER will pass through the transition "Evaluate Patient Health," where the implementation of this could involve visual analysis, blood testing, an MRI, or other options chosen during the normal run-time of the system. This feature, combined with Ripple-Down Rules, allows the careflow system to evolve, as opposed to most rigid business workflow systems, which are static and unchanging after compilation.

Another piece of the flexibility puzzle is the interface in which users are allowed to make changes. It is taken for granted that physicians and nurses must be able to adjust dosing regimens and treatment. However, there are two other potential barriers to such a system. If the user interface is too complex or requires an onerous amount of time or effort, staff will continue to work 'off-system' even though the system provides a method for exceptions. Also, one cannot neglect the physical realities of the system's deployment. If physicians are deployed with substandard hardware, or a lack of hardware, requiring multiple users to queue for access to the system at a limited amount of terminals, more 'off-system' changes are likely. It has been described in the literature how substandard hardware allows users to make mistakes in the entry of prescriptions and requirements, or in signing off on a course of treatment. This requires verification later, wasting time and money, and potentially endangering the health of the patient. Thus, flexibility extends beyond the actual software. Another example, noted in real life was the speed of the network in the hospital, which limited the implementation of a system that performed adequately in the lab conditions. In this case, workers continued to use informal paper records, which were especially vulnerable to being lost. If health care workers gain an initially negative impression of the workflow system, then no matter how well flexibility is implemented, it will not gain major use.

As noted, the construction of proper exception handling system in a careflow management system

usually depends on extensive *a priori* knowledge. However, not all possible exceptions can be predicted, and some outcomes outside the scope of the system may not be true 'exceptions' at all in that they are common or expected. Another example often discussed is the use of older medications normally superceded by newer drugs. Since the patients were stable on the older medications, a change was considered unwise by providers. The system lacked a proper input for this override; with proper "Ripple Down Rules" implementation, this would be an easily managed exception, and have the benefit of being immediately available to all other users of the system from that point onwards.

One additional consideration would be the difficulties inherent in transitioning between an existing workflow system to a new one implementing worklets and Ripple-Down Rules. It is difficult to change processes midflow. Several suggestions on this matter can be offered: one avenue of approach is to simply let all extant processes complete naturally under the old system while spawning new processes with the updated system. This may be difficult or impossible depending on the changes in the interface of the system, the average length of a process (which may range up to several months in the health care field) or other factors. In conclusion, the most logical approach appears to be extending upon the work in implementing 'worklets' within a current workflow system, allowing the end users of the system to make extensive customization to the process on-the-fly. This observation is based on support from the literature and feedback from healthcare providers themselves. Such a system would likely be based on the open-source YAWL (Yet Another Workflow Language). YAWL is written and maintained in Java, with source code available from a central repository and many already-compatible worklet extensions. Thus, it would make a logical starting point for any project centered around flexibility.

CASE HANDLING WORKFLOWS FOR HEALTHCARE

Case handling (van der Aalst, 2005) is a way to provide flexibility to workflow management systems, and would be an ideal option for the use of healthcare. In a hospital setting there are many trained professionals, all of them having different processes for different situations. An implementation using a contemporary workflow management system would result in surgeons that are blind from the information available, just doing the tasks specified for the activities in their in-trays (worklists). An important part of case handling is to avoid the blind surgeon metaphor.

What's Wrong with WFMSs?

Workflow management systems (WFMSs) are too restrictive and have problems dealing with change. Staff members in hospitals should not be forced into doing tasks. Workers will use their judgment and determine what would be the next best task to execute. Let us say a surgeon decided to do a procedure that was not an option in the existing workflow. He/she cannot be restricted to actions. The addition to the process would have to be added to the workflow system during runtime. There are four problems which make WFMS inflexible.

The fundamental principle of straight-jacketed work is vital for the WFMS, which can hardly ever match up with the way workers organize their tasks. Usually activities are performed at a far more fine-grained level than proposed by a process model. So the problem with straight-jacketing an activity would be that a worker would have to ignore what the task a process model would want to execute, stop the simulation and update the current workflow.

Typical WFMSs make no distinction between authorization and distribution of work, which means a worker is only offered to a task he is authorized to do. This will lead to large in-trays (worklists) for employees with higher status, as their role may include many others. This means that a worker, let's say a surgeon, can certainly execute the same task as a nurse and hence the surgeon's in-tray will include the nurses tasks and his/her own. A worker's role may be limited to the execute role. Roles are needed for the distribution of work. If the in-tray is overcrowded it would be pretty bothersome to execute every task, especially if it is not needed.

A WFMS that supports a strong control-flow orientation will exclude the context of tasks to be performed, most notably data created at earlier points in the process. This leads to context tunneling, which means a worker can only see the data that is deliberately provided. Whenever a new piece of data is added to the system, it is important that it can be available to all tasks. Information cannot be withheld from a worker, it will be the deciding factor in what to execute next.

The push-oriented nature of routing leaves hardly any decision to the user, so that he does not even have a means of making small adjustments to the process. Workflows that support routing can become very inflexible, and small errors can snowball into greater problems. This completely goes against flexibility in workflows. This means that you would have to stop the system every time you need to make a change in the process. When a worker decides to go against a predefined process, the new process has to be added during runtime. Data should also be added or removed during the runtime. If users are forced to go around the system frequently, the system is more an annoyance than a plus.

What is Case Handling?

There are three ways to give a workflow more flexibility: dynamic change, worklets and case handling. Unlike workflow management, which uses predefined process control structures to determine what should be done during a workflow and the user in a case handling system is controlling the case and decides how the business goal is reached. Case handling focuses on the case and not on the routing or the activities. The case and data are the products that are being created based on the information in the workflow.

Case handling systems have several ideas in common with the Activity Theory. The Activity Theory states that people invent new tools to work more efficiently and whenever a new tool is introduced, there is a new way to execute an activity. All activities have a motive and a goal that must be accomplished at the end. All activities are intervened by artifacts like tools and knowledge. Individual activities are a part of collection according to the work practice that takes place. The similarity can be seen in the features of case handling. Case handling has four basic features which will improve typical WFMS:

- To avoid context tunneling all the data in the case must be available to the worker.
- The ability to decide which activities are executed based on the information available rather than the activities already executed. The idea here is how the goal is going to be reached.
- Separate work distribution from authorization and allow for additional types of roles, not just the execute role.
- It will allow workers to view and add or change information in the workflow before or after activities have been executed, which means data can be altered at any moment during runtime.

The data that is available to the user is free, mandatory and/or restricted. Free data objects can be changed at anytime during the case. Mandatory data objects need to be available for a specific activity to be completed. If a data object is restricted then it can only be used in that activity. This basically solves the problem of context tunneling. The data can be global and viewed by everyone using the system or it can be restricted for just one worker to use during an activity.

Case Handling allows the user a number of choices. The user can complete the case in any way possible and this also means every case can be unique. It's very important that the worker is not forced into doing an activity, which would promote routing. In case handling three roles are available for each process and each activity which include: the execute role, the redo role, and the skip role.

- The *execute role* is the role that is needed to carry out the activity or to start a process. All WFMS have this role.
- The *redo role* is necessary to undo activities and the case will go back to the previous state before the execution of the activity and when an activity is undone all the following activities are undone too. If there was a mistake, this will allow the user to go back and pick the correct activity to execute.
- The *skip role* gives you the option not to execute an activity at the moment. It can be done later in the simulation or never. A task you might want to skip would be prescribing a medication which does not need to be done every time.

Case handling systems are supposed to be flexible. It is very important that the user can update data during runtime. A good example of this would be a change in blood pressure. It can be changed the instant that it is known and it will be available to all the following tasks that need it.

For a Healthcare system, the case is the end product. The workflows will mostly revolve around what the worker observes and the patient's information. Workflow management systems focus on the control flow, while case handling systems rely on the data. Control flow is not a good quality to have when you're working in a medical setting because information is always changing and it needs to be available to the user. In a case handling system, the decisions are made by the worker and not the system. The case handling paradigm is a great way to provide flexibility in WFMS and it will help construct an efficient system for Healthcare purposes.

YAWL – YET ANOTHER WORKFLOW LANGUAGE

In this section we provide reasoning for the selection of YAWL over CPNTools as a workflow (careflow) modeling tool. Petri net based workflow languages have the following positive properties: graphical representation, formal semantics, are state-based and event-based, and have an abundance of analysis techniques to assess their correctness and performance.

Petri nets can also be extended by multi-level abstractions/hierarchies, time inscriptions, data types, to increase their practical expressiveness. However, to model practical workflow (careflow) systems with Petri nets, one has also to consider availability and effective support for specific workflow patterns such as cancellation pattern, advanced synchronization patterns and patterns involving multiple instances of a sub-process. These patterns are notoriously difficult to model with Petri nets and yet they are frequent in workflow systems.

As a result of these diverse requirements and practical modeling expectations, it is rational to start with Petri net based modeling tool that incorporates extensions with abstractions, hierarchical modeling, time annotations, and selected workflow patterns. YAWL is such a workflow language. It is based on rigorous analysis of existing workflow management systems and related standards using a comprehensive set of workflow patterns. YAWL is inspired by Petri nets but it is a completely new language with independent semantics. In Figure 1 we show symbols used as modeling elements of YAWL. Each specification is composed of tasks (atomic or composite), conditions (called places), one unique input place

and one unique output place. Each task (atomic or composite) can have multiple instances. By extending Petri nets with these parameters, we directly support multiple instances' patterns. AND/XOR/OR Splits and Joins patterns are also supported and therefore advanced synchronization patterns can be realized. A notion to remove tokens from places irrespective of how many tokens are present is denoted with dashed rounded rectangles and lines. The moment when the task executes all tokens are being removed. This construct supports the cancellation pattern. Using the elements presented one can model wide range of workflow (careflow) systems. YAWL supports 19 of the 20 widely used workflow (careflow) patterns (van der Aalst and ter Hofstede. 2005).

CASE STUDY: CAREFLOW PROCESS FOR CUTANEOUS MELANOMA

This section describes a workflow (careflow) process model for a diagnosis and treatment of Cutaneous Melanoma (CM) based on medical guidelines, Clinical Effectiveness V4, provided by the University of Texas M.D. Anderson Cancer Center. The algorithm for CM has been developed using YAWL modeling and simulation environment that is based on Petri net formalism. In order to keep the example manageable, the careflow process for the diagnosis and for treatment of the CM is divided into three phases (sub-processes): clinical presentation, evaluations, and actual treatment followed by surveillance. Each of these three sub-processes is captured by composite tasks. A number of simplifying assumptions were made; for example, we assume that the patient medical histories such as clinical and/or pathological reports are available to start the diagnosis process.

Clinical Presentation Sub-Process

The sub-process starts with the composite task of Clinical Presentation when the skin ulcer status is evaluated based on the pathological results and the physical examination. The ulcerated status is defined based on any one of the following "Clark Levels", namely Clark I, Clark II-III, Clark IV-V, or N0M0. Clark I indicates no ulceration or mitosis, Clark II-III is less than 1.0 mm in size, not ulcerated and less than 1mitosis per mm². Clark III-IV is less than 1.0 mm in size, ulcerated or at least 1 mitosis per mm². N0M0 means equal to or greater than 1.0 mm in size, any ulceration status, any mitotic index. This task is completed when the Clark level is declared by the owner/executor of the process. Then the control of the process is handed over to the next composite task, the Evaluation sub-process.

Evaluation Sub-Process

After the Clark level has been confirmed, there may or may not be a need for additional test or diagnosis to be performed. Depending on the Clark level the medical guideline for CM suggests further evaluation such as chest X-ray (CHR) in cases of Clark levels II-III, IV-V and N0M0. Clark I status does not require further diagnosis steps. In case of ulcerated status N0M0, an ultrasound procedure for the tumor is recommended along with LDH (Lactate DeHydrogenase) blood. The owner/executor of this composite task could be a pathologist or a physician. He/she provides further suggestions in terms of a note to "what additional steps to be performed" before the patient is subjected to the treatment sub-process.

Treatment and Surveillance Sub-Process

This sub-process takes into consideration the previous clinical and pathological results and furthers the treatment and follow up procedures based on

the patient's standings. Based on the ulceration status and evaluations, treatments such as incisions ranging from 05-1 cm margins or SNLD - Selective Lymph Node Dissection – based on results of sentinel lymph node evaluation or sometimes LM – Lymphatic mapping – and Sentinel Lymph Node biopsy, are suggested as curing treatment. The owner/executor of this sub-process (composite task) also proposes post-operative procedures based on patient's situation. These procedures range from annual physical examination or a skin survey every 3, 4, 6 months or certain post-operative procedures ranging from CT of chest to radiation therapy or brain MRI, and the likes. The completion of this composite task leads to a conclusion of the whole careflow process. As a result the careflow is being terminated. In Figure 3 we show top level YAWL Careflow for cutaneous melanoma. In Figure 4 we show YAWL's GUI (Graphical User Interface) with a running case.

Flexibility in Careflow Systems can be accomplished by several techniques such as *worklets* – form of dynamic flexibility and dynamic exception handling, *Adaptive Workflows*, frequently implemented with nested nets, *declarative approach* as opposed to procedural approach, *history-dependent* Petri Nets, *High-level Nets* with Nets and Rules as Tokens, *Petri Net Transformations* – include various forms of Petri net morphisms and Petri net reductions, *Exception Handling* – it includes the LPM – the Learning Process Model, *Workflow Patterns* with various forms of careflow behavioral inheritance. In Figure 5, Figure 6, and Figure 7 we show various workflow patterns applicable in development of careflow systems.

INTER-ORGANIZATIONAL CAREFLOW SYSTEMS

Inter-Organizational Careflows (IOCF) become important as they provide solution for data sharing, heterogeneity in resources and work coordination

Figure 3. YAWL Careflow for Cutaneous Melanoma

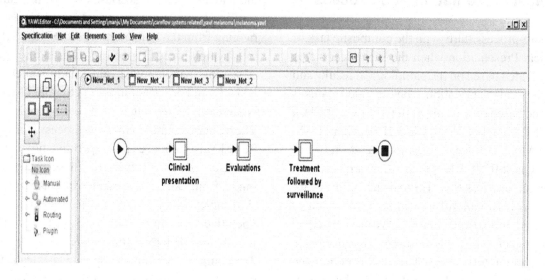

Figure 4. YAWL's GUI with running case

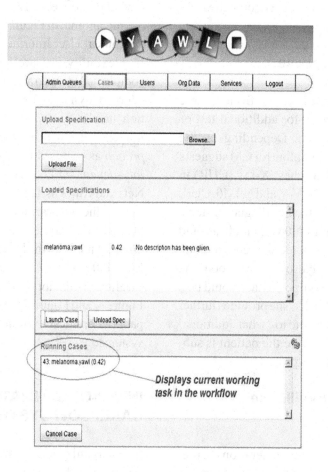

Figure 5. Multiple Instance Patterns

Multiple Instances Without Synchronization

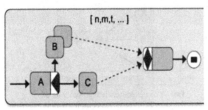

Tasks B and C are executed in parallel after task A. Task B is a multiple instance task of which between n and m instances will be created. Note that there is no synchronization between instances of B and C.

Multiple Instances With a Priori Run Time Knowledge

Same solution as Multiple Instances With a Priori Design Time Knowledge except that n is replaced by XQuery expressions. These expressions are evaluated at run time to help determine how many instances of task B are to be created.

Multiple Instances With a Priori Design Time Knowledge

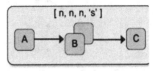

After task A, n instances of task B are created. When all such created instances are completed, task C can start.

Multiple Instances Without a Priori Run Time Knowledge

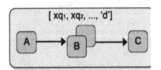

After completion of task A, the XQueries xq 1 and xq 2 are evaluated to help determine the number of instances to be created of task B. The 'd' indicates that new instances may be created dynamically (to a maximum of the value of xq 2).

Note that synchronization of all created threads takes place before execution of task C which is not prescribed by the original pattern. To avoid this, a similar solution as described in Multiple Instances Without Synchronization may be used.

at a global level. However, a secured computing infrastructure such as Multilevel Security (MLS) or Role-Based Access Control (RBAC) is needed to support today's vast healthcare organizations.

We present an algorithm to incorporate MLS features into IOCFs using Bell-LaPadula security model (Griew and Currell, 1995). In this model security labels of subject and object are verified before the subject can access the object. The algorithm reduces the careflow nets of participating healthcare organizations using the reduction rules while preserving the communication patterns between healthcare organizations. We also

present an algorithm to identify implicit places (behaviorally redundant places) in the IOCFs with MLS features. Our method and algorithms are illustrated by a running example.

The Internet, which is the primary medium for conducting e-commerce, is by design an open non-secure medium. Inter-Organizational Workflows allow data sharing and work coordination at the global level as the globalization of business becomes a common practice. However, the prolific use of Inter-Organizational Workflows for critical and strategic applications makes security an essential and integral part. Another major problem

Figure 6. Advanced Branching and Synchronization Patterns

Multiple Choice

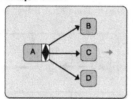

Synchronizing Merge

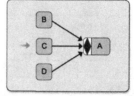

Task B, task C, task D or any combination thereof is executed after task A. Note that such a choice typically involves predicates for the various arcs. Currently such conditions are specified in XPath.

Task A can execute when at least one of the tasks B, C, or D has completed and there is no possibility of another incoming branch becoming active in the foreseeable future, given the current state of the workflow. Note that this solution in YAWL does not impose any restrictions on the corresponding graph (e.g., it doesn't assume the existence of a corresponding multichoice).

Multiple Merge

See solution to Simple Merge.

Discriminator

There are two different solutions to this.

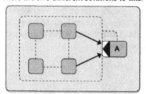

The first thread that completes, triggers A and leads to cancellation of the other threads.

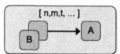

When t threads are completed, or if the number of threads is less than t when all threads are completed, task A can be initiated. Any remaining threads of task B are cancelled. This provides a solution to the n-out-of-m join. Note: the original pattern description did not prescribe cancellation of the "other threads".

Figure 7. Cancellation Pattern

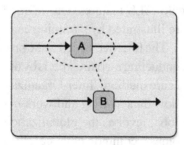

Execution of task B means cancellation of task A. In fact, any region can be chosen for cancellation so cancellation sets allow for cancellation of a single task, a whole case, and anything in between.

with Inter-Organizational Workflows is that they often use heterogeneous and distributed hardware and software systems to execute a given workflow. This gives rise to decentralized security policies and mechanisms that need to be managed.

Inter-organizational workflows merged with multilevel security provide the necessary security. However sophisticated techniques are required to review, analyze, and test this approach for correct behavior. Workflows are case-based (van der Aalst and Berens, 2001), i.e., every piece of work is executed for a specific case. Cases are handled by executing tasks in a specific order. Workflow process definition specifies which tasks need to be executed and in what order. Each task has pre and post conditions: the preconditions should hold before the task is executed, and the post conditions should hold after execution of the task. Most work items are executed by a resource. A resource is either a machine or a person. Resources are allowed to deal with specific work items.

Workflow has three dimensions: the case dimension, the process dimension and the resource dimension. The case dimension signifies the fact that all cases are handled individually. Cases do not directly influence each other. Clearly they influence each other indirectly via the sharing of resources and data. In the process dimension, the workflow process, i.e., the tasks and the routing along these tasks, is specified. In the resource dimension, the resources are grouped into roles and organizational units. A workflow management system (WfMS) is a software system that supports the modeling, execution, and administration of business processes. Before a workflow can be executed it has to be described in a way that WfMS is able to understand. This description is called workflow specification.

In this section we address the following practical problem of contemporary electronic commerce (including IOCFs): how to design correct and secure electronic commerce enterprise that involves many organizations cooperating infrequently through synchronous or asynchronous message passing. Both correctness and security are critical features of such system. The above problem is difficult because complex communication patterns between organizations may lead to inter-organizational workflow systems that are not correct in terms of soundness and consistency. Adding requirements of MLS to such systems constitutes additional level of complexity (Khadka and Mikolajczak, 2007).

IOWFs were previously analyzed and classified by several authors (van der Aalst, 1999). These papers provide a methodology of IOWFs modeling and analysis using Petri nets. In this paper we model workflows and IOWFs using Petri nets. We also apply methodologies of Petri nets and software engineering of distributed computing systems. Security features of MLS are expressed and integrated in terms of Petri nets on top of IOWFs. Such merging of IOWFs and MLS features and related analysis' techniques constitute main elements of novelty through incremental system development, i.e. first functionality and then security (Gami and Mikolajczak, 2007b).

MULTI-LEVEL SECURITY

Multi-level security (MLS) is a concept involving mandatory access control (MAC), i.e. the system enforces security policy regardless of the actions of system users or administrators. MLS systems strive to enforce the security restrictions with incredibly high reliability so as to not leak any data at all.

Access control decisions are based on clearance level for users/subjects and classification level for information/objects in the system. The term multilevel is used because both people and information are classified into different levels of trust and sensitivity. These are referred to as security labels or security levels.

In addition to hierarchical clearance levels (e.g. Secret, Top Secret, Unclassified) information is marked by a classification level depending upon its sensitivity level. This marking (classification level) indicates another restriction placed on the distribution of a particular classified data item. A security label may include classification level identifiers in addition to a hierarchical clearance level.

A system with classification levels generally acquires a large number of distinct security levels: one for every legal combination of a hierarchical clearance level with zero or more classification levels. In Figure 8 we show a system that contains Top Secret (T), Secret (S) and Unclassified (U) hierarchical clearance levels. Information has been classified with compartments A and B. The arrows in the lattice show security levels that can be read by which other security levels.

Figure 8. Security lattice for Unclassified (U), Secret (S), Top Secret (T) users with compartments A, B

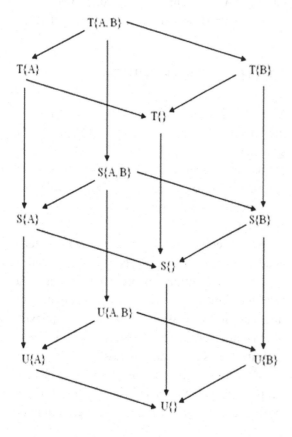

Two security levels can be compared based upon their clearance levels and classification levels. Given two security levels, first their clearance levels are compared. If the clearance levels are different then hierarchical ordering of clearance levels is used to determine which security level has higher precedence over the other. This is followed by comparison of their classification levels to determine the reading and writing rights. For example in Figure 8, if we have to compare two security labels T{A,B} and S{A} then we conclude that T{A,B} has higher precedence than S{A} based on hierarchical ordering of classification level. Then we compare classification levels of two given security labels. We conclude that T{A,B} can read data labeled S{A} since it contains the A compartment. If we have to compare security labels T{} and S{A} then we first conclude that T{} has higher precedence than S{A} based on hierarchical ordering of classification level. Then we compare classification levels of two given security labels. We conclude that T{} cannot read data labeled S{A} since it does not contain the A compartment.

If clearance levels are same then the classification levels determine the higher precedence as well as the reading and writing rights. There is also a supremum security level comprising of highest clearance level and all the classification levels. In Figure 8, if a user has Top Secret clearance with access to both compartments A and B, i.e. a supremum security label of T{A, B}, then he/she has the permission to read any data on the system. There is also an infimum security level formed by lowest clearance level and zero classification levels. In Figure 8 U{} is the infimum security level. The interrelationships between these levels generally based upon reading and writing rules form a directed acyclic graph, with nodes representing the security levels. We call this graph to be a security lattice.

Today's globally spread businesses use heterogeneous and distributed hardware and software systems to execute a given workflow. This gives rise to decentralized security policies and mechanisms that need to be managed. The prolific use of inter-organizational workflows for critical and strategic applications gives rise to a major concern regarding security and a need for a more reliable security mechanism.

The Bell-LaPadula model also called the multi-level model, was proposed in 1970s. It is a formal state transition model of computer security policy that describes a set of access control rules. In this model, the entities in a computer system are divided into abstract sets of subjects and objects. A "subject" is somebody (user) who wants access to an "object" (information, data file, system). The concept of a secure state is defined, and it is proven that each state transition preserves security by moving from secure state to secure state, thereby inductively proving that the system is secure.

A system state is defined to be "secure" if the only permitted access modes of subjects to objects are in accordance with a specific security policy. In order to determine whether or not a specific access mode is allowed, the clearance of a subject is compared to the classification of the object, and a determination is made as to whether the subject is authorized for the specific access mode. The Bell-LaPadula model supports mandatory access control by determining the access rights from the security levels associated with subjects and objects.

The concept of a secure state is defined by two properties: the simple security (ss) property and the *-property.

1. *ss-property* allows all low-level information to be available at a higher level. It restricts high-level information to be available at a lower level. A subject is allowed to read an object only if the former's security label is identical or higher than latter's security label (no read up).

2. *-property* ensures there is no write down. A subject with a higher security label should not write an object of lower security label.

These two restrictions ensure there is no flow of information from higher security label to lower security label subjects/objects. However these two properties are not sufficient to ensure that security is not compromised since it could be possible that leakage of information can occur through indirect means via covert channels.

In some situations, special devices are required to make lower security label information available at higher security label and vice-versa. We can use downgraders and starlight link for this purpose. Downgraders are devices that allow lower security label information to flow to higher security label but not vice versa. Starlight link is a secured mechanism that allows higher security label to write to lower security label.

Within an organization there are various subjects with hierarchical security levels ranging from high to low level. Also most organizations have various classification levels for information, depending upon its sensitivity. Bell-LaPadula security model requires identification of subjects and objects in the system and assigning security labels to them. This can be easily done because of the way organizations are composed. Thus we use Bell-LaPadula model to incorporate MLS in IOWF.

MERGING MULTILEVEL SECURITY INTO INTERORGANIZATIONAL WORKFLOWS

Now we present an algorithm to merge multilevel security into an inter-organizational workflow (Gami and Mikolajczak, 2007b).

Algorithm - Merging MLS into IOWF
Input: IOWF and MLS lattice

Output: IOWF with MLS features

Step 1. Identify a set of subjects A={A_1, A_2... A_p} where p ≥ 1 for any one of the participating workflow.

Step 2. Determine a set of hierarchical clearance levels {X_1, X_2... X_m} for subjects, where 1 ≤ m ≤ p and X_j has higher precedence than X_i for j > i.

Step 3. Identify a set of objects B = {B_1, B_2... B_q} where q ≥ 0 in the same participating workflow.

Step 4. Determine a set of classification levels {Y_1, Y_2... Y_n} for objects depending upon its sensitivity, where 0 ≤ n ≤ q.

Step 5. Combine clearance levels and classification levels to obtain security lattice with security labels S_k = X_i{Y_1,Y_2,..., Y_j} where i ≤ m, j ≤ n, k ≤ $m2^n$, as nodes.

Step 6. Assign security labels to subjects and objects taking into account Bell-LaPadula security model and the working of the participating workflow, to form a security lattice of applicable security labels. If A is a set of all subjects and S is the set of all possible security labels, then there exists a many-to-one function f_1: A → S, i.e. each element in set A has a corresponding element in set S. If B is a set of all objects and S is the set of all possible security labels, then there exists a many-to-one function f_2: B→S, i.e. each element in set B has a corresponding element in set S.

Step 7. Repeat steps 1 to 6 for all participating organizations.

Step 8. Combine security lattices of participating organization taking into account which security label can read which other security label, to obtain security lattice for the complete IOWF. If S_1 and S_2 are two security labels such that S_1 can read S_2 then introduce an arrow from S_1 to S_2 in the security lattice indicating reading right.

Step 9. Compare security label of subject with security label of object it is trying to access. Grant access only if the subject is cleared to access that object, otherwise deny access.

CORRECTNESS OF INTERORGANIZATIONAL WORKFLOWS

In IOWFs each business partner has a private workflow process that is connected to the workflow processes of some of the other partners. It involves communication between the workflows of all participating organizations. Error in design of IOWF are thus difficult to detect and can result in some serious consequences. Therefore, there is need to detect the correctness of the IOWF. There are two concepts to verify the correctness of IOWF namely soundness and consistency. A workflow is sound if and only if, for any case, the process terminates properly, i.e., termination is guaranteed, there are no dangling tasks and there is no deadlock in the workflow. Consistency deals with verifying whether the implementation of IOWF meets the original specification.

In order to check the consistency of IOWF, instead of checking all possible firing sequence the concept of implicit places is used to avoid state explosion. A place in a net system is a constraint on the firing of its output transitions. If the removal of a place does not change the behavior of the original net system, that place represents a redundancy in the system and can be removed. A place whose removal preserves the behavior of the system is called an implicit place, also called a redundant place. An implicit or redundant place always contains sufficient tokens to allow for the firing of transitions connected to it.

Behavior of a net system implies sequences of fireable transitions and marking of places in the net system. The behavior of the net system can be represented by the reachability graph.

Implicit places allow for the efficient verification of consistency. The generalized concept of implicit place set can be described as follows:

Let (PN, M) be a marked Petri net with PN = (P, T, F) and P_1⊆P. P_1 is an implicit place set if and only if for every reachable state M' and any transition t∈T: if each place in (•t \ P_1) contains a token in state M', then each place in (•t∩P$_I$) contains a token in M'. Place p in P is an implicit place if and only if {p} is an implicit place set.

In Figure 9 p$_5$ is implicit as it does not influence the behavior of the workflow. A token is placed in p$_5$ when transition t$_1$ fires. Then transition t$_2$ fires followed by t$_3$. Even if p$_5$ was removed, it would have not affected the flow of transition firings, as can be seen from the reachability graphs. The set {p$_5$} is implicit place set for the workflow in Figure 10. Removal of implicit place is significant especially in larger workflows because it eliminates redundant places.

FUTURE RESEARCH DIRECTIONS

Computerization of careflow processes in health-care industry can dramatically reduce medical errors and therefore improve quality of service. Currently these are mostly research and academic efforts. Deciding which standard and system to select will be an important next step. Finally broad industrial adaptation of careflow systems in healthcare industry will be the next even more important step. Use of careflow systems will also improve education and training of medical personnel taking into account graphical representation of tasks and conditions as well as dynamic nature of Petri net based environments. Future careflow systems should be graphical, based on some version of Petri nets, and use easy–to-follow graphical user interface. Such systems must be also presented on several levels of abstraction to allow graphical representation of various details. To accomplish this last objective will require effective use of Petri net morphisms to model careflow systems with different precision and,

Figure 9. Left two figures: Workflow with implicit places and its reachability graph. Right two figures: Workflow with removed implicit places and its reachability graph

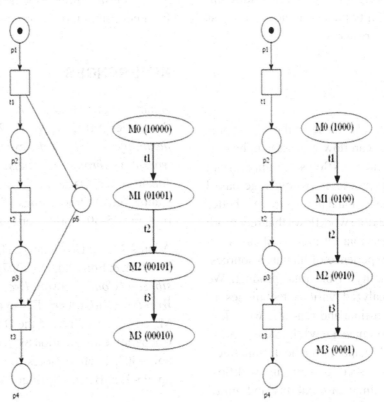

Figure 10. Example Workflow

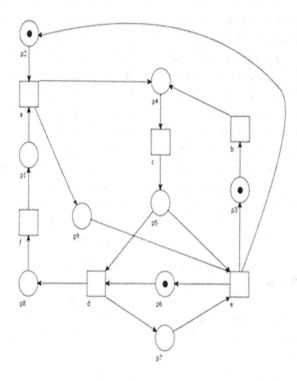

perhaps, from different perspectives. Future approaches to flexibility include issues of process patterns and query patterns.

CONCLUSION

We explored in this chapter several forms of process flexibility for careflow processes in healthcare domain. Rigid workflows are appropriate in manufacturing processes. Knowledge-based systems and organizational procedures are better represented by flexible workflows that rely more on historic and test data for processed cases, on knowledge and experience of human resources, as well as on quality of the final product. We reviewed and analyzed various techniques to accomplish design-time and run-time workflow flexibility. We presented YAWL implementation of the Cutaneus Melanoma medical guidelines. We also addressed security issue in workflow systems by indicating that flexibility and multi-

level security can be modeled separately within Petri net computational model.

REFERENCES

Adams, M., ter Hofstede, A. H. M., Edmond, D., & van der Aalst, W. M. P. (2005). *Facilitating flexibility and dynamic exception handling in workflows through worklets*. In Orlando Bello, Johann Eder, Oscar Pastor & Jo~ao Falc~ao e Cunha, (eds.), Proceedings of the CAiSE'05 Forum, pp. 45-50, Porto, Portugal, FEUP Edicoes.

Adams, M., ter Hofstede, A. H. M., van der Aalst, W. M. P., & Edmond, D. (2007). *Dynamic, Extensible and Context-Aware Exception Handling for Workflows*. In Curbera, F., Leymann, F., & Weske, M., eds, Proceedings of the OTM Conference on Cooperative information Systems (CoopIS 2007), vol. 4803, Lecture Notes in Computer Science, pp. 95-112. Berlin: Springer-Verlag.

Adams, M., ter Hofstede, A.H.M., Edmond, D., &. van der Aalst, W.M.P. (2006). Worklets: A Service-Oriented Implementation of Dynamic Flexibility in Workflows. In Meersman, R. & Tari, Z. et al., (eds.), *On the Move to Meaningful Internet Systems*, OTM Confederated International Conferences, 14th International Conference on Cooperative Information Systems (CoopIS 2006), vol. 4275, Lecture Notes in Computer Science, pp. 291-308. Berlin: Springer-Verlag.

Arrow, K., et al. (2009). Toward a 21-st Century Healthcare System. *Recommendations for Health Care Reform, Annals of Internal Medicine, 150,* 493-495. Retrievied from www.annals.org, on March 3 2009.

Ferraialo, D. F., Kuhn, D. R., & Chandramouli, R. (2007). *Role-Based Access Control* (2nd ed.). Norwood, MA, USA: Artech House.

Gami, N., & Mikolajczak, B. (2007a). *Integration of Multilevel Security Features into Loosely Coupled Inter-Organizational Workflow*, Proc. Fourth International Conference on Information Technology: New Generations, ITNG '07, Las Vegas, Nevada, USA.

Gami, N., & Mikolajczak, B. (2007b). *Consistency of Loosely Coupled Inter-Organizational Workflow with Multi-level Security Features*, Proc. of the 5th International Workshop on Modeling, Simulation, Verification and Validation of Enterprise Information Systems (MSVVEIS 2007) in conjunction with the 9th International Conference on Enterprise Information Systems, Funchal, Madeira - Portugal.

Girault, C., & Valk, R. (2003). *Petri Nets for Systems Engineering: a Guide to Modeling, Verification, and Applications* (pp. 278–281). Berlin, New York: Springer-Verlag.

Griew, A. & Currell, R., (1995), *A Strategy for Security of the Electronic Patient Record*, Institute for Health Informatics, Aberystwyth, Version 2.1.

Khadka, B., & Mikolajczak, B. (2007). *Transformation of Live Sequence Charts to Colored Petri Nets*, Proceedings of the 5th Symposium on Design, Analysis, and Simulation of Distributed Systems, DASD 2007, Summer Computer Simulation Conference SCSC'07, San Diego, CA, USA.

Mikolajczak, B., & Wang, Z. (2003). *Conceptual Modeling of Concurrent Systems through Stepwise Abstraction and Refinement using Petri Net Morphisms*. Proc. of the 22nd Int. Conference on Conceptual Modeling. ER'2003, Chicago, Illinois. [Springer-Verlag.]. *Lecture Notes in Computer Science, 2813,* 433–445. doi:10.1007/978-3-540-39648-2_34

Rinderle, S., Reichert, M., & Dadam, P. (2004). Correctness Criteria for Dynamic Changes in Workflow Systems: A Survey. *Data & Knowledge Engineering, 50*(1), 9–34. doi:10.1016/j.datak.2004.01.002

Sadiq, S., Sadiq, W., & Orlowska, M. (2001). *Pockets of Flexibility in Workflow Specification.* In Proceedings of the 20th International Conference on Conceptual Modeling (ER 2001). vol. 2224. Lecture Notes in Computer Science. pp. 513-526. Berlin, Springer-Verlag.

Schonenberg, M. H., Mans, R. S., Russell, N. C., Mulyar, N. A., & van der Aalst, W. M. P. (2007). *Towards a Taxonomy of Process Flexibility (Extended Version)*, BPM Center Report BPM-07-11.

van der Aalst, W.M.P. (1999). Inter-organizational Workflows: An Approach based on Message Sequence Charts and Petri Nets, *Systems Analysis - Modeling - Simulation, 34(3),* 335-367.

van der Aalst, W. M. P., Adams, M., ter Hofstede, A. H. M., Pesic, M., & Schonenberg, H. (2009), *Flexibility as a Service*. In L. Chen, (ed.) Database Systems for Advanced Applications (DASFAA 2009), (LNCS, vol.5667, pp. 320-334). Berlin: Springer-Verlag.

van der Aalst, W. M. P., & Berens, P. J. S. (2001). Beyond workflow management: Product-driven case handling. In Ellis, S., Rodden, T., & Zigurs, I. (eds.), *International ACM SIGGROUP Conference on Supporting Group Work*, pp. 42-51, New York: ACM Press.

van der Aalst, W. M. P., & ter Hofstede, A. H. M. (2005). YAWL: Yet Another Workflow Language. *Information Systems*, *30*(4), 245–275. doi:10.1016/j.is.2004.02.002

van der Aalst, W. M. P., ter Hofstede, A. H. M., Kiepuszewski, B., & Barros, A. P. (2003). Workflow patterns. *Distributed and Parallel Databases*, *14*(3), 5–51. doi:10.1023/A:1022883727209

van der Aalst, W. M. P., Weske, M., & Gruenbauer, D. (2005). Case Handling: A New Paradigm for Business Process Support. *Data & Knowledge Engineering*, *53*(2), 129–162. doi:10.1016/j.datak.2004.07.003

ADDITIONAL READING

American Diabetes Association. (2000). Standards of Medical Care for Patients with Diabetes Mellitus. *Diabetes Care*, *26*(Supplement 1.).

Atluri, V., & Huang, W. K. (1996). *An Extended Petri Net Model for Supporting Workflows in a Multilevel Secure Environment*. Proc. of the 10th IFIP WG 11.3 Working conference on Database Security. pp.199-216.

Atluri, V., & Huang, W. K. (1996). *An Authorization Model for Workflows*, Proceedings of the Fifth European Symposium on Research in Computer Security. Rome-Italy.(LNCS vol. 1146, pp. 44-64). New York: Springer-Verlag.

Barkley, J. (1995). *Implementing Role-Based Access Control using Object Technology*, First ACM Workshop on Role-Based Access Control, Gaithersburg, Maryland.

Barkley, J. (1995), *Application Engineering in Health Care*, Proceedings of the 2nd Annual CHIN Summit.

Bellazzi, R. (2003). Electronic management of systems in Diabetes Mellitus: impact on patient outcomes. *Disease Management & Health Outcomes*, *11*(3), 159–171. doi:10.2165/00115677-200311030-00003

Borgida, B., & Murata, T. (1999). *Tolerating exceptions in workflows: a unified framework for data and processes*. Proceedings of the International Joint Conference on Work Activities. Coordination and Collaboration (WACC'99). pp.59–68. San Francisco:ACM Press.

Casati, F. (1998). *A discussion on approaches to handling exceptions in workflows*, CSCW Workshop on Adaptive Workflow Systems, Seattle, USA.

Dustdar, S. (2004). Caramba - a process-aware collaboration system supporting ad hoc and collaborative processes in virtual teams. *Distributed and Parallel Databases*, *15*(1), 45–66. doi:10.1023/B:DAPD.0000009431.20250.56

Ellis, C. A., Keddara, K., & Rozenberg, G. (1995). *Dynamic change within workflow systems*.In Comstock, N., Ellis, C., Kling, R., Mylopoulos, K., & Kaplan, S., (eds). Proceedings of the Conference on Organizational Computing Systems. (ACM SIGOIS, pp. 10-21). Milpitas, California. New York: ACM Press.

Ferraiolo, D., & Kuhn, R. (1995). *An Introduction to Role-based Access Control* (1995). NIST/ITL Bulletin. Retrieved 10/1/10 from: http://csrc.nist.gov/groups/SNS/rbac/.

Ferraiolo, D., Sandhu, R., Gavrila, S., Kuhn, R. D., & Chandramouli, R. (2001). Proposed NIST Standard for Role-Based Access Control. *ACM Transactions on Information and System Security*, *4*(3), doi:10.1145/501978.501980

Ferraiolo, D.F., Cugini, J.A., & Kuhn, D.R. (1995). *Role-Based Access Control (RBAC): Features and Motivations*, 11th Annual Computer Security Applications Proceedings.

Ferraiolo, D. F., Gilbert, D. M., & Lynch, N. (1993). *An Examination of Federal and Commercial Access Control Policy Needs*, Proceedings of the 16th NIST-NSA National Computer Security Conference, Baltimore, Maryland.

Ferraiolo, D. F., & Kuhn, D. R. (1992). *Role-Based Access Controls*. Proceedings of the 15th NIST-NSA National Computer Security Conference, Baltimore, Maryland.

George, M., & Pyke, J. (2003). Staffware White Paper: Dynamic Process Orchestration. Precedence research, Staffware Plc. Version 1. Retrieved 10/1/2010 from http://is.tm.tue.nl/bpm2003/download/WP%20Dynamic%20Process%20Orchestration%20v1.pdf.

Hagen, H., & Alonso, G. (2000). Exception handling in workflow management systems. *IEEE Transactions on Software Engineering, 26*(10), 943–958. doi:10.1109/32.879818

Hensinger, C., Reichert, M., Bauer, T., Strzeletz, T., & Dadam, D. (2000). *ADEPT workflow - advanced workflow technology for the efficient support of adaptive, enterprise-wide processes.* Conference on Extending Database Technology. Konstanz, Germany.

Joeris, G. (1999). Defining flexible workflow execution behaviors. In Dadam, D. & Reichert, M., (eds, *Enterprise-wide and Cross-enterprise Workflow Management: Concepts, Systems, Applications*, vol. 24, CEUR Workshop Proceedings, Paderborn, Germany.

Kang, B. H., Preston, P., & Compton, P. (1998). *Simulated expert evaluation of multiple classification ripple down rules.* Proceedings of the 11th Workshop on Knowledge Acquisition, Modeling and Management. Banff, Alberta, Canada.

Knorr, K. (2001). *Multilevel Security and Information Flow in Petri Net Workflows.* Proceedings of the 11th Conference on Advanced Information Systems Engineering. Heidelberg.

Li, X., Hu, J., Bu, L., Zhao, J., & Zheng, G. (2005). *Consistency Checking of Concurrent Models for Scenario-Based Specifications*, Proceedings of 12th International SDL Forum. pp. 298-312. Grimstad, Norway.

Mikolajczak, B. (2004) *Stepwise Abstractions of Workflow Systems using Petri Net Morphisms*, Proceedings of the IEEE Int. Conference on Networking, Sensing and Control, Taipei, Taiwan, IEEE Computer Society Press.

Mikolajczak, B., & Bauskar, B. (2004). *Modeling Inheritance Anomaly in Concurrent Object-Oriented Systems Using Colored Petri Nets*, Proc. of the IEEE Int. Conference Systems, Man, Cybernetics SMC'04. The Hague: IEEE Computer Society Press.

Mikolajczak, B., & Bauskar, B. (2006). *Abstract Node Method for Integration of Object Oriented Design with Colored Petri Nets.* Proc. of the Third International Conference on Information Technology: New Generation ITNG. pp. 680-687. Las Vegas, Nevada, IEEE Computer Society Press.

Mikolajczak, B., & Joshi, S. (2004). *Modeling of Information Systems Security Features by Colored Petri Nets.* Proc. of the IEEE Int. Conference Systems, Man, Cybernetics SMC'04. The Hague, Netherlands. IEEE Computer Society Press.

Mikolajczak, B., & Joshi, S. (2005). *Specifying Selected Security Features in Inter-Organizational Workflows*, Proc. of the International Conference on Intelligent Agents, Web and Internet Commerce IAWTIC. Vienna, Austria, IEEE Computer Society Press.

Mikolajczak, B., & Wang, Z. (2003). *Conceptual Modeling of Information Systems with General Morphisms of Petri Nets*, Int. Symposium Intelligent Information Processing and Web Mining, IIS'03, Zakopane, Poland. M.A. Klopotek et al. ed., Advances in Soft Computing. pp. 535-540. Springer, Physica Series.

Muller, R., Greiner, U., & Rahm, E. (2004). AgentWork: A workflow system supporting rule-based workflow adaptation. *Data & Knowledge Engineering*, *51*(2), 223–256. doi:10.1016/j.datak.2004.03.010

Myong, H. K., Froscher, N. J., Eppinger, J. B., & Moskowitz, S. I. (1997). *An Architecture for Multilevel Secure Interoperability*. Washington, DC: Proceedings from Center for High Assurance Computer Systems, Information Technology Division.

National Electronic Library for Healthcare. UK, National Service framework: a practical aid to implementation in primary care: chronic disease management. URL: Retrieved 10/1/10 from: www.nelh.nhs.uk/nsf/inprimarycare/pdf_files/nsf_chronicdisease.pdf.

Panzarasa, S., Maddè, S., Quaglini, S., Pistarini, C., & Stefanelli, M. (2002). Evidence-based careflow management systems: the case of post-stroke rehabilitation. *Journal of Biomedical Informatics*, *35*(2), 123–139. doi:10.1016/S1532-0464(02)00505-1

Pesic, M., Schonenberg, M. H., Sidorova, N., & van der Aalst, W. M. P. (2007). *Constraint-Based Workflow Models: Change Made Easy*. In Curbera, F., Leymann, F.& Weske, M., (eds). Proceedings of the OTM Conference on Cooperative information Systems (CoopIS 2007).(LNCS vol. 4803,pp. 77-94). Berlin: Springer-Verlag.

Quaglini, S., Stefanelli, M., Lanzola, G., Caporusso, V., & Panzarasa, S. (2001). Flexible guideline-based patient careflow systems. *Artificial Intelligence in Medicine*, *22*(1), 65–80. doi:10.1016/S0933-3657(00)00100-7

RBAC (2004). *Role-Based Access Control () Role Engineering Process*, Version 3.0, Developed for: the Healthcare RBAC Task Force Developed by: Science Applications International Corporation (SAIC).

RBAC (2004). *Core and Hierarchical Role Based Access Control () profile of XACML*. Version 2.0. Committee Draft 01.

Richards, D. (2001). *Combining cases and rules to provide contextualized knowledge-based systems*. Modeling and Using Context, Third International and Interdisciplinary Conference, CONTEXT 2001. vol. 2116. Lecture Notes in Artificial Intelligence. pp. 465-469, Dundee, UK, Berlin, Springer-Verlag.

Russell, N., van der Aalst, W. M. P., & ter Hofstede, A. H. M. (2006). *Workflow Exception Patterns*. In Dubois, E. and Pohl, K., eds, Proceedings of the 18th International Conference on Advanced Information Systems Engineering (CAiSE'06).(LNCS vol. 4001. pp. 288-302). Berlin:Springer-Verlag.

Sandhu, R., Coyne, E., Feinstein, H.L., Youman, Ch., E. (1996). Role-Based Access Control Models. *IEEE Computer, 29(2),* 38-47.

Sandhu, R., Ferraialo, D., & Kuhn, R. The NIST Model for Role-Based Access Control: Towards a Unified Standard. Proceedings, 5th ACM Workshop on Role Based Access Control, July 26-27, 2000, Berlin,pp.47-63. - initial proposal for the current INCITS 359-2004 RBAC standard.

Sperl-Hillen, J., O'Connor, P. J., Carlson, R. R., Lawson, T. B., Halstenson, C., Crowson, T., & Wuorenma, J. (2000). Improving diabetes care in a large health care system: an enhanced primary care approach. *The Joint Commission Journal on Quality Improvement*, *26*(11), 615–622.

Strong, D. M., & Miller, S. M. (1995). Exceptions and exception handling in computerized information processes. *ACM Transactions on Information Systems*, *13*(2), 206–233. doi:10.1145/201040.201049 van der Aalst, W. M. P. (2001). Exterminating the dynamic change bug: A concrete approach to support workflow change. *Information Systems Frontiers, 3*(3), 297–317. doi:10.1023/A:1011409408711

van der Aalst, W. M. P., & Pesic, M. (2006). *DecSerFlow: Towards a Truly Declarative Service Flow Language*. In M. Bravetti, M. Nunez, & G. Zavattaro, (eds), International Conference on Web Services and Formal Methods (WS-FM 2006). (LNCS vol. 4184.pp. 1-23). Berlin: Springer-Verlag.

Weigand, H., & van den Heuvel, W.-J. (2002). Cross-organizational workflow integration using contracts. *Decision Support Systems, 33*, 247–265. doi:10.1016/S0167-9236(02)00015-5

Zielstroff, R. D. (1998). Online Practice guidelines: Issues, obstacles, and future prospects. *Journal of the American Medical Informatics Association, 5*(3), 227–236.

KEY TERMS AND DEFINITIONS

Careflow Systems: Workflow management systems as applied to healthcare management processes.

Case-Handling Systems: Workflow systems able to handle differently various cases of a workflow.

Circumspectness: Property of a workflow to have a designated owner for every exception that can be raised during the workflow execution.

Colored Petri Nets: Computational graphical model for parallel and distributed systems with formal behavioral semantics that can be hierarchical and can incorporate complex logical and time dependencies.

Consistency: Workflow property that deals with verifying whether the implementation of. Inter-organizational Workflow meets the original specification of the system.

Exception Handling: Subsystem of a workflow system that assigns an owner to every exception that can arise during the workflow execution.

Flexibility of Workflow Systems: Feature of workflow systems with capabilities to be modified at design or at run time of the system.

Multi-Level Security: Computer system security that takes into account reading and writing privileges on several security levels.

Role-Based Access Control: Security strategy that allows access to a personnel with proper role.

Soundness: Property of a workflow system to be able to reach the output of the workflow from every reachable state of the workflow.

Worklets: Small workflow sub-processes that implement a new or changed version of one major task of a workflow.

Section 3
Certification and Evaluation of Security

Chapter 6
Information Security Standards for Health Information Systems:
The Implementer's Approach

Evangelos Kotsonis
Adacom SA, Greece

Stelios Eliakis
Athens University of Economics and Business, Greece

ABSTRACT

Current developments in the field of integrated treatment show the need for IS security approaches within the healthcare domain. Health information systems are called to meet unique demands to remain operational in the face of natural disasters, system failures and denial-of-service attacks. At the same time, the data contained in health information systems are strictly confidential and, due to the ethical, judicial and social implications in case of data loss, health related data require extremely sensitive handling. The purpose of this chapter is to provide an overview of information security management standards in the context of health care information systems and focus on the most widely accepted ISO/IEC 27000 family of standards for information security management. In the end of the chapter, a guide to develop a complete and robust information security management system for a health care organization will be provided, by mentioning special implications that are met in a health care organization, as well as special considerations related to health related web applications. This guide will be based on special requirements of ISO/IEC 27799:2008 (Health informatics — Information security management in health using ISO/IEC 27002).

INTRODUCTION

While security of personal information is considered important to all individuals, corporations, institutions and governments, there are special requirements in the health sector that need to be met to ensure confidentiality, integrity, auditability and availability of personal health information. This type of information is considered by many as the most security demanding, since confidentiality, availability and integrity is considered to be critical for such information in several contexts and environments. Protecting confidentiality is essential if the privacy of subjects of care is to be

DOI: 10.4018/978-1-61692-895-7.ch006

maintained. Integrity of health information must be protected to ensure patient safety, and an important component of this protection is ensuring that the information's entire life cycle is fully auditable. Availability of health information is also critical to effective health care delivery.

Because of this critical nature of requirements that characterizes health care information, all health organizations should examine whether they have established information systems that satisfy privacy, safety, security and availability requirements, regardless of their size, location and model of service delivery (Sunyaev, 2009).

When addressing these special information security needs of the health sector, a security approach should accordingly take into consideration the unique operating environment in health organizations (ISO 27799:2008). If the understanding of the security requirements is not the same for all involved parties and the security mechanisms that will be implemented do not comply with some globally accepted rules and practices, then the system that will be designed will not necessarily achieve the desired security level. Thus, it will be very difficult to interoperate with other systems, which, in the context of health care, could have lethal consequences.

Additionally, it is of general agreement that security issues should be considered very early in an e-health development process, in order to avoid risks and to facilitate the achievement of the overall e-health system (Sunyaev A., 2009). It is therefore clear that the role and contribution of international standards to the design and implementation of security in health care information systems is dominant. Standards-setting and professional regulatory organizations have been busy addressing the problems of medical privacy and the security of healthcare information from their own perspectives, but until recently a unified approach was not available in the form of an international standard, focused on managing information security in health organizations. This gap has been filed by ISO/IEC 27799:2008, which

was issued by the International Organization for Standardization.

The purpose of this chapter is to provide an overview of information security management standards in the context of health care information systems and focus on the most widely accepted family of standards for information security management which is the ISO/IEC 27000 family of standards.

In the following section, an overview of standard organizations and standardization processes will be provided. Following, the ISO/IEC 27000 family of standards will be described and a focus on ISO 27001:2005, ISO 27002:2005 and ISO 27799:2008 will be provided. In the end of this chapter, a guide to develop a complete and robust information security management system for a health care organization will be provided by mentioning special implications, which are met in a health care organization in general, and special considerations related to health related web applications. This guide will be based on special requirements of ISO/IEC 27799:2008.

BACKGROUND ON STANDARDS AND CERTIFICATIONS

"Standardization is the process of developing and agreeing upon technical standards. A standard is a document that establishes uniform engineering or technical specifications, criteria, methods, processes, or practices" (Tsohou, 2009). Standards may fall into one of the following categories: International standard (a standard adopted by an international standards organization and made available to the general public), European standard (a standard adopted by a European standards organization and made available to the general public), and National standard (a standard adopted by a national standards organization and made available to the general public) (Guijarro, 2009).

The development of standards for software in healthcare has been an essential step for creating architectures for rational health information exchange (Department of Health and Human Services, 2000). Healthcare information technology (HIT) has utilized a number of standards that are considered to be generic purpose standards and have been used in other industries for a long time (such as XML for message formats and the ISO/IEC 17799:2005 Security Standards or NIST-800 Series Security Framework). In addition, a number of standards have been developed which are used almost exclusively by healthcare. Healthcare IT standards include messaging standards such as the various versions of HL7.

There are at least six principal organizations which have developed health related international standards including ASTM-E31, ANSI-HL7, CEN-TC 251, ISO-TC 215, NEMA-DICOM, and IEEE. ASTM, the American Society for Testing and Materials based in the United States, is mainly used by commercial laboratory vendors. Its committee E31 is focused in developing e-health standards. ANSI, the American National Standards Institute operating in the United States, is developing HL7 which is a family of standards for the exchange, integration, sharing and retrieval of electronic health information. CEN, the European Committee for Standardization, has formed the Technical Committee CEN/TC 251 Health Informatics, which has created a series of European pre-standards and standards covering the electronic exchange of medical data principally focused on Electronic Health Records. ISO, the International Organization for Standardization, develops e-health standards through the technical committee ISO TC215, which involves a number of other organizations such as CEN and HL7. The American College of Radiology (ACR) and the National Electrical Manufacturers Association (NEMA) have published DICOM, a standard that addressed the methods for data transfer in digital medical images in the United States. Finally IEEE, the Institute of Electrical and Electronics Engineers, is establishing a series of standards related with medical device communications.

ISO 27000 STANDARDS FOR HEALTHCARE INFORMATION SYSTEMS

Standards set specifications, formats, terminology and others to enable information exchange. There are standards which have been developed for the same purpose offering two or more solutions, but none of them can be considered to be universally acceptable. Thus, it is not easy to select the best or most relevant standard. On the other hand, the existence of multiple standards is also important as it leads to competition and helps promote the quality of the e-health system environment (Chheda, 2008). The International Organization for Standardization (ISO) (Standardization) standards and guides for conformity assessment represent an international consensus on best practices. Their use contributes to the consistency of conformity assessment worldwide and so facilitates trade (Tsohou, 2009).

Information security management is a continuous, everlasting process that allows an organization to achieve the desired level of confidentiality, integrity and availability of its information and services. "An information security management system (ISMS) refers to that part of the overall management system, based on a business risk approach, to establish, implement, operate, monitor, review, maintain and improve information security". (Tsohou, 2009)

ISO/IEC JTC 1 SC 27 maintains an expert committee dedicated to the development of international management systems standards for information security, also known as the Information Security Management System (ISMS) family of standards. Through the use of the ISMS family of standards, organizations can develop and implement a framework for managing security of their information assets. Also, organizations can use the standards of the ISMS family to prepare for an independent assessment of their ISMS, applied to the protection of information assets, such as financial information, intellectual property, and employee details or information entrusted to them by customers or third parties. (ISO/IEC 27000:2009).

The ISMS family of standards that ISO has published intended to assist organizations of all types and sizes to implement and operate an effective and operating ISMS. Each international standard that belongs to the ISMS family of standards has specific purpose and contents which is utilized by the rest of the standards that belong to the family.

The most important international standards of the ISMS family of standards are the following:

- ISO/IEC 27000:2009, Information security management systems — Overview and vocabulary. This standard provides an overview of information security management systems and defines terms which are related to the overall ISMS family of standards (ISO/IEC 27000:2009)
- ISO/IEC 27001:2005, Information security management systems — Requirements - specifies the requirements for establishing, implementing, operating, monitoring, reviewing, maintaining and improving a documented ISMS within the context of the organization's overall business risks (ISO/IEC 27001:2005)
- ISO/IEC 27002:2005, Code of practice for information security management - This standard establishes guidelines and general principles for initiating, implementing, maintaining, and improving information security management in an organization. (ISO/IEC 27002:2005)

Additionally, ISO has prepared and published a series of international standards purposed to provide guidelines on several aspects of the previously mentioned baseline standards. The most important of these additional standards are the following:

- ISO/IEC 27003:2009, Information security management system implementation guidance. This standard guides the design of an ISO/IEC 27001:2005-compliant ISMS, leading up to the initiation of an ISMS implementation project.(ISO/IEC 27003:2009)
- ISO/IEC 27004:2009, Information security management — Measurement. Measures and measurement methods are provided in this standard that can be used to examine the effectiveness of an implemented information security management system (ISMS) and controls or groups of controls, as specified in ISO/IEC 27001:2005.(ISO/IEC 27004:2009)
- ISO/IEC 27005:2008, Information security risk management. This standard provides guidelines for Information Security Risk Management in an organization, supporting in particular the requirements of an ISMS according to ISO/IEC 27001:2005. (ISO/IEC 27005:2008)

Finally, in the context of ISMS, ISO has published a number of industry specific international standards. In the case of healthcare information systems, the corresponding international standard is ISO/IEC 27799:2008. This standard provides guidance specifically focused to healthcare organizations and other custodians of personal health information that will assist them to understand how best to protect the confidentiality, integrity and availability of health related information by implementing ISO/IEC 27002:2005 (ISO/IEC 27799:2008).

In the rest of this section, the three most important International Standards are going to be described, as they are the ones which can form the basis for the development of a certified health ISMS.

ISO/IEC 27001:2005 – The Requirements

ISO/IEC 27001:2005 is the formal set of specifications against which organizations may seek independent certification of their Information Security Management System (ISMS). It applies to all types of organizations (e.g. commercial, enterprises, government agencies), regardless of type, size and nature.

ISO/IEC 27001:2005 specifies requirements for the establishment, implementation, monitoring and review, maintenance and improvement of a management system - an overall management and control framework - for managing an organization's information security risks. For the development of this framework, the standard proposes the application of a system of processes, together with interactions between these processes, and their management. Such a system is further referred to as a "process approach", which is structured in the circular "Plan-Do-Check-Act" (PDCA) model (Tsohou, 2009).

An ISO/IEC 27001:2005 compliant ISMS therefore incorporates several Plan-Do-Check-Act (PDCA) cycles. Information security controls are not merely specified and implemented as one-off activities but are continually reviewed and adjusted to take account of changes in the security threats, vulnerabilities and impact of information security failures, using review and improvement activities, which are also specified within the management system.

The requirements set by ISO/IEC 27001:2005 do not mandate the implementation of specific information security controls. Instead, several security controls are noted in an appendix (annex), with references to ISO/IEC 27002:2005. These security controls are provided indicatively and organizations adopting ISO/IEC 27001:2005 are free to choose the specific information security controls that are applicable to their particular information security needs.

ISO/IEC 27002:2005 – The Code of Practice

ISO/IEC 27002:2005, the latest version of "Information technology - Security techniques - Code of practice for information security management", to give it its full title, is an internationally-accepted standard of good practice for information security. Tens or hundreds of thousands of organizations worldwide follow ISO/IEC 27002:2005.

ISO/IEC 27002:2005 is a code of practice - a generic, advisory document, not truly a standard or formal specification such as ISO/IEC 27001:2005. It lays out a reasonably well structured set of suggested controls that can be used to address information security risks, covering confidentiality, integrity and availability aspects (ISO/IEC 27002:2005).

ISO/IEC 27002:2005 is highly interrelated to ISO/IEC 27001:2005, as it provides further details for the implementation of security controls that are included in the annex of ISO/IEC 27001:2005. It is intended to serve as a single reference point for identifying a range of controls, suitable for different contexts and environments where information systems are used.

The control objectives and controls that ISO/IEC 27001:2005 proposes intend to meet the requirements identified by a formal risk assessment. Therefore organizations that adopt ISO/IEC 27002:2005 must first assess their own information security risks and then apply suitable controls, using the standard for guidance (ISO/IEC 27002:2005).

The structure of the best practice includes 39 control objectives, aimed to protect information assets against threats to confidentiality, integrity and availability. These control objectives indicate what has to be achieved to satisfy 11 specified control clauses. Additionally, for each one of the control objectives, a number of suggested controls is mentioned. These controls are indicative controls that are considered sufficient to achieve each corresponding objective. The implementation of each of these controls is not mandatory; rather they are mentioned as alternatives to the users during the implementation of the ISMS. The decision for the control that is suitable for each environment should be based on a risk assessment process and the users are free to mitigate identified risks by implementing controls that are not mentioned in ISO/IEC 27002:2005.

ISO/IEC 27799:2008 – The Healthcare Perspective

The special requirements and the diverse environment of health organizations were taken into consideration by ISO, which in June 2008 published the first final version of ISO/IEC 27799:2008. The purpose of ISO/IEC 27799:2008 is to provide assistance in the development process of an ISMS explicitly in a health organization, based on guidelines and control objectives that were provided in ISO/IEC 27002:2005.

ISO 27799:2008 defines guidelines to support the interpretation and implementation of ISO/IEC 27002:2005 in health informatics and is a companion to that standard. It specifies a set of detailed controls for managing health information security and provides health information security best practice guidelines (ISO/IEC 27799:2008).

The purpose of ISO/IEC 27799:2008 is not to substitute ISO/IEC 27002:2005 in the context of health care. Rather it is designed to be used as a focused and fine grained guideline that can be used as a guide to healthcare organizations and other custodians of personal health information, to indicate how to protect confidentiality, integrity and availability of such information by implementing controls mentioned in ISO/IEC 27002:2005, which is a generic guide.

Health information may be met in different formats (words and numbers, sound recordings, drawings, video and medical images), stored in various media (printing or writing on paper or electronic storage) and transmitted by multiple methods (by hand, via fax, over computer networks or by post). ISO/IEC 27799:2008 applies to health information in all its aspects; whatever form, media or transmit method, as the outmost objective is the protection of health information (ISO/IEC 27799:2008).

The standard is written like an implementation guideline/book, something an experienced consultant might espouse. The first section of the standard provides an overview on health information security. This overview includes the definition of security goals for health information security, as well as placing the information security within information governance, corporate governance and clinical governance. Additionally, in order to define the exact scope of the ISMS that will be developed, ISO/IEC 27799:2008 provides a definition of the health information that should be protected and finally, it includes a description of threats and vulnerabilities that might affect health information security.

The second section of ISO/IEC 2799:2008 describes a practical action plan for implementing ISO/IEC 27002:2005 in the context of health information security management systems. In this section, a taxonomy of ISO/IEC 27001:2005 and ISO/IEC 27002:2005 standards is provided, as well as a first definition of the importance of management commitment in the implementation of ISO/IEC 27002:2005. In the rest of the section, the user is provided with guidance on establishing and then operating an ISMS in a health environment, through the creation of a circular "Plan-Do-Check-Act" (PDCA) model (Tsohou, 2009).

The third section of the standard contains specific advice on the 11 security control clauses and 39 main security control categories described in ISO/IEC 27002:2005, which is adjusted to the special requirements of health information. Based on these control clauses and objectives, minimum requirements are stated where appropriate and, in a few cases, normative guidelines are set out describing the proper application of certain ISO/IEC 27002:2005 security controls to the protection of health information. These minimum requirements are considered to be essential to the protection of personal health information and even in the standard it is stated that compliance with these requirements are a prerequisite for achieving compliance with the standard itself (ISO/IEC 27799:2008).

Finally, the standard contains 3 informative annexes. In these annexes, the standard initially provides an overview of threats to health information security and how they can affect confidentiality, integrity or availability of information. Except from these threats, the standard also describes in these annexes specific tasks and related documents that the ISMS, which is under development, should contain and also suggests a set of support tools that could be utilized as an aid to implementation process.

ISO/IEC 27799:2008 A PRACTICAL APPROACH

The purpose of this chapter is to constitute an explanatory guide on the process of implementing a health ISMS, compliant with ISO/IEC 27799:2008. According to ISO/IEC 27000:2009, the establishment, operation, maintenance and improvement of an effective health ISMS should be based on a process based Plan – Do – Check – Act (PDCA) cycle.

The activities and documents mandated for ISO/IEC 27001:2005 certification are described in generic manner in the standard itself, while a more structured approach with specific steps for each phase of the PDCA cycle is provided in ISO/IEC 27799:2008. In this chapter the structure of activities that is provided by ISO/IEC 27799:2008 is followed, in order to be able to meet requirements set by both international standards. In the following sections the actions that are included in each phase of the PDCA cycle will be described in detail, intended to provide proper guidance during the implementation of an ISO/IEC 27799:2008 compliant ISMS in a health organization.

Planning

The first phase of the PDCA cycle is the phase where the health ISMS is created and established. All the subsequent phases of each PDCA cycle depend on what is specified, defined and documented in this phase, as this is when the system is defined in terms of environment, boundaries, people involved, status and purpose. The documents that are developed during the planning phase are used as reference, in the form of high level guidelines and policies for the development of the entire ISMS. Thus, special care and significant effort must be given during this phase.

In the planning phase, six (6) discrete implementation steps can be distinguished. These steps are provided in the following list:

- Obtain and document management support.
- Define the scope of the health ISMS
- Define Information Security Policy
- Create the structure of the ISMS management
- Assess the risks of the organization
- Manage identified risks

Through the actions that are required for each of these steps, certain documents are produced. The generated documents will be used as the basic documentation of the entire ISMS that will be developed.

In the rest of this section, the user will be provided with guidelines for the implementation of the above mentioned steps, and special requirements that exist in the context of a health organization will be explicitly stated and taken into consideration.

Management Support

It is clearly stated in all international standards that management support is vital for the development of a concrete and operational system with the complexity of an ISMS. Evident support from the management of the health organization is necessary prior to the initiation of the ISMS establishment efforts. Management of the organization must be actively involved in the implementation process and support all efforts by providing strategic instructions and required resources.

The involvement of the management should be documented in the form of written and verbal statements of commitment, in which the importance of health information security and recognition of its benefits should be mentioned (ISO/IEC 27799:2008). Through this statement, the management should set the health information security goals that the health ISMS is implemented to fulfill. Through these goals, the management should communicate the importance of meeting the information security objectives and conforming to the information security policy. Finally, the statement should also contain the responsibilities that the management has according to the law and point out the need for continual improvement (ISO/IEC 27001:2005).

The main goals/objectives of an ISMS should be the protection of confidentiality, integrity and availability of information. In the context of a health ISMS, these objectives can be translated as follows (Farn, 2007):

* Protecting Personal Information; - Confidentiality
* Preventing Mistakes in Healthcare Practice; - Integrity
* Maintaining the Functions of the Healthcare Organs (The Continuity of Healthcare Services) – Availability.

According to ISO/IEC 27799:2008, the information security goals that a health organization should meet are not restricted solely to the assurance of confidentiality, integrity and availability of health information. Even if these attributes of information are of major importance, the following considerations should also be taken into account

when defining the goals of health information security:

* honoring legislative obligations as expressed in applicable data protection laws and regulations protecting a subject of care's right to privacy,
* maintaining established privacy and security best practices in health informatics,
* maintaining individual and organizational accountability among health organizations and health professionals,
* supporting the implementation of systematic risk management within health organizations,
* meeting the security needs identified in common healthcare situations,
* reducing operating costs by facilitating the increased use of technology in a safe, secure, and well managed manner that supports – but does not constrain – current health activities,
* maintaining public trust in health organizations and the information systems these organizations rely upon,
* maintaining professional standards and ethics as established by health-related professional organizations (insofar as information security maintains the confidentiality and integrity of health information),
* operating electronic health information systems in an environment appropriately secured against threats,
* facilitating interoperability among health systems, since health information increasingly flows among organizations and across jurisdictional boundaries (especially as such interoperability enhances the proper handling of health information to ensure its continued confidentiality, integrity and availability).

Additionally, the management should establish and document a control procedure of the system.

Through this procedure, the management should seek to achieve the following goals:

- Ensure that ISMS objectives and goals are established and met
- Specify the criteria for accepting risks and for acceptable risk levels and ensure that they are followed
- Ensure that internal audits of ISMS are conducted
- Conduct management reviews of the ISMS

Health ISMS Scope Definition

Following the management's documented commitment for support of the health ISMS, the limits and boundaries of the ISMS should be formally defined. Provided that health organizations are usually large units with multiple processes and different departments, it is hard to achieve the necessary level of compliance in one attempt. Thus, it is recommended to prefer an incremental and iterative process to achieve total coverage and full benefit, during the definition of the scope of a health ISMS (ISO/IEC 27799:2008).

The scope should be clearly documented in the form of a scope statement, which will be publicized within the organization. This statement will define the boundary of the compliance activity in terms of people, processes, platforms and applications (ISO/IEC 27799:2008). Additionally, this document should be publicized widely, reviewed and adopted by all organization's information, clinical and corporate governance groups (ISO/IEC 27799:2008).

Due to the integrated future e-health, the interconnection of health information systems is expected to be increased. This fact makes security approaches in healthcare especially challenging, as health organizations can no more act as if their systems were isolated islands of information (Sunyaev, 2009). The strategic goal of every health unit may differ, functions and services provided may vary and even business and operational objectives

and structure may have nothing in common across various health organizations. This complexity and interconnectivity between different functions and departments of health information systems, may transform scope definition in a quite complex and demanding task.

To aid the scope definition of a health ISMS, it is essential to use certain criteria that will cover all aspects of the organization and ensure that objectives and boundaries of the ISMS are clearly defined. When developed, these criteria will indicate the exact expectations anticipated by the ISMS. Visibility, balance between technical and business involvement, degree of local or central relevance, management overhead that the ISMS will introduce can only be a fragment of expectations that the ISMS will be called to satisfy, and they should all be reflected in a properly defined scope (ISO/IEC 27799:2008).

A very useful tool for the determination of the acceptance criteria that can and should be used during the scope definition would be a summary level gap analysis. This analysis could be performed on a sampling basis to gain an initial understanding on the work that would be required to achieve compliance to the scope that is formulated.

Information Security Policy Definition

After the definition of the scope of the ISMS of a health organization, ISO/IEC 27001:2005 mandates the development of an information security policy document. This document is also mentioned as ISMS policy and is considered to be a superset of the information security policy Sunyaev, 2009). This document should be communicated across the organization to users in a form that is relevant, accessible and understandable to the intended reader, while special care should be taken not to disclose sensitive information (ISO/IEC 27001:2005).

The information security policy document should state management commitment and set out the organization's approach to managing information security (ISO/IEC 27001:2005). This policy will be used as a reference to all policies that will be developed in the context of the ISMS and this is the document that the rest of the policies will be based upon.

The contents of the information security policy document are specifically defined in ISO/IEC 27001:2005 and ISO/IEC 27799:2008. Although, in ISO/IEC 27799:2008 additional factors that should be concerned are mentioned to cover special requirements of the healthcare sector, the definition of this document is almost the same and should contain the following information:

- The sense of direction and principles for action with regard to information security. To define this, a framework for setting objectives and goals of the ISMS with reference to the decided scope and management commitment should be provided.
- Explanation of legislative, regulatory and contractual requirements that the ISMS should meet.
- Responsibilities for information security management, including reporting information security incidents.

As the security policy will constitute the policy of policies for the system, it should be carefully developed to provide the proper guidelines for the development of the ISMS. Special care should be taken for special factors that should be taken into consideration when developing health care information systems. Such factors are the following:

- Consent: clinicians have access to sensitive healthcare information of patients, but in the same time the patients have the right to allow or deny access to these records. This very right of the patients to determine the access rights to their medical data can be legitimately overcome in cases of healthcare priorities which are usually linked to

the incapacity of the certain subjects of care to express their preferences.
- Responsibilities: In a health organization, a number of different roles and responsibilities may exist. Respectively, arrangements and authority limits are also complicated and they can also be temporary and constantly changing (e.g. in the case of students, on call staff or support staff).
- Information Sharing: Health organizations are usually distributed or are required to exchange sensitive patient information for multiple and different purposes (e.g. for the treatment of a patient or for research or medical trials reasons).

During the development of the information security policy of a health ISMS, the above factors should be taken into consideration. This means that a health ISMS policy should state generic exclusions and procedures that would be required when restrictions in access to medical data should be overcome or information sharing should be allowed. Additionally, in the case where health organizations obtain support for third party organizations, controls and procedures should cover the interactions and specify responsibilities of each party (ISO/IEC 27799:2008).

ISMS Management Structure

After the definition of the ISMS scope and the preparation of the information security policy, the task that follows is the development of the structure of the ISMS. This structure should be decided and security responsibilities should be assigned to roles that are included and described in the structure of the ISMS. This structure should be appropriately designed to enforce and ensure coordination between stakeholders and departments of the organization. This coordination is an essential requirement to the timely establishment of the system and the achievement of the established objectives.

Allocation of Security Responsibilities

Each entity that will be included in the ISMS structure should be accompanied with a documented set of security responsibilities. Responsibilities for protection of individual assets and roles related to specific security processes (e.g. business continuity planning) or sites/information processing facilities should be clearly identified and, if required, be supplemented with more detailed guidance. When defining security responsibilities, the following should not be omitted:

- Assets and security processes
- Entity responsible for each asset or security process
- Details of responsibilities
- Authorization levels

Individuals with security responsibilities may delegate tasks to others, but the responsibility itself is not transferable. Therefore the individuals remain responsible and should monitor the correct performance of delegated tasks.

A special requirement for a health organization when defining responsibilities and ISMS structure is to clearly define access rights that facilitate access by subjects of care (e.g. requests should be made to obtain personal health information in any case). This kind of responsibility definition is required to facilitate reporting and to ensure timely delivery of information.

Coordination of Activities

The management structure of the ISMS can be configured to better match existing structure of the organization. Nevertheless, ISO/IEC 27799:2008 mandates the creation of two new entities in the organization chart, the Information Security Officer and the Information Security Management Forum.

The Information Security Officer will be responsible for health information security within the organization and will participate in the Information Security Management Forum.

The Information Security Management Forum (ISMF) will be in the heart of the ISMS, purposed to coordinate security activities, to oversee and to direct information security. The ISMF should involve members from the full range of information assurance and information governance functions. Managers, users, administrators, application designers, auditors, security personnel and specialists skilled in areas such as insurance, legal issues, human resources, IT or risk management should be present in the ISMF.

The ISMF will have to meet regularly (ISO/IEC 27799:2008 dictates that the ISMF should meet at least on a monthly basis) and the Information Security Officer should report to the ISMF and provide it with secretariat services. Finally, the Information Security Officer will be responsible to collate, publish and comment on the reports received by ISMF members (ISO/IEC 27799:2008).

Risk Analysis

The next step, following the definition of ISMS structure and allocation of security responsibilities, will be to locate and assess all information security risks that the organization faces. This assessment is performed via a structured risk analysis. Risk Analysis (RA) is a methodology for the assessment of risks, which involves the identification and valuation of assets and the assessment of threats and vulnerabilities. (Gritzalis D.,2003). In the context of a healthcare organization, assets include health information, IT services, hardware, software, communication facilities, media, IT facilities and medical devices that have value to the organization (ISO/IEC 13335-1:2004). A threat is a potential cause of an unwanted incident, that may result in harm to a system or organization (ISO/IEC 13335-1:2004) and vulnerabilities are weaknesses of assets or groups of assets that can be exploited by one or more threats (ISO/IEC 13335-1:2004). The risk is the combination of the probability of an event and its consequences and can be estimated by combining threats, vulnerabilities, assets, asset values, and security controls that are currently applied (ISO/IEC 27799:2008).

Healthcare organizations may find selecting a risk analysis methodology a quite competitive task (Vorster, 2005). Currently, there are numerous methodologies available, some of which are qualitative, while others are quantitative in nature (Vorster, 2005). Due to the special requirements, especially in the evaluation of risks that healthcare organizations face, information risk analysis in healthcare ought to consider qualitative as well as quantative factors. Financial losses should not be the primary consideration, but may be taken into account where there is evidence of large sums being paid for negligence.

A health care organization can choose from a number of standardized methodologies as a guide to identify and evaluate information security risk. NIST 800 30 (Stoneburner G., 2002), CRAMM (Zeki, 2002), OCTAVE (Alberts C., 2002) and ISO/IEC 13335-1:2004 are some of these methodologies, but when it comes to determine an ideal methodology there is no silver bullet. All the above mentioned methodologies are supported by automated tools, which can save the analyst from a large amount of work and guide them during the risk analysis process, according to the methodology it complies with. In general, risk analysis methodologies usually follow four stages (Gritzalis D., 2003), followed by the risk management stage, when the mitigation of identified risk is decided. The stages that are included in the risk analysis and management phases can be considered to be the following:

- Identification of assets
- Valuation and classification of information assets
- Threat and vulnerability evaluation
- Risk evaluation
- Risk management

The risk analysis cannot typically be delivered by any single individual, rather it is an activity designed to reach consensus, so that all viewpoints are collected and taken into consideration in evaluation of asset values, threats, vulnerabilities and risks (ISO/IEC 27799:2008).

In the rest of this section, guidance will be provided for the performance of each of the risk analysis stages, in respect to special requirements present in the healthcare sector.

Identification of Assets

The first step to an effective risk analysis is to identify the assets that are included in the scope of the analysis, which is the same with the scope of the health ISMS itself. As mentioned in ISO/IEC 27799:2008, in the context of health information security, assets include health information, IT services, hardware, software, communication facilities, media, IT facilities and medical devices that record or report data.

Health information can be met in various types, each one of which has different confidentiality, availability and integrity requirements. ISO/IEC 27799:2008 defines the following types of health information:

- personal health information;
- pseudonymized data derived from personal health information via some methodology for pseudonymous identification;
- statistical and research data, including anonymized data derived from personal health information by removal of personally identifying data;
- clinical/medical knowledge not related to any specific subjects of care, including clinical decision support data (e.g. data on adverse drug reactions);
- data on health professionals, staff and volunteers;
- information related to public health surveillance;
- audit trail data, produced by health information systems that contain personal health

information, or pseudonymous data derived from personal health information, or that contain data about the actions of users with regard to personal health information;

- System security data for health information systems, including access control data and other security related system configuration data for health information systems.

In order to identify the assets within the scope of the risk analysis, the analyst should use as a starting point the following:

- Patient care systems, applications and devices that store and process health information (e.g., pharmacy, infection control, cancer registry, MRI, CTI, Ultrasound), whether they are standalone systems or connected to the network
- Business systems and applications that store, process, or transmit health information to support billing, customer service and general administrative operations, (e.g., supply chain, state submissions, credentialing)
- Infrastructure components, such as routers and firewalls, that are connected to or facilitate the transmission of health information to/from the types of systems described above

In complex information systems it may be useful to designate groups of assets, which act together to provide a particular function as 'services'. In this case the service owner is responsible for the delivery of the service, including the functioning of the assets, which provide it. In order to detect possible grouping capabilities of a set of assets, the following clauses may be utilized:

- Assets that are under the same direct management control
- Assets that have the same function or mission objective

- Assets that have essentially the same operating characteristics and security needs
- Assets that reside in the same general operating environment.

Especially for the case of medical devices that report or record data, special care should be taken. These devices often operate within special environments and electromagnetic emissions occur during their operation. Therefore, it is important to uniquely identify such devices in the inventory of assets. These devices may have "on-board" computers that are used to manage the equipment and to gather, store and analyze results and may be connected to external or internal networks through dial-up connections or local area network connections. It is not necessary to gather and report on each individual device, rather, it is important to group and gather information on types of devices.

All assets should be clearly identified and an inventory of important assets should be drawn up and maintained (ISO/IEC 17799:2005). The inventory of assets should include all information related to each asset including:

- Type of asset (e.g. information, software, physical, services, people, intangible asset)
- Format (e.g. electronic document, printed document, hardware, network equipment, database)
- Location

According to ISO/IEC 27002:2005, all assets should be owned by a designated part of the organization. The term 'owner' identifies an individual or entity that has approved management responsibility for controlling the production, development, maintenance, use and security of the assets. The term 'owner' does not mean that the person actually has any property rights to the asset (ISO/IEC 17799:2005). The asset owner should be responsible to ensure that information and assets that they own are appropriately classified and should periodically review access restrictions and classifications.

In the case of medical data and personal health information ownership should remain on the subject of care, and custodians should be designated for each asset. Specific rules should be defined and documented for the acceptable use of health information assets.

Valuation and Classification of Information Assets

Accountability for assets helps to ensure that appropriate protection is maintained. Health information assets should be classified to indicate needs, priorities and expected degree of protection when handled (ISO/IEC 17799:2005). The classification scheme that will be developed must be documented and rules and guidelines that will define how information of each class should be treated should be specified and communicated across the organization.

Classification and valuation of assets in general should be based on the security attributes of the assets. The security attributes refer to the assets' confidentiality, integrity and availability. Most commonly, classification schemes are based solely on confidentiality requirements and the other two security attributes are taken into consideration during the risk analysis. However, when performing information classification in healthcare related assets, availability and integrity of information are essential for the ongoing provision of service, thus classification in respect of availability and integrity should also be applied to assets (ISO 27799:2008).

In regards to confidentiality, special requirements that are pointed in ISO/IEC 27799:2008 should be taken into consideration when developing a classification scheme for health information. These special requirements are enhanced by the fact that confidentiality of personal health organization is subjective, context dependent and can

shift over the lifetime of an individual's health record (ISO 27799:2008).

Due to the sensitivity of personal health information, it is very important for users of health information systems to know when the data they are accessing contains personal health information. Therefore procedures for labeling and handling of confidential information are considered to be extremely important. These procedures should cover all information handling aspects for each of the classifications level, by defining how information should be processed, stored, transmitted and destroyed. Finally, special care should be taken to clearly mention the requirements that should be met to declassify confidential information, and a review process should be established to continuously examine if the classification level meets the security requirements of each asset.

Threat and Vulnerability Evaluation

As previously mentioned, there is a close relationship and interdependency between assets, vulnerabilities and threats. This relationship, together with metrics like impact of an attack or probability of vulnerability exploitation constitutes the overall information security risk of the organization. In order to determine these metrics, the asset evaluation and classification information is utilized in the next phase of the risk analysis which includes the determination of threats and vulnerabilities that are related to the assets of the ISMS.

A threat is a potential cause of a security incident that may cause an information system or organization to be lost or damaged (JIPDEC, 2004). The scale of the threat is determined by evaluating the probability of its occurrence for each factor or information asset. Threats can be identified by investigating on ways that someone could exploit vulnerabilities that exist on the assets of the system to perform attacks against the security of the information system.

Common threat sources can be categorized in natural threats, human threats and environmental threats (Stoneburner G., 2002). ISO/IEC 27799:2008 contains a full annex with 25 healthcare specific threats that should not be omitted when determining threats that a health information system may face.

Vulnerabilities are weak points and security holes, which are specific to an information asset. Vulnerabilities do not cause any damage but they allow threats to exist or to be exploited and cause damage or any kind of failure. Vulnerabilities can easily be identified if they are considered in relation to the characteristics and attributes of information assets (JIPDEC, 2004). Evaluation of vulnerabilities can be explained as the evaluation of the weakness level of an information asset. Although the extent to which assets should be categorized will differ for different organizations, vulnerabilities are typically categorized as "Low", "Medium" or "High". The same categorization applies to threats (JIPDEC, 2004).

Risk Evaluation

In the final step of the risk analysis, the definition and evaluation of risk should be performed. As stated above, the risk is a function of a number of factors, including asset value, threats, vulnerabilities, impact and existing security controls. From the number of factors that are involved in the evaluation of risk, it may seem that this estimation is a difficult task, but if previous stages of the risk analysis have been completed in an accurate and correct manner, at this stage, the following information will have already been defined and formally documented:

- Inventory of assets
- Asset values and classification
- Evaluated threats that assets face
- Existing vulnerabilities of assets

By combining the above mentioned information, the analyst can develop a business impact analysis document, as a first step toward risk evalu-

ation. The business impact analysis document will depict the amount of damage that a security incident would have on the organization. Also, in the business impact analysis, the dependency of business processes upon IT services, hardware, software, media and locations will be understood.

After collecting all the above information, the analyst will have the task to evaluate identified risks, as combinations of assets, threats, vulnerabilities and existing controls. The risk levels that will be used for the classification of risks should be determined in advance and specific rules or formulas should be developed to formalize the process of risk evaluation. Risk assessment automated tools can provide significant assistance in this part of the procedure as they already contain standard based formulas of risk calculation based on information provided for the risk factors mentioned above.

Risk Management

After the completion of the identification and evaluation of risks, the risk management planning is performed. Risk management responds to the risk analysis by identifying which controls should be strengthened, which controls are already effectively in place and which additional controls the organization needs to implement in order to reduce the residual level of risk to an acceptable level (ISO 27799:2008). The decisions related to risk management are based upon and should reflect the organization's appetite for risk and should be properly justified on cost – benefit basis.

Risk appetite, at the organizational level, is the amount of risk exposure, or potential adverse impact from an event that an organization is willing to accept or retain. Once the risk appetite threshold has been breached, risk management and business controls are implemented to bring the exposure level back within the accepted range (Tipton, 2007). To determine the risk appetite of the organization and accordingly develop an effective risk management plan, special care should be taken to ensure the alignment of responsibility for information security with the authority to make risk management decisions (ISO 27799:2008).

To establish the organization's risk appetite and determine the acceptable level of risk, specific criteria should be defined, based on objective decision parameters. Such criteria can be developed by taking into consideration resource availability, priorities in risk mitigation, level of complexity or difficulty in mitigating each risk and previous experience or events that occurred in the past. Especially for health organizations, ISO/IEC 27799:2008 defines a set of considerations that should not be omitted when defining the risk appetite of the health care organizations, which is provided in the following list:

- health sector, industry or organizational standards;
- clinical or other priorities;
- cultural fit;
- reactions of subjects of care;
- coherence with IT, clinical, and corporate risk acceptance strategy;
- cost;
- effectiveness;
- type of protection;
- number of threats covered;
- risk level at which the controls become justified;
- risk level that led to the recommendation being made;
- alternatives already in place;
- additional benefits derived.

Taken together, these factors will yield a cost benefit assessment that can underpin the necessary business case for seeking funding. Based on the risk appetite and the results of the risk evaluation, the organization should decide on the management of each risk. Although most information security professionals focus on reducing risk through contingency planning, many alternatives exist and should be taken into consideration. These alternatives are provided in the following list (Tipton, 2007):

- Accept risk. A decision is made to continue operations as-is, with a consensus to accept inherent risks.
- Transfer risk. A decision is made to transfer risk, for example, from one business unit to another or from one business area to a third party (e.g. insurer).
- Mitigate risk. The organization has a core competency that allows the elimination or reduction of risk through establishment or improvement in controls and processes.
- Share risk. Attempts are made to share risk through partnerships or outsourcing.

The decision of whether a risk will be accepted, transferred, mitigated or shared will be made by the ISMF of the health organization and it will be formally recorded for periodic review and re-assessment. The document that will include decisions on risk management should have the form of a risk treatment plan. The role of the risk treatment plan is to provide direction on how the organization will address each risk. The point is to produce a plan that specifies and provides a rationale behind each action. The risk treatment plan should contain a priority list of how to address organizational risks to each asset. Necessary controls will be allocated to each asset and the actions that will address the risk as well as the priority in which actions will be performed will also be described. Overall, the risk treatment plan should contain the following information for each risk that was identified (Calder, 2009):

- What decision the organization made for the management of this risk;
- What controls are already in place;
- What additional controls are considered necessary;

Table 1. Example structure of a statement of applicability (Arnason S.T., 2008)

Control Reference	Description	Implement	Justify	Procedure Approach	Comment
A.10.7.2	A paper shredder has been added. New process for secure disposal of media has been implemented.	Fully		Please refer to the control and policy document.	To reduce the risk of unauthorized access to sensitive information. See the result from the risk treatment plan.

- The timeframe for the implementation of the controls.

The risk treatment plan document may contain the Statement of Applicability document. The statement of applicability is the document from which an auditor will begin the process of confirming whether or not appropriate controls are in place and operative. It is a formal statement as to which of the selected mitigation security controls are applicable to the organization and which are not (Calder, 2009). In Table 1 an example structure of the statement of applicability is provided.

The first column is a reference to the corresponding control in the ISO/IEC 27001:2005 standard. The second column describes required actions and includes a reference to the risk treatment plan. The third column describes the status of implementation of the selected control; possible values for this column are "full", "partial", or not at all. The fourth column provides a justification on the decision for selecting or excluding a control. The fifth column indicates relevant procedures or policies and the last column is provided for additional comments (Calder, 2009).

After its initial development, both the risk treatment plan and the statement of applicability document will be maintained by the information security officer or similar officer on behalf of the ISMF. These documents should be provided to the clinical and corporate governance functions to form a key part of the governance documentation set (ISO 27799:2008).

Documentation Summary of the Plan Phase

The plan phase produces documents relevant to the ISMS implementation. First and foremost is the need for a plan phase guideline document to ensure the organization is capturing and executing all the relevant steps for the plan phase. The essential documents that should be prepared during the planning phase are the following:

- Scope statement
- Information security policy of the organization
- Organizational security policy
- Inventory of assets and system assets to be protected
- Business impact analysis
- Risk assessment plans and risk assessment report(s)
- Standards and procedural guidelines and templates that will be followed. Such procedures may contain the following:
  - Procedures for identifying information assets
  - Asset valuation and classification procedures
  - Asset handling guidelines
  - Risk management procedures
- Contractual agreements (including service level agreements and acceptable use agreements)
- Risk treatment plan
- Statement of applicability

In addition, the health care organization can document and materialize priorities in meeting clinical needs. This information can be developed in cooperation with clinical and corporate governance functions and used by the ISMF as backup material in support of risk acceptance decisions that will be made (ISO 27799:2008).

Doing

During the planning phase, the ISMS is actually designed and materialized. In the "Do" phase the documents that guide the implementation of the ISMS are produced, with implementation being the focus of the phase. The core purpose of the "Do" phase is the implementation of the Risk Treatment Plan that was generated in the end of the "Plan" phase, based on the risk analysis that was performed.

The "Do" phase can be implemented in a number of different ways. The main goals that ISO/IEC 27799:2008 indicates to be achieved are the following:

- Creating and scheduling a risk treatment plan
- Allocating resources
- Selecting and implementing security controls
- Training and educating
- Managing operations
- Managing resources
- Managing security incidents:

In order to achieve the above mentioned goals the organization must develop a number of policies, procedures, guides and standards, and implement the technical security controls that are defined and prioritized in the risk treatment plan.

For the proper delivery of the required artifacts, prior to any additional action, the organization should first develop an ISMS implementation program, in which the implementation schedule will be detailed. In this plan, tasks, required re-

sources and estimated durations will be included, to ensure the availability of human and non human resources that will be required during the ISMS implementation.

Often formatted as a Gant chart, this plan should be made available to clinical and other staff, to minimize interruptions to operations upon integration of information security improvements in every day operations. An effort to combine this integration with planned changes in IT facilities and health care service provision would increase the effectiveness of the ISMS. Finally, special care should be taken to depict in the implementation schedule known periods of unusual healthcare activity such as the influx of a new batch of interns and trainees, as such activities may affect the progress of ISMS implementation.

In the rest of the chapter, a brief guide of developing policies, standards, guides and procedures will be provided and additionally specific instructions for the implementation of controls in health care organizations will be mentioned, based on clause 7 of ISO/IEC 27799:2008.

Policy Development

The ISMS policy and the organizational security policy support that security (or information assurance) is a necessary part of organizational existence and operations. These policies are high level and do not identify specific security controls. Therefore, the initial step in the do phase is to develop policies for each security control or classification of security controls that in turn find justification in Statement of Applicability.

The term security policy appears in the literature with several different meanings. There are differences regarding the content of the policy, the language in which it is expressed (e.g. formal notation, structured text, natural language, etc.) and the level of abstraction (Gritzalis D., 2003). Based on the contents and the purpose of a policy document, it can be categorized in one of five categories, "Policy", "Standard", "Baseline",

"Guideline", or "Procedure", as described in the following list (Harris, 2008):

- A Policy is an overall general statement produced by senior management (or a selected policy board or committee) that dictates what role security plays within the organization. It is usually point specific and covers a single area to specify requirements or rules that must be met. For example, an "Acceptable Use" policy would cover the rules and regulations for appropriate use of the computing facilities.

- A Standard is typically a collection of system-specific or procedural-specific requirements that must be met by everyone. Standards refer to mandatory activities, actions or rules that can give a policy its support and reinforcement in direction. For example, a standard may exist that describes how to harden a Windows workstation for placement on an external (DMZ) network. People must follow this standard exactly if they wish to install a Windows workstation on an external network segment. Standards could be internal, or be externally mandated (government laws and regulations).

- A Baseline can either refer to a point in time that can be used as a comparison for future changes or it can refer to the minimum level of protection required.

- A Guideline is typically a collection of system specific or procedural specific "suggestions" for best practice that can be used in cases where a specific standard does not apply. Whereas standards are specific mandatory rules, guidelines are general approaches that provide the necessary flexibility for unforeseen circumstances

- Procedures spell out how the policy, standards, and guidelines will actually be implemented in an operating environment. They are detailed step-by-step tasks that should be performed to achieve a certain

goal. The steps can apply to users, IT staff, operations staff, security members, and others who may need to carry out specific tasks. For example, if a policy states that all individuals who access confidential information must be properly authenticated, the supporting procedures will explain the steps for this to happen by defining the access criteria for authorization, how access control mechanisms are implemented and configured, and how access activities are audited. Procedures are considered the lowest level in the policy chain because they are closest to the computers and users (compared to policies) and provide detailed steps for configuration and installation issues, thus they should be detailed enough to be both understandable and useful to a diverse group of individuals.

Security policies, standards, guidelines, and procedures must be developed with a realistic view to be most effective. Highly structured organizations usually follow guidelines in a more uniform way. Less structured organizations may need more explanation and emphasis to promote compliance. The more detailed the rules are, the easier it is to know when one has been violated. However, overly detailed documentation and rules can prove to be more burdensome than helpful. On the other hand, many times, the more formal the rules, the easier they are to enforce. The business type, its culture, and its goals must be evaluated in order to make sure that the proper language is used when writing security documentation (Harris, 2008).

Implications in Developing Policies in a Health Care Context

As previously mentioned, the context in which health care organizations and health care information systems operate creates various implications and affects in different ways the requirements that a health ISMS should cover. When defining the security policies in such a system, there are a number of contextual elements which should be taken into consideration.

These contextual elements can be summarized in two strong points of interest that the policy development team should have in mind when developing policies (Gritzalis D., 2003). The first point is the importance of social and ethical values that affect the operation of the entire health care organization. These values pose ethical considerations and social priorities that should not be overlooked. Especially for policies that are related to confidentiality of medical data, special clauses should be included to create multiple layers of protection for the medical records. These clauses should be carefully selected not to affect the timely access of authorized personnel to medical records.

The second point of interest is the diversity and complexity of a healthcare organization. Different interests and concerns of stakeholders, extended distribution of decision power and special organizational structure form a labyrinth of conflicting interests that raise the difficulty of developing an applicable and robust policy. The policy development team should try to level the usability of policies and procedures with the decision power of each party related to each procedure and describe, in a formal and structured way, who can do what and why within the boundaries of the ISMS.

It is obvious that the policy development may prove to be a quite demanding task. Due to the complexity that the completion of this task requires, the policy development should not be expected to be completed immediately. Rather, the policies and procedures that constitute the integral parts of a health ISMS are constantly evolving by remaining in the focus of the PDCA cycle. During the first cycles, the changes will probably be radical and the corrections may be quite a lot, but as the time passes and the system reaches a level of maturity, the changes and improvements of the policies and procedure will be reduced until they reach their stable versions.

Methodologies and resources exist for the development of security policies. Generic guidelines and specific health care related guides exist and can be used as assisting documents in the development of the security policies of a health ISMS. Methods based on security cookbooks, risk analysis, management and socio technical methodologies are provided in the bibliography (Gritzalis D., 2003) and are constantly evolving to meet synchronous environments.

Selection of Security Controls

Once security requirements and risks have been identified and decisions for the treatment of risks have been made, appropriate controls should be selected and implemented to ensure risks are reduced to an acceptable level. In Annex A of ISO/IEC 27001: 2005 and in ISO/IEC 17799:2005 a set of suggested controls that can be used for risk mitigation is provided. Controls can either be selected by the above mentioned standards or from other controls sets or new controls can be designed to meet specific needs as appropriate (ISO/IEC 17799:2005).

However, in a health care organization where personal health information has to be protected and the environment is significantly different from any other organization, certain control clauses and control categories should be implemented. In ISO/IEC 27799:2008, minimum requirements and normative guidelines are set out to describe the proper application of certain security controls within the boundaries of health information. These control clauses and control categories constitute additions in controls set out in ISO/IEC 27002:2005 and have been categorized in the following eleven clauses:

- Security policy
- Organization of information security
- Asset management
- Human resources security
- Physical and environmental security

- Communications and operations management
- Access control
- Information systems acquisition, development and maintenance
- Information security incident management
- Business continuity management
- Compliance

The above clauses that are mentioned in ISO/IEC 27799:2008 consider the entire information system of the organization and all the aspects of such an information system, including policies, people, facilities, applications, hardware and devices. However, several requirements enforced by each clause can be adjusted to dictate specific requirements that a health related web application should cover in order to be part of a certified health ISMS. In the rest of this section, such an adjustment will be attempted, depicting certain requirements that must be covered by health related web applications. These requirements will be presented in a clause by clause basis, according to the structure of the ISO 27000 family of standards.

Security Policy

The objective of the security policy clause is "to provide management direction and support for the information security in accordance with business requirements and relevant laws and regulations. Management should set a clear policy direction in line with business objectives and demonstrate support for and commitment to information security through the issue and maintenance of an information security policy across the organization" (ISO/IEC 17799:2005).

The actual requirement that is posed by this clause is the existence of a documentation set that provides management directions, expresses management's understanding of information security and sets the objectives and goals of the ISMS. Such documents should have been developed during the planning phase and the policy development phases.

In order for the developed policies to maintain their effectiveness and applicability, it is necessary to establish and follow a formal review process. Through this process, the policies of the health ISMS will be adjusted to incorporate changes in the organization, the environment or changes in the requirements that should be met. During the determination of this review process, the context of a health care organization should be taken into account. Health care specific regulation, addition or alteration in health care units of the organization, virus out brakes and pandemics that may increase risk or apply the need for changes in security safeguards and comments from staff and patients, are only a fraction of the variables that may ultimately affect the security policies or procedures of the organization.

Without the existence of a formal documented security policy set, a web application should not be accepted for use by a health organization that targets to certification. The functional and non functional requirements of a custom web application or even a properly configured off the self application should be defined to ensure that the application complies with the security policy of the organization. Without using policies as points of reference, a decision whether the application is compliant with them cannot be taken and cannot be justified. Thus, it is important to initially ensure that formal policies do exist prior initiating any requirement analysis of a web application related to health information system and secondly, but equally important is to take into consideration every policy, procedure, guide and standard set by the security policies, when designing and implementing an application.

Organizing Information Security

When it comes to organization issues, the most important differentiation of a health care organization are the high level of third party participation in numerous activities and the sensitivity of the information that flows within the organization. Pharmaceutical companies, external practitioners and doctors must be able to cooperate without significant disruption, to provide health treatment to patients. Different level of information access should be provided to each stakeholder and special care should be taken to protect the patient data that should be owned by the patients themselves.

It is obvious that the development of a management structure is not an easy task to be completed in a health care organization, while the responsibilities and rights of each stakeholder should reflect legal, regulatory, operational and security requirements. These requirements and the way that they will be fulfilled should be a topic of discussion in every meeting of the Information Security Management Forum of the organization, where every party related to the security of the organization should be represented.

The existence and high level of involvement of external parties should be explicitly stated and identified during the risk assessment and the information that crosses the jurisdictional boundaries of the organization should also be protected. Formal agreements should be signed with all parties that have access to confidential information, regardless whether they are employees of the organization or external cooperating organizations. Such agreements should initially include definitions that state the confidential nature and value of personal health information, describe the security precautions and measures that each party should follow, define the level of access to each service and/or information and state the penalties exacted in the event of any failure to comply with the agreement clauses. Additionally, these agreements should contain the obligations of each party related to reporting to the ISMF, the expected service level related to the service that is provided and a description of the required representation of each party in health organization meetings and working groups.

The nature and capabilities of web applications can be considered to be suitable to environments with multiple stakeholders, who are geographically dispersed and are characterized by high level of mobility. However, the above mentioned considerations should also be reflected in the application when it resides within the boundaries of a health ISMS. The management structure and the roles that are defined should be depicted within the application, accompanied by a description of the responsibilities and rights of each role. The clauses of agreements that are signed between relying parties should also be mapped in certain areas of each application, either in the form of acceptable use screens or in the form of references to formal documents of the health ISMS that the application belongs to. These clauses should also contain the reporting and auditing requirements that are agreed between parties, in order for the application to be developed with appropriate auditing and reporting functionalities, which allow both parties to comply with the agreement terms and conditions.

Asset Management

Asset management in the context of a health care organization is considered to be a sensitive and critical issue. Assets that reside within a health ISMS are immediately related to personal health information. Regardless if they are in intangible or tangible form, an attack against the assets of a health care organization can lead to disclosure of personal health information, or to loss of integrity of such information. Such attack can lead to faults in patient treatment decisions, or to service disruptions, which is considered to be a serious problem in health environment, where delays can have severe impact in the health of a patient.

Medical databases, servers that are used to transmit and receive medical information and devices that are used to read digitalized medical records can all be considered as a single category of assets that can be met in a health care organization. These assets should be protected against loss of integrity, confidentiality or availability as they are used supportively in every day operations in a health organization, so it is important to be recognized and uniquely identified. Also, a designated custodian should have the responsibility for each one of these assets and rules for acceptable use should be identified, documented and implemented to maintain their currency and availability.

Labeling and handling guides should also be enforced in health related data. Health data continuously flow within the organization and is exchanged with third party organizations. These data may exist in more than one form, depending on their use. For example health information for a patient may exist in a digital record, in their health card or in a hard copy of a medical record that is used for treatment. To be able to preserve security of health data, labeling and handling procedures should be established primarily to uniquely identify such data and secondly to define acceptable use rules that should be followed by anyone that handles medical data.

The second category of assets that should be mentioned contains medical devices that record or report data. Such devices have different requirements in term of availability and integrity of data as they typically reside in restricted areas. The fact that they reside in protected areas provides an adequate level of protection against confidentiality breach, but as medical data are generated through these devices, accuracy and integrity should also be taken into serious consideration. Additionally, these devices often have special requirements in power and resources that are needed to operate, while they cannot be replicated to ensure their availability. Finally, medical devices may require special security considerations and special handling rules, due to their sensitivity or due to the environment in which they operate and to the electromagnetic emissions that occur during their operation.

Health related web applications within the boundaries of a health ISMS should take into serious consideration all the above special requirements that exist in a health organization. The most important remarks that should not be omitted while developing applications that utilize,

store or process health information can be summarized as follows:

- Acceptable use of the health information that is utilized within the application should be mentioned within the application.
- Special countermeasures for ensuring currency and integrity of all information should be taken during development. Integrity checks, continuous update of utilized information and utilization of multiple information sources (for cross checking reasons) can be considered to be only a reference of potential techniques that can be utilized for ensuring integrity and currency of health information.
- Information classification levels should be implemented and access and authorization rights should be based on these classification levels, in accordance with security policies and the sensitivity of each piece of information, as indicated by the classification process.
- Confidential information or security sensitive assets should be uniquely identified and labeling should be used for the recognition of different classification levels. Additionally labels should uniquely identify records of subjects of care that may need special handling. Such cases may be considered to be the following:
  - Subjects of care that are at elevated risk of non authorized access (e.g. employees of the organization, politicians, celebrities, newsmakers, etc.)
  - Subjects of care that are related to employees of the organization or personnel that may be called to treat them (e.g. neighbors, colleagues, relatives, etc.)
- Availability requirements should be seriously taken into consideration, as the need for current health related information is often critical and availability issues may

have severe impact for the health of the subject of care. The development of specific hardware and software standards, and their integration in the policy set of the organization, can assist in ensuring availability of a health related web application.

Human Resources Security

One characteristic that human resources department of a health organization has to deal with is the large number of temporary staff (contractors, volunteers, students, etc.). Such employees should have access to personal health information for a certain period of time and may move from one department to another or move between institutions or organizations. To enable control and management of the required access rights, the management of external or temporary human resources should be governed by rules and policies that will define the entire lifecycle of the employment.

Prior to employment, specific roles and responsibilities for temporary or short term staff should be defined and laid down in the organization's information security policy and in corresponding job descriptions. Additionally, in order to know how and where to contact health professional staff, screening procedures should be applied and followed to maintain currency on contact information, whilst relationships with academic institutions or professional bodies may assist this task. Finally, prior to employment all employees that process or have access to personal health information should formally agree on clauses that depict their responsibilities related to information security. The formal agreement can have the form of terms and conditions of employment, which should refer to the possible penalties that the employee may face when breach of information security is identified. Such terms should not be applicable for a limited timeframe but should survive the completion of the employment and have a permanent character.

During the employment, it is important that all employees remain informed for any change in the policies, procedures or handling rules related

to health information that are accessed. Management should ensure that all changes are properly published and that their enforcement is monitored. Additionally, the management should take special care for defining disciplinary processes that comply with the policies of the organization and are reflected in the agreements signed by the employees. Finally, special care should be taken by management to avoid disclosure of sensitive information that may take place when a subject of care and the staff of the organization have personal relationships (neighbors, friends, colleagues, relatives, etc.), in order to avoid been accused for confidentiality breach.

Finally, any termination of employment should also be performed with special care. The removal of access rights should be formally interpreted in documented procedures, which should be followed during termination of employment. Similar procedures should also be used to handle change of roles that employees have. These procedures should ensure that at each point of time, each employee has access to assets on a need-to-have basis and that access is forbidden to confidential information, unless it is necessary. Also, care should be taken for cases where transactions that are bound to a certain staff member take place well after the time of care (e.g. the sign off of medical transcriptions when the staff member's employment is terminated). Because of the high risk that the exposure of confidential information poses to the organization, health organizations should consider immediate termination of access rights following the supply of a resignation notice, notice of dismissal, etc.

All the above mentioned changes and alterations in access rights, prior, during and upon termination of employment should also be mapped to a health related web application. Role based authentication and authorization should be implemented to facilitate the support of temporary staff and the rotation of employees and various stakeholders of the organization. The roles and rights of each role should correspond to roles and responsibilities set out by the organization's policies, guides and procedures. Application should also include functionalities like immediate removal of rights of an employee, tracking of pending transactions that are bound to an individual employee prior termination and ability to assign transactions between employees, based on the procedures of the organization. Finally, the application should facilitate the recording and reporting of auditing information that should be in a form, which can be utilized to support disciplinary process, even in court. Technologies such as time stamping and digital signing can be used to ensure integrity and non repudiation of electronic transactions.

Physical and Environmental Security

When considering the physical and environmental security, the different characteristics of certain areas of a health care organization should be taken into consideration. Within such an organization the areas can be categorized based on the following factors/questions:

- Who has access to this area (e.g. subjects of care, doctors, staff, visitors, relatives of the subjects of care)?
- Is health information recorded or reported in this area?
- Is health information of multiple subjects of care collected, gathered or processed within this area?
- Are special precautions needed for access to this area?

The requirements set by answering the above mentioned questions may classify each area and indicate specific requirements for access control, device handling guides or information handling procedures. The remote areas that remain within the scope of the health organization (e.g. ambulances or external laboratories) should not be omitted during the definition of the scope of the ISMS and physical and environmental security

safeguards should also be considered for these cases.

As web applications may be accessed from different areas and remote locations, care should be taken to ensure confidentiality of information. Guides should be developed to assist users during the use of both the application itself and the equipment that is needed for accessing the application. Clauses that should be included in such guides may instruct the following:

- Applications that contain confidential information should not be accessed from computers available for public use (e.g. internet café).
- Confidential information should not be accessed through portable devices within public places, unless it is necessary for the treatment of subjects of care.
- Care should also be taken during disposal of devices upon which applications that have access to medical information are installed.
- Encryption can be utilized to protect local files that are stored in portable devices (e.g. temporary files or local database files that may be utilized within an application).
- Servers that are used to store, process and transmit confidential information should be appropriately protected in terms of availability, integrity and confidentiality, both in physical and electronic aspects.

Communications and Operations Management

The change management process is an integral part of every complex and medium to large scaled infrastructure. The purpose of change management is to ensure that no disruption is going to take place during planned or unplanned changes and that no unnecessary changes take place within the infrastructure. In the case of health care organizations, where disruption is often not acceptable, the change management process and relevant procedures should be carefully planned to include comprehensive testing to minimize related risks. However, it is important to restrict use of actual personal health information during any phase of testing.

Significant importance should be awarded to the close monitoring of the infrastructure and the supporting network of the health organization. Such monitoring is required to enable better planning of changes and potential risks that these changes might create. Segregation of duties should be enforced, where appropriate, to reduce risk of unauthorized modification or misuse of personal health information. Accordingly, the health information systems should be clearly separated from test, development or other operation environment for the same cause.

Different handling and separation should also apply to backup of health information. Encryption techniques should be enforced in databases that hold health information, while media in transit and backup copies of this information should all be encrypted and protected from any kind of breach to their integrity and confidentiality. Encryption should also be used in email, or any other electronic communication, when health information is included within the conversation.

In respect to monitoring, logging and auditing, health information systems that store and process personal health information special requirements arise. Audit logs are used to ensure accountability for subjects of care and also provide a strong incentive to users of such systems to conform to policies on the acceptable use of personal health information. Audit records should be created every time that a user accesses, creates, updates or archives personal health information via the system. In each one of these records, the following information should be included:

- Unique identifier of the user that made the change
- Unique identifier of the data subject (e.g. subject of care)

- Kind of function performed (record creation, access, update, etc.)
- Time and date of performance

Logs should be retained for a certain period and protected against tampering and integrity loss, while log analysis should be performed in a periodic manner to ensure that the identification of data access, which occurred during specified period of time, will be possible when required.

A health related web application should also reside within a clearly separated system and its development and testing should be performed in compliance with the change management and testing procedures of the organization. Such an application should support encryption functionalities for the data that are processed through it, while segregation of duties should be enforced to avoid developers and testers being able to gain access to confidential data for the period that the application is in the operating environment. Logging, monitoring and auditing facilities should be supported by a health related web application, in accordance to requirements stated above, and special care should be taken for ensuring confidentiality and integrity of electronic transmission of health data that take place through the web application.

Access Control

Access control is the ultimate and most common countermeasure that is utilized to protect confidentiality and integrity of information. The existence of an access control policy is mandated by ISO/IEC 27799:2008. This policy shall be used for the governance of access at least to health information data. The access control policy shall reflect professional, ethical, legal and subject of care related requirements and should take account of the tasks performed by health professionals and the tasks' workflow. This policy should contain at least the following information:

- Definition of who has access to health information, in order to be used as a point of reference during authorization provisioning decisions.

- Requirements for user registration, both in terms of information that will be required and registration process.
- Definition of authentication levels according to the levels of access that will become available to each user.
- Definition of password complexity requirements.
- Definition of user responsibilities, in respect to the rights and ethical responsibilities of health professionals, as agreed in law and as accepted by members of health professional bodies.
- Definition of specific and clear requirements and processes that will be needed to override the normal access control rules in emergency situation.

A health related web application should support the implementation of every aspect of the access control policy of a health organization, thus it is very important to be able to satisfy all above clauses of the access control policy.

The users of a health related web application should fulfill specific criteria in order to have access to any private part of the application. As mentioned in ISO/IEC 27799:2008, users of health information systems should only access personal health information when a healthcare relationship exists between the user and the data subject, or when the user is carrying out an activity on behalf of the data subject or when there is a need for specific data to support such an activity (ISO/IEC 27799:2008).

In order to decide if a user belongs to one of these categories and provide the suitable access rights, a formal registration process should be followed. During the registration process, specific information that will be used to identify the user as a person and their role in the system will be gathered. ISO/IEC 27799:2008 mentions that the following information should be collected, and reviewed in short periods, for each user that is registered in a system:

- The accurate capture of a user's identity (e.g. full name, date of birth, current residence address)
- The accurate capture, after verification of a user's enduring professional credentials and job title
- The assignment of an unambiguous user identifier

This information are the least needed that should be collected during the user registration process and should be periodically reviewed to ensure that they are complete, accurate and that access provided is still required.

Based on the registration process, the user will be provided with a certain level of access in sectors of the system that contain confidential information. The decision on what the user's privileges will be must be based on his role and purpose. The decision of what privileges will be awarded to each user should be a combination of the following decisive factors:

- The professional credentials and job title of the user that were established during registration. This strategy of privilege management is referred as "role based access control" and targets to restrict user's access privileges to just those required to fulfill one or more well defined roles.
- The user's participation in teams (e.g. clinical teams) or groups that perform operations which require access to certain health information. This method is mentioned as Workgroup based access control.
- The legitimate delegation of privileges related to access to a user (e.g. a specialist) by a user who has a legitimate relationship to a subject of care's personal health information (e.g. a family physician). This

method of privilege awarding is called discretionary access control.

A health care related web application should support all the above strategies/methods of privilege management and create mappings of users to roles and these roles to specific functions of the application. Additionally, users (e.g. health professionals, supporting staff, etc.) should be associated with subjects of care.

Finally, the health related web application should also support a number of different authentication methods and techniques that provide different level of assurance. The decision on which authentication method should be used will be based on the information that is accessed or protected. Single factor or two factor authentication should be mandated for the authentication for both users and subjects of care when it is necessary to access their own records, while special emphasis should be given to the nature of the authentication method, especially for handicapped subjects of care, and to provisions for access by substitute decision makers (ISO/IEC 27799:2008).

Information Systems Acquisition, Development and Maintenance

The assurance of operational continuity in an organization with the level of complexity similar to that of a health organization can be an extremely resource demanding task. Most organizations often follow reactive approaches or are conservative when deciding changes to old systems that are used in everyday operations or are utilized for the provision of critical services. This conservative approach results to old, out of date systems with low performance that are unable to meet constantly evolving requirements.

However, due to the criticality that characterizes most of the health care applications, the adoption of a demanding acquisition, development and maintenance procedure is necessary. The security requirements that each acquired information system should satisfy should be targeted to

protect integrity, confidentiality and availability. Message integrity should be ensured, input data should be validated for correctness prior being stored, and cryptography should be used to protect the confidentiality of created records.

Special care should be taken to ensure adequate identification of records that correspond to subjects of care and duplicate records should be detected and removed with great care from systems, databases and applications. Verification of the correctness of each record should be performed both during creating a new record for a subject of care and during the retrieval of the record. Great care should be exercised in the design of this operation of an application or system to ensure that health professionals can trust the system to provide the information needed to confirm that each record retrieved matches the individual under treatment.

Information Security Incident Management

Information security incidents include corruption or unintentional disclosure of personal health information or the loss of availability of health information systems, where such a loss adversely affects patient care or contributes to adverse clinical events (ISO/IEC 27799:2008).

Implications that are related to health care organizations should allow the forensic data collection, but in the same time protect the privacy of subjects of care and inter-jurisdictional requirements should be considered when applied. In any case, upon the occurrence of a security incident, the organization should inform the subject of care for the fact of the occurrence, the potential disclosure of personal health information and for the consequences that the incident may have to their care.

Business Continuity Management

Business continuity planning in healthcare is especially challenging for the information security professional, as any plan should also need to be suitably integrated with the organization's plans for handling power failures, implementing infection control and dealing with other clinical emergencies.

Business continuity should be taken into account when developing health related applications. Crisis situations should be the most common scenario when testing business continuity planning, while power failures or staff shortage should be key components in each of these scenarios.

Compliance

Audit programs should be developed in the organization to ensure compliance of each part of a health ISMS with requirements set by regulatory, legislative or certification bodies. Health organizations' audit programs should be formally structured to cover all requirements, all areas of risk and all implemented controls, within a 12 month or 18 month cycle.

The subject of any audit should not omit special data protection and consent that is required for access to personal information, and should examine all information processing facilities for compliance with security policies and standards and technical compliance.

Check-Act

After the establishment of the controls and policies of the health ISMS, the latter enters the final stage of each PDCA cycle. This final stage is constituted of the Check and Act phases.

In the Check phase, the ISMS enters a period of monitoring and continuous reviewing. The process of monitoring and reviewing intends to assess the effectiveness of the ISMS, both in achieving and maintaining the current level of security, and in improving the security level of the organization, in accordance with the information security strategy and the organization's goals.

Monitoring and reviewing of the ISMS is implemented mainly through planned or unplanned audits of different nature. Such audits can be differentiated based on characteristics of the audit team (e.g. small or large teams, coming either from within the organization or are invited by external organization or from other business units), or based on the purpose of the audit itself (e.g. internal review, or certification audit). The main categories of such ISMS reviews, as mentioned in ISO/IEC 27799:2008 are the following:

- Self assessment. This kind of review is performed mainly for internal reasons and is implemented by a small team residing within the boundaries of the organization. The purpose of such audit reviews is the indication of the effectiveness of the ISMS and the suggestion of corrective actions.
- Peer review. This review is similar to self assessment with the difference that different organizational loyalties of the peer reviewers give rise to an increase in objectivity and thus result in assurance.
- Independent audit. The result of independent audits is a report which brings a degree of benchmarking, produced by objective and experienced reviewers.
- Certification audit. A certification audit is a formal process that encompasses a scoping session, a document review and then the audit of the compliance itself and results in the certification of the organization for compliance with a specific standard (e.g. ISO 27001:2005 or ISO/IEC 27799:2008).

Through the review process that is performed in the Check phase, a series of improvements or corrections may be produced. These results are returned to the Information Security Management Forum for further consideration and the ISMF decides the corrective actions that will be taken in response to these results. These actions, which constitute the Act phase of the PDCA cycle, are governed by the corrective and preventive actions procedures that should constitute integral part of the ISMS.

FUTURE RESEARCH DIRECTIONS

The current chapter intends to provide an overview of all requirements related to design, develop and maintain a robust Information Security Management System in a health care organization, based on the requirements set by ISO 27000 family of standards and on special clarifications provided in ISO 27799:2008 for health care organizations. The future step in this chapter's research is to break up each of the tasks, which are mentioned as required, and define best practices and special requirements that a health organization may follow as a guide to perform each task. When this work is completed for all tasks, either of high or low level of complexity, a complete guide for ISMS development in health care organizations will be available for use.

CONCLUSION

Throughout this chapter, a comprehensive review of the implementation process of a health Information Security Management System was provided. As a guide to implementation, the international standards of the ISO 27000 family were used, and certification requirements that are set by them were explicitly stated and pointed out. Additionally, implications, which appear in health related organizations, were also stated, based on ISO/IEC 27799:2008, alongside with a more specific guidance on requirements that a health related web application should fulfill when residing within a health ISMS, which is certified for compliance with ISO/IEC 27001:2005 or ISO/IEC 27799:2008.

From this overview of the ISO 27000 family of standards and the analysis of requirements that relate to security it is obvious that the road to establishment of a solid, effective and secure health ISMS may seem an extremely demanding process, but it is also a fact that the proposed approach of continuous development through a PDCA cycle offers a structured and manageable method to radically reach the desired level of maturity, effectiveness and security.

REFERENCES

Alberts, C., & Dorofee, A. (2002). *Managing Information Security Risks - The OCTAVE Approach.* Carnegie Mellon Software Engineering Institute.

Anderson, R. (1996). An Update on the BMA Security Policy. Cambridge University Computer Lab. Retrieved 10/1/2010, from http://www.cl.cam.ac.uk/~rja14/bmaupdate/bmaupdate.html.

Arnason, S. T., & Willet, K. (2008). *How to Achieve 27001 Certification: An Example of Applied Compliance Management.* Boca Raton, FL: Auerbach Publications.

Calder, A. (2009). *Information Security based on ISO 27001/ISO 27002. A Management Guide.* Second edition. Zaltbommel, NL: Van Haren Publishing.

Chheda, N. (2008). Standardization and certification: The truth just sounds different. Retrieved 15/12/2009, from http://www.nainil.com/research/whitepapers/Standardization_and_Certification.pdf.

Department of Health and Human Services. (2000). *Uniform Data Standards for Patient Medical Record Information.* National Committee on Vital and Health Statistics Report to the Secretary of U.S.

Farn, K., Hwang, J., & Lin, S. (2007). *Study on Applying ISO/DIS 27799 to Healthcare Industry's ISMS.* In Proceedings of the 6th Conference on WSEAS international Conference on Applied Computer Science - Volume 6 (Hangzhou, China, April 15 - 17, 2007).

Gritzalis, D., & Kokolakis, S. (2003). Security policy development for Healthcare Information Systems. In B. Blobel, *Advanced health telematics and Telemedicine.* 105-110. Amsterdam: IOS Press.

Guijarro, L. (2009). ICT standardisation and public procurement in the United States and in the European Union: Influence on egovernment deployment. *Telecommunications Policy, 33*(5-6), 285–295. doi:10.1016/j.telpol.2009.02.001

Harris, S. (2008). *CISSP Certification All-in-One Exam Guide*, Fourth Edition. Osborne: McGraw-Hill.

ISO 27799:2008 (2008) *Health Informatics - Information security management in health using ISO/IEC 27002.* Retrieved: 15/12/2009 from http://www.iso.org/iso/iso_catalogue/catalogue_tc/catalogue_detail.htm?csnumber=41298.

ISO/IEC. ISO 27799:2008. (2008) *Health informatics — Information security management in health using ISO/IEC 27002.* Retrieved 10/01/2010, from http://www.iso.org/iso/catalogue_detail?csnumber=41298.

ISO/IEC 13335-1:2004 (2004) *Information technology — Security techniques — Management of information and communications technology security — Part 1: Concepts and models for information and communications technology security management.* Retrieved 15/12/2009 from http://www.iso.org/iso/iso_catalogue/catalogue_tc/catalogue_detail.htm?csnumber=39066.

ISO/IEC 17799:2005 (2005) *Information technology — Security techniques — Code of practice for information security management.* Retrieved 15/12/2009 from http://www.iso.org/iso/iso_catalogue/catalogue_tc/catalogue_detail.htm?csnumber=39612.

ISO/IEC 27000:2009 (2009) *Information technology — Security techniques — Information security management systems — Overview and vocabulary.* Retrieved: 15/12/2009 from http://www.iso.org/iso/iso_catalogue/catalogue_tc/catalogue_detail.htm?csnumber=41933.

ISO/IEC 27001:2005. (2005) *Information technology — Security techniques — Information Security Management Systems — Requirements,* Retrieved: 10/01/2010 from http://www.iso.org/iso/catalogue_detail.htm?csnumber=42103.

ISO/IEC 27002:2005. (2005.). *Information technology -- Security techniques — Code of practice for information security management.* Retrieved: 10/01/2010, from http://www.iso.org/iso/iso_catalogue/catalogue_tc/catalogue_detail.htm?csnumber=50297.

ISO/IEC 27003:2010. (2010) *Information technology — Security techniques — Information security management system implementation guidance.* Retrieved: 03/02/2010 from http://www.iso.org/iso/iso_catalogue/catalogue_tc/catalogue_detail.htm?csnumber=42105.

ISO/IEC 27004:2009. (2010) *Information technology — Security techniques — Information security management — Measurement.* Retrieved 15/12/2009 from http://www.iso.org/iso/iso_catalogue/catalogue_tc/catalogue_detail.htm?csnumber=42106.

ISO/IEC 27005:2008. (2008) *Information technology — Security techniques — Information security risk management.* Retrieved 15/12/2009 from http://www.iso.org/iso/iso_catalogue/catalogue_tc/catalogue_detail.htm?csnumber=42107.

ISO/IEC TR 13335-3:1998 (1998) *Information technology — Guidelines for the management of IT Security — Part 3: Techniques for the management of IT Security.* Retrieved: 15/12/2009 from http://www.iso.org/iso/catalogue_detail.htm?csnumber=21756.

Janczewski, L., & Shi, F. X. (2002). Development of Information Security Baselines for Healthcare Information Systems in New Zealand. [Elsevier.]. *Computers & Security, 21*, 172–192. doi:10.1016/S0167-4048(02)00212-2

JIPDEC. (2004, 11 08). *ISMS User's Guide for Medical Organizations*. Japan. Retrieved 10/01/2010 from http://www.isms.jipdec.jp/doc/JIP-ISMS114-10E.pdf.

Osama Salah, G. H. (2009). *Mandatory Information Security Management System Documents Required for ISO/IEC 27001 Certification*. Retrieved from http://www.iso27001security.com/ISO27k_mandatory_ISMS_documents.rtf.

SANS. (n.d.). *Information Security Policy Templates*. Retrieved 10/1/2010, from SANS.org: http://www.sans.org/security-resources/policies/#name.

Stoneburner, G., Goguen, A., & Feringa, A. (2002). *Risk Management Guide for Information Technology Systems*. Recommendations of the National Institute of Standards and Technology Retrieved 10/01/2010 from http://csrc.nist.gov/publications/nistpubs/800-30/sp800-30.pdf.

Sunyaev, A., Atherton, M., Mauro, C., Leimester, J., & Krcmar, H. (2009). Characteristics of IS Security Approaches with Respect to Healthcare. Proceedings of the Fifteenth Americas Conference on Information Systems. San Francisco, California.

Sunyaev, A., Gottlinger, S., Mauro, C., Leimester, J., & Krcmar, H. (2009). *Analysis of the Applications of the Electronic Health Card in Germany. WI 2009 - Proceedings of Wirtschaftsinformatik 2009 - Business Services:onzepte* (pp. 749–758). Vienna, Austria: Technologien und Anwendungen.

Tipton, H. F., & Krause, M. (2007). *Information Security Management Handbook* (6th ed.). Boca Raton, FL: Auerbach Publications. doi:10.1201/9781439833032

Tsohou, A. Kokolakis. S., Lambrinoudakis C., Gritzalis S. (2009). *Information Systems Security Management: A review and a classification of the ISO standards*. e-Democracy 2009 3rd Conference on Electronic Democracy – Next Generation Society: Technological and Legal Issues. Athens, Greece.

Vorster, A., & Labuschagne, L. (2005). A framework for comparing different information security risk analysis methodologies. Proceedings of the 2005 annual research conference of the South African institute of computer scientists and information technologists on IT research in developing countries (pp. 95 - 103). South African Institute for Computer Scientists and Information Technologists.

Zeki, Y. (2002). A qualitative risk analysis and management tool - CRAMM. Retrieved 10/1/2010, from SANS Institute InfoSec Reading Room: http://www.sans.org/reading_room/whitepapers/auditing/a_qualitative_risk_analysis_and_management_tool_cramm_83?show=83.php&cat=auditing.

KEY TERMS AND DEFINITIONS

Asset: Anything that has value to the organization.

Availability: The property of being accessible and usable upon demand by an authorized entity.

Confidentiality: The property that information is not made available or disclosed to unauthorized individuals, entities, or processes.

Health Professional: Person who is authorized by a recognized body to be qualified to perform certain health duties.

Healthcare Organization: Generic term used to describe many types of organizations that provide healthcare services.

Healthcare: Any type of service provided by professionals or paraprofessionals with an impact on health status.

Information Security Management System (ISMS): The part of the overall management system, based on a business risk approach, to establish, implement, operate, monitor, review, maintain and improve information security.

Information Security: Preservation of confidentiality, integrity and availability of information; in addition, other properties such as authenticity, accountability, non-repudiation and reliability can also be involved.

Integrity: The property of safeguarding the accuracy and completeness of assets.

Risk Analysis: Systematic use of information to identify sources and to estimate the risk.

Risk Management: Coordinated activities to direct and control an organization with regard to risk.

Statement of Applicability: Documented statement describing the control objectives and controls that are relevant and applicable to the organization's ISMS.

Subject of Care: One or more persons scheduled to receive, receiving, or having received a health service.

Chapter 7
Statistical Models for EHR Security in Web Healthcare Information Systems

Stelios Zimeras
University of the Aegean, Greece

Anastasia N. Kastania
Athens University of Economics & Business, Greece

ABSTRACT

Security is an important requirement for health information systems. Security is important for several reasons, most of which have a foundation in economics. Firstly, equipment is expensive to get, install, and integrate into the infrastructure of an organization. Secondly, the operations of an organization are based on the applied technology infrastructure, which means that disruption of operations quickly turns into unnecessary costs and, when applicable, potential loss of revenue. The adoption of digital patient records, increased regulation, supplier consolidation, and the increasing demand for information, highlights the need for better information security. Electronic health (e-Health) has become an important area of concern. A comprehensive EHR (Electronic Health Record) at the point of care could be created by collecting and sharing data among all sites at which patient receives care, as well as by incorporating information supplied by the patient. One of the greatest incentives to adopting EHRs will be reaching a critical mass of information sharing investors in health care information technology. In this work the authors examine the security properties of the EHR, with a special emphasis on software reliability. The authors focus on modelling and studying the reliability feature of the EHR. Special attention is given on exploiting the mathematical foundations of reliability modelling in a service-oriented architecture. Statistical measures called web metrics can be introduced to assess the performance of these systems.

INTRODUCTION

Security and privacy are important requirements for health information systems. During the last

DOI: 10.4018/978-1-61692-895-7.ch007

decade much attention has been given to the different aspects of information systems security. Security is important for several reasons: (1) equipment is expensive to buy, install, and integrate into the infrastructure of an organization; (2) the operations of an organization are dependent on applied technological infrastructure, which means that disruption of operations quickly turns into unnecessary costs and potential loss of revenue and (3) laws in most computer-dependent nations enforce protection of data and proprietary information stored on computer systems.

Every feature of health care and the medical profession is penetrated by computing and networking architectures. An issue of growing importance in the healthcare sector is information security and privacy. The EHR (Electronic Health Record), as defined by Cambridge Health Informatics Ltd (2001), is a summary lifelong record holding electronically details of potentially all of patient's interactions with the healthcare system (Singleton et al, 2001). A comprehensive EHR at the point of care could be created by collecting and sharing data among all points of care, where a patient is treated, as well as by integrating data supplied by the patient. Data must be built on common words (data and terminology), structures and organizations (in terms of interoperability) in order to be shared and used by possibly heterogeneous institutions. A growing body of research is focused on developing mechanisms to address privacy and security concerns related to Internet and mobile healthcare applications.

Using composition in designing and building software systems is one of the distinguishing features of the component-based and service-oriented approaches. Reliability is a particular expression of the broader concept of dependability. Other dependability aspects are, for example, availability and safety. The quality of the flow of service delivered by a system is referred to as reliability. In the literature two definitions of reliability exist: (i) the probability that the system performs its proper functions under specified conditions of time and (ii) the probability that the system successfully completes its operation when it is invoked (also known as "reliability on demand").

In this work we focus on studying and modelling the reliability of Web applications for healthcare, which implement Service Oriented Architectures and exchange EHR of patients. We give particular emphasis on the reliability of a service-oriented architecture based on the mathematical foundations, which characterize its essential elements, and model how the reliability of the whole application is affected by the system and the EHR growth. When Web healthcare IT chooses the Web Services paradigm, then software and system reliability demands for secure Web Services and proper use of EHRs. The main features that make Web Services attractive, such as accessibility to data, powerful software connections, platform independence and open run-time environments are the threats for sensitive patient information.

In the following section we provide background information related to EHR with respect to information sources that contribute to a patient's EHR and applications that process EHR data in a larger scale (i.e. for many patients) in order to draw useful knowledge. Then we proceed by presenting the needs for security and quality in healthcare and focus on a crucial aspect of healthcare systems' quality, namely the software reliability. For this reason, we present several statistical models that can be used for measuring software reliability and estimating the viability of the Healthcare application.

BACKGROUND ON ELECTRONIC HEALTH RECORDS

A carefully designed Health Information System which includes various fields related to patient care could be used as a tool for extracting statistical information concerning patients' health. The use of information systems for this purpose is a practice that is being studied recently. The Utrecht study (Grobee et. al., 2005) combined the traditional epidemiological studies with the strength of the Electronic Health Record that is being kept in Primary Health Care Facilities. Another study was carried out in 2004 (Majeed, 2004) which

Figure 1. Creation of an electronic health record (Mantas, 2002)

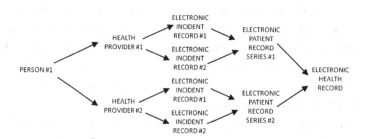

concludes that the data files stored in electronic form are potentially available for process and analysis. Thiru et. al. (2003) exploited information from Electronic Health Records, processed it using statistical methods and identified several cases of coronary disease. Mansson et. al. (2004) studied the applicability of data extraction from an Electronic Health Record and concluded that collecting data is possible in various formats. In 1994, Fuke et. al. (2004) used an Electronic Health Record to identify diabetic patients with or without coronary disease. Utilizing a reformed Information System for Primary Health Care Units to improve organization of patients' health data is expected to assist Primary Health Care workers in their everyday practice. In addition, such a reformed Information System could be based not only on health data fields, but also on secondary information that may be correlated with specific health conditions. Data extraction from an Information System is an invaluable process for research in general and for conducting epidemiological studies in particular. Developing a unique Electronic Health Record for registering patients injured by accidents aims to be used as a tool for the surveillance of various parameters on the specified population, as well as for extracting epidemiological information from the database of the EHR.

An important area of focus and activity in multiple domains is Electronic health (e-Health). The EHR is expected to replace paper medical records as the primary source of information for health care, and still comply with all clinical, legal and administrative requirements. Development of a fully functional interoperable EHR system remains a major challenge. Recent research has proposed prototype service-oriented architecture (SOA) models for EHR in various contexts including clinical decision support, collaborative medical (mammogram) image analysis, and health clinic setting.

The Healthcare Information and Management Systems Society (HIMSS) define the EHR in any care delivery setting as a "longitudinal electronic record of patient health information. The EHR includes information about patient demographics, problems, progress notes, vital signs, medications, laboratory data, immunizations, radiology reports and past medical history. The clinician's workflow is automated by the EHR. A complete record of a clinical patient encounter is produced by the EHR. Its interface supports other care-related activities - quality control, evidence-based decision support and outcomes reporting" (Figure 1). A comprehensive EHR at the point of care could be created by collecting and sharing data among all sites at which a patient receives care, as well as by incorporating data supplied by the patient. To share and use data from heterogeneous institutions, data must be created and stored by means of common words (data and terminology), structures, and organizations (interoperability) (Daskalaki et. al., 2001; Mantas, 2002; Shortliffe, 1999).

One of the greatest motivations for the adoption of EHRs is the creation of an information

Figure 2. Sources of health-related data (Mantas, 2002)

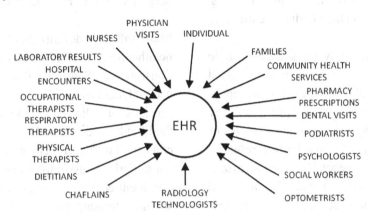

repository, which can be used for large scale population studies and in the same time will be a valuable resource for various investors of health care industry. The electronic record must contain eight key attributes (Daskalaki et. al., 2001): (1) Provision of reliable, real-time, and secure access to medical advice when and where it is needed. (2) Capture and management of episodic and longitudinal electronic health record information. (3) Function as clinicians' basic information resource when providing patient care. (4) Assistance in evidence based care services. (5) Support for continuous quality improvement, utilization review, risk management and performance management. (6) Capture information necessary for reimbursement. (7) Support of public health reporting, public health initiatives and clinical research through provision of longitudinal data. (8) Support of clinical trials support.

The key benefits from the use of EHR are: (1) Improvement in patient care by allowing clinical decisions to be made by means of using up-to-date documents. (2) Reduction in errors. (3) Removal of lost patient charts. (4) Strengthening both inside and external communication. A wide range of possibly heterogeneous health information sources is responsible for the complexity of the EHR since data are generated each time an individual visits a healthcare provider. Figure 2 identifies some of the data sources for an EHR as listed by the Institute of Medicine.

SECURITY IN HEALTHCARE

Every feature of health care and medical profession is influenced by computing and networking techniques. An issue of growing importance in the healthcare sector is information security and privacy. The need for better data security is pointed out by increased regulation, provider consolidation and the adoption of digital patient records. We critically assess the research literature on information security and privacy in healthcare, published in both information and non-information systems disciplines including health informatics, public health, law, medicine and popular trade publications and reports. Security is essential in healthcare for lessening the business costs of dealing with electronic attacks both for those in public health and for those related to electronic-commerce (business sector). Security is also of primary importance from a patient's perspective due to the importance of having reliable data available in order to reach accurate and effective medical decisions, while at the same time protecting patient's privacy.

Security of healthcare information is also tied with community protection and personal safety.

Securing medical information against hackers, crackers, pranksters and busybodies is extremely important.

A lot of stakeholders may access the electronic medical records. These records can also be used (possibly anonymized) for various official purposes such as prediction and cost analysis. They may also be accessed by law enforcement agencies or social work departments. A multitude of research projects utilize medical records in an anonymized or in a semi-anonymized form. The intra and extra organizational uses of the electronic patient records demonstrate the need for implementing legal protection measures. Simultaneously, the existence of a variety of functions, which can be performed by using electronic medical records, including research, diagnosis, preventive and curative treatments and administration, calls for stricter security measures, in order to defend for example against social engineering attacks.

Availability, confidentiality and security are the concepts involved in the traditional model of information security. (1) The concept of Availability requires that information has to be available for those who are entitled to handle it or access it, when they need it. There are various threats related to availability which arise from intentional or accidental infrastructure damage (might be network, software or hardware-related) or denial of service attacks. (2) The concept of Integrity requires information to be defended against deliberate or unexpected mutation and corruption. Threats include viruses, non-replicating malware (for example, Trojan horses), errors in structural integrity, illegal or inadvertent modification, fraudulent misuse or logical corruption. (3) The concept of Confidentiality requires that information should not be available for those who are not entitled to access or process it. Disclosure and unauthorized access by hackers are threats related to violation of the right to privacy. Solutions include access control, passwords and encryption.

QUALITY OF HEALTHCARE

Many different definitions of quality exist in the healthcare sector from which the following definition from the US Institute of Medicine is commonly used: "Quality is the extent to which health care services for individuals and populations increase the likelihood of wanted health outcomes and are consistent with current professional knowledge". An underlying assumption is made through this statement concerning the relativity of quality as an understanding. Furthermore, according to this reasoning quality assessment is connected with the processes and outcomes of patient care as these are produced given the current convention and medical scientific knowledge. There is also a need to conduct systematic research on groups of patients to assess the quality of health care services in medical practice. According to Fowles et. al. (2008) quality can relate to the structure, process and outcome of health care delivery with the most popular aspects looked at being effectiveness and patient experiences. Broadly, the term quality in health care can also include other aspects such as continuity of care, access, acceptability, appropriateness and timeliness (Figure 3).

Performance improvements are motivated by reporting systems and quality assessment. Another approach is the adoption of standardized quality-related performance indicators used to calculate provider reimbursement. In primary care the linkage of conditions that need improvement with quality measures has been proven successful (Wang et. al., 2003; Ash and Bates, 2005; Fowles et. al., 2008; Donabedian, 1988; McCarthy et al., 1999). McGlynn et. al. (2003) defines an evaluation model measuring or describing something, usually with an intention to answer a question or to make a decision. It implies a series of criteria to be measured and judgments to be made, going beyond data collection and study alone.

Web applications include product, usage and development characteristics and are subjected to constant growth. Requirements engineering

Figure 3. Aspects of quality

methods need adjustment when dealing with Web applications development. The present work focuses on utilizing different aspects having as an aim to contribute in the design and development of Web applications Certification Frameworks and various Web quality seals (Wyatt, 2001).

Websites can be classified (Kastania and Zimeras, 2009) by using three classes: (a) The Web typology or digital business models: In this category the website is analyzed using specific types of web models and is characterized as one of them (electronic business models) (Davidson, 2002): (b) The "stages of development models": In this category the models distinguish different development stages according to the functionality of the website. As a consequence the website is categorized according to its functionality (Timmers, 2000); (c) The use of a Scoring system: Specific characteristics of the Web site are scored. According to the total score the Web site can be compared to other Web sites. Eliot uses binary scoring (Cockburn and Wilson, 1996) giving one mark for each one of five functionality levels assigned in six categories (information and business operations, information and marketing of products/services, transactions, customer services, ease of use and innovation). Elliot (2002) developed a scoring system for evaluating seventy-six characteristics of a web site coded in Likert Scale (from

1 to 9) organized in sections (web site design, web site functionality, web site value for the customer) with different weighting scores per section and subsection and with different characteristics per sector.

Quality dimensions are: the operational characteristics, reliability and resistibility, conformity to requirements, duration of life and modifiability, service before and after product delivery, aesthetics and appearance, and finally perception (transcendental, objective, and subjective). Ten quality principles related to cultural web sites are: transparency, effectiveness, maintenance, accessibility, user centeredness, responsiveness, multilingualism, interoperability, management, and perseverance (Minerva, 2004). SERVQUAL (Parasuraman et. Al., 1988) approach consists of five dimensions (tangibles, reliability, responsiveness, assurance and empathy) which are the most beneficial for service quality as ranked by customers across all industries.

Web application security has certain characteristics that make it necessary to employ security techniques. Issues about security are: confidentiality, authorization, authentication, accountability, integrity. Web application security (Kotsis, 2006) needs to be assured: (a) on the client side (desktop security, protection of personal information) (b) during request/responses (network security, secure message exchange, non-repudiation) and (c) at the service provider level (host-security, service availability). Use of encryption, digital signatures and certificates are a necessity as well as secure client-server interaction.

SOFTWARE RELIABILITY

Software reliability has many directions by means of mathematical and statistical techniques. Reliability specifically refers to the progression of the service delivered by a system. Reliability is defined in the literature as the probability that the system performs its proper functions under specified conditions of time (Lyu, 1996) and as the probability that the system successfully completes its mission when it is invoked (Goseva-Popstojanova et al., 2001). Also it could be defined as the probability that the software will not cause a failure of the system for a specific period of time under specified conditions.

The technique is to apply statistical models on the previous failure data to predict future behaviour of a system. Major statistical distributions are used in software reliability modelling such as exponential, gamma, Weibull, binomial, Poisson, normal, log normal, Bayes, and Markov distributions. By applying these distributions to data collected from systems failures fitting processes could be introduced based on maximum likelihood or least squares estimates. Also statistical methods like Chi-squared or goodness-of-fit are required to be introduced, in order to check the effectiveness of the selected model.

Three main definitions have to be introduced, in order to make the notion of software reliability understandable: fault, error, and failure. An incorrect statement introduced somewhere in the software (Goseva-Popstojanova, 2001) is a fault. An unexpected state in which a system may enter on delivering a fault (for example, an internal variable assumes an unexpected value) is an error. When an error circulates up to the system output (for example, an output variable assumes an unexpected value) (Cortellessa and Grassi, 2007) a failure occurs.

In this paragraph, the most popular and related proposed reliability distributions are introduced. Specifically, they describe the software failure rate models, which are used to explore the program failure rate per failure at the failure intervals. Software reliability models rely on two types of data, either the number of failures per time period or the time between failures. The failure rate could be defined as the total number of failures within a subject population divided by the number of life units spend by that population, during a precise measurement period under specified conditions and failures. The event or inoperable state, is a state in which any item or part of any item does not or would not function as previously mentioned (Wallace and Coleman, 2001).

Exponential distributions are used almost exclusively, that is, the probability distribution function pdf of X: $f(x) = \lambda e^{-\lambda t}$. This distribution can be chosen as a failure distribution if and only if assuming a constant hazard rate can be justified, that is, hazard rate $= \lambda$ (Mann, 1974). Having defined the pdf $f(x)$, we can calculate the probability that the system fails in a given time interval [t1, t2], where this probability is the area under the curve between the endpoints of the interval. Evaluation of the integral is given by:

$$\Pr\left(\text{failure between } t_1 \text{ and } t_2\right) = \int_{t_1}^{t_2} f(t)dt$$

(see Figure 4).

The system survives until it fails the first time, so we could define the reliability (survival) function $R(t)$ as $R(t)=1-F(t)=P(T>t)$ (Figure 5).

Alternative models using an exponential distribution include the Jelinski-Moranda, Musa Basic, Non-homogeneous Poisson process (NHPP), De-eutrophication, Schneidewind, hyper-exponential models and Goel-Okumoto. For

Figure 4. pdf $f(x) = \lambda e^{-\lambda t}$

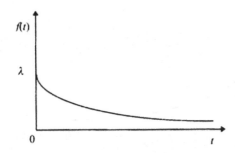

these, subsequent failure rates are not influenced by failures in the past (memory is not essential) (Wallace and Coleman, 2001). A common form of the gamma distribution (exponential, log normal or normal), depending on the value of β, is the Weibull model. Variations include the Rayleigh model and the S-shaped reliability growth model. The logarithmic model is used by Musa assuming that the contribution of errors is different for the calculation of the error rate. The binomial distribution is used by Shooman and Bayesian statistics are used by Littlewood-Verrall (Wallace and Coleman, 2001; Lyu, 1996; Wallace and Coleman, 2001).

Software Reliability Failure Rate Models

1. Jelinski-Moranda model

$$f(t_i) = \phi[N - (i-1)] \exp\{-\phi(N - (i-1))t_i\}$$

$$R(t_i) = 1 - F(t_i) = \exp\{-\phi(N - i + 1)t_i\}$$

$$\lambda(t_i) = \phi\{N - (i-1)\}$$

2. Schick-Wolverton model

$$f(t_i) = \phi[N - (i-1)]t_i \exp\left\{-\frac{1}{2}[\phi(N - (i-1))t_i^2]\right\}$$

$$R(t_i) = 1 - F(t_i) = \exp\left\{-\frac{1}{2}[\phi(N - i + 1)t_i^2]\right\}$$

$$\lambda(t_i) = \phi\{N - (i-1)\}t_i^2$$

3. J-M geometric model

$$f(t_i) = Dk^{i-1} \exp\left(-Dk^{i-1}t_i\right)$$

$$R(t_i) = 1 - F(t_i) = \exp\{-Dk^{i-1}t_i\}$$

$$\lambda(t_i) = \exp\{-Dk^{i-1}\}$$

4. Weibull model

$$f(t_i) = \left[\frac{\beta(t - \gamma)^{\beta-1}}{\theta^\beta}\right] \exp\left\{-\left[\frac{t - \gamma}{\theta^\beta}\right]\right\}$$

$$R(t_i) = 1 - F(t_i) = \exp\left\{-\left[\frac{t - \gamma}{\theta^\beta}\right]\right\}$$

$$\lambda(t_i) = \frac{\beta(t - \gamma)^{\beta-1}}{\theta^\beta}$$

where: φ is a constant, the contribution any one fault makes to the overall program; N is the number of initial faults in the program; t_i is the time between the $(i-1)^{th}$ and the ith failures; D is the initial program failure rate; k is the parameter of geometric function (0<k<1); p is the probability of removing a failure when it occurs. Certain assumptions should be considered for the models as (1) Reliability predictions must consider in a similar nature that the software is handled. (2) Every fault has the same chance within a severity rating as any other fault in that class. (3) The failures when faults are detected are independent. The models require data for their implementations (Wallace and Coleman, 2001; Lyu, 1996; Wallace and Coleman, 2001).

Figure 5. Distribution function and reliability function for exponential pdf

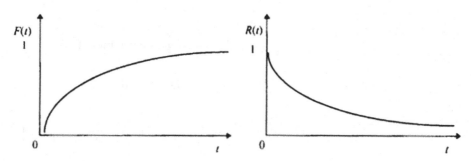

Software reliability growth models have been grouped into two classes of models: concave and S-shaped. The main characteristic of these models is the asymptotic behaviour. There are many different representations of software reliability models. Let M(t) be the (random) number of failures experienced by time t where $E[M(t)]=\mu(t)$. An example equation for $\mu(t)$ is the Goel-Okumoto (G-O) model: $\mu(t) = a(1-e^{-bt})$, where a is the expected total number of failure in the system and b is the rate at which the failure rate decreases [33].

The GO-model is one of the most popular non-homogeneous Poisson process (NHPP) model which a strong influence on the software reliability modeling perspective. The usual assumptions of the GO-model are: (1) A Poisson distribution is followed by the number of faults in time t. (2) All faults are having the same chance of being detected and are independent. (3) Immediate removal of all detected faults is performed.

For most models, $\mu(t) = aF(t)$, where *a* is the expected total number of failures in the system and F(t) is a cumulative distribution function. Also F(0) = 0, so no failures are discovered before the test starts, and $F(\infty) = 1$, so $\mu(\infty) = a$ and *a* is the total number of failures discovered after an infinite amount of testing (Wood, 1996). Software reliability growth model examples are given in Table 1.

Fitting f(x) functions to the data means estimating its parameters from the data. For estimating the parameters two main approaches could be

proposed: (1) the direct (maximum likelihood technique) and (2) the indirect (least square technique). In the direct approach the data are imported directly into the proposed equations, where alternatively in the indirect approach the data would introduce a describing function and estimations of the parameters would be achieved by fitting of the best curve.

Considering the Goel-Okumoto (G-O) model: $\mu(t) = a(1-e^{-bt})$, applying the maximum likelihood technique, estimating b could be found by solving the equation (Wood, 1996):

$$\sum_{i=1}^{k} \frac{n_i \left[t_i \left(e^{-bt_i} \right) - t_{i-1} \left(e^{-bt_{i-1}} \right) \right]}{\left(e^{-bt_{i-1}} - e^{-bt_i} \right)} = \frac{t_k e^{-bt_k} \sum_{i=1}^{k} n_i}{\left(1 - e^{-bt_k} \right)}$$

where k is the current number of failures, and t_i is the cumulative test time at the end of the ith failure. The parameter a can be estimated by solving the equation

$$a = \frac{\sum_{i=1}^{k} n_i}{\left(1 - e^{-bt_k} \right)}$$

where b could be obtained by the above equation. Considering the least-squared method the b parameter could be obtained by minimizing the equation (Wood, 1996):

Table 1. Software Reliability Growth Model Examples (Wood, 1996)

Model Name	Model Type	$\mu(t)$	Comments
Goel-Oku moto (G-O)	Concave	$a(1-e^{-bt})$ $a>=0,\ b>0$	Also called Musa model or exponential model
G-O S-Shaped	S-Shaped	$a(1-(1+bt)e^{-bt})$ $a>=0,\ b>0$	Modification of G-O model to make it S-shaped (Gamma function instead of exponential)
Hossain-Dahiya/G-O	Concave	$a(1-e^{-bt})/(1+ce^{-bt})$ $a>=0,\ b>0,\ c>0$	Solves a technical condition with the G-O model. Becomes same as G-O as c approaches).
Gompertz	S-Shaped	$a(b^d)$ and $d=c^t$ $a>=0,\ 0<=b<=1,\ 0<c<1$	Used by Fujitsu, Namazu Works
Pareto	Concave	$a(1-(1+t/\beta)^{1-\alpha}$ $a>=0,\ b>0,\ 0<=\alpha<=1$	Assumes failures have different failure rates and failures with highest rates removed first
Weibull	Concave	$a(1-e^{-d})$ and $d=bt^c$ $a>=0,\ b>0,\ c>0$	Same as G-O for c=1
Yamada Exponential	Concave	$a(1-e^{-rad})$ and $d=1-e^{-\beta t}$ $a>=0,\ r\alpha>0,\ \beta>0$	Attempts to account for testing effort
Yamada Raleigh	S-Shaped	$a(1-e^{-rad})$, $d=1-e^{-f}$, $f=\beta t^2/2$ $a>=0,\ r\alpha>0,\ \beta>0$	Attempts to account for testing effort
Log Poisson	Infinite Failure	$(1/c)\ln(c\alpha t+1)$ $c>0,\ \alpha>0$	Failure rate decreases but does not approach 0

$$\sum_{i=1}^{w}\left(\ln\left(\left(\frac{f_i - f_{i-1}}{t_i - t_{i-1}}\right)\right) - \ln\left(b\right) - \ln\left(a - f_i\right)\right)^2$$

where k is the current number of failures of testing, t_i is the cumulative test time at the end of the ith failure and f_i is the cumulative number of failures (Wood, 1996). Usually, the above two equations have to be solved numerically.

FUTURE RESEARCH DIRECTIONS

The need for a means to objectively determine software quality arises from the desire to apply the techniques of contemporary engineering fields to the development of software. A large number of software reliability growth models have been proposed to analyse the reliability of a software application based on the failure times by proposing appropriate failure rate models. As a result, the estimates of the residual number of faults, failure rate, reliability obtained from these models tend to explain the real situations.

Modelling involves estimation techniques, which may be applied upon choosing the appropriate model. Considering estimation techniques proposed research directions could be the application of deterministic (maximum likelihood, bootstrapping) and stochastic (MCMC) approaches, as well as the comparison between them by means of advanced statistical techniques (like Analysis of Variance).

CONCLUSION

Computing and networking techniques and technologies are gradually penetrating every feature of health care and medical practice. Information security and privacy in healthcare is an issue of growing importance. The adoption of digital patient records, increased regulation, supplier consolidation, and the increasing demand for information between patients, providers and payers, all point towards the need for better data security.

A crucial sphere of concern and action is electronic health (e-Health). A growing body of research is focused on developing mechanisms to address privacy and security concerns related to Internet and mobile technology based healthcare applications.

According to Mantas (2002), quality can apply to the structure, process and outcome of care delivery and the most popular aspects looked at are patient experiences and effectiveness. The term quality, when applied to healthcare, includes aspects such as access, appropriateness, acceptability, timeliness and continuity of care. Kastania and Zimeras (2009) defined a model of assessment as describing or measuring something, usually with a goal such as making a recommendation or answering a question. It implies a series of criteria to be measured and judgments to be made, going beyond data collection and analysis alone. Web applications include product, use and development characteristics and are subjected to constant growth. Quality, Performance, Security and Testing are some of the most fundamental characteristics of web sites security evaluations. Herein, we have focused on modelling and analysis of the reliability feature of the software, with a particular emphasis on the mathematical formulation of reliability modelling of a service-oriented architecture. It could be defined as the probability that the software will not cause the failure of the system under specified conditions for a specified time. Wide extent of models could be introduced (based on exponential distribution), where in this work we have examined the properties of the Goel-Okumoto (G-O) model, which is one of the most popular model from the inhomogeneous Poisson models.

REFERENCES

American National Standards Institute/American Institute of Aeronautics and Astronautics. ANSI/AIAA (1993). *Recommended Practice for Software Reliability*, R-013-1992. Washington, DC.

Ash, J. S., & Bates, D. W. (2005). Factors and forces impacting EHR system adoption: report of a 2004 ACMI discussion. *Journal of the American Medical Informatics Association, 12*, 8–12. doi:10.1197/jamia.M1684

Baresi, L., Ghezzi, C., & Guinea, S. (2004). Smart monitors for composed services, *Proc. of 2nd International Conference on Service Oriented Computing (ICSOC'04)*. New York, NY, USA.

Cockburn, C., & Wilson, T. D. (1996). Business Use of the World Wide Web. *Information Journal of International Management, 26*(2), 83–102. doi:10.1016/0268-4012(95)00071-2

Cortellessa, V., & Grassi, V. (2007). Reliability Modelling and Analysis of Service-Oriented Architectures.In Luciano Baresi &· Elisabetta Di Nitto (Eds.) *Test and Analysis of Web Services*, 339- 362, Berlin:Springer-Verlag.

Daskalaki, A., Lazakidou, A., Philipp, C., Jacob, C., & Berlien, H. P. (2001). Introducing electronic health record into laser medicine. *Medical Informatics, 5*, 85–86.

Davidson, R. (2002). Development of an Industry Specific Web Site Evaluation Framework for the Australian Wine Industry. *School of Commerce Research Paper Series*, 02-9.

Donabedian, A. (1988). The quality of care. How can it be assessed? *JAMA, 260, 12* 1743-1748

Elliot, S. (2002). *Electronic Commerce B2C Strategies and Model*. Chichester: John Wiley & Sons.

Fowles, J. B., Weiner, J. P., & Chan, K. S. (2008). *Performance Measures Using Electronic Health records: Five Case Studies (Vol. 92)*. The Commonwealth Fund.

Fuke, D., Hunt, J., Siemenczuk, J., Estoup, M., Carroll, M., Payne, N., & Touchette, D. (2004). Cholesterol management of patients with diabetes in a primary care practice- based research network. *The American Journal of Managed Care, 10*(2), 130–136.

Goseva-Popstojanova, K., Mathur, A. P., & Trivedi, K. S. (2001). Architecture-based approach to reliability assessment of software systems. *Performance Evaluation, 45*, 179–204. doi:10.1016/S0166-5316(01)00034-7

Grobee, D., Hoes, A., Verheij, T., Schrijvers, A., van Ameijden, E., & Numans, M. (2005). The Utrecht Health Project: Optimization of routine healthcare data for research. *European Journal of Epidemiology, 20*, 285–287. doi:10.1007/s10654-004-5689-2

Kastania, A., & Zimeras, S. (2009). (in press). Evaluation of Web based applications, *Special Issue "Web-based Applications in Health Care and Biomedicine" of the Annals of Information Systems Series*. New York. *Springer Publications.*

Kotsis, G. (2006). Performance of Web applications. In Kappel, G., Proll, B., Reich, S., & Retschitzegger, W. (Eds.), *Web Engineering.* Chichester: John Wiley & Sons.

Lyu, M. R. (1996) (Editor), *Handbook of Software Reliability Engineering*, New York: IEEE Computer Society Press.

Lyu, M. R. (1996). *Handbook of Software Reliability Engineering. IEEE Computer Society Press and McGraw Hill*. Editor.

Majeed, A. (2004). Sources, uses, strengths and limitations of data collected in primary care in England. *Health Statistics Quarterly, 21*, 5–14.

Mann, N. R., Schafer, Ray, E., & Singpurwalla, Nozer, D. (1974). *Methods for Statistical Analysis of Reliability and Life Data*, John Wiley & Sons.

Mansson, J., Nilsson, G., Bjorkelund, C., & Strender, L. E. (2004). Collection and retrieval of structured clinical data from electronic patient records in general practice. A first-phase study to create a health care database for research and quality assessment. *Scandinavian Journal of Primary Health Care, 22*(1), 6–10. doi:10.1080/02813430310003660

Mantas, J. (2002). Electronic health record. In Mantas, J., & Hasman, A. (Eds.), *Textbook in health informatics: A nursing perspective* (pp. 250–257). Amsterdam: IOS Press.

McCarthy, D. B., Shatin, D., Drinkard, C. R., Kleinman, J. H., & Gardener, J. S. (1999). Medical records and privacy: empirical effects of legislation. *Health Services Research, 34*, 417–425.

McGlynn, Elizabeth A., Asch, Steven, M., Adams, John, Keesey, Joan, Hicks, Jennifer, DeCristofaro, and Alison, Kerr, Eve, A. (2003). The Quality of Health Care Delivered to Adults in the United States. *The New England Journal of Medicine, 348*, 2635–2645. doi:10.1056/NEJMsa022615

Minerva e-Europe European Cultural Website Quality Principles (2004). Retrieved 10/1/10 from: http://www.minervaeurope.org/userneeds/qualityprinciples.htm.

Parasuraman, A., Zeithaml, V. A., & Berry, L. L. (1988). SERVQUAL: a multiple item scale for measuring consumer perceptions of service quality. *Journal of Retailing, 64*(1), 12–40.

Shortliffe, E. (1999). The evolution of electronic medical records. *Academic Medicine, 74*(4), 414–419. doi:10.1097/00001888-199904000-00038

Singleton, P., Hunnable, J., & Mason, R. (2001). Gaining Patient Consent to Disclosure. A Consultancy Project for the NHS Executive. London: Department of Health. Retrieved on 10/1/2010 from: http://www.dh.gov.uk/prod_consum_dh/groups/dh_digitalassets/@dh/@en/documents/digitalasset/dh_4131403.pdf

The Healthcare Information and Management Systems Society. http://www.himss.org

Thiru, K., Donnan, P., & Sullivan, F. (2003). A validated logistic regression model to identify coronary heart disease patients within primary care databases in the United Kingdom. *AMIA... Annual Symposium Proceedings / AMIA Symposium. AMIA Symposium*, 1030.

Timmers, P. (2000). *Electronic Commerce: Strategies and Models for Business-to- Business Trading*. Son, U.K.: John Wiley.

Wallace, D., & Coleman, C. (2001). Application and Improvement of Software Reliability Models, In Proceedings of NASA Office of Safety and Mission Assurance Software Assurance Symposium Symposium (OSMA SAS '01), Morgantown, West Virginia, USA.

Wang, S., Middleton, B., Prosser, L., Bardon, C., Spurr, C., & Carchidi, P. (2003). Academic publication proves that EMRs are cost effective: A cost-benefit analysis of electronic medical records in primary care. *The American Journal of Medicine, 114*(5), 397–403. doi:10.1016/S0002-9343(03)00057-3

Wood, A. (1996). *Software Reliability Growth Models*, Technical Report 96.1.

Wyatt, D. Jeremy, (2001). *Development of an Evaluation Methodology for NSW Health Clinical Information Access Program* (CIAP). Sydney: New South Wales Health department. Retrieved 10/1/10 from http://www.health. nsw.gov.au/health-publicaffairs/ publications/ ciap/01_773CIAP.pdf.

KEY TERMS AND DEFINITIONS

Failure Rate: The frequency with which an engineered system or component fails.

Health Care Informatics Systems: Systems that combine information science, computer science and health care. They are dealing with the resources, devices, and methods that are required in order to optimize the acquisition, storage, retrieval, and use of information in health and biomedicine. Health informatics tools include not only computers but also clinical guidelines, formal medical terminologies, and information and communication systems.

Healthcare Quality: Quality is the extent to which health care services for individuals and populations increase the likelihood of wanted health outcomes and are consistent with current professional knowledge.

Software Reliability: The probability of failure-free operation of a computer program in a specified environment for a specified time.

Section 4
Trust in Healthcare Networks (and Communities)

Chapter 8
Identity Management and Audit Trail Support for Privacy Protection in E–Health Networks

Liam Peyton
University of Ottawa, Canada

Jun Hu
University of Ottawa, Canada

ABSTRACT

E-health networks can enable integrated healthcare services and data interoperability in the form of electronic health records accessible via Internet technology. Efficiency and quality of care can be improved for example by: streamlining administrative processes involving prescriptions and insurance payments; providing remote access to specialists through telemedicine; or correlating data from clinics, pharmacies and emergency rooms to detect potential adverse events. However, a major requirement to enable adoption of e-health networks is the ability to address issues around security, privacy and trust in a systematic manner. In particular, privacy legislation, regulatory guidelines, and organizational policies require that a framework for privacy protection must be established. Federated identity management can be used to systematically protect patient and health care provider identities in a single sign on framework that controls access to patient data, but an audit trail and reporting mechanism is needed in order to ensure and validate compliance. In this chapter, the authors use example e-health scenarios to analyze the legal, business and technical issues that need to be addressed.

INTRODUCTION

E-health networks can enable integrated healthcare services and data interoperability in the form of electronic health records accessible via Internet technology. Efficiency and quality of care can be improved for example by: streamlining admin-istrative processes involving prescriptions and insurance payments; providing remote access to specialists through telemedicine; or correlating data from clinics, pharmacies and emergency rooms to detect potential adverse events. However, a major requirement to enable adoption of e-health networks is the ability to address issues around security, privacy and trust in a systematic manner. In particular, privacy legislation, regulatory

DOI: 10.4018/978-1-61692-895-7.ch008

guidelines, and organizational policies require that a framework for privacy protection must be established.

The Liberty Alliance project is a consortium of technology vendors and consumer-facing enterprises which is developing an open standard and set of specifications for federated identity management (Tourzan and Koga, 2006). A "Circle of Trust" (CoT) (Shin et al, 2004) is a key concept in which federated identity management is used to create a business to business (B2B) network of cooperating enterprises that provide integrated services to users. These cooperating enterprises have trust relationships and operational agreements established amongst them. Health care networks involve separate cooperating enterprises (physician, hospital, pharmacy, lab, insurance, etc.). Federated identity management is a mechanism that could be leveraged to systematically protect patient and health care provider identities in a single sign on framework that controls access to patient data.

An example scenario of how a CoT could streamline and improve health care services based on an ePrescription service and the processing of insurance payments is described and analyzed in (Peyton et al, 2007). Another scenario based on a CoT shows how data could be integrated from pharmacies, clinics and emergency rooms to support data mining for the detection of adverse events (Hu et al, 2008). Another significant scenario for e-health networks and federated identity management is a telemedicine consultation in which a remote expert is given permission in order to assist in the care of a patient (Peyton and Hu, 2007; Peyton, Hu and Zhan, 2007). This scenario is significant, since it emphasizes the dynamic nature of health care and the balance that must be struck between protecting sensitive health information and ensuring information is immediately available to health care providers as needed in order to provide the highest possible quality of care.

We will use a telemedicine scenario in which physicians consult and provide health services through an online collaborative medical consultation system to highlight the business, legal and technical issues that must be addressed in order to manage privacy compliance in an e-health network. In particular, we review and evaluate the architecture of a Circle of Trust (CoT) focusing on three components defined by the Liberty Alliance framework (Discovery Service, Identity Mapping Service, Interaction Service) as well as a fourth component (Audit Service) that has been proposed as an extension to address potential privacy breaches in Liberty Alliance (Alsaleh and Adams, 2006).

BACKGROUND

A number of researchers have investigated collaborative on-line medical consultation. CoMed (Sung et al., 2000) is a desktop conferencing application, which allows interactive real-time cooperation among several medical experts. A Web-based medical collaboration environment in the context of the regional healthcare network of Crete is described in (Tsiknakis et al, 2002) that provides integrated services for virtual workspaces, annotations, e-mail, and on-line collaboration. The development of a provincial telemedicine center in China is described in (Xiaomin et al, 2002). A web-based system to provide tele-consultation for severe acute respiratory syndrome (SARS) patients in Shanghai Infection Hospital and Xinhua Hospital is described in (Zhang et al, 2005). A summary of legal issues related to telemedicine is given in (White, 2002).

Europe has comprehensive privacy legislation known as the European Union Directive on Privacy and Electronic Communication (European Union, 2002) and Canada has a similar legislation known as the Personal Information Protection and Electronic Documents Act (PIPEDA, 2000). In Ontario, Canada, there is specific legislation for health information in the form of the Personal Health Information Privacy Act (PHIPA, 2004) within the context of PIPEDA. PHIPA specifies the legal responsibilities of health information custodians in terms of how they are to handle personal health information and specifically allows the sharing of information within the "circle of care" for a patient. The United States is not as stringent as Europe, but does have similar legislation in the area of health care (HIPAA, 1996). In general, Asia and particularly China has a slightly different emphasis in their approach to privacy. A good overview of Chinese law as it relates to privacy is given in (Maisog, 2009). China has not clearly defined privacy as a fundamental right, but the legal protection of privacy rights has gradually increased (Lu, 2005). In the Chinese Constitution, Article 38 states that the personal dignity of citizens of the People's Republic of China is inviolable. The General Principles of Criminal Law states that if others intentionally violate citizen's right to privacy and cause serious consequences, there should be criminal penalties.

A discussion of Circle of Trust (CoT) and federated identity management is provided in (Shin et al, 2004). In a CoT, an individual's identity and personal information is maintained and protected by an Identity Provider, which enables cooperating enterprises within the CoT to use the individual's personal information in a systematic manner when the individual's permission is obtained. This paper focuses on the Liberty Alliance federated identity management framework support for a CoT, whose architecture is described in (Tourzan and Koga, 2006), and whose approach to security and privacy is described in (Landau, 2003). The data services template (Kellomäki and Kainulainen, 2006) is critical to our analysis of the audit service. The interaction service specification (Aarts and Madsen, 2006) is also relevant for securing the consent of the individual. The details of the discovery service (Hodges and Cahill, 2006) and identity mapping service (Hodges et al, 2006) are also relevant to

the manner in which the audit service supports pseudonymous identity.

In (Gates and Slonim, 2004) the importance of audits for ensuring trust is emphasized with respect to identity management and the concept of user "owned" data. Potential privacy breaches within the Liberty Alliance framework in support of a CoT were identified in (Alsaleh and Adams, 2006), and an audit trail service was proposed as an extension to the Liberty Alliance framework. To address privacy requirements for identity management, it is important to distinguish between anonymous and pseudonymous identity (Koch and Möslein, 2005). In the case of pseudonymous identity, one can link events across sessions to an identity, without actually knowing the identity or any identity data. This is the key to the Liberty Alliance framework and the proposed audit trail service.

Languages such as (XACML, 2009) and (P3P, 2002) can be used to define privacy policies within a Circle of Trust. In addition, flexible, access control is needed to support collaborations. Role-based (Sandhu et al, 1996) access control is well known, while team-based (Thomas, 1997) and context aware access control (Covington et al, 2001) models are particularly suitable for collaboration. In (Yip at al, 2006), an extensible information security specification format is used to enforce business rules and information security policies based on audit trails. The design of a system for auditing HIPAA compliance by monitoring the data flow and the work flow of medical imaging system is presented in (Chen et al, 2005). Methods for logging events to an audit trail are well known with tools like AspectJ and Log4J. These tools make it possible to incorporate systematic logging with low overhead, even without modifying the existing code base of a system (Davies et al, 2003). Log files have been used in system management (Wei et al, 2005) and system security enhancement (Kowalski, 2006). Collecting log files into a data warehouse enables monitoring of data access and troubleshooting of abnormal patterns of access (Andrews and Zhang, 2000).

TELEMEDICINE SCENARIO IN A CIRCLE OF TRUST ARCHITECTURE

In this section we lay out the essential components of a Circle of Trust (COT) architecture in support of a telemedicine scenario based on the Liberty Alliance framework. The scenario describes a collaborative online medical consultation service which allows specialists from a Cardiology Research Center to view patient records remotely at the request of their physician. The CoT architecture includes federated identity management to protect patient identity and personal health information, integrated access control mechanisms to facilitate delegation of responsibility when physicians are consulting, and a distributed audit service to support validation of personal information usage.

Scenario

A doctor, D1, at a Local Clinic, conducts an examination and orders laboratory tests from the Regional Hospital for a patient, P1. The doctor would like to consult a cardiology specialist, S1, working at a Cardiology Research Center. The clinical record with associated lab tests and images (e.g. radiographs or skin photographs) will need to be shared and the recommendations and observations from the consulted specialist should be added to the patient's record. There are tools and technologies (such as chat, whiteboard, conferencing, file sharing) that can readily be used to share such information over the Internet, but the information is of a sensitive nature and access needs to be carefully controlled. The general principles that should be adhered to are:

1. The doctor should only be accessing information of patients they are treating.

Figure 1. Circle of trust for medical consultation scenario

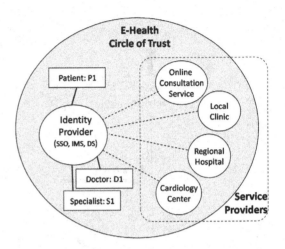

2. The doctor should be able to share information remotely with registered specialists as needed.
3. Patient identity should be protected and only necessary information should be shared and only at the time it is needed.

The technical challenge that we address here is how to register users from many different organizations, control access to information in a manner that adheres to the three principals and provide an audit mechanism so that regulatory agencies can ensure that the principles are being adhered to.

Single Sign On

Figure 1 shows how the relevant medical organizations affiliated together into a Circle of Trust (CoT) based on business agreements and Liberty Alliance architecture. The Online Consultation Service is a service provider for physicians who want to consult with specialists. The Regional Hospital provides patient records and lab test results. The Cardiology Center provides specialized equipment and experts and stores aggregated data concerning treatments and trends. The Identity Provider provides a single sign on (SSO) service

Figure 2. Team-based access to patient medical record in a circle of trust

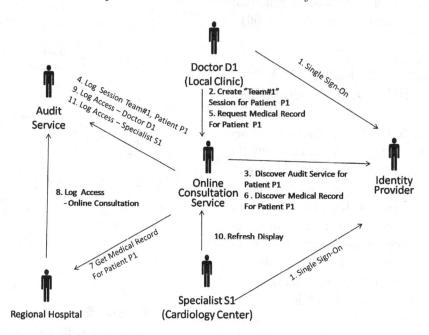

for the CoT so that users need to authenticate or "log in" only once. The identity of the patient is masked through a system of pseudonyms that the Identity Provider provides by means of an identity mapping service (IMS). Access control policies at the different organizations define what information can be shared under what circumstances. The Identity Provider also provides a discovery service (DS) that helps users discover and connect to services in a secure manner.

Access Control for Dynamic Data Sharing

Figure 2 shows the steps that the doctor and a cardiology specialist follow in order to share a patient's medical data via the Online Consultation Web Site as well as the interaction with a distributed audit service to log data access events.

The steps are as follows:

1. The Doctor and Specialist are redirected to the Identity Provider to perform a single sign on to the CoT the first time they attempt to access any service in the CoT.

2. The doctor initiates a collaborative session via the Online Consultation Service, and defines the "circle of care" Team#1 who can view the consultation (includes Specialist).

3. The Online Consultation Service knows of the Patient, Doctor and Specialist only through pseudonyms and can only perform actions on their behalf using security credentials provided by the Identity Provider. Using the Discovery Service of the Identity Provider, patient permission for consultation is provided along with an End Point Reference (EPR) for the Audit Service.

4. Using the EPR, an audit event is logged for the online consultation session for Patient P1, and the members of Team#1 that are allowed to participate.

5. The doctor requests the Medical Record for patient P1.

6. The Online Consultation Service obtains an EPR for the Regional Hospital service in order to obtain the Medical Record for P1.

7. The Online Consultation Service obtains the Medical Record for Patient P1, and is now responsible for controlling and logging access to the Medical Record.

8. The Regional Hospital logs an audit event to record the Medical Record access by the Online Consultation Service (on behalf of Doctor D1 and Team#1).

9. The Online Consultation service logs an audit event when the Medical Record for Patient P1 is displayed to Doctor D1

10. The Specialist refreshes their display in order to see the latest information shared by Doctor D1.

11. The Online Consultation service logs an audit event when the Medical Record for Patient P1 is displayed to Specialist S1.

Access control for the above scenario is defined by using a combination of role and team based access control. Access to the Medical Record is defined by an Access Control List (ACL), which defines what Roles are allowed to access the file and what actions they can take. In this case, a Doctor, who is the Primary Physician for a Patient, can read and modify the medical record and both can also create a "Team" group to temporarily share access to the Medical Record for the duration of a consultation session. The role of Consulting Specialist can read and add to the medical record, but not modify the record, nor create a "Team" Group. When the physician creates a group "Team#1", his role is "Primary Physician" and the cardiology specialist is added to the group in the role of "Consulting Specialist". When the Online Consultation Service requests access to the Medical Record for Patient P1 on behalf of the Primary Physician, the Regional Hospital checks that Doctor D1 is the Primary Physician for the patient before allowing Access. From that point on, the Online Consultation Service is

responsible for controlling and logging access. Note that Team#1 only exists for the duration of the collaboration session, so the Specialist will not have access after the session provided by the Online Consultation Service ends.

Audit Service

By providing a log of all access to patient data, the Audit Service provides a useful tool for protecting privacy by providing a mechanism for transparency so that regulatory agencies and patients can monitor who is accessing what patient data and for what purpose. It is important to note that no patient data is stored by the Audit Service. A reference to the type of information access is recorded but not the actual information. Similarly, the End Point Reference provides a pseudonym for the patient that is meaningful only to the Audit Service. No real identify information is available. The Audit Service is essential to ensure trust and confidence in the system by providing a mechanism for regulatory agencies and patients to validate how data is being shared and with whom. Sophisticated monitoring and analysis of data sharing and access control can be provided if the audit logs from all services are collected and consolidated into a Audit Data Mart as shown in Figure 3.

The Audit Data Mart stores all Access events in a multi-dimensional star schema that allows access to be analyzed and reported along different dimensions in detail for each access as well as in aggregate along different dimensions such as Time (minute, hour, day, month, year), Health Worker (role, service, hospital, region, province), Access Type (Primary Physician, Consulting Specialist, Attending Nurse), and Medical Record (type, location). Note that patient identity is masked, and that no health information is stored in the data mart. Only the data that identifies the access event and the type of information accessed is stored. Having a multi-dimensional storage is a flexible format for defining reports and analyses on the data that make it easy for regulatory agencies to

Figure 3. Collecting access events into an audit data mart

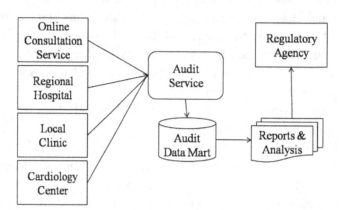

Figure 4. Star schema of audit data mart

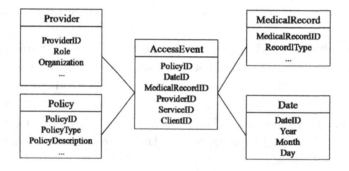

monitor and mine the type of access that is taking place.

Figure 4 is the star schema showing the dimension model for our scenario. The AccessEvent fact table records the detailed information from the logs. It has a multipart primary key which consists of the PolicyID of the policy under which access was allowed, DateID of the date the access occurred, MedicalRecordID of the patient's record that was accessed, ProviderID of the person that accessed the record, ServiceID of the e-health service that provided the record and ClientID of the e-health service which requested the record. Each of these IDs links to a dimension with attributes along which aggregation can occur. The Provider dimension can aggregate providers according to role (Primary Physician, Consulting Specialist, Attending Nurse, E-Health Service,

etc.) and organization (Local Clinic, Regional Hospital, Cardiology Center, etc). The Medical-Record can aggregate records according to type (lab test result, prescription, etc.). The Policy dimension also aggregates records according to type (TeamConsult, Clinical, Research, etc.). Finally, the Date dimension can aggregate records according to day, month, and year.

In our scenario, there would be three rows in the Access Fact table. One to log that the Regional Hospital provided Patient P1's medical record to the Online Consultation Service on behalf of Doctor D1 under the TeamConsult policy. One to log that the Online Consultation Service provided the record to the Local Clinic on behalf of Doctor D1 under the Clinical policy. Lastly, another to indicate that the Online Consultation Service provided the record to the Cardiology Center on behalf of Specialist S1 under the Clinical policy.

By maintaining a log of access control events, one can analyze and report on the data in many different ways. One would be able to present a view of all accesses related to a particular MedicalRecordID, or analyze the access of a particular doctor or specialist, or analyze what data sharing is occurring between what e-health services and which organizations.

PRIVACY PROTECTION

The scenario we have described needs to be analyzed carefully to ensure that privacy is protected. More formally, using the terms defined by the Liberty Alliance, we need to examine what is taking place whenever a web service in the network behaves as an Attribute Provider in response to requests from a Web Service Client. In our scenario, the Regional Hospital is an Attribute Provider that will provide the Medical Record for Patient P1. The Online Consultation Service is a Web Service Client when it initially requests the Medical Record for Patient P1. The Online Consultation Service also acts as an Attribute Provider when responding to requests from Doctor D1 or Specialist S1. As outlined in (Landau, 2003), a number of privacy breaches are possible:

1. The Regional Hospital could fail to obtain Patient P1's consent before giving access to P1's data to the Online Consultation Service (on behalf of Doctor D1 and Team#1). The Regional Hospital has to ensure that there is patient consent to share their Medical Record. Typically, Patient P1 would sign a form authorizing Doctor D1 as their primary physician, giving them permission to access their Medical Record. In this scenario, that consent should include the right for Doctor D1 to expand the "circle of care" identified

as Team#1 as needed and be able to share the Medical Record with Team#1 electronically.

2. An Attribute Provider might release a Patient P1's attributes to an unauthorized Web Service Client. Care must be taken by the Regional Hospital to ensure that the Online Consultation Service is certified. Simultaneously, Doctors and Specialists must be educated to ensure that they cannot be fooled into using an unauthorized service.

3. An Attribute Provider might fail to properly enforce access-control and privacy policies. It is the responsibility of the Online Consultation Service to ensure that the primary physician, Doctor D1, can only add registered, qualified specialists in Team#1 who are relevant to the current care of Patient P1.

4. A registered user of the Online Consultation Service could obtain Patient P1's data for purposes not allowed by the relevant privacy legislation. For example, Doctor D1 is authorized to view Patient P1's Medical Record for the purpose of providing care or treatment. If the doctor accesses Patient P1's Medical Record for any other purpose (example: personal curiosity), the patient's privacy is breached.

An Audit Service can be used to provide transparent verifiable evidence to a regulatory agency to certify compliance or investigate possible privacy breaches. However, even in the absence of any privacy violations (malicious or otherwise), privacy legislation gives a patient the right to see and question how his / her data is being used. The Audit Service does not prevent privacy breaches but it can act as a deterrent as well as allow patients and regulatory agencies to monitor how data is being shared (Peyton et al, 2007). Figure 5 provides more detail on the Audit Service and the role of an Interaction Service for obtaining consent. The utilized steps are the following:

Figure 5. Interacting with the Identity Provider, Interaction Service and Audit Service

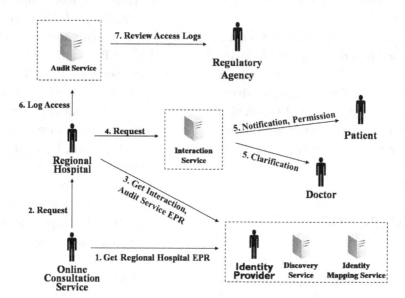

1. The Online Consultation Service gets an End Point Reference (EPR) for the Regional Hospital from the Discovery Service provided by the Identity Provider. The EPR is created from the encrypted opaque identifier maintained by the Identity Mapping Service for the Regional Hospital which only the Online Consultation Service can use. The Identity Mapping Service, in effect, has a different pseudonym for Patient P1, for each Web Service Client that might want to interact with the Regional Hospital. Since there is a different pseudonym for each client, there is no way for clients to share and collate information amongst them about Patient P1. They each have a different pseudonym for Patient P1. Only the Identity Mapping Service knows the real identity of P1.

2. The Regional Hospital receives a request for Patient P1's Medical record and must decide whether or not the request is allowed. This is a policy decision point, and the result of that decision will be logged to the Audit Service.

3. The Regional Hospital interacts with the Discovery Service in the usual manner to obtain an EPR for the Interaction Service if needed and an EPR for the Audit Service.

4. If permission from Patient P1 is required and has not yet been given, the Regional Hospital can make a request to the Interaction Service.

5. The Interaction Service can notify Patient P1 that there is a request from the Online Consultation Service on behalf of Doctor D1 to access their Medical Record and share it with Team#1. It can interact with him / her to obtain permission, including passing on a request for clarification from Patient P1 to Doctor D1. Note that both the Regional Hospital and the Online Consultation Service does not know the identity of the Patient or how to contact him / her. The Interaction Service is a special trusted service which is authorized to interact with Patient P1.

6. The Regional Hospital logs an access audit event with the Audit Service indicating that the Online Consultation Service accessed Patient P1's Medical Record on behalf of Doctor D1 and Team#1.

7.   Later, a Regulatory Agency can review the logged access events as part of a routine audit, or perhaps at the request of the patient.

Organizational control of the various services is an important consideration. It is reasonable to assume that the Discovery Service and Identity Mapping Service could be provided by a single trusted organization, the Identity Provider, since their operations are closely linked. In an e-health network, one could imagine a separate government regulated agency would be responsible for managing and safeguarding identity.

In principle, the Interaction Service could be provided by the Identity Provider. However, it is important that the Identity Provider is not involved in the services being provided during the interaction. The Identity Provider is being trusted with safeguarding the identity of the patients and their identity information. Because of that sensitive role, it is better for the Identity Provider not to be aware of any personal health information. It is when identity information is combined with personal health information that privacy can be compromised. As a result, it is preferable if a separate organization provides the Interaction Service. It is even possible that different organizations will provide different interaction services for different purposes.

The Audit Service must be provided by a different organization than the Identity Provider. The Audit Service can log requests from all Attribute Providers in the Circle of Trust. As well, the EPR used allows the Audit Service to recognize and correlate all data sharing requests related to a specific patient across all Attribute Providers without knowing the identity. This provides a comprehensive, consolidated audit trail of the patient's data and how it is being shared. This is important for privacy compliance. The single audit trail makes it straight forward for a patient to see who is using his / her data for what purpose as is required by privacy legislation. It also enables a Regulatory Agency to document compliance or

investigate alleged privacy breaches by validating the data sharing that occurs against the established policies and permissions of a given patient and the stated privacy practices of an Attribute Provider. However, if that information was ever combined with the identity information maintained by the Identity Provider it would be a complete breach of privacy. This is why the Audit Service must record the patient's audit trail in a privacy preserving manner (Peyton et al, 2007).

The Audit Service could be maintained by a privacy oversight organization, but it might also make sense for it to be maintained or at least be accessible by an organization responsible for monitoring public health services and the quality of care provided. Privacy is just one aspect of quality of care.

FUTURE RESEARCH DIRECTIONS

When extended with an Audit Service, the Liberty Alliance framework provides adequate infrastructure for privacy protection in e-health networks, but there are still organizational issues which must be addressed. Trusted organizations, with appropriate regulatory oversight, must be found or created within the healthcare system to host the Identity Provider, Interaction Service and Audit Service.

In addition, every organization that hosts an Attribute Provider service must be convinced or required to log its events to the Audit Service. Again this is more a regulatory issue than a technical one as technology to incorporate systematic logging with low overhead is well understood (Davies et al, 2003)..

It is worth emphasizing that the Audit Service does not guarantee privacy protection but rather ensures transparency and accountability by providing a historical record of data access events. This can be used to provide patients with an account of how their data is being used and the ability to challenge it, as required by privacy legislation. It also provides the means for a Regulatory Agency to validate compliance or investigate alleged breaches of privacy.

With respect to privacy compliance for the Audit Service itself, access control restrictions to the Audit Service must be carefully considered and the patient's identity should not be easily deducible by a party having direct access to the audit trail records, remembering of course, that no attribute values are stored, just the names of the attributes. More research is needed, but at a minimum, access control mechanisms should ensure that under no circumstances is it possible to modify or delete records once they have been logged to the Audit Service. Attribute Providers should only be able to add or log events. They should have no ability to read events that are logged to the Audit Service (not even their own). Patients should have the right to view all events logged relating to the access and use of their data (and only their data). With appropriate authorization and responsibility, designated officials within the Regulatory agency should be able to query all records.

CONCLUSIONS

E-health networks can enable integrated healthcare services and data interoperability in the form of electronic health records accessible via Internet technology. However, in order to address issues of privacy and trust, mechanisms are required to systematically control access to medical information shared over the Internet. We have illustrated in a simple scenario mechanisms that can be used to:

- address how to register users from many different organizations and mask patient identity, in a federated identity management framework based on standards from the Liberty Alliance project;
- support authorized dynamic sharing of information by integrating team and role-based access control;

- provide sophisticated monitoring and analysis of access using an Audit Service to build an Audit Data Mart.

REFERENCES

P3. (2002). *The Platform for Privacy Preferences 1.0 Specification*. World Wide Web Consortium Recommendation. Accessed 2009/12 http://www.w3.org/TR/P3P/.

Aarts, R., & Madsen, P. (Eds.). (2006). *Liberty ID-WSF Interaction Service Specification*, Ver. 2.0. Liberty Alliance Project. New Jersey. Accessed 2009/12 http://www.projectliberty.org/resource_center/specifications/liberty_alliance_id_wsf_2_0_specifications.

Alsaleh, M., & Adams, C. (2006). *Enhancing Consumer Privacy in the Liberty Alliance Identity Federation and Web Services Frameworks*. Proceedings of the 6th Workshop on Privacy Enhancing Technologies (PET 2006). Cambridge, United Kingdom.

Andrews, J. H., & Zhang, Y. (2000). *Broad-spectrum studies of log file analysis*, Proceedings of the 2000 International Conference on Software Engineering. Limerick, Ireland.

Chen, X., Zhang, J., Wu, D., & Han, R. (2005). *HIPPA's compliant Auditing System for Medical Imaging System*. Proceedings of the 2005 IEEE Engineering in Medicine and Biology 27th Annual Conference. Shanghai, China.

Covington, M., Long, W., Srinivasan, S., Dey, A., Ahamad, M., & Abowd, G. D. (2001). *Securing context-aware applications using environment roles*, ACM Symposium on Access Control Model and Technology. pp. 10-12, Chantilly, VA.

Davies, J., Huismans, N., Slaney, R., Whiting, S., Webster, M., & Berry, R. (2003). *An Aspect Oriented Performance Analysis Environment*. International Conference on Aspect Oriented Software Development. Accessed 2009/12 http://aosd.net/archive/2003/program/davies.pdf.

European Union. (2002). *Directive on Privacy and Electronic Communications*. European Parliament, Brussels. Accessed 2009/12 http://ec.europa.eu/justice_home/fsj/privacy/law/index_en.htm.

Gates, C., & Slonim, J. (2004). *Owner Controlled Information. New Security Paradigms Workshop*. Ascona, Switzerland: ACM Press.

HIPAA. (1996), *Health Insurance Portability and Accountability Act*. United States Congress. Accessed 2009/12 http://aspe.hhs.gov/admnsimp/pl104191.htm.

Hodges, J., Aarts, R., Madsen, P., & Cantor, S. (Eds.). (2006). *Liberty ID-WSF Authentication, Single Sign-On, and Identity Mapping Services Specification Ver2.0*. Liberty Alliance Project. New Jersey. Accessed 2009/12.http://www.projectliberty.org/resource_center/specifications/liberty_alliance_id_wsf_2_0_specifications.

Hodges, J., & Cahill, C. (Eds.). (2006). *Liberty ID-WSF Discovery Service Specification. Ver2.0*. Liberty Alliance Project. New Jersey. Accessed 2009/12 http://www.projectliberty.org/resource_center/specifications/liberty_alliance_id_wsf_2_0_specifications.

Hu, J., Peyton, L., Turner, C., & Bishay, H. (2008). *A Model of Trusted Data Collection for Knowledge Discovery in B2B Networks*. Proceedings of the 3rd Intern'l MCETECH Conference on e-Technologies. pp. 60-69. Montreal, Canada Retrieved from http://doi.ieeecomputersociety.org/10.1109/MCETECH.2008.22.

Kellomäki, S., & Kainulainen, J. (Eds.). (2006). *Liberty ID-WSF Data Services Template ver.2.1*. Liberty Alliance Project. New Jersey. Accessed 2009/12 http://www.projectliberty.org/resource_center/specifications/liberty_alliance_id_wsf_2_0_specifications.

Koch, M., & Möslein, K. M. (2005). Identity Management for Ecommerce and Collaborative Applications. *International Journal of Electronic Commerce, 9*(3), 11–29.

Kowalski, K. (2006). *Analysis of Log Files Intersections for Security Enhancement*. The Third Intern'l Conference on Information Technology: New Generations. pp. 452-457.Las Vegas, Nevada.

Landau, S. (Ed.). (2003). *Liberty ID-WSF Security and Privacy Overview, version 1.0*. Liberty Alliance Project. Accessed 2009/12 http://www.projectliberty.org/resource_center/specifications/liberty_alliance_id_wsf_2_0_specifications.

Lu, Y. (2005). Privacy and data privacy issues in contemporary China. *Ethics and Information Technology, 7*, 7–15. doi:10.1007/s10676-005-0456-y

Maisog, M. (2009). *Personal Information Protection in China*. (originally published on DataGuidance Website), Hunton & Williams LLP, New York. Accessed 2009/12 www.huntonfiles.com/files/webupload/PrivacyLaw_Personal_Information_Protection_in_China.pdf.

Peyton, L., & Hu, J. (2007). A Service Oriented Architecture for Managing Privacy Compliance in Collaborative Environments. [Geneva, Switzerland: Inderscience Publishers.]. *International Journal of Business Process Integration and Management, 2*(4), 292–301. doi:10.1504/IJBPIM.2007.017754

Peyton, L., Hu, J., Doshi, C., & Seguin, P. (2007). *Addressing Privacy in a Federated Identity Management Network for E-Health*. 8th World Congress on the Management of eBusiness. Toronto. Retrieved from http://doi.ieeecomputersociety.org/10.1109/WCMEB.2007.34.

Peyton, L., Hu, J., & Zhan, B. (2007). *Addressing Trust and Privacy in Telemedicine*. The Symposium on E-Commerce and E-Business in China (SEEC) at the Ninth International Conference on E-Commerce (ICEC 2007). Minneapolis, United States.

PHIPA. (2004). *Personal Health Information Protection Act*, Government of Ontario, Canada. Accessed 2009/12 http://www.e-laws.gov.on.ca/html/statutes/english/elaws_statutes_04p03_e.htm.

PIPEDA. (2000). *The Personal Information Protection and Electronic Documents Act*, Department of Justice, Canada. Accessed 2009/12 http://laws.justice.gc.ca/en/P-8.6/text.html.

Sandhu, R. S., Coyne, E. J., Feinstein, H. L., & Youman, C. E. (1996). Role-based access control models. *IEEE Computer, 29*, 38–47.

Shin, D., Ahn, G., & Shenoy, P. (2004). *Ensuring Information Assurance in Federated Identity Management*. pp. 821-826. IEEE Intl. Conference on Performance, Computing, and Communications.

Sung, M. Y., Kim, M. S., Kim, E. J., Yoo, J. H., & Sung, M. W. (2000). CoMed: a real-time collaborative medicine system. *International Journal of Medical Informatics*, (Issue 57), 117–126. doi:10.1016/S1386-5056(00)00060-5

Thomas, R. K. (1997). *Team-based Access Control (TMAC): A Primitive for Applying Role-based Access Controls in Collaborative Environments*. Proceedings of the second ACM workshop on Role-based access control (RBAC '97). pp. 13-19. New York: ACM.

Tourzan, J., & Koga, Y. (Eds.). (2006). *Liberty ID-WSF Architecture Overview, version 2.0*, Liberty Alliance Project. Accessed 2009/012 http://www.projectliberty.org/resource_center/specifications/liberty_alliance_id_wsf_2_0_specifications.

Tsiknakis, M., Katehakis, D., & Orphanoudakis, S. (2002). An open, component-based information infrastructure for integrated health information networks. *International Journal of Medical Informatics, 68*(issue 1), 3–26. doi:10.1016/S1386-5056(02)00060-6

Wei, P., Tao, L., & Sheng, M. (2005). *Mining Logs Files for Data Driven System Management*. Proceedings of the Second International Conference on Autonomic Computing ICAC 2005. Seattle, United States.

White, P. (2002). Legal issues in teleradiology. *The British Journal of Radiology, 75*, 201–206.

XACML. (2009). *Sun's XACML Implementation*. Accessed 2009/012 http://sunxacml.sourceforge.net/.

Xiaomin, W., Weidong, Z., & Yulin, W. (2002). *The development and application of a provincial telemedicine center*. Proceedings of the second joint EMBS/BMES Conference. pp. 1843-1844. Accessed 2009/012 http://ieeexplore.ieee.org/stamp/stamp.jsp?arnumber=1053055&isnumber=22474.

Yip, F. Ray, P. Paramesh, N. (2006). *Enforcing Business Rules and Information Security Policies through Compliance Audits: XISSF - A Compliance Specification Mechanism*. First IEEE/IFIP International Workshop on Business-Driven IT Management (BDIM '06). pp. 81-90. Accessed 2009/012 http://ieeexplore.ieee.org/stamp/stamp.jsp?arnumber=1649214&isnumber=34578.

Zhang, J., Sun, J., Yang, Y., Chen, X., Meng, L., & Lian, P. (2005). Web-based electronic patient records for collaborative medical applications. *Computerized Medical Imaging and Graphics, 29*(2), 115–124. doi:10.1016/j.compmedimag.2004.09.005

KEY TERMS AND DEFINITIONS

Access control: The mechanisms put in place to control who can access what information under what circumstances.

Audit: A mechanism for verifying compliance with regulations, typically based on a system of audit trail records that document what business processing actions have taken place.

Circle of Trust: A "Circle of Trust" is a key concept in which federated identity management is used to create a business to business network of cooperating enterprises that provide integrated services to users. These cooperating enterprises have trust relationships and operational agreements established amongst them to ensure that patient data and privacy is protected and respected.

E-Health Network: E-health networks are business to business networks that provide integrated healthcare services and data interoperability in the form of electronic health records accessible via Internet technology

Privacy: The legal protections that regulate what is to be considered personal information and control under what circumstances that information can be collected and shared. Typically, implied or explicit consent of the person is required.

Telemedicine: Telemedicine is the provision of health care service, such as consultations, remote medical procedures and examinations over the Internet or by phone.

Chapter 9
Certification and Security Issues in Biomedical Grid Portals:
The GRISSOM Case Study

Charalampos Doukas
University of the Aegean, Greece

Ilias Maglogiannis
University of Central Greece, Greece

Aristotle Chatziioannou
National Hellenic Research Foundation, Greece

ABSTRACT

User authentication and data security are very important aspects for the deployment and proper function of biomedical grid portals, since both sensitive data issues and controlled access to grid resources must be addressed. This chapter discusses certification and security issues in biomedical grid portals and presents the security infrastructure of GRISSOM (Grids for In Silico Systems biology and Medicine) platform. The platform consists of a web-based portal and a Web Service that enables statistical analysis of microarray cDNA data with the use of EGEE Grid infrastructure. The security infrastructure addresses user authentication and access issues, data encryption, Grid secure access and Web Service Security. The appendix of the chapter contains code snapshots on how to implement secure authentication in Web Services and create user SSL certificates on demand.

INTRODUCTION

In the field of bioinformatics, DNA microarray experiments are becoming a standard technique in order to examine patterns of gene expression. As this technology matures and the cost drops significantly, the amount of experimental data produced by laboratories around the world constantly increases, leading to the problem of finding powerful and easy to use analysis tools and platforms. The GRISSOM (Grids for In Silico Systems biology and Medicine) portal is a web-based platform that provides a concrete environment for data normalization, statistical gene selection, clustering and annotation of microarray data exploiting the Grid infrastructure of a project called EGEE (Enabling Grids for E-sciencE, http://public.eu-egee.org/).

DOI: 10.4018/978-1-61692-895-7.ch009

The EGEE project is funded by the European Commission and aims to develop a service grid infrastructure available to scientists 24 hours-a-day including a Greek portion (HellasGrid), allowing the execution of parallel algorithms. Running the analysis algorithms in a parallel and distributed fashion, decreases the amount of time needed to complete without the occupation of the end user's equipment, offering large scalability. Raw data are uploaded from the user and through an easy to use step-by-step web environment he/she defines the analysis parameters before submitting it to the GRID infrastructure. The analysis is monitored automatically from the GRISSOM platform and the user is properly informed about the status of his experiment. The platform includes also access to external biological repositories and meta-data analysis resources. A web service has been created that provides access to the aforementioned resources and functionality through various application programming interfaces.

The web-based access to the computational resources of the GRID and the handling of biological data introduces many issues concerning authentication, encryption and integrity. This book chapter aims at presenting the certification and security mechanisms developed and deployed specially at the GRISSOM platform for enabling the secure transactions between users and a generic GRID infrastructure. More specifically, the chapter presents an assessment of the risk factors introducing potential vulnerability at all levels (system reliability with respect to result's correctness, system functional robustness, malicious software protection) and data protection. In addition, it discusses the development and deployment of a user registration and authentication mechanism for achieving secure access and data confidentiality against the services and the security infrastructures of a GRID Infrastructure (GSI – Globus Security Infrastructure) and monitoring services. A proper web-based mechanism for the automated provision of user certificates is also presented among with technical details for the secure communication

between the platform modules and the integration with the GRID services. Finally, the appendix of the chapter contains code snapshots on how to implement secure authentication in Web Services and create user SSL certificates on demand.

BACKGROUND

Information on Biomedical Grid Portals

Most Biomedical Grid portals are Web applications that provide a front-end interface to accessing various grid computational and storage resources, along with access to special biological repositories that contain information like biological datasets and metadata, tools for meta-analysis (e.g., gene annotation), etc. Although the architecture of Web applications vary, many biomedical grid applications leverage similar sets of software components (see Figure 1). The Web Server (examples: Apache, IIS) processes incoming web requests, often routing them to other pieces of software. This is the outer layer of software for most Web applications, serving up static content when requested or delivering content dynamically generated by an individual application. The Web Application Container (examples: ASP/ASP.NET and J2EE/servlet containers like Tomcat, JBoss, Weblogic, Websphere) is a layer of software/ libraries to facilitate writing, deploying and running Web applications. This typically abstracts away details like communicating with the Web server and process lifetime management so Web application authors can focus on exposing useful functionality through dynamically-generated content. Other technologies like CGI and PHP, which run as modules in the web server provide some similar capabilities. The Web Applications themselves (e.g., Grid portals) usually runs in a Web Application Container and often communicate to some backend Data Layer when generating content. The Data Layer is usually a

Figure 1. Typical Architecture Scheme for Biomedical Grid Portals

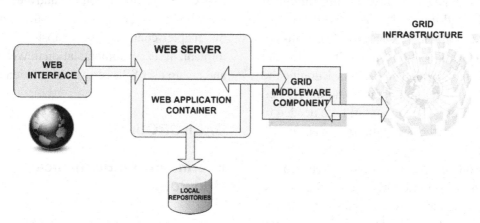

back-end database, but could also be a file system or other storage mechanism. Special middleware mechanisms are finally utilized to provide access to grid resources and proper functionality for data management.

Figure 1 illustrates the aforementioned major components of biomedical grid portals and how they interact in order to provide users with functionalities and services that utilize grid resources.

Several implementations of biomedical and life sciences grid portals exist in literature (Krishnan, 2004). The most important of them are summarized below.

The BRIDGES (BioMedical Research Informatics Delivered by Grid Enabled Services project, http://www.nesc.ac.uk/hub/projects/bridges) project has been funded by the UK Department of Trade and Industry to develop a computational infrastructure to support the needs of Cardiovascular Functional Genomics (CFG) project (Cardiovascular Functional Genomics project, http://www.brc.dcs.gla.ac.uk/projects/cfg) who are investigating possible genetic causes of hypertension, one of the main causes of cardiovascular mortality. The key component of BRIDGES architecture is a special data hub, which represents both a local data repository, together with data made available via externally linked Grid accessible data sets. The BIG (Biomedical Imaging Grid) is a Web-based Grid portal for management of biomedical information (data and images) in a distributed environment. BIG is an interactive environment that deals with complex user's requests, regarding the acquisition of biomedical data, the "processing" and "delivering" of biomedical images, using the power and security of Computational Grids.

The cancer Biomedical Informatics Grid, or caBIG, is a virtual informatics infrastructure that connects data, research tools, scientists, and organizations to leverage their combined strengths and expertise in an open federated environment with widely accepted standards and shared tools. The underlying service oriented infrastructure that supports caBIG is referred to as caGrid. The main application community motivating the need for caGrid is the cancer research community. However, the infrastructure has been designed and implemented as a general middleware system that can support other biomedical application domains. caGrid is built as a service-oriented architecture on top of Grid Service technologies; more specifically, on the Web Services Resource Framework (WSRF) standards. It also draws from the model driven architecture paradigm to enable syntactic and semantic interoperability among resources and rich metadata driven discovery and query of distributed resources. In essence, caGrid combines Grid computing, service oriented architecture, and model driven architecture in an integrated framework providing the technology that enables collaborating institutions to share information and analytical resources efficiently and securely.

The MediGRID platform (Beronov et al., 2008) demonstrates the feasibility and usefulness of grid services in medicine and life sciences by applying such services in biomedical research with multidimensional data and by correlating genotypic and phenotypic data. It has a modular setup: The four methodological modules (middleware, ontology, resource fusion and eScience) plan to incrementally develop and provide a Grid infrastructure while taking into account the need of the biomedical users. The user communities are represented in three research modules for biomedical informatics, image processing and clinical research.

SECURITY REQUIREMENTS FOR BIOMEDICAL GRID PORTALS

In the field of information security, three core principles are confidentiality, integrity and availability. A variety of mechanisms can be employed to achieve these three elements of information security, but many systems (at minimum) rely on a combination of mechanisms from the following broad categories. These principles in the context of Grid based distributed systems are discussed in this section.

Authentication is "the process of verifying an identity claimed by or for a system entity". Authentication requirements can be divided into Grid portal account creation and subsequent run-time authentication, as when the authorized user attempts to use the portal for job submission or data access. Some Grid portals are architected to multiplex all users onto a single Grid account/ID (e.g., "CMS"), while other portals are predicated on the portal user already having a Grid account (and the goal of the Grid portal in this case is to perform Grid computations on a per-user basis

as that particular user). In both cases, most web portals and applications will require user identification at portal registration time and authentication of user identities to (1) limit system access (authorization) based on this identity and to (2) tie a record of system actions to this identity (for auditing).

When only a single account/ID exists for the entire portal, the Grid portal requirements for user registration and identification are stringent. An organization (in this case the people who have control over the Grid portal) should manage user identifiers by (i) uniquely identifying each user; (ii) verifying the identity of each user; (iii) receiving authorization to issue a user identifier from an appropriate organizational official.; (iv) ensuring that the user identifier is issues to the intended party; (v) disabling the user identifier after a defined time period of inactivity; and (vi) archiving user identifiers.

When jobs and/or data access via the Grid portal take place based on a per-user pre-existing account, account creation is not as critical, because presumably an attacker could not launch jobs just by having a Grid portal account. After the account has been created on the Grid portal, there are a number of alternatives for authenticating to the Grid portal to access the Grid for either job execution or data access. The HTTP protocol includes Basic and Digest authentication, which is built into most web browsers and web servers. Since these are basically plaintext protocols, Basic and Digest authentication should generally be avoided especially for password-based security mechanisms.

Another very popular approach is forms-based authentication in which the security token (often a password) is entered in a web form for input to the web application. Forms-based authentication gives a great deal of flexibility and control to the web application designer, but because of the plaintext nature of HTTP, care must be taken to protect the submission of the security token (usually SSL). Because of the relatively unconstrained nature of form input data, careful input checking must be done to avoid security vulnerabilities. A common problem with password-based authentication is that user-chosen passwords are often relatively weak and easy to crack.

In contrast, certificate-based authentication, most often via SSL is often considered a stronger way to establish the client's identity. Other strong forms of authentication including smart cards and biometrics exist as well, but SSL has the advantage of being built into most web servers and browsers. Among the challenges with PKI-based X.509 (Adams and Farrell, 1999) certificates is that the user's certificate must usually be physically located on a particular machine and establishing proper trust hierarchies through various different certificate authorities (CAs) can be difficult to setup and get right. In most cases the web application would be interested in authenticating its users, but it can also be important for users to verify the identity of the web application. The most common way to do this is via the certificate based server authentication of SSL/HTTPS. Many attackers exploit users' confusion about the web application's identity to trick them into revealing sensitive information.

Authorization is the process by which a "right or a permission is granted to a system entity to access a system resource". The goals of authorization or access control are to restrict system access to those users or entities, which actually need it. In addition to preventing unwelcome, unwanted system usage, access control is also used to limit the possible actions that are allowed by a properly authenticated user. Typically, this means following the principle of least privilege: a user should only be granted the lowest authorization level needed to carry out the desired action. Giving all users administrative-level access may be an easy way to ensure that valid user requests aren't rejected, but it's hardly a secure configuration.

Authorization is most commonly managed through access control lists (user-centric) or capabilities (resource-centric). Simple lists can be fine when the set of users and resources is small, but gets to be difficult to manage as these sets grow. One way to combat this complexity is role-based access control, in which users are assigned roles and these roles are used as the unit of authorization. Another variation is to assign attributes to the users and then restrict access to resources based on the attributes presented. Access to a resource is usually not all-or-nothing, and authorization incorporates what action or operation is intended as well. Important considerations for web application authorization involve out-of-the box (default) security and ease of proper configuration. The default configuration for a newly-installed web application should be very restrictive, but often this is not the case. Many default configurations allow access to everyone, or include default guest or administrator accounts with well known passwords. Properly configuring access control mechanisms can also be challenging for web applications. A highly sophisticated, securely programmed authorization mechanism is worthless if it is not configured correctly so care must be taken to enable administrators to easily allow access only to those that need it.

Auditing is the process of verifying that security requirements have been satisfied, with corrections suggested where they haven't been met. Essential to effective auditing is that actions are traced and logged through all parts of the system. With web applications, this means that logging of significant operations must happen in the web server, web application and data layer, in addition to the web application itself. Events of interest include: errors, failures, state accesses, authentication, access control and other security checks, in addition to application-specific operations and actions. Care must be taken to protect the integrity of logging and trace data, even (and perhaps especially) in the case of system failures. Logs that are tampered with or destroyed are useless in performing an effective audit. Auditing of log and trace data can either be done manually or it can be automated and often a combination of both is used. Either way, auditing should be done on a regular basis. Automated systems that continually monitor, detect, and in some cases even correct (or at least recommend corrections for) security problems can be particularly useful for maintaining a secure web application. Web applications should be careful to ensure that errors or failures somewhere in the system do not introduce security vulnerabilities. Attackers, for instance, are often able to exploit the detailed error information provided by web applications to gain unauthorized access.

Web-based applications, in contrast to desktop-based application clients, have a challenge with regard to where client-related state information is stored. A desktop application would store state locally on the client machine, but because of the relatively stateless nature of the web browser, client state in web applications tends to be stored remotely on the server. The challenge then becomes securely managing and associating session state with an authenticated client identity. Unlike the other areas mentioned above, session state management is not strictly a security concern. However, the potential for security vulnerabilities in this area as well as its unique relevance to web applications merit its discussion here. Many web application containers include built-in session management capabilities, and in most cases it is desirable to leverage this functionality where possible. When session state management must be built by the web application, care must be taken to ensure that session state can not be tampered with and is securely (i.e., cryptographically) and consistently mapped to an authentication token. From the client perspective, session identifiers are often included in cookies that are automatically saved and presented by the web browser. Such information could also be presented elsewhere in user input data. Care must be taken to protect the integrity and confidentiality of these session identifiers as attackers can use this information to gain unauthorized access to the system.

BASIC GRID SECURITY MECHANISMS

The Globus Toolkit

The Globus Toolkit (GT, http://www.globus.org/toolkit/) contains a collection of components that have been proven to be useful and were selected from solutions that had been used in different grid applications. These solutions showed a potential for reusing because of their usefulness and generality. These solutions were then generalized in order to become useful for a wide variety of applications. The Globus Toolkit is thus a collection of standard building blocks and tools that does not give a complete solution for any grid project, and very few of the GT components include user interface elements that are immediately useful to the application. GT provides solutions to the most common problems and promotes standard solutions. A grid application typically must assemble together a subset of these components, components from other sources, either off-the-shelf or specially tailored for the application, and application-specific code. These components must be organized and integrated by architects and system integrators according to the requirements of the specific application. Standard mechanisms used in the GT include SSL/TLS, LDAP v3, X.509 Proxy Certificates, SOAP, HTTP, and GridFTP. Reference implementations of new and proposed standards may also be provided, e.g. WSRF, DAI, WS-Agreement, WSDL 2.0, WSDM, SAML, and XACML.

OGSA Security Framework

Open Grid Services Architecture (OGSA) is a service-oriented architecture (SOA) that represents an evolution towards a grid system architecture based on Web services concepts and technologies, autonomic computing principles and open standards for integration and interoperability. The first implementation of OGSA mechanisms corresponds to version 3 of the Globus toolkit, GT3. OGSA builds on concepts and technologies from both the grid and Web services. It was created in order to meet the challenges related to the integration of services across virtual organizations (VOs) running on top of different native platforms (Foster et al., 2002). Security arises at various levels of the OGSA architecture. The OGSA security model stipulates that security mechanisms should be pluggable and discoverable by service requesters from a service description, enabling service providers to select their preferred mechanisms. The Global Grid Forum's OGSA 1.0 (The Open Grid Services Architecture, Version 1.0, Global Grid Forum, 29 January 2005) document targets security requirements including authentication and authorization, security infrastructures, perimeter security solutions, isolation, delegation, policy exchange, intrusion detection and protection, and secure logging. It also specifies security services associated with message integrity, confidentiality and privacy, auditing, intrusion prevention and access control.

The Grid Security Infrastructure

The Grid Security Infrastructure (GSI) is the portion of the Globus Toolkit that implements security functionality. Its security model constitutes a de facto standard for grid security. GSI maps to local security mechanisms and gateways are used in order to translate from the common GSI infrastructure into the local site mechanisms. It supports the following features:

- A public-key system. GSI is based on public-key cryptography and thus supports privacy, integrity, and authentication. Both grid users and grid services need to have a X.509 certificate and a private key. User certificates can be managed in several ways. Certificates are issued by Certification Authorities that both users and services must trust.

- Mutual authentication through digital certificates. GSI supports three authentication methods: (i) X.509 certificates; (ii) username and password; (iii) anonymous authentication. GSI uses X.509 certificates to guarantee a strong authentication and X.509 identity and proxy certificates (Tueche et al., 2001) in order to provide a globally unique identifier. GSI relies on trusted third parties for signing users and host certificates. It commonly uses the Transport Layer Security (TLS) protocol for authentication, and defines a common credential format based on X.509 identity certificates. Authentication is provided by the conjunction of an X.509 certificate and an associated private key. GSI certificates are issued by a trusted party called the Certification Authority (CA).

- Credential management. Certificate management is supported by MyProxy (Novotny et al., 2001), a remote client–server system in which clients can store credentials with access control policies in an online repository for later retrieval. Typically, users store long-lived credentials in the repository, which are thereafter used for providing short-lived credentials for grid sessions. MyProxy uses X.509 certificates and can be combined with a Certification Authority service that automatically stores its own certificates, to be used for ID/password sign-on. A command-line interface is provided allowing users to introduce user ID and password to obtain grid proxy credentials on their local services.

- Credential delegation and single sign-on. These features are implemented with the help of proxy certificates (Tueche et al., 2001). Proxy certificates are similar to X.509 digital certificates except that they are signed by an end user, and whereas X.509 certificates are intended for assigning long-term identities, proxy certificates are used for short-term delegation of rights. They allow a user to create and delegate a set of credentials to another user without the involvement of an administrator. Users generate delegated proxy certificates with short life spans that get passed from one component to another and form the basis of authentication, access control and logging. For single sign-on, the user signs in once in order to create the proxy certificate, which is thereafter used for all subsequent authentications. Proxy certificates may be created locally by the user and used by subsequent clients. Thereafter the proxy certificate can be used to authenticate to a remote service. Proxy certificates can thus be used to create other proxy certificates, allowing thus a chain of delegations.

For single sign-on, the user signs in once in order to create the proxy certificate which is thereafter used for all subsequent authentications. Proxy certificates may be created locally by the user and used by subsequent clients. Thereafter the proxy certificate can be used to authenticate to a remote service. Proxy certificates can thus be used to create other proxy certificates, allowing thus a chain of delegations. These delegations can also be restricted with the help of the policy specified in a restricted proxy certificate. Restricted proxies represent an extension of the X.509 certificates to carry restriction policies, enabling grantors to delegate only a portion of the rights they possess.

Authorization and access control was initially based on a simple access control list placed in a flat file called the Gridmap. GT2 used the Gridmap file to map a user to a user ID on a remote resource during job submission. GT3 extended this idea by allowing Gridmap files to be associated with services and factories, and consequently applying access control policies to those services and factories.

THE GRISSOM PORTAL IN BRIEF

The main purpose of the GRISSOM (GRids for In Silico Systems BiOlogy and Medicine) platform (http://www.grissom.gr) is to provide experts with a powerful, labor-free, rapid computational pipeline efficient for analysis of huge volumes of DNA microarray data, through the enactment of multiple independent analysis workflows for the same or multiple datasets that are implemented in parallel, by exploiting the GRID infrastructure. The user-friendly design of GRISSOM enables a wide range of users with different levels of expertise, to perform versatile analyses through its web-based interface. The platform supports several microarray experiment analysis steps, including data importing, preprocessing, statistical analysis and clustering while real time help is available for every step. Annotated output results are exportable, can be submitted for Pathway Analysis exploiting Gene Ontology Terms and can be integrated upon request to the GRISSOM repository. The analysis pipeline adopted by GRISSOM is based upon Gene ARMADA (Chatziioannou et al., 2009) application, which has been extensively tested and used in several multi-level analysis studies (Tzouvelekis et al., 2007; Welboren et al., 2009). The major architectural components of the platform are illustrated in Figure 2 and namely are the web interface, the grid infrastructure, the Biomart annotation web service module, the GRISSOM Web Service, and the distributed database respectively.

Web Interface

Key component of the GRISSOM platform is the web server that transparently interfaces with the end users. Implemented using PHP scripts over a MySQL database, this portal provides a rich collection of useful tools for data upload/download, experimental parameters setting, results annotation and visualization. Utilizing the gLite (Laure et al., 2006) and Globus (Foster and Kesselman,

Figure 2. Architectural and functional components of the GRISSOM Platform

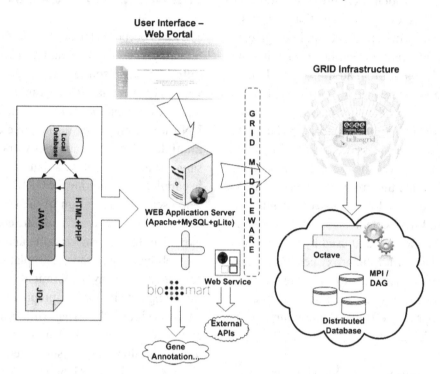

1997) toolkits this web server functions as a grid UI (user interface), communicating with the GRID infrastructure for job submission and monitoring. When a user submits a new experiment, an analysis is enacted, where input data together with the analysis parameters, are transferred to Grid storage elements and a description of the job is created using the JDL language.

Instead of using MPI computing, parallel workflows are implemented simultaneously through the utilization of distributed computing methodologies, based in the instantiation of distinct computing jobs, written in Python and Octave Forge mathematical language, as derived by a special Directed Acyclic Graph (DAG) scheduler for job management in the Grid. The results of the analysis (differentially expressed gene lists) are retrieved by the server for visualization, further meta-analysis or storage to the repository upon user's request.

Grid Infrastructure Access

Job execution upon the Grid infrastructure is instantiated by the DagMan (Directed Acyclic Graph Manager) system, which is a tool of the Condor platform (Tannenbaum et al., 2002). Based on the dimensionality of the problem, two or more nodes (number proportional to number of conditions) are added to the graph in order to perform normalization steps in parallel.

Normalization steps are selected to be parallelized because of the high computational cost ($\approx O(n3logn)$). After the end of data normalization, data are mustered and merged in a single OctaveForge data structure in order to perform the final statistical testing. This final step is significantly faster and running it on a single node is not posing serious limitations from a computing cost's perspective.

Annotation through Biomart Web Service

In order to facilitate meta-analysis and massive annotation of experiment-related platforms and genes, GRISSOM integrates an interface for the BioMart system (Haider et al., 2009). BioMart is a query-oriented data management system which provides data-mining searches of complex descriptive biological or other data. BioMart provides transparent access through the use of web services or APIs written in Perl and Java. These web services were integrated into the GRISSOM application and adapted to querying the EBI ArrayExpress (Brazma et al., 2001) and Ensembl databases (Hubbard et al., 2002).

Porting GRISSOM to Other Workflows through Web Services

Web Services are emerging as a promising technology to build distributed applications. Service Oriented Architecture (SOA) (Newcomer and Lomow, 2005) enables the concept of loosely-coupled, open-standard, language- and platform-independent systems. The loosely-coupled features allow service providers to modify backend functions while maintaining the same interface to clients. The core service functions are encapsulated and remain transparent to clients. The open-standard approach supports collaboration and integration with other services.

Web Services are platform, programming language, tool and network infrastructure independent, fostering the reuse of existing back-end infrastructure. The basic SOA includes three service components: provider, requester and registry. The current implementation of Web Services mainly utilizes XML technologies and obeys W3C defined standards. WSDL (Web Service Description Language) is commonly defined by the service provider for invoking the service. SOAP (Simple Object Access Protocol) is adopted as message transfer protocol between requester

and provider. UDDI (the Universal Description, Discovery and Integration) is used for service registration and discovery.

GRISSOM provides web service based access to its functionality and repository resources, facilitating its integration in other application environments, through the creation of appropriate workflows. Access pertains experiment management (submission and monitoring) and query submission for experiment retrieval from the GRISSOM repository. Each of the aforementioned functionalities can be invoked through the developed Web Service and is described through the appropriate WSDL representation of the Service.

Distributed Database

The GRISSOM application integrates a local repository of microarray data, complying to MIAME and miniML (MIAME Notation in Markup Language) (Brazma et al., 2001) annotation systems. The compatibility of the local repository with these standards for microarray data exchange ensures the unobstructed access to published data from public repositories such as NCBI GEO (Barrett et al., 2008) and ArrayExpress (Brazma et al., 2001). Therefore, GRISSOM is suitable not limited only to proprietary genomic data analysis but also can be used to easily reproduce already published microarray experiments. The repository architecture comprises three parts: Firstly, a MySQL database at the UI that contains information about executed analyses such as parameters, size, data and MIAME or GEO- miniM information. Secondly a data repository that resides in the GRID Storage Elements containing raw and processed data from every microarray experiment analysis referenced in the main database. The third part comprises the Bioconductor annotation files and the interconnections to other public repositories for annotation (Biomart) and meta-analysis tasks.

SECURITY ASPECTS OF THE GRISSOM PORTAL

The GRISSOM portal as already described involves both the management of biological data and the utilization of the EGEE infrastructure. Thus both access control and data encryption schemes must be applied to ensure proper usage of grid computational resources and security. Based on the presented architectural scheme of GRISSOM platform, two basic security mechanisms have been developed and deployed; the user access and authentication mechanism and the access mechanism to EGEE infrastructure (see Figure 5).

User Access, Authentication and Data Encryption

Access to GRISSOM platform is provided to registered users only. The registration process requires the submission of various personal information (mostly for communication purposes), in addition to the login details (i.e. username and password). The registration form is enhanced with a user feedback mechanism that requires the input of alphanumeric string illustrated in an image. The latter is a common mechanism utilized in order to avoid any automatic software generated registrations. Upon completion, a verification email is sent to the user that contains an activation link and a personal digital certificate. The certificate is generated real time on the platforms application server using the X.509 public key infrastructure cryptography standard (Adams and Farrell, 1999; Housley et al., 2002). The generation on the server provides better certificate management. The latter is required to be imported to the user's web browser in order to enable access to the platform's main functionality. In order to verify that a user has successfully authenticated into the portal and can browse through the GRISSOM platform PHP Sessions have been utilized. Sessions are the way of saving the state and user specific variables across subsequent page requests. This is achieved by handing a unique and difficult-to-guess identity value (session id) to the browser (either in a cookie or the URL) which the browser submits with every new request. The session is alive as long as the browser keeps sending the id with every new request. The ability to restrict and maintain user actions within unique sessions is critical to web security.

All data exchanged between the user's side and the GRISSOM platform is secured through the use of the Secure Socket Layer (SSL) (Thomas, 2000) protocol. The latter is a cryptographic protocol that provides security and data integrity for communications over TCP/IP networks such as the Internet. OpenSSL (http://www.openssl.org/) has been used for the implementation of the latter protocol that is embedded into the platform hosting server. Through the aforementioned mechanisms both maximum user access control and data encryption are guaranteed.

Access and Resources Restriction

In order to assure proper utilization of GRISSOM resources and functionality, every user account that is created is restricted to specific access in portal's area and functions in conjunction to grid resources quota that have been applied. Regarding the latter, each user cannot submit more than 10 microarray analysis experiments per day. In addition, a 200Mb size limit for each experimental dataset uploaded to the grid and a total 1Gb size limit per user for storage occupation in the GRISSOM distributed repository are applied.

Secure Access to HellasGrid Infrastructure

The second security mechanism concerns the communication between the GRISSOM platform and the EGEE (Enabling Grids for E-sciEnce, http://public.eu-egee.org/) infrastructure and is based on the security directions introduced by EGEE. More specifically, the authentication model for EGEE is

Figure 3. The EGEE Security System (source http://glite.web.cern.ch/glite/security/) used to implement client authentication to Grid resources

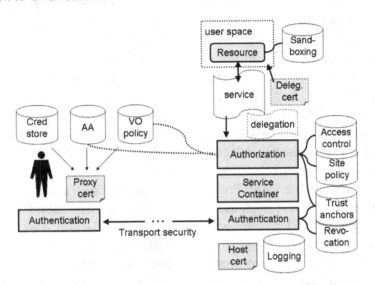

based on the concept of trusted third parties (TTPs): entities that are not related to any relying party except through a trust relationship. Underlying that trust relationship is the digital signature of the TTP, based on conventional asymmetric cryptography. X.509v3 public key certificates are utilized to express identity assertions. These certificates are issued by Certification Authorities (CAs). Different types of CAs exist, as well as different means of delivering certificates to end-entities. Whatever the delivery mechanism or operational mode of the CA, the authentication is based on at least the distinguished name (DN) of the subject contained therein. The authorisation of a user on a specific Grid resource can be done in two different ways. The first is simpler, and relies on the grid-mapfile mechanism. The second way relies on the Virtual Organisation Membership Service (VOMS) and the LCAS/LCMAPS mechanism, which allow for a more detailed definition of user privileges. More information can be found in EGEE Security Architecture document, available online at: https://edms.cern.ch/document/487004/ (see Figure 3).

The Grid Security Infrastructure (GSI) in EGEE provides a delegation capability: an exten-sion of the standard SSL protocol which reduces the number of times the user must enter his pass-phrase. If a Grid computation requires that sev-eral Grid resources be used (each requiring mu-tual authentication), or if there is a need to have agents (local or remote) requesting services on behalf of a user, the need to re-enter the user's passphrase can be avoided by creating a proxy. A proxy consists of a new certificate and a private key. The key pair that is used for the proxy, i.e. the public key embedded in the certificate and the private key, may either be regenerated for each proxy or obtained by other means. The new cer-tificate contains the owner's identity, modified slightly to indicate that it is a proxy. The new certificate is signed by the owner, rather than a CA, and it also includes a time notation after which the proxy should no longer be accepted by others. Proxies have limited lifetimes.

In GRISSOM we have utilized MyProxy platform (Novotny et al., 2001) to address the certificate management issue. MyProxy is open source software for managing X.509 Public Key Infrastructure (PKI) security credentials (cer-tificates and private keys). MyProxy combines an online credential repository with an online certificate authority to allow users to securely obtain credentials when and where needed. Users run myproxy-logon to authenticate and obtain credentials, including trusted CA certificates and Certificate Revocation Lists (CRLs). Storing credentials in a MyProxy repository allows users to easily obtain RFC 3820 proxy credentials, without worrying about managing private key and certificate files. It can be used to delegate credentials to services acting on their behalf (like a grid portal) by storing credentials in the MyProxy repository and sending the MyProxy passphrase to the service. Users can also use MyProxy to renew their credentials, so, for example, long-running jobs don't fail because of expired credentials. A professionally managed MyProxy server can provide a more secure storage location for private keys than typical end-user systems. MyProxy can be configured to encrypt all private keys in the repository with user-chosen passphrases, with server-enforced policies for passphrase quality. By using a proxy credential delegation protocol, MyProxy allows users to obtain proxy credentials when needed without ever transferring private keys over the network.

Web Services Security Issues

The Web Services Security (WS-Security) specification (WS-Security specification, 2004) describes enhancements to SOAP messaging to provide quality of protection through message integrity, message confidentiality, and single message authentication. These mechanisms can be used to accommodate a wide variety of security models and encryption technologies. WS-Security provides a set of mechanisms to help developers of Web Services secure SOAP message exchanges. Specifically, it describes enhancements to the existing SOAP messaging to provide quality of protection through the application of message integrity, message confidentiality, and single message authentication to SOAP messages. These

basic mechanisms can be combined in various ways to accommodate building a wide variety of security models using a variety of cryptographic technologies.

WS-Security defines a SOAP Header element to carry security-related data. In case XML Signature is used, the header can contain the information defined by XML Signature that describes how the message was signed, the key that was used, and the resulting signature value. Likewise, if an element within the message is encrypted, the encryption information such as that conveyed by XML Encryption can be contained within the WS-Security header. WS-Security does not specify the format of the signature or encryption. Instead, it specifies how one would embed the security information laid out by other specifications within a SOAP message. WS-Security is primarily a specification for an XML-based security metadata container.

WS-Security also provides a general-purpose mechanism for associating security tokens with messages (see Figure 4). However, no specific type of security token is required by WS-Security. It is designed to be extensible (e.g. support multiple security token formats) to accommodate a variety of authentication and authorization mechanisms. For example, a requestor might provide proof of identity and a signed claim that they have a particular business certification. A Web service, receiving such a message could then determine what kind of trust they place in the claim.

Additionally, WS-Security describes how to encode binary security tokens and attach them to SOAP messages. Specifically, the WS-Security profile specifications describes how to encode Username Tokens, X.509 Tokens, SAML Tokens, REL Tokens and Kerberos Tokens as well as how to include opaque encrypted keys as a sample of different binary token types. With WS-Security, the domain of these mechanisms can be extended by carrying authentication information in Web services requests. WS-Security also includes extensibility mechanisms that can be used to further describe the credentials that are included

Figure 4. Typical Message flow of WS-Security implementation and token association

with a message. WS-Security is a building block that can be used in conjunction with other Web service protocols to address a wide variety of application security requirements.

Message integrity is provided by leveraging XML Signature and security tokens to ensure that messages have originated from the appropriate sender and were not modified in transit. Similarly, message confidentiality leverages XML Encryption and security tokens to keep portions of a SOAP message confidential (Figure 5).

In order to provide secure access to the developed GRISSOM Web Service we have utilized the Apache Rampart module (http://ws.apache.org/rampart/). Apache Rampart is the Axis2 module that provides WS-Security functionality to Axis2 Web services and their clients. Rampart currently implements WS-Security, WS-SecurityPolicy, WS-SecureConversation and WS-Trust specifications. Authentication is performed through configuring the Web Service to accept client requests proceeded by credential authentication (i.e. username and password) through secure channel and encryption (usually HTTPS). To pass the aforementioned user credentials in this manner, the utilized WS-Security defines the UsernameToken element. The adopted schema for the element is as follows:

```
<xs:element name="UsernameToken">
  <xs:complexType>
    <xs:sequence>
```

```
<xs:element ref="Username"/>
  <xs:element
    ref="Password"
    minOccurs="0"/>
</xs:sequence>
<xs:attribute name="Id"
  type="xs:ID"/>
<xs:anyAttribute
  namespace="##other"/>
</xs:complexType>
</xs:element>
```

This schema fragment references two other types: Username and Password. The latter are essentially variables that contain extra attributes as needed. Password contains an attribute named Type that indicates how the password is being passed around. The password is not passed as plain text but in encrypted format:

```
<wsse:UsernameToken>
  <wsse:Username>charalampos
  </wsse:Username>
  <wsse:Password
    Type="wsse:PasswordDigest">
    KE6QugOpkPyT3Eo0SEgT
    30W4Keg=</wsse:Password>
  <wsse:Nonce>5uW4ABku/m6/
  S5rnE+L7vg==</wsse:Nonce>
  <wsu:Created xmlns:wsu=
    "http://schemas.xmlsoap.org/
    ws/2002/07/utility">
```

Figure 5. GRISSOM Security mechanisms flowchart

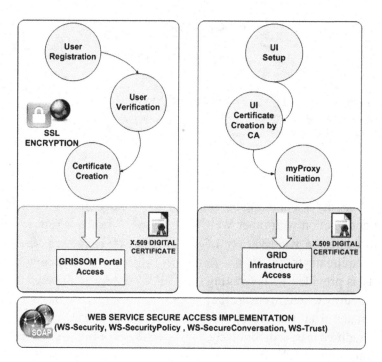

```
        2009-12-03T00:44:02Z
     </wsu:Created>
   </wsse:UsernameToken>
```

In general, WS-Security allows for a SOAP message to identify the caller, sign the message, and encrypt message contents. Whenever possible, existing specifications are reused to reduce the amount of invention required to securely deliver a SOAP message.

The Appendix contains sample code for configuring a Web Service to request authentication based on credentials and utilizing the Rampart API, among with client code that authenticates and connects to the service respectively.

Evaluation of the GRISSOM Portal

The Open Web Application Security Project (OWASP) has compiled a list of ten of the most common security vulnerabilities afflicting Web applications, including Grid portals (The Ten Most

Critical Web Application Security Vulnerabilities, 2004) which include the following:

- **Unvalidated Parameters:** In case input data contained in web requests is not properly checked (by the application) before being processed. Attackers can craft parameters to hijack the application or cause it to behave in dangerous, unexpected ways. Injection Flaws, Buffer Overflows, and XSS Flaws are all specific types of Unvalidated Parameter vulnerabilities.

- **Broken Access Control:** Access control mechanisms sometimes work inconsistently or incorrectly, allowing unintended access to resources. This is particularly troublesome for web application administrative interfaces.

- **Broken Authentication and Session Management:** Authentication problems can range from weak authentication mechanisms that are easily broken (plain text secrets to retrieve forgotten passwords), to insufficient session protection (exploiting access to one set of session information to gain access to someone else's) to forged sessions or session cookies (allowing session impersonation).

- **Cross-Site Scripting Flaws:** It involves exploiting an unvalidated parameter vulnerability to send a script to the web application that is in turn delivered to and executed by the end user's web browser.

- **Buffer Overflows:** They can occur when specially crafted input results are injected in the execution of arbitrary code on the target server. This is particularly problematic if the server is running as root or an administrator account as the malicious code will also have those privileges. In general, Java applications do not suffer from this type of vulnerability.

- **Injection Flaws:** In contrast to the other unvalidated parameter attacks, injection flaws refer to when injected code or command strings are passed through the web application directly to some backend system like SQL databases.

- **Improper Error Handling:** It applies when error messages are displayed to the user and in some way reveal details about how the system or application works (the attacker could then exploit this knowledge). This is typically a problem when very detailed stack traces are displayed to the user giving some information of the structure of the code and its operation. Attackers can also probe for inconsistencies in error messages returned ("file not found" vs. "access denied") to gain a better understanding of the application.

- **Insecure Storage:** Refers to storage of sensitive data (passwords, account information, etc.) without proper encryption or access control mechanisms. This could be on disk, in a database, or in memory.

Usually one of the other exploits is needed to actually gain access to this insecure data.

- **Denial of Service (DoS) Attacks:** They can happen when the sheer volume of requests to the web application overwhelms the capacity, denying access to legitimate users. This is usually an even more troublesome problem, because it's very hard for web applications to distinguish between legitimate and malicious requests.

- **Insecure Configuration Management:** It can be caused from unpatched software to unchanged insecure default settings to outright configuration mistakes of third party software.

In order to secure the GRISSOM portal against the aforementioned vulnerabilities a number of measures have been taken, including form input data validation, special access control at every portal web page, robust authentication management, update notification and patch installation of the major third party software components the portal consists of (e.g., the Apache Web Server and the MySQL Database) for addressing scripting flaws, buffer overflows and injection flaws. Finally software and hardware firewalls deployed within and outside the infrastructure provide protection from DoS attacks.

SUMMARY AND CONCLUSIONS

The web-based access to the computational resources of the GRID and the handling of biological data introduces many issues concerning authentication, encryption and integrity. This book chapter has presented the certification and security mechanisms developed and deployed specially at the GRISSOM platform for enabling the secure transactions between users and a generic GRID infrastructure. An assessment of the risk factors introducing potential vulnerability at all levels (system reliability with respect to result's correctness, system functional robustness, malicious software protection) and data protection has also been presented. In addition, the development and deployment of a user registration and authentication mechanism for achieving secure access and data confidentiality against the services and the security infrastructures of a GRID Infrastructure (GSI – Globus Security Infrastructure) and monitoring services has been discussed. Finally, the following appendix contains code examples for secure web services authentication and real time SSL certificates generation using tools available by the open source community.

FUTURE WORK DIRECTIONS

Future work of the GRISSOM platform includes the enhancement of the portal with new tools and repositories for providing users with more functionality on processing biological data. This means that security mechanisms of the portal must be extended and upgraded. The latter would include:

- The incorporation of better certificate management mechanisms: While more users are registered to the platform a better certificate management system might be needed that will incorporate automated certificate revocation and notification and access restriction based on specified user roles.

- Intrusion detection system: The introduction of an intrusion detection system will enable the notification of the platform's administrators in case a security compromise is detected, either externally or internally by the platform's users.

- Automated auditing system: An auditing procedure will be designed for manually or automatically inspecting potential vulnerabilities of the system. This will also include procedures for automatically retriev-

ing crucial information regarding security updates of the major software components the platform relies on.

REFERENCES

Adams, C., Farrell, S. (1999). *Internet X.509 Public Key Infrastructure: Certificate Management Protocol*. RFC 2510.

Barrett, T., Troup, D. B., Wilhite, S. E., Ledoux, P., Rudnev, D., & Evangelista, C. (2008). *NCBI GEO: archive for high-throughput functional genomic data*. Nucleic Acids Res.

Beronov, K., Dzhimova, O., Delgado, A., Vossberg, M., Krefting, D., et al. (2008). *Virtual endovascular correction and hemodynamic analysis over the MediGRID-portal*. eMBEC 2008 IFMBE Proceedings ECIFMBE 2008. 4th European Conference of the International Federation for Medical and Biological Engineering.

Brazma, A., Hingamp, P., Quackenbush, J., Sherlock, G., Spellman, P., & Stoeckert, C. (2001). Minimum information about a microarray experiment (MIAME)-toward standards for microarray data. *Proc. Nat Genet.*, *29*(4), 365–371. doi:10.1038/ng1201-365

Chatziioannou, A., Moulos, P., & Kolisis, F. (2009). Gene ARMADA: an integrated multi-analysis platform for microarray data implemented in MATLAB. *BMC Bioinformatics*, *10*, 354. .doi:10.1186/1471-2105-10-354

Foster, I., & Kesselman, C. (1997). Globus: a Metacomputing Infrastructure Toolkit. *International Journal of High Performance Computing Applications*, *11*(2), 115–128. doi:10.1177/109434209701100205

Foster, I., Kesselman, C., Nick, J., & Tuecke, S. (2002). *The physiology of the grid*. Global Grid Forum.

Haider, S., Ballester, B., Smedley, D., Zhang, J., Rice, P., Kasprzyk, A. (2009). *BioMart Central Portal--unified access to biological data.* Nucleic acids research.

Housley, R. et al. *RFC3280 (2002): Internet X.509 Public Key Infrastructure Certificate and Certificate Revocation List (CRL) Profile.* Retrieved from http://www.ietf.org/rfc/rfc3280.txt

Hubbard, T., Barker, D., Birney, E., Cameron, G., Chen, Y., & Clark, L. (2002). The Ensembl genome database project. *Nucleic Acids Research, 30*(1), 38–41. doi:10.1093/nar/30.1.38

Krishnan, A. (2004). A Survey of life sciences applications on the grid. *New Gen. Comput., 22*(2), 111–126. doi:10.1007/BF03040950

Laure, E., Fisher, S.M., Frohner, A., Grandi, C., Kunszt, P., Krenek, A., Mulmo, O., Pacini, F., Prelz, F., White, J., Barroso, M., Buncic, P., Hemmer, F., Meglio, A, & Di, ., &Edlund, A. (2006). Programming the Grid with gLite. *Computational Methods In Science And Technology, 12*(1), 33–45.

Newcomer, E., & Lomow, G. (2005). *Understanding SOA with Web Services.* Addison Wesley.

Novotny, J., Tuecke, S., & Welch, V. (2001). *An Online Credential Repository for the Grid: MyProxy.* Proceedings of the Tenth International Symposium on High Performance Distributed Computing (HPDC-10). (pp. 104-111). IEEE Press.

Tannenbaum, T., Wright, D., Miller, K., & Livny, M. (2002). Condor - A Distributed Job Scheduler in Thomas Sterling, (Ed.). *Beowulf Cluster Computing with Linux.* Boston: The MIT Press.

The Open Grid Services Architecture. *Version 1.5* (2006). Retrieved 25 July 2009 from http://www.ogf.org/documents/GFD.80.pdf

The Ten Most Critical Web Application Security Vulnerabilities. The Open Web Application Security Project (OWASP). (2004). Retrieved 25 July 2009 from http://www.owasp.org/documentation/topten.html.

Thomas, S. A. (2000). *SSL and TLS essentials securing the Web.* New York: Wiley.

Tueche, S. et al. (2001). *Internet X.509 public key infrastructure proxy certificate profile.* IETF draft.

Tzouvelekis, A., Harokopos, V., Paparountas, T., Oikonomou, N., Chatziioannou, A., & Vilaras, G. (2007). Comparative expression profiling in pulmonary fibrosis suggests a role of hypoxia-inducible factor-1alpha in disease pathogenesis. *American Journal of Respiratory and Critical Care Medicine, 176*(11), 1108–1119. doi:10.1164/rccm.200705-683OC

Welboren, W. J., van Driel, M. A., Janssen-Megens, E. M., van Heeringen, S. J., Sweep, F. C., Span, P. N., & Stunnenberg, H. G. (2009). ChIP-Seq of ERalpha and RNA polymerase II defines genes differentially responding to ligands. *The EMBO Journal, 28*(10), 1418–1428. doi:10.1038/emboj.2009.88

WS-Security Specification (2004). Retrieved 25 July 2009 from http://www-128.ibm.com/developerworks/library/specification/ws-secure/

KEY TERMS AND DEFINITIONS

Biomedical Grid Portals: Biomedical Grid portals are Web applications that provide a front-end interface to accessing various grid computational and storage resources, along with access to special biological repositories that contain information like biological datasets and metadata, tools for meta-analysis (e.g., gene annotation), etc.

GRISSOM Portal: The GRISSOM (Grids for In Silico Systems biology and Medicine) portal is a web-based platform that provides a concrete environment for data normalization, statistical gene selection, clustering and annotation of microarray data exploiting the Grid infrastructure of a project called EGEE (Enabling Grids for E-sciencE, http://public.eu-egee.org/). Running the analysis algorithms in a parallel and distributed fashion, decreases the amount of time needed to complete without the occupation of the end user's equipment, offering large scalability. Raw data are uploaded from the user and through an easy to use step-by-step web environment he/she defines the analysis parameters before submitting it to the GRID infrastructure. The analysis is monitored automatically from the GRISSOM platform and the user is properly informed about the status of his experiment. The platform includes also access to external biological repositories and meta-data analysis resources.

HellasGrid: Hellasgrid main objective is the development of a National Strategy on Grid technologies and the coordination of the related communities' activities & actions, so as to provide a seamless electronic infrastructure environment throughout Greece and facilitate the communities' participation in pan-European and international efforts.

The EGEE Project: The EGEE project brings together experts from more than 50 countries with the common aim of building on recent advances in Grid technology and developing a service Grid infrastructure which is available to scientists 24 hours-a-day. The project provides researchers in academia and business with access to a production level Grid infrastructure, independent of their geographic location. The EGEE project also focuses on attracting a wide range of new users to the Grid.

Web Service Security: The Web Services Security (WS-Security) specification (see WS-Security specification) describes enhancements to SOAP messaging to provide quality of protection through message integrity, message confidentiality, and single message authentication. These mechanisms can be used to accommodate a wide variety of security models and encryption technologies.

Web Services: Web Services are emerging as a promising technology to build distributed applications. It is an implementation of Service Oriented Architecture (SOA) that supports the concept of loosely-coupled, open-standard, language - and platform-independent systems. The loosely-coupled features allow service providers to modify backend functions while maintaining the same interface to clients. Web Services are accessed through the HTTP/HTTPS protocols and utilize XML (eXtendible Markup Language) for data exchange. This in turn implies that Web Services are independent of platform, programming language, tool and network infrastructure. Services can be assembled and composed in such a way to foster the reuse of existing back-end infrastructure.

APPENDIX A

A password callback example that is utilized within the GRISSOM Web Service in order to securely authenticate usernames is presented. The provided code is in Java™ and uses the Apache Rampart WS-Security module and Apache Axis for Web Services implementation. Information on how to obtain and install Rampart and Axis modules can be found in http://ws.apache.org/rampart/ and http://ws.apache.org/axis2/ respectively.

Server Side

GRISSOM_WS_AuthHandler.java

```java
import org.apache.ws.security.WSPasswordCallback;
import javax.security.auth.callback.Callback;
import javax.security.auth.callback.CallbackHandler;
import javax.security.auth.callback.UnsupportedCallbackException;
import java.io.IOException;
public class GRISSOM_WS_AuthHandler implements CallbackHandler {
  public void handle(Callback[] callbacks) throws IOException,
      UnsupportedCallbackException {
    for (int i = 0; i < callbacks.length; i++) {

      //When the server side need to authenticate the user
      WSPasswordCallback pwcb = (WSPasswordCallback)callbacks[i];

      if(pwcb.getIdentifer().equals("a username") && pwcb.getPass
      word().equals("the password")) {
        //If authentication successful, simply return
        return;
      } else {
              throw new UnsupportedCallbackException(callbacks[i], "authenti-
cation has failed");
      }

    }
  }
}
```

WS-Security_policy.xml

```xml
<wsp:Policy wsu:Id="UsernameTokenOverHTTPS" xmlns:wsu="http://docs.oasis-open.
org/wss/2004/01/oasis-200401-wss-wssecurity-utility-1.0.xsd" xmlns:wsp="http://
schemas.xmlsoap.org/ws/2004/09/policy">
  <wsp:ExactlyOne>
    <wsp:All>
      <sp:TransportBinding xmlns:sp="http://schemas.xmlsoap.org/
        ws/2005/07/securitypolicy">
        <wsp:Policy>
          <sp:TransportToken>
            <wsp:Policy>
              <sp:HttpsToken RequireClientCertificate="false"/>
            </wsp:Policy>
          </sp:TransportToken>
            <sp:AlgorithmSuite>
              <wsp:Policy>
                <sp:Basic256/>
              </wsp:Policy>
            </sp:AlgorithmSuite>
              <sp:Layout>
                <wsp:Policy>
                  <sp:Lax/>
                </wsp:Policy>
              </sp:Layout>
              <sp:IncludeTimestamp/>
        </wsp:Policy>
      </sp:TransportBinding>
<sp:SignedSupportingTokens xmlns:sp="http://schemas.xmlsoap.org/
 ws/2005/07/securitypolicy">
  <wsp:Policy>
    <sp:UsernameToken sp:IncludeToken="http://schemas.xmlsoap.org/
      ws/2005/07/securitypolicy/IncludeToken/AlwaysToRecipient" />
  </wsp:Policy>
</sp:SignedSupportingTokens>
  <ramp:RampartConfig xmlns:ramp="http://ws.apache.org/rampart/policy">
  <ramp:passwordCallbackClass> GRISSOM_WS_AuthHandler</
  ramp:passwordCallbackClass>
  </ramp:RampartConfig>
  </wsp:All>
  </wsp:ExactlyOne>
</wsp:Policy>
```

Activation of the Rampart module through adding the following code into the Web Service's WSDL file:

```
<service>
  <module ref="rampart"/>
  <parameter name="GRISSOM_WS" locked="false"> SecureService</parameter>
  <operation name="add">
    <messageReceiver class="org.apache.axis2.rpc.receivers.RPCMessageReceiv-
er"/>
  </operation>
  <wsp:Policy wsu:Id="UsernameTokenOverHTTPS" xmlns:wsu="http://docs.
oasis-open.org/wss/2004/01/oasis-200401-wss-wssecurity-utility-1.0.xsd"
xmlns:wsp="http://schemas.xmlsoap.org/ws/2004/09/policy">
  .....
  </wsp:Policy>
</service>
```

Client Side

The following code has to be added to the client application in order to authenticate to the GRISSOM Web Service before consuming any services:

```
...
ConfigurationContext ctx = ConfigurationContextFactory.createConfigurationCont
extFromFileSystem("path/to/rampart/module", null);

  SecureServiceStub stub = new SecureServiceStub(ctx,"https://www.grissom.
gr:8080/axis2/services/GRISSOM_WS");

  ServiceClient sc = stub._getServiceClient();

  sc.engageModule("rampart");

  Options options = sc.getOptions();
  options.setUserName("the username");
  options.setPassword("the password");
...
```

APPENDIX B

Apendix B contains PHP sample code for generating user certificates by using OpenSSL (http://www.openssl.org/).

```
//path were each client certificate will be generated
$path = "/etc/ssl/client/".$username;
//assume we have our certification authority certificates in /etc/ssl
$cert = "/etc/ssl/";
//create the folder if it does not exist
if(!file_exists($path)) {
        mkdir($path, '0777');
}
//change permission to writeable
exec('chmod 777 '.$path);
//copy certification authority certificate temporarily to user's path
exec('cp '.$cert.'ca.key '.$path.'/ca.key');
exec('cp '.$cert.'ca.crt '.$path.'/ca.crt');
exec('chmod 777 '.$cert.'ca.crt');
exec('chmod 777 '.$cert.'ca.key');
//generate key
exec('openssl genrsa -out '.$path.'/'.$_POST['lastname'].'.key 1024');
exec('openssl req -new -key '.$path.'/'.$last.'.key -out
'.$path.'/'.$last.'.csr -subj \'/C='.$country.'/ST='.$state.'/L='.$state.'/
CN='.$first.' '.$last.'/emailAddress='.$email.'/challengePassword='.$passwo
rd.'\'');
//sign certificate
exec('openssl x509 -req -days 365 -CA '.$path.'/ca.crt -CAkey '.$path.'/ca.key
-CAcreateserial -in '.$path.'/'.$last.'.csr -out '.$path.'/'.$last.'.crt');
//export certificate
exec('openssl pkcs12 -export -clcerts -in '.$path.'/'.$last.'.crt -in-
key '.$path.'/'.$last.'.key -out '.$path.'/'.$last.'.p12 -password
pass:'.$password.'');
```

Chapter 10
Health 2.0 and Medicine 2.0:
Safety, Ownership and Privacy Issues

Anastasius Moumtzoglou
P&A Kyriakou Children's Hospital, Greece

ABSTRACT

The collaborative nature of Medicine 2.0/Health 2.0 and its emphasis on personalized health care clearly outlines it with respect to e-health and Web 2.0. The Semantic Web uses the notion that the meaning of a concept relates to other concepts. Therefore, it amplifies many of the existing challenges, but also offers new opportunities for the quality problems of Web 2.0 and enhances the potential to translate information into knowledge. Perhaps the most exciting expectation is that people will use the semantic web to search for healthcare providers of the highest quality, using services that take into account their own preferences and employ decentralized data from different sources. On the other hand, the Semantic Web magnifies privacy and may raise concerns about disintermediation between patients and health professionals and over reliance on virtual interactions. Therefore, the perspective of the chapter is to consider the key debates that occur in the literature with respect to the terms Medicine 2.0 and Health 2.0 acknowledging that any authentic solution to health problems has to originate from patient-centered care.

INTRODUCTION

The importance of healthcare information and communications technology (ICT) has grown in an exponential manner over the last 15 years (Institute of Medicine, 2001). Moreover, national strategies with respect to health information infrastructures are emerging across different parts of the world (National Committee on Vital and Health Statistics, 2001; Office of Health and the Information Highway, 1999; Australian Health Information Council, 2004; Department of Health and Children, 2005). Their vision is to improve the safety, quality and effectiveness of patient care by supporting clinical practice, resource management, research and training through the availability of relevant evidence and information. In addition, these strategies ensure interoperability

DOI: 10.4018/978-1-61692-895-7.ch010

and data protection, and incorporate a commitment to promote consumer empowerment and patient self-care through the provision of electronic information and/or telemedicine facilities.

However, e-health definitions vary from the speculative and diffuse to the most detailed. Most definitions conceptualize e-health as a wide range of medical informatics applications, which allow the management and distribution of health care. They include the dissemination of health-related information, storage and exchange of clinical data, inter-professional communication, computer-based support, patient-provider interaction, education, health service management, health communities and telemedicine. They also vary with respect to the targeted functions, stakeholders, contexts and theoretical issues. Most of them incorporate a wide range of specified medical informatics applications or terms that are more general. Nevertheless, the majority emphasizes the communicative functions of e-health and specifies the use of networked digital technologies, especially the Internet, thus differentiating e-health from the field of medical informatics. Finally, some definitions explicitly target health professionals or patients while most of them involve applications for all stakeholder groups. In terms of the functional capacity, most definitions conceptualize e-health as a broad range of medical informatics applications, which facilitate the organization and delivery of health care. In terms of the stakeholders, many definitions emphasize applications for providers--particularly those stressing exchange of clinical and administrative data. Several definitions emphasize the changing educational context of health care; particularly patient empowerment, and point to the capacity of e-health to facilitate shared decision-making. Overall, we might divide e-health into four domains:

- public health policy and prevention
- information service for citizens
- integrated patient care and patient health records
- telecare and independent-living services

We might also relate it to electronic communication as most definitions associate it with the use of networked digital information and communications technologies, especially the Internet, differentiating e-health from its parent domain of medical informatics. One component of electronic communication is when patients use new technologies to try out information about their health and health care options (Pagliari et al., 2005). The potential of the Internet to store large volumes of information provides an unprecedented opportunity to provide high-quality, interactive evidence-based information. Interactive components permit the provision of personalized information to users and provide decision, peer, or behavior modification support.

Health information and interactive components constitute an interactive health communication application (IHCA). Initially, IHCAs were developed on non-Web-based platforms such as CD-ROM (Murray et al., 2005). Lately, the relative prominence has moved toward Internet interventions (Ritterband et al., 2003), including accuracy, completeness, readability, disclosure, and references (Eysenbach et al., 2002). However, we know little about the user perspective on health websites but we do know that patients bring forth different criteria for the value of traditional, non-Web-based information materials (Coulter et al., 1998). Overall, patients are likely to use different criteria to assess the quality of health websites. Although we have made steps developing criteria to evaluate more interactive online health behavior modification and disease management programs (Evers et al., 2005), these also neglect the user perspective. Thus, the perspective of the chapter is to assess, in a patient-centered discourse, the key debates that exist in the literature with respect to the terms Medicine 2.0 and Health 2.0.

BACKGROUND

The term Web 2.0 was first used in front of a wide audience by Eric Knorr, executive editor of InfoWorld, in the December 2003 special issue of the business IT magazine CIO, with the title 'Fast Forward 2010 - The Fate of IT', in his article '2004 - The Year of Web Services'. However, the concept of Web 2.0 began with a conference brainstorming session between O'Reilly and MediaLive International and became popular following the O'Reilly Media Web 2.0 conference in 2004. O'Reilly defined Web 2.0 by a series of case examples, and visualized Web 2.0 as a set of principles and practices that put together a solar system of sites, at a varying distance from the core, which illustrate some or all of the following principles (O'Reilly, 2005):

- the Web as platform
- harnessing collective intelligence
- data is the next Intel inside
- end of the software release cycle
- lightweight programming models
- software above the level of a single device
- rich user experiences

Web 2.0 refers to a perceived second generation of web development and design that facilitates communication, reliable information sharing, interoperability, and collaboration on the World Wide Web. The term Web 2.0 refers to new ways of using the Internet as a platform for interactive applications. The main difference from the original World Wide Web is greater user involvement in developing and managing content, which changes information nature and value. Therefore, a distinguishing feature of Web 2.0 is the concept of online social networking, which emphasizes the creation of value through mass user participation. Constant development, enrichment, and evolution because of user interaction (the alleged perpetual beta) characterize these technologies. Users assist with their development and are part of the collec-

tive intelligence, which is harnessed to make the services better and more responsive.

Conn (2007) proposed that the first three of these principles are essential to health care. 'The web as platform' principle requires that the software of a Web 2.0 company has to be Web-based, and provide a structured service so that the more people use it, the better it becomes; O'Reilly described it as 'the architecture of participation'. 'Harnessing collective intelligence' is the second key principle, which is also referred to as 'the wisdom of crowds'. Conn's interpretation of this principle is that Web 2.0 developers must make powerful applications with user participation designed into the systems in order to benefit of this wisdom. That way, participation becomes an integral part of making the underlying database more valuable. Doherty (2008) considers the principle of harnessing collective intelligence, through the use of Web 2.0 technologies by health consumers. He explores a Web 2.0 pedagogical model that would connect medical, health science students, and health consumers, in order to improve student education through collaborative learning opportunities and convenient access to various sources of information and expertise. 'Data is the next Intel inside' highlights that specialized data enhanced through the service provider analysis and service users contributions become the primary asset of a Web 2.0 company. Overall, we might distinguish five key aspects, which emerge from Web 2.0 in health, health care, and medicine. These aspects include (Eysenbach, 2008):

- social networking
- participation
- apomediation
- collaboration
- openness

However, there are difficulties in the application of Web 2.0 principles to health and medicine. Like many important concepts, Web 2.0 does not have a definite boundary, but rather, a gravitational centre. Critics have claimed that its definition is too amorphous (McFredries, 2006) and have attempted to narrow it (O'Reilly, 2006). At the same time, other authors argue that Web 2.0 does not actually exist but merely uses 'Web 1.0' technologies and concepts. Overall, researchers view Web 2.0 as incorporating search tools and Podcasts (Giustini, 2006; Sandars & Schroter, 2007), which many leading websites encompass (Meattle, 2007); Web 2.0 and the Internet might be synonymous. Notwithstanding this skepticism, the use of Web 2.0 tools for health continues to grow. Therefore, the term Medicine 2.0, which opposes the traditional structure in health care, has entered standard nomenclature. It implies that the healthcare systems need to proceed from hospital-based treatment to health promotion and patient empowerment. However, interactive health communication applications (IHCAs) overlap significantly with components of Medicine 2.0. There are elements, like health and medical education, which remain common for e-health and Medicine 2.0. In addition, the academic literature does not consider the emphasis on personalized health care a salient matter. These ambiguities imply that Medicine 2.0 is not an independent research field. However, we argue that Medicine 2.0 has certain characteristics that permit analysis different from e-health. These characteristics include its collaborative nature and its emphasis on personalized health care.

The terms Medicine 2.0 and Health 2.0 are highly similar and subsume five main salient areas:

- the participants involved (doctors, patients, etc)
- its impact on both traditional and collaborative practices in medicine
- its ability to provide personalized health care
- its ability to promote continuing medical education
- its associated method- and tool-related issues, such as possible inaccuracy in end-user-generated content

Overall, both terms refer to a number of related concepts, which include telemedicine, electronic medical records, and the use of the Internet by patients themselves. A key concept is that patients should have a greater understanding and power into information generated about them, while traditional models of medicine assume that the physician is responsible for the patient record, on either paper or a proprietary computer system. Physicians are the gatekeepers of this information. This model operates reasonably well in acute care and general practice, where information about blood results would be of little sense to a layperson. However, in complex chronic diseases, and psychiatric disorders, patients are at risk of not well-coordinated care. Collected data might contain the opinions of healthcare professionals and is not shared with the patient in a variety of diverse places. Medical ethics increasingly consider such actions as medical paternalism. In response to the fragmented definitions for Health 2.0, Klepper and Sarasohn-Kahn(2008) attempted to develop an image of its working parts, that is, the kind of information it might receive and generate, which users would be and what impacts might be. Their vision tries to reveal the way innovators might aggregate and reformulate data sets from disparate resources creating new market value for purchasers, clinicians and patients.

It is worthwhile mentioning that we ignore the term Web 2.0 in the scholarly debate. We usually refer to 'apomediation', a new socio-technological term, we coined to avoid the term Web 2.0 (Eysenbach, 2007; Eysenbach, 2008). Apomediation (the Latin apo- means separate, detached, and away from) characterizes the 'third way' for users to identify reliable information and services. Other ways include the use of intermediaries, for example, health professionals giving 'relevant' information to a patient, and disintermediation, which refers to bypassing 'middlemen'. Apomediation, which is prevalent in Web 2.0, is an alternative information seeking strategy. People rely less on traditional experts and authorities as gatekeepers and receive 'guidance' from apomediaries, which include (Eysenach, 2007; Eysenbach, 2008):

- consumer ratings
- technologies like PICS or MedPICS labels and its RDF successors
- collaborative filtering and recommender systems
- social networking sites
- social bookmarking
- blogs
- wikis
- communication tools
- folksonomies

An intermediary stands in between the consumer and information. Therefore, it is different with respect to an apomediary. As a result, the reliability and quality of the intermediary conclusively determines the credibility and quality of consumers' information. Apomediation means that there are agents (people, tools) who 'stand by' to guide a consumer to high quality information and services.

While these distinctions are not absolute and combinations of both practices are possible (i.e. people moving back and forth between apomediation and intermediation models), we have hypothesized that they affect how people assess credibility (Eysenbach, 2008). In the health context, the traditional role of the intermediary is to guide consumers to relevant and credible information. Thus, the main problem of bypassing the intermediary is that consumers may 'get lost' in the vast amount of irrelevant information. Apomediation theory argues that apomediaries can support users navigate through the invasion of information.

Types of Web 2.0 Technology in Health Care

Social networking is crucial to various Web 2.0 and Medicine 2.0 applications and involves the explicit

modeling of connections between people. Moreover, it is a powerful tool, which engages users to enter, update, and manage personal information. However, the evolving technology infrastructure of Web 2.0 includes server-software; content-syndication; messaging-protocols; standards-oriented browsers with plugins and extensions; various client-applications. Web 2.0 is mostly about the benefits of free Internet software (Giustini, 2006). Its essential elements include Really Simple Syndication (RSS), which disseminates cognizance of additional information; blogs to discuss recent trends; wikis to share knowledge; and podcasts to obtain information available 'on the move' (Kamel Boulos, 2006; McLean et al., 2007).

RSS is a family of web feed formats used to communicate updated works in a standardized format (Libby, 1999). An RSS document includes the text, and metadata, such as publishing dates, and authorship. It benefits publishers by letting them syndicate content automatically, and readers with timely updates from favored websites or aggregate feeds from multiple sites into a single spot. Software called an 'RSS reader', 'feed reader' or 'aggregator' can read RSS feeds. A standardized XML file format, used for the distribution of information, allows readability from many different programs. The user subscribes to a feed by entering into the reader the feed's URL or by clicking an RSS icon in a browser. As a result, the RSS reader checks the user's subscribed feeds regularly, and downloads any updates, providing an interface, which monitors and reads the feeds. Several attempts at web syndication, which did not gain widespread popularity, preceded the RSS formats. RDF Site Summary was the first version of RSS that Guha created at Netscape in March 1999 for use on the My.Netscape.Com portal. This was Netscape's contribution in RSS development for eight years. The RSS-DEV Working Group and Winer emerged to fill the gap. In September 2002, Winer released a radical, new version of the format RSS 2.0 that honored with the title Really Simple Syndication. However, Winer and the RSS-DEV

Working Group had Netscape's involvement, and they could not make a valid declaration on the RSS name or structure. This fueled an ongoing debate in the syndication development community as to the actual publisher of RSS. In December 2005, the Microsoft Internet Explorer and Outlook teams announced the adoption of the feed icon while in January 2006, Rogers Cadenhead introduced the RSS Advisory Board without Dave Winer's participation. He desired to maintain the development of the RSS structure and resolve ambiguities. In June 2007, the board revised their specification in order to verify that namespaces may increase key elements with namespace attributes.

Many professional and educational services in health care adopt wikis, blogs and podcasts because of their enjoyment of use, rapidity of deployment, and the opportunity for information sharing and ease of collaboration. Group collaboration lies behind the notion of wikis, which are dynamic web pages, whose visitors can edit, update or change their content. Wikis allow for asynchronous group socialization, communication and collaboration, and constitute an archiving, brainstorming, and collaboration tool. We can think of a health community wiki as a collaborative website authored by a group of patients or healthcare professionals.

Blog is an abbreviation of 'Web Log', which provides a resource rich multimedia environment without replacing personal homepages and bulletin boards. Blogs have become popular manifestations of Web 2.0 because they bypass the need for authors to program in hypertext markup language (HTML). Therefore, they allow easy self-publishing of information on any topic, mainly reflecting the author's personal thoughts. Moreover, blogs can compensate for search engine inadequacies in publication and can be useful for those who wish to understand the progress of an issue quickly. Overall, it is straightforward to set up your own blog, and search for blogs using search engines. Conversations can be traced using trackback software (Kamel Boulos & Wheeler,

2007) while one can use blogrolls (lists of recommended sites) to find other relevant blogs (a way similar to following hypertext links from trusted websites). Blogs may be tracked with RSS (Really Simple Syndication, or Rich Site Summary, or RDF Site Summary), which is a Web 2.0 syntax for syndicating content. Information delivery and personal expression is not limited to written text. There are many blogs with health focus. Patients share their own health and disease experiences (eg, 'my Breast Cancer blog' - cancerspot.org), and health professionals offer advice to patients (eg, Clinical Cases and Images - casesblog.blogspot. com). There also are blogs devoted to health informatics as well as aggregations of leading health and medical informatics blogs.

Podcasting, a word formed by joining 'broadcasting' and 'iPod' (Apple Computer's MP3 player), implies that we can distribute podcasts, listened to on almost any device, via RSS feed. Podcasts are repositories of audio and video files, which subscribers receive without their intervention, providing the potential for mobile-learning experiences. The syndication aspect of delivery is what differentiates podcasts from other files while it is relatively easy to perform all activities within a health professions' learning environment. Their implementation in health care includes audio broadcasts by patients or health professionals on health related topics.

The underlying ranges of technologies most of these applications work through cover (Murray, 2008):

- AJAX (Asynchronous JavaScript and XML) programming
- Cascading Style Sheets (CSS)
- folksonomies
- syndication
- user-generated content
- mashups

Paradoxically, some of the previous applications' disadvantages apply to their openness and ease of use. The process of collaboration leads to a Darwinian paradigm of survival of the fittest content within a Web page. Moreover, the veracity of these resources requires careful monitoring, moderation, and operation in a closed and secure digital world. Therefore, we need to build the pedagogical evidence base about the different aspects of these tools in the education of healthcare professionals. Wikis, blogs, podcasts, and vodcasts carry the capacity of complementing, improving, and adding new collaborative dimensions to current continuing professional development and education. The main reason is that they offer information sharing, collaboration features, and provide users the added benefit of reducing the technical expertise required to use these features. They allow users to perform collaborative tasks themselves with few delivery obstacles (Abram, 2007), and concentrate on the learning task. Therefore, such technology is a 'transparent technology' (Rosser et al., 2007).

Issues, Controversies, Problems

The use of Web 2.0 in healthcare has raised criticism of doctors' limitations to use Google as a diagnostic tool. Tang & Ng (2006) argue that Google is more effective only for conditions with unique symptoms and signs we can easily use as a search term. Moreover, concerns exist about the effects of patients obtaining information online (Ojalvo, 1996) and the quality of user-generated content leading to misinformation (The Economist, 2007). Finally, partly due to inadequate definition, and the novelty of the endeavor, little empirical evidence exists about the use of Web 2.0. However, a research, which examined physician practice, suggested that 245,000 physicians in the U.S are using Web 2.0, beyond the stage of the early adopter, for their practice (Manhattan Research, 2007). Hughes (2008) argues there are four major issues in the literature on Health/Medicine 2.0. These include the lack of clear definitions; issues around the loss of control over information;

safety and the danger of inaccurate information; and issues of ownership and privacy. The first main field of contention is the lack of agreement on the Web 2.0 concept (Skiba et al., 2006), which has dribbled into the Medicine 2.0 and Health 2.0 domains (Versel, 2008). The situation is further complicated by authors, who speculate that some Web 2.0 tools will become redundant (Giustini, 2007). However, we assume that patients will use Medicine 2.0 tools, even though some researchers have argued that Medicine 2.0 and Health 2.0 may have a different bearing for different audiences (Eysenbach, 2008). Hughes (2008) supports that the terms currently have a high degree of intersection and that both terms imply something more complex than the simple application Web 2.0 to a health care context. The following main argument deals with doctor-patient collaboration, encompassing doctors' resistance to use Medicine 2.0. Their concerns arise from the undesirable behavior of patients, which includes not consulting a physician, consulting a physician too late or coming to the wrong conclusion about their disease management even if accurate information is available. Ferguson (2007) calls these doctors 'e-patient resistant clinicians' and suggests a sense of loss of control, paternalism, or lack of training driving their behaviors. However, the issue is prominent in Medicine 2.0, where we recognize amplifying effects to this behavior, such as lack of training for doctors (Sandars & Schroter, 2007) or the difficulty of advising patients on use of Medicine 2.0 tools (Goh, 2006).

Overall, doctors need to accept the emergence of Medicine 2.0 but their current training is not sufficient to do so (Hughes, 2008). Forty or fifty years ago, there was a tendency to believe that we could objectively describe the traits, which define 'professions', identifying their members' specialist skills and an ethic of compassion and service to the community. Later social scientists examined carefully the professions; as a result, they queried their altruism and emphasized their ability to define their own role (Freidson, 1970).

Nowadays, patients replace the traditional model whereby the doctor took the decision with the informed or shared decision-taking model. In that model, we introduce the understanding, values and preferences of the patient into the equation and he/she shares in, or takes, the decision. These changes define a new medical professionalism. Doctors lose control, patients and other healthcare workers gain it, and the potential for both conflict and collaboration is greater. Doctors' privileged access to people's bodies, privileged access to information about them, and control over dangerous drugs, instruments, or other materials are diminishing, and the corresponding rights and responsibilities of patients are being emphasized.

Patient-centered care introduces mutual respect and partnership for quality patient care, rather than an accusation. A patient-centered environment of care is safe, clean, safeguards patient privacy (Frampton et al., 2008) but also requires specific competencies. Relevant competencies for doctors' patient-centered professionalism include (Askham, & Chisholm, 2006):

- guidance of patients to appropriate sources of information on health and healthcare
- effective education on health protection and disease prevention
- clear and unambiguous statement of information on risk
- patients' role preferences
- support for self-care and self-management of chronic conditions

The third main consideration is the possibility of misinformation although studies preceding the rapid growth in Medicine 2.0 have found little support for this issue (Crocco et al., 2002). Esquivel (2006) argues that in an Internet-based cancer support group, most information was accurate and the moderators corrected most false or misleading statements quickly. Eysenbach (2008), examining the effect of information accuracy and reliability in relation to e-health, notes that patients will tend to use both experts and Medicine 2.0 information to make their health decisions, as apomediaries work as filtering processes for distributed information, further reducing information risk (Eysenbach, 2008). However, many practitioners and researchers remain to be convinced, despite this preliminary evidence of low risk (Giustini, 2006; Tang & Ng, 2006).

The fourth and final argument relates to privacy and ownership issues (Karkalis & Koutsouris, 2006; Kamel Boulos & Burden, 2007). This applies not only to patients but also to doctors who may use social networking sites (Sandars et al., 2008) and may include patient groups driving the research agenda. Therefore, we should consider models of identity management and authorization schemes in the context of Medicine 2.0 research. This tends to accentuate e-health trends (Ferguson, 2007), and highlights the patient groups who claim ownership over the input of specific sites.

Solutions and Recommendations

Whereas web 1.0 and 2.0 were nascent technologies, web 3.0 promises to be a sophisticated web, which will produce better pathways for information retrieval and create a greater role for cognitive processing of information (Giustini, 2007). We also call it semantic web, due to a term coined by Sir Tim Berners-Lee in his landmark study in Scientific American (Berners-Lee et al., 2001). Berners-Lee stresses that we need semantic interpretation to demonstrate the hidden meaning of web documents. He argues that access to an extensive network of data should help to answer humanity's most difficult problems. A semantic net is a knowledge representation system based on Artificial Intelligence, which Quillian introduced earlier in the late-60s. Semantic nets use the relationship of a concept to other concepts in order to derive a meaning. Therefore, they require that individuals and organizations produce machine-processable documents for the software to aggregate this knowledge and draw inferences.

A fundamental feature of web 3.0 is that it uses data about data, so called metadata, and it enables computers to talk to each other. Until 1999, we used many different ways to attach metadata to web documents. However, the World Wide Web Consortium (W3C) unified the different approaches forming the Resource Description Framework (RDF), the current standard to transfer metadata (Swick & Brickley, 2000; Klyne & Carroll, 2003; Lassila & Swick, 1999). We can express RDF in extensible Markup Language (XML) syntax (Lassila & Swick, 1999), which is an XML file. The difference between XML and RDF is that while XML-Schemas tell computers how something looks like, RDF explains to a machine what it is, providing the meaning of the concepts and their relationships. If the perspective of the semantic web becomes a reality, it will have a profound impact on the way people obtain information and interact with the web. Specifically, it will improve the ability of search engines to disseminate accurate and related searches on the web. A better 'understanding' of the background leads to automatic translations and ranked results not only by relevance, but also by quality. In addition to such search engines, new software agents will be able to autonomously conduct searches, interpret and aggregate knowledge published by independent sources, and to a certain extent may make independent 'reasoning'.

While it is difficult to predict whether and when the Semantic Web will work according to its proponents' prediction, the challenges and opportunities of the Semantic Web for health and healthcare line up around three major issues (Eysenbach, 2003):

- increased access to information and knowledge
- quality issues
- accessibility issues

Accessibility and quality issues of health information on the Web 2.0 were also hot topics in the medical literature. Empirical studies suggest that it is difficult for consumers to distinguish health information of high quality amongst the stream of information (Eysenbach et al., 2002). The Semantic Web amplifies many of the existing challenges, but also offers new opportunities for the quality problems of Web 2.0 because we can classify data in a machine processable format. Web 2.0 provides a multitude of information but does not improve knowledge. The Semantic Web enhances the potential to translate information into knowledge, and empowers patients with information that meets their individual information needs. Its proponents argue that individuals' starting point will be a web-based personal health record while they will gather information using intelligent agents (Nikolopoulos, 2008). For example, if a journal publishes original research results about a disease, the agent will automatically generate a link to that article, if the web-based health record contains the same diagnosis. Moreover, the Semantic Web allows queries for which there is not yet an answer. For example, it might reveal an effective treatment for a disease. One might also anticipate that medical journals will publish 'semantic nets' for each article.

Perhaps the most exciting prospect is that people will use their own preferences and decentralized data from different sources to rank healthcare providers. The Semantic Web leaves nothing to implication, further increasing the transparency for patients. In the future, patients could publish their experiences with respect to the provision of health care on their homepages and rate providers, and treatments. They could also feed them, in anonymized form, into the Semantic Web, so that agents can aggregate this information, which could help patients to make informed choices on their health and healthcare.

On the other hand, the Semantic Web magnifies privacy concerns as the publication of consumers' experiential information in a machine-processable format, increases the option to gather, link, and interpret information but also increases the possibility of its misuse. Even if we assume that data in health records remains protected, the substantial amount of publicly available knowledge on the web may be sufficient for a third party to compile a health profile of an individual. Finally, the Semantic Web raises concerns about disintermediation between patients and health professionals and over reliance on virtual interactions (Jadad, 1999).

However, the Semantic Web can represent trust relationships among individuals and organizations, a prerequisite for successful knowledge management on the web. The basic concept is that we should base web quality management on a collaborative design, which includes health professionals and consumers. If they use metadata, search engines will analyze trust relationships and rate their results according to quality and trust criteria of the individual user. Yet, one of the most challenging questions is to develop algorithms that enable intelligent agents to calculate a `trust score'. The components of trust might be user preferences and prior experiences with individuals or organizations, and reputation. One hypothesis is to use the web diversity for calculating trust scores, taking into account that the software will investigate and analyze the complex relationship between trustors and trustees online.

'Access' is a remarkably broad term, which refers to physical accesses but also the findability or readability of information. An access barrier can be anything that prevents the user's access, findability, make use of, or even comprehension of the meaning of a document on the web. Therefore, we may distinguish accessibility into the following levels (Eysenbach, 2003):

- physical accessibility
- findability
- readability, comprehensibility
- design and usability

It is unlikely that the Semantic Web will increase physical accessibility to the Internet. However, the conditions of access and qualitative factors affecting access, like convenience, and privacy will play an increasingly prominent role. Findability, as a barrier, means that people cannot find the relevant information but the Semantic Web can improve information access at this level if we enrich information with machine-processable statements. One of the problems of readability is that we enter and manage health information on the web using textual representation, which we cannot tailor for illiteracy or different target audiences (Eysenbach, 2002). The Semantic Web may help people with different educational or sociocultural background if we represent the knowledge about how to take a drug or its side effects. Design and the usability is a potential barrier of accessibility, which includes accessibility for particular user groups. Finally, the Semantic Web has the potential to deliver access to disabled users because it may provide specific information for the user's needs and benefit from the metadata. It also allows annotators to give additional information to improve accessibility of information.

FUTURE RESEARCH DIRECTIONS

The benefits of the Semantic Web include knowledge representation, knowledge integration, and knowledge discovery. The Semantic Web languages enable knowledge representation by means of a knowledge base, which consists of ontology and individuals. In order to understand why we need the semantic web in healthcare, we have to observe shifts of the online habits of doctors to searching, due to numerous reams of unorganized information in web 2.0. Consequently, medical librarians argue that it is necessary to build better mechanisms for information retrieval (Robu et al., 2006; Lorence & Spink, 2004). Despite its constant accessibility, Google's search results are indicative of an approaching mess with information overload leading doctors back to PubMed, Clinical Evidence, and the Cochrane Library. However, in a period of greater personalization, the latest information technologies will treat patients' health problems according to their genetic profiles.

On the other hand, the Semantic Web magnifies privacy concerns, promotes concerns about disintermediation, and strengthens patient-centered care. Partnership between informed and respected patients and their families, and a coordinated healthcare team (The Institute for Alternative Futures, 2004) are necessary. However, we know comparatively little about doctors and patients partnership in knowledge, and the effects of patient knowledge. A good deal of research evidence is available about what patients want. However, we still need to know more about the extent of involvement they desire differing kinds of patient in differing situations. We also need to ask to what degree the doctors take into account the views of patients, and whether they serve their best interests. Furthermore, we have to ask the extent of patients' involvement in setting or monitoring their best interests, and draw up codes of practice for doctors and appraise them or review their capability to practise against the codes. We need to know more about what kind of regulation or monitoring would make patients trust doctors, develop, and explore new educational initiatives to train healthcare professionals about the core competencies required for supporting patient-centeredness. We have to establish clear assessment criteria, validity, and reliability of methods for assessing doctors' relevant competences, and develop and implement methods for obtaining and using standardized patient feedback. We should pay greater attention to the role models, which doctors encounter in their training because the process we provide health care undermines the patient's role.

Clinicians must learn about the principles and practice of developing health literacy, enabling shared decision-making, and supporting self-care. In order to do this effectively they must be exceptional listeners, encourage patients to tell them about their beliefs and preferences, show compassion and respect for patients' dignity and autonomy, willingness to involve patients in decisions and respect their preferences, and welcome feedback from patients. They must learn how to obtain appropriate written information for patients, and they must develop attitudes of empathy and openness. They also need to guide their patients to reliable information sources and understand what outcomes are of importance to them. Finally, they have to ask them about the role they prefer to play in decisions about their treatment. This dimension necessitates advances in information and social technologies that support patients and providers, as well as the cultural shifts.

CONCLUSION

Medicine 2.0 describes the participants involved; the impact on novel collaborations and practice; the ability to provide personalized health care; the use in medical education; its associated methods and tools. However, there are four major tensions between stakeholders, which include the scope, definition, and existence of the field, the patient-doctor relationship, the methods and tools, which relate to information accuracy, ownership and privacy. The Semantic Web, a proposed solution to accessibility and quality of information issues, makes substantial reuse of existing ontologies but also presents substantial research challenges. Therefore, we need engineering methods to ensure that the structures conform to sound design requirements, and empirical analysis to understand and predict the resulting behaviors.

REFERENCES

Abram, S. (2007). Earning the right to give advice. *SirsiDynix One Source, 3,* Retrieved July 25, 2009, from http://www.imakenews.com/sirsi/e_article000805034.cfm?x=b9vt0Kw,b2rpPgSw.

Askham, J., & Chisholm, A. (2006). *Patient-Centred Medical Professionalism: Towards an agenda for research and action.* London: Picker Institute Europe.

Australian Health Information Council. (2004). *Strategic Plan for Information Management and Information and Communication Technology (IM&ICT) in Health.* Canberra, Australia.

Berners-Lee, T., Hendler, J., & Lassila, O. (2001). The semantic web. a new form of web content that is meaningful to computers will unleash a revolution of new possibilities. [from http://www.scientificamerican.com/article.cfm?id=the-semantic-web.]. *Scientific American, 284*(5), 28–37. Retrieved July 25, 2009.

Conn, J. (2007). *Health 2.0: The next generation of Web enterprises.* Retrieved July 25, 2009, from http://www.modernhealthcare.com/apps/pbcs.dll/article?AID=/20071211/FREE/312110003/1029/FREE.

Coulter, A., Entwistle, V., & Gilbert, D. (1998). *Informing Patients. An Assessment of the Quality of Patient Information Materials.* London: King's Fund Publishing.

Crocco, A. G., Villasis-Keever, M., & Jadad, A. R. (2002). Analysis of cases of harm associated with use of health information on the internet. *Journal of the American Medical Association, 287*(21), 2869–2871. doi:10.1001/jama.287.21.2869

Department of Health and Children. (2004). *Health Information: A National Strategy.* Dublin, Retrieved July 25, 2009, from http://www.dohc.ie/publications/pdf/nhis.pdf?direct=1.

Doherty, I. (2008). Web 2-0 - A Movement Within The Health Community. *Health Care and Informatics Review Online, 12*(2), 49–57.

Esquivel, A., Meric-Bernstam, F., & Bernstam, E. V. (2006). Accuracy and self correction of information received from an internet breast cancer list: content analysis. *British Medical Journal, 332*(7547), 939–942. doi:10.1136/bmj.38753.524201.7C

Eysenbach, G. (2003). The Semantic Web and healthcare consumers: a new challenge and opportunity on the horizon? *International Journal of Healthcare Technology and Management, 5(3/4/5),* 194-212.

Eysenbach, G. (2007). From intermediation to disintermediation and apomediation: new models for consumers to access and assess the credibility of health information in the age of Web2.0. *Studies in Health Technology and Informatics, 129,* 162–166.

Eysenbach, G. (2008). Medicine 2.0: Social networking, collaboration, participation, apomediation, and openness. *Journal of Medical Internet Research, 10*(3), e22. doi:10.2196/jmir.1030

Eysenbach, G. (2008). Credibility of health information and digital media: new perspectives and implications for youth. In Metzger, M. J., & Flanagin, A. J. (Eds.), *Digital Media, Youth, and Credibility. The John D and Catherine T MacArthur Foundation Series on Digital Media and Learning.* Cambridge, MA: MIT Press.

Eysenbach, G., Powell, J., Kuss, O., & Sa, E. R. (2002). Empirical studies assessing the quality of health information for consumers on the world wide web: a systematic review. *Journal of the American Medical Association, 287,* 2691–2700. doi:10.1001/jama.287.20.2691

Ferguson, T. (2007). *ePatients: How they can help us heal health care.* E-patients net. Retrieved July 25, 2009, from http://www.e-patients.net/e-Patients_White_Paper.pdf.

Frampton, S., Guastello, S., Brady, C., Hale, M., Horowitz, S., Bennett Smith, S., & Stone, S. (2008). *Patient-centered care improvement guide*. Camden, ME: Picker Institute, Inc.

Freidson, E. (1970). *The Profession of Medicine*. New York: Atherton Press.

Giustini, D. (2006). How Web 2.0 is changing medicine. *British Medical Journal, 333*, 1283–1284. doi:10.1136/bmj.39062.555405.80

Giustini, D. (2007). Web 3.0 and medicine. *British Medical Journal, 335*(7633), 1273–1274. doi:10.1136/bmj.39428.494236.BE

Goh, S. H. (2006). The internet as a health education tool: sieving the wheat from the chaff. *Singapore Medical Journal, 47*(1), 3–5.

Institute of Medicine. (2001). *Crossing the Quality Chasm: A New Health System for the 21st Century*. Washington, DC: National Academies Press.

Jadad, A. R. (1999). Promoting partnerships: challenges for the internet age. *BMJ (Clinical Research Ed.), 319*, 761–764.

Kamel Boulos, M. N., & Burden, D. (2007). Web GIS in practice V: 3-D interactive and real-time mapping in Second Life. *International Journal of Health Geographic's, 6*, Retrieved July 25, 2009, from http://www.pubmedcentral.nih.gov/articlerender.fcgi?artid=2216085.

Kamel Boulos, M. N., Maramba, I., & Wheeler, S. (2006). Wikis, blogs and podcasts: a new generation of Web-based tools for virtual collaborative clinical practice and education. *BMC Medical Education, 6*, 41. doi:10.1186/1472-6920-6-41

Kamel Boulos, M. N., & Wheeler, S. (2007). The emerging Web 2.0 social software: an enabling suite of sociable technologies in health and health care education. *Health Information and Libraries Journal, 24*, 2–23. doi:10.1111/j.1471-1842.2007.00701.x

Karkalis, G. I., & Koutsouris, D. D. (2006). *E-health and the Web 2.0*. The International Special Topic Conference on Information Technology in Biomedicine, October 26-28, Greece.

Klepper, B., & Sarasohn-Kahn, J. (2008). A Broad Vision of Health 2-0 - Reformulating Data for Transparency- Decision Support- and Revitalized Health Care Markets. *Health Care and Informatics Review Online, 12*(2), 45–48.

Klyne, G., & Carroll, J. J. (2003). *Resource Description Framework (RDF): concepts and abstract syntax*. The World Wide Web Consortium (W3C). Retrieved July 25, 2009, from http://www.w3.org/TR/2003/WD-rdf-concepts-20030123/.

Lassila, O., & Swick, R. R. (1999). *Resource Description Framework (RDF) model and Syntax specification*. The World Wide Web Consortium (W3C), Retrieved July 25, 2009, from http://www.w3.org/TR/REC-rdf-syntax/.

Libby, D. (1999). *RSS 0.91 Spec, revision 3*. Netscape Communications. Retrieved July 25, 2009, from http://web.archive.org/web/20001204093600/my.netscape.com/publish/formats/rss-spec-0.91.html.

Lorence, D. P., & Spink, A. (2004). Semantics and the medical web: a review of the barriers and breakthroughs in effective healthcare query. *Health Information and Libraries Journal, 21*, 109–116. doi:10.1111/j.1471-1842.2004.00491.x

Manhattan Research. LLC. (2007). *Physicians and Web 2.0: 5 Things You Should Know about the Evolving Online Landscape for Physicians*. Retrieved July 25, 2009, from http://www.manhattanresearch.com/TTPWhitePaper.aspx.

McFredries, P. (2006). Technically Speaking The Web, Take Two. *IEEE Spectrum Magazine, 43*(6), 68. doi:10.1109/MSPEC.2006.1638049

McLean, R., Richards, B., & Wardman, J. (2007). The effect of Web 2.0 on the future of medical practice and education: Darwikinian evolution or folksonomic revolution? *The Medical Journal of Australia, 187*, 174–177.

Murray, E., Burns, J., See, T. J., Lai, R., & Nazareth, I. (2005). Interactive Health Communication Applications for people with chronic disease. *Cochrane Database of Systematic Reviews, 4*, CD004274.

Murray, P. (2008). Web 2.0 and social technologies: what might they offer for the future of health informatics? *Health Care and Informatics Review Online, 12*(2), 5–16.

National Committee on Vital and Health Statistics. (2001). *Information for Health: A Strategy for Building the National Health Information Infrastructure*. Washington, DC: U.S. Department of Health and Human Services.

Nikolopoulos, K. (2008). *Healthcare and Emerging Rich Web Technologies – The WEB 2.0/Semantic Web Challenge and Opportunity*. OBBeC. Retrieved July 25, 2009, from http://www.obbec. com/specialreports/86-healthcare-it/1828-healthcare-and-emerging-rich-web-technologies-the-web-20semantic-web-challenge-and-opportunity.

O'Reilly, T. (2005). *What is Web 2.0. Design Patterns and Business Models for the Next Generation of Software*. O'Reilly Media, Retrieved July 25, 2009, from http://www.oreillynet.com/ pub/a/oreilly/tim/news/2005/09/30/what-is-web-20.html.

O'Reilly, T. (2006). *Web 2.0 compact definition: trying again*. O'Reilly radar, Retrieved July 25, 2009, from http://radar.oreilly.com/ archives/2006/12/web-20-compact-definition-tryi.html.

Office of Health and the Information Highway. (1999). *Canada Health Infoway: Paths to Better Health*. Ottawa: Health Canada.

Ojalvo, H. E. (1996). Online advice: Good medicine or cyber-quackery? *ACP Observer,* Retrieved July 25, 2009, from http://www.acponline.org/ journals/news/dec96/cybrquak.htm.

Pagliari, C., Sloan, D., Gregor, P., Sullivan, F., Detmer, D., & Kahan, J. (2005). What is eHealth (4): a scoping exercise to map the field. *Journal of Medical Internet Research, 7*(1), e9. doi:10.2196/ jmir.7.1.e9

Quillian, M. R. (1968). Semantic memories. In Minsky, M. M. (Ed.), *Semantic Information Processing* (pp. 216–270). Cambridge: MIT Press.

Ritterband, L., Gonder-Frederick, L. A., Cox, D. J., Clifton, A. D., West, R. W., & Borowitz, S. (2003). Internet interventions: In review, in use, and into the future. *Professional Psychology, Research and Practice, 34*(5), 527–534. doi:10.1037/0735-7028.34.5.527

Robu, I., Robu, V., & Thirion, B. (2006). An introduction to the semantic web for health sciences librarians. *Journal of the Medical Library Association, 94*, 198–205.

Rosser, J., Lynch, P., Cuddihy, L., Gentile, D., Klonsky, J., & Merrell, R. (2007). The impact of video games on training surgeons in the 21st century. *Archives of Surgery, 142*(2), 181–186. doi:10.1001/archsurg.142.2.181

Sandars, J., Homer, M., Pell, G., & Croker, T. (2008). Web 2.0 and social software: the medical student way of e-learning. *Medical Teacher, 14*, 1–5. doi:10.1080/01421590701798729

Sandars, J., & Schroter, S. (2007). Web 2.0 technologies for undergraduate and postgraduate medical education: an online survey. *Postgraduate Medical Journal, 83*(986), 759–762. doi:10.1136/ pgmj.2007.063123

Skiba, B., Tamas, A., & Robinson, K. (2006). *Web 2.0: hype or reality...and how will it play out? A strategic analysis*. Arma Partners. Retrieved July 25, 2009, from http://www.armapartners.com/files/admin/uploads/W17_F_1873_8699.pdf.

Swick, R. R., & Brickley, D. (2000). *PICS Rating Vocabularies in XML/RDF*, The World Wide Web Consortium (W3C), Retrieved July 25, 2009, from http://www.w3.org/TR/rdf-pics.

Tang, H., & Ng, J. (2006). Googling for a diagnosis-use of Google as a diagnostic aid: internet based study. *British Medical Journal, 333*, 1143–1145. doi:10.1136/bmj.39003.640567.AE

The Economist. (2007). Health 2.0: Technology and society: Is the outbreak of cancer videos, bulimia blogs and other forms of "user generated" medical information a healthy trend? *The Economist, Sept.*, 73-74.

The Institute for Alternative Futures. (2004). *Patient-Centered Care 2015: Scenarios, Vision, Goals & Next Steps*. Camden, ME: The Picker Institute.

Versel, N. (2008). Health 2.0. Will its promise be realized? *Managed Care Magazine, 17*(3), 49–52.

ADDITIONAL READING

Al-hakim, L. (Ed.). (2007). *Web Mobile-Based Applications for Healthcare Management*. Hershey, PA: IRM Press.

Dunbrack, L. (2008). *Describing the Health 2.0 Landscape in the United States*. Framingham, MA: IDC.

KEY TERMS AND DEFINITIONS

Apomediation: An information seeking strategy where people rely less on experts and authorities, and receive 'guidance' from networked collaborative filtering processes.

Health 2.0/Medicine 2.0: Participatory healthcare, which integrates patients and stakeholders while summarizing health information.

Intelligent Agents: Expert or knowledge-based systems embedded in computer-based information systems, which help users find information of interest.

Patient-Centered Care: Quality healthcare achieved through a partnership between a coordinated healthcare team, informed and respected patients and their families.

Semantic Web: An evolving extension of the World Wide Web, which defines and links web data, in a way that machine can use it.

Social Networking: The explicit modeling of online networks, which allow users share opinions, insights, experiences and perspectives.

Web 2.0: A number of technologies, which include user-generated web content, information and multimedia sharing, online collaboration and social networking.

Section 5
Security in Wireless and Mobile Healthcare Applications

Chapter 11
Securing and Prioritizing Health Information in TETRA Networks

Konstantinos Siassiakos
University of Piraeus, Greece

Athina Lazakidou
University of Peloponnese, Greece

ABSTRACT

Cost reduction pressures and the need for shortened in-patient stays are promoting the use of wireless patient monitoring systems in hospitals. Their contribution to better process management, superior flexibility and increased efficiency within hospitals is further underlining the appeal of wireless net-working options for patient monitoring systems. Wireless connectivity has encouraged an overall rise in productivity through improved workflow and data management. Wireless patient monitors have also supported enhanced flexibility within the hospital environment by enabling remote monitoring of patients. TETRA technology provides several ways of protecting the privacy and security of communication, such as authentication, air interface encryption and end-to-end encryption. The objective of this chapter is to study how simply can a healthcare professional collect physiological data from mobile and/or remote patients and how securely and reliably health information can be transferred from emergency places to hospitals through a TETRA network.

INTRODUCTION

Today's healthcare professionals need to be connected to the network always. Continuous connectivity is the watchword of these demanding users, who need to communicate over the network seamlessly and stay connected everywhere in emergency cases.

Telemedicine applications, including those based on wireless technologies, span the areas of emergency health care: telecardiology, teleradiology, telepathology, teledermatology, teleophthalmology, teleoncology, and telepsychiatry. In addition, health telematics applications, enabling the availability of prompt and expert medical care, have been exploited for the provision of healthcare services at understaffed areas, such as rural

DOI: 10.4018/978-1-61692-895-7.ch011

health centers, ambulance vehicles, ships, trains, and airplanes, as well as for home monitoring.

The primary problem with tiny, low power sensors is to establish and maintain wireless links in the presence of so many high power devices that radiate noise. This noise will change through out the day so that a continuously adapting routing technique is needed. Unfortunately, several challenges exist such as:

1. Deploying sensors to provide proper sensor coverage.
2. Balancing resource usage to maximize sensor lifetime.
3. Communicating messages reliably among the nodes (i.e. healthcare provider, patient, emergency vehicles) using multihop paths.
4. Prioritizing routing messages, e.g., emergency call vs. outgoing patients.
5. Authenticating data links as well as securing the data to ensure patience confidentiality.

BACKGROUND

High quality health care requires individuals to share sensitive personal information with their doctors and other healthcare professionals. This information is necessary to make the most accurate diagnoses and provide the best treatment. It may be shared with others, such as insurance companies, pharmacies, researchers, and employers, for many reasons. If patients are not confident that this information will be kept confidential, they will not be forthright and reveal accurate and complete information. If healthcare providers are not confident that the organization that is responsible for the healthcare record will keep it confidential, they will limit what patients add to the record. Either of these actions is likely to result in inferior healthcare. The privacy and security of personal health information has become a major public concern.

Safety is always a first priority, followed closely by concern for the environment. Effective communication during an emergency evacuation, shut-down or man-down alarm is a clear instance where the right wireless communications technology is required.

A wireless communications system is also a tool that will be used to help protect investments and personnel against criminal or even terrorist threat. However, today's criminals are tech-savvy, thus any system must be secure, against potential mis-use, if it was to fall into the wrong hands.

Requirements fall into six key areas: Flexibility & Scalability; Efficient Communications, Reliability and System Availability; Data Communications; User Environment & Interface; and Operations and Maintenance. So what is TETRA and how does it meet expectations in each of these vital areas?

The most common information security problem within the healthcare systems is the access of the employees (inside threat). Specifically people who work in a hospital have the ability to view protected health information (PHI) of anybody. This raises the probability for a legal action, which cause major impacts. It is conceivable how important it is to enforce security policies. It is important to introduce security policies, which guide the decisions made by people who have the authority and set the boundaries under which the staff could operate. Apart from the inside threat, damage in a healthcare system may occur by an outside threat such as hackers. In this case it is very important to develop mechanisms which minimize the risk. So we must not allow any insecure Internet connection in the internal network of the healthcare system.

The *first security risk* is the failure to protect sensitive data beyond encryption.

The *second security risk* is the inability to accurately manage mobile computer assets. Under HIPAA, healthcare organizations must be able to audit how many computers they have in their inventory, where they are assigned, who is logging into them, what software is installed and where the computer is located.

The *third security risk* is sensitive information on public terminals. Nursing stations, public information terminals and help stations allow for greater risk of data breaches. Unattended stationary computers should always be monitored and protected with an authentication prompt.

The *fourth security risk* is difficulty in implementing a comprehensive data security plan. Healthcare facilities must have a comprehensive data security plan including asset tracking and recovery software that has cable locks, encryption software and secure passwords. Plan updates and constant checking on effectiveness of applied security controls should be done to ensure maximum effectiveness.

The *fifth security risk* is reluctance to create a data breach policy. In the event of a data breach there should be a standard procedure in place for timely notification of supervisors, law enforcement, patients and the media.

TETRA NETWORKS

Terrestrial Trunked Radio (TETRA) comprises a suite of open digital trunked radio standards defined by the European Telecommunications Standards Institute (ETSI) to meet the needs of the most demanding of Professional Mobile Radio (PMR) users. TETRA is an Interoperability standard that allows equipment from multiple vendors to interoperate with each other. TETRA is used by PMR users such as Public Safety, Transportation, Utilities, Government, Commercial & Industrial, Oil & Gas and Military. TETRA is also used by Public Access Mobile Radio (PAMR) Operators.

The Professional Mobile Radio market, which includes Private and Public Access Mobile Radio (PMR and PAMR), has traditionally been scattered in many dimensions in terms of technologies, frequency allocation etc. The first clear change

towards international standardization was the introduction of the analogue MPT1327 trunked radio standard, that lead to a market success in most parts of the world. Terrestrial Trunked Radio (TETRA) is the first truly open digital private mobile radio standard. TETRA is opening an even more international Professional Mobile Radio market. The high level of user involvement in the creation of the standard ensures that it will meet the needs of the demanding users.

Each communication channel is divided into four separate time slots, enabling a number of operations to be carried out, simultaneously, from one terminal. A key feature is bandwidth on demand, which means that if a situation only calls for two-way voice operation, only one time slot will be used. However, if full-motion video images, or voice and data are required, multiple time slots might be used. TETRA will only use as much bandwidth as is necessary for each operation.

This technology also boasts near-perfect security, offering high levels of encryption - security, which is difficult to achieve on traditional mobile radio systems. TETRA's network infrastructure can cover large, sparsely populated areas with a minimal number of base stations, or it can cover densely populated areas, with high volumes of traffic, utilizing a greater number of base stations.

To ensure an open multivendor market, TETRA specifies the following essential interfaces:

- **Air Interface** ensures the interoperability of terminal equipment from different manufacturers.
- **Terminal Equipment Interface (TEI)** facilitates the independent development of mobile data applications.
- **Inter-System Interface (ISI)** allows the interconnection of TETRA networks from different manufacturers.
- **Direct Mode Operation (DMO)** guarantees communication between terminals also beyond network coverage.

Figure 1. Interfaces specified by TETRA

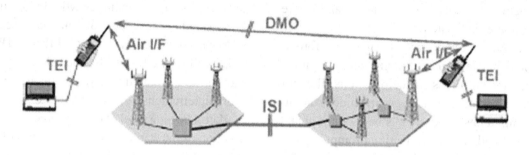

TETRA terminals can act as mobile phones (cell phones), with a direct connection to the PSTN. It is common also for them to operate in a group calling mode in which a single button push will connect the user to a dispatcher and all the other users in a group. It is also possible for the terminal to act as a one-to-one walkie-talkie but without the normal range limitation, since the call still uses the network. Emergency buttons, provided on the terminals, enable the users to transmit emergency signals, to the dispatcher, overriding any other activity taking place at the same time.

TETRA uses Time Division Multiple Access (TDMA) with four user channels on one radio carrier and 25 kHz spacing between carriers. Both point-to-point and point-to-multipoint transfer can be used. Digital data transmission is also included in the standard though at a low data rate.

TETRA Mobile Stations (MS) can communicate Direct Mode or using Trunked infrastructure (Switching and Management Infrastructure or SwMI) made of TETRA Base Stations (TBS). As well as allowing direct communications in situations where network coverage has been lost, Direct Mode or DMO also includes the possibility of using one (or a chain) of TETRA terminals as relays for a signal. This functionality is called DMO gateway (from DMO to TMO) or DMO Repeater (DMO to DMO). In rescue situations this feature could allow direct communications underground or in areas of bad coverage.

In addition to voice and dispatch services, the TETRA system supports several types of data communication. Status messages and short data services (SDS) are provided over the system's main control channel, while Packet Data or Circuit switched data communication uses specifically assigned traffic channels. All traffic is normally encrypted. TETRA provides both over the air encryption and end-to-end encryption.

The main advantages of TETRA over other technologies (such as GSM) are:

- much lower frequency, which gives longer range and permits very high levels of *geographic* coverage with a smaller number of transmitters, thus cutting infrastructure costs.

- high spectral efficiency; 4 channels in 25 kHz and no guard bands, compared to GSM with 8 channels in 200 kHz and guard bands.

- very fast call set-up; a one to many group call is generally set-up within 0.5 seconds (typical less than 250 msec for a single node call) compared with the many seconds (typically 7 to 10s) that are required for a GSM network.

- operation at high speeds (>400 km/h); TETRA was used during the French TGV train speed record on 3 April 2007 at 574.8 km/h.

- the system contains several mechanisms, designed into the protocols and radio parameters, to ensure communication success even during overload situations (e.g. during major public events or disaster situations), thus calls will always get through unlike in cellular systems. The system also supports a range of emergency calling modes.
- TETRA infrastructure is usually separate from (but connected to) that of the public (mobile) phone networks, resulting in (normally) no call charges for the system owners, substantially more diverse and resilient communications and easy customization and integration with data applications (vehicle location, GIS databases, dispatch systems etc).
- unlike most cellular technologies, TETRA networks typically provide a number of fall-back modes such as the ability for a base station to process local calls. So called Mission Critical networks can be built with TETRA where all aspects are fail-safe/multiple-redundant.
- in the absence of a network mobiles/portables can use 'direct mode' whereby they share channels directly (walkie-talkie mode).
- gateway mode - where a single mobile with connection to the network can act as a relay for other nearby mobiles that are out of range of the infrastructure.
- TETRA also provides a point-to-point function that traditional analogue emergency services radio systems did not provide. This enables users to have a one-to-one trunked 'radio' link between sets without the need for the direct involvement of a control room operator/dispatcher.
- unlike the cellular technologies, which connect one subscriber to one other subscriber (one-to-one) then TETRA is built to do one-to-one, one-to-many and many-

to-many. These operational modes are directly relevant to the public safety and professional users.
- TETRA supports both air-interface encryption and End-to-end encryption
- Rapid deployment (transportable) network solutions are available for disaster relief and temporary capacity provision.
- Equipment is available from many suppliers around the world, thus providing the benefits of competition.
- Network solutions are available in both the older circuit-switched (telephone like) architectures and flat, IP architectures with soft (software) switches.

EFFICIENT COMMUNICATIONS

Effective communication is critical in increasing operational efficiency and employee productivity. Each user will have different needs, communicating on a one-to-one or one-to-many basis. However, for most organisations there are clear priorities. The prime example is for emergency communications, as this is crucial to ensure safety of personnel and assets. Group communication is the next most important requirement, while support for individual and telephony calls is typically a lower priority. The safety of personnel is critical in this upstream facility, which covers more than 280 square kilometres. Features like emergency and priority calling are vital in overriding all other calls and ensuring an instant reaction to critical situations. Emergency scenarios are pre-configured on the system and are activated automatically in response to incidents. TETRA is unique in supporting critical emergency communications and offers the group call capabilities required for maintenance, production, safety and security staff.

Furthermore, TETRA's independence from public or cellular networks assures the ability to carry critical communications when other sys-

Table 1. Characteristics of TETRA calls

TETRA Call Type	Characteristics
Emergency Call	Emergency calls can support a set of key elements for handling emergency operations, including: special handling (and prioritisation) of emergency calls; automatic alarm capability (to raise the alarm if, for example, a user cannot talk); special dispatch console features; and an easily accessible emergency button on terminals.
Group Call	Group calls are critical to business efficiency. At a refinery for example, talk groups can be assigned to different functions: production workers, maintenance, fire etc. These talk groups are typically controlled by a dispatcher.
Individual Call	Individual calls are private calls between two users, or one user and the dispatch console.
Telephony	Telephone (interconnect) calls are typically used by management functions and may employ a gateway to permit connections between a user and a PABX or public telephone network (PSTN).
Priority Call	Priority call assignment by user or group can be set by the network manager. Emergency calls always take the highest priority, regardless of who initiates them. Pre-emptive priority calls can take priority too, and can be made by supervisors and key personnel, so that important operational information is relayed without delay.
Announcement Call	Announcement call is a valuable extension to the group call service, allowing announcements to be broadcast to multiple talk groups.
Advanced Calls	TETRA supports several other advanced call types, including: Recent User Priority; Dynamic Regrouping Services; and Site Wide Calls.

tems typically fail. A full range of voice services designed to ensure efficient operations is also available with TETRA. These include faster call set-up than with traditional telephone systems, and group calling for seamless work-group collaboration on an all-informed basis, often coordinated by one or more dispatch operators.

Wireless data is growing strongly. In cellular networks for example, it now accounts for almost one-third of overall user revenue in developed countries, an increase of some 20% in the last year. For healthcare organisations, wireless data can improve efficiency in several areas:

- Remote monitoring solutions – e.g. for corrosion monitoring (SCADA)
- Faster decision making, based on instant update of process data, enables a faster response and can help the identification and prevention of potential problems
- Maintenance inspections and operator rounds –collecting status data and records
- Business-process-driven schedule and dispatch of personnel, vehicles and other assets
- Alerts of emergency situations

- Location solutions – help users find missing or broken-down vehicles and manage the workforce.

Integrated Voice and Data

An integrated voice and data network such as TETRA means users only need to carry one device for all their communication needs. Standard TETRA portables and mobiles have a small display and simple keypad for text entry. This makes them ideal for basic transactions such as database enquiries and text messaging. More specialised devices are available for use in vehicles, which handle complex enquiries and email. There are also handheld PDAs and other mobile units available. Location Solutions are the most commonly used TETRA data application today.

SECURITY FUNCTIONS

TETRA contains a wealth of security functions designed to protect users' information. This information can consist of the users' speech and data traffic and also other information that relates to the identities and operations of the users themselves. When describing these TETRA security functions it is important to make a distinction between the different categories of functions and their specific application.

In TETRA the following categories can be identified:

- **Security Mechanisms:** These are independent self-contained functions that aim to achieve a specific security objective such as confidentiality of information or authentication of mobile terminals. Security mechanisms are the main building blocks for a security system.

- **Security Management Features:** These are functions that are used to control, manage and operate the individual security mechanisms. They form the heart of the resulting security and should guarantee that the security features are integrated into a consistent security system. Furthermore they are used to realize interoperability of the security mechanisms over different networks. Key management is the most essential security management function.

- **Standard Cryptographic Algorithms:** These are standardized system specific mathematical functions that are used, normally in combination with parameters called "cryptographic keys", to provide an adequate security level for the security mechanisms and the security management features. Standardized cryptographic algorithms are offered in TETRA to support interoperability between different TETRA systems.

- **Lawful Interception Mechanisms:** These are functions that are used within some communication systems to provide the lawfully required access to information and communication, with the aim to fulfill national regulatory requirements. It is essential that such functions do not undermine the regular security of the system. Therefore these functions should be controlled through security management features.

- **Evaluation of Security Mechanisms:** It is very important to be aware of the different roles and objectives of these classes. In certain proprietary systems the first two classes are often confused. This results in a "knot" of security features, which is difficult to analyze and even harder to correctly implement and control in an operational environment. But also mechanisms and algorithms get confused. Sometimes one tends to assess security provided by a certain mechanism only by the strength of the algorithm used, ignoring the environment in which it is used.

WIRELESS HEALTH MONITORING

A wireless sensor network (WSN) is a communication network composed of wireless sensor devices. These devices essentially are low cost, low power, multi-functional, small sized and communicate over short distances (Akyildiz et al, 2002). Typically these devices serve as nodes in a wireless network and are deployed randomly in a given area. Nodes establish connectivity with each other dynamically after deployment and do not follow a pre-determined topology. Therefore wireless sensor networks are self-organizing in nature and are suitable for military surveillance, control communication and monitoring disaster areas.

One application of WSN is in remote healthcare monitoring of patients. Wireless Sensor nodes are placed on patients and thus acquire critical data for remote monitoring by health care providers. Significant amount of research has been done in the area of Wireless Body Area Sensor Networks (WBASN) with many researchers proposing various types of sensor nodes. An example of a wearable health monitoring device that integrates a number of sensor devices onto a wearable motherboard can be found in (Sungmee Park et al., 2002). MIT project called Mithril (DeVaul et al, 2003), Carnegie Mellon University's e-textile project (Martin et al, 2003) are a few examples of such systems. Stanford university's lifeguard project comprise of physiological sensors (ECG/Respiration electrodes, Pulse Oximeter, Blood Pressure Monitor, Temperature probe), a wearable device with built-in accelerometers (CPOD), and a base station (Pocket PC). The CPOD acquires and logs the physiological parameters measured by the sensors (http://lifeguard.stanford.edu).

Several efforts have been made recently to provide an efficient mobile healthcare monitoring system. Authors in (Krco et al, 2003) propose Mobihealth project, which is an application of WSN for healthcare monitoring using GSM and UMTS technologies. Researchers in (Mandellos et al, 2004) provide solution for emergency healthcare monitoring in ambulances utilizing GSM and Wireless LANs. The authors in (Rasid, 2005) point out the use of Bluetooth technology for multi channel biomedical signal transmission via GPRS. Thus it is evident that many such projects have been implemented to date; however very little effort has been done to provide security and patient privacy when dealing with WBASNs.

Healthcare monitoring systems are traditionally complex systems involving not only data collection using WSN but also data propagation to healthcare provider, large databases and complex expert and knowledge based systems. Therefore, security and patient privacy is a very sensitive and important issue in design of such systems.

UTILIZATION OF TETRA NETWORK FOR HEALTH INFORMATION TRANSFER

The *TETRA* network has many advantages over traditional analog communication systems. Digital coding and transmission greatly enhances the sound quality and practically eliminates the problems with cracks and sound distortions. Contrary to analog networks, when using *TETRA*, one may address a voice connection to a single user or to a group of users.

Another important feature of the *TETRA* network is the possibility to associate the connections with certain priority numbers so that the low-priority connections can be terminated in case the network is overloaded.

The most important aspect is that the advanced communication solutions have the potential to save more lives; the lives of the public and those who work for the emergency services. The new generation of communications has been designed specifically for the emergency services, are generally being implemented to support multi-agency operation, and include unique features demanded by emergency service users.

In an emergency, every second counts. A life could be saved if a rescue crew can get an early, accurate diagnosis. Fast diagnosis could depend on being able to monitor and record the patient's vital signs and transmit the data wirelessly to a medical expert for consultation.

The proposed system enables the transmission of critical biosignals (ECG, blood pressure, heart rate, temperature), and still images of the patient, from the emergency site or ambulance to an emergency call center. It enables physicians to direct pre-hospital care in a more efficient way, improving patients' outcome and reducing mortality.

Using a TETRA network, such a solution can be used to monitor and transmit hospital quality diagnostics to remote specialists. Patient medical data, including motion picture images from inside the ambulance in transit will be transmitted to the medical center. Experts at the hospital can suggest proper treatment earlier, saving vital minutes. Knowing the history of the patient's condition during the trip to hospital will also cut delays when the patient arrives in the emergency room.

The integration of data into the voice channel enhances the functionality of automated vehicle tracking systems and digitized mapping. Telemetry enables ambulance crews to transmit heart rhythms and other patient monitoring to hospital casualty units. Video enables also emergency units to view accident scenes remotely. Digitizing of the mobile network has the added benefit of improving the speed of traditional manual in-house processes such as: patient report forms, database management and vehicle management.

CONCLUSION

Cost and return on investment is always a consideration. The TETRA network can enable existing information and resources to be extended out to the point of care, helping medical professionals deliver top medical care in a more timely and efficient manner. In medicine, time savings equals hospital savings. Instant access to clinical and drug information or the ability to electronically prescribe drugs can save several minutes per situation and decrease errors. Improved care in less time enables more patients to be treated and better results for patient and hospital.

Using a TETRA network can benefit not only ambulance crews, but also medical personnel at remote locations. They can be sure that accurate patient diagnostic information is transmitted securely and reliably, allowing them to determine the correct treatment as soon as possible. Not every chest pain is a heart attack: more than 40% of patients admitted to hospital with chest pains are eventually diagnosed as having non-cardiac or non-life threatening symptoms. Transporting a patient for such an "unnecessary" hospital admission is not only expensive but can also delay an ambulance from more critical emergencies.

Provide discussion of the overall coverage of the chapter and concluding remarks.

Wireless telemedicine technologies provide promising solutions for forthcoming healthcare applications. The new technological trends, together with more work and needed efforts in the areas of interoperability, standards, security, and legal issues at both the national and international levels, will facilitate wider application of health-care telematics, including wireless, for the whole health-care sector. The proposed type of TETRA Network for medical purposes will improve our quality of life. We strongly believe that the proposed system will save the lives of many patients transported by ambulance in emergencies.

REFERENCES

Akyildiz, A., Su, W., Sankarasubramaniam, Y., & Cayirci, E. (2002). A Survey on Sensor Networks. *IEEE Communications Magazine, 40*(8), 102–114. doi:10.1109/MCOM.2002.1024422

Berreti, D. (1998). *Default set of BSS Parameters for Cosmote Network and set of BSS parameters for umbrella cells, Nokia Productivity Services.* Athens, Greece: Technical Report, Nokia Telecommunications.

Bhargava, A., & Zoltowski, M. (2003). *Sensors and wireless communication for medical care.* In Proceedings of the 14th International Workshop on Database and Expert Systems Applications, DEXA'03, Prague, Czech Republic.

Chakravorty, R. (2006). A *programmable service architecture for mobile medical care.* In Proceedings of the 4th Annual IEEE International Conference on Pervasive Computing and Communications Workshops (PerCom '06), Pisa, Italy.

Dimitriadou, E., Ioannou, K., Panoutsopoulos, I., Garmpis, A., & Kotsopoulos, S. (2005). Priority to Low Moving Terminals in TETRA Networks. *WSEAS Transactions on Communications, 4*(11), 1228–1236.

Dunlop, J. (1999). *Digital Mobile Communications and the TETRA System*. New York: John Wiley & Sons.

Hong, D., & Rappaport, S. (1986). Traffic model and performance analysis for cellular mobile radio telephone systems with prioritized and non prioritized handoff procedures. *IEEE Transactions on Vehicular Technology, 35*, 77–92. doi:10.1109/T-VT.1986.24076

Ioannou, K., Louvros, S., Panoutsopoulos, I., Kotsopoulos, S., & Karagiannidis, G. (2002). Optimizing the Handover Call Blocking Probability in Cellular Networks with High Speed Moving Terminals. *IEEE Communications Letters, 6*(10), 422–424. doi:10.1109/LCOMM.2002.802048

Jafari, R., Dabiri, F., Brisk, P., & Sarrafzadeh, M. (2005). *CustoMed: A power optimized customizable and mobile medical monitoring and analysis system*. In Proceedings of ACM HCI Challenges in Health Assessment Workshop in Conjunction with Proceedings of the Conference on Human Factors in Computing Systems (CHI '05), Portland, Oregon, USA.

Jea, D., & Srivastava, M. B. (2006). *A remote medical monitoring and interaction system*. In Proceedings of the 4th International Conference on Mobile Systems, Applications, and Services (MobiSys '06), Uppsala, Sweden.

Krco, S., & Delic, V. (2003). *Personal Wireless Sensor Network for Mobile Health Care Monitoring*. In Proceedings of the IEEE TELSIKS 2003, Nis, Serbia-Montenegro.

Kyriacou, E., Pavlopoulos, S., Koutsouris, D., Andreou, A., Pattichis, C., & Schizas, C. (2001). *Multipurpose Health Care Telemedicine System*. In Proceedings of the 23rd Annual International Conference of the IEEE/EMBS, Istanbul, Turkey.

Lin, Y., Jan, I., Ko, P., Chen, Y., Wong, J., & Jan, G. (2004). A wireless PDA-based physiological monitoring system for patient transport. *IEEE Transactions on IT in Biomedicine, 8*(4), 439–447. doi:10.1109/TITB.2004.837829

Mandellos, G., Lymperopoulos, D., Koukias, M., Tzes, A., Lazarou, N., & Vagianos, C. (2004). *A Novel Mobile Telemedicine System for Ambulance Transport: Design and Evaluation*. Proceedings of the 26th Annual International Conference of the IEEE Engineering in Medicine and Biology Society, San Francisco, CA, USA.

Martin, J. E. T., & Jones, M. Shenoy, R. (2003). *Towards a design framework for wearable electronic textiles*. In Proceedings of the 7th IEEE International Symposium on Wearable Computers. New York. USA.

Pattichis, C., Kyriacou, E., Voskarides, S., Pattichis, M., Istepanian, R., & Schizas, C. (2002). Wireless Telemedicine Systems: An Overview. *IEEE Antennas and Propagation, 44*(2), 143–153. doi:10.1109/MAP.2002.1003651

Pavlopoulos, S., Kyriacou, E., Berler, A., Dembeyiotis, S., & Koutsouris, D. (1998). Novel emergency telemedicine system based on wireless communication technology—AMBULANCE. *IEEE Transactions on Information Technology in Biomedicine, 2*(4), 261–267. doi:10.1109/4233.737581

Rappaport, T. S. (1999). *Wireless Communications: Principles and Practice*. Upper Saddle River, NJ: Prentice Hall.

Rasid, M., & Woodward, B. (2005). Bluetooth Telemedicine Processor for Multichannel Biomedical Signal Transmission via Mobile Cellular Networks. *IEEE Transactions on Information Technology in Biomedicine, 9*(1), 35–43. doi:10.1109/TITB.2004.840070

Stavroulakis, P. (2007). *TErrestrial Trunked RAdio - TETRA: A Global Security Tool. Signals and Communication Technology.* Berlin: Springer-Verlag.

Sungmee Park, K., & Jayaraman, S. (2002). *The wearable motherboard: a framework for personalized mobile information processing.* In Proceedings of the 39th ACM/IEEE Design Automation Conference. New Orleans, LA, USA.

Varshney, U. (2005). Pervasive Healthcare: Applications, Challenges And Wireless Solutions, *Communications of the Association for Information Systems*: 16, Article 3. Retrieved from http://aisel.aisnet.org/cais/vol16/iss1/3 (10/1/2010).

Varshney, U. (2006). Patient monitoring using infrastructure oriented wireless LANs. *International Journal of Electronic Healthcare*, 2(2), 149–163.

Varshney, U. (2006). Using wireless technologies in healthcare. *International Journal of Mobile Communications*, 4(3), 354–368.

Zander, J. Kim, S.-L. (2001). *Radio Resource Management for Wireless Networks.* Norwood, MA: Artech House.

WEBSITES

Key Factors for Personal Health Monitoring & Diagnosis Devices. Retrieved from http://www.mocomed.org/workshop2002/beitraege/Schwaibold.pdf

Performance Issued in a Secure Health Monitoring Wireless Sensor Network, Retrieved from http://www.comp.brad.ac.uk/het-net/tutorials/WP01.pdf

Terrestrial Trunked Radio Definition, in Wikipedia, Retrieved from http://en.wikipedia.org/wiki/Terrestrial_Trunked_Radio

The TETRA Security Functions, in TETRA Security, TETRA MoU Association, Retrieved from http://www.tetra-association.com/

Vendor Identifies Top Five Healthcare Data Security Risks. Retrieved from http://www.healthcare-itnews.com/story.cms?id=8913&page=2

Wireless Health Monitoring in the near Future, Retrieved from http://www.mobilemag.com/content/100/104/C3888/

Wireless Mobile Medicine: Better, Stronger, Faster, Retrieved from http://www.masshightech.com/stories/2004/08/16/focus3-Wireless-mobile-medicine:-Better,-stronger,-faster.html

Wireless Technology Choices Abound for Medical Monitoring. Retrieved from http://www.rtcmagazine.com/home/article.php?id=100281&pg=3

Wireless Transmission of Emergency Medical Care Data. Retrieved from http://ieeexplore.ieee.org/iel4/5909/15760/00731511.pdf

KEY TERMS AND DEFINITIONS

Confidentiality: Confidentiality has been defined by the International Organization for Standardization (ISO) in ISO-17799 as "ensuring that information is accessible only to those authorized to have access" and is one of the cornerstones of information security. Confidentiality is one of the design goals for many cryptosystems, made possible in practice by the techniques of modern cryptography. Confidentiality also refers to an ethical principle associated with several professions (e.g., medicine, law, religion, professional psychology, and journalism). In ethics, and (in some places) in law and alternative forms of legal dispute resolution such as mediation, some types of communication between a person and one of these professionals are "privileged" and may not be discussed or divulged to third parties. In those jurisdictions in which the law makes provision for such confidentiality, there are usually penalties for its violation.

Data Integrity: Data integrity is a term used in computer science and telecommunications that can mean ensuring data is "whole" or complete, the condition in which data is identically maintained during any operation (such as transfer, storage or retrieval), the preservation of data for their intended use, or, relative to specified operations, the a priori expectation of data quality. Put simply, data integrity is the assurance that data is consistent and correct.

Health Information: The recorded information in any format (e.g., oral, written, or electronic) regarding the physical or mental condition of an individual, health care provision, or health care payment.

Information Security: Information security means protecting information and information systems from unauthorized access, use, disclosure, disruption, modification or destruction. The terms information security, computer security and information assurance are frequently incorrectly used interchangeably. These fields are interrelated often and share the common goals of protecting the confidentiality, integrity and availability of information; however, there are some subtle differences between them.

TETRA: Terrestrial Trunked Radio (TETRA) is a set of standards developed by the European Telecommunications Standardization Institute (ETSI) that describes a common mobile radio communications infrastructure throughout Europe. This infrastructure is targeted primarily at the mobile radio needs of public safety groups (such as police and fire departments), utility companies, and other enterprises that provide voice and data communications services.

Section 6
Legal Aspects of Security in Healthcare

Chapter 12

Online Advertising in Relation to Medicinal Products and Health Related Services:
Data & Consumer Protection Issues

Eleni Tzoulia
LL.M. Heidelberg, Germany

ABSTRACT

This study examines special issues of online advertising in relation to medicinal products and health related services. It demonstrates that the marketing of medicinal products over the internet puts consumers at a number of risks related to both their privacy and their health. It endeavours to answer the question whether the existing EU legislation can efficiently protect the individual, who may be induced to disclose his/her health related information to and be involved in transactions with entities of questionable origin for the purchase of medicinal products online.

INTRODUCTION

Industrialization and mass production, which have long characterized international economy, as well as the rapid growth of the services sector in our days, have tipped the balance between supply and demand. As a consequence, firms today need to act in ways that would increase demand for their products as much as possible. With this in mind, firms utilize marketing strategies, specifically merchandising (using the product itself), pricing and display, including the proper communications policy (Kloss, 2003). In view of the above distinc-

tions, advertising is among the communication policies of a firm.

Interactivity, the application of digital technology and multimedia – including the absence of all space and time restrictions (Mantzoufas, 2007) – increased the popularity of the internet. Although initially used for communication, research and military purposes (Mayer, 1996; Argyropoulos, 2001), the internet evolved into an excellent trading platform. Today cyberspace hosts a kind of commercial activity which, notwithstanding differences, truly reflects the conventional way of doing business. What is more, the internet has evolved into a powerful marketing tool.

DOI: 10.4018/978-1-61692-895-7.ch012

In their efforts to maximize profits and sustain themselves in the market, firms often utilize unfair advertising practices, e.g. passing off or trademark infringement, trade/competitor libel, misleading advertising, unsolicited commercial communication, etc.

This study examines special issues of online advertising in relation to medicinal products and health related services. It outlines the development of the pharmaceutical industry in the light of rising competition as more and more players joined the industry. To be able to cope with the competition, pharmaceutical firms utilize various marketing/advertising means which fail to stand the scrutiny of law. This study shows that the internet is fertile ground for unfair commercial practices, and in this light the key question it endeavours to answer is whether existing EU laws can ensure the protection of consumers against data theft and health risks. Indeed, while surfing the internet, a user may inadvertently disclose his/her medical record to subsequently receive via e-mail solicitations for health-related transactions, or advertisements, by questionable providers.

BACKGROUND: ONLINE ADVERTISING OF MEDICINAL PRODUCTS AND SERVICES

Advertising on the Internet

According to the terminology introduced in Directive 2000/31/EC with respect to E-commerce, online advertising is a form of "commercial communication". Under article 2, section f, "commercial communication" means any *"form of communication designed to promote, directly or indirectly, the goods, services or image of a company, organization or person pursuing a commercial, industrial or craft activity or exercising a regulated profession."* It is clearly stated that domain names or electronic-mail addresses of a company, organization or person do not constitute

commercial communication; the same applies to communications relating to goods, services or image of the company without financial consideration. The above definition aims on the one hand to distinguish among commercial, private and political modes of communication, while on the other hand it is broad enough to bring under the regulatory scope of the Directive all forms of electronic marketing (banners, frames, linking, web sponsoring, power shopping, virtual malls, online auctions, email marketing, etc.) (Marinos, 2002).

For the purposes of this study the advertising of products and services on the internet is distinguished as direct and indirect, depending on whether the advertisement reaches the user or the user 'bumps into' it. In their indirect version, electronic ads can be found on the web pages of producers and/or providers of various products/services. In fact, in bibliography commercial web sites are often considered as a form of advertisement. This attitude in Germany was heavily criticized mainly on the grounds of the proportional implementation of the separation rule (Trennungsgebot) in German law on unfair competition. This rule dictates that any advertisement must be clearly distinct from the rest of the content of the publication or of the Radio-TV broadcast, with a view to avoid misleading the consumers (Heyms & Pries, 2002; Lettl, 2004). The solution came from the EU Directive on e-commerce where in article 6 it provides that the commercial communication shall be clearly identifiable as such. Therefore, it is rather awkward to consider such web pages as advertisements in themselves, but rather as platforms upon which advertisements are hosted, either in banners or in hyperlinks. Argyropoulos (2001) describes these web pages as "virtual windows showcasing information" (p. 32).

It has already been mentioned that the rise of market competition inspires some companies to utilize unfair practices in the promotion of their products. These companies take advantage of digital technologies and the globalizing effect of the internet to launch misleading advertising campaigns. A commercial practice which finds fertile ground on the internet is direct advertising, i.e. targeting specific consumers on the basis of their various traits/interests. This practice is an effective marketing tool, in terms of time and cost, as it focuses on specific consumer groups and ignores others (Iyer, Soberman & Villas-Boas, 2004). These companies use various techniques to monitor internet user behaviour by gathering related information concerning the users' personal and professional life, gender, physical and psychological health, purchase history and interests in general. Subsequently, this information is processed into a consumer profile per user monitored. The profiles are matched with proper electronic ads which are communicated to target users by email, or the users are induced to visit specific web pages (Igglezakis, 2003).

In view of the above, the term 'direct electronic advertising' is understood as unsolicited commercial communication by email (spam), in the form of simple advertising emails or of electronic brochures (newsletters) sent via email. Under the same advertising category come even the 'pop ups' and the so called interstitials. The pop ups are a form of web advertising which appears in a new browser window as soon as a user reaches a web page. The content of these windows is irrelevant to the original information pursued by the internet user. The "pop unders", which constitute a version of "pop ups", are a form of advertising in a new browser window which becomes visible after closing the browser window of a web site originally visited (Micklitz, & Schirmbacher 2006). The interstitials, on the other hand, are advertisements appearing on the active browser window before the expected content is displayed, which interrupts the user's search (Heyms & Pries, 2002). Another form of consumer manipulation is "keyword advertising", which is made possible with the use of meta-tags to trigger hyperlinks to web pages (ads) that are not

related to the search term the user entered into a search engine. Furthermore, Google uses Adsense technology, a cookie which stores information on which sites carrying AdSense ads the user has visited, to provide interest-based advertising. "Adsense for content" automatically crawls the content of the web pages visited by the user and, using factors such as keyword analysis, word frequency, font size and the overall link structure of the web, it determines what each web page is about. Then it delivers ads relevant to the user's interests each time the user browses a website participating in AdSense network. The "AdSense for search" technology, on the other hand, allows website publishers to provide Google search to their visitors and to earn money by displaying on the search results pages Google ads, matched with the search term given by the reader ("Google AdSense Help", n.d.).

Personal Data Outside Time and Space

One of the main characteristics of the internet, which makes it so popular among consumers and service/product providers, is that it can reach instantly all users regardless of their location on the planet. The idea of physical borders breaks down when talking about surfing on the internet. Each web page is identified with a unique address and can be accessed from any part of the world with basically the same transmission speeds and message quality (Johnson & Post, 1998). Moreover, the internet is a melting pot of services (email, newsgroups, chat rooms, the World Wide Web, blogs, forums etc.) and multimedia (text, graphics, video, animation and sound) which were created by various entities set up in different parts of the world and are subject to different jurisdictions.

Furthermore, time acquires a relative dimension in cyberspace. In this "brave" new environment which lends itself to technological experimentation, scores of innovative applications make their debut everyday. The skyrocketing popularity and commerce potential of the internet drives electronic service providers into a perpetual quest for state-of-the-art technologies in the hope to elicit/capture the interest of users-consumers who become all the more demanding. However, the faster the internet technology becomes obsolete and is replaced, the faster the regulatory framework governing the application of these technologies falls into disuse. In the last decade the European law-making demonstrates a certain mystification in the face of technological developments, which finds expression in regular reviews of Community regulations, giving the Member States short notice to adapt and mandating the Member States and the Commission to review the efficiency of individual regulations in the context of the evolution of the society of information (Mitrou, 2002).

In the maelstrom of cyberspace personal data are more vulnerable in relation to an off-line environment, for two reasons. On the one hand technology makes theft/capture and processing of personal data easier, thus exposing the public to a variety of dangers such as identity theft, and, on the other hand, it is more difficult to police and sanction such practices from a legal point of view. Indeed, user information travels the internet in the form of strings of bits. Information in digital form (data) becomes a commodity which is independent of its storage medium. This is made possible by technologies which resize it to extremely small packages, transmit and store it equally fast for later processing. This, however, increases the chances for data theft (Marinos, 1998).

There are numerous technological applications which are used for unauthorized collection of user information. A 'cookie', for example, is the oldest and most popular technology on the internet whose function is to track user information. Cookies are small pieces of text stored on a user's computer and sent back to the websites from where they originated in the first place. Cookies are not by definition malicious software (malware). They can hold session data, as in a shopping card, they can be used to store login

credentials and they can provide customization or personalization (McKinley, 2008). They are therefore used by servers to identify and remember the visitors of each web page, so that the next time a user browses the same content they can facilitate his/her navigation, saving his/her time (Theodorides, 2005). Nevertheless, cookies are not altogether harmless. One of the main user tracking concerns arises when a third party, other than the web-site the user is visiting, is allowed to store data on the user's system. This is possible when the user visits a web page, where content from another site (e.g. an advertisement) is being referenced. The third party content is loaded by the browser, and their server may be able to set their own cookies for their domain. For instance, when a user visits a web site "A", which hosts an advertisement coming from a different domain "B", the server at "B" sends the user's browser a cookie containing a small bit of data, a number indicating a unique user in their system, and stores which site the user is coming from. When the user then visits web site "C", which also uses ads from "B", the user's cookie is sent to the server at "B", effectively letting the server at "B" know that the user is viewing "C" (McKinley, 2008). Web bugs function in a similar manner. They are electronic tags, often invisible because they typically appear in the form of graphics only 1-by-1 pixel in size, embedded on web pages or email messages to monitor people's surfing habits (Smith, 1999).

Another malware is the so called *Trojan horse*, which "is an application that claims to provide a set of features, but instead contains a payload that performs more malicious tasks behind the user's back, much like the mythical gift to the defenders of Troy that contained warriors who took over the city from within its walls. Trojan horse applications can perform a number of different tasks, from using the target computer to illicitly store files to acting as spyware, software that quietly gathers data about how the target computer is configured, what software is installed, and even what Web sites the target user visits on the Internet" (Simons & Causey, 2002).

Also, another method for unauthorized collection of personal data is to "infect" a computer with spyware (e.g. Alexa). Under this category of malicious software comes the *adware*, i.e. a software package designed to infiltrate a computer during the installation of an application the user has downloaded for free from the internet (e.g. a peer-to-peer application such as Kazaa). Adware packages act in the background by repeatedly presenting to the user advertisements or "hassle" users to visit other web pages (pop-ups). The keyloggers are one of the most dangerous types of spyware. They have been designed to covertly log (note) user key strokes and send this information to third parties without the user being aware.

As mentioned earlier, cyberspace is an environment without physical borders, where the conventional notion of territorial jurisdiction does not apply. Digitized personal data, which have been 'harvested' in an unauthorized manner, travel cross-border, even across the Atlantic, to reach other territorial jurisdictions where the level of personal data protection may be very low. These countries are known in international bibliography as "data havens" (Igglezakis, 2003). In the face of this situation the European law is trying to catch up with technological developments by issuing a series of directives designed to protect the individuals from unauthorized collection (e.g. via mail, telephone, the internet) and processing of their personal data (EU Directives 95/46/EC, 97/66/EC, 2006/24/EC).

Promotion of Medicinal Products and Health Related Services on the Internet: The Growth of the Pharmaceutical Industry

The beginnings of the modern pharmaceutical industry can be traced in Switzerland of the 19th century, when firms processing chemical substances in the Rhine valley discovered the antiseptic qualities of various dyestuffs. Also, the discovery and widespread popularity of penicillin in the 1940's, the increasing application of research results and of scientific knowledge in the area of industrial development led to the establishment of pharmaceutical companies which, over the following decades, evolved into major pharmaceutical players throughout the world (e.g. Hoffman-La Roche, Sandoz, Ciba-Geigy, Novartis).

The pharmaceutical industry expanded rapidly during the sixties and seventies as a result of new discoveries and the flourishing of the global economy, which encouraged new investments in health care. Actually, over the last decades new scientific discoveries and technological innovations have made the repeated introduction of new medicines possible, while more and more pharmaceutical firms have joined the competition, in this way intensifying it. Today consumers are better informed and require of the pharmaceutical companies to deliver products that are effective and priced reasonably.

Having these developments in mind, pharmaceutical companies tend to spend considerable amounts of money in advertising, marketing and lobbying. In the USA alone the cost of the promotional campaign of the pharmaceutical industry is in the range of 19 billion dollars a year. This campaign does not involve only the print and electronic media (Radio & TV), but also medical representatives whose task is to inform medical practitioners and related health providers about new medicinal products. Furthermore, in some countries pharmaceutical companies utilize lobbyists to influence politicians and representatives of the public sector ("The History and Analysis of the Pharmaceutical Industry", n.d.).

The Introduction of Pharmaceutical Companies on the Internet: The Problems

It is obvious, in view of the above, that consumers have no or very little choice in their purchase of medicinal products. This situation is peculiar to the pharmaceutical sector. In other words, it is at the informed decision of the medical practitioner or chemist – both qualified professionals – to prescribe or recommend medicines to patients. Consequently, the promotional campaigns of the pharmaceutical companies target the above mentioned professionals who act as "middlemen" between the industry and consumers. However, the introduction of pharmacies on the internet – the result of ruthless competition – gave consumers direct access to health products, thus decreasing the mediation of medical practitioners and chemists as regards the choice of medicines.

However, despite the benefits the consumers reap from the internet presence of pharmaceutical companies and pharmacies, there are significant risks involved. An individual who purchases medicinal products and health related services online belongs to a vulnerable group of people who share the following characteristics: they are internet users, consumers and usually in need of medical attention. Further below it will be demonstrated that the marketing of medicinal products over the internet puts in danger both the consumers' privacy and health. Specifically, the internet users may be induced to disclose their vital/personal information to subsequently become targets of unsolicited mail for the purchase of such products, most of which are of questionable origin and effectiveness, to say the least.

LEGAL IMPLICATIONS FROM THE ELECTRONIC PROMOTION OF MEDICINAL PRODUCTS

Protection of Personal Data

In connection with the broad distinction between direct and indirect advertising which was introduced earlier, we can also identify two major categories in relation to the measures adopted for the promotion of medicinal products on the internet: a) those applying to commercial sites or "electronic pharmacies" (Koehler & Arndt, 2001), and b) the electronic communication known as spam, pop-ups, etc. Electronic pharmacies operate over the internet but may be physically established in or outside the European Union. Internet users access the sites of electronic pharmacies mainly in search of medicinal products that are available for online order. Usually there are no restrictions in regards to the visitor's place of residence. Visitors can also come into contractual agreements with the vendors; in which case they may be required to disclose personal information. However, the same information can also be obtained by way of cookies sent from the vendor's server and stored to the user's computer without the user being aware of the particular transaction between the vendor's server and the user's computer. The question is whether this 'harvesting', storage and processing of user information is legal, or under what circumstances such practices would be warranted, especially in view of the fact that the information could be used for direct advertising.

First of all, the information in question is health related, i.e. about the physical and mental health of the user and, pursuant to article 8 (1) of Directive 95/46/EC on the protection of individuals against the processing of personal data and on the free movement of such data, constitutes a category of sensitive personal information. Under this category comes all information revealing a person's medical condition (impairment, disability), mental condition (neurosis, psychopathic disorders, psychosis), medical history (diseases, hospital stay, medication or drugs used), nutritional or other needs, and sex life (e.g. sexually transmitted diseases, homosexuality) (Armamentos & Sotiropoulos, 2005). Pursuant to the same Directive (Art. 8 (1)) the processing[1] of sensitive information is prohibited in principle. However, this prohibition does not apply under certain circumstances of which those that have a direct bearing on medicinal products are set out in section a, paragraph 2 and paragraph 3 of the same article. Specifically, the processing of sensitive information is not prohibited when the person ("data subject") has given his/her explicit consent, subject to a contrary regulation by any member-state (EU Directive 95/46/EC: article 8, paragraph 2, section a). Also, the processing of personal data is excluded from the prohibition *"where processing of the data is required for the purpose of preventive medicine, medical diagnosis, the provision of care or treatment or the management of health-care services, and where those data are processed by a health professional ... or by another person also subject to an equal obligation or secrecy"* (ibid: article 8, paragraph 3).

In addition, pursuant to Article 5 of Directive 2002/58/EC concerning the processing of personal data and the protection of privacy in the electronic communications sector, the confidentiality of communications becomes an obligation of the Member States: *"In particular, they shall prohibit listening, tapping, storage or other kinds of interception or surveillance of communications and the related traffic data by persons other than users, without the consent of the users concerned ..."*. This prohibition seems to apply to the use of spy software for unauthorised practices, e.g. the tapping of personal data, storage and processing of the same for subsequent compilation of user profiles. Nevertheless, the same Directive allows for two exceptions. Specifically, Article 5 (3), in combination with recitals 24 and 25 of the Preamble, allows the use of cookies, including that of any spy software, *"on condition the user is provided with clear and comprehensive information in accordance with Directive 95/46/EC, inter alia about the purposes of the processing, and is offered the right to refuse such processing by the data controller."* This represents an "opt out" system where the function of the spyware stored in the user's terminal may be terminated as soon as the informed consent of the user is requested (Igglezakis, 2003). The second exception to the prohibition concerning the confidentiality of communications is laid down in Article 5 (2).

In the light of recital 23, this exception stipulates that communications are recorded legally *"for the purpose of providing evidence of a commercial transaction or of any other business communication"* on condition the user/subscriber has agreed to the recording and the duration of the same which cannot exceed the period necessary to establish beyond any reasonable doubt evidence for the transaction.

Article 13 of Directive 2002/58/EC provides an answer to the question whether the data which have been collected by means of spy software can be utilized in direct advertising practices. According to paragraph 1 of the same article, the use of electronic mail for the purposes of direct marketing is allowed only on condition the users have given their prior explicit consent. In other words, this Directive introduces an "opt in" system which, in principle, prohibits spamming, unless users have given their prior consent. Paragraph 3 of the above mentioned article applies to all other forms of direct marketing. It enjoins the Member States to adopt at least[2] one "opt out" system, i.e. one that would allow such marketing methods on condition the user can refuse them *ex post* (Micklitz & Schirmbacher, 2006; Lettl, 2004). The same system is utilized when direct marketing by email is made possible on the basis of data collected legally from natural or legal persons in the context of commercial transactions. At this point it should be noted that Directive 2005/29/EC concerning unfair business-to-consumer commercial practices in the internal market had no material effect on the regulations discussed in this paragraph. Although the said Directive acknowledges that direct advertising is unfair (Arts. 8 & 9), i.e. those practices which utilize aggressive commercial practices, harassment, coercion or inducement which are likely to impair the consumer's free will. In addition, in Appendix 1, item (26), the same Directive says that "persistent unwanted solicitation" by phone, email, etc. constitutes unfair practice, and goes on

"…without prejudice to Article 10 of Directive 2002/58/EC." (see also Gamerith (2003)).

In summary, the storage and processing of consumers' personal data in the context of online pharmacies is allowed in Europe on condition that customers have previously given their informed consent. The use of this information (data), especially for direct advertising by email or by other means, should in principle be prohibited in view of the sensitive nature of the data collected, unless the customer/user has explicitly allowed such advertising ("opt in" system). It should be noted that according to Article 8 (2a) of Directive 95/46/EC, the above mentioned rules lay down the minimum of protection and it is up to the Member States to institute stricter regulations altogether prohibiting, contrary to the users' explicit consent, the processing of sensitive personal data, hence of the advertising which results from this processing. In this case there is doubt as to whether the exception laid down in Article 8 (3) (Directive 95/46/EC) could apply, i.e. that the processing of personal data is allowed regardless of the users' consent when such processing is carried out for the provision of care and health related services to users, where the processing is carried out by health professionals subject to professional secrecy. In any case, the term "online pharmacies", in reference to firms marketing medicinal products over the internet, is rather a euphemism (Koehler & Arndt, 2001).

CONSUMER PROTECTION ISSUES

Introduction

The term "electronic commerce" is used in bibliography in a broad sense. However, certain commercial transactions are referred to as 'business-to-business' (b2b) and 'business-to-consumer' (b2c). The former type of commercial transaction takes place in extranets between businesses or between suppliers and wholesalers. The latter, b2c, de-scribes commercial activities between a business and end customers. When b2c is taking place over electronic systems (e-commerce) the commercial transactions can be distinguished into *online* and *offline*. In the case of online transactions, both the execution of contracts and performance take place online. The purchase of digitized products (e.g. software, music, e-books or tickets, etc.), including internet telephony (VoIP), internet Radio & TV, come under this type of transaction. On the other hand, offline transactions are those which involve negotiations and execution of contracts over the internet and performance in a conventional way (Koehler & Arndt, 2001; Igglezakis, 2003). Under the latter type of transactions comes the purchasing of medicinal products over the internet. In this case both advertising and contractual agreements, including payment, take place online but the delivery of products (performance) takes place by mail or courier.

There are a number of legal issues associated with consumer protection in the context of the above mentioned transactions, but the detailed review of these issues here is beyond the scope of this paper. In brief, however, the European legislation has dealt with the execution of electronic contracts between consumers and e-businesses, particularly in connection with sending and receiving declarations of intent, and faulty declarations; the right [of the consumers] to rescind and return the goods; the use of general transaction terms; the validation of electronic signatures; and unfair commercial practices with an emphasis on misleading advertising[3].

However, this paper will examine specific concerns in relation to cross-border sales of medicinal products for human use made through internet pharmacies. It is true that the pharmaceutical sector has always been under state intervention on the grounds of public health. Strict specifications do not apply only to the production of medicines; the circulation of the same is subject also to approvals and permits, while consumption – even in the absence of prescription – is subject to restrictions (e.g. expiration dates, dosing). Also, both the value and effectiveness of medicines are monitored even after the medicines have been placed in the market, while if undesirable effects or side effects are reported or if proved that the medicinal products fall short of the contents listed and approved, these products are banned and withdrawn from the market. For instance, owing to side effects, the Bayer product Lipitor, for cholesterol lowering, was recently withdrawn from the market; the same for the pain killer medicine, Vioxx, of the American firm Merck (Stefanou, 2005; Koenig, Mueller & Trafkowski, 2000).

Until recently the framework which regulates the marketing and sale of medicines in the European Union has been a patchwork of national laws, particularly as regards distance sales (over the internet). Directive 97/7/EC on distance sales and Directive 2000/31/EC on electronic commerce fail to provide a solution. With a view to consumer protection, article 14 of the former Directive allows the Member States of the EU to introduce or maintain a ban on the marketing/advertising of certain goods or services, especially of medicinal products. In that way, directive 97/7/EC enables the establishment of big differences between the national legislations of member states in relation to advertising of medicines. On the other hand, the E-commerce Directive – especially Recital 21 combined with Article 2(h) – drives a sharp distinction between the marketing of medicinal products and its coordinated field (Nett, 2002).

Directive 2001/83/EC of the European Parliament and of the Council of 6 November 2001 on the Community code relating to medicinal products for human use aims to streamline laws, regulations and administrative provisions of the Member States to facilitate marketing authorisations for medicinal products. The same Directive includes provisions for the advertising of medicines. Specifically, it defines the Title 'Advertising of Medicinal Products' as "*any form of ... canvassing activity or inducement designed to promote the prescription, supply, sale or consumption of medicinal products;*

it shall include the particular: the advertising of medicinal products to the general public, ..., the provision of inducements to prescribe or supply medicinal products by the gift, offer or promise of any benefit or bonus, ..." (Article 86). The same Directive prohibits the advertising of medicinal products which failed to acquire marketing authorization in compliance with Community legislation[4], while it also prohibits the advertising of prescription medication to the general public (Article 87). According to Article 88, it will be at the discretion of the Member States to ban on their territory "advertising to the general public of medicinal products the cost of which may be reimbursed."

The DocMorris Case

The interpretation of the above mentioned provisions is made clear in the judgment of the European Court of Justice (ECJ) in the case of DocMorris[5], which sheds more light on the status of internet pharmacies in the European Union. The DocMorris was Europe's first mail order pharmacy with main offices set up in the Netherlands. Its activities, among others, include online marketing and sale over-the-counter (non-prescription) and prescription drugs via the internet both in the Netherlands and Germany. The German Association of Apothecaries (Deutscher Apothekerverband eV) instituted proceedings against DocMorris at the Court of First Instance in Frankfurt (Landgericht Frankfurt am Main) on the grounds the distance selling and advertising of medicinal products by DocMorris violated the German law which are available only through traditional pharmacies. The applicant also stated that German law requires the physical presence of the customer when the medicines are purchased, and this because customers should be provided with the proper instructions. In its reference for a preliminary ruling the ECJ examined the compatibility of the German prohibition with Community law in the light of the principle of the free movement of goods (Article 28 EC) and Directive 2001/83/EC. The ECJ was also asked, and ruled accordingly, about two questions. The first question is whether pharmacies operating lawfully in one Member State are authorized to engage in cross-border distance selling (e.g. via the internet) of medicinal products which do not circulate widely in other Member States (country of delivery). The second question is whether a national prohibition on distance advertising of medicinal products is compatible with Community law.

The Principle of the Country of Origin

Incidentally, to elucidate the grounds for and the operative part of the Court's judgment on the DocMorris case, the content of the principle of the free movement of goods in the European Union must be made clear particularly in the context of Articles 28 EC and 30 EC. Article 28 EC prohibits quantitative restrictions on imports among the Member States and all measures having equivalent effect. Quantitative restrictions are national regulations which prohibit or limit by quotas the import of goods from other Member States (Geiger, 2004; Oppermann, 2005). However, various judgments by the ECJ shed more light on the meaning of 'measures of equivalent effect' (in terms of quotas).

The interpretation of such 'measures' was given in the Dassonville case (Case no. 8/74) where the ECJ said that: *"All trading rules enacted by Member States which are capable of hindering, directly or indirectly, actually or potentially, intra-community trade are to be considered as measures having an effect equivalent to quantitative restrictions."* On the basis of the above formula, as clarified by the ECJ also in the case of Cassis de Dijon (Case no. 120/78 of 20 Feb. 1979), it is concluded that measures which have effects equivalent to quantitative restrictions (quotas) can be adopted as national legislative provisions applying not to the importation of products but

to the promotion and sale of such products in the national markets (Oppermann, 2005). Whether these provisions introduce discrimination against foreign products or apply indiscriminately, even to domestic products, is irrelevant. In addition, the effect of such national regulations on intra-Community commerce can be overlooked only for the reasons listed in Article 30 EC[6], and on condition that the principle of proportionality is maintained. It should be noted that the ECJ, in its ruling on the Cassis de Dijon case, accepted that intra-Community commerce can be restricted by national legislation for reasons of consumer protection and honesty of the transactions.

From the above mentioned case laws derives the country-of-origin principle. According to this principle a product which has lawfully been produced and/or put to circulation in a Member State of the European Union can also be sold in any other Member State. What is more, it is enough for a product to meet the necessary conditions in order to be placed in the market of the country of origin, i.e. products produced in other countries but placed in the market of another Member State, or produced in the country of origin exclusively for export purposes are also included (Blasi, 2004). On the other hand, restrictions on the free movement of goods by the legal system of the country of delivery can be justified on exceptional grounds provided for by Community law (Hucke, 2001; Blasi, 2004).

Nevertheless, in its judgement of the Keck case (in Joined Cases C-267/91 and C-268/91, 24 Nov. 1993), the ECJ seems to have changed its mind in regards to the broad application of the term 'measures of equivalent effect' in comparison to previous case law. In the Keck case the Court's grounds (no. 16) were that *"...the application to products from other Member States of national provisions restricting or prohibiting certain selling arrangements is not such as to hinder directly or indirectly, actually or potentially, trade between Member States ... so long as those provisions apply to all relevant traders ... and so long as they affect in the same manner, in law and in fact, the marketing of domestic products and of those from other Member States."*

Although the above judgment does show that the ECJ backtracked in relation to the brevity it had shown in previous interpretations of the term 'measures of equivalent effect', the case laws produced to that date remain harmless (Grandpierre, 1999; Heermann, 1999). The judgement in question refers to provisions which govern the distribution and sale of products in a Member State, and such provisions are in force regardless of the origin of the products. Also, the ECJ states that such provisions continue to function as measures of equivalent effect on condition it is proved that despite their apparent neutral nature they prohibit access or obstruct the trade of foreign products in a national market in favour of the domestic products (Blasi, 2004). Therefore, it could be said that in the Keck case the Court intervened by correcting the '*Dassonville formula*', crossing out the word "potentially" (Tzoulia, 2006).

Electronic Pharmacies in the European Union Today

Coming back to the DocMorris case we should look at the judgment of the ECJ in terms of the issue of compatibility with the European Law of the German prohibition affecting distance selling of medicinal products, on the one hand, and related advertising, on the other hand.

Looking at the first part of the issue, the ECJ distinguishes between authorised and not authorised medicinal products in the context of the German market. It resorts to article 6 (1) of Directive 2001/83/EC to state that as far as the second category of products (unauthorised) is concerned the German prohibition on distance selling is compatible with Community law, i.e. with the provisions of Article 28 EC. This is true because the relevant German law sets into force a secondary Community law which requires prior

authorization before a medicine is placed in the market of a Member State.

Notwithstanding the above, the ECJ has dealt with the German provision in the light of measures of equivalent effect and in connection with medicinal products authorized in Germany. The Court concluded that the prohibition of distance selling of medicinal products, even if it applies indiscriminately to foreign and domestic traders, raises obstacles to the cross-border business of pharmacies established outside Germany, while it favours pharmacies operating in the German territory. This is true because the prohibition bans the cross-border mail-order pharmacy operations, which benefits domestic pharmacies in spite of the fact that they lose an alternative marketing tool. Finally, the Court ruled that the negative effect of the German provision on intra-Community commerce may be justified with reference to prescription products, and on the grounds of protecting consumers and public health.

In regards to the second issue, i.e. to what extent the prohibition on the distance advertising of medicinal products is incompatible with Community law, the Court's ruling was based on the provisions of Article 86, Directive 2001/83/EC, which define advertising of medicinal products. According to these provisions, advertising to the general public of non-authorized or prescription medicinal products is prohibited. However, the advertising of medicinal products available over the counter is permitted. The Court, fending off the argument that it is electronic advertising *per se* which induces customers to commercial transactions, where the pharmacist can not be physically present, thought that the above mentioned provisions could also apply to online marketing (Koch, 2004; Koenig, Mueller & Trafkowski, 2000).

In view of the above conclusions, it follows that the operation of electronic pharmacies, i.e. online advertising and sale by mail-order of medicinal products, is in principle free in the European Union. Community law prohibits such firms to sell medicinal products which have not been authorised in other Member States. At the same time, with a view to consumer protection and public health, Community law allows Member States to prohibit the electronic advertising and sale of prescription medicines. These restrictions do not apply to over-the-counter medicinal products.

It should be noted that the DocMorris case modernized German legislation in regards to the sale and advertising of medicines. Currently, it is legal to operate internet pharmacies in Germany, while under certain conditions the German law condones advertising and sale of prescription medicines. The same is true in Great Britain, Spain, Holland and Denmark (Pickering, 2007). In Greece, however, the National Organization for Medicines prohibits the electronic advertising of prescription medicinal products (National Organization for Medicines Decrees no. 39600 & 53425, 2001).

Private International Law Issues

In view of the above, it is obvious that internet advertising and sale of medicines, notwithstanding the benefits to the pharmaceutical industry and to end consumers, carries certain risks for the latter. The European Union seems to be aware of all the side effects of electronic marketing and sale of medicines in cyberspace. Therefore, the EU is scrupulously attempting, on the one hand, to ensure a high level of consumer protection in cases where the consumers decide, or are induced or simply invited, to engage in the relevant commercial transactions and, on the other hand, not raise obstacles to the intra-Community free movement of personal data and medicinal products. It is also true that in so far as Community law applies, even when rectifying the law of a Member State, the satisfaction of competing interests is more like a Solomon's solution.

Nevertheless, it has been surreptitiously mentioned that Community space can not be isolated in cyberspace, while the development of legal relationships in cyberspace is more than likely to

manifest elements of extraterritoriality (Mitrou, 2002; Perakis, 1999). This means that the personal data of EU consumers are at risk of theft, possibly for cross-border communication to third parties who launch direct advertising campaigns. On the other hand, it is a fact that internet pharmacies established outside the EU are accessible by and available for business to EU consumers. Therefore, it is worth considering whether the legislative and regulatory measures of the Community designed for the protection of the EU citizens are ineffective in cyberspace.

Although it is outside the scope of this paper to elaborate on this issue, it is absurd to believe that the key to solving the globalizing effect of the internet lies in the self-regulation of the internet content. Having a complex and transnational character, the legal relationships forged on the internet must not be left at the mercy of rules of professional ethics and self-appointed legal instruments (Mitrou, 2002; Hoeren, 1998). The mechanisms for alternative problem-solving, e.g. mediation or arbitration, and the suppressive application of technology to maintain order on the internet (e.g. flagging and blocking of web pages), or the preventive measure of labelling web sites, are no more than substitutes of justice, to which one must always resort to obtain redress (Hoeren, 1998; Rossnagel, 2002).

In the light of the subject matter, private international law can guarantee the application of the European standards for consumer protection. Consequently, if an e-advertisement (direct or indirect) from outside Community space constitutes a risk to EU consumers (inducing them to execute agreements or mislead them to purchase goods or services), the principle of "place of the act", i.e. the rule of private international law (common in most EU legal systems) which sets the law applicable to acts of unfair competition involving elements of extraterritoriality, shall give cause to proceedings in the jurisdiction where the affected consumer is domiciled. The same rule shall apply if a medicine that has been purchased via an internet pharmacy set up in a third country resulted in the harm of an EU citizen, i.e. in a case of tort[7]. Please note that offences against the person also constitute tort, committed in terms of illegal access to and unauthorised processing of personal information and harassment of the person via direct advertising messages (Perakis, 1999; Mankowski, 1999).

Directive 95/46/EC provides more examples of the 'transposition' of the European legal order over the law of third countries in regards to the protection of personal data. The Community legislator proves very ingenious with the extension of the scope of the directive to the processing of personal data by a controller or by the controller's representative or even by means of equipment located inside Community territory (Article 4 of Directive 95/46/EC). On the other hand, the transfer of personal data to third countries is conditional upon the existence there of an acceptable level of data protection, which forces one's arm for international dialogue and cooperation[8].

Lastly, one could argue that to the extent the EU appears to the international community as a unified legal order, not only on account of harmonising substantial law but also of the private international law of the Member States, the risks which underline commercial activities with third countries are mitigated. Furthermore, the EU instruments keeping up with technological developments and the regulation of more and more aspects of online activities could ensure the protection of the EU citizen in cyberspace.

CONCLUSION

This chapter attempted to examine an aspect of online marketing and the problems associated with internet advertising of medicinal products. The author hopes to have shown that although this particular commercial communication contributes to the intra-Community movement of medicinal products, at the same time it invades the private sphere of citizens, in addition to pos-

ing a public health risk. The European legal order has been balancing conflicting interests to this date, having achieved a minimum of consumer/data protection in all Member States, liberating at the same time the pharmaceutical industry in the European Union. In terms of the risks associated with the e-commerce activities of pharmaceutical firms / pharmacies established in third countries, this paper is in favour of further regulation and harmonization by the EU.

REFERENCES

Argyropoulos, A. (2001). *Electronic Crime*. Athens – Komotini: Sakkoulas Publications.

Armamentos, P., & Sotiropoulos, B. (2005). *Personal data – Interpretation of Law 2472/1997*. Athens, Thessaloniki: Sakkoulas Publications.

Blasi, M. (2004). *Das Herkunftslandprinzip der Fernseh- und der E-Commerce Richtlinie*. Berlin, Köln, München: Carl Heymanns Verlag.

Criminal proceedings against Bernard Keck and Daniel Mithouard, Joined cases C-267/91 and C-268/91, ECJ (1993).

Deutscher Apothekerverband eV v. 0800 DocMorris NV and Jacques Waterval, Case C-322/01, ECJ (2003).

Gamerith, H. (2003). Neue Herausforderungen für ein europäisches Lauterkeitsrecht. *Wettbewerb in Recht und Praxis, 2*, 143–172.

Geiger, R. (2004). *Vertrag über die Europäische Union und Vertrag zur Gründung der Europäischen Gemeinschaft*. München: Verlag C. H. Beck.

Google AdSense Help. (n.d).*About AdSense - AdSense Help*. Retrieved 10/1/2010 from https://www.google.com/adsense/support/bin/topic.py?hl=en-uk&topic=13488.

Graf von Bernstoff, C. (2000). Ausgewählte Rechtsprobleme im Electronic Commerce. *Recht der Internationalen Wirtschaft, 1*, 14–20.

Grandpierre, A. (1999). *Herkunftsprinzip kontra Marktortanknüpfung, Auswirkungen des Gemeinschaftsrechts auf die Kollisionsregeln im Wettbewerbsrecht. Frankfurt/M.* Berlin, Bern, New York, Paris, Wien: Verlag Peter Lang.

Greek National Organization for Medicines Decrees no. 39600 & 53425 (2001).

Heermann, P. W. (1999). Artikel 30 EGV im Lichte der „Keck" – Rechtssprechung: Anerkennung sonstiger Verkaufsmodalitäten und Einführung eines einheitlichen Rechtsfertigungssystems. *Gewerblicher Rechtsschutz und Urheberrecht. Internationaler Teil, 7*, 575–587.

Heyms, S., & Pries, C. (2002). *Werbung online – Eine Betrachtung aus rechtlichen Sicht.* Berlinq: Erich Schmidt Verlag.

Hoeren, T. (1998). Internet & Recht – Neue Paradigmen des Informationsrechts. *Neue Juristische Wochenschrift, 39*, 2849–2854.

Hucke, A. (2001). *Erforderlichkeit einer Harmonisierung des Wettbewerbsrechts im Europa.* Baden – Baden: Nomos Verlagsgesellschaft.

Igglezakis, I. (2003). *The legal framework of e-commerce.* Athens, Thessaloniki: Sakkoulas Publications.

Iyer, G., Soberman, D., & Villas-Boas, M. (2004). *The targeting of advertising.* Retrieved 10/1/2010 from http://library.nyenrode.nl/INSEAD/2004/2004-020.pdf.

Johnson, D. R., & Post, D. G. (1998). *The New 'Civic Virtue' of the Internet: A Complex Systems Model for the Governance of Cyberspace.* Retrieved 10/1/2010 from http://www.temple.edu/lawschool/dpost/Newcivicvirtue.html

Kloss, I. (2003). *Werbung. Lehr-, Studien- und Nachschlagewerk.* Oldenbourg: Oldenbourg - Verlag.

Koch, B. (2004). Die erste Bewertung der Entscheidung "DocMorris" des EuGH. *Europäische Zeitschrift für Wirtschaftrecht, 2*, 50–51.

Koehler, M., & Arndt, H.-W. (2001). *Recht des Internet.* Heidelberg: C.F. Mueller Verlag.

Koenig, C., Mueller, E.–M., Trafkowski, A. (2000). Internethandel mit Arzneimitteln und Wettbewerb im EG-Binnenmarkt. *Europäisches Wirtschafts- und Steuerrecht, 3*, 97 - 105.

Kornilakis, P. (2007). The Internet and Civil Law. *Armenopoulos, 7*, 993–998.

Lettl, T. (2004). *Das neue UWG.* München: Verlag C.H.Beck.

Mankowski, P. (1999). Internet und Internationales Wettbewerbsrecht. *Gewerblicher Rechtsschutz und Urheberrecht. Internationaler Teil, 11*, 909–921.

Mantzoufas, P. (2007). Taking risks in the information society and protection of personal data. *Armenopoulos, 7*, 1088–1109.

Marinos, M. T. (1998). Licensing databases – information as commodity. *Commercial Law Review, 1*, 16–36.

Marinos, M. T. (2002). *Unfair Competition.* Athens: Publications P.N. Sakkoulas, Law & Economy.

Mayer, F. C. (1996). Recht und Cyberspace. *Neue Juristische Wochenschrift, 28*, 1782–1791.

Micklitz, H. W., & Schirmbacher, M. (2006). Distanzkommunikation im europäischen Lauterkeitsrecht. *Wettbewerb in Recht und Praxis, 2*, 148–168.

Mitrou, L. (2002). *Law in the Society of Information*. Athens, Thessaloniki: Sakkoulas Publications.

Nett, C. (2002). *Wettbewerb im E-commerce: Die Auswirkungen des Herkunftslandprinzips der E-Commerce Richtlinie auf das Lauterkeitsrecht der Mitgliedstaaten*. Retrieved 10/1/2010 from http://deposit.ddb.de/cgi-bin/dokserv?idn=965274187&dok_var=d1&dok_ext=pdf&filename=965274187.pdf.

Oppermann, T. (2005). *Europarecht*. München: Verlag C. H. Beck.

Perakis, E. (1999). Contemporary issues on advertising. *Enterprise and Company Law*, *3*, 251–263.

Pickering, G. (2007). *Internet pharmacy in the European Union*. Retrieved 10/1/2010 from http://www.reedsmith.com/_db/_documents/Internet__Pharmacy_article.pdf

Procureur du Roi v Benoît and Gustave Dassonville, Case 8-74, ECJ (1974).

Rewe-Zentral AG v Bundesmonopolverwaltung für Branntwein, Case 120/78, ECJ (1979).

Rossnagel, A. (2002). Weltweites Internet - globale Rechtsordnung? *Multimedia und Recht*, *2*, 67–71.

Simons, C., & Causey, J. (2002). *Microsoft Windows XP Networking Inside Out*. Microsoft Press.

Stefanou, K. (2005). Protecting human health and consumer safety in the European legal order and the European standardization policy. *Enterprise and Company Law*, *12*, 1248–1264.

Theodorides, K. (2005). The traps of cyberspace (I). *Hellenic Review of European Law*, *2*, 471–483.

Tzoulia, E. (2006). *The principle of origin and online advertising*. Unpublished master's thesis, Ruprecht – Karls Universitaet, Heidelberg.

KEY TERMS AND DEFINITIONS

Direct Advertising: A marketing strategy used by firms in the form of targeting their advertisements at specific segments of the market that have already expressed a preference for their products.

European Law: A body of treaties, legislative acts and court judgments which operates alongside the legal systems of the European Union's member states. It has direct effect within the EU's member states and, where conflict occurs, takes precedence over national law. The primary source of EU law is the EU's treaties. These are power-giving treaties which set broad policy goals and establish institutions that, amongst other things, can enact legislation in order to achieve those goals. The legislative acts of the EU come in two forms: regulations and directives. Regulations become law in all member states the moment they come into force, without the requirement for any implementing measures, and automatically override conflicting domestic provisions. Directives require member states to achieve a certain result while leaving them discretion as to how to achieve the result. The details of how they are to be implemented are left to member states.

Indirect Advertising: Advertising that addresses the market as a whole and that is not targeted to a specific audience.

Internet Pharmacy: Company trading with pharmaceutical products which operates over the internet.

Medicinal Products: According to Directive 2001/83/EC a medicinal product is defined in the European Union as any substance or combination of substances presented for treating or preventing disease in human beings. Any substance or combination of substances which may be administered to human beings with a view to making a medical diagnosis or to restoring, correcting or modifying physiological functions in human beings is likewise considered a medicinal product.

Online Advertising: A form of promotion for goods and services that uses the Internet and World Wide Web to deliver marketing messages to attract customers.

Personal Data: Any information relating to an identified or identifiable natural person ('Data Subject'), according to Directive 95/46/EC; an identifiable person is one who can be identified, directly or indirectly, in particular by reference to an identification number or to one or more factors specific to his physical, physiological, mental, economic, cultural or social identity.

Pharmaceutical Industry: Branch of companies that develop, produce, and market drugs licensed for use as medications.

Principle of "Place of the Act": The Rome II Regulation has introduced a new European regime for determining the applicable law in all cases of non-contractual liability with an international element. If the act of unfair competition affects markets or consumers in general, then the applicable law is that of the state or states where competitive relations are affected.

Unfair Advertising Practices: Marketing methods that prove to be harmful to the consumers and liable to restriction.

ENDNOTES

[1]   According to article 2 (a) of Directive 95/46/EC 'processing' shall mean any collection, recording, organization, storage, adaptation or alteration, retrieval, consultation, use, disclosure … etc of 'personal data'.

[2]   Directive 2002/58/EC was transposed on Greek law 3471/2006 which introduces stricter regulations. Article 11 of the home law provides for an "opt in" system for all kinds of unsolicited communication / direct marketing of products (Kornilakis, 2007).

[3]   Directive 97/7/EC of the European Parliament and of the Council of 20 May 1997 on the Protection of Consumers in respect of Distance Contracts. Directive 1999/93/EC of the European Parliament and of the Council of 13 December 1999 on a Community framework for electronic signatures. Directive 2000/31/EC of the European Parliament and of the Council of 8 June 2000 on certain legal aspects of information society services, in particular electronic commerce, in the Internal Market. Directive 2005/29/EC of the European Parliament and of the Council on unfair business-to-consumer commercial practices in the internal market. See also Graf von Bernstorff (2000).

[4]   Anabolic steroids, illegal and psychotropic substances, diet pills, etc.

[5]   Case C-322/01 Deutscher Apothekerverband eV v. 0800 DocMorris NV (2003).

[6]   In other words for reasons of "public morality, public policy or public security, the protection of health and life of humans, animals or plants; the protection of national treasures possessing artistic, historic or archaeological value; or the protection of industrial and commercial property."

[7]   Under Greek law acts of unfair competition come under tort (art. 26 of Civil Code). See also Marinos (2002).

[8]   Articles 25 and 26 of Directive 95/46/EC. See Mitrou (2002) in regard to an agreement with the USA on "Safe Harbor Principles".

Section 7
Case Studies:
How Healthcare Professionals
and Students Perceive Security

Chapter 13
Password Sharing and How to Reduce It

Ana Ferreira
Cintesis, Portugal & University of Kent, UK

Ricardo Correia
Cintesis, Portugal

David W Chadwick
University of Kent, UK

Henrique Santos
University of Minho, Portugal

Rui Gomes
Hospital Prof. Doutor Fernando Fonseca, Portugal

Diogo Reis
Hospital S. Sebastião, Portugal

Luis Antunes
Instituto de Telecomunicações, Portugal

ABSTRACT

Password sharing is a common security problem. Some application domains are more exposed than others and, by dealing with very sensitive information, the healthcare domain is definitely not exempt from this problem. This chapter presents a case study of a cross section of how healthcare professionals actually deal with password authentication in typical real world scenarios. It then compares the professionals' actual practice with what they feel about password sharing and what are the most frequent problems associated with it. Further, this chapter discusses and suggests how to solve or minimize some of these problems using both technological and social cultural mechanisms.

DOI: 10.4018/978-1-61692-895-7.ch013

INTRODUCTION

Health care is an industry sector considered to be exposed to high risks regarding information security. Nevertheless, today's technology and good practices provide a range of controls to mitigate (up to a certain level) most of those risks, especially those related to electronic health records. The biggest risk faced is a lack of understanding of the complex environments that our health services present and ensuring that users understand and comply with local policies. Convergence towards a viable universal solution is not imminent. Therefore trust in e-health is decidedly more fragile as compared with many other industry sectors. This can be explained by the constant challenges in system interconnectivity and an environment of continual changes in legislation (Croll & Croll, 2006).

A hospital is an environment in which sensitive information is the base of clinical decisions, so there is the need for a correct balance between the usability of information technologies and the security of the information (Kurtz, 2003). Hospital Information Systems (HIS) need to tackle security concerns regarding confidentiality (e.g. access control, and secure communications), integrity (e.g. data consistency, error correction, redundancy, and accidental or malicious alterations) and availability (e.g. continuous access to information by authorised users).

Confidentiality, which involves access control and secure communications, has been defined as ensuring that information is accessible only to those authorised to have access (ISO, 2000).

Access control relates specifically to confidentiality, and is a step performed after the identification and authentication of users is finished. Its purpose is to guard access to the patient records in the Information Systems (IS). Access control should start with a clear and succinct definition of an access policy (Blobel, 2000). This may seem easy to achieve, but usually does not exist, either because it can be very complex or simply because

no one thought it was necessary to articulate it. In the healthcare environment, processes and people acting upon them may change very often and are, therefore, difficult to track. The primary cause of security breaches is insiders and the consequences in a healthcare environment can be more damaging than in any other organisation. Security should enable and not intrude in the daily workflow; otherwise people will try to bypass it just to do their work more easily. So, it is very important to assess and understand the reality of a working environment in a hospital.

Of the few published studies on the specific issue of password management and security in healthcare systems, a previous survey (Stanton & Stam, 2005) showed that end users do not comply with the regular security procedures that are necessary to keep their user accounts' information safe. This behaviour is closely related to the organization goals, so end users from organizations whose missions depend mainly upon security, behave better in performing security procedures. Nevertheless, training, awareness and knowledge of monitoring can also help in improving users' behaviour. Unfortunately, the downside of this is the fact that end users need to remember their chosen or assigned passwords so they tend to write them somewhere in order not to forget them. Furthermore, all the awareness and training of end users seems to be of little effect when it comes to password sharing behaviours.

This chapter addresses the topic of password sharing as follows. The Background section introduces some concepts related to Electronic Medical Record security. Password Sharing section confronts and analyses case study results of what happens in practice in terms of sharing passwords. It then compares this to what the healthcare professionals say happens and what their opinions and views on these issues are. The next section (Discussion and Recommendations) discusses the results in more detail and presents some recommendations for possible solutions to the problem of password sharing, in terms of both technological and social and cultural changes. The chapter ends with the conclusions of this research.

BACKGROUND

Information Security

Information security is usually defined by three main characteristics: *confidentiality* as the prevention of unauthorized disclosure of information; *integrity* as the prevention of unauthorized modification of information; and *availability* as the prevention of unauthorized withholding of information or resources (Gollman, 1999; Harris, 2003). In specific environments, like healthcare, some authors and even standards like the ISO 27000 family, highlight other security properties, like Authenticity (the clear identification of the author of a piece of information), but these can usually be considered as variants of the three main properties (e.g. authenticity can be considered to be part of integrity (Pfleeger & Pfleeger, 2007). Another important variant is the difference between privacy and confidentiality. Privacy relates to the right an individual to protect his or her private information from unwarranted disclosure, whilst confidentiality relates to the provision of mechanisms to protect information from unauthorized access (Gollman, 1999).

The complexity of information security systems make it very difficult to build a fully secure system (Schneier, 2004). This complexity is related to 3 contributing factors: the technology itself and the risks inherent in using it; the difficulty of classifying information in terms of both organization and users' security requirements; and facilitating the ease of understanding and use of the information technology by humans. The end users of the system are usually not technological experts and this is one of the most problematic factor to consider (Schneier, 2004) when it comes to access control. These contributing factors coupled with the fact that attackers are always finding new ways to exploit potential vulnerabilities in existing technology make it very difficult to build secure information systems. To make matters worse, potential solutions often have conflicting aims, for example: assuring the privacy of information, whilst needing to be able to access it for audit or law enforcement purposes; making it easy for an authorised user to gain access to information but complex for an unauthorised one.

Electronic Medical Record - EMR

A patient record is a set of documents containing clinical and administrative information regarding one particular patient. It supports communication and decision making in daily practice, and is used by different users for different purposes (Wyatt, 1994). It exists to memorise and communicate the data existing on a particular individual, in order to help deliver care to him or her. Records are not only an information resource but also a communication mechanism which enables communication between health professionals and between the past and the present (Dick & Steen, 1997) (Nygran, Wyatt & Wright, 1998). Patient records, the patient and published best practice are the three sources needed for the practice of evidence-based medicine (Wyatt & Wright, 1998). They are used for immediate clinical decisions (either by the author, or by others), future clinical decisions, quality improvement, education, clinical research, management and reimbursement, and to act as evidence in a court case (Wyatt, 2005). Many different names are given when patient records are computerised. Some of the acronyms found in the literature are confusing and others are redundant. Terms like Computerised Patient Record (CPR), Computerised Medical Record (CMR), Patient Health Record (PHR), Electronic Medical Record (EMR) and Electronic Patient Record (EPR) have been used in the past. Electronic Health Record (EHR) has turned out to be the most generic term, although each one of the others represents a different concept in the current understanding of EHR (Waegemann, 2002). This chapter uses the term Electronic Medical Record (EMR), which means an organised collection of all medical records about an individual patient stored in the various computer systems and databases of all the providers who have provided health care to that patient within their organisation.

For decades, medical records' technology was remarkably stagnant. Occasional breakthroughs consisted of new systems of colour-coded chart tags and rolling lateral file cabinets (Bodenheimer & Grumbach, 2003). In 1997 it was stated that after 30 years of work and millions of dollars in research and implementation of computer systems in healthcare in the USA, patient records were still predominantly paper records (Dick & Steen, 1997). Between 1991 and 1998 the European Union provided 47 Million Euros of direct funding support to research projects on EMRs whose budgets totalled 76 Million Euros (Iakovidis, 1998). As a result of some of these efforts, EMRs were implemented in the healthcare institutions of each country, although at very different speeds. During the 80s and the 90s the free market in provision gave rise to a considerable fragmentation (Beolchi, 2002).

Generically the main requirements an electronic medical record must fulfil are:

- be fast enough to give instantaneous replies;
- have a simple interface, which is easy to use;
- be trustworthy regarding the information it delivers;
- be versatile to adapt itself to user requirements;
- be extensible to include new features as they arise.

Problems of EMR Confidentiality and Healthcare Professionals

The introduction of EMR systems within healthcare organizations has the main goal of integrating heterogeneous patient information that is usually scattered over different locations (Waegemann, 2003; Cruz-Correia et al, 2005). This is why the EMR is becoming an essential source of information and an important support tool for the healthcare professional. There is also an increasing need to access healthcare information at remote locations (MRI, 2005). This and the distributed nature of the information stress the need for information security requirements to be taken seriously (Bakker, 2004).

One obstacle mentioned by healthcare professionals for the use and integration of EMR within healthcare is the lack of controls to assure patient privacy (Knitz, 2005). As stated earlier, in order to protect a patient's privacy it is essential to at least provide for information confidentiality. Healthcare professionals report that using EMR has problems in terms of security due to its ease of distribution and wider online access (Miller, Hillman & Given, 2004). If they do not comprehend the technology or how the system can or cannot protect patient information it will be more difficult for them to agree on using it, or to help improve its flaws and integrate it efficiently within their daily work.

On the other hand, healthcare professionals normally bypass system controls in order to hasten and make the completion of their tasks easier (Lehoux, 2006) (Adams & Sasse, 1999). When they do this, they do not realize that they could be doing more harm than good. Sharing passwords is similar to sharing identities, to masquerading as another identity and performing tasks as another person. So anyone that is using another person's password will be associated to that identity. When something wrong happens, when for example someone inserted the wrong information about a patient's medication and the patient gets worse, who is the responsible party? If multiple human users are using the same user account, then the audit trail is unable to determine precisely which human user did what to which information and when. It thus becomes impossible to find the source of any security breach. However, the account holder—the person to whom the username and password was originally issued – will be held responsible if he/ she was supposed to be the sole user of the account and password sharing is officially forbidden by the organization. In this case this user is officially the only person using that username/password combination. Users typically will not want to be held responsible for unauthorized actions that they have not undertaken, and once this is made known to them, they will be unlikely to want to share their account passwords again.

Users usually have no problem in understanding that certain computer accounts should only be accessed by themselves and that their usernames and passwords should not be divulged to anyone else. If you ask users if they would be willing to give their bank debit or credit card and PIN number to someone else, they would invariably say "certainly not". Thus they have no problem in understanding that some accounts should be for their sole use only.

Password sharing may happen if there is the assumption that only registered healthcare professionals are using the system. But are they the only users? How can the systems' administrators check if there are no intruders in the system if everyone uses the same identity? The current user may be someone from outside that is trying to do harm. The intruder may only access confidential information but could, even worse, change and/ or delete it. Sharing passwords distributes them and makes it easier for them to be discovered by outsiders or by insiders that are not authorized to access the EMR. It is therefore not only bad practise but also potentially dangerous practise.

Password sharing in healthcare needs a proper study and improvements in password usage must be properly adapted to the human users of EMR as well as to the technical functionalities of the EMR itself. The next section presents two studies that help to understand what really happens in practice regarding sharing passwords and reveals what healthcare professionals' feel about it.

PASSWORD SHARING

This section presents a review of published studies about password sharing from the healthcare practice and from healthcare professionals' perspectives. It also includes results from an analysis of user access logs of a real EMR system as well as from studies that explored the users' perceptions and opinions in relation to password sharing.

Literature Review

A literature review was performed according to the following steps:

1. Build search queries to select published articles of the subject in study (see Table 1).
2. Filter the published papers based on their titles and abstracts.
3. Select related papers and papers that are referenced by the ones selected in B.
4. Get the full papers.
5. Read and summarize the full papers.

A large number of papers regarding password sharing and password authentication problems were found in the initial search (see Table 1). From this list of papers there was a further selection in order to choose the papers relating to healthcare practice as well as papers regarding healthcare professionals' perspectives and views on these topics.

For the healthcare practice theme, from the 183 papers obtained from the search, after performing steps A to E, only 10 papers were selected for review, from which 9 full papers were obtained. From these 9 papers, 5 papers were found from the initial search queries while 4 papers were found as references in step C. 5 of the 9 papers were directly related to the healthcare domain while 4 were from different domains.

For the healthcare professionals' perspectives in relation to password sharing, 10 papers were selected for review. 9 papers were directly

Table 1. Database search query results

Database	Query	No of articles
PUBMED		
	password sharing	5
	authentication password	8
	password problems	15
SCOPUS		
	"sharing password"	6
	"password authentication" problems	67
IEEE Xplorer		
	sharing password	8
	password problems	2
ISI		
	"password sharing"	7
	"authentication password"	9
ACM portal		
	"password sharing"	17
	"authentication password" problems	39
	Total	**183**

selected from the search queries while 1 was selected from referenced articles (step C). Only 8 full papers were obtained, read and summarized. From these 8 papers, only 7 papers were included in this review (one of the papers related to the professionals practice and not to their views and perspectives on the subject) - 3 papers related to the healthcare domain while the other 4 were related to other domains.

In Table 2 and Table 3: * refers to papers not from the healthcare domain; [+] refers to papers obtained not directly from the search query.

What Happens in Practice

Results from the literature review, regarding password sharing in healthcare practice, showed that for most healthcare information systems, passwords are the first line of defence in keeping patient and administrative records private and secure. However, this defence is only as strong as the passwords employees choose to use. In more

detail, the published articles focused mainly on three themes that are discussed below: password sharing, constraints of the healthcare domain and attitudes of healthcare professionals.

Password Sharing

A U.S. survey of non-malicious, low technical knowledge behaviour related to password creation and sharing showed that password "hygiene" (i.e. the good practices to use passwords) was generally poor but varied substantially across different organization types (e.g., military organizations versus telecommunications companies) (Stanton & Stam, 2005). The set of studied items included three items pertaining to password management behaviour (e.g., frequency of changing the password), three items pertaining to password sharing behaviour (e.g., sharing with others in the work group) and three items pertaining to organizational support of security-related behaviour (e.g. "My company/ org. provides training programs to help employees improve their awareness"). Their results showed that improvements in basic hygiene behaviours (e.g., frequent changes to one's password) are associated with training, awareness, knowledge of monitoring, and rewards; on the other hand, researchers did not find improvement in relation to password sharing behaviours.

Current systems for banking authentication require that customers do not reveal their access codes, even to their family members. A study of banking and security in Australia showed that the practice of sharing passwords does not conform to this requirement (Singh et al, 2007). For married and de facto couples, password sharing is seen as a practical way of managing money and a demonstration of trust. Sharing Personal Identification Numbers (PINs) is a common practice among remote indigenous communities in Australia. In areas with poor banking access, this is the only way to access cash. People with certain disabilities have to share passwords with carers, and PIN numbers with retail clerks.

Table 2. Summary of objectives and methods from the reviewed papers

Paper	Objective	Methods & participants	Year
A	Find a better solution for user authentication besides passwords	Survey	2003
B	Collect problems from users and staff	Online tracking system - 278	2007
C	Investigate the use of the digital pen (DP) system to collect data in a clinical trial.	Qualitative (semi-structured interviews; focus group) Quantitative (questionnaire) - 134	2008
D*	Assess how people deal with money and banking in the context of their relationships	Qualitative (open-ended interviews and focus groups) – 108	2007
E*	Family Accounts - a new user account model for shared home computers	Group interview; system use; questionnaires – 38	2008
F*	Assess students' best practices on password security	Survey	2008
G*+	Assess user behaviours and perceptions relating to password systems	Web based questionnaire – 139	1999

Table 3. Summary of the problems and solutions and/or recommendations relating to passwords

Paper	Problems	Possible solutions and/or recommendations
A	The need to remember multiple passwords	Single sign on with biometrics
B	4% (11 reports) were password problems (forget password or application not available on all computers)	Improve future implementations based on paper obtained results
C	Most of the technical problems of the system occurred during setup-password access	Improve future systems based on paper obtained results
D*	Sharing of passwords	Design security systems for banking based on observed social and cultural practices of password and pin sharing
E*	• A family who used password-protected profiles mentioned that everyone except the mother had forgotten their passwords, so they relied on her to remain logged in. • Only one study participant claimed to never use someone else's profile, while seven of nineteen (37%) claimed to use someone else's profile at least weekly. • A majority of the participants in the multiple profiles group mentioned that they use other family members' profiles for quick tasks due to convenience, if the computer is already logged in.	This user account model is the most appropriate model for using shared computers
F*	Passwords have many problems	Practices and attitudes should be improved; develop a web application to help students gaining experience with passwords
G*+	4 major factors influence effective password use: multiple passwords; password content; perceived compatibility with work practices; users' perceptions of organizational security and information sensitivity	• Designers of security mechanisms are the key to successful security systems; • Unless security departments understand how the mechanisms they design are used in practice, there will remain the danger that mechanisms that look secure on paper will fail in practice

Constraints of the Healthcare Domain

The access to patient data is not as simple as it may appear at first glance. The processes of healthcare delivery are very dynamic, and so some authors claim that the problem of access control with access control mechanisms (ACM) is too rigid to represent the staff's role and affiliate/membership in the complex real world. Consequently, it may have been natural for a hospital to prioritize resolving that problem.

To Hirose (Hirose, 1998), this problem is caused by the security system representing neither the patient-doctor relation nor the clinical situation at the points of care. He suggested that one possible solution to this problem is to implement an access control method based on the "relation and situation" model on a multi-axial ACM. In his words, "our method holds user declaration of relation/situation as the access reason, then allows flexible data access as needed at the point-of-care. As the result, EMR system records (who, when, where, why, whose, what, and how) on each access, and has the ability of accurately audit without any maintenance cost" (Hirose & Sasaki, 2001).

This interesting solution includes a health professional / patient relation and situation model that includes the following possible classifications:

- in charge of pre-examination
- in charge
- as a member of the treating team
- on behalf of (when the staff in charge is off duty)
- on night coverage
- as a request for consultation
- in an ambulance
- in an emergency
- as an auditor

Also it includes time classifications:

- constant (e.g. main doctor or treating team staff)
- periodical (e.g. anaesthetist or ICU staff)
- intermittent (e.g. some kinds of therapeutic support)
- unsettled (ex. consultation)

Attitudes of Healthcare Professionals

In a 2006 paper, Cazier et al. presented the results of a study of actual healthcare workers' password practices (Lazier & Medlin, 2006). They have examined the passwords created by 90 employees of a healthcare agency through an empirical analysis of the passwords, the factors of length and strength. The results of this study show that a very small percentage of employees are using most of the best practices as recommended by governmental, educational and private organizations. Most users (64%) did not use both upper and lowercase passwords. The vast majority (78%) of those who do use upper and lowercase passwords, do so only in logical places, such as in capitalizing a name.

In addition to using a mix of upper- and lowercase letters, most experts recommend having a combination of letters and numbers. In this case, less than a fourth (24%) used both letters and numbers. Of those who used letters and numbers, the vast majority (82%) only used numbers at either the beginning or end of the word. Also, the great majority of the employees, 59%, appear to be using common words that can be found in any English language dictionary, thus making them very susceptible to dictionary attacks or password guessing. Of even greater concern, 43% of all passwords appear to be the name of a person. Another common threat is having the user name the same (4.4%) or similar (11%) to the password.

The authors concluded by stating that most employees in this healthcare agency were not very security savvy when they created their passwords. Also it appears that they do not completely understand the ramifications of a password breach (like possible access to patients' accounts by a hacker) and how their choice of a weak password could affect the security of their agency's system.

A Case Study

Methods

Three different Information Systems implemented in hospitals were used in this study: (1) a Virtual Patient Record (VPR), (2) an Obstetrics and Gynaecology Departmental Patient Record (ObsGyn.

care), and (3) a Hospital Information System (HIS). The first two information systems are being used in a Central Hospital with more than 1300 beds, whilst the third one is running in a smaller regional hospital with about 300 beds.

The accesses and actions taken place in each of these systems are logged in databases. The collected log data of the three information systems referred to sessions from October 2004 until December 2007. The suspicious behaviour that was searched for was users working for more than 24 hours (in some cases doctors work for 24 hours consecutively). All user sessions that started less than 10 hours from the end of the last session were considered to be referring to the same working day.

Results

The number of suspicious cases found in VPR was 508; the calculated working days ranged from 24 to 63 hours (average = 29 hours). These working days referred to 139 of 1434 logins (r_{VPR}=9.7%). In 72 logins (r_{VPR}^{1}=5.0%) the suspicious behaviour only occurred once; in 57 logins (r_{VPR}^{2}=4.0%) occurred 2 to 9 times; and in 10 logins (r_{VPR}^{10}=0.7%) occurred 10 to 56 times. The 10 logins that more frequently have suspicious behaviour referred to the following medical specialties: Anaesthesiology (4 logins), Emergency (2 logins), Infectious Diseases (2 login), Cardiothoracic Surgery (1 login), Gastroenterology (1 login).

Regarding ObsGyn.care, the number of suspicious cases found was 58; the calculated working days ranged from 24 to 48 hours (average = 27.5 hours). These working days referred to 28 of 266 logins ($r_{O\&G}$=10.5%). In 16 logins ($r_{O\&G}^{1}$=6.0%) the suspicious behaviour only occurred once; in 12 logins ($r_{O\&G}^{2}$=4.5%) occurred 2 to 9 times; and never ($r_{O\&G}^{10}$=0%) occurred more than 10 times.

Regarding HIS, the number of suspicious cases found was 315; the calculated working days ranged from 24 to 91 hours (average = 34.5 hours). The working days referred to 77 of 346 logins (r_{HIS}=22.3%). In 26 logins (r_{HIS}^{1}=7.5%) the suspicious behaviour only occurred once; in 43 logins (r_{HIS}^{2}=12.4%) occurred from 2 to 9 times; and in 8 logins (r_{HIS}^{10}=2.3%) occurred from 10 to 22 times.

The rate of suspicious cases is very similar in the VPR and Obs.care (r_{VPR}=9.7%; $r_{O\&G}$=10.5%), and is double in the HIS case (r_{HIS}=22.3%). However, in the VPR there were more recurring cases than in the Obs.care IS (r_{VPR}^{10}=0.7%; $r_{O\&G}^{10}$=0%), see Table 4.

Discussion

Although technical solutions exist to provide secure access control, they demand a clear definition of permissions for each group of actors. Healthcare organisations must comply with current legislation, ethical rules and internal processes, which are very difficult to objectively define as access control rules. The number of shared passwords found may probably just represent the tip of the iceberg. However, it is sufficient to generate apprehension.

Table 4. Comparison of password sharing among three Information Systems; number and ratio per month of cases of suspected working days (SWD); number and percentage of suspected logins, and percentages grouped the frequency of SWDs

Information System	SWD		Suspicious Logins N (%)			
	N	Per month	Total	*Once*	*Until 10 times*	*10 or more*
VPR	508	14	139 (9.7)	*72 (5.0)*	*57 (4.0)*	*10 (0.7)*
ObsGyn.care	58	2	28 (11)	*16 (6.0)*	*12 (4.5)*	*0 (0.0)*
HIS	315	105	77 (22)	*26 (7.5)*	*43 (12)*	*8 (2.3)*

The analyses of these results made the developer team of HIS change some features of the system, namely the creation of a timeout function so that the interface logs out automatically after a specific idle time. This way the interface locks out and makes the next user insert his/her credentials again. The plan is to make a new analysis of the HIS system in the future, in order to evaluate the impact of the timeout function on login and password sharing.

Healthcare Professionals' Perspectives

Results from the literature review, regarding healthcare professionals' perspectives about password sharing, showed that in both healthcare and other domains, problems with password usage are very similar (Table 3 and Table 4). These include password sharing on a regular basis as well as password forgetting. Although most studies conclude that the obtained results will help to improve the design and definition of password authentication mechanisms, this can only be achieved if the development phases focus on end users' needs and workflows. In order to further explore health care professionals' perspectives a study was carried on. It included a qualitative method (focus groups) to gain lot of information regarding this issue, followed by a quantitative method (a structured questionnaire) to further explore specific issues that came up during the focus groups' discussions.

Focus-Groups

The main objective of focus groups (FG) is to gather opinions and experiences related to specific topics. This is obtained through sampling groups (comprising 6 to 8 people) of the required population, who meet to discuss a set of topics amongst themselves. The discussion can last on average from one to one and a half hours, and is guided by a skilled moderator who records the discussions.

The data is first transcribed and then analysed in a qualitative manner.

Methods

Population
The selection of participants was made from postgraduate students at the Faculty of Medicine of the University of Porto. Students were chosen from the following Masters Courses: Medical Informatics and Evidence and Decision in Healthcare; and from the Doctoral Programs in Clinical Studies and Healthcare Services Research. Both healthcare professionals (HCPs) and informatics' professionals are enrolled on the Masters Courses, but only HCPs were selected and put into groups according to their professional backgrounds (i.e. segmentation). One of these groups however had HCPs with mixed backgrounds. The doctoral program only enrols medical doctors and so these comprised one of the groups. The reason for grouping participants according to professional backgrounds facilitates discussions because all the participants in a group have similar experiences and backgrounds, usually at the same level (Morgan, 1996).

The HCP were contacted and selected at the beginning of their courses (during their first lectures). They were gathered in a room without knowing that they were going to participate in a focus group or what the topic of discussion was going to be.

Line of Discussion
The list below presents the line of discussion that was followed by the moderator:

1. The participants were given the main theme to discuss and other information regarding the process that would be followed during the course of the focus group. Each participant was asked to give their consent to participating.

2. Each participant was initially asked to give details about their profession and work location, as well as the use of EMR within their practice.

3. After that they were all asked to discuss amongst themselves:

   a. The use of paper records or EMR, what are the advantages or disadvantages of each

   b. access control issues in general

   c. access control mechanisms they use on a daily basis when accessing any system

   d. the problems and benefits of giving different access levels to different groups of users

   e. access control policies to EMR: who defines them, what should be improved

At the end they were asked to give their opinions about the best access control solutions they think should be used to control the access to EMR.

Data Collection and Analysis

Data was collected by audio recording the whole conversation while the conversations of the third and fourth group were also recorded with a video camera (see Table 5).

Regarding the analysis, only one person was involved during the whole process. The discussions from each focus group were transcribed into 4 separate word documents. Each document was then divided into smaller ones, containing only the dialogues belonging to each one of the participants, so that the data could be more easily related to a specific participant.

All documents were inserted into the qualitative analysis software, QSR NVivo 7 (NVivo, 2009), and the coding was done using this tool to register and structure data in a more automatic way. The coding started after each focus group documents were generated and was done separately for each focus group.

The data analysis was performed in phases. In the first phase, codes were generated from the data itself (in vivo coding), using a line-by-line coding strategy. These codes comprise the core ideas that were found within the text. Line-by-line coding helps to identify gaps, define actions and explicate both actions and meanings and leads to developing theoretical categories. On a second phase, a more focused and structured coding was done and codes started to fit and be grouped into categories. The third phase was based on axial coding where relations between categories and sub-categories became more visible and so they were organized as such.

Results

Four groups were arranged with a total of 26 participants: one group with 4 nurses (FG1), one group with 5 health technicians (FG2) (3 radiologists, 1 pharmacist and 1 neurophysiologist), another group with 7 people from mixed backgrounds

Table 5. Description of each focus group data collection

FG	Segmentation	Date & Time	Recording	Audio	Video	Moderators
FG1	Yes	11/01/2008 18h:20m	44m:28s	Y	N	2
FG2	Yes	11/01/2008 19h:20m	37m:22s	Y	N	2
FG3	No	21/02/2008 19h:00m	54m:44s	Y	Y	1
FG4	Yes	26/06/2008 19h:00m	40m:16s	Y	Y	1

Table 6.Healthcare institutions for the FG participants

FG	University hospital	Health centre	Hospital	Hospital centre (2 or more hospitals)	Private clinic
FG1	1	1	2		
FG2	2		2	1	
FG3	1	1	3	1	1
FG4	4	1	1	4	
TOTAL	**8**	**3**	**8**	**6**	**1**

(FG3) (1 doctor, 3 nurses and 3 health technicians) and the last group with 10 medical doctors (FG4). Table 6 shows the participants' affiliations.

Figure 1 shows one of the main categories (access control) and sub-categories related to the topic of shared logins and passwords that came up during the focus group discussions.

From all the focus group discussions 16 different people (6 nurses, 3 health technicians and 7 doctors) talked about shared logins and passwords. 14 state that passwords are shared on a regular basis while 2 state that each professional has his own password and to use others they need to know them and it is their responsibility.

From the 14 that stated that passwords are shared on a regular basis: 3 people said that the professionals usually left the applications open and so others could still access and use the application with another person's login and password; 3 people said they needed to use a colleague's password because the system had some problems or theirs was not available at the moment; 2 people said that as they work in a team of two, they both used each other's passwords at some point; 2 people said that there was an habit of password sharing within the clinical environment; 2 people said that it was common to enter several computers at the same time with the same password; 1 person said that some applications only needed a login to access while another said that there were usually generic passwords within the applications.

Some quotes from the focus groups discussions relating to password sharing:

Figure 1. Main category and sub-categories related to the topic of shared logins and passwords, generated from the focus groups discussions

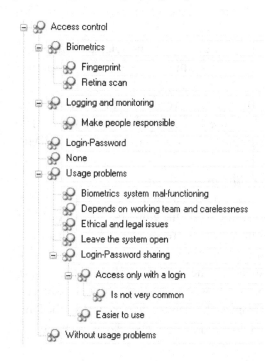

"In the beginning I didn't have a login, I had a colleague beside me and I never used his credentials without him being around..." (nurse)

"...something that happened to me was that because the IT service was not available and did not give me a login and password, my superiors told me to use another person's login and password... this is not right is it? Because I'm recording

something I did in someone else's name... it is ethically incorrect..." (nurse)

"...there is not much security at a clinical level... there is the habit of using each others' logins..." (technician)

"...It depends on the working team...where I work (health centre or hospital) no one is careful to keep their passwords secret..." (nurse)

"...people leave the applications open all the time..." (technician)

"...well, actually in my case, we usually work in pairs so the doctor with another team member... so with my password or hers..it's easier to medicate the patient, to visit the patient...is easier..."(doctor)-- "In my Unit is similar..." (nurse)

"...sometimes...to access the system we just need to provide the login...and it is possible, without a password..and is easy because the login everybody knows...it's the ID number of the professional..." (nurse).

Discussion

Although healthcare professionals are bound to preserve patients' confidentiality and deal with very sensitive information on a daily basis they refer that passwords are shared on a regularly so that they can perform their job more easily, or because they neglect the closing of the application they are using, or even because the system was unavailable and professionals needed to access it using other people's credentials.

These results show not only problems related with the technology and system efficiency and performance, but also with human processes and workflows. These problems need to be addressed both in terms of making sure system availability is guaranteed for a 24/7 period as well as changing cultural and social interactions to guarantee that healthcare professionals have more difficulty in

sharing their identity. This can be done by allowing them an easier and regular access to the systems, without hindering those from achieving their main goals (i.e. to treat patients with the best resources possible available) and making them bypass the security controls.

Structured Questionnaires

These are questionnaires containing different sets of questions, organized in a specific order. A sample of the population is selected and the questions are applied either face to face or people are left to complete them in their own time. The questionnaires can be oriented to focus on specific information. They can, for instance, be based on previously obtained information such as from focus group discussions, as they were in this specific study. The data is analysed quantitatively.

Methods

Construction of the Questionnaire

Questions were constructed based directly on the categories resulting from the focus groups, with the exception of Section 3 where the topics were related to legislation and patient rights to access their medical record. Section 3 also contained questions about a hypothetical scenario.

Population

Questionnaires were tested and corrected with 5 different people from different backgrounds before they were applied to the population in the study.

Healthcare professionals from different healthcare institutions and backgrounds were approached in a random fashion at their working place during working hours. They were asked to answer the questionnaire and they could either refuse to do it, do it immediately or do it later in their own time.

Data Collection and Analysis

Data was collected from the respondents, who were completely unaided in this. The data was subsequently analysed and summarized by the SPSS statistical program.

Results

27 valid questionnaires were received and analyzed. Questionnaires were received from 12 medical doctors, 6 nurses and 9 healthcare professionals. 16 participants were female while 11 were male. 14 participants worked in a hospital, 5 in a health centre, 1 in a laboratory, 2 in an academic institution, 1 in a public healthcare institution and 4 in a private healthcare institution. In terms of academic education, 23 respondents had a BSc and 4 had an MSc. Also, 16 had some informatics' proficiency, 7 had had some informatics' education and 3 had had none (1 respondent did not answer this question).

The questionnaire was divided into four sections and was based on the categories generated from the focus groups' discussions. The questionnaire was designed to further explore some the issues that are more relevant to this study. Section 1 contained 9 generic questions regarding EMR; Section 2 had 11 questions regarding access control to EMR; Section 3 had 4 questions about a fictitious scenario of patients using an Automatic Teller Machine to access their medical records; and Section 4 had 7 demographic questions.

The answers obtained from Section 1 of the questionnaire showed that 21 HCP had used EMR during the course of their work whilst 6 respondents never had and 17 HCP used the EMR daily or almost every day whilst 3 used EMR between 1 and 3 times per week. The responses from the second set of questions focused on those 21 respondents that have used EMR during the course of their work. 19 respondents said they logged in to the EMR with a password, 4 of them used passwords together with biometrics, 1 respondent used biometrics alone and 1 did not use any kind of mechanism.

Table 7 summarises the responses from the most common issues when users authenticate to the EMR with username and password. 15 said this mechanism was easy to use, 4 said they usually share their usernames and passwords, 3 continually forget their passwords and 2 had no opinion on the subject.

Discussion

Although many references were made during the focus groups' discussions in relation to sharing passwords as a common practice amongst the healthcare professionals, only 4 people from the 21 that use EMR for their work agreed that they share passwords. This can mean that when people are asked about the fact itself they may not want to refer it as something they do but when discussing it on an informal way amongst other professionals, this is regularly mentioned, even if in the third person as "something that happens regularly".

Again, healthcare processes and workflows need to be analysed in depth so this issue can be tackled and corrected according to user needs and goals when using the systems.

DISCUSSION AND RECOMMENDATIONS

Interpretation of the Studies

The studies showed that healthcare professionals are aware of what happens in practice and that sharing passwords is a common behaviour. Although

Table 7. Issues regarding the use of login and password as authentication mechanisms

Issues of login-password	No of respondents
Accesses easily	15
Shares passwords	4
Forgets many times	3
No opinion	2

some see it as a wrong behaviour others feel that it can be a useful strategy to fasten and facilitate the team work. The use of passwords as an authentication mechanism is very easy to implement and use but may not be the most efficient mechanism to protect information. It is also very difficult to control, in practice, who shares passwords with whom since the records can only show the identity that accessed and when. This means only an identity can be verified and not who physically accessed the system. A brief study of the access control logs can be one first step to verify if this problem may or may not exist. If the problem is suspected to exist, then other measures can be introduced according to the system's objectives and security level. These measures are further discussed in this section where some technical and well as social and cultural recommendations are presented.

How to Reduce Password Sharing

The issue of password sharing can be addressed from two different perspectives. One is the technological perspective; the other is the human perspective. Whilst different technologies can be used to help to stop the problem of password sharing, without the active involvement of the human users, many technological solutions might fail. Consequently this section will first address the human aspects of password sharing, and then it will turn to the different technologies that might be used to help to address the issue.

Social and Cultural Suggestions

It is abundantly clear that password sharing can only be reduced through the active involvement of the human users. Unless users are willing to acknowledge that password sharing is a problem that needs to be addressed, then little progress will be made in eradicating it (other than by technologically eliminating the need for passwords). EMR are a critical resource to organizations in the health sector. If these records were to become publicly available and broadcast on the Internet, or were to be tampered with by intruders without the knowledge of the health care professionals, this could have life threatening consequences to the patients. They thus need to be strongly protected.

- A critical success factor in reducing password sharing is therefore user education (Adams & Sasse, 1999). Primarily users need to be informed why password sharing is a problem. If the users do not perceive that a problem exists, then they will not be motivated to address it. The educator needs to explain to the users that computer resources and the information that is stored on them are valuable resource to the organization;

- Part of the task of user education is to instil in users the fact that this principle should apply to all the computer accounts that they possess, and not just to their bank accounts. Consequently users should not divulge to third parties their usernames and passwords of any accounts that grant access to computer systems;

- Organizations need to have detailed audit trails recording who accessed and processed which information and when. If there is a breach in the security, it is the audit trail that will inform that and lead back to the source of the breach. (For example, a doctor or a patient will not usually know if some unauthorized person read or copied the patient's medical record, but the audit trail should have a record of this. If each access is uniquely recorded in the audit trail, and each user has a unique account protected by its own username and password, then the audit trail can lead us back to the user account which was responsible for the breach in security);

- Clearly for non-sharing of passwords to be effective, organizations need to have sensible policies for the allocation of new accounts to users, and simple procedures to follow that are not unduly onerous or deemed to be unnecessary;

- Staff should know how to apply for new accounts (so education is important) and the procedure should be fast and efficient, so as to not de-motivate staff. (Ideally this procedure will be one that is automatically carried out when a new member of staff joins the organization, and the account username and password will be issued along with keys to doors, uniforms and other equipment that is necessary for the person to perform their roles.

- The policies for new account creation should not be too restrictive or exclusive, otherwise users may be forced into sharing their passwords so that others who are refused their own accounts, can still do their jobs in the normal way);

- If the organization is licensing software or services from third parties, and pays a license fee per user account, then the organization should purchase sufficient licenses so that all users can have their own account and consequently do not need to share the same account password. (Skimping or cheating on licenses will not encourage users to not share their account passwords on other accounts which are not so restricted);

- The culture of the organization may need to be addressed. A culture that allows staff to share confidential information between them without proper authorization will have difficulty in preventing its staff from sharing their usernames and passwords;

- The organization should also have a set of sanctions that are applied to staff who break the agreed norms of information protection and handling. Staff will be knowledgeable about the policies and correct procedures to follow, and will actively follow them;

- When passwords are lost or forgotten, which invariably they will be, there needs to be a simple, quick and efficient procedure for replacing them. Some IT Help Desks find that password replacements are the single most costly procedure that is undertaken, due to the scale of the problem. The administrator should have a single command that they can issue, which will automatically generate the new password, and print it off for the staff member to take away with them. This should be a random one-time use password that requires the user to register his/her own preferred and easy to remember password after using this newly generated password to login;

- The organization needs to have a clear and easy to understand password policy that is made known to staff and that has been agreed with them. Password policies should contain rules for the length and content of passwords, and the frequency at which they should be changed. Sample password policies are available on the Internet e.g. at http://www.sans.org/resources/policies/Password_Policy.pdf and http://password-manager.hitachi-id.com/docs/password-policy-guidelines.html. But beware. Some organizations make impossible demands on their users. They require passwords to be strong, i.e. long, in a mixture of lower/upper case, numbers, letters and non-alphanumeric characters, so that they cannot be easily cracked, and they also require them to be changed frequently to give hackers less time to crack them. This combination makes it extremely difficult for users to remember what their original strong passwords are (since they cannot be dictionary words), and the frequent change of passwords means that if a user does eventually manage to memorize his password, then no sooner has he done this than the password has to be replaced with another one. If passwords are to be very strong then they should be granted a long lifetime measured in years rather than months, since the time taken to crack them will typically be measured in millions of years;

- Users should not have to remember multiple strong passwords as this is beyond their mental capacities. (Adams & Sasse, 1999) presents the results of a survey into user's attitudes and perceptions of passwords, and reasons for why they often break the rules.

Technical Suggestions

Technology can help alleviate the problem of password sharing, by employing various techniques that either help users to stop sharing passwords, or remove the need to use passwords. In the former category we have single sign on systems and resource management mechanisms. In the latter category we have biometric authentication, and the use of various hardware devices that do not use conventional passwords for authentication.

Helping Users to not Share Passwords

There are several techniques that can be employed to discourage users from sharing their passwords:

- **Single Sign On (SSO) is one option**. With SSO, the user's username and password are used to grant the user access to all (or as many as possible) of his accounts and applications. This has a number of benefits. Firstly it makes easier for users to move between systems, services and machines because once he has logged into the first of these, he can move seamlessly between them all without needing to login again. Clearly a user is unlikely to give his SSO username and password to a colleague, if this means his colleague is simultane-

ously granted access to all of his accounts. Secondly the use of just one SSO password encourages the user to utilize a much stronger password comprising more characters and more entropy than in the case where the user is burdened with having to remember many different passwords for many accounts. This adds to the overall security of the system. (However, SSO also has its disadvantages. One can regard SSO as the user putting all his computer account eggs into one basket – if an attacker gains access to one account he has access to all of them. Furthermore SSO is operationally difficult to achieve since a user's employer typically will not have access to all the user's accounts and therefore is not in a position to enable SSO to all of them. SSO is also technically difficult to achieve. This is because most organizations will have a number of legacy systems and applications which will be very difficult and costly to provide with SSO functionality);

- **Ensuring each system is scalable to the number of users that are envisaged** is also an important factor in helping users to stop password sharing. If the system itself cannot support the number of current or envisaged users, then the system administrator will be forced to make multiple users share the same account and password;

- **If the amount of resources that can be consumed by a single user account is limited**, or is charged for, then **this also discourages users from sharing their account passwords**. For example, the account could have a maximum session time, or CPU usage. If a user is likely to be restricted in his future actions because of the resources consumed by one of his colleagues to whom he has shared his account password, then the user will be less likely to share his password with others in future.

Removing the Need for Passwords

Password based authentication is relatively easy for users to understand and use, and it is easy to implement. This is why password based systems are so prevalent today. However, from a security perspective, user passwords are a very poor authentication technique. This is because passwords are easy to forge using password cracker software, they are easy to share, and users are usually unaware when they are stolen. Many alternative authentication techniques exist, which rely on either the biometric characteristics of the user or the user possessing a hardware token of some sort.

- There are many different **biometric authentication techniques** in use today (Harris, 2003), which might rely on physical user characteristics, like fingerprints, voice or iris scanning, or behavioural characteristics, like keystroke dynamics, pointer dynamics or gait (Magalhães & Santos, 2008), to name a few. Despite the characteristic being used, they all share the following properties: universality (everyone should possess the characteristic; uniquely (no users share the same biometric characteristic); continuity (the characteristic should remain unchanged); and must be measurable in computer terms (Jain & Ross, 2006). Observing these properties the biometric technique should be able to differentiate between one user and another.

- Various different types of **hardware device** can be used for user authentication. These rely on a secret computation being performed in the hardware, and the answer is provided as the user's authentication token to the system being accessed. The answer can be a onetime password or a digital signature. If the hardware device is something the user permanently needs to have in his possession, such as a mobile phone or identity card, then using this as the authentication hardware device makes it much less likely the user will share it. To stop hardware devices from being stolen and used by the thief they are usually protected with a PIN. The user has to enter the PIN into the device before it will reveal the secret to him. Entering the wrong PIN a small number of times will usually lock the device from further use. This is to protect it from being used by a thief who would otherwise try every PIN combination until he found the correct one.

CONCLUSION

This chapter presents a number of cases and experiences relating with password sharing in healthcare. The idea was to give an overview of what happens in practice and what may be able to be improved regarding this important issue. Further, the authors wanted to provide a set of suggestions to aid organizations in their quest to reduce the frequency of password sharing that is either surreptitiously or knowingly carried out by their employees. Whilst technical solutions can be employed, the most cost effective solutions are usually not technical but rather are social and cultural. The most important factor is user education. Users are typically intelligent rational human beings, and when something is properly and effectively communicated to them, such as the negative aspects of password sharing, they are usually willing to comply with the request to cease such activity.

REFERENCES

Adams, A., & Sasse, M. A. (1999). Users are not the enemy. *Communications of the ACM, 42*(12), 40–46. doi:10.1145/322796.322806

Bakker, A. (2004). Access to EHR and access control at a moment in the past: a discussion of the need and an exploration of the consequences. *International Journal of Medical Informatics, 73*(3), 267–270. doi:10.1016/j.ijmedinf.2003.11.008

Beolchi, L. (2002). *Telemedicine Glossary* (4th ed.). Belgium: European Commission.

Blobel, B. (2000). Authorisation and access control for electronic health record systems. *International Journal of Medical Informatics, 73*(3), 251–257. doi:10.1016/j.ijmedinf.2003.11.018

Bodenheimer, T., & Grumbach, K. (2003). A Spark to Revitalize Primary Care? *JAMA: the Journal of the American Medical Association, 290*, 259–264. doi:10.1001/jama.290.2.259

Cazier, J., & Medlin, B. (2006). How secure is your information system? An investigation into actual healthcare worker password practices. *Perspectives in Health Information Management, 3*(8).

Croll, P., & Croll, J. (2006). Investigating risk exposure in e-health systems. *International Journal of Medical Informatics, 76*(5-6), 460–465. doi:10.1016/j.ijmedinf.2006.09.013

Cruz-Correia, R., Vieira-Marques, P., Costa, P., Ferreira, A., Oliveira-Palhares, E., Araújo, F. (2005). Integration of Hospital data using Agent Technologies – a case study. *AICommunications special issue of ECAI, 18(3)*, 191-200.

Dick, R., & Steen, E. (1997). *The Computer-based Patient Record: An Essential Technology for HealthCare*. Washington: National Academy Press.

Gollman, D. (1999). *Computer Security* (1st ed.). New York: John Wiley & Sons.

Harris, S. (2003). *CISSP Certification All-in-One Exam Guide* (2nd ed.). New York: McGraw-Hill Osborne Media.

Hirose, Y. (1998). Access control and system audit based on patient-doctor relation and clinical situation model. *Medinfo '98, 2*, 1151-1155.

Hirose, Y., Sasaki, Y., & Kinoshita, A. (2001). Human resource assignment and role representation mechanism with the cascading staff-group authoring and relation/situation model. *Medinfo, 10*(1), 740–744.

Iakovidis, I. (1998). From electronic medical record to personal health records: present situation and trends in European Union in the area of electronic healthcare records. *Medinfo, 9*, 18–22.

Institute, M. R. (2005). *7th annual survey of electronic health record trends and usage for 2005*. Medical Records Institute.

International Organization for Standardization. International Standard ISO/IEC 17799. (2000). Information technology - Code of practice for information security management. Geneva: ISO2000.

Jain, A., & Ross, A. (2006). Biometrics: A tool for information security. *IEEE Transactions on Information Forensics and Security, 1*(2), 125–143. doi:10.1109/TIFS.2006.873653

Knitz, M. (2005). *HIPPA compliance and electronic medical records: are both possible?* Graduate research report: Bowie State University.

Kurtz, G. (2003). EMR confidentiality and information security. *Journal of Healthcare Information Management, 17*(3), 41–48.

Lehoux, P. (2006). *The Problem of Health Technology: Policy Implications for Modern Health Care* (1st ed.). Routledge.

Magalhães, S., Santos, H. M. D., et al. (2008). Keystroke Dynamic and Graphical Authentication Systems. *Encyclopedia of Information Science and Technology*, Second ed. M. Khosrow-Pour. USA, Information Science Reference, 1, 2313 - 2318.

Miller, R., Hillman, J., & Given, R. (2004). Physician use of IT: results from the Deloitte Research Survey. *Journal of Healthcare Information Management, 18*(1), 72–80.

Morgan, D. (1996). Focus Groups. *Annual Review of Sociology, 22*, 129–152. doi:10.1146/annurev.soc.22.1.129

NVIVO 7.(2009). *QSR International*. Retrieved from: http://www.qsrinternational.com/. (13th April 2009).

Nygren, E., Wyatt, J., & Wright, P. (1998). Helping clinicians to find data and avoid delays. *Lancet, 352*, 1462–1466. doi:10.1016/S0140-6736(97)08307-4

Pfleeger, C. P., & Pfleeger, S. L. (2007). *Security in Computing* (4th ed.). Prentice Hall.

Schneier, B. (2004). *Secrets and Lies: digital security in a networked world*. Wiley.

Singh, S., Cabraal, A., Demosthenous, C., Astbrink, G., Furlong, M., et al. (2007). *Password sharing: implications for security design based on social practice*. In Proceedings of the SIGCHI conference on Human factors in computing systems, pp. 895-904.

Stanton, J., & Stam, K. (2005). Analysis of end user security behaviors. *Computers & Security, 24*(2), 124–133. doi:10.1016/j.cose.2004.07.001

Waegemann, C. (2002). *Status Report 2002: Electronic Health Records.*

Waegemann, C. (2003). EHR vs. CPR vs. EMR. *Healthcare Informatics online.*

Wyatt, J. (1994). Clinical data systems, Part 1: Data and medical records. *The Lancet, 344*, 1543 7.

Wyatt, J. (2005). *Clinical data capture and presentation*. Porto: Medical Informatics Summer School.

Wyatt, J., & Wright, P. (1998). Design should help use of patients' data. *Lancet, 352*, 1375–1378. doi:10.1016/S0140-6736(97)08306-2

ADDITIONAL READING

Brogan, M., Lin, C., Pai, R., & Kalet, I. (2007). *Implementing A Mandatory Password Change Policy at an Academic Medical Institution*. Proceedings of AMIA Symposium, 884.

Bruce, P. (2003). Rx for password headaches: biometric authentication solution lets physicians be their passwords. *Health Management Technology*. St. Vincent Hospitals and Health Care Center Inc.'s solution.

Cruz-Correia, R., Vieira-Marques, P., Ferreira, A., Almeida, F., Wyatt, J., & Costa-Pereira, A. (2007). Reviewing the integration of patient data: how systems are evolving in practice to meet patient needs. *BMC Medical Informatics and Decision Making, 7*, 14. doi:10.1186/1472-6947-7-14

Cruz-Correia, R., Vieira-Marques, P., Ferreira, A., Oliveira-Palhares, E., Costa, P., & Costa-Pereira, A. (2006). Monitoring the integration of hospital information systems: how it may ensure and improve the quality of data. *Studies in Health Technology and Informatics, 121*, 176–182.

Ferreira, A., Cruz-Correia, R., Antunes, L., & Chadwick, D. (2008). Security of Electronic Medical Records. In Lazakidou, A., & Siassiakos, K. (Eds.), *Handbook of Research on Distributed Medical Informatics and E-Health*. Medical Information Science Reference.

Ferreira, A., Cruz-Correia, R., Antunes, L., Farinha, P., Oliveira-Palhares, E., Chadwick, D. W., & Costa-Pereira, A. (2006). *How to break access control in a controlled manner?* Proceedings of the 19th IEEE Symposium on Computer-Based Medical Systems, pp. 847-851.

Ferreira, A., Cruz-Correia, R., Antunes, L., Palhares, E., Marques, P., Costa, P., & Costa-Pereira, A. (2004). *Integrity for Electronic Patient Record Reports*. Proceedings of the 17th IEEE Symposium on Computer-Based Medical Systems, 4-9.

Ferreira, A., Cruz-Correia, R., & Costa-Pereira, A. (2004). *Securing a Web-based EPR: An approach to secure a centralized EPR within a hospital*. Proceedings of the 6th International Conference on Enterprise Information Systems, 3, 54-9.

Ferreira, A., Cruz-Correia, R., & Costa-Pereira, A. (2007). *Why teach computer security to medical students?* Proceedings of the 12th MEDINFO Congress, 129, 1469-1470. Amsterdam: IOS Press

Hart, D. (2008). Attitudes and practices of students towards password security. *Journal of Computing Sciences in Colleges, 23*(5), 169–174.

Littlejohns, P., Wyatt, J., & Garvican, L. (2003). Evaluating computerised health information systems: hard lessons still to be learnt. *BMJ (Clinical Research Ed.), 326*, 860–863. doi:10.1136/bmj.326.7394.860

Miller, R., & Sim, I. (2004). Physicians' use of electronic medical records: barriers and solutions. *Health Affairs, 23*(2), 116–126. doi:10.1377/hlthaff.23.2.116

Proctor, R., Lien, M., Vu, K., Schultz, E., & Salvendy, G. (2002). Improving computer security for authentication of users: Influence of proactive password restrictions. *Behavior Research Methods, Instruments, & Computers, 34*(2), 163–169.

KEY TERMS AND DEFINITIONS

Authentication Mechanism: A mechanism that allows the users to identify and prove who they say they are to an information system (e.g. with a login and password).

Electronic Medical Record: A set of documents within an information system, containing clinical and administrative information, regarding one particular patient in order to support the healthcare professional in his/her daily practice in treating the patient.

Information Security: Usually defined by 3 characteristics: confidentiality – prevent access from unauthorized users; integrity – prevent modification from unauthorized users; availability – provide access to authorized users whenever is needed; as well as auditing – register and control of who does what within the system; and accountability – make users responsible for what they did within the system. The last two are only possible if we can identify and trust that identities are not shared.

Login: A unique tag that identifies a user of an information system (it can be a number or a word).

Password Sharing: The act of giving the login and password to be used by another user and not keeping them private. In this way, users can act on other people's behalf.

Password: A word or string of characters that is uniquely related with a login and proves the identity of a user to the information system (this piece of information has to be kept private and proves to the system that the user identified by that login and that password is who he says he is, because this combination is unique).

Privacy: The right an individual has of keeping his/her information private. He/she controls who can access what. Confidentiality provides for privacy as it relates to the means and mechanisms put into place to guarantee that the information is kept private.

Security Breach: Security incident that violates the protection of some information. Violation may happen in terms of confidentiality (unauthorized access), integrity (unauthorized modification) and availability of information (deny of access to the information) (e.g. password sharing can constitute a breach of any of the characteristics above).

Chapter 14
Behavioral Security:
Investigating the Attitude of Nursing Students Toward Security Concepts and Practices

Stelios Daskalakis
National and Kapodistrian University of Athens, Greece

Maria Katharaki
National and Kapodistrian University of Athens, Greece

Joseph Liaskos
National and Kapodistrian University of Athens, Greece

John Mantas
National and Kapodistrian University of Athens, Greece

ABSTRACT

Information and computer security are gaining continuous attention in the context of modern organizations across all domains of human activities. Emphasizing on behavioral factors toward the applicability of security measures and practices is an area under research, aiming to look beyond the strict technical peculiarities and investigate human attitudes in regards to security consciousness and familiarity. The aim of this chapter is to shed light on those aspects in relation with healthcare, by empirically assessing the intention of undergraduate nursing students to apply security concepts and practices. A research theoretical framework is proposed based on an empirical synthesis of constructs adopted from well established theories as the Health Belief Model and the Protection Motivation Theory along with a variety of previous research works. The model is then empirically tested and validated against a sample of 149 undergraduate nursing students. Data analysis was performed using partial least squares. The research findings highlighted the significant effects of perceived benefits, general security orientation and self-efficacy to behavioral intention along with the positive effect of general controllability to self-efficacy of nursing students in applying security concepts and practices, whereas a series of other constructs did not prove to be significant. The study outcomes contribute to further observations related with behavioral

DOI: 10.4018/978-1-61692-895-7.ch014

security. Despite the fact that the current empirical study was conducted under a specific context and settings, implications are discussed, regarding the security readiness of nursing students prior their engagement to a real healthcare environment.

INTRODUCTION

In today's knowledge-based economy, Information and Communication Technology (ICT) is no longer an optional 'add-on' or a 'nice to have' supporting tool for existing organizational practices. Instead, it tends to be a necessity for every organization that struggles to remain competitive in its corresponding marketplace and expand its scope of business influence. The same necessity applies not only to business-oriented organizations, but to every institutional entity that provides services of any kind. This evolution of ICT in organizations acts as a framework for promoting the quality of services provided, and consequently achieving operational excellence.

Despite the obvious direct and indirect advantages, there are also several security related concerns in current information-oriented organizations (Herath & Rao, 2009). Ensuring information integrity requires continuous monitoring and the protection of information assets is a first class priority within modern organizational structures. Information Systems (IS) are playing a key role in information security, as they are the actual medium for data handling (Ng & Xu, 2007). With regards to IS software applications, they are mainly classified either as "*preventive/ protective*" or "*beneficial*", depending on their operational use (Chenoweth, Minch, & Gattiker, 2009; Dinev & Hu, 2005). Typical examples of beneficial applications include word processing, spreadsheets and other similar software. On the contrary, preventive software includes a diversity of applications that provide protection over certain types of threats (Chenoweth et al., 2009; Dinev & Hu, 2005). Typical examples of such software include firewalls, intrusion prevention or detection

systems, anti malware (ad-aware, spyware, virus, worm, etc.) software and other.

BACKGROUND

Security and Behavioral Aspects

Information security is not only about infrastructure, software or networks (Aytes & Connolly, 2003; Rhee, Kim, & Ryu, 2009; Ng & Rahim, 2005; Ng & Xu, 2007; Workman, Bommer, & Straub, 2008). Users and their attitudes are of equal importance (Herath & Rao, 2009; Rhee et al., 2009; Stanton et al., 2005) since they play a dominant role at the implementation of information security policies and countermeasures. If *human factors* are neglected, information security issues are restricted into a technical perspective which is not realistic and may end up in erroneous conclusions regarding the *information security readiness* within organizations, institutions or any other kind of user communities. Inline with this ascertainment, a series of research works identify the importance of end-users attitudes, beliefs and behaviors in implementing effective information security (Aytes & Connolly, 2003; Herath & Rao, 2009; Ng & Rahim, 2005; Ng & Xu, 2007; Stanton et al., 2005; Workman et al., 2008; Yeo, Rahim, & Ren, 2008).

Research on *information security behavior* is still in its infancy and researchers urge to identify pathways towards in-depth investigation of behavior in regards to information security (Stanton et al., 2005, p. 125). Several attempts may be identified in the literature, which empirically adapt theories and assess dimensions from a variety of scientific domains, mainly emphasizing on constructs from "psychology, criminology and sociology" (Mishra & Dhillon, 2006, p.21).

Related work in the field of applicability of research theories to information security (Chenoweth et al., 2009; Gurung, Luo, & Liao, 2009; LaRose, Rifon, Liu, & Lee, 2005; Ng & Xu., 2007; Pahnila, Siponen, & Mahmood, 2007; Siponen, Pahnila, & Mahmood, 2007; Workman et al., 2008) brings on the foreground two theoretical frameworks that are dominant in the healthcare domain, the *Health Belief Model* and the *Protection Motivation Theory*. According to the National Cancer Institute (2005):

"The Health Belief Model (HBM) addresses the individual's perceptions of the threat posed by a health problem (susceptibility, severity), the benefits of avoiding the threat, and factors influencing the decision to act (barriers, cues to action, and self-efficacy)" (p.12).

The dimensions and characteristics of the Health Belief Model are summarized and presented by Frost, Zuckerman and Zuckerman (2008) and other research works (University of Twente Health Belief Model; National Cancer Institute, 2005, p.14), consisting of: perceived threat, perceived susceptibility, perceived severity, perceived benefits, barriers to action, cues to action and self-efficacy (Frost et al., 2008, p.2). Similarly, Protection Motivation Theory, as defined by Rogers (1975), represents a synthesis from the Health Belief Model, the Theory of Reasoned Action and the self-efficacy Theory (Cismaru, 2006, p.2). Key constructs include: perceived severity, perceived vulnerability, threat appraisal, coping appraisal, response efficacy and self-efficacy (Frost et al., 2008, p.2; University of Twente Protection Motivation Theory).

Healthcare Considerations

Since ICT seems to play a key role at the healthcare industry, there is an urgent need to modern-ize healthcare information systems, in order to provide standardized interoperability methods (Daskalakis, 2007) and create consciousness to healthcare stakeholders in regards to technology (Levett-Jones et al., 2009). This is also underlined by the growing evolution of Health Informatics, an interdisciplinary field that combines medical, nursing, informatics and other scientific professions. A variety of initiatives at the education (undergraduate and graduate curricula) of physicians and nurses, seek to introduce, train and create awareness on ICT aspects to future healthcare professionals. Information and computer security is also gaining attention within the healthcare domain, as an effect of the respective technology penetration in the field. Especially after the realization of technologies such as Electronic Health Record (EHR) and Telemedicine, a variety of information security issues related to patient confidentiality and privacy are becoming more significant (Vaast, 2007, p.134; Adams & Blandford, 2005, p.176).

Research Aim

The purpose of the current study is to analyze the attitudes, perceptions and beliefs of nursing students regarding information and computer security conceptualization, adoption and use. By assessing *behavioral aspects of security* in this specific target group, we can potentially identify their *educational needs* regarding *information security awareness and knowledge*. More important, though, is to be able to reach further conclusions since nursing students will inevitably use information systems infrastructure for accomplishing everyday tasks in their future professional occupation at a variety of healthcare organizations. Consequently, their behavioral security attitude is of great importance as a pre-stage to their future professional work in healthcare institutions, practicing nursing and interacting with IS of all kinds, requiring the applicability of proper security measures and practices.

The aim of this study is twofold: Firstly to combine appropriate dimensions from well established behavioral theories and conclude on a comprehensive research model related with the assessment of *security concepts and practices* of nursing students. Secondly, to empirically investigate the actual information and ICT security beliefs and attitudes of nursing students. The conduction of an appropriate field study would assist in drawing conclusions regarding the 'security readiness' of nurses and in proposing suitable actions towards the adoption of security concepts and practices in the healthcare environment.

The structure of this chapter is organized as follows. "Section 2-Methods", describes the methodology applied in order to formulate an appropriate research model, aiming to assess generic security perceptions in a healthcare context, focusing on nursing undergraduate students. Research procedure and data analysis are also presented. "Section 3-Results", provides a detailed analysis in terms of demographics data along with the formulation of a structural equation model, based on partial least squares. At last, "Section 4-Discussion", contains a thorough discussion on the findings, the limitations and the future orientation of the current research work.

METHODS

Research Model and Hypotheses Definition

The formulation strategy of an appropriate research model in order to empirically investigate the attitudes of undergraduate nursing students in regards to security concepts and practices was based on several factors. Primarily, a thorough literature review on related work and previous research studies on behavioral security was performed. The review revealed the extensive use of the Health Belief Model (HBM) and the Protection Motivation Theory (PMT) as base

theories for conducting empirical studies. Other theoretical frameworks, like the Theory of Planned Behavior, the General Deterrence Theory, the Theory of Reasoned Action, and the Innovation Diffusion Theory were also utilized (Mishra & Dhillon, 2006); however, HBM and PMT proved to be the dominant ones. The literature research concentrated on a total of eleven (11) field studies. Six out of the eleven field studies utilize PMT either in its original proposition or as a basis for extension. Furthermore, three studies are explicitly focusing on the investigation of the use of preventive technologies, specifically antispyware (Chenoweth et al., 2009; Diven & Hu, 2005; Gurung et al., 2009), two studies are researching on the attitude of computer users (Ng & Rahim, 2005) and employees (Ng & Xu, 2007) behavior respectively, two studies investigate the use of information security policies adherence from an organizational perspective (Pahnila et al.,2007; Siponen et al., 2007) and four out of the eleven studies attempt to provide empirical studies on more generic issues like online safety behavior (LaRose et al., 2005), behavior related with self-efficacy (Rhee et al., 2009) and the reinforcement of security measures in organizations (Herath & Rao, 2009; Workman et al., 2008).

In the context of the empirical study described in this chapter, the investigation strategy was decided to focus on generic security perceptions of nursing students with respect to information and information technology security concepts and practices. Thus, the scope of this research is beyond the solely examination of a specific preventive technology or software application that belongs to this category (like antispyware), but instead to investigate it as part of the context of participants' generic security perceptions and practices attitude. Furthermore, the study did not emphasize on information security policies or in the use of specific beneficial technologies. On the other hand, the work presented in this chapter based the security perceptions upon three main axes, combining concepts from general informa-

Figure 1. Schematic representation of constructs adoption

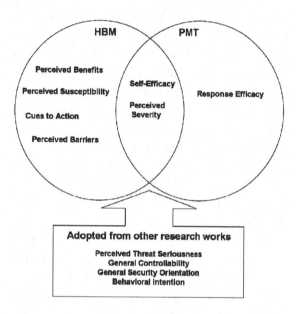

easily perceived by non-technical computer users like nurses than other, more advanced software applications like antispyware.

In order to formulate an appropriate *research framework*, both in terms of *theoretical model* conceptualization but also in terms of defining a comprehensive set of measures for the assessment of fraud, privacy and malware issues, a synthesis of dimensions and characteristics was conducted from a variety of research works of the literature. Initially, a formulation of an appropriate research framework is attempted. In that context, the current study adapted the modeling of the Health Belief Model as proposed by Ng and Xu (2007) and as it appears at Grosser (1982) and enriched it with additional constructs that appeared in other well established theories and previous research works (Figure 1). In specific, apart from the HBM and the additional constructs proposed by Ng & Xu (2007), the formulated model is also influenced from PMT, the conceptual works of Rhee et al. (2009) and the works of LaRose et al. (2005) and Chenoweth et al. (2009) (Table 1).

The following sections provide a detailed description on the constructs adopted along with the hypothesized relationships amongst them.

tion security but also from vertical computer and IT related security, emphasizing in fraud, privacy, and virus related issues, as influenced from the research work of LaRose et al. (2005). With respect to fraud, the assessment mainly emphasized on issues related with loss of banking/credit card data during unsafe internet interaction, influenced by LaRose et al. (2005) and the combination of empirical characteristics. Concerning privacy related issues, we encapsulate the perception formulated by Fernando and Dawson (2009), who reach the conclusion, based on the literature, that " 'privacy' concerns control over access to oneself and associated information, including health information, while 'security' refers to all measures that protect information privacy" (p.2). With respect to malware related issues, an attempt to investigate the comprehension and use of preventive technologies was included, mainly influenced by the empirical work of Ng and Xu (2007). The usefulness, need and perceived added value of using an antivirus software was selected for evaluation since antivirus concepts are more

Perceived Susceptibility

Initially defined at the Health Belief Model, perceived susceptibility encompasses *"one's opinion of chances of getting a condition"* (University of Twente, Health Belief Model). The current construct appears in previous empirical studies related with information security (LaRose et al., 2005; Ng & Xu, 2007). In the context of the current study, we hypothesize the following:

H1 (+): Perceived Susceptibility positively affects behavioral intention to apply security concepts and practices

Table 1. Constructs and relationships of the current study

Construct /Relationship	Source
Perceived Susceptibility (PSC) / PSC→BI*	Health Belief Model, LaRose et al. (2005), Ng and Xu (2007)
Perceived Barriers (PBAR) / PBAR→ BI	Health Belief Model, Ng and Xu (2007)
Perceived Benefits (PB) / PB→BI	Health Belief Model, LaRose et al. (2005), Ng and Xu (2007)
Cues to Action (CTA) / CTA→BI	Health Belief Model, Ng and Xu (2007)
Response Efficacy (RE) / RE→BI	Chenoweth et al. (2009), LaRose et al. (2005), Protection Motivation Theory
General Security Orientation(GSO) / GSO → BI	Ng & Xu (2007)
Perceived Severity (PS) / PS→BI	Chenoweth et al. (2009), Health Belief Model, LaRose et al. (2005), Ng and Xu (2007), Protection Motivation Theory
Perceived Threat (Seriousness) (PTS) / PTS→BI	LaRose et al. (2005), Health Belief Model
General Controllability (GC) / GC→SE	Rhee et al. (2009)
Self-Efficacy SE) / SE→BI	Chenoweth et al. (2009), Health Belief Model, Ng and Xu (2007), Protection Motivation Theory, Rhee et al. (2009) * Dinev and Hu (2005) also include the notion of Self Efficacy but with a different relationship (affecting Perceived Behavioral Control)
BI: Behavioral Intention	

Perceived Barriers

The current construct was also defined as part of the Health Belief Model. According to the National Cancer Institute (2005), perceived barriers are related with "beliefs about the material and psychological costs of taking action" (p.14). In the context of the current study we hypothesize the following, inline with other research works (Ng & Xu, 2007):

H2 (-): Perceived Barriers negatively affects behavioral intention to apply security concepts and practices

Perceived Benefits

According to the definition provided by the University of Twente, perceived benefits are related with "one's belief in the efficacy of the advised action to reduce risk or seriousness of impact" (University of Twente, Health Belief Model). In a similar manner, the National Cancer institute defines perceived benefits as the "beliefs about the effectiveness of taking action to reduce risk or seriousness" (National Cancer Institute, 2005, p.14). In the context of the current study, we hypothesize the following, inline with other research works (LaRose et al., 2005; Ng & Xu, 2007):

H3 (+): Perceived Benefits positively affects behavioral intention to apply security concepts and practices

Cues to Action

Cues to Action are defined as "Factors that activate 'readiness to change'" (National Cancer Institute (2005), p.14) or "Strategies to activate 'readiness'" (University of Twente, Health Belief Model). Being part of the Health Belief Model, it has been well appreciated in previous research works in the field of information security (Ng & Xu, 2007) along with its importance in the healthcare domain (Vaast, 2007), whereas in the context of the current study we hypothesize the following:

H4 (+): Cues to Action positively affect behavioral intention to apply security concepts and practices

Response Efficacy

Adopted from the Protection Motivation Theory, the current construct contributes to the research theory to be proposed, as it appears in a variety of previous empirical studies in the field of information security (Chenoweth et al., 2009; Gurung et al., 2009; LaRose et al., 2005; Pahnila et al., 2007; Siponen et al., 2007; Workman et al., 2008). Response efficacy is defined by the University of Twente as "the individual's expectancy that carrying out recommendations can remove the threat" (University of Twente Protection Motivation Theory). Thus, we hypothesize the following:

H5 (+): Response efficacy will positively affect behavioral intention to apply security concepts and practices

General Security Orientation

Such a dimension was solely adopted from Ng and Xu (2007). Since we aim to assess generic security perceptions from nursing students, this construct was evaluated as necessary in order to examine the students' "predisposition and interest concerning practicing computer security" (Ng & Xu, 2007, p. 427). The hypothesis formulated is as follows:

H6 (+): General Security Orientation will positively affect behavioral intention to apply security concepts and practices

Perceived Severity

Perceived severity holds a substantive role in both the Health Belief Model and the Protection Motivation Theory. As defined by the University of Twente, perceived severity is related with "one's opinion of how serious a condition and its

consequences are" (University of Twente Health Belief Model). A plethora of researchers investigate such a construct in the context of information security studies (Chenoweth et al., 2009; Gurung et al., 2009; LaRose et al., 2005; Ng & Xu, 2007). Chenoweth et al. (2009) assess perceived severity in the context of antispyware, "as a measure of the perceived magnitude of what might happen if a respondent's computer is infected with spyware" (p.5). Ng and Xu (2007) encapsulate it, as part of their adaptation of the Health Belief Model (p.425) and Workman et al. (2008) refer and hypothesize the "perceived severity of threat" (p.2803). In the context of the study described in this chapter, the relevant formulated hypothesis is as follows:

H7 (+): Perceived Severity positively affects behavioral intention to apply security concepts and practices

Perceived Threat Seriousness

The current construct was solely adopted from LaRose et al. (2005), who propose a synthesis of constructs from Protection Motivation Theory and Social Cognitive Theory. The empirical investigation conducted at the current study attempts to utilize it from a 'generic threat perspective' in contrast with perceived severity that was selected to represent a 'personal threat perception' at an individual level. Thus, the hypothesis formulated is as follows:

H8 (+): Perceived Threat Seriousness positively affects behavioral intention to apply security concepts and practices

General Controllability

General controllability was solely adopted from Rhee et al. (2009) as it was assessed as a key construct under inclusion in the proposed model. It is investigated under the notion of information security threats and as Rhee et al. (2009) point out, it "can be defined as an individual's belief in the availability of technological means and solutions to control information security threats in general" (p.4). The importance of controllability is also highlighted by Dinev and Hu (2005) who refer to Pavlou and Fygenson (2005) in order to state that controllability is related with "the individual's judgments about the availability of resources and opportunities to perform the behavior" (Pavlou & Fygenson, 2005, as cited in Dinev & Hu, 2005). The formulated hypothesis, in the context of the current study, closely follows the proposition of Rhee et al. (2009, p.4). Consistent with those authors, the following is under investigation:

H9 (+): General Controllability of information security threats positively affects self-efficacy

Self-Efficacy

Self-Efficacy is a dominant dimension under investigation in a variety of research works from a diversity of disciplines. Information technology and its acceptance are also interrelated with the idea of computer self-efficacy (Igbaria & Iivari, 1995). As Igbaria and Iivari (1995) point out, it is related with the "belief in one's capabilities of using a computer in the accomplishment of specific tasks" (p. 587). The generic perception of self-efficacy, as a behavioral attribute, has gained attention in a plethora of studies related with information security (Chenoweth et al., 2009; Dinev & Hu, 2005; Gurung et al., 2009; Levett-Jones et al., 2009; Ng & Rahim, 2005; Ng & Xu, 2007; Pahnila et al., 2007; Rhee et al., 2009; Siponen et al., 2007; Workman et al., 2008) and is highlighted at both the Health Belief Model and the Protection Motivation Theory (National Cancer Institute, 2005; Norman, Boer, & Seydel, 2005; University of Twente Health Belief Model; University of Twente Protection Motivation Theory). In specific, the importance of self-efficacy is highlighted by Levett-Jones et al. (2009), who reach the conclusion that it is

related with "the actual beliefs that people hold about their capabilities that are powerful influences on how they perform" (p.613). In a shorter description, the National Cancer Institute (2005) defines self-efficacy as the "confidence in one's ability to take action" (p. 14). In the context of the current study, self-efficacy was deemed to be an integral part of the research model in order to observe the attitude and confidence of nursing students toward security concepts and practices. Thus, the hypothesis formulated is as follows:

H10 (+): Self-Efficacy positively affects behavioral intention to apply security concepts and practices

Behavioral Intention

The inclusion of behavioral intention as a construct in the current proposed model attempts to reflect the investigation of nursing students' behavioral intention to apply security concepts and practices. As described by Venkatesh (Personal web page, Theoretical Models), the notion of behavioral intention is "the degree to which a person has formulated conscious plans to perform or not perform some specified future behavior" whereas the same author emphasizes the "correlation" of intention to use with the actual use (Venkatesh et al., 2003, as cited in Pahnila et al., 2007). In the context of the current study, the inclusion of the specific construct was also influenced by the empirical work of Ng and Xu (2007) who propose an adaptation of the Health Belief Model, having the dimension of behavior as a key dependent variable. Similarly, Grosser (1982) describes the *"Likelihood of taking action"* as the main dependent variable of the Health Belief Model (p.1058). Consistent with them, we encapsulate the current dimension as a key dependent construct, in order to adequately examine the abovementioned hypotheses.

Overall, the synthesized dimensions from the Health Belief Model as outlined by Grosser (1982) along with the modeling of Ng and Xu (2007), the Protection Motivation Theory and the research works of Chenoweth et al. (2009), Rhee et al. (2009) and LaRose et al. (2005) in conjunction with their interrelations, formulate the proposed research model of the current study.

Sample Analysis and Procedure Administration

The sample synthesis was formulated solely from undergraduate students of the second and third year of their study at the Faculty of Nursing at the National and Kapodistrian University of Athens, Greece. The choice of this concrete target group was dictated by the particular characteristics they have, compared to their colleagues of the first year, in terms of knowledge and skills gained by the modules "Introduction to Informatics" and "Introduction to Health Informatics" being taught in the first year undergraduates (first and second semester accordingly). The selected target group is supposed to demonstrate a relative easiness in computing, and ICT usefulness in both nursing and clinical practice overall. In addition, the majority of the selected students use ICT, e.g. to accomplish university coursework, to communicate through email messaging or through other modern channels of communication like social networking websites. With regards to the research instrument, a questionnaire was designed with structure, format and content clear, friendly and accurate, facilitating its completion from the participants. The questionnaire structure was based on a series of constructs including items with corresponding questions of standardized scales adopted from previous studies. Further questions were also introduced based on the specific characteristics of the undergraduate students.

In detail, perceived susceptibility (coded as PSC) was qualified by three items, PSC1, PSC2 and PSC3 that were influenced by LaRose et al. (2005) and refined in the context of the current study, giving information on the fraud, malware and private susceptibility, respectively. Response

Efficacy (coded as RE) was attributed by two items, RE1 and RE2 influenced by LaRose et al. (2005) and refined in the context of the current study and a third one, RE3, which was purely adopted from LaRose et al. (2005). Continuously, Perceived Threat Seriousness (coded as PTS) was attributed by four questions. The PTS1 and PTS3 items were influenced from LaRose et al. (2005) and refined in order to reflect the scope of the current study, while PTS2 was adopted from LaRose et al. (2005). The last item, PTS4, was self-developed and aimed to indicate the students' attitude towards unsafe internet sites. Perceived Severity (coded as PS) was qualified by three questions, PS1, PS2 and PS3. PS1 was influenced by LaRose et al. (2005) and Ng and Xu (2007) and refined in the context of the current study. PS2 was adopted from Ng and Xu (2007) whereas PS3 was self-developed. Similarly, General Security Orientation (coded as GSO) was attributed by four items, GSO1, GSO2, GSO3 and GSO3 respectively. GSO1 was influenced by the research work of Ng and Xu (2007) and refined in order to reflect the scope of the current study and GSO4 was adopted directly from the same authors. With respect to items GSO2 and GSO3, these were also adopted from Ng and Xu (2007), based on the work of Jayanti and Burns 1998 (Ng & Xu, p.430). Furthermore, General Controllability (coded as GC) was attributed by three items, GC1, GC2 and GC3, all adopted from Rhee et al. (2009). Likewise, Self Efficacy (coded as SE), was attributed by four items, SE1, SE2, SE3 and SE4 which were also adopted from Rhee et al (2009). Perceived Benefits (coded as PB) was attributed by two questions, PB1 and PB2 which were adopted from LaRose et al. (2005). Continuously, Perceived Barriers (PBAR) was attributed by three questions, PBAR1, PBAR2 and PBAR3. Whereas the first item was purely adopted from Ng and Xu (2007), the rest of the items were influenced from the research work of Ng and Xu (2007) but initially based on Champion (1984) and Woon, Tan and Low (2005) (Ng

& Xu, 2007, p.430). Cues to Action (CTA) was assessed by four questions; the three of them, CTA1, CTA2 and CTA3 were influenced by Ng and Xu (2007) and refined in order to reflect the scope of the current study whereas CTA4 was clearly a self-developed metric. Behavioral Intention (coded as BI), at last, was assessed by four questions, BI1, BI2, BI3 and BI4, all adopted from Rhee et al. (2009).

It should be noted that all questions used a seven-point Likert scale representing a range from exceptional disagreement (1) to exceptional agreement (7), while the choice 'do not know/do not answer' was also given to the students. A final comments section was included at the end of the questionnaire, inviting the respondents to provide free text comments of any kind, related either with the process or with the context of attitude toward security concepts and practices.

Following the development of the research instrument, the final questionnaire, along with demographic related questions, was administered to students in paper form at the end of their class, providing a sample of 149 undergraduate students. In order to preserve the confidentiality, questionnaire completion was anonymous, thus no personal information was attached to participants' responses. Additionally, data collection was for research purposes only. The completed questionnaires were returned back to the researchers directly after the completion without any intermediaries.

Data Analysis

The Cronbach's alpha (α) coefficient (Cronbach, 1951) was used to assess the internal consistency of the thirty seven (37) items so much in whole as much in each part of the research model. Students' questionnaire responses were processed according to the statistical software SPSS 16.0 for Windows (SPSS, 2007). Demographic analysis and descriptive analysis of the 37-items was performed, while a Mann-Whitney test (Mann & Whitney, 1947) was utilized in order to assess the differences between

the population means of female-male and 2nd-3rd year of study on their responses.

The responses were also analyzed using a Structural Equation Model, based *on partial least squares (PLS)*. The application of a *structural equation modeling* (SEM) technique, and particularly the use of partial least squares, closely follows the strategy of previous research works (Herath & Rao, 2009; Ng & Rahim, 2005; Rhee et al., 2009; Workman et al., 2008). The current data analysis method is well suited for its predictive nature (Gefen, Straub, & Boudreau, 2000; Iivari, 2005). The statistical analysis software package used was SmartPLS M3 v2 (Ringle, Wende, & Will, 2005).

RESULTS

Reliability Assessment

With regards to the questionnaire internal consistency, the total alpha for all the 37-items was 0.879 (>0.80), demonstrating consistency in the survey responses (Carlbring et al., 2007). The change in Cronbachs' alpha (α) would be seen if a particular item was deleted as Table 2 outlines.

None of the items would substantially affect reliability if they were deleted, since Cronbach's alpha is more than 0.87.

Demographics

Table 3 presents the demographics data generated. In specific, 13.4% of the subjects were male, and 86.6% were female. Such a difference may be explained by the fact that nursing science, traditionally, is primarily preferred by women than men. Additionally, 49% of the subjects were second year students, and 51% were third year students of the Faculty. The average age of the responders was 20.18 years old, but ranged from 18 years to 37 years. Only a 2.7% of the sample was above

Table 2. Cronbachs' alpha if Item Deleted

Items	Cronbachs' alpha (α) if Item Deleted		Items	Cronbachs' alpha (α) if Item Deleted
PSC1	0.880		SE1	0.874
PSC2	0.879		SE2	0.874
PSC3	0.880		SE3	0.873
RE1	0.880		SE4	0.874
RE2	0.878		PB1	0.876
RE3	0.880		PB2	0.877
PTS1	0.877		PBAR1	0.875
PTS2	0.879		PBAR2	0.879
PTS3	0.877		PBAR3	0.875
PTS4	0.877		CTA1	0.877
PS1	0.877		CTA2	0.873
PS2	0.878		CTA3	0.873
PS3	0.878		CTA4	0.874
GSO1	0.871		BI1	0.875
GSO2	0.871		BI2	0.883
GSO3	0.871		BI3	0.883
GSO4	0.872		BI4	0.882
GC1	0.875			
GC2	0.876			
GC3	0.876			

PSC: Perceived Susceptibility, PS: Perceived Severity, PTS: Perceived Threat Seriousness, PBAR: Perceived Barriers, GC: General Controllability, SE: Self-Efficacy, PB: Perceived Benefits, RE: Response Efficacy, CTA: Cues to Action, GSO: General Security Orientation, BI: Behavioral Intention

Table 3. Generated demographics data

	Frequency	Percentage (%)
Gender		
male	20	13.4
female	129	86.6
Total	*149*	*100*
Age		
18-23	133	89.3
24-29	2	1.3
30-35	3	2.0
36-41	1	0.7
not answered	10	6.7
Total	*149*	*100*
Year of study		
second year	73	49
third year	76	51
Total	*149*	*100*

30 years old and it is notable that a 6.7% of the sample didn't state its age.

Table 4 outlines the descriptive statistics for all constructs' items, indicating the low scores, in terms of the seven Likert scale responses of the participants, with regard to their efficacy to keep their computer safe from all online threats by their own (RE3), being constantly mindful about computer security (GSO4), feeling confident handling virus infected files (SE1) and the perceived barriers from exercising care in security issues (PBAR1, PBAR2 and PBAR3). Similarly, participants answered with a low score on the action taken by the university to organize security talks (CTA2), a fact that could be possibly explained either from the lack of such initiatives or the lack

Table 4. Descriptive statistics of constructs' items

Items	Mean	SD	Items	Mean	SD
PSC1	4.86	1.72	SE1	3.41	2.08
PSC2	5.44	1.86	SE2	4.19	1.80
PSC3	5.09	1.80	SE3	5.07	1.71
RE1	4.12	2.05	SE4	5.24	1.67
RE2	6.13	1.63	PB1	5.89	1.20
RE3	3.95	2.23	PB2	5.50	1.47
PTS1	5.99	1.75	PBAR1	2.86	1.86
PTS2	5.63	1.38	PBAR2	3.18	1.94
PTS3	5.49	1.58	PBAR3	3.46	1.91
PTS4	5.83	1.22	CTA1	4.09	1.86
PS1	6.30	1.39	CTA2	3.85	2.50
PS2	5.46	1.61	CTA3	4.30	2.09
PS3	6.38	0.94	CTA4	4.13	2.12
GSO1	4.01	1.96	BI1	5.44	1.50
GSO2	4.82	1.87	BI2	5.70	1.36
GSO3	4.86	1.90	BI3	4.96	1.81
GSO4	3.87	1.91	BI4	5.42	1.40
GC1	4.23	1.97			
GC2	4.49	1.78			
GC3	5.16	1.53			

PSC: Perceived Susceptibility, **PS**: Perceived Severity, **PTS**: Perceived Threat Seriousness, **PBAR**: Perceived Barriers, **GC**: General Controllability, **SE**: Self-Efficacy, **PB**: Perceived Benefits, **RE**: Response Efficacy, **CTA**: Cues to Action, **GSO**: General Security Orientation, **BI**: Behavioral Intention

of notifications to students with respect to such informative talks.

Based on Table 4, a general interpretation of the answers concerning the eleven constructs of the proposed model shows that: Perceived Susceptibility (PS) ranges in a high level, which means that the participating students consider that it is highly possible for them to face security issues. Response Efficacy (RE) related to protection software downloading and installation is in high levels; however the ability both to switch to a different computer or operating system and to keep safe from all online threats, ranges from low to medium level. Perceived Threat Seriousness (PT) ranges in high levels, since most threats are considered as serious. Perceived Severity (PS)

ranges in high levels, meaning that most of the security issues should have a major impact to our sample. General Security Orientation (GSO) which corresponds to the extent students are concerned and keep informed about security issues while they try to take action to prevent security incidents, ranges in medium levels. General Controllability (GC) ranges in medium to high levels, but in general nursing students seem to trust the ICT potential to prevent and control security threats. Self-Efficacy (SE) is in rather low levels as far as the handling of virus infected files is concerned (they do not feel self-efficient to handle such files), and ranges from rather medium to even high levels as far as the understanding of terms / words, using programs, and learning advanced skills relating to information security are concerned. Perceived Benefits (PB) in applying security programs or practices ranges in high levels. Cues to Action (CTA) from the institution, regarding organization of security talks, sending of alert messages, emails, reminders, range from low to rather medium levels, which means they are not initiated enough to take specific security measures. Behavioral Intention (BI) ranges in high levels, meaning that nursing students are willing to enforce security procedures, add additional measures, buy more software, learn more so as to strengthen information security. Perceived Barriers (PBAR) range in low or rather medium levels, which means that exercising care to security issues, is not considered inconvenient, time-consuming, or difficult by nursing students.

Analyzing further the participants' responses, a non-parametric Mann–Whitney U test was performed to assess the differences on the 37-item responses between male-female and second-third year of study. The statistical significant results of Mann-Whitney test are highlighted at Table 5 (grouping variable gender) and Table 6 (grouping variable year of study). According to the findings, the test indicates a statistically significant difference between male and female on their response on self efficacy to handling virus infection (SE1), understanding security issues (SE2) and learning how to protect their information system (SE4) by installing appropriate software applications. This difference could be explained further by gender differences. In particular, male participants felt

more confident on the above aspects than the respective female responders.

According to Table 6, seven items, PSC2, PTS2, PTS3, GC1, BI1, BI2 and BI3 proved to have significant differences between the group of second and third year students. In regards to those items, significance may be explained by the fact that the year of study influences the level of participants' perceptions on those attributes. Such differences on their response may be attributed to the fact that senior students have an advanced consciousness regarding security concepts and practices as opposed to second year students, as they may have also experienced cases of privacy and personal data violations.

Partial Least Squares

For the partial least squares analysis, an assessment of the *measurement* and the *structural model* was conducted, consistent with past research works (Chea & Luo, 2007; Chin, 1998; Gefen et al., 2000; Iivari, 2005; Roldán & Leal, 2003). Findings are described in the following sections.

Measurement Model

The process of investigating the measurement model involved the assessment of individual item loadings, internal consistency, convergent validity and discriminant validity (Iivari, 2005; Roldán & Leal, 2003). The following sections present the findings for each of those parts.

Table 5. Mann-Whitney, Grouping Variable: Gender

	SE1	SE2	SE4
Mann-Whitney U	740.50	722.00	835.50
Wilcoxon W	9125.50	9107.00	9220.50
Z	-3.11	-3.21	-2.61
Asymp. Sig. (2-tailed)	0.00*	0.00*	0.01**
* Correlation is significant at the 0.01 level (2-tail) ** Correlation is significant at the 0.05 level (2-tail)			

Individual Item Loadings

The initial data analysis produced inadequate individual item loading for RE3 (below 0.5), thus the decision was to drop the current item (Shepherd, Tesch, & Hsu, 2006, p.208), and rerun the PLS analysis. The findings, in terms of individual item loadings, are presented at Table 7.

Overall, the values of the remaining thirty six (36) individual item loadings can be considered reliable, as they exceed the threshold value of 0.7 (Chin, 1998). In certain cases item loadings are below 0.7, namely PBAR3 with 0.667, PTS1 with 0.601, PTS2 with 0.581 and PS2 with 0.507. However, those four loadings exceed the acceptable level of 0.5 (Shepherd et al., 2006; Chin,

Table 6. Mann-Whitney results, grouping variable: Year

	PSC2	PTS2	PTS3	GC1	BI1	BI2	BI3
Mann-Whitney U	2345.00	2110.50	2229.00	2237.00	2278.00	2294.00	2123.00
Wilcoxon W	5271.00	5036.50	5155.00	5163.00	5204.00	5220.00	5049.00
Z	-1.69	-2.62	-2.12	-2.07	-1.95	-1.91	-2.53
Asymp. Sig. (2-tailed)	0.09***	0.01**	0.03**	0.04**	0.05***	0.06***	0.01**
** Correlation is significant at the 0.05 level (2-tail). *** Correlation is significant at the 0.10 level (2-tail).							

Table 7. Individual item loadings values

Item	Loading value		Item	Loading value		Item	Loading value	
PSC1	0.775		PS1	0.882		PTS1	0.601	
PSC2	0.927		PS2	0.507		PTS2	0.581	
PSC3	0.784		PS3	0.749		PTS3	0.847	
						PTS4	0.774	
PBAR1	0.937		GC1	0.846				
PBAR2	0.942		GC2	0.807		SE1	0.785	
PBAR3	0.667		GC3	0.76		SE2	0.767	
						SE3	0.882	
PB1	0.932		RE1	0.83		SE4	0.801	
PB2	0.877		RE2	0.729				
CTA1	0.745		GSO1	0.865		BI1	0.905	
CTA2	0.78		GSO2	0.882		BI2	0.858	
CTA3	0.886		GSO3	0.89		BI3	0.765	
CTA4	0.808		GSO4	0.803		BI4	0.806	
PSC: Perceived Susceptibility, **PS**: Perceived Severity, **PTS**: Perceived Threat Seriousness, **PBAR**: Perceived Barriers, **GC**: General Controllability, **SE**: Self-Efficacy, PB: Perceived Benefits, **RE**: Response Efficacy, **CTA**: Cues to Action, **GSO**: General Security Orientation, **BI**: Behavioral Intention								

1998), with two of them producing values greater than 0.6.

Internal Consistency and Convergent Validity
Internal consistency is related with the investigation of construct validity and the assessment of the values of Cronbachs' alpha and composite reliability (Roldán & Leal, 2003). Convergent validity investigates the values of the Average Variance Extracted (AVE) (Fornell & Larcker, 1981). Table 8 outlines the findings of the current study in relation with the above metrics.

The assessment of internal consistency was based on the threshold value of 0.7 (Fornell & Larcker, 1981 as cited in Iivari, 2005, p.15). In particular, all constructs produced reliable values in terms of Cronbachs' alpha, except perceived severity (PS) and response efficacy (RE). With regards to Composite reliability, all values exceeded 0.7, thus considered reliable. With the notable exception of perceived severity (PS) and response efficacy (RE), in relation with their Cronbachs' alpha values, and based on the fact that all constructs produced adequate composite

reliability results, internal consistency results were considered reliable.

Concerning Convergent validity, the assessment was based on the cut-off value of 0.5 for AVE, as proposed by Fornell and Larcker (1981) (Chin, 1998). All constructs produced values greater than 0.5, thus achieving adequate convergent validity.

Discriminant Validity
Discriminant validity was assessed by comparing the value of the square root of the AVE of each construct with the correlations (Chea & Luo, 2007; Chin, 1998; Iivari, 2005), in order to observe whether "*the diagonal elements were significantly greater than the off-diagonal elements in the corresponding rows and columns*" (Barclay et al., 1995, as cited in Roldán & Leal, 2003, p.76). Based on the study findings (Table 9), the model proved to have adequate discriminant validity.

Structural Model

With regards to the structural model, a bootstrapping technique was applied (500 resamples), consistent with past research works (Chin, 1998;

Table 8. Internal Consistency and Convergent validity values

	Cronbachs' Alpha	Composite Reliability	AVE
BI	0.8541	0.902	0.6978
CTA	0.8314	0.8808	0.6498
GC	0.7411	0.8467	0.6484
GSO	0.8833	0.9194	0.7407
PB	0.7832	0.9005	0.8191
PBAR	0.8381	0.8914	0.7368
PS	0.5844	0.7647	0.5316
PSUSC	0.7872	0.8701	0.6922
PTS	0.7031	0.7983	0.5038
RE	0.3647	0.757	0.61
SE	0.8195	0.8803	0.6484

PSC: Perceived Susceptibility, **PS**: Perceived Severity, **PTS**: Perceived Threat Seriousness, **PBAR**: Perceived Barriers, **GC**: General Controllability, **SE**: Self-Efficacy, **PB**: Perceived Benefits, **RE**: Response Efficacy, **CTA**: Cues to Action, **GSO**: General Security Orientation, **BI**: Behavioral Intention

Iivari, 2005). The evaluation was based on a two-tail test with three significant levels of p< 0.1(*), p<0.05 (**) and p<0.01(***). The overall findings are presented at Table 10. The R^2 value produced was found to be equal to 0.479, thus explaining 47.9% of the variance in the construct of BI.

The findings of the structural model highlight the strong significant relationships of perceived benefits and general security orientation with behavioral intention to apply security concepts and practices. Furthermore, general controllability was found to have a strong effect on self-efficacy, which in turn affects behavioral intention. On the other hand, perceived susceptibility, perceived barriers, cues to action, response efficacy, perceived severity and perceived threat seriousness did not prove to have a significant relationship in the context of the current study. Parts of the findings appear to be aligned with previous research works whereas other results did not comply with similar research studies. In particular, Ng and Xu (2007) research findings comply with the current ones in a sense that they also identified that cues to action, perceived barriers, and perceived severity did not demonstrate any effect on behavioral intention. The results of this study are also aligned with Ng and Xu (2007) in regards to the significant effects of perceived

benefits and self-efficacy to behavioral intention. The positive effect of general controllability to self-efficacy is also aligned with the findings of Rhee et al. (2009).

On the other hand, Ng and Xu (2007) identified general security orientation as insignificant in relation with behavioral intention, as opposed to the current study which produced a very strong effect. Similarly, perceived susceptibility, identified as insignificant in the current study, was appreciated in the context of the research work of Ng and Xu (2007). Differences were also identified in relation with the empirical work of LaRose et al. (2005), where perceived threat seriousness and response efficacy were found to be significant whereas, in the current study, did not confirm.

FUTURE RESEARCH

The current study possesses a series of limitations. Primarily the sample size, although adequate for performing a thorough statistical analysis, needs further enrichment in order to deduce observations on a larger part of the stakeholders' population. In addition, the participants constitute a sample with particular characteristics (related with young age, majority of female responders along with the

Table 9. Discriminant validity results

	BI	CTA	GC	GSO	PB	PBAR	PS	PSUSC	PTS	RE	SE
BI	**0.8353**	0	0	0	0	0	0	0	0	0	0
CTA	0.243	**0.8061**	0	0	0	0	0	0	0	0	0
GC	0.2956	0.3215	**0.8052**	0	0	0	0	0	0	0	0
GSO	0.5955	0.2386	0.2578	**0.8606**	0	0	0	0	0	0	0
PB	0.4318	0.1491	0.4032	0.2052	**0.905**	0	0	0	0	0	0
PBAR	-0.1701	-0.0831	-0.0875	-0.2212	-0.0868	**0.8583**	0	0	0	0	0
PS	0.2563	-0.0264	0.1088	0.2596	0.2734	-0.1538	**0.7291**	0	0	0	0
PSUSC	0.0706	0.0648	0.0239	-0.0099	0.1124	0.0714	0.0936	**0.8319**	0	0	0
PTS	0.2428	0.1992	0.0108	0.1535	0.2782	-0.0851	0.3725	0.2788	**0.7097**	0	0
RE	0.3014	0.1537	0.1514	0.4494	0.141	-0.1446	0.1703	0.0318	0.1461	**0.781**	0
SE	0.4553	0.1865	0.2641	0.5495	0.2224	0.0132	0.1207	-0.0512	0.1156	0.2679	**0.8052**

Table 10. Results of the structural model

Causal Relationship	Path Coefficient	Significance
PSC→BI	0.034	NS
PBAR→BI	-0.044	NS
PB→ BI	0.275	***
CTA→BI	0.059	NS
RE→BI	0.008	NS
GSO→BI	0.418	***
PS→BI	0.027	NS
PTS→BI	0.049	NS
GC→SE	0.264	***
SE→BI	0.145	*
R² of BI: 0.479		
Significance levels: p<0.1(*), p<0.05(**), p<0.01(***) *NS: Non-Significant*		

early and daily exposure to computers, internet and technology) contributing in the effect and interpretation of their responses. Thus, the supported hypotheses as much as the unsupported ones, as outlined from the structural model, can be justified further, based on the limitations implied by the above characteristics.

Furthermore, the constructs and hypotheses formulated were based on empirical synthesis. Despite the use of well known theoretical frameworks such as the Health Belief Model and the Protection Motivation Theory and the rest of the research works, the synthesis of dimensions may need further extensions with specific inclusions of key constructs that currently were not investigated. This limitation is also part of the paucity of empirical studies on behavioral security currently at the literature. As research efforts progress in time, the investigation of further dimensions will be further promoted and encouraged.

Overall, despite the above limitations, the work presented in this chapter aims to contribute further in the area of behavioral security. Such limitations also form the basis for future work in the current field. Initially, further enrichment of the sample may be applied, both in terms of

size but also in terms of diversity of participants. Future increase of the sample size would lead us to more representative results whereas the inclusion of separate stakeholder groups, either per age, gender or per year of study, would assist us in generating findings that would offer a comparative analysis amongst the different behaviors. In addition, further research studies in the context of generic security concepts and practices, with the same instrument, may be applied to real healthcare settings. This would provide the opportunity to observe actual security behaviors of nursing or other healthcare staff under the use of a series of information systems and the applicability of security concepts and practices on them. By applying the research strategy outlined in the current chapter, findings may be combined with respective outcomes from related work in the field. However, such a combination may prove to be irrelevant in terms of the research context of the various studies. Thus, a comparative analysis may be performed, under the same research context, between nursing students and nurses employed in healthcare organizations. It would then be of great interest to compare student perceptions with respective behaviors of healthcare professionals and comment on similarities and differences. Such an investigation would assist us to draw conclusions regarding the behavioral security attitude both from an educational and from a professional healthcare perspective.

CONCLUSION

This chapter focused on behavioral aspects and attitudes of stakeholders with respect to security concepts and practices. It specialized in healthcare, in an attempt to investigate the perceptions of undergraduate nursing students regarding information security conceptualization, adoption and use. In order to assess their attitudes, a theoretical model was formulated and proposed, based on a variety of previous theories and research works. An empirical investigation was then conducted, attempting to explore the actual 'security readiness' of 149 nursing students, in regards to their beliefs on both information and IT security. A thorough data analysis was conducted and a structural equation model was formulated. The results revealed the positive effect of perceived benefits, general security orientation and self-efficacy to behavioral intention along with the very strong effect of general controllability to self-efficacy. The rest of the formulated hypotheses did not prove to be significant.

With respect to the relationships that were not confirmed, it may be explained by the fact that undergraduate nursing students, most possibly, do perceive the notion of susceptibility, severity, threat seriousness and the obvious barriers towards a behavior that would apply the necessary security concepts and practices. However, mainly due to their age, their attitude does not encapsulate the appropriate consciousness regarding information and computer security. Their early exposure to personal computers and informatics may have led to an immature behavior in cases where security is involved. Such an ascertainment may also be supported by their comments during the questionnaire completion which included statements of the type "I am very interested in applying security on my personal computer but mainly I ask my brother or my friends to do so, primarily because I am bored to perform such a task" or "Having an antivirus is not enough. The computer needs constant updating and…it is really a boring thing to do!". Further observations are related with the low appreciation in terms of cues to action. The set of questions assessing this specific construct were formulated from the University perspective and the actions it takes to inform the student community. The responders' attitude toward those questions and the unsupported hypothesis of cues to action in relation with behavioral intention could be explained by the lack of actions taken by the university or lack of notifications to students with respect to these actions. Consequently, it may be deduced that further initiatives should take place and current ones need to be further advertised amongst the students' communities in order to achieve a broader visibility and exposure. It should not be neglected that undergraduate nursing students constitute the future healthcare staff in relative organizations. Thus, by gaining the appropriate skills while also fostering an appropriate behavioral security attitude will also assist them to apply such knowledge in a future professional setting. Moreover, the information resulted from the analysis could be the start point for further research on academic teaching and research staff towards security issues, in order to further check and improve the channels of communication and the actions taken with respect to security issues promotion.

ACKNOWLEDGMENT

The authors would like to sincerely thank the undergraduate nursing students who participated at the current study.

REFERENCES

Adams, A., & Blandford, A. (2005). Bridging the gap between organizational and user perspectives of security in the clinical domain. *International Journal of Human-Computer Studies*, *63*(1-2), 175–202. doi:10.1016/j.ijhcs.2005.04.022

Aytes, K., & Connolly, T. (2003). *A research model for investigating human behavior related to computer security*. In Proceedings of the 9th Americas Conference on Information Systems. Tampa, Florida USA, 2027-2031.

Barclay, D., Higgins, C., & Thompson, R. (1995). The partial least squares (PLS) approach to causal modeling: Personal computer adoption and use as an illustration. *Technology Studies*, *2*, 285–309.

Carlbring, P., Brunt, S., Bohman, S., Austin, D., & Richards, J, L-Göran, Ö., & Andersson, G. (2007). Internet vs. paper and pencil administration of questionnaires commonly used in panic/agoraphobia research. *Computers in Human Behavior*, *23*(3), 1421–14. doi:10.1016/j.chb.2005.05.002

Champion, V. L. (1984). Instrument development for Health Belief Model constructs. *ANS. Advances in Nursing Science*, *6*(3), 73–85.

Chea, S., & Luo, M. M. (2007). *Cognition, emotion, satisfaction and post-adoption behaviors of e-service customers*. In Proceedings of the 40th Annual Hawaii International Conference on System Sciences (HICSS'07). Big Island, Hawaii, USA, 154b.

Chenoweth, T., Minch, R., & Gattiker, T. (2009). *Application of Protection Motivation Theory to adoption of protective technologies*. In Proceedings of the 42nd Hawaii International Conference on System Sciences. Waikoloa, Big Island, Hawaii USA, 1-10.

Chin, W. W. (1998). The partial least squares approach for structural equation modeling. In Marcoulides, G. A. (Ed.), *Modern methods for business research* (pp. 295–336). Mahwah, NJ: Lawrence Erlbaum Associates.

Cismaru, M. (2006). Using Protection Motivation Theory to Increase the Persuasiveness of Public Service Communications. Public Policy Paper Series. *The Saskatchewan Institute of Public Policy*, *40*, 1-27. Retrieved September 20, 2009, from: http://www.uregina.ca/sipp.

Cronbach, L. (1951). Coefficient alpha and the internal structure of tests. *Psychometrica*, *16*, 297–334. doi:10.1007/BF02310555

Daskalakis, S. (2007). *Application integration and interoperability of Healthcare Information Systems*. Unpublished doctoral dissertation, National and Kapodistrian University of Athens, Athens, Greece.

Dinev, T., & Hu, Q. (2005). *The centrality of awareness in the formation of user behavioral intention toward preventive technologies in the context of voluntary use*. In Proceedings of the 4th Annual Workshop on HCI Research in MIS (SIGHCI'05). Las Vegas, Nevada, USA, paper 10.

Fernando, J. I., & Dawson, L. L. (2009). The health information system security threat lifecycle: An informatics theory. *International Journal of Medical Informatics*..doi:10.1016/j.ijmedinf.2009.08.006

Fornell, C., & Larcker, D. F. (1981). Evaluating structural equation models with unobservable variables and measurement error. *JMR, Journal of Marketing Research*, *18*, 39–50. doi:10.2307/3151312

Frost, R., Zuckerman, M., & Zuckerman, E. (2008). *Health Promotion Theories and Models for Program Planning and Implementation*. College of Public Health, University of Arizona. Retrieved September 20, 2009, from: http://www.azrapeprevention.org/agency_updates/2008/2008_01_UA.pdf

Gefen, D., Straub, D. W., & Boudreau, M. (2000). Structural equation modeling techniques and regression: Guidelines for research practice. *Communications of AIS*, *4*(7), 1–79.

Grosser, R. L. (1982). Health belief model aids understanding of patient behavior. *AORN Journal*, *35*(6), 1056–1059. doi:10.1016/S0001-2092(07)62466-1

Gurung, A., Luo, X., & Liao, Q. (2009). Consumer motivations in taking action against spyware: an empirical investigation. *Information Management & Computer Security*, *7*(3), 276–289. doi:10.1108/09685220910978112

Herath, T., & Rao, H. R. (2009). Encouraging information security behaviors in organizations: Role of penalties, pressures and perceived effectiveness. *Decision Support Systems*, *47*, 154–165. doi:10.1016/j.dss.2009.02.005

Igbaria, M., & Iivari, J. (1995). The effects of self-efficacy on computer usage. *International Journal of Management Science*, *23*(6), 587–605.

Iivari, J. (2005). An empirical test of the DeLone-McLean Model of information system success. *The Data Base for Advances in Information Systems*, *36*(2), 8–27.

Jayanti, R. K., & Burns, A. C. (1998). The antecedents of preventive health care behavior: An empirical study. *Journal of the Academy of Marketing Science*, *26*(1), 6–15. doi:10.1177/0092070398261002

LaRose, R., Rifon, N., Liu, S., & Lee, D. (2005). *Understanding online safety behavior: A multivariate model*. In Proceedings of the 55th Annual Conference of the International Communication Association. New York City, USA.

Levett-Jones, T., Kenny, R., Van der Riet, P., Hazelton, M., Kable, A., Bourgeois, S., & Luxford, Y. (2009). Exploring the information and communication technology competence and confidence of nursing students and their perception of its relevance to clinical practice. *Nurse Education Today*, *29*, 612–616. doi:10.1016/j.nedt.2009.01.007

Mann, H. B., & Whitney, D. R. (1947). On a test of whether one of two random variables is stochastically larger than the other. *Annals of Mathematical Statistics*, *18*, 50–60. doi:10.1214/aoms/1177730491

Mishra, S., & Dhillon, G. (2006). *Information Systems security governance research: A behavioral perspective*. In Proceedings of the 3rd Annual Symposium on Information Assurance (ASIA '06). Albany, NY, 18-26.

National Cancer Institute. (2005). *Theory at a Glance: A Guide for Health Promotion Practice*. (2nd ed.) NIH Publication No. 05-3896: US Department of Health and Human Services. Retrieved September 10, 2009, from: http://tinyurl.com/y4648y.

Ng, B. Y., & Rahim, M. A. (2005). *A sociobehavioral study of home computer users' intention to practice security*. In Proceedings of the 9th Pacific Asia Conference on Information Systems. Bangkok, Thailand, 234-247.

Ng, B. Y., & Xu, Y. (2007). *Studying users' computer security behavior using the Health Belief Model*. In Proceedings of the 11th Pacific Asia Conference on Information Systems. Auckland, New Zealand, 423-437.

Norman, P., Boer, H., & Seydel, E. R. (2005). Protection motivation theory. In *Predicting Health Behaviour: Research and Practice with Social Cognition Models* (pp. 81–126). Maidenhead: Open University Press.

Pahnila, S., Siponen, M., & Mahmood, A. (2007). *Which factors explain employees' adherence to information security policies? An empirical study*. In Proceedings of the Pacific Asia Conference on Information Systems (PACIS 2007). Auckland, New Zealand.

Pavlou, P. A., & Fygenson, M. (2005). Understanding and predicting electronic commerce adoption: An extension of the Theory of Planned Behavior. *Management Information Systems Quarterly*, *30*(1), 115–143.

Rhee, H.-S., Kim, C., & Ryu, Y. U. (2009). Self-efficacy in information security: Its influence on end users' information security practice behavior. *Computers & Security*..doi:10.1016/j.cose.2009.05.008

Ringle, C. M., Wende, S., & Will, A. (2005). SmartPLS 2.0 (M3), University of Hamburg. Retrieved from: http://www.smartpls.de.

Rogers, R. W. (1975). A protection motivation theory of fear appeals and attitude change. *The Journal of Psychology*, *91*, 93–114. doi:10.1080/00223980.1975.9915803

Roldán, L. J., & Leal, A. (2003). A validation test of an adaptation of the DeLone and McLean's Model in the Spanish EIS Field. In Cano, J. J. (Ed.), *Critical reflections on information systems. A systemic approach* (pp. 66–84). Hershey, PA: Idea Group Publishing.

Shepherd, M. M., Tesch, D. B., & Hsu, J. S. C. (2006). Environmental traits that support a learning organization: The impact on information system development projects. *Comparative Technology Transfer and Society*, *4*, 196–218. doi:10.1353/ctt.2006.0022

Siponen, M., Pahnila, S., & Mahmood, A. (2007). Employees' adherence to Information Security policies: An empirical study. In IFIP International Federation for Information Processing, 232, *New Approaches for Security, Privacy and Trust in Complex Environments*, eds. Venter, H., Eloff, M., Labuschagne, L. Eloff, J. von Solms, R., (Boston: Springer), 133-144.

SPSS, Inc. (2007). *SPSS for Windows, Version 16.0.*

Stanton, J. M., Stam, K. R., Mastrangelo, P., & Jolton, J. (2005). Analysis of end user security behaviors. *Computers & Security*, *24*(2), 124–133. doi:10.1016/j.cose.2004.07.001

University of Twente. Health Belief Model. Retrieved September 21, 2009, from http://www.cw.utwente.nl/theorieenoverzicht/Theory%20clusters/Health%20Communication/Health_Belief_Model.doc/

University of Twente. Protection Motivation Theory. Retrieved September 21,2009, from http://www.tcw.utwente.nl/theorieenoverzicht/Theory%20clusters/Health%20Communication/Protection_Motivation_Theory.doc/

Vaast, E. (2007). Danger is in the eye of the beholders: Social representations of Information Systems security in healthcare. *The Journal of Strategic Information Systems*, *16*, 130–152. doi:10.1016/j.jsis.2007.05.003

Venkatesh, V. Personal web page, Theoretical Models. Retrieved September 21, 2009, from http://www.vvenkatesh.com/organizations/Theoretical_Models.asp

Venkatesh, V., Morris, G. M., Davis, B. G., & Davis, D. F. (2003). User acceptance of information technology: Toward a unified view. *Management Information Systems Quarterly*, *27*(3), 425–478.

Woon, I. M. Y., Tan, G. W., & Low, R. T. (2005). *A Protection Motivation Theory approach to home wireless security*. In Proceedings of the 26th International Conference on Information Systems. Las Vegas, Nevada, USA, paper 31.

Workman, M., Bommer, W. H., & Straub, D. (2008). Security lapses and the omission of information security measures: A threat control model and empirical test. *Computers in Human Behavior*, *24*, 2799–2816. doi:10.1016/j.chb.2008.04.005

Yeo, C. A., Rahim, M. M., & Ren, Y. Y. (2008). Use of persuasive technology to change end-users' IT security aware behavior: A pilot study. *World Academy of Science. Engineering and Technology, 46*, 232–238.

KEY TERMS AND DEFINITIONS

Behavioral Security: Behavioral security is building and enforcing procedures to prevent the misusing of computer hardware and software. [Kendall KE, Kendall JE. Systems analysis and design. 6th edition, Pearson Prentice Hall, 2005]

Health Belief Model: The Health Belief Model (HBM) is a psychological model that attempts to explain and predict health behaviors. This is done by focusing on the attitudes and beliefs of individuals. [University of Twente, http://www.cw.utwente.nl/theorieenoverzicht/Theory%20 clusters/Health%20Communication/Health_Belief_Model.doc/]

Nursing: The field of nursing care concerned with the promotion, maintenance, and restoration of health. [MeSH database, Medline]

Partial Least Squares: Is a linear regression method that forms components (factors, or latent variables) as new independent variables (explanatory variables, or predictors) in a regression model. The components in partial least squares are determined by both the response variable(s) and the predictor variables. A regression model from partial least squares can be expected to have a smaller number of components without an appreciably smaller R-square value. [http://www.statsoft.com/textbook/statistics-glossary/p/]

Protection Motivation Theory (PMT): was originally proposed to provide conceptual clarity to the understanding of fear appeals. The Protection Motivation Theory proposes that we protect ourselves based on four factors: the perceived severity of a threatening event, the perceived probability of the occurrence, or vulnerability, the efficacy of the recommended preventive behavior, and the perceived self efficacy. [Rogers, R. W. (1975). A protection motivation theory of fear appeals and attitude change. Journal of Psychology, 91, 93-114.]

Compilation of References

Aarts, R., & Madsen, P. (Eds.). (2006). *Liberty ID-WSF Interaction Service Specification*, Ver. 2.0. Liberty Alliance Project. New Jersey. Accessed 2009/12 http://www.projectliberty.org/resource_center/specifications/liberty_alliance_id_wsf_2_0_specifications.

Abram, S. (2007). Earning the right to give advice. *SirsiDynix One Source, 3*, Retrieved July 25, 2009, from http://www.imakenews.com/sirsi/e_article000805034.cfm?x=b9vt0Kw,b2rpPgSw.

Adams, D., & Beckett, D. (1998). 4D Triggers 2000. *Summit, 98*, 2–17.

Adams, A., & Sasse, M. A. (1999). Users are not the enemy. *Communications of the ACM, 42*(12), 40–46. doi:10.1145/322796.322806

Adams, A., & Blandford, A. (2005). Bridging the gap between organizational and user perspectives of security in the clinical domain. *International Journal of Human-Computer Studies, 63*(1-2), 175–202. doi:10.1016/j.ijhcs.2005.04.022

Adams, C., Farrell, S. (1999). *Internet X.509 Public Key Infrastructure: Certificate Management Protocol.* RFC 2510.

Adams, M., ter Hofstede, A. H. M., Edmond, D., & van der Aalst, W. M. P. (2005). *Facilitating flexibility and dynamic exception handling in workflows through worklets.* In Orlando Bello, Johann Eder, Oscar Pastor & Jo~ao Falc~ao e Cunha, (eds.), Proceedings of the CAiSE'05 Forum, pp. 45-50, Porto, Portugal, FEUP Edicoes.

Adams, M., ter Hofstede, A. H. M., van der Aalst, W. M. P., & Edmond, D. (2007). *Dynamic, Extensible and Context-Aware Exception Handling for Workflows*. In Curbera, F., Leymann, F., & Weske, M., eds, Proceedings of the OTM Conference on Cooperative information Systems (CoopIS 2007), vol. 4803, Lecture Notes in Computer Science, pp. 95-112. Berlin: Springer-Verlag.

Adams, M., ter Hofstede, A.H.M., Edmond, D., &. van der Aalst, W.M.P. (2006). Worklets: A Service-Oriented Implementation of Dynamic Flexibility in Workflows. In Meersman, R. & Tari, Z. et al., (eds.), *On the Move to Meaningful Internet Systems*, OTM Confederated International Conferences, 14th International Conference on Cooperative Information Systems (CoopIS 2006), vol. 4275, Lecture Notes in Computer Science, pp. 291-308. Berlin: Springer-Verlag.

Agrawal, R., & Johnson, C. (2007). Securing electronic health records without impeding the flow of information. *International Journal of Medical Informatics, 76*, 471–479. doi:10.1016/j.ijmedinf.2006.09.015

Agrawal, R., & Srikant, R. (1994). *Fast algorithms for mining association rules*. Proceedings of the 1994 Very Large Data Bases. Santiago, Chile.

Agrawal, R., Kiernan, J., Srikant, R., & Xu, Y. (2002). *Hippocratic databases*. Proceedings of the 2002 Very Large Data Bases. Hong Kong, China.

Akyildiz, A., Su, W., Sankarasubramaniam, Y., & Cayirci, E. (2002). A Survey on Sensor Networks. *IEEE Communications Magazine, 40*(8), 102–114. doi:10.1109/MCOM.2002.1024422

Alberta Health Services. (n.d). Engaging the Patient in Healthcare: An overview of Personal Health Record Systems and Implications for Alberta, *White Paper*.

Alberts, C., & Dorofee, A. (2002). *Managing Information Security Risks - The OCTAVE Approach*. Carnegie Mellon Software Engineering Institute.

Alhaqbani, B., & Fidge, C. (2008). *Access Control Requirements for Processing Electronic Health Records*. (. *Lecture Notes in Computer Science, 4928*, 371–382. doi:10.1007/978-3-540-78238-4_38

Allman, M. (2000). A Web Server's View of the Transport Layer. *ACM Computer Communication Review, 30*(5), 10–20. doi:10.1145/505672.505674

Alsaleh, M., & Adams, C. (2006). *Enhancing Consumer Privacy in the Liberty Alliance Identity Federation and Web Services Frameworks*. Proceedings of the 6th Workshop on Privacy Enhancing Technologies (PET 2006). Cambridge, United Kingdom.

American National Standards Institute/American Institute of Aeronautics and Astronautics. ANSI/AIAA (1993). *Recommended Practice for Software Reliability*, R-013-1992. Washington, DC.

Anderson, J. G. (2007). Social, Ethical and Legal Barriers to E-health. *International Journal of Medical Informatics, 76*, 480–483. doi:10.1016/j.ijmedinf.2006.09.016

Anderson, R. (1996). *A security policy model for clinical information systems*. The Proceedings of the 1996 IEEE Symposium on Security and Privacy. Oakland, CA.

Anderson, R. (1996). An Update on the BMA Security Policy. Cambridge University Computer Lab. Retrieved 10/1/2010, from http://www.cl.cam.ac.uk/~rja14/bmaupdate/bmaupdate.html.

Andrews, J. H., & Zhang, Y. (2000). *Broad-spectrum studies of log file analysis*, Proceedings of the 2000 International Conference on Software Engineering. Limerick, Ireland.

Argyropoulos, A. (2001). *Electronic Crime*. Athens – Komotini: Sakkoulas Publications.

Armamentos, P., & Sotiropoulos, B. (2005). *Personal data – Interpretation of Law 2472/1997*. Athens, Thessaloniki: Sakkoulas Publications.

Arnason, S. T., & Willet, K. (2008). *How to Achieve 27001 Certification: An Example of Applied Compliance Management*. Boca Raton, FL: Auerbach Publications.

Arrow, K., et al. (2009). Toward a 21-st Century Healthcare System. *Recommendations for Health Care Reform, Annals of Internal Medicine, 150*, 493-495. Retrievied from www.annals.org, on March 3 2009.

Ash, J. S., & Bates, D. W. (2005). Factors and forces impacting EHR system adoption: report of a 2004 ACMI discussion. *Journal of the American Medical Informatics Association, 12*, 8–12. doi:10.1197/jamia.M1684

Askham, J., & Chisholm, A. (2006). *Patient-Centred Medical Professionalism: Towards an agenda for research and action*. London: Picker Institute Europe.

Atluri, V., & Huang, W. (1996). *An Authorization Model for Workflows*. Paper presented at the 4th European Symposium on Research in Computer Security, (. *Lecture Notes in Computer Science, 1146*, 44–64.

Au, M., Huang, Q., Liu, J., Susilo, W., Wong, D., & Yang, G. (2008). Traceable and Retrievable Identity-Based Encryption. In Bellovin, S.M., Gennaro, R., Keromytis, A.D., Yung, M. (eds.) *ACNS 2008. (LNCS*, vol. 5037,pp. 94–110). Heidelberg: Springer-Verlag.

Australian Health Information Council. (2004). *Strategic Plan for Information Management and Information and Communication Technology (IM&ICT) in Health*. Canberra, Australia.

Aytes, K., & Connolly, T. (2003). *A research model for investigating human behavior related to computer security*. In Proceedings of the 9th Americas Conference on Information Systems. Tampa, Florida USA, 2027-2031.

Bakker, A. (2004). Access to EHR and access control at a moment in the past: a discussion of the need and an exploration of the consequences. *International Journal of Medical Informatics, 73*(3), 267–270. doi:10.1016/j.ijmedinf.2003.11.008

Barclay, D., Higgins, C., & Thompson, R. (1995). The partial least squares (PLS) approach to causal modeling: Personal computer adoption and use as an illustration. *Technology Studies, 2,* 285–309.

Baresi, L., Ghezzi, C., & Guinea, S. (2004). Smart monitors for composed services, *Proc. of 2nd International Conference on Service Oriented Computing (ICSOC '04).* New York, NY, USA.

Barrett, T., Troup, D. B., Wilhite, S. E., Ledoux, P., Rudnev, D., & Evangelista, C. (2008). *NCBI GEO: archive for high-throughput functional genomic data.* Nucleic Acids Res.

Bellifemine, F., Caire, G., & Greenwood, D. (2007). *Developing Multi-Agent Systems with JADE.* Wiley Series in Agent Technology, John Wiley & Sons. doi:10.1002/9780470058411

Beolchi, L. (2002). *Telemedicine Glossary* (4th ed.). Belgium: European Commission.

Berman, J. J. (2002). Confidentiality Issues for Medical Data Miners. *Artificial Intelligence in Medicine, 26*(1-2), 25–36. doi:10.1016/S0933-3657(02)00050-7

Berner, E. (2008). Ethical and Legal Issues in the Use of Health Information Technology to Improve Patient Safety. *HEC Forum, 20*(3), 243–258. doi:10.1007/s10730-008-9074-5

Berners-Lee, T., Hendler, J., & Lassila, O. (2001). The semantic web. a new form of web content that is meaningful to computers will unleash a revolution of new possibilities. [from http://www.scientificamerican.com/article.cfm?id=the-semantic-web.]. *Scientific American, 284*(5), 28–37. Retrieved July 25, 2009.

Beronov, K., Dzhimova, O., Delgado, A., Vossberg, M., Krefting, D., et al. (2008). *Virtual endovascular correction and hemodynamic analysis over the MediGRID-portal.* eMBEC 2008 IFMBE Proceedings ECIFMBE 2008. 4th European Conference of the International Federation for Medical and Biological Engineering.

Berreti, D. (1998). *Default set of BSS Parameters for Cosmote Network and set of BSS parameters for umbrella cells, Nokia Productivity Services.* Athens, Greece: Technical Report, Nokia Telecommunications.

Bethencourt, J., Sahai, A., & Waters, B. (2007). *Ciphertext-Policy Attribute-Based Encryption.* In Proceedings of the 2007 IEEE Symposium on Security and Privacy. Oakland, California.

Bhargava, A., & Zoltowski, M. (2003). *Sensors and wireless communication for medical care.* In Proceedings of the 14th International Workshop on Database and Expert Systems Applications, DEXA'03, Prague, Czech Republic.

Bhatti, R., Moidu, K., & Ghafoor, A. (2006). *Policy-based security management for federated healthcare databases (or RHIOs).* In Proceedings of the 2006 International Workshop on Healthcare Information and Knowledge Management. Arlington, VA.

Blasi, M. (2004). *Das Herkunftslandprinzip der Fernseh- und der E-Commerce Richtlinie.* Berlin, Köln, München: Carl Heymanns Verlag.

Blobel, B., Nordberg, R., Davis, J. M., & Pharow, P. (2006). Modelling privilege management and access control. *International Journal of Medical Informatics, 75*(8), 597–623. doi:10.1016/j.ijmedinf.2005.08.010

Blobel, B. (2002). *Information Systems. Studies in Health Technology and Informatics. Analysis, design and implementation of secure and interoperable distributed health information systems* (*Vol. 89*). Amsterdam: IOS Press.

Blobel, B. (2004). Authorisation and access control for electronic health record systems. *International Journal of Medical Informatics, 73,* 251–257. doi:10.1016/j.ijmedinf.2003.11.018

Blobel, B., & Roger-France, F. (2001). A systematic approach for analysis and design of secure health information systems. *International Journal of Medical Informatics, 62*(3), 51–78. doi:10.1016/S1386-5056(01)00147-2

Blobel, B., & Holena, M. (1997). *Comparison, evaluation, and possible harmonisation of the HL7, DHE, and CORBA middleware*. In Dudeck, J. Blobel, B. Lordieck, W. Bórkle, T. (Eds.), New technologies in hospital information systems, Series Studies in Health Technology and Informatics, vol. 89, pp. 40—47, Amsterdam: IOS Press.

Bodenheimer, T., & Grumbach, K. (2003). A Spark to Revitalize Primary Care? *JAMA: the Journal of the American Medical Association, 290*, 259–264. doi:10.1001/jama.290.2.259

Boneh, D., & Franklin, M. (2001). Identity-Based Encryption from the Weil Pairing. In *Advances in Cryptology - CRYPTO 2001*,(LNCS 2139, pp. 213-229). Heidelberg: Springer-Verlag.

Brazma, A., Hingamp, P., Quackenbush, J., Sherlock, G., Spellman, P., & Stoeckert, C. (2001). Minimum information about a microarray experiment (MIAME)-toward standards for microarray data. *Proc. Nat Genet., 29*(4), 365–371. doi:10.1038/ng1201-365

Byun, J. W., Bertino, E., & Li, N. (2005, June). *Purpose Based Access Control of Complex Data for Privacy Protection*. Paper presented at the 10th ACM Symposium on Access Control Models and Technologies (SACMAT'05), Stockholm, Sweden.

Calder, A. (2009). *Information Security based on ISO 27001/ISO 27002. A Management Guide*. Second edition. Zaltbommel, NL: Van Haren Publishing.

Care2X Integrated Healthcare Environment (n.d.). Retrieved July 15, 2009, from http://www.care2x.org/.

Carlbring, P., Brunt, S., Bohman, S., Austin, D., & Richards, J, L-Göran, Ö., & Andersson, G. (2007). Internet vs. paper and pencil administration of questionnaires commonly used in panic/agoraphobia research. *Computers in Human Behavior, 23*(3), 1421–14. doi:10.1016/j.chb.2005.05.002

Casati, F., Castano, S., & Fugini, M. (2001). Managing workflow authorization constraints through active database technology. *Information Systems Frontiers, 3*(3), 319–338. doi:10.1023/A:1011461409620

Cazier, J., & Medlin, B. (2006). How secure is your information system? An investigation into actual healthcare worker password practices. *Perspectives in Health Information Management, 3*(8).

Ceri, S., & Widom, J. (1998). Applications of active databases. In Widom, J., & Ceri, S. (Eds.), *Triggers and Rules for Advanced Database processing* (pp. 259–261). San Francisco, California.

Chakravorty, R. (2006). *A programmable service architecture for mobile medical care*. In Proceedings of the 4th Annual IEEE International Conference on Pervasive Computing and Communications Workshops (PerCom '06), Pisa, Italy.

Champion, V. L. (1984). Instrument development for Health Belief Model constructs. *ANS. Advances in Nursing Science, 6*(3), 73–85.

Chatziioannou, A., Moulos, P., & Kolisis, F. (2009). Gene ARMADA: an integrated multi-analysis platform for microarray data implemented in MATLAB. *BMC Bioinformatics, 10*, 354..doi:10.1186/1471-2105-10-354

Chea, S., & Luo, M. M. (2007). *Cognition, emotion, satisfaction and post-adoption behaviors of e-service customers*. In Proceedings of the 40th Annual Hawaii International Conference on System Sciences (HICSS'07). Big Island, Hawaii, USA, 154b.

Chen, Y.-C., Chen, L.-K., Tsai, M.-D., Chiu, H.-C., Chiu, J.-S., & Chong, C.-F. (2008). Fingerprint verification on medical image reporting system. *Computer Methods and Programs in Biomedicine, 89*(3), 282–288.

Chen, X., Zhang, J., Wu, D., & Han, R. (2005). *HIPPA's compliant Auditing System for Medical Imaging System*. Proceedings of the 2005 IEEE Engineering in Medicine and Biology 27th Annual Conference. Shanghai, China.

Chenoweth, T., Minch, R., & Gattiker, T. (2009). *Application of Protection Motivation Theory to adoption of protective technologies*. In Proceedings of the 42nd Hawaii International Conference on System Sciences. Waikoloa, Big Island, Hawaii USA, 1-10.

Chheda, N. (2008). Standardization and certification: The truth just sounds different. Retrieved 15/12/2009, from http://www.nainil.com/research/whitepapers/Standardization_and_Certification.pdf.

Chilmark Research. (2008). *iPHR Market Report: Analysis & Trends of Internet-based Personal Health Records' Market*. Retrieved November 25, 2009, from http://chilmarkresearchstore.com/iphr-market-report-2008.html.

Chin, W. W. (1998). The partial least squares approach for structural equation modeling. In Marcoulides, G. A. (Ed.), *Modern methods for business research* (pp. 295–336). Mahwah, NJ: Lawrence Erlbaum Associates.

Choe, J., & Yoo, S. K. (2008). Web-based secure access from multiple patient repositories. *International Journal of Medical Informatics*, *77*(4), 242–248. doi:10.1016/j.ijmedinf.2007.06.001

Choi, Y. B., Capitan, K. E., Krause, J. S., & Streeper, M. M. (2006). Challenges Associated with Privacy in Health Care Industry: Implementation of HIPAA and the Security Rules. *Journal of Medical Systems*, *30*(1), 57–64. doi:10.1007/s10916-006-7405-0

Cismaru, M. (2006). Using Protection Motivation Theory to Increase the Persuasiveness of Public Service Communications. Public Policy Paper Series. *The Saskatchewan Institute of Public Policy, 40*, 1-27. Retrieved September 20, 2009, from: http://www.uregina.ca/sipp.

Cockburn, C., & Wilson, T. D. (1996). Business Use of the World Wide Web. *Information Journal of International Management*, *26*(2), 83–102. doi:10.1016/0268-4012(95)00071-2

Conn, J. (2007). *Health 2.0: The next generation of Web enterprises*. Retrieved July 25, 2009, from http://www.modernhealthcare.com/apps/pbcs.dll/article?AID=/20071211/FREE/312110003/1029/FREE.

Conrick, M., & Newell, C. (2006). Issues of Ethics and Law. In Conrick, M. (Ed.), *Health Informatics: Transforming Healthcare with Technology*. Melbourne, Australia: Thomson Social Science Press.

Corporation, I. B. M. (2005). *IBM Websphere Workflow - Getting Started with Buildtime V. 3.6*. Retrieved October 20, 2007, from http://publibfp.dhe.ibm.com/epubs/pdf/h1262860.pdf.

Cortellessa, V., & Grassi, V. (2007). Reliability Modelling and Analysis of Service-Oriented Architectures. In Luciano Baresi &· Elisabetta Di Nitto (Eds.) *Test and Analysis of Web Services*, 339- 362, Berlin:Springer-Verlag.

Coulter, A., Entwistle, V., & Gilbert, D. (1998). *Informing Patients. An Assessment of the Quality of Patient Information Materials*. London: King's Fund Publishing.

Covington, M., Long, W., Srinivasan, S., Dey, A., Ahamad, M., & Abowd, G. D. (2001). *Securing context-aware applications using environment roles*, ACM Symposium on Access Control Model and Technology. pp. 10-12,Chantilly, VA.

Criminal proceedings against Bernard Keck and Daniel Mithouard, Joined cases C-267/91 and C-268/91, ECJ (1993).

Crocco, A. G., Villasis-Keever, M., & Jadad, A. R. (2002). Analysis of cases of harm associated with use of health information on the internet. *Journal of the American Medical Association*, *287*(21), 2869–2871. doi:10.1001/jama.287.21.2869

Croll, P., & Croll, J. (2006). Investigating risk exposure in e-health systems. *International Journal of Medical Informatics*, *76*(5-6), 460–465. doi:10.1016/j.ijmedinf.2006.09.013

Cronbach, L. (1951). Coefficient alpha and the internal structure of tests. *Psychometrica*, *16*, 297–334. doi:10.1007/BF02310555

Cruz-Correia, R., Vieira-Marques, P., Costa, P., Ferreira, A., Oliveira-Palhares, E., Araújo, F. (2005). Integration of Hospital data using Agent Technologies – a case study. *AI Communications special issue of ECAI, 18(3)*, 191-200.

Daskalaki, A., Lazakidou, A., Philipp, C., Jacob, C., & Berlien, H. P. (2001). Introducing electronic health record into laser medicine. *Medical Informatics*, *5*, 85–86.

Daskalakis, S. (2007). *Application integration and interoperability of Healthcare Information Systems.* Unpublished doctoral dissertation, National and Kapodistrian University of Athens, Athens, Greece.

Davidson, R. (2002). Development of an Industry Specific Web Site Evaluation Framework for the Australian Wine Industry. *School of Commerce Research Paper Series*, 02-9.

Davies, J., Huismans, N., Slaney, R., Whiting, S., Webster, M., & Berry, R. (2003). *An Aspect Oriented Performance Analysis Environment.* International Conference on Aspect Oriented Software Development. Accessed 2009/12 http://aosd.net/archive/2003/program/davies.pdf.

Department of Health and Human Services. (2000). *Uniform Data Standards for Patient Medical Record Information.* National Committee on Vital and Health Statistics Report to the Secretary of U.S.

Department of Health and Children. (2004). *Health Information: A National Strategy.* Dublin, Retrieved July 25, 2009, from http://www.dohc.ie/publications/pdf/nhis.pdf?direct=1.

Deutscher Apothekerverband eV v. 0800 DocMorris NV and Jacques Waterval, Case C-322/01, ECJ (2003).

Dick, R., & Steen, E. (1997). *The Computer-based Patient Record: An Essential Technology for HealthCare.* Washington: National Academy Press.

Dimitriadou, E., Ioannou, K., Panoutsopoulos, I., Garmpis, A., & Kotsopoulos, S. (2005). Priority to Low Moving Terminals in TETRA Networks. *WSEAS Transactions on Communications*, 4(11), 1228–1236.

Dinev, T., & Hu, Q. (2005). *The centrality of awareness in the formation of user behavioral intention toward preventive technologies in the context of voluntary use.* In Proceedings of the 4th Annual Workshop on HCI Research in MIS (SIGHCI'05). Las Vegas, Nevada, USA, paper 10.

Dodds, D. J. (1982). Reducing dictionary size by using a hashing technique. [New York: ACM Press.]. *Communications of the ACM*, 25(6), 368–370. doi:10.1145/358523.358547

Doherty, I. (2008). Web 2-0 - A Movement Within The Health Community. *Health Care and Informatics Review Online*, 12(2), 49–57.

Donabedian, A. (1988). The quality of care. How can it be assessed? *JAMA, 260, 12* 1743-1748

Dunlop, J. (1999). *Digital Mobile Communications and the TETRA System.* New York: John Wiley & Sons.

Eddy, A. (2000). A Critical Analysis of Health and Human Services' Proposed Health Privacy Regulations in Light of the Health Insurance Privacy and Accountability Act of 1996. *Annals of Health Law, 9*, 1–72.

Elliot, S. (2002). *Electronic Commerce B2C Strategies and Model.* Chichester: John Wiley & Sons.

Emig, C., Schandua, H., & Abeck, S. (2006). *SOA-aware authorization control.* Paper presented at the International Conference on Software Engineering Advances, Papeete, Tahiti, French Polynesia.

Esquivel, A., Meric-Bernstam, F., & Bernstam, E. V. (2006). Accuracy and self correction of information received from an internet breast cancer list: content analysis. *British Medical Journal, 332*(7547), 939–942. doi:10.1136/bmj.38753.524201.7C

European Union. (2002). *Directive on Privacy and Electronic Communications.* European Parliament, Brussels. Accessed 2009/12 http://ec.europa.eu/justice_home/fsj/privacy/law/index_en.htm.

Eysenbach, G. (2007). From intermediation to disintermediation and apomediation: new models for consumers to access and assess the credibility of health information in the age of Web2.0. *Studies in Health Technology and Informatics, 129*, 162–166.

Eysenbach, G. (2008). Medicine 2.0: Social networking, collaboration, participation, apomediation, and openness. *Journal of Medical Internet Research, 10*(3), e22. doi:10.2196/jmir.1030

Eysenbach, G., Powell, J., Kuss, O., & Sa, E. R. (2002). Empirical studies assessing the quality of health information for consumers on the world wide web: a systematic review. *Journal of the American Medical Association, 287*, 2691–2700. doi:10.1001/jama.287.20.2691

Eysenbach, G. (2008). Credibility of health information and digital media: new perspectives and implications for youth. In Metzger, M. J., & Flanagin, A. J. (Eds.), *Digital Media, Youth, and Credibility. The John D and Catherine T MacArthur Foundation Series on Digital Media and Learning*. Cambridge, MA: MIT Press.

Eysenbach, G. (2003). The Semantic Web and healthcare consumers: a new challenge and opportunity on the horizon? *International Journal of Healthcare Technology and Management, 5(3/4/5)*, 194-212.

Farn, K., Hwang, J., & Lin, S. (2007). *Study on Applying ISO/DIS 27799 to Healthcare Industry's ISMS*. In Proceedings of the 6th Conference on WSEAS international Conference on Applied Computer Science - Volume 6 (Hangzhou, China, April 15 - 17, 2007).

Feinstein, H., Sandhu, R., Coyne, E., & Youman, C. (1996). Role-based access control models. *IEEE Computer, 29*(2), 38–47.

Ferguson, T. (2007). *ePatients: How they can help us heal health care*. E-patients net. Retrieved July 25, 2009, from http://www.e-patients.net/e-Patients_White_Paper.pdf.

Fernando, J. I., & Dawson, L. L. (2009). The health information system security threat lifecycle: An informatics theory. *International Journal of Medical Informatics.*. doi:10.1016/j.ijmedinf.2009.08.006

Ferraialo, D. F., Kuhn, D. R., & Chandramouli, R. (2007). *Role-Based Access Control* (2nd ed.). Norwood, MA, USA: Artech House.

Ferraiolo, D., & Kuhn, R. (1992). *Role-Based Access Control*. In proceedings of the 15th National Computer Security Conference, Balmy, Baltimore, USA.

Ferreira, A., Cruz-Correia, R., Antunes, L., & Chadwick, D. (2007). *Access Control: How can it improve patient's healthcare? Medical and Care Compunetics 4* (pp. 65–77). Amsterdam: IOS Press.

FIPA. (n.d.). *The Foundation for Intelligent Physical Agents Agent Communication Language Specifications*. (n.d.). Retrieved July 17, 2009, from http://www.fipa.org/repository/aclspecs.html

Fornell, C., & Larcker, D. F. (1981). Evaluating structural equation models with unobservable variables and measurement error. *JMR, Journal of Marketing Research, 18*, 39–50. doi:10.2307/3151312

Foster, I., & Kesselman, C. (1997). Globus: a Metacomputing Infrastructure Toolkit. *International Journal of High Performance Computing Applications, 11*(2), 115–128. doi:10.1177/109434209701100205

Foster, I., Kesselman, C., Nick, J., & Tuecke, S. (2002). *The physiology of the grid*. Global Grid Forum.

Fowles, J. B., Weiner, J. P., & Chan, K. S. (2008). *Performance Measures Using Electronic Health records: Five Case Studies* (*Vol. 92*). The Commonwealth Fund.

Frampton, S., Guastello, S., Brady, C., Hale, M., Horowitz, S., Bennett Smith, S., & Stone, S. (2008). *Patient-centered care improvement guide*. Camden, ME: Picker Institute, Inc.

Freidson, E. (1970). *The Profession of Medicine*. New York: Atherton Press.

Frost, R., Zuckerman, M., & Zuckerman, E. (2008). *Health Promotion Theories and Models for Program Planning and Implementation*. College of Public Health, University of Arizona. Retrieved September 20, 2009, from: http://www.azrapeprevention.org/agency_updates/2008/2008_01_UA.pdf

Fuke, D., Hunt, J., Siemenczuk, J., Estoup, M., Carroll, M., Payne, N., & Touchette, D. (2004). Cholesterol management of patients with diabetes in a primary care practice- based research network. *The American Journal of Managed Care, 10*(2), 130–136.

Gamerith, H. (2003). Neue Herausforderungen für ein europäisches Lauterkeitsrecht. *Wettbewerb in Recht und Praxis, 2*, 143–172.

Gami, N., & Mikolajczak, B. (2007a). *Integration of Multilevel Security Features into Loosely Coupled Inter-Organizational Workflow*, Proc. Fourth International Conference on Information Technology: New Generations, ITNG '07, Las Vegas, Nevada, USA.

Gami, N., & Mikolajczak, B. (2007b). *Consistency of Loosely Coupled Inter-Organizational Workflow with Multi-level Security Features*, Proc. of the 5th International Workshop on Modeling, Simulation, Verification and Validation of Enterprise Information Systems (MS-VVEIS 2007) in conjunction with the 9th International Conference on Enterprise Information Systems, Funchal, Madeira - Portugal.

Gantz, J., & Rochester, B. J. (2005). *Pirates of the Digital Millennium*. New Jersey: Prentice Hall.

Garson, K., & Adams, C. (2008). *Security and privacy system architecture for an e-hospital environment*. In proceedings of the 7th symposium on Identity and trust on the Internet. Gaithersburg, Maryland: ACM, Gold-schmidt, P. G. (2005). HIT and MIS: implications of health information technology and medical information systems. *Communications of the ACM, 48*, 68–74.

Gates, C., & Slonim, J. (2004). *Owner Controlled Information. New Security Paradigms Workshop*. Ascona, Switzerland: ACM Press.

Gefen, D., Straub, D. W., & Boudreau, M. (2000). Structural equation modeling techniques and regression: Guidelines for research practice. *Communications of AIS, 4*(7), 1–79.

Geiger, R. (2004). *Vertrag über die Europäische Union und Vertrag zur Gründung der Europäischen Gemeinschaft*. München: Verlag C. H. Beck.

Girault, C., & Valk, R. (2003). *Petri Nets for Systems Engineering: a Guide to Modeling, Verification, and Applications* (pp. 278–281). Berlin, New York: Springer-Verlag.

Giustini, D. (2006). How Web 2.0 is changing medicine. *British Medical Journal, 333*, 1283–1284. doi:10.1136/bmj.39062.555405.80

Giustini, D. (2007). Web 3.0 and medicine. *British Medical Journal, 335*(7633), 1273–1274. doi:10.1136/bmj.39428.494236.BE

Goh, S. H. (2006). The internet as a health education tool: sieving the wheat from the chaff. *Singapore Medical Journal, 47*(1), 3–5.

Gollman, D. (1999). *Computer Security* (1st ed.). New York: John Wiley & Sons.

Google AdSense Help. (n.d). *About AdSense - AdSense Help*. Retrieved 10/1/2010 from https://www.google.com/adsense/support/bin/topic.py?hl=en-uk&topic=13488.

Gornshtein, D., & Tamarkin, B. (2004). *Locking conflicts resolution in Oracle RAC environments. A Technical White Paper*, WisdomForce Technologies, Revision 1.0, Retrieved 1/1/2010, from http://www.wisdomforce.com/resources/docs/locking.rac.pdf.

Goseva-Popstojanova, K., Mathur, A. P., & Trivedi, K. S. (2001). Architecture-based approach to reliability assessment of software systems. *Performance Evaluation, 45*, 179–204. doi:10.1016/S0166-5316(01)00034-7

Graf von Bernstoff, C. (2000). Ausgewählte Rechtsprobleme im Electronic Commerce. *Recht der Internationalen Wirtschaft, 1*, 14–20.

Grain, H. (2006). Consumer issues in Informatics. In Conrick, M. (Ed.), *Health Informatics: Transforming Healthcare with Technology*. Melbourne, Australia: Thomson Social Science Press.

Grandison, T., & Davis, J. (2007). *The Impact of Industry Constraints on Model-Driven Data Disclosure Controls*. The Proceedings of the 2007 International Workshop on Model-Based Trustworthy Health Information Systems. Nashville, Tennessee.

Grandpierre, A. (1999). *Herkunftsprinzip kontra Marktor-tanknüpfung, Auswirkungen des Gemeinschaftsrechts auf die Kollisionsregeln im Wettbewerbsrecht. Frankfurt/M.* Berlin, Bern, New York, Paris, Wien: Verlag Peter Lang.

Greek National Organization for Medicines Decrees no. 39600 & 53425 (2001).

Griew, A. & Currell, R., (1995), *A Strategy for Security of the Electronic Patient Record*, Institute for Health Informatics, Aberystwyth, Version 2.1.

Grimson, J., Grimson, W., Berry, D., Stephens, G., Felton, E., & Kalra, D. (1998). A CORBA-based integration of distributed electronic healthcare records using the synapses approach. *IEEE Transactions on Information Technology in Biomedicine, 2*, 124–138. doi:10.1109/4233.735777

Gritzalis, D., & Lambrinoudakis, C. (2004). A security architecture for interconnecting health information systems. *International Journal of Medical Informatics, 73*(3), 305–309. doi:10.1016/j.ijmedinf.2003.12.011

Gritzalis, D. (2000). *Security and Reliability in ICT. Laboratorial exercises 1.5.* Computer Science Laboratory. Athens University of Economics and Business.

Gritzalis, D., Lambrinoudakis, C., Lekkas, D., & Deftereos, S. (2005). Technical guidelines for enhancing privacy and data protection in modern electronic medical environments. *IEEE Transactions on Information Technology in Biomedicine, 9*(3), 413–423. doi:10.1109/TITB.2005.847498

Gritzalis, D. (1994). *Information System Security in high vulnerability environments.* Doctoral dissertation, University of the Aegean, Greece.

Gritzalis, D., & Kokolakis, S. (2003). Security policy development for Healthcare Information Systems. In B. Blobel, *Advanced health telematics and Telemedicine.* 105-110. Amsterdam: IOS Press.

Grobee, D., Hoes, A., Verheij, T., Schrijvers, A., van Ameijden, E., & Numans, M. (2005). The Utrecht Health Project: Optimization of routine healthcare data for research. *European Journal of Epidemiology, 20*, 285–287. doi:10.1007/s10654-004-5689-2

Grosser, R. L. (1982). Health belief model aids understanding of patient behavior. *AORN Journal, 35*(6), 1056–1059. doi:10.1016/S0001-2092(07)62466-1

Guijarro, L. (2009). ICT standardisation and public procurement in the United States and in the European Union: Influence on egovernment deployment. *Telecommunications Policy, 33*(5-6), 285–295. doi:10.1016/j.telpol.2009.02.001

Gurung, A., Luo, X., & Liao, Q. (2009). Consumer motivations in taking action against spyware: an empirical investigation. *Information Management & Computer Security, 7*(3), 276–289. doi:10.1108/09685220910978112

Gyongyi, J., & Garcia-Molina, H. (2005). *Web spam taxonomy.* In proceedings of the First International Workshop on Adversarial Information Retrieval on the Web (AIRWeb). In the 14th International World Wide Web Conference *Nippon Convention Center (Makuhari Messe), Chiba, Japan.*, New York: ACM Press.

Hafner, M., Memon, M., & Alam, M. (2008). Modeling and Enforcing Advanced Access Control Policies in Healthcare Systems with SECTET. In H. Giese (ed.), *MoDELS Workshops*,(LNCS, Vol. 5002, pp132-144). Heidelberg: Springer-Verlag.

Haider, S., Ballester, B., Smedley, D., Zhang, J., Rice, P., Kasprzyk, A. (2009). *BioMart Central Portal--unified access to biological data.* Nucleic acids research.

Hand, D. J., Mannila, H., & Smyth, P. (2001). *Principles of Data Mining (Adaptive Computation and Machine Learning).* MIT Press.

Harris, S. (2003). *CISSP Certification All-in-One Exam Guide* (2nd ed.). New York: McGraw-Hill Osborne Media.

Harris, S. (2008). *CISSP Certification All-in-One Exam Guide*, Fourth Edition. Osborne: McGraw-Hill.

Heckle, R. R., & Lutters, W. G. (2007). *Privacy implications for single sign-on authentication in a hospital environment.* In Proceedings of the 3rd Symposium on Usable privacy and security. Pittsburgh, Pennsylvania. USA.

Heermann, P. W. (1999). Artikel 30 EGV im Lichte der „Keck" – Rechtssprechung: Anerkennung sonstiger Verkaufsmodalitäten und Einführung eines einheitlichen Rechtsfertigungssystems. *Gewerblicher Rechtsschutz und Urheberrecht. Internationaler Teil, 7*, 575–587.

Heimrich, T., & Specht, G. (2002). Enhancing ECA Rules for Distributed Active Database Systems. A.B. Chaudhri et al. (Eds.). Web Databases and Web Services 2002, LNCS 2593, (pp. 199–205). Berlin Heidelberg 2003:Springer-Verlag.

Hellenic Data Protection Authority (HDPA). (2006). *Law 3471/2006.*

Herath, T., & Rao, H. R. (2009). Encouraging information security behaviors in organizations: Role of penalties, pressures and perceived effectiveness. *Decision Support Systems, 47*, 154–165. doi:10.1016/j.dss.2009.02.005

Heyms, S., & Pries, C. (2002). *Werbung online – Eine Betrachtung aus rechtlichen Sicht.* Berlinq: Erich Schmidt Verlag.

HIMSS. (2009). *Patient Identity Integrity.* A White Paper by the HIMSS Patient Identity Integrity Work Group. Retrieved 10/1/2010 from http://www.himss.org/content/files/PrivacySecurity/PIIWhitePaper.pdf.

HIPAA. (1996), *Health Insurance Portability and Accountability Act.* United States Congress. Accessed 2009/12 http://aspe.hhs.gov/admnsimp/pl104191.htm.

Hirose, Y., Sasaki, Y., & Kinoshita, A. (2001). Human resource assignment and role representation mechanism with the cascading staff-group authoring and relation/situation model. *Medinfo, 10*(1), 740–744.

Hirose, Y. (1998). Access control and system audit based on patient-doctor relation and clinical situation model. *Medinfo '98, 2*, 1151-1155.

Hodges, J., & Cahill, C. (Eds.). (2006). *Liberty ID-WSF Discovery Service Specification. Ver2.0.* Liberty Alliance Project. New Jersey. Accessed 2009/12 http://www.projectliberty.org/resource_center/specifications/liberty_alliance_id_wsf_2_0_specifications.

Hodges, J., Aarts, R., Madsen, P., & Cantor, S. (Eds.). (2006). *Liberty ID-WSF Authentication, Single Sign-On, and Identity Mapping Services Specification Ver2.0.* Liberty Alliance Project. New Jersey. Accessed 2009/12. http://www.projectliberty.org/resource_center/specifications/liberty_alliance_id_wsf_2_0_specifications.

Hoeren, T. (1998). Internet & Recht – Neue Paradigmen des Informationsrechts. *Neue Juristische Wochenschrift, 39*, 2849–2854.

Hong, D., & Rappaport, S. (1986). Traffic model and performance analysis for cellular mobile radio telephone systems with prioritized and non prioritized handoff procedures. *IEEE Transactions on Vehicular Technology, 35*, 77–92. doi:10.1109/T-VT.1986.24076

Hornig, C. (1984). *A Standard for the Transmission of IP Datagrams over Ethernet Networks*, Retrieved June 13, 2009, from http://www.ietf.org/rfc/rfc894.txt.

Housley, R. et al. *RFC3280 (2002): Internet X.509 Public Key Infrastructure Certificate and Certificate Revocation List (CRL) Profile.* Retrieved from http://www.ietf.org/rfc/rfc3280.txt

Hu, J., Peyton, L., Turner, C., & Bishay, H. (2008). *A Model of Trusted Data Collection for Knowledge Discovery in B2B Networks.* Proceedings of the 3rd Intern'l MCETECH Conference on e-Technologies. pp. 60-69. Montreal, Canada Retrieved from http://doi.ieeecomputersociety.org/10.1109/MCETECH.2008.22.

Hubbard, T., Barker, D., Birney, E., Cameron, G., Chen, Y., & Clark, L. (2002). The Ensembl genome database project. *Nucleic Acids Research, 30*(1), 38–41. doi:10.1093/nar/30.1.38

Hucke, A. (2001). *Erforderlichkeit einer Harmonisierung des Wettbewerbsrechts im Europa.* Baden – Baden: Nomos Verlagsgesellschaft.

Hung, P. C. K. (2005). *Towards a Privacy Access Control Model for e-Healthcare Services.* Paper presented at the 3rd Annual Conference on Privacy, Security and Trust. The Fairmont Algonquin, St. Andrews, New Brunswick, Canada.

Iakovidis, I. (1998). From electronic medical record to personal health records: present situation and trends in European Union in the area of electronic healthcare records. *Medinfo*, *9*, 18–22.

Ibraimi, L., Tang, Q., Hartel, P., & Jonker, W. (2009). *Efficient and Provable Secure Ciphertext-Policy Attribute-Based Encryption Schemes.*(LNCS, Vol. 5451, pp. 1-12) Berlin: Springer.

Igbaria, M., & Iivari, J. (1995). The effects of self-efficacy on computer usage. *International Journal of Management Science*, *23*(6), 587–605.

Igglezakis, I. (2003). *The legal framework of e-commerce*. Athens, Thessaloniki: Sakkoulas Publications.

IHE. (2006). *IHE Patient Care Coordination Technical Framework: Basic patient privacy consents*. Retrieved 10/12/2009 from http://wiki.ihe.net/index.php?title=Basic_Patient_Privacy_Consents.

Iivari, J. (2005). An empirical test of the DeLone-McLean Model of information system success. *The Data Base for Advances in Information Systems*, *36*(2), 8–27.

Information Society in Greece. (2005). *ICT applications in health and welfare*, Action Line Measures, Technical Report of Measure 2.6, Retrieved November 27, 2008, from http://www.infosoc.gr/infosoc/en-UK/epktp/priority_actions/customerservice/hiddenchannel01/metro6.htm.

Ingres 9.2 Security Guide. (2008). *Introduction to Ingres Security: User Authentication Remote Users Installation Passwords*. pp.9.

Ingres II Enterprise Edition. (1998). *Database Administration's Guide. Release Notes for Ingres Release 2.0/9808* (pp. 328–333). Computer Associates International, Inc.

Institute, M. R. (2005). *7th annual survey of electronic health record trends and usage for 2005*. Medical Records Institute.

Institute of Medicine. (2001). *Crossing the Quality Chasm: A New Health System for the 21st Century*. Washington, DC: National Academies Press.

International Organization for Standardization. International Standard ISO/IEC 17799. (2000). Information technology - Code of practice for information security management. Geneva: ISO2000.

Ioannou, K., Louvros, S., Panoutsopoulos, I., Kotsopoulos, S., & Karagiannidis, G. (2002). Optimizing the Handover Call Blocking Probability in Cellular Networks with High Speed Moving Terminals. *IEEE Communications Letters*, *6*(10), 422–424. doi:10.1109/LCOMM.2002.802048

Ishac, J., & Allman, M. (2001). *On the performance of TCP spoofing in satellite networks*. NASA/TM—2001-211151.

ISO 27799:2008 (2008) *Health Informatics - Information security management in health using ISO/IEC 27002*. Retrieved: 15/12/2009 from http://www.iso.org/iso/iso_catalogue/catalogue_tc/catalogue_detail.htm?csnumber=41298.

ISO 7498-2. (1989). *Information processing systems — Open Systems Interconnection — Basic Reference Model — Part 2: Security Architecture*. Retrieved February 12, 2009, from http://webstore.iec.ch/preview/info_isoiec13888-2%7Bed1.0%7Den.pdf.

ISO/IEC 13335-1:2004 (2004) *Information technology — Security techniques — Management of information and communications technology security — Part 1: Concepts and models for information and communications technology security management*. Retrieved 15/12/2009 from http://www.iso.org/iso/iso_catalogue/catalogue_tc/catalogue_detail.htm?csnumber=39066.

ISO/IEC 17799. (2005). *Information technology-Security techniques-Code of practice for information security management*. Retrieved February 12, 2009, from http://www.iso.org/iso/en/prods-services/popstds/information-security.html.

ISO/IEC 17799:2005 (2005) *Information technology — Security techniques — Code of practice for information security management*. Retrieved 15/12/2009 from http://www.iso.org/iso/iso_catalogue/catalogue_tc/catalogue_detail.htm?csnumber=39612.

ISO/IEC 27000:2009 (2009) *Information technology — Security techniques — Information security management systems — Overview and vocabulary*. Retrieved: 15/12/2009 from http://www.iso.org/iso/iso_catalogue/catalogue_tc/catalogue_detail.htm?csnumber=41933.

ISO/IEC 27001:2005. (2005) *Information technology — Security techniques — Information Security Management Systems — Requirements*, Retrieved: 10/01/2010 from http://www.iso.org/iso/catalogue_detail.htm?csnumber=42103.

ISO/IEC 27002:2005. (2005.). *Information technology -- Security techniques — Code of practice for information security management*. Retrieved: 10/01/2010, from http://www.iso.org/iso/iso_catalogue/catalogue_tc/catalogue_detail.htm?csnumber=50297.

ISO/IEC 27003:2010. (2010) *Information technology — Security techniques — Information security management system implementation guidance*. Retrieved: 03/02/2010 from http://www.iso.org/iso/iso_catalogue/catalogue_tc/catalogue_detail.htm?csnumber=42105.

ISO/IEC 27004:2009. (2010) *Information technology — Security techniques — Information security management — Measurement*. Retrieved: 15/12/2009 from http://www.iso.org/iso/iso_catalogue/catalogue_tc/catalogue_detail.htm?csnumber=42106.

ISO/IEC 27005:2008. (2008) *Information technology — Security techniques — Information security risk management*. Retrieved: 15/12/2009 from http://www.iso.org/iso/iso_catalogue/catalogue_tc/catalogue_detail.htm?csnumber=42107.

ISO/IEC TR 13335-3:1998 (1998) *Information technology — Guidelines for the management of IT Security — Part 3: Techniques for the management of IT Security*. Retrieved: 15/12/2009 from http://www.iso.org/iso/catalogue_detail.htm?csnumber=21756.

ISO/IEC. ISO 27799:2008. (2008) *Health informatics — Information security management in health using ISO/IEC 27002*. Retrieved 10/01/2010, from http://www.iso.org/iso/catalogue_detail?csnumber=41298.

Iyer, G., Soberman, D., & Villas-Boas, M. (2004). *The targeting of advertising*. Retrieved 10/1/2010 from http://library.nyenrode.nl/INSEAD/2004/2004-020.pdf.

Jadad, A. R. (1999). Promoting partnerships: challenges for the internet age. *BMJ (Clinical Research Ed.)*, *319*, 761–764.

JADE. (n.d.). *Java Agent DEvelopment Framework*. Retrieved July 17, 2009, from http://jade.tilab.com.

Jafari, R., Dabiri, F., Brisk, P., & Sarrafzadeh, M. (2005). *CustoMed: A power optimized customizable and mobile medical monitoring and analysis system*. In Proceedings of ACM HCI Challenges in Health Assessment Workshop in Conjunction with Proceedings of the Conference on Human Factors in Computing Systems (CHI '05), Portland, Oregon, USA.

Jain, A., & Ross, A. (2006). Biometrics: A tool for information security. *IEEE Transactions on Information Forensics and Security*, *1*(2), 125–143. doi:10.1109/TIFS.2006.873653

Janczewski, L., & Shi, F. X. (2002). Development of Information Security Baselines for Healthcare Information Systems in New Zealand. [Elsevier.]. *Computers & Security*, *21*, 172–192. doi:10.1016/S0167-4048(02)00212-2

Japanese Ministry of Internal Affairs, Communications Information, and Communications Policy. (JMIA-CICP) (2003). *Personal Data Protection Law*. Retrieved 10/12/2009 from http://www.kantei.go.jp/jp/it/privacy/houseika/hourituan/index.html.

Jayanti, R. K., & Burns, A. C. (1998). The antecedents of preventive health care behavior: An empirical study. *Journal of the Academy of Marketing Science*, *26*(1), 6–15. doi:10.1177/0092070398261002

Jea, D., & Srivastava, M. B. (2006). *A remote medical monitoring and interaction system*. In Proceedings of the 4th International Conference on Mobile Systems, Applications, and Services (MobiSys '06), Uppsala, Sweden.

JIPDEC. (2004, 11 08). *ISMS User's Guide for Medical Organizations*. Japan. Retrieved 10/01/2010 from http://www.isms.jipdec.jp/doc/JIP-ISMS114-10E.pdf.

Johnson, D. R., & Post, D. G. (1998). *The New 'Civic Virtue' of the Internet: A Complex Systems Model for the Governance of Cyberspace.* Retrieved 10/1/2010 from http://www.temple.edu/lawschool/dpost/Newcivicvirtue.html

Juric, M. B., Mathew, B., & Sarang, P. (2006). *Business Process Execution Language for Web Services.* Packt Publishing Ltd.

Kamel Boulos, M. N., Maramba, I., & Wheeler, S. (2006). Wikis, blogs and podcasts: a new generation of Web-based tools for virtual collaborative clinical practice and education. *BMC Medical Education, 6,* 41. doi:10.1186/1472-6920-6-41

Kamel Boulos, M. N., & Wheeler, S. (2007). The emerging Web 2.0 social software: an enabling suite of sociable technologies in health and health care education. *Health Information and Libraries Journal, 24,* 2–23. doi:10.1111/j.1471-1842.2007.00701.x

Kamel Boulos, M. N., & Burden, D. (2007). Web GIS in practice V: 3-D interactive and real-time mapping in Second Life. *International Journal of Health Geographic's, 6,* Retrieved July 25, 2009, from http://www.pubmedcentral.nih.gov/articlerender.fcgi?artid=2216085.

Kapsalis, V., Hadellis, L., Karelis, D., & Koubias, S. (2006). A dynamic context-aware access control architecture for e-services. *Journal of Computer Security, 25,* 507–521. doi:10.1016/j.cose.2006.05.004

Kara, S., & Kayis, B. (2004). Manufacturing flexibility and variability: an overview. *Journal of Manufacturing Technology Management, 15,* 466–478. doi:10.1108/17410380410547870

Karkalis, G. I., & Koutsouris, D. D. (2006). *E-health and the Web 2.0.* The International Special Topic Conference on Information Technology in Biomedicine, October 26-28, Greece.

Kastania, A., & Zimeras, S. (2009). (in press). Evaluation of Web based applications, *Special Issue "Web-based Applications in Health Care and Biomedicine" of the Annals of Information Systems Series.* New York. *Springer Publications.*

Katsikas, S. (1995). *The administration of risk in Information Systems. Information security, technical, legal and social issues.* Athens: EPY Editions.

Katsikas, S., Gritzalis, S., Spinellis, D. et al. (1997). *Trusted Third Party Services for Health Care in Europe.* CEC/DG XIII/INFOSEC, Project 20820, final report.

Kellomäki, S., & Kainulainen, J. (Eds.). (2006). *Liberty ID-WSF Data Services Template ver.2.1.* Liberty Alliance Project. New Jersey. Accessed 2009/12 http://www.projectliberty.org/resource_center/specifications/liberty_alliance_id_wsf_2_0_specifications.

Khadka, B., & Mikolajczak, B. (2007). *Transformation of Live Sequence Charts to Colored Petri Nets,* Proceedings of the 5th Symposium on Design, Analysis, and Simulation of Distributed Systems, DASD 2007, Summer Computer Simulation Conference SCSC'07, San Diego, CA, USA.

Kim, D.-K., Ray, I., France, R., & Li, N. (2004). *Modeling Role-Based Access Control Using Parameterized UML Models.* In proceedings of the 7th International Conference Fundamental Approaches to Software Engineering, FASE 2004, Barcelona, Spain.

Klepper, B., & Sarasohn-Kahn, J. (2008). A Broad Vision of Health 2-0 - Reformulating Data for Transparency-Decision Support- and Revitalized Health Care Markets. *Health Care and Informatics Review Online, 12*(2), 45–48.

Kloppmann, M., Koenig, D., Leymann, F., Pfau, G., Rickayzen, A., von Riegen, C., et al. (2005). *WS-BPEL Extension for People - BPEL4People, IBM Corporation and SAP AG.* Retrieved November 30, 2009, from http://download.boulder.ibm.com/ibmdl/pub/software/dw/specs/ws-bpel4people/BPEL4 People_white_paper.pdf.

Kloss, I. (2003). *Werbung. Lehr-, Studien- und Nachschlagewerk.* Oldenbourg: Oldenbourg - Verlag.

Klyne, G., & Carroll, J. J. (2003). *Resource Description Framework (RDF): concepts and abstract syntax.* The World Wide Web Consortium (W3C). Retrieved July 25, 2009, from http://www.w3.org/TR/2003/WD-rdf-concepts-20030123/.

Knitz, M. (2005). *HIPPA compliance and electronic medical records: are both possible?* Graduate research report: Bowie State University.

Knuth, D. (1973). *The Art of Computer Programming, Sorting and Searching.* Addison Wesley Series in Computer Science and Information Processing. 3, 506-542. Reading, MA: Addison-Wesley.

Koch, M., & Möslein, K. M. (2005). Identity Management for Ecommerce and Collaborative Applications. *International Journal of Electronic Commerce, 9*(3), 11–29.

Koch, B. (2004). Die erste Bewertung der Entscheidung "DocMorris" des EuGH. *Europäische Zeitschrift für Wirtschaftrecht, 2,* 50–51.

Koehler, M., & Arndt, H.-W. (2001). *Recht des Internet.* Heidelberg: C.F. Mueller Verlag.

Koenig, C., Mueller, E.–M., Trafkowski, A. (2000). Internethandel mit Arzneimitteln und Wettbewerb im EG-Binnenmarkt. *Europäisches Wirtschafts- und Steuerrecht, 3,* 97 - 105.

Kohavi, R. (1995). *A Study of Cross-validation and Bootstrap for Accuracy Estimation and Model Selection.* In Proceedings of the 14th International Joint Conference on Artificial Intelligence,(pp. 1137-1 143). San Francisco:Morgan Kaufmann.

Kornilakis, P. (2007). The Internet and Civil Law. *Armenopoulos, 7,* 993–998.

Kotsis, G. (2006). Performance of Web applications. In Kappel, G., Proll, B., Reich, S., & Retschitzegger, W. (Eds.), *Web Engineering.* Chichester: John Wiley & Sons.

Koufi, & V., Vassilacopoulos, G. (2008). *HDGPortal: A Grid Portal Application for Pervasive Access to Process-Based Healthcare Systems.* Paper presented at the 2nd International Conference in Pervasive Computing Technologies in Healthcare, Tampere, Finland.

Kowalski, K. (2006). *Analysis of Log Files Intersections for Security Enhancement.* The Third Intern'l Conference on Information Technology: New Generations. pp. 452-457.Las Vegas, Nevada.

Krco, S., & Delic, V. (2003). *Personal Wireless Sensor Network for Mobile Health Care Monitoring.* In Proceedings of the IEEE TELSIKS 2003, Nis, Serbia-Montenegro.

Krishnan, A. (2004). A Survey of life sciences applications on the grid. *New Gen. Comput., 22*(2), 111–126. doi:10.1007/BF03040950

Kulkarni, D., & Tripathi, A. (2008). *Context-Aware Role-based Access Control in Pervasive Computing Systems,* Paper presented at the 13th ACM Symposium on Access Control Models and Technologies (SACMAT'08). Estes Park, Colorado, USA.

Kurtz, G. (2003). EMR confidentiality and information security. *Journal of Healthcare Information Management, 17*(3), 41–48.

Kyriacou, E., Pavlopoulos, S., Koutsouris, D., Andreou, A., Pattichis, C., & Schizas, C. (2001). *Multipurpose Health Care Telemedicine System.* In Proceedings of the 23rd Annual International Conference of the IEEE/EMBS, Istanbul, Turkey.

Landau, S. (Ed.). (2003). *Liberty ID-WSF Security and Privacy Overview, version 1.0.* Liberty Alliance Project. Accessed 2009/12 http://www.projectliberty.org/resource_center/specifications/liberty_alliance_id_wsf_2_0_specifications.

LaRose, R., Rifon, N., Liu, S., & Lee, D. (2005). *Understanding online safety behavior: A multivariate model.* In Proceedings of the 55th Annual Conference of the International Communication Association.New York City, USA.

Lassila, O., & Swick, R. R. (1999). *Resource Description Framework (RDF) model and Syntax specification.* The World Wide Web Consortium (W3C), Retrieved July 25, 2009, from http://www.w3.org/TR/REC-rdf-syntax/.

Lauer, G. (2009). *Health Record Banks Gaining Traction in Regional Projects.* Retrieved December 9, 2009, from http://www.ihealthbeat.org/features/2009/health-record-banks-gaining-traction-in-regional-projects.aspx.

Laure, E., Fisher, S.M., Frohner, A., Grandi, C., Kunszt, P., Krenek, A., Mulmo, O., Pacini, F., Prelz, F., White, J., Barroso, M., Buncic, P., Hemmer, F., Meglio, A, & Di,., &Edlund, A. (2006). Programming the Grid with gLite. *Computational Methods In Science And Technology, 12*(1), 33–45.

Lee, G., Kim, W., Kim, D.-k., & Yeh, H. (2004). *Effective Web-Related Resource Security Using Distributed Role Hierarchy.* In proceedings of the 5th International Conference on Advances in Web-Age Information Management, WAIM 2004. Dalian, China.

Lehoux, P. (2006). *The Problem of Health Technology: Policy Implications for Modern Health Care* (1st ed.). Routledge.

Lettl, T. (2004). *Das neue UWG.* München: Verlag C.H.Beck.

Levett-Jones, T., Kenny, R., Van der Riet, P., Hazelton, M., Kable, A., Bourgeois, S., & Luxford, Y. (2009). Exploring the information and communication technology competence and confidence of nursing students and their perception of its relevance to clinical practice. *Nurse Education Today, 29,* 612–616. doi:10.1016/j.nedt.2009.01.007

Lia, Q., Zhangb, X., Xua, M., & Wu, J. (2009). Towards secure dynamic collaborations with group-based RBAC model. *Journal of Computer Security, 28,* 260–275. doi:10.1016/j.cose.2008.12.004

Libby, D. (1999). *RSS 0.91 Spec, revision 3.* Netscape Communications. Retrieved July 25, 2009, from http://web.archive.org/web/20001204093600/my.netscape.com/publish/formats/rss-spec-0.91.html.

Lin, Y., Jan, I., Ko, P., Chen, Y., Wong, J., & Jan, G. (2004). A wireless PDA-based physiological monitoring system for patient transport. *IEEE Transactions on IT in Biomedicine, 8*(4), 439–447. doi:10.1109/TITB.2004.837829

Linden, H., Kalra, D., Hasman, A. & Talmon, J. (2009). Inter-organizational future proof EHR systems. A review of the security and privacy related issues. *International journal of medical informatics, 7 8*pp. 141–160.

Liu, S.-l., Guo, B.-a., & Zhang, Q.-s. (2009). An identity-based encryption scheme with compact ciphertexts. *Journal of Shanghai Jiaotong University (Science), 14*(1), 86–89. doi:10.1007/s12204-009-0086-3

Liu, D. R., & Shen, M. (2003). Workflow modeling for virtual processes: An order-preserving process - view approach. *Information Systems, 28*(6), 505–532. doi:10.1016/S0306-4379(02)00028-5

Lopez, D. M., & Blobel, B. F. M. E. (2009). A development framework for semantically interoperable health information systems. *International Journal of Medical Informatics, 78*(2), 83–103. doi:10.1016/j.ijmedinf.2008.05.009

Lorence, D. P., & Spink, A. (2004). Semantics and the medical web: a review of the barriers and breakthroughs in effective healthcare query. *Health Information and Libraries Journal, 21,* 109–116. doi:10.1111/j.1471-1842.2004.00491.x

Lu, Y. (2005). Privacy and data privacy issues in contemporary China. *Ethics and Information Technology, 7,* 7–15. doi:10.1007/s10676-005-0456-y

Lusignan, S. d., Chan, T., Theadom, A., & Dhoul, N. (2007). The roles of policy and professionalism in the protection of processed clinical data: A literature review. *International Journal of Medical Informatics, 76*(4), 261–268. doi:10.1016/j.ijmedinf.2005.11.003

Lyu, M. R. (1996). *Handbook of Software Reliability Engineering. IEEE Computer Society Press and McGraw Hill.* Editor.

Magalhães, S., Santos, H. M. D., et al. (2008). Keystroke Dynamic and Graphical Authentication Systems. *Encyclopedia of Information Science and Technology,* Second ed. M. Khosrow-Pour. USA, Information Science Reference, 1, 2313 - 2318.

Maisog, M. (2009). *Personal Information Protection in China.* (originally published on DataGuidance Website), Hunton & Williams LLP, New York. Accessed 2009/12 www.huntonfiles.com/files/webupload/PrivacyLaw_Personal_Information_Protection_in_China.pdf.

Majeed, A. (2004). Sources, uses, strengths and limitations of data collected in primary care in England. *Health Statistics Quarterly, 21*, 5–14.

Malin, B., Mathe, J., Duncavage, S., Werner, J., Ledeczi, A., & Sztipanovits, J. (2007). *Implementing a Model-Based Design Environment for Clinical Information Systems.* Proceedings of the 2007 ACM/IEEE International Workshop on Model-Based Trustworthy Health Information Systems. Nashville, TN.

Mandellos, G., Lymperopoulos, D., Koukias, M., Tzes, A., Lazarou, N., & Vagianos, C. (2004). *A Novel Mobile Telemedicine System for Ambulance Transport: Design and Evaluation.* Proceedings of the 26th Annual International Conference of the IEEE Engineering in Medicine and Biology Society, San Francisco, CA, USA.

Manhattan Research. LLC. (2007). *Physicians and Web 2.0: 5 Things You Should Know about the Evolving Online Landscape for Physicians.* Retrieved July 25, 2009, from http://www.manhattanresearch.com/TTPWhitePaper.aspx.

Mankowski, P. (1999). Internet und Internationales Wettbewerbsrecht. *Gewerblicher Rechtsschutz und Urheberrecht. Internationaler Teil, 11*, 909–921.

Mann, H. B., & Whitney, D. R. (1947). On a test of whether one of two random variables is stochastically larger than the other. *Annals of Mathematical Statistics, 18*, 50–60. doi:10.1214/aoms/1177730491

Mann, N. R., Schafer, Ray, E., & Singpurwalla, Nozer, D. (1974). *Methods for Statistical Analysis of Reliability and Life Data*, John Wiley & Sons.

Mansson, J., Nilsson, G., Bjorkelund, C., & Strender, L. E. (2004). Collection and retrieval of structured clinical data from electronic patient records in general practice. A first-phase study to create a health care database for research and quality assessment. *Scandinavian Journal of Primary Health Care, 22*(1), 6–10. doi:10.1080/02813430310003660

Mantas, J. (2002). Electronic health record. In Mantas, J., & Hasman, A. (Eds.), *Textbook in health informatics: A nursing perspective* (pp. 250–257). Amsterdam: IOS Press.

Mantzoufas, P. (2007). Taking risks in the information society and protection of personal data. *Armenopoulos, 7*, 1088–1109.

Marinos, M. T. (1998). Licensing databases – information as commodity. *Commercial Law Review, 1*, 16–36.

Marinos, M. T. (2002). *Unfair Competition.* Athens: Publications P.N. Sakkoulas, Law & Economy.

Marjanovic, O. (2005). Towards IS supported co-ordination in emergent business processes. *Business Process Management Journal, 11*(5), 476–487. doi:10.1108/14637150510619830

Martin, J. E. T., & Jones, M. Shenoy, R. (2003). *Towards a design framework for wearable electronic textiles.* In Proceedings of the 7th IEEE International Symposium on Wearable Computers. New York. USA.

Mayer, F. C. (1996). Recht und Cyberspace. *Neue Juristische Wochenschrift, 28*, 1782–1791.

McCarthy, D. B., Shatin, D., Drinkard, C. R., Kleinman, J. H., & Gardener, J. S. (1999). Medical records and privacy: empirical effects of legislation. *Health Services Research, 34*, 417–425. McGlynn, Elizabeth A., Asch, Steven, M., Adams, John, Keesey, Joan, Hicks, Jennifer, DeCristofaro, and Alison, Kerr, Eve, A. (2003). The Quality of Health Care Delivered to Adults in the United States. *The New England Journal of Medicine, 348*, 2635–2645. doi:10.1056/NEJMsa022615

McFredries, P. (2006). Technically Speaking The Web, Take Two. *IEEE Spectrum Magazine, 43*(6), 68. doi:10.1109/MSPEC.2006.1638049

McKenzie, A. M. (1973). *TELNET Protocol Specification.* Retrieved 1/1/2010, from ftp://ftp.rfc-editor.org/in-notes/rfc495.txt.

McLean, R., Richards, B., & Wardman, J. (2007). The effect of Web 2.0 on the future of medical practice and education: Darwikinian evolution or folksonomic revolution? *The Medical Journal of Australia, 187*, 174–177.

Micklitz, H. W., & Schirmbacher, M. (2006). Distanzkommunikation im europäischen Lauterkeitsrecht. *Wettbewerb in Recht und Praxis, 2*, 148–168.

Mikolajczak, B., & Wang, Z. (2003). *Conceptual Modeling of Concurrent Systems through Stepwise Abstraction and Refinement using Petri Net Morphisms.* Proc. of the 22nd Int. Conference on Conceptual Modeling. ER'2003, Chicago, Illinois. [Springer-Verlag.]. *Lecture Notes in Computer Science, 2813*, 433–445. doi:10.1007/978-3-540-39648-2_34

Miller, R., Hillman, J., & Given, R. (2004). Physician use of IT: results from the Deloitte Research Survey. *Journal of Healthcare Information Management, 18*(1), 72–80.

Minerva e-Europe European Cultural Website Quality Principles (2004). Retrieved 10/1/10 from: http://www.minervaeurope.org/userneeds/qualityprinciples.htm.

Mirkovic, J., Dietrich, S., Dittrich, D., & Reiher, P. (2004). *Internet Denial of Service: Attack and Defense Mechanisms*, pp. 19-20, 45, 51-52, and 297, New Jersey: Prentice Hall.

Mishra, S., & Dhillon, G. (2006). *Information Systems security governance research: A behavioral perspective.* In Proceedings of the 3rd Annual Symposium on Information Assurance (ASIA '06). Albany, NY, 18-26.

Mitrou, L. (2002). *Law in the Society of Information.* Athens, Thessaloniki: Sakkoulas Publications.

Miyazaki, S., & Masuda, M. (2005). Methods of Transposition of Nurses between Wards. *JSME International Journal Series C, 48*(1), 2–7. doi:10.1299/jsmec.48.2

Morgan, D. (1996). Focus Groups. *Annual Review of Sociology, 22*, 129–152. doi:10.1146/annurev.soc.22.1.129

Motta, G. H. M. B., & Furuie, S. S. (2003). A contextual role-based access control authorization model for electronic patient record. *IEEE Transactions on Information Technology in Biomedicine, 7*(3), 202–207. doi:10.1109/TITB.2003.816562

Mourtou, E. (2009). An Evaluation of the Flexibility of the Information Management System in a Greek Public Hospital. *The Journal on Information Technology in Healthcare, 7*(5), 304–314.

Mourtou, E. (2007). *The technological innovation in the management of intra hospital procedures and the implementation of innovation on patient electronic medical record.* Doctoral dissertation, University of Patras, Greece.

Mourtou, E., & Pavlidis, G. (2005). Coding of Medical and Surgical Equipment and Supplies in Pharmacies of Greek Public Hospitals. *Proceedings of the 10th International Symposium on Health Information Management - iSHIMR 2005* pp. 150-159) Thessalonica, Greece: South East European Centre.

Murray, E., Burns, J., See, T. J., Lai, R., & Nazareth, I. (2005). Interactive Health Communication Applications for people with chronic disease. *Cochrane Database of Systematic Reviews, 4*, CD004274.

Murray, P. (2008). Web 2.0 and social technologies: what might they offer for the future of health informatics? *Health Care and Informatics Review Online, 12*(2), 5–16.

National Cancer Institute. (2005). *Theory at a Glance: A Guide for Health Promotion Practice.* (2nd ed.) NIH Publication No. 05-3896: US Department of Health and Human Services. Retrieved September 10, 2009, from: http://tinyurl.com/y4648y.

National Committee on Vital and Health Statistics. (2001). *Information for Health: A Strategy for Building the National Health Information Infrastructure.* Washington, DC: U.S. Department of Health and Human Services.

National Institute of Standards and Technology (NIST). (n.d.). *Role Based Access Control (RBAC) and Role Based Security.* Retrieved December 10, 2009, from http://csrc.nist.gov/groups/SNS/rbac/.

NCSC. (1998). *Glossary of Computer Security Terms.* In Aqua Book. Retrieved 20/5/2009, from http://www. marcorsyscom.usmc.mil/ sites/ia/references/national/ NCSC-TG-004% 20Glossary.html.

NEMA. (2004). *Break-glass - an approach to granting emergency access to healthcare systems.* Retrieved from http://www.medicalimaging.org/documents/Break-Glass_-_Emergency_Access_to_Healthcare_Systems. pdf.

Nett, C. (2002). *Wettbewerb im E-commerce: Die Auswirkungen des Herkunftslandprinzips der E-Commerce Richtlinie auf das Lauterkeitsrecht der Mitgliedstaaten.* Retrieved 10/1/2010 from http://deposit.ddb.de/ cgi-bin/dokserv?idn=965274187&dok_var=d1&dok_ ext=pdf&filename=965274187.pdf.

Newcomer, E., & Lomow, G. (2005). *Understanding SOA with Web Services.* Addison Wesley.

Ng, B. Y., & Rahim, M. A. (2005). *A socio-behavioral study of home computer users' intention to practice security.* In Proceedings of the 9th Pacific Asia Conference on Information Systems. Bangkok, Thailand, 234-247.

Ng, B. Y., & Xu, Y. (2007). *Studying users' computer security behavior using the Health Belief Model.* In Proceedings of the 11th Pacific Asia Conference on Information Systems. Auckland, New Zealand, 423-437.

Nikolopoulos, K. (2008). *Healthcare and Emerging Rich Web Technologies – The WEB 2.0/Semantic Web Challenge and Opportunity.* OBBeC. Retrieved July 25, 2009, from http://www.obbec.com/specialreports/86-healthcare-it/1828-healthcare-and-emerging-rich-web-technologies-the-web-20semantic-web-challenge-and-opportunity.

Norman, P., Boer, H., & Seydel, E. R. (2005). Protection motivation theory. In *Predicting Health Behaviour: Research and Practice with Social Cognition Models* (pp. 81–126). Maidenhead: Open University Press.

Novotny, J., Tuecke, S., & Welch, V. (2001). *An Online Credential Repository for the Grid: MyProxy.* Proceedings of the Tenth International Symposium on High Performance Distributed Computing (HPDC-10). (pp. 104-111). IEEE Press.

NVIVO 7.(2009). *QSR International.* Retrieved from: http://www.qsrinternational.com/. (13th April 2009).

Nygren, E., Wyatt, J., & Wright, P. (1998). Helping clinicians to find data and avoid delays. *Lancet, 352,* 1462–1466. doi:10.1016/S0140-6736(97)08307-4

O'Reilly, T. (2005). *What is Web 2.0. Design Patterns and Business Models for the Next Generation of Software.* O'Reilly Media, Retrieved July 25, 2009, from http:// www.oreillynet.com/pub/a/oreilly/tim/news/2005/09/30/ what-is-web-20.html.

O'Reilly, T. (2006). *Web 2.0 compact definition: trying again.* O'Reilly radar, Retrieved July 25, 2009, from http:// radar.oreilly.com/archives/2006/12/web-20-compact-definition-tryi.html.

Office of Health and the Information Highway. (1999). *Canada Health Infoway: Paths to Better Health.* Ottawa: Health Canada.

Office of the Privacy Commissioner of Canada (OPCC). (2010). *Personal Information Protection and Electronic Documents* Act. Retrieved 10/1/2010 from http://www. priv.gc.ca/information/02_05_d_08_e.cfm.

Ohno-Machadoa, L., Silveira, P. S. P., & Vinterbo, S. (2004). Protecting patient privacy by quantifiable control of disclosures in disseminated databases. *International Journal of Medical Informatics, 73*(7-8), 599–606. doi:10.1016/j.ijmedinf.2004.05.002

Ojalvo, H. E. (1996). Online advice: Good medicine or cyber-quackery? *ACP Observer,* Retrieved July 25, 2009, from http://www.acponline.org/journals/news/dec96/ cybrquak.htm.

Oppermann, T. (2005). *Europarecht.* München: Verlag C. H. Beck.

Osama Salah, G. H. (2009). *Mandatory Information Security Management System Documents Required for ISO/IEC 27001 Certification.* Retrieved from http://www. iso27001security.com/ISO27k_mandatory_ISMS_documents.rtf.

P3. (2002). *The Platform for Privacy Preferences 1.0 Specification*. World Wide Web Consortium Recommendation. Accessed 2009/12 http://www.w3.org/TR/P3P/.

Pagliari, C., Sloan, D., Gregor, P., Sullivan, F., Detmer, D., & Kahan, J. (2005). What is eHealth (4): a scoping exercise to map the field. *Journal of Medical Internet Research*, 7(1), e9. doi:10.2196/jmir.7.1.e9

Pahnila, S., Siponen, M., & Mahmood, A. (2007). *Which factors explain employees' adherence to information security policies? An empirical study*. In Proceedings of the Pacific Asia Conference on Information Systems (PACIS 2007). Auckland, New Zealand.

Parasuraman, A., Zeithaml, V. A., & Berry, L. L. (1988). SERVQUAL: a multiple item scale for measuring consumer perceptions of service quality. *Journal of Retailing*, 64(1), 12–40.

Patrick, J. (2009). *A Critical Essay on the Deployment of an ED Clinical Information System Systemic Failure or Bad Luck?* Retrieved 10/12/2009 from http://www.it.usyd.edu.au/~hitru/essays/The%20Story%20of%20the%20Deployment%20of%20an%20ED%20Clinical%20Information%20System6.0.pdf.

Patterson, A. D., Gibson, G., & Katz, H. R. (1998). *A case for redundant arrays of inexpensive disks (RAID)*. University of California Berkley.

Pattichis, C., Kyriacou, E., Voskarides, S., Pattichis, M., Istepanian, R., & Schizas, C. (2002). Wireless Telemedicine Systems: An Overview. *IEEE Antennas and Propagation*, 44(2), 143–153. doi:10.1109/MAP.2002.1003651

Pavlopoulos, S., Kyriacou, E., Berler, A., Dembeyiotis, S., & Koutsouris, D. (1998). Novel emergency telemedicine system based on wireless communication technology—AMBULANCE. *IEEE Transactions on Information Technology in Biomedicine*, 2(4), 261–267. doi:10.1109/4233.737581

Pavlou, P. A., & Fygenson, M. (2005). Understanding and predicting electronic commerce adoption: An extension of the Theory of Planned Behavior. *Management Information Systems Quarterly*, 30(1), 115–143.

Pear, R. (2007). *Warnings over privacy of US Health Network*. Retrieved 10/1/2010 from http://www.nytimes.com/2007/02/18/washington/18health.html.

Peleg, M., Beimel, D., Dori, D., & Denekamp, Y. (2008). Situation-Based Access Control: Privacy management via modeling of patient data access scenarios. *Journal of Biomedical Informatics*, 41(6), 1028–1040. doi:10.1016/j.jbi.2008.03.014

Perakis, E. (1999). Contemporary issues on advertising. *Enterprise and Company Law*, 3, 251–263.

Peyton, L., & Hu, J. (2007). A Service Oriented Architecture for Managing Privacy Compliance in Collaborative Environments. [Geneva, Switzerland: Inderscience Publishers.]. *International Journal of Business Process Integration and Management*, 2(4), 292–301. doi:10.1504/IJBPIM.2007.017754

Peyton, L., Hu, J., & Zhan, B. (2007). *Addressing Trust and Privacy in Telemedicine*. The Symposium on E-Commerce and E-Business in China (SEEC) at the Ninth International Conference on E-Commerce (ICEC 2007). Minneapolis, United States.

Peyton, L., Hu, J., Doshi, C., & Seguin, P. (2007). *Addressing Privacy in a Federated Identity Management Network for E-Health*. 8th World Congress on the Management of eBusiness. Toronto. Retrieved from http://doi.ieeecomputersociety.org/10.1109/WCMEB.2007.34.

Pfleeger, C. P., & Pfleeger, S. L. (2007). *Security in Computing* (4th ed.). Prentice Hall.

PHIPA. (2004). *Personal Health Information Protection Act*, Government of Ontario, Canada. Accessed 2009/12 http://www.e-laws.gov.on.ca/html/statutes/english/elaws_statutes_04p03_e.htm.

Pickering, G. (2007). *Internet pharmacy in the European Union*. Retrieved 10/1/2010 from http://www.reedsmith.com/_db/_documents/Internet_Pharmacy_article.pdf

PIPEDA. (2000). *The Personal Information Protection and Electronic Documents Act*, Department of Justice, Canada. Accessed 2009/12 http://laws.justice.gc.ca/en/P-8.6/text.html.

Power, K. (2009). Global Mobile Healthcare An Electronic Framework for Portability of Health Records, *Medical Tourism Magazine*. Retrieved October 20, 2009, from http://www.medicaltourismmag.com/issue-detail. php?item=223&issue=10.

Procureur du Roi v Benoît and Gustave Dassonville, Case 8-74, ECJ (1974).

Quillian, M. R. (1968). Semantic memories. In Minsky, M. M. (Ed.), *Semantic Information Processing* (pp. 216–270). Cambridge: MIT Press.

Rappaport, T. S. (1999). *Wireless Communications: Principles and Practice*. Upper Saddle River, NJ: Prentice Hall.

Rash, M. C. (2005). Privacy concerns hinder electronic medical records. *The Business Journal of the Greater Triad Area*. Retrieved 10/1/2010 from http://www.bizjournals. com/triad/stories/2005/04/04/focus2.html.

Rasid, M., & Woodward, B. (2005). Bluetooth Telemedicine Processor for Multichannel Biomedical Signal Transmission via Mobile Cellular Networks. *IEEE Transactions on Information Technology in Biomedicine*, 9(1), 35–43. doi:10.1109/TITB.2004.840070

Rewe-Zentral AG v Bundesmonopolverwaltung für Branntwein, Case 120/78, ECJ (1979).

Rhee, H.-S., Kim, C., & Ryu, Y. U. (2009). Self-efficacy in information security: Its influence on end users' information security practice behavior. *Computers & Security.*. doi:10.1016/j.cose.2009.05.008

Rinderle, S., Reichert, M., & Dadam, P. (2004). Correctness Criteria for Dynamic Changes in Workflow Systems: A Survey. *Data & Knowledge Engineering*, 50(1), 9–34. doi:10.1016/j.datak.2004.01.002

Ringle, C. M., Wende, S., & Will, A. (2005). SmartPLS 2.0 (M3), University of Hamburg. Retrieved from: http://www.smartpls.de.

Ritterband, L., Gonder-Frederick, L. A., Cox, D. J., Clifton, A. D., West, R. W., & Borowitz, S. (2003). Internet interventions: In review, in use, and into the future. *Professional Psychology, Research and Practice*, 34(5), 527–534. doi:10.1037/0735-7028.34.5.527

Robu, I., Robu, V., & Thirion, B. (2006). An introduction to the semantic web for health sciences librarians. *Journal of the Medical Library Association*, 94, 198–205.

Rogers, R. W. (1975). A protection motivation theory of fear appeals and attitude change. *The Journal of Psychology*, 91, 93–114. doi:10.1080/00223980.1975.9915803

Roldán, L. J., & Leal, A. (2003). A validation test of an adaptation of the DeLone and McLean's Model in the Spanish EIS Field. In Cano, J. J. (Ed.), *Critical reflections on information systems. A systemic approach* (pp. 66–84). Hershey, PA: Idea Group Publishing.

Rosser, J., Lynch, P., Cuddihy, L., Gentile, D., Klonsky, J., & Merrell, R. (2007). The impact of video games on training surgeons in the 21st century. *Archives of Surgery*, 142(2), 181–186. doi:10.1001/archsurg.142.2.181

Rossnagel, A. (2002). Weltweites Internet - globale Rechtsordnung? *Multimedia und Recht*, 2, 67–71.

Rostad, L., & Edsburg, O. (2006). *Proceedings from 2006 Annual Computer Security Applications Conference*. Miami Beach, FL.

Rothschild, A. S., Dietrich, L., Ball, M. J., Wurtz, H., Farish-Hunt, H., & Cortes-Comerer, N. (2005). Leveraging systems thinking to design patient-centered clinical documentation systems. *International Journal of Medical Informatics*, 74(5), 395–398. doi:10.1016/j. ijmedinf.2005.03.011

Sadiq, S., Sadiq, W., & Orlowska, M. (2001). *Pockets of Flexibility in Workflow Specification*. In Proceedings of the 20th International Conference on Conceptual Modeling (ER 2001). vol. 2224. Lecture Notes in Computer Science. pp. 513-526. Berlin, Springer-Verlag.

Safran, C., Bloomrosen, M., Hammond, W. E., Labkoff, S., Markel-Fox, S., & Tang, P. C. (2007). Toward a National Framework for the Secondary Use of Health Data: An American Medical Informatics Association White Paper. *Journal of the American Medical Informatics Association, 14*(1), 1–9. doi:10.1197/jamia.M2273

Sahai, A., & Waters, B. (2005). *Fuzzy Identity-Based Encryption Advances in Cryptology*. In proceedings of the 24th Annual International Conference on the Theory and Applications of Cryptographic Techniques (Eurocrypt 2005). LNCS, 3494, 457-473. Aarhus / Denmark.

Sandars, J., Homer, M., Pell, G., & Croker, T. (2008). Web 2.0 and social software: the medical student way of e-learning. *Medical Teacher, 14*, 1–5. doi:10.1080/01421590701798729

Sandars, J., & Schroter, S. (2007). Web 2.0 technologies for undergraduate and postgraduate medical education: an online survey. *Postgraduate Medical Journal, 83*(986), 759–762. doi:10.1136/pgmj.2007.063123

Sandhu, R. S., Coynek, E. J., Feinsteink, H. L., & Youmank, C. E. (1996). Role-Based Access Control Models. *IEEE Computer, 29*(2), 38–47.

Sandhu, R. S., & Samarati, P. (1994). Access control: principles and practice. *IEEE Communications Magazine, 32*(9), 40–49. doi:10.1109/35.312842

Sandhu, R. S., Coyne, E. J., Feinstein, H. L., & Youman, C. E. (1996). Role-based access control models. *IEEE Computer, 29*, 38–47.

Sandhu, R., Ferraiolot, D., & Kuhnt, R. (2000). *The NIST Model for Role-Based Access Control: Towards A Unified Standard*. In Proceedings of the 5th ACM Workshop on Role Based Access Control, Berlin, Germany.

Sanghwan, K., Sangho, L., & Jongkun, L. (2006). *Computational Engineering in Systems Applications, IMACS Multiconference on Beijing* (Vol. 1, pp. 59–64). Deadlock Analysis of Petri Nets Based on the Resource Share Places Relationship.

SANS. (n.d.). *Information Security Policy Templates*. Retrieved 10/1/2010, from SANS.org: http://www.sans.org/security-resources/policies/#name.

Schneier, B. (2004). *Secrets and Lies: digital security in a networked world*. Wiley.

Schonenberg, M. H., Mans, R. S., Russell, N. C., Mulyar, N. A., & van der Aalst, W. M. P. (2007). *Towards a Taxonomy of Process Flexibility (Extended Version)*, BPM Center Report BPM-07-11.

Schumacher, R. (2005). High Performance SQL Server DBA. In Ed. Burleson D. Kittrell (Eds.) *Tuning & Optimization Secrets*, NC: Rampant TechPress.

Shamir, A. (1985). *Identity-Based Cryptosystems and Signature Schemes*. In Proceedings of Crypto'84 and In G. R. Blakley and D. Chaum, (ed.), Advances in Cryptology, LNCS 196, 47–53. Berlin:Springer–Verlag.

Shepherd, M. M., Tesch, D. B., & Hsu, J. S. C. (2006). Environmental traits that support a learning organization: The impact on information system development projects. *Comparative Technology Transfer and Society, 4*, 196–218. doi:10.1353/ctt.2006.0022

Shin, D., Ahn, G., & Shenoy, P. (2004). *Ensuring Information Assurance in Federated Identity Management*. pp. 821-826.IEEE Intl. Conference on Performance, Computing, and Communications.

Shin, Y. N., Lee, Y. J., Shin, W., & Choi, J. (2008). *Designing Fingerprint-Recognition-Based Access Control for Electronic Medical Records Systems*. In Proceedings of the 22nd International Conference on Advanced Information Networking and Applications Workshops, AINAW 2008. Okinawa, Japan.

Shortliffe, E. (1999). The evolution of electronic medical records. *Academic Medicine, 74*(4), 414–419. doi:10.1097/00001888-199904000-00038

Simons, C., & Causey, J. (2002). *Microsoft Windows XP Networking Inside Out*. Microsoft Press.

Simpson, J. A., & Weiner, E. S. C. (1989). *Oxford English Dictionary*. Oxford, UK: Oxford University Press.

Singh, S., Cabraal, A., Demosthenous, C., Astbrink, G., Furlong, M., et al. (2007). *Password sharing: implications for security design based on social practice.* In Proceedings of the SIGCHI conference on Human factors in computing systems, pp. 895-904.

Singleton, P., Hunnable, J., & Mason, R. (2001). Gaining Patient Consent to Disclosure. A Consultancy Project for the NHS Executive. London: Department of Health. Retrieved on 10/1/2010 from: http://www.dh.gov.uk/prod_consum_dh/groups/dh_digitalassets/@dh/@en/documents/digitalasset/dh_4131403.pdf

Siponen, M., Pahnila, S., & Mahmood, A. (2007). Employees' adherence to Information Security policies: An empirical study. In IFIP International Federation for Information Processing, 232, *New Approaches for Security, Privacy and Trust in Complex Environments*, eds. Venter, H., Eloff, M., Labuschagne, L. Eloff, J. von Solms, R., (Boston: Springer), 133-144.

Skiba, B., Tamas, A., & Robinson, K. (2006). *Web 2.0: hype or reality...and how will it play out? A strategic analysis.* Arma Partners. Retrieved July 25, 2009, from http://www.armapartners.com/files/admin/uploads/W17_F_1873_8699.pdf.

Stallings, W., & Brown, L. (2008). *Computer security: principles and practice.* Upper Saddle River, NJ: Pearson international ed.

Stanton, J., & Stam, K. (2005). Analysis of end user security behaviors. *Computers & Security, 24*(2), 124–133. doi:10.1016/j.cose.2004.07.001

Stanton, J. M., Stam, K. R., Mastrangelo, P., & Jolton, J. (2005). Analysis of end user security behaviors. *Computers & Security, 24*(2), 124–133. doi:10.1016/j.cose.2004.07.001

Stavroulakis, P. (2007). *TErrestrial Trunked RAdio - TETRA: A Global Security Tool. Signals and Communication Technology.* Berlin: Springer-Verlag.

Stefanou, K. (2005). Protecting human health and consumer safety in the European legal order and the European standardization policy. *Enterprise and Company Law, 12,* 1248–1264.

Stonebraker, M. (1992). The Integration of Rule Systems and Database Systems. *IEEE Transactions on Knowledge and Data Engineering, 4*(5), 415–423. doi:10.1109/69.166984

Stoneburner, G., Goguen, A., & Feringa, A. (2002). *Risk Management Guide for Information Technology Systems.* Recommendations of the National Institute of Standards and Technology Retrieved 10/01/2010 from http://csrc.nist.gov/publications/nistpubs/800-30/sp800-30.pdf.

Sung, M. Y., Kim, M. S., Kim, E. J., Yoo, J. H., & Sung, M. W. (2000). CoMed: a real-time collaborative medicine system. *International Journal of Medical Informatics,* (Issue 57), 117–126. doi:10.1016/S1386-5056(00)00060-5

Sungmee Park, K., & Jayaraman, S. (2002). *The wearable motherboard: a framework for personalized mobile information processing.* In Proceedings of the 39th ACM/IEEE Design Automation Conference. New Orleans, LA, USA.

Sunyaev, A., Gottlinger, S., Mauro, C., Leimester, J., & Krcmar, H. (2009). *Analysis of the Applications of the Electronic Health Card in Germany. WI 2009 - Proceedings of Wirtschaftsinformatik 2009 - Business Services: onzepte* (pp. 749–758). Vienna, Austria: Technologien und Anwendungen.

Sunyaev, A., Atherton, M., Mauro, C., Leimester, J., & Krcmar, H. (2009). Characteristics of IS Security Approaches with Respect to Healthcare. Proceedings of the Fifteenth Americas Conference on Information Systems. San Francisco, California.

Swanson, M., Bartol, N., Sabato, J., Hash, J., & Graffo, L. (2003). *Security Metrics Guide for Information Technology Systems, NIST Special Publication 800-55, Computer Security Division, Information Technology Laboratory, National Institute of Standards and Technology.* Gaithersburg, MD: U.S. Department of Commerce, Technology Administration, National Institute of Standards and Technology.

Swick, R. R., & Brickley, D. (2000). *PICS Rating Vocabularies in XML/RDF,* The World Wide Web Consortium (W3C), Retrieved July 25, 2009, from http://www.w3.org/TR/rdf-pics.

Tanase, M. (2003). *IP Spoofing: An Introduction*. Retrieved 10/4/2009, from http://www.securityfocus.com/infocus/1674.

Tang, P. C., Ash, J. S., Bates, D. W., Overhage, J. M., & Sands, D. Z. (2006). Personal Health Records: Definitions, Benefits, and Strategies for Overcoming Barriers to Adoption. *Journal of the American Medical Informatics Association, 13*(2), 121–126. doi:10.1197/jamia.M2025

Tang, H., & Ng, J. (2006). Googling for a diagnosis-use of Google as a diagnostic aid: internet based study. *British Medical Journal, 333*, 1143–1145. doi:10.1136/bmj.39003.640567.AE

Tannenbaum, T., Wright, D., Miller, K., & Livny, M. (2002). Condor - A Distributed Job Scheduler in Thomas Sterling, (Ed.). *Beowulf Cluster Computing with Linux*. Boston: The MIT Press.

The Economist. (2007). Health 2.0: Technology and society: Is the outbreak of cancer videos, bulimia blogs and other forms of "user generated" medical information a healthy trend? *The Economist, Sept.*, 73-74.

The Healthcare Information and Management Systems Society. http://www.himss.org

The Institute for Alternative Futures. (2004). *Patient-Centered Care 2015: Scenarios, Vision, Goals & Next Steps*. Camden, ME: The Picker Institute.

The Open Grid Services Architecture. *Version 1.5* (2006). Retrieved 25 July 2009 from http://www.ogf.org/documents/GFD.80.pdf

The Ten Most Critical Web Application Security Vulnerabilities. The Open Web Application Security Project (OWASP). (2004). Retrieved 25 July 2009 from http://www.owasp.org/documentation/topten.html.

Theodorides, K. (2005). The traps of cyberspace (I). *Hellenic Review of European Law, 2*, 471–483.

Thiru, K., Donnan, P., & Sullivan, F. (2003). A validated logistic regression model to identify coronary heart disease patients within primary care databases in the United Kingdom. *AMIA... Annual Symposium Proceedings / AMIA Symposium. AMIA Symposium*, 1030.

Thomas, S. A. (2000). *SSL and TLS essentials securing the Web*. New York: Wiley.

Thomas, R. K. (1997). *Team-based Access Control (TMAC): A Primitive for Applying Role-based Access Controls in Collaborative Environments*. Proceedings of the second ACM workshop on Role-based access control (RBAC '97). pp. 13-19. New York: ACM.

Timmers, P. (2000). *Electronic Commerce: Strategies and Models for Business-to- Business Trading*. Son, U.K.: John Wiley.

Tipton, H. F., & Krause, M. (2007). *Information Security Management Handbook* (6th ed.). Boca Raton, FL: Auerbach Publications. doi:10.1201/9781439833032

Tourzan, J., & Koga, Y. (Eds.). (2006). *Liberty ID-WSF Architecture Overview, version 2.0*, Liberty Alliance Project. Accessed 2009/012 http://www.projectliberty.org/resource_center/specifications/liberty_alliance_id_wsf_2_0_specifications.

Tsiknakis, M., Katehakis, D., & Orphanoudakis, S. (2002). An open, component-based information infrastructure for integrated health information networks. *International Journal of Medical Informatics, 68*(issue 1), 3–26. doi:10.1016/S1386-5056(02)00060-6

Tsohou, A. Kokolakis. S., Lambrinoudakis C., Gritzalis S. (2009). *Information Systems Security Management: A review and a classification of the ISO standards*. e-Democracy 2009 3rd Conference on Electronic Democracy – Next Generation Society: Technological and Legal Issues. Athens, Greece.

Tueche, S. et al. (2001). *Internet X.509 public key infrastructure proxy certificate profile*. IETF draft.

Tzoulia, E. (2006). *The principle of origin and online advertising*. Unpublished master's thesis, Ruprecht–Karls Universitaet, Heidelberg.

Tzouvelekis, A., Harokopos, V., Paparountas, T., Oikonomou, N., Chatziioannou, A., & Vilaras, G. (2007). Comparative expression profiling in pulmonary fibrosis suggests a role of hypoxia-inducible factor-1 alpha in disease pathogenesis. *American Journal of Respiratory and Critical Care Medicine, 176*(11), 1108–1119. doi:10.1164/rccm.200705-683OC

University of Twente. Health Belief Model. Retrieved September 21, 2009, from http://www.cw.utwente.nl/theorieenoverzicht/Theory%20clusters/Health%20Communication/Health_Belief_Model.doc/

University of Twente. Protection Motivation Theory. Retrieved September 21, 2009, from http://www.tcw.utwente.nl/theorieenoverzicht/Theory%20clusters/Health%20Communication/Protection_Motivation_Theory.doc/

USA Department of Health and Human Services (HHS). (1996). *Health Insurance Portability and Accountability* act. Retrieved 10/1/2010 from http://www.hhs.gov/ocr/hipaa/.

Vaast, E. (2007). Danger is in the eye of the beholders: Social representations of Information Systems security in healthcare. *The Journal of Strategic Information Systems, 16*, 130–152. doi:10.1016/j.jsis.2007.05.003

van der Aalst, W. M. P., & ter Hofstede, A. H. M. (2005). YAWL: Yet Another Workflow Language. *Information Systems, 30*(4), 245–275. doi:10.1016/j.is.2004.02.002

van der Aalst, W. M. P., ter Hofstede, A. H. M., Kiepuszewski, B., & Barros, A. P. (2003). Workflow patterns. *Distributed and Parallel Databases, 14*(3), 5–51. doi:10.1023/A:1022883727209

van der Aalst, W. M. P., Weske, M., & Gruenbauer, D. (2005). Case Handling: A New Paradigm for Business Process Support. *Data & Knowledge Engineering, 53*(2), 129–162. doi:10.1016/j.datak.2004.07.003

van der Aalst, W. M. P., Adams, M., ter Hofstede, A. H. M., Pesic, M., & Schonenberg, H. (2009), *Flexibility as a Service*. In L. Chen, (ed.) Database Systems for Advanced Applications (DASFAA 2009), (LNCS, vol.5667, pp. 320-334). Berlin: Springer-Verlag.

van der Aalst, W. M. P., & Berens, P. J. S. (2001). Beyond workflow management: Product-driven case handling. In Ellis, S., Rodden, T., & Zigurs, I. (eds.), *International ACM SIGGROUP Conference on Supporting Group Work*, pp. 42-51, New York: ACM Press.

van der Aalst, W.M.P. (1999). Inter-organizational Workflows: An Approach based on Message Sequence Charts and Petri Nets, *Systems Analysis - Modeling - Simulation, 34(3)*, 335-367.

van der Linden, H., Kalra, D., Hasman, A., & Talmon, J. (2009). Inter-organizational future proof EHR systems: A review of the security and privacy related issues. *International Journal of Medical Informatics, 78*(3), 141–160. doi:10.1016/j.ijmedinf.2008.06.013

Varshney, U. (2006). Patient monitoring using infrastructure oriented wireless LANs. *International Journal of Electronic Healthcare, 2*(2), 149–163.

Varshney, U. (2006). Using wireless technologies in healthcare. *International Journal of Mobile Communications, 4*(3), 354–368.

Varshney, U. (2005). Pervasive Healthcare: Applications, Challenges And Wireless Solutions, *Communications of the Association for Information Systems*: 16, Article 3. Retrieved from http://aisel.aisnet.org/cais/vol16/iss1/3 (10/1/2010).

Venkatesh, V., Morris, G. M., Davis, B. G., & Davis, D. F. (2003). User acceptance of information technology: Toward a unified view. *Management Information Systems Quarterly, 27*(3), 425–478.

Venkatesh, V. Personal web page, Theoretical Models. Retrieved September 21, 2009, from http://www.vvenkatesh.com/organizations/Theoretical_Models.asp

Versel, N. (2008). Health 2.0. Will its promise be realized? *Managed Care Magazine, 17*(3), 49–52.

Vorster, A., & Labuschagne, L. (2005). A framework for comparing different information security risk analysis methodologies. Proceedings of the 2005 annual research conference of the South African institute of computer scientists and information technologists on IT research in developing countries (pp. 95 - 103). South African Institute for Computer Scientists and Information Technologists.

Waegemann, C. (2002). *Status Report 2002: Electronic Health Records.*

Waegemann, C. (2003). EHR vs. CPR vs. EMR. *Healthcare Informatics online.*

Wager, K., & Wickham, L. F. Gloser. P.J. (2005). *Managing Health Care Information Systems. A practical Approach for Health Care Executives.*(pp. 81-83). San Francisco: Jossey-Bass.

Wagner, M. (2009). *Electronic Medical Records: The Good, Bad, And Ugly.* Retrieved 10/12/2009 from http://www.darkreading.com/shared/printableArticle.jhtml?articleID=222002718.

Wallace, D., & Coleman, C. (2001). Application and Improvement of Software Reliability Models, In Proceedings of NASA Office of Safety and Mission Assurance Software Assurance Symposium Symposium (OSMA SAS '01), Morgantown, West Virginia, USA.

Wang, S., Middleton, B., Prosser, L., Bardon, C., Spurr, C., & Carchidi, P. (2003). Academic publication proves that EMRs are cost effective: A cost-benefit analysis of electronic medical records in primary care. *The American Journal of Medicine, 114*(5), 397–403. doi:10.1016/S0002-9343(03)00057-3

Weaver, A. C., Dwyer, S. J., III, & Snyder, A. M. (2003). *Federated, secure trust networks for distributed healthcare it services.* Proceedings of the 2003 IEEE International Conference on Industrial Informatics. Alberta, Canada.

Wei, P., Tao, L., & Sheng, M. (2005). *Mining Logs Files for Data Driven System Management.* Proceedings of the Second International Conference on Autonomic Computing ICAC 2005. Seattle, United States.

Welboren, W. J., van Driel, M. A., Janssen-Megens, E. M., van Heeringen, S. J., Sweep, F. C., Span, P. N., & Stunnenberg, H. G. (2009). ChIP-Seq of ERalpha and RNA polymerase II defines genes differentially responding to ligands. *The EMBO Journal, 28*(10), 1418–1428. doi:10.1038/emboj.2009.88

White, P. (2002). Legal issues in teleradiology. *The British Journal of Radiology, 75,* 201–206.

Wiederhold, G., & Bilello, M. (1998). *Protecting Inappropriate Release of Data from Realistic Databases.* In Proceedings of DEXA '98 Workshop on Security and Integrity of Data Intensive Applications.

Wiljer, D., Urowitz, S., Apatu, E., DeLenardo, C., Eysenbach, G., & Harth, T. (2008). Patient accessible electronic health records: exploring recommendations for successful implementation strategies. *Journal of Medical Internet Research, 10*(4), e34. doi:10.2196/jmir.1061

Wirth, N. (1986). *Algorithms and Data structures,* Prentice-Hall series in automatic computation, 257-279., London: Prentice-Hall.

Wold, G. H., & Shriver, R. F. (1994). Risk analysis techniques. *Disaster Recovery Journal, 7*(3), 46–52.

Wong, R. (2006). *An overview of Data Protection Laws around the world.* Retrieved 10/1/2010 from http://pages.britishlibrary.net/rwong/dpa.html.

Wood, A. (1996). *Software Reliability Growth Models,* Technical Report 96.1.

Woon, I. M. Y., Tan, G. W., & Low, R. T. (2005). *A Protection Motivation Theory approach to home wireless security.* In Proceedings of the 26th International Conference on Information Systems.Las Vegas, Nevada, USA, paper 31.

Workman, M., Bommer, W. H., & Straub, D. (2008). Security lapses and the omission of information security measures: A threat control model and empirical test. *Computers in Human Behavior, 24,* 2799–2816. doi:10.1016/j.chb.2008.04.005

WS-Security Specification (2004). Retrieved 25 July 2009 from http://www-128.ibm.com/developerworks/library/specification/ws-secure/

Wu, S., Sheth, A., Miller, J., & Luo, Z. (2002). Authorization and Access Control of Application Data in Workflow Systems. *Journal of Intelligent Information Systems, 18*(1), 71–94. doi:10.1023/A:1012972608697

Wyatt, J. (2005). *Clinical data capture and presentation.* Porto: Medical Informatics Summer School.

Wyatt, J., & Wright, P. (1998). Design should help use of patients' data. *Lancet, 352,* 1375–1378. doi:10.1016/S0140-6736(97)08306-2

Wyatt, D. Jeremy, (2001). *Development of an Evaluation Methodology for NSW Health Clinical Information Access Program* (CIAP). Sydney: New South Wales Health department. Retrieved 10/1/10 from http://www.health.nsw.gov.au/health-publicaffairs/ publications/ciap/01_773CIAP.pdf.

Wyatt, J. (1994). Clinical data systems, Part 1: Data and medical records. *The Lancet, 344,* 1543 7.

XACML. (2009). *Sun's XACML Implementation.* Accessed 2009/012 http://sunxacml.sourceforge.net/.

Xiaomin, W., Weidong, Z., & Yulin, W. (2002). *The development and application of a provincial telemedicine center.* Proceedings of the second joint EMBS/BMES Conference. pp. 1843-1844. Accessed 2009/012 http://ieeexplore.ieee.org/stamp/stamp.jsp?arnumber=1053055&isnumber=22474.

Yeo, C. A., Rahim, M. M., & Ren, Y. Y. (2008). Use of persuasive technology to change end-users' IT security aware behavior: A pilot study. *World Academy of Science. Engineering and Technology, 46,* 232–238.

Yip, F. Ray, P. Paramesh, N. (2006). *Enforcing Business Rules and Information Security Policies through Compliance Audits: XISSF - A Compliance Specification Mechanism.* First IEEE/IFIP International Workshop on Business-Driven IT Management (BDIM '06). pp. 81-90. Accessed 2009/012 http://ieeexplore.ieee.org/stamp/stamp.jsp?arnumber=1649214&isnumber=34578.

Zander, J. Kim, S.-L. (2001). *Radio Resource Management for Wireless Networks.* Norwood, MA: Artech House.

Zeki, Y. (2002). A qualitative risk analysis and management tool - CRAMM. Retrieved 10/1/2010, from SANS Institute InfoSec Reading Room: http://www.sans.org/reading_room/whitepapers/auditing/a_qualitative_risk_analysis_and_management_tool_cramm_83?show=83.php&cat=auditing.

Zhang, J., Sun, J., Yang, Y., Chen, X., Meng, L., & Lian, P. (2005). Web-based electronic patient records for collaborative medical applications. *Computerized Medical Imaging and Graphics, 29*(2), 115–124. doi:10.1016/j.compmedimag.2004.09.005

Zhang, G., & Parashar, M. (2004, January). *Context-Aware Dynamic Access Control for Pervasive Applications.* Paper presented at the Communication Networks and Distributed Systems Modeling and Simulation Conference (CNDS 2004). San Diego, California, USA.

Zhang, Y., & Paxson, V. (1998). *Detecting Backdoors.* Retrieved May 20, 2009, from http://www.icir.org/vern/papers/backdoor/.

About the Contributors

Anargyros Chryssanthou studied Applied Informatics in Athens University of Economics and Business. He holds an MSc in Information Security and Computer Crime from the University of Glamorgan (Wales – UK). He has written and presented several articles in national conferences, concerning various aspects of computer security, from network forensics to cryptography, security management and ISO implementations of Information Security Management Systems (ISMS). He worked in the past as a Database Reporting Specialist for Coca Cola Hellenic Bottle and Company and designed several commercial database applications. He is currently employed by the Hellenic Data Protection Authority as an ICT Auditor, where his duties include auditing the use of personal data by companies of the public and the private sector. He is currently working most on spam issues as well as on privacy and security issues of the Greek medical sector. His research interests include network security, cryptography, with special interest on steganography, which was the subject of his MSc thesis, and computer forensics, where he is currently aiming on building a concise forensic methodology on investigating electronic crime in general and privacy violations in particular.

Ioannis Apostolakis was born in Chania of Crete and studied Mathematics in the University of Athens. He has a MSc in Informatics, Operational Research and Education issues and also a PhD in Health Informatics. He had Post Doctoral studies in Medical Informatics. He had been for several years scientific researcher in the Department of clinical therapeutics in the University of Athens. He has research and educational activities in issues of Health Informatics and Education. He is working as Visiting Professor at National School of Public Health, Greece. More information is available at http://www.iapostolakis.gr

Iraklis Varlamis is a lecturer at the Department of Informatics and Telematics of Harokopio University of Athens. He received his Ph.D. in Computer Science from Athens University of Economics and Business, Greece. From 1999-2004, he was member of the DB-NET (http://www.db-net.aueb.gr/) research group (Head: Associate Prof. Vazirgiannis) and since 2005 he is collaborating with the WIM (http://wim.aueb.gr) research group (Head: Associate Prof. Vassalos). His research interests vary from data-mining and the use of semantics in web mining to virtual communities and their applications in education and healthcare. He has published several articles in international journals and conferences, concerning web document clustering, the use of semantics in web link analysis and web usage mining, word sense disambiguation using thesauruses, virtual communities in healthcare etc. He has lectured databases and data mining, information systems and software technology as a lecturer and visiting lecturer at Harokopio University of Athens, Athens University of Economics and Business, the University of Peloponnese, the University of Central Greece, and the University of Aegean. More information is available at http://www.dit.hua.gr/~varlamis

* * *

Luís Antunes obtained a PhD in Computer Science at University of Porto. Currently he is an Auxiliary Professor at the Computer Science Department at University of Porto. Most of his research is on Computational Complexity and Cryptography. He is in the Coordination Committee of the first Health Informatics Master course in Portugal and has a strong collaboration with the Medical School of Porto University. He supervises several Master and PhD students in areas such as Access Control and Information Measures for Cryptography protocols.

Rafae Bhatti received the BS degree in electronics engineering from Ghulam Ishaq Khan Institute of Engineering Sciences and Technology (GIKI), Pakistan, in 1999 and the MS and PhD degrees in computer engineering from Purdue University in 2003 and 2006, respectively. This work was done when he was a postdoc at IBM Almaden Research Center. His PhD research is in the area of information systems security, in particular access management in federated systems and specification of XML-based security protocols for Web-based information systems. His recent work focuses on designing privacy and security technologies for application in the healthcare delivery. His work on XML-based access control framework for the Role-Based Access Control (RBAC) model has recently been cited by the OASIS consortium in their official announcement of the RBAC standard. He is a member of the IEEE and the IEEE Computer Society. He currently works at Oracle.

David W. Chadwick is a Professor of Information Systems Security at the University of Kent. He is the leader of the Information Systems Security Research Group (ISSRG) at Kent and a member of IEEE and ACM. His group are the creators of PERMIS (www.openpermis.org), an open source X.509 and SAML supported role based authorisation infrastructure which is part of the US NMI software suite. It is currently integrated with Globus Toolkit, Shibboleth, Apache and OMII-UK and is currently being integrated into the UK's National Grid Service.

Aristotelis A. Chatziioannou received a Diploma in Electrical & Computer Engineering and a Ph.D. in Metabolic Engineering and Medical Informatics from the National Technical University of Athens (NTUA) Greece in 1996 and 2005 respectively. From June 2004 up to August 2005 he was with Al. Fleming Biomedical Science Research Center as an expert in Bioinformatics. Since September of 2005 he is with the Institute of Biological Research & Biotechnology in the National Hellenic Research Foundation, where he holds the position of the Principal Investigator (elected Research Assistant Professor) of the group of Metabolic Engineering and Bioinformatics. He has designed and directed and co-developed GRISSOM, the first Grid-based platform at European level, for the analysis and interpretation of DNA microarray experiments. His published work includes 16 journal papers, 3 book chapters and more than 50 papers in conference proceedings. His scientific activities include metabolic engineering, genomics, biological ontologies, bioinformatics, computational biology, biomedical image processing. He is also associate Editor of the journal Frontiers in Systems Biology.

Ricardo João Cruz Correia obtained a PhD in Medical Informatics at University of Porto. Currently he is an Assistant Professor at the Department of Biostatistics and Medical Informatics at the Faculty of Medicine of the University of Porto. His research interest is the electronic patient records and on the integration of heterogeneous healthcare information systems. He supervises several Master students in areas such as Patient Records Integration, Telemedicine, Clinical Decision Support Systems and Information Flow in clinical departments.

Stelios Daskalakis holds a PhD in Health Informatics from the National and Kapodistrian University of Athens (Greece). He is a research associate of the Health Informatics Laboratory at the Faculty of Nursing of the aforementioned University. His research interests focus on human/ behavioral and social aspects of technology adoption in a variety of domains including SOA (Service-Oriented Architectures) and enterprise interoperability, health informatics and e-Learning. The area of his research analysis emphasizes on quantitative methods, in particular partial least squares path modeling. He has participated both as presenter and reviewer in international conferences and has authored a series of scientific papers appearing in international conferences and journals. He also possesses substantial IT industry experience, having served as a Senior IT Consultant/Architect in leading multinational information technology organizations.

Charalampos Doukas has received the Diploma in Information & Communication Systems Engineering from the University of the Aegean Greece in 2005 and is currently a PhD student at the same department. His main interests include video and image processing of medical data, medical ontologies and semantics, medical data classification and data transmission over heterogeneous networks. He has published more than 25 papers in international scientific conferences, 8 journal papers and 4 book chapters. He is member of the Technical Chamber in Greece, member of Hellenic Artificial Intelligence Society, member of IEEE EMBS Greek Society and peer reviewer in scientific journals like IEEE Transactions on Information Technology in Biomedicine and IEEE Transactions in Medical Imaging. He is currently working as an external researcher at the University of the Aegean and at National Hellenic Research Institute.

Stelios Eliakis is a Researcher and a PhD Candidate at the Department of Management Science and Technology of the Athens University of Economics and Business (AUEB). He holds a B.Sc. in informatics and a M.Sc. in Information Systems from AUEB. His research areas are IS Security, e-business integration, electronic services, interoperability, Web Services and RFID. He has participated in several national and European projects such as SMART (FP6), MeDAS and HERMES (the Greek e-Government case). He has published his work in international conferences such as MIMI2007, ETFA2008 and MCIS2009.

Ana Ferreira is an IT specialist at Porto Faculty of Medicine; she is a CISSP and is pursuing a PhD in Computer Science with a joint supervision between the University of Porto and the University of Kent, aiming at improving access control to healthcare information systems. Other main interests include information security for healthcare, wireless networks, usability, users' awareness and education.

Alejandro Enrique Flores obtained his Bachelor Degree in Honors Business Management and Informatics Technology from the University of Talca, Chile. He is lecture at the University of Talca,

Chile since 2003 and candidate for Doctor of Philosophy at the University of Wollongong. His main research interest includes Health Informatics and information security.

Rui Gomes has served in the last 10 years as Chief Information Officer (CIO) under public healthcare organizations. He was responsible for the information and communications department and usually works with several national and international projects and committees. Rui is pursuing an Electronic Engineering degree at Coimbra University and is working at the Hospital Fernando Fonseca in Lisbon. His major teaching and research interest is information security management for healthcare, services management and business continuing plans.

Tyrone Grandison received his B.Sc. and M.Sc. degrees from the University of the West Indies, Jamaica in 1997 and 1998, respectively, and a Ph.D. degree from the Imperial College of Sciences, Technology and Medicine in the University of London, United Kingdom in 2003. His research interests include security-sensitive and privacy-aware data disclosure, large-scale text analytics, security and trust management and fundamental data protection science for new frameworks, models, methodologies, opportunities for industry verticals. Currently, he leads the Data Disclosure team in the Health Informatics department at the IBM Almaden Research Center. Tyrone is a Distinguished Engineer of the Association of Computing Machinery (ACM), Senior Member of the Institute of Electrical and Electronics Engineers (IEEE) and has been recognized by the National Society of Black Engineers (i.e. Pioneer of the Year 2009) and the Black Engineer of the Year Award Board (i.e. Modern Day Technology Leader 2009, Minority in Science Trailblazer 2010).

Jun Hu is a systems analyst at Health Canada and a Ph.D. candidate in Computer Science at the University of Ottawa. Her research interests are in application architecture, distributed data mining and privacy. She has a M.Sc. (2006) and B.Sc. (2004) in Computer Science from the University of Ottawa.

Anastasia N. Kastania was born in Athens, Greece. She received her B.Sc. in Mathematics and her Doctor of Philosophy Degree in Medical Informatics from the National Kapodistrian University of Athens. Research productivity is summarized in various articles (monographs or in collaboration with other researchers) in International Journals, International Conference Proceedings, International Book Series and International Book Chapters. She works at the Athens University of Economics and Business since 1987 and currently, she is Visiting Assistant Professor (PD 407/80) of Applied Informatics in the Department of Accounting and Finance, Athens University of Economics and Business. She has participated in many Research Projects in Greece and in European Union. She is the writer of many didactic books in the areas of Informatics and Statistics. She is also a Visiting Researcher at the Bioinformatics and Medical Informatics Team, Centre of Basic Research, Biotechnology Division, Foundation for Biomedical Research of the Academy of Athens.

Maria Katharaki (Ph.D. in OR) is a Visiting Lecturer in Quantitative Analysis in Decision Making, Faculty of Economics, National and Kapodistrian University of Athens, Greece. Her research interests are mainly in the areas of Quantititative Analysis, Decision Making Processes, Organizations' Performance Assessment and Evaluation Techniques. Her current research includes topics of e-learning programs evaluation, human resources management, and assessment of healthcare technology acceptance. She has published a range of quantitative research on the topics of performance assessment and management of organizations (healthcare units, tax offices, universities). She is an author of two books related to quantitative analysis in decision making and marketing issues. She has also served as a scientific expert and advisor in governmental bodies related with healthcare management and public administration initiatives.

Evangelos Kotsonis currently works as a Senior Security Consultant for Adacom SA, one of the largest security companies in Greece. In Adacom SA, he is called to perform a number of variable tasks, including requirement analysis, presales oriented tasks, project management tasks and also marketing activities. He holds a B.Sc. in informatics and a M.Sc. in Information Systems from AUEB. Also, he is a Certified Information Security Auditor of ISACA and holds a specialization on ISO27001 Audit by TUV Austria Hellas. Finally, he holds a number of certifications and specialization related to security products that certify both his technical and sales capabilities and knowledge. Evangelos has also participated in a number of different projects and engagements, including in all research, government, banking and corporate sectors, thus obtaining a large number of experiences from different environments and diverse requirements.

Vassiliki Koufi received her B.Sc. in Informatics from the University of Piraeus (2001) and her M.Sc. in Data Communication Systems from Brunel University, UK (2003). Since 2003, she is a Ph.D candidate in the Department of Digital Systems at the University of Piraeus and works as a network engineer in the Network Management Center at the University of Piraeus. Since February 2009 she is teaching fellow at the Department of Digital Systems, University of Piraeus. Ms. Koufi has been actively involved in several projects concerning the development of healthcare information systems and other web-based applications as well as the development and management of telecommunication services and applications. She has published several research papers in internationally refereed journals, conferences and books. Her research interests include ubiquitous and pervasive healthcare, context-aware healthcare information systems, process-oriented web-based and cloud-based healthcare information systems, healthcare information systems security, personal health records systems and security issues arising in these systems.

Athina Lazakidou is Lecturer in Health Informatics at the University of Peloponnese, Department of Nursing (Greece) and visiting lecturer in informatics at the Hellenic Naval Academy. She has been visiting lecturer at the Computer Science Dept. (Univ. Cyprus 2000-2002) and at the Nursing Dept. (Univ. Athens 2002-2007). She holds a diploma in computer science (1996) from the Athens University of Economics and Business (Greece). In 2000, she received her PhD in medical informatics from the Department of Medical Informatics, University Hospital Benjamin Franklin at the Free University of Berlin (Germany). She is also an internationally known expert in the field of computer applications in health care and biomedicine, with six books and numerous papers to her credit. She is editor of the Handbook of Research on Informatics in Healthcare and Biomedicine and Handbook of Research on Distributed Medical Informatics and E-Health, the best authoritative reference sources for breakthroughs in computer applications for healthcare and biomedicine. Her research interests include health informatics, e-learning in medicine, software engineering, graphical user interfaces, (bio)medical databases, clinical decision support systems, hospital and clinical information systems, electronic medical record systems, telematics, and other Web-based applications in healthcare and biomedicine.

Joseph Liaskos holds a PhD in Health Informatics from the National and Kapodistrian University of Athens (Greece). He is a research associate at the University of Athens, Faculty of Nursing, Laboratory of Health Informatics. His research interests cover Electronic Health Records, Nursing Informatics, Education and Training in Health Informatics. He has participated both as presenter and reviewer in international conferences, and has authored a series of scientific papers in international conferences, journals, and books. He has been working in European and National Research Projects for the past ten years.

Ilias G. Maglogiannis received a Diploma in Electrical & Computer Engineering (1996) and a Ph.D. in Biomedical Engineering and Medical Informatics from the National Technical University of Athens (2000) Greece. He worked as Researcher at the Biomedical Engineering Laboratory in NTUA, as Lecturer at the Dept of Information and Communication Systems Engineering in University of the Aegean and now is Assistant Professor at the Dept of Computer Science and Biomedical Informatics in the State University of Central Greece (www.dib.ucg.gr). He has worked in several European and National Research programs in Biomedical Engineering and Informatics and has published three books, fifty journal papers and more than seventy international conference papers. His scientific activities include biomedical informatics, medical image processing and telemedicine. He is a member of IEEE - Societies: Engineering in Medicine and Biology, Computer, Communications, SPIE - International Society for Optical Engineering, ACM, the Technical Chamber of Greece, the Greek Computer Society and the Hellenic Organization of Biomedical Engineering and a national representative for Greece in the IFIP technical committee TC 12.

Flora Malamateniou was born in Athens, Greece. She received the B.Sc degree in Statistics from the University of Piraeus in 1993 and the M.Sc and the Ph.D degree in Health Informatics from the University of Athens in 1995 and 1999, respectively. She has worked as a senior researcher at Research Academic Computer Technology Institute, Greece during 2000-2004 and at Informatics and Telematics Institute Centre for Research and Technology, Greece during 2004-2008. She has been actively involved in many national and EU-funded R&TD projects and in the European IST programmes, E2R I/II, TENCompetence, iCLASS, C-CARE and LIMBER. Currently, she is an Assistant Professor at the Department of Digital Systems of the University of Piraeus. Her current research interests include process-oriented, web-based healthcare information systems, pervasive healthcare, virtual healthcare records, information security and workflow systems.

John Mantas is a Professor of Health Informatics at the School of Health Sciences of the University of Athens and Director of the Health Informatics Laboratory at the Faculty of Nursing of the aforementioned University. He was a Former Dean of the Faculty (2001-2005) while he currently serves as a member of the Governing Board of the Cyprus University of Technology. He also serves as a Vice President of the European Federation for Medical Informatics (EFMI) for the period 2008-2010 and as the Chair of the Workgroup on Education of the International Medical Informatics Association (IMIA) for the period 2004-2007 and as the Co-Chair for the period 2007-2010 respectively. He is a member of editorial boards of scientific journals and author of over 120 publications in international and national scientific journals and international conferences, with more than 300 citations registered in international indexes.

Boleslaw Mikolajczak, professor and chair of the Computer and Information Department, College of Engineering, University of Massachusetts, Dartmouth, MA 02747, USA, is a researcher in formal conceptual modeling of computational processes, sequential as well as parallel and distributed. For the first he applies finite state machines. For the second he uses various forms of Petri nets. He is an author of several books, many journal and conference publications devoted to studies of models of computations and their applications to software and systems' development. In particular, he is an author of an algorithm, both sequential and parallel, that computes all generalized homomorphisms (or partitions) between two finite state machines. This algorithm leads to optimized decompositions of model-based software systems. Recently he applied conceptual modeling techniques to medical guidelines modeling with colored Petri nets. The objective of this research is to improve quality of medical procedures from patients perspective and efficiency of these procedures.

Anastasius Moumtzoglou is an Executive Board Member of the European Society for Quality in HealthCare (ESQH), and President of the Hellenic Society for Quality & Safety in HealthCare (HSQSH). He holds B.A in Economics (National & Kapodistrian University of Athens), MA in Health Services Management (National School of Public Health), MA in Macroeconomics (The University of Liverpool), and Ph.D. in Economics (National & Kapodistrian University of Athens), He works for 'P. & A. Kyriakou' Children's Hospital and teaches the module of quality at the graduate and postgraduate level. He has written three books, which are the only ones in the Greek references. He has also served as a scientific coordinator and researcher in Greek and European research programs. In 2004, he was declared "Person of Quality in Healthcare", with respect to Greece. His research interests include healthcare management, quality, knowledge management, pensions, and the dualism of the labor market.

Efstratia Mourtou is the head of Informatics Department of St. Andrew General Hospital, Patras, Greece, and recently she is a tutor of the Hellenic Open University and a tutor of the Technological Educational Institute of Patras. She teaches "Health Informatics", "Biostatistics", "Peculiarities & Challenges of hospitals", and maths. She has been active in several research projects such as: design ICT manuals for medical staff, planning the development of hospital informatics, statistical evaluation of hospital's chemotherapy expenditure, codification of Medical Equipment and Supplies. She has many publications in International Journals and Conferences in the field of Hospital Information Systems.

Eleni Mytilinaiou was born in Athens, Greece. She received a Diploma of Engineering in Computer Engineering and Informatics from the University of Patra (1997) and an M.Sc. in Network-Centric Information Systems from the University of Piraeus (2008). Since 2008 she is a Ph.D candidate in the Department of Digital Systems at the University of Piraeus while she works as a department leader of the New Technologies department at the Athens Urban Transportation Organization. She has been actively involved in several projects concerning the development of information systems, web-based applications and telecommunication applications in the field of transportation. Her research interests include ubiquitous and pervasive healthcare, context-aware healthcare information systems, process-oriented web-based and cloud-based healthcare information systems and healthcare information systems security.

Liam Peyton, Ph.D., P.Eng., is a principal investigator for the Intelligent Data Warehouse laboratory and Associate Professor at the University of Ottawa which he joined in 2002 after spending 10 years as an industry consultant and instructor specializing in business process automation, performance management, and software development methodologies. He has degrees from Aalborg University (Ph.D. 1996), Stanford University (M.Sc. 1989), and McGill University (B.Sc. 1984).

Diogo Reis is an IT specialist at Healthcare Center of Entre o Douro e Vouga. He is also the responsible for the electronic patient record system, and radiology information system being used in Healthcare Center of Entre o Douro e Vouga. His main interests are the electronic patient records and integration of healthcare information systems. He is pursuing is MSc in Health Informatics at the Medical School of Porto University.

Henrique M. D. Santos received his PhD in Computer Engineering, at the University of the Minho, Portugal. Currently he is an Associate Professor at the Information Technology and Communications group, at the University of Minho, being responsible for several graduate and postgraduate courses, as well as the supervision of several dissertations, mainly in the Information Security and Computer Architecture areas. He is also the president of the ALGORITMI Research Centre, at the University of Minho, and president of a national Technical Committee (CT 136) for information system security standards. During the second semester of 1990, under an ERASMUS program, he was teaching at the University of Bristol, United Kingdom, where it was recognized as University Academic staff.

Konstantinos Siassiakos holds a diploma (1995) of Electrical and Computer Engineer from the Department of Electrical and Computer Engineering Studies, University of Patras, Greece, and a Ph.D. (2001) diploma from the Department of Electrical and Computer Engineering, National Technical University of Athens, Greece. He currently works as visiting lecturer at the University of Piraeus at the Department of Informatics and at the Technological Educational Institute of Halkida in Greece. He has worked as an IT consultant at Ministry of Development (General Secretariat of Industry) on the Operational Programme 'Competitiveness' and as a researcher at the Department of Technology Education & Digital Systems, University of Piraeus. He has participated in various european Research and Development projects. His research interests include web-based learning systems in medicine and other areas, educational technologies, human computer interaction, quality assurance, management information systems in health organisations and other areas, business process reengineering, and e-government technologies.

Willy Susilo obtained his Bachelor Degree in Computer Science from Universitas Surabaya, Indonesia with a "Summa Cum Laude" predicate. He received his Master Degree in Computer Science and Doctor of Philosophy from University of Wollongong in 1996 and 2001, resp. His main research interest include cryptography and computer security, in particular the design of signature schemes. He was appointed as a Professor and Head of School of Computer Science and Software Engineering (SCSSE) in 2009. Prior to this role, he was the deputy director of ICT Research Institute and the Academic Program Director for UoW (Singapore). He is the director of Centre for Computer and Information Security Research (CCISR).

Eleni Tzoulia was born in Athens, Greece on July 2, 1981. She graduated from the Democritus University of Thrace in 2003 with a bachelor degree in law. In 2006 she earned a master degree in European economic law from the Ruprecht-Karls University of Heidelberg. In the same year she started a traineeship in the Secretariat General of the European Parliament in Brussels, while in 2007 she joined the office of the European Ombudsman in Strasbourg as a trainee legal officer. After returning to Greece in 2008 she was recruited by the Technological Educational Institute of Crete as a lecturer of law for the Finance and Insurance Department of Agios Nikolaos. Since 2005 she is a licensed Attorney at law, registered in the bar association of Heraklion, Crete.

George Vassilacopoulos was born in Athens, Greece, received his Ph.D. degree from the University of London, U.K. and he is currently a Professor at the Department of Digital Systems of the University of Piraeus. He has been an advisor of health informatics to the Greek Minister of Health, a member of the board of two major Athens hospitals and an advisor of informatics to the National Ambulance Service of Greece. He has actively participated in several research and development projects at both National and European levels. His research interests include healthcare information systems, workflow systems, healthcare systems security, web-based healthcare information systems and electronic patient records. He has authored numerous publications in these areas in international journals and refereed conferences. He is a member of BCS and IEEE.

Khin Than Win (MBBS,PhD, DCS,IDCS, MS-CIS) is a Senior Lecturer in the School of Information Systems and Technology. She is a medical doctor with PhD in Information Technology (Health Informatics). Her background in medicine and knowledge of computing motivate her to be involved in health informatics research area. She supervises several honours and post graduate research students in health informatics. She has published several academic papers (peer reviewed) in health informatics.

Stelios Zimeras was born in Piraeus, Greece. He received his B.Sc. in Statistics from University of Piraeus, Depart. of Statistics and Insurance Sciences, and his her Doctor of Philosophy Degree in Statistics from University of Leeds, U.K. Research productivity is summarized in various articles (monographs or in collaboration with other researchers) in International Journals, International Conference Proceedings, International Book Series and International Book Chapters. Since 2008 he is Assistant Professor at the University of the Aegean, Depart. of Statistics and Actuarial – Financial Mathematics. He has participated in many Research Projects in Greece and in European Union. He is the writer of many papers in the areas of Informatics and Statistics.

Index

A

access control 23, 25, 26, 27, 28, 31, 33, 34, 35, 38, 39, 40, 41, 164, 165, 173, 244, 261

access levels 43

access permissions 1, 2, 4, 7, 9, 10, 11, 12, 14, 16, 17, 18, 21, 46, 47, 48, 49, 50, 51, 53, 54, 55, 56, 58, 59, 60, 61, 65

accountability 28, 43

active enforcement 68, 75, 76, 82

adaptive careflow nets 85, 86

adaptive careflows 85

adaptivity 86, 88

address resolution protocols (ARP) 29

administrative processes 160

advertising 226, 227, 228, 230, 231, 232, 233, 234, 235, 236, 237, 238, 239, 240

advertising, direct 240

advertising, indirect 240

advertising, online 226, 227, 236, 240, 241

advertising, unfair practices in 227, 233, 241

agents 55, 56, 57, 61, 62, 63, 64, 65

agents, intelligent 211

American College of Radiology (ACR) 115

apomediaries 201, 204

apomediation 199, 200, 201, 208, 211

assets 127, 129, 132, 134, 144

asset tracking software 215

attribute-based encryption (ABE) 1, 12, 14, 17, 21

auditing 214

audit log 68, 75, 78, 81

audits 160, 161, 164, 165, 167, 168, 169, 170

audit trail and reporting mechanism 160

audit trails 246, 257

authentication 213, 215, 219

authentication mechanism 263

authenticity 28, 43

availability 114, 120, 135, 144

B

backend data layers 175

behavioral security 285

bioinformatics 174

biomedical grid portals 174, 175, 176, 177, 191

biomedical imaging grid (BIG) 176

biomedical research informatics delivered by grid enabled services (BRIDGES) project 176

biometrics 13, 18, 22

blogs 201, 202, 203, 209, 211

boundedness 92

BPM process engine 52, 58

business process execution language (BPEL) 48, 52, 53, 54, 55, 57, 58, 61, 62, 65

business process management (BPM) 52, 56, 58, 59

business to business (B2B) network 161, 171, 173

C

cable locks 215

Cardiovascular Functional Genomics (CFG) project 176

careflow (CF) systems 84, 85, 86, 88, 91, 92, 97, 98, 105, 107, 110, 111

case-handling systems 111

ciphertexts 12, 20, 21